script **ALAN MOORE**

story **ALAN MOORE & MALCOLM McLAREN**

sequential adaptation **ANTONY JOHNSTON**

art & covers **FACUNDO PERCIO**

tarot card design **PAUL DUFFIELD**

color **HERNAN CABRERA**

letters **JAYMES REED**

WILLIAM CHRISTENSEN editor-in-chief

MARK SEIFERT creative director

JIM KUHORIC managing editor

DAVID MARKS director of events

ARIANA OSBORNE production assistant

COLLECTING FASHION BEAST #1-10

Dedicated to the memory of Malcolm McLaren.
Too fast to live, too young to die.

www.avatarpress.com   www.twitter.com/avatarpress   www.facebook.com/avatarpresscomics
FASHION BEAST COLLECTED. July 2013. Published by Avatar Press, Inc., 515 N. Century Blvd. Rantoul, IL 61866. ©2013 Avatar Press, Inc. Fashion Beast and all related properties TM & ©2013 Malcolm McLaren. Deep in Vogue TM & ©2013 Malcolm McLaren. All characters as depicted in this story are over the age of 18. The stories, characters, and institutions mentioned in this magazine are entirely fictional. Printed in Canada.

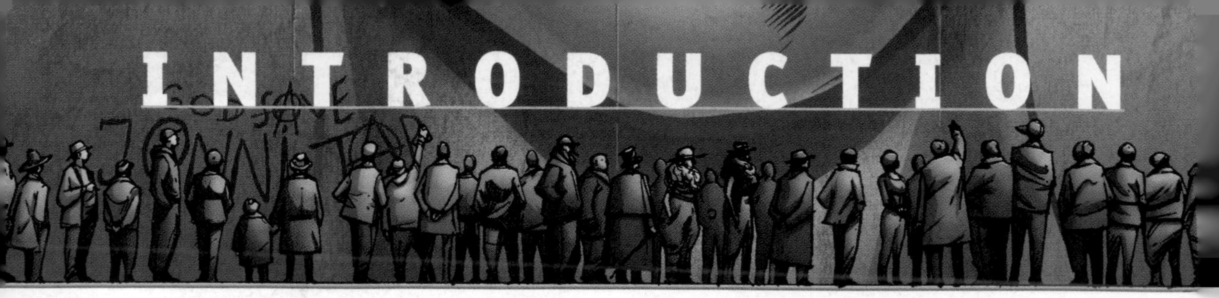

INTRODUCTION

While not in the habit of writing fore- or after-words for my own work, with this current volume being in such an unusual category of that work and having such an unusual history, an exception seems to be called for. For one thing, *Fashion Beast* is a comic-book adaptation of a thoroughly unlikely film that never was, written by someone who is dependably apoplectic regarding the idea of comic-books being adapted into films. It's also the first of my works that I've been able to read as if it were written by someone else, so much time having elapsed since its inception that, with everything save for the barest plot outline forgotten, much of this book seems completely new to me. While I've personally found this creative amnesia to be very enjoyable, I realise that it poses difficulties when it comes to an unravelling of the project's complicated history: frankly, the twentieth century was a bit of a blur, and the account below can only with charity be called even 'highly subjective'.

For example, I no longer properly recall the exact year or even decade when the idea first arose. My best guess would be in the last, guttering years of the 1980s, with Margaret Thatcher still clinging grimly to power, but if someone were to make an argument for the first dazed and traumatised years of the 1990s, with John Major still clinging grimly to Edwina Curry, I wouldn't offer much resistance. What I do recall is answering the telephone to find myself in conversation with one of the most intriguing and influential figures in modern popular culture, the always-incendiary Malcolm McLaren; the man who had, arguably, invented Punk as a Situationist prank.

At that point in his strikingly diverse career, Malcolm's magpie attentions had alighted on the medium of cinema as a new area to which he could apply his radical creative strategies. One of the most noticeable and effective of these, a tactic he employed in almost everything he did, was that of the surprising synthesis or mash-up. It was around this period that he had only recently successfully fused contemporary techno dance beats with firstly opera and secondly the waltz in the sublime grooves of, respectively, *Fans* and *Waltz Darling*. His latest ideas for cultural cross-fertilisation, he informed me, centred on the similarities between comics and cinema as two distinctly different visual storytelling media. Reasoning that a capable comic creator might possibly bring something fresh to a screenplay, he'd decamped to a bustling and thriving comic-shop in Saint Mark's Place and had asked the coolest-looking thirteen year-old kid that he could find who his favourite comic writer was. According to Malcolm, this unusually insightful and right-thinking young man had replied, without hesitation, "Alan Moore: left hand of God".

BY ALAN MOORE

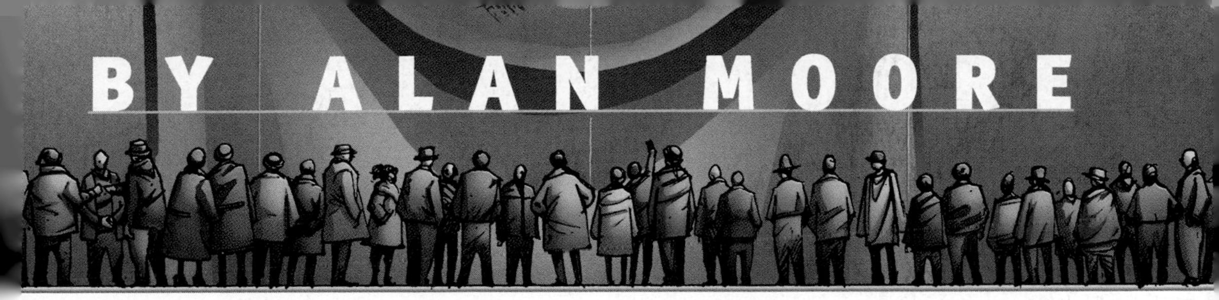

In the unlikely event that I ever write a characteristically unassuming and self-effacing autobiography, this will almost certainly be its title.

The subversive impresario invited me to meet with him in London to discuss some film ideas he had, and whether I might like to be involved in writing any of them. While I confess that I had no ambitions or genuine creative interest in the world of cinema, I had always idly wondered what it would be like to write within that form. More persuasively, I was keen to meet and if possible work with Malcolm McLaren, to my mind one of the most effervescent pop-culture intellects of the twentieth century. Thus it was that a week or so later I found myself rendezvousing with this self-consciously Mephistophelean figure in the lobby of the London hotel he was staying at. Arriving a few minutes early, I walked in on the last few shots of a photo-session for the avowedly sensationalistic *Sun*. A cheerily salacious newspaper photographer was coaxing Malcolm into a variety of poses to accompany a feature on the previous day's multi-million pound court settlement with members of the Sex Pistols. "Fantastic. That's fantastic. Now, can you turn your pockets inside-out and look miserable? Lovely." Always with a touch of the uproarious English pantomime tradition in his carefully composed patchwork persona... perhaps Aladdin's uncle proffering new lamps for old... Malcolm was gleefully playing along with this, although not for a moment could anyone have the impression that, in this encounter with the tabloid press, he was the one being manipulated.

When the photographer was gone we talked, and I was able to gain an impression of him in repose, between performances as the public Malcolm McLaren, the knowingly Dickensian loveable-villain cartoon that he himself had engineered for popular consumption. At least as tall as I am and considerably better-dressed, he had a bird-like quality... most probably the magpie mentioned earlier, but certainly some manner of ingenious corvid... and when standing he resembled nothing more than an anthropomorphic candle, with that orange blaze of cerebral combustion rising from the human wax. In conversation he was effortlessly entertaining and incisive both, a smoothly flowing stream of arcane details on a dozen different subjects, fascinating linkages and promising juxtapositions all delivered in those sinuous and slightly nasal tones, the most persuasive and most archetypal tradesman at the modern world's fluorescent street-bazaar. He was charming in a thoroughly archaic sense, immensely likeable and also very funny. Having by chance only just watched Alex Cox's *Sid and Nancy* on the previous evening, I asked Malcolm how he felt about the somewhat unflattering portrait painted of him in that movie, where essentially the inference is of McLaren as a saturnine Svengali, calculatedly manipulating both the life and death of a naive Sid Vicious. His reply was evidently heartfelt and emphatic: "I would never, *never*..." He paused briefly, for effect. "...have dressed in clothes like that." (More recently, I heard a far more sympathetic version of the pointless Vicious/Spungen tragedy, in which the Pistols' manager and instigator was engaged in a doomed struggle to divert his self-destructive charge from their perhaps inevitable end. All stories by their nature are at second hand and therefore unreliable, but I thought this interpretation more closely resembled the seemingly conscientious and engaging individual I met.)

His film ideas were typically idiosyncratic. First there was *Surf Nazis,* with an aboriginal protagonist possessing the ability to summon waves, a talent which presumably would serve him in good stead during his confrontation with the titular board-waxing National Socialists. A second sketchy outline, with a working title that eludes me at the moment, took as its unlikely starting point the poet Oscar Wilde's surprisingly successful tour of Wild West mining camps and from there bloomed into the tale of a female performer much more in the mode of a late 19th century Madonna prototype than of the divine Oscar, visiting the girl- and entertainment-starved encampments of the Gold Rush. While I'm sure that in the right hands both of the above conceptions could be worked into original and entertaining feature films, I was equally sure at the time that those hands in every likelihood were not my own. His third and final concept... possibly he'd left the best till last... was a bizarre and riotous conglomerate of the tortured life of Christian

Dior fused with both the fable "Beauty and the Beast" and Jean Cocteau's haunting and luminous film adaptation of that story, with the instantly engrossing working title *Fashion Beast.*

Despite not having any prior interest (fairly obviously) in the fashion industry or its mythology, I immediately grasped the narrative connections and allusions that a story like this would make possible, and the idea's potential to be realised as a film of relevance, originality and substance. I think Malcolm was pleased, perhaps because of his own background in the rag trade, that out of the three proposals this one had especially stirred my enthusiasm. We talked for a while about the fashion business, and I learned that Malcolm was familiar with my home town from his days knee-deep in schmatte, when he'd found out that the sole remaining individual who still made cobbler's lasts (a foot-shaped wooden armature for building shoes around) in the whole British Isles was based in the historic shoe-town of Northampton, trading under the impressive handle of 'The Last Man'.

He asked me if I could complete a first-draft screenplay by a given date, there being serious time constraints, and while I was uncertain whether I'd be able to accomplish this not having previously worked on anything of quite this nature, I told him I thought that it was doable, on the condition he ignore his own perfectly sound advice imparted in the sleeve-notes of *The Great Rock 'n' Roll Swindle,* and trust a hippy. Probably against his better judgement he accepted this proviso, and I set to work constructing the preliminary detailed, structured outline of the work in hand known as a treatment. All the major features of the narrative were already in place in this proposal. Malcolm had suggested that two of the principal characters might be "a girl who looks like a boy who looks like a girl" and "a boy who looks like a girl who looks like a boy", and seemed to like the resultant Doll Seguin and Johnny Tare. He also acceded to my notion of setting the story in an unspecified 'everycity' during a similarly unspecified epoch with elements of both the past and future, in order to recreate the timelessness of the original fairytale. The only alterations that he made, as I recall, were to suggest that the screenplay also achieve the flamboyant street-level energy of *Flashdance* and the gut-punching emotional darkness of *Chinatown.* At the time, I confess to thinking of these latter two inclusions as possibly crackpot whims on Malcolm's part, although as I attempted to apply the required sensibilities to my emerging drama I began to see how the suggested elements could work and realised that rather than crackpot whims they were instead more probably valuable insights.

The screenplay was completed on time and to Malcolm's satisfaction, but unfortunately other factors had arisen by that point which meant that *Fashion Beast* (like almost all projected feature films) would not be made. If I was disappointed it was more on Malcolm's behalf than my own. For my part I'd been well-paid for my time, I'd had the opportunity to explore a new medium and best of all I'd had the chance to work with and observe a thoroughly unique creative mind in action. It was only a pity that, in the relatively barren cultural landscape of those times, more of Malcolm McLaren's genuinely interesting and galvanising ideas had failed to see the light of day.

And there the matter rested for some several years. I bumped into the man once in the intervening time, a chance encounter on one of my only reluctant excursions to a London club where we spoke briefly, exchanged fond regards and, in my recollection of the meeting, didn't mention *Fashion Beast* at all. The decades steadily clicked up, and my receding memories of Johnny, Doll, Celestine and the salon gradually evaporated or else were supplanted by more pressing and immediate concerns. When Avatar's William Christensen gave me a call to announce that he'd lately discovered a copy of *Fashion Beast*'s screenplay, and proposed a comic adaptation, I could think of no immediate reason why that wouldn't work provided Malcolm was on board with the idea. As it turned out he was, which led to what would sadly prove to be our final lively conversation. He called me one evening and we both agreed it would be very satisfying to see *Fashion Beast* emerge at last, albeit in a different form to that originally intended. Our enthusiasm thus established, each of us caught up with what the other one was currently involved in. I remember Malcolm telling me of an extremely promising new form of music he was at that time investigating, very young French artists who were prising sound-chips from outdated Gameboy consoles and reusing them in their own compositions. I have no clear idea what that would have sounded like, but based on my appraisal of Malcolm's unerring instincts, I imagine that it would at least have been completely new and fascinating. I was also both encouraged and impressed to find him still compulsively seeking the cultural edge, still convinced in the burning necessity of innovation. He was living proof that even the most doggedly bohemian agendas can be made to succeed with sufficient thought, sufficient energy.

Now, here we are: 2013, with the complete work finally emerging in a new shape, a new century. If I at any point had worries or concerns about how well-received the piece might be, these weren't in any way connected with the talents handling the project. Antony Johnson has long been my preferred choice in the adaptation of my work from one form to another, and in *Fashion Beast* has handled many tricky, cinema-specific scenes with marvellous imagination and aplomb. The overlay of different soundtracks in the opening scenes, which at the time had seemed like an acoustic feat which could be readily accomplished by someone of Malcolm's proven track-record, is an excellent example of the intelligent solutions which Antony provides to difficulties that might otherwise prove insurmountable. As for Facundo Percio, while this is the first time that I've been privileged to see his work, I'm equally admiring. His skilful approximation of the cinematic pace of *Fashion Beast* in his essential visual storytelling is a masterful achievement, while in his realisation of Celestine's universe and its inhabitants he's conjured a convincing landscape of near-future dread that at the same time resonates with fairytale and fable in precisely the same way that I'd originally intended. Given my earlier comments on this being the first work of mine that I've been able to appreciate as if somebody else had been the author, then I'd have to say that on the strength of what these two gents have accomplished, I'm quite good.

No, my brief anxieties regarding *Fashion Beast* concerned the way in which the story might have aged, given the intervening years between inception and completion. Would our speculative late '80s fantasy upon a fashion world about which I at least knew precious little still hold any relevance or meaning for a modern audience in a modern world? However, during my proof-reading of the comic's individual

issues, I began to realise just how prescient that speculative fantasy had been. When we'd commenced the work, the country of the catwalk seemed at worst a frivolous diversion from the more substantial issues of a given era, without any of the morbid, gothic touches that infuse the atmosphere of *Fashion Beast*. That was, of course, before the shooting of Gianni Versace highlighted the violence and obsession stalking on the margins of the industry, and before Alexander McQueen's suicide revealed the darkness and despair that's at its colourful and florid heart. In many ways, the story seems more relevant to the peculiar climate into which it has emerged than to the different landscape in which it was first conceived and written.

But then, of course, Malcolm was always ahead of his time. And though he isn't here to see his concept's birthing after a protracted labour, or at least not in the flesh, his pyrotechnic and eclectic methods have embedded themselves deep enough into the marrow of contemporary culture to ensure him an invisible yet potent immortality. And in so far as his abiding cultural presence might be capable of holding probable opinions, I like to think that he'd be as delighted as myself that our unlikely beast could still prove fashionable. Thank you very much for your time, and I hope that you'll enjoy this autumn collection.

Alan Moore,
Northampton,
June 14th, 2013.

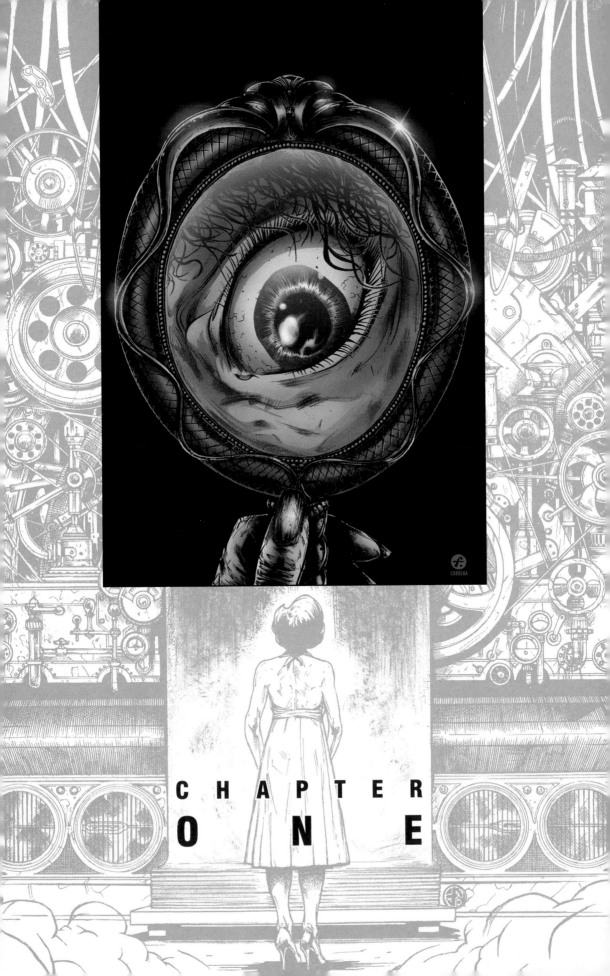

CHAPTER
ONE

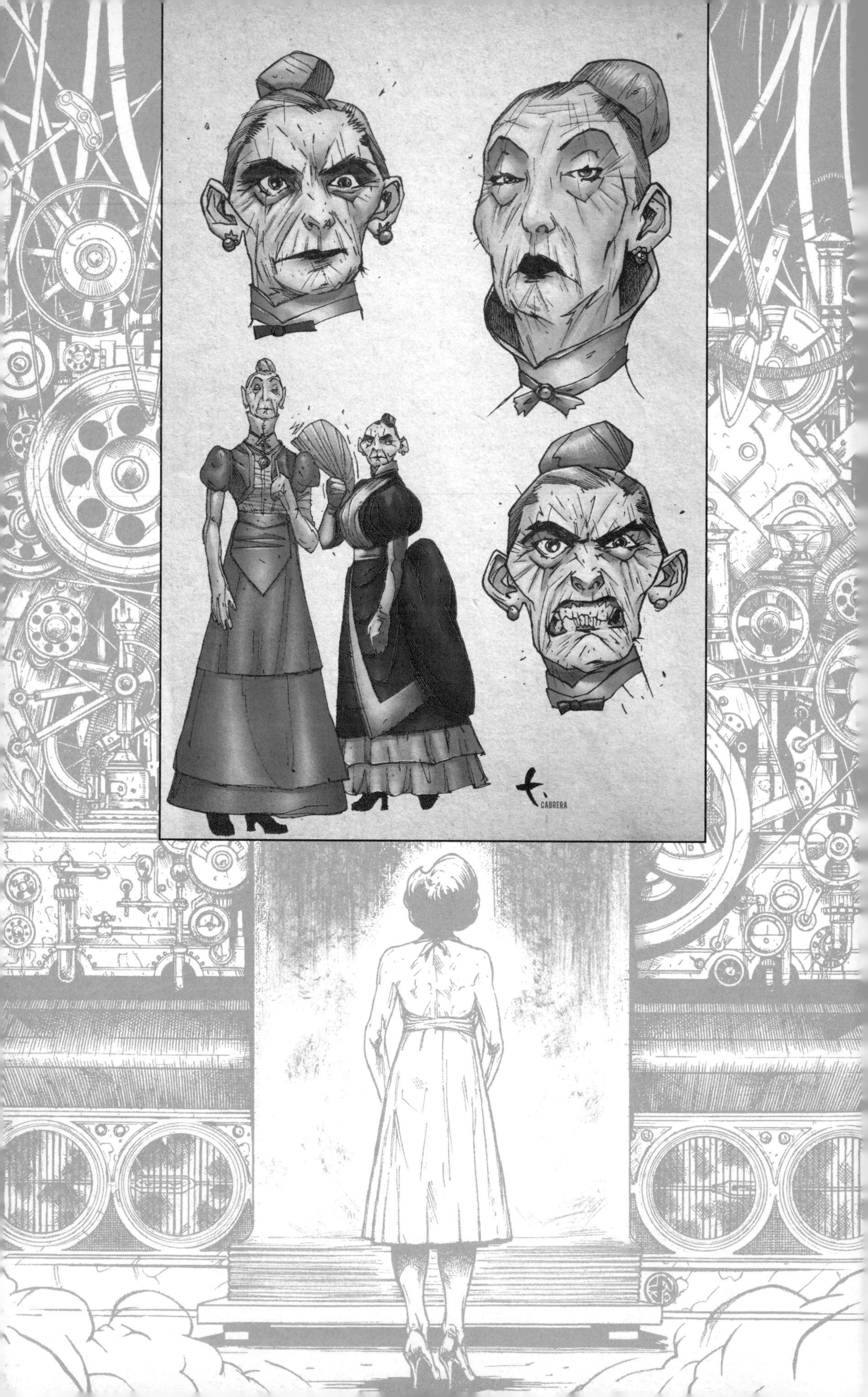
CABRERA

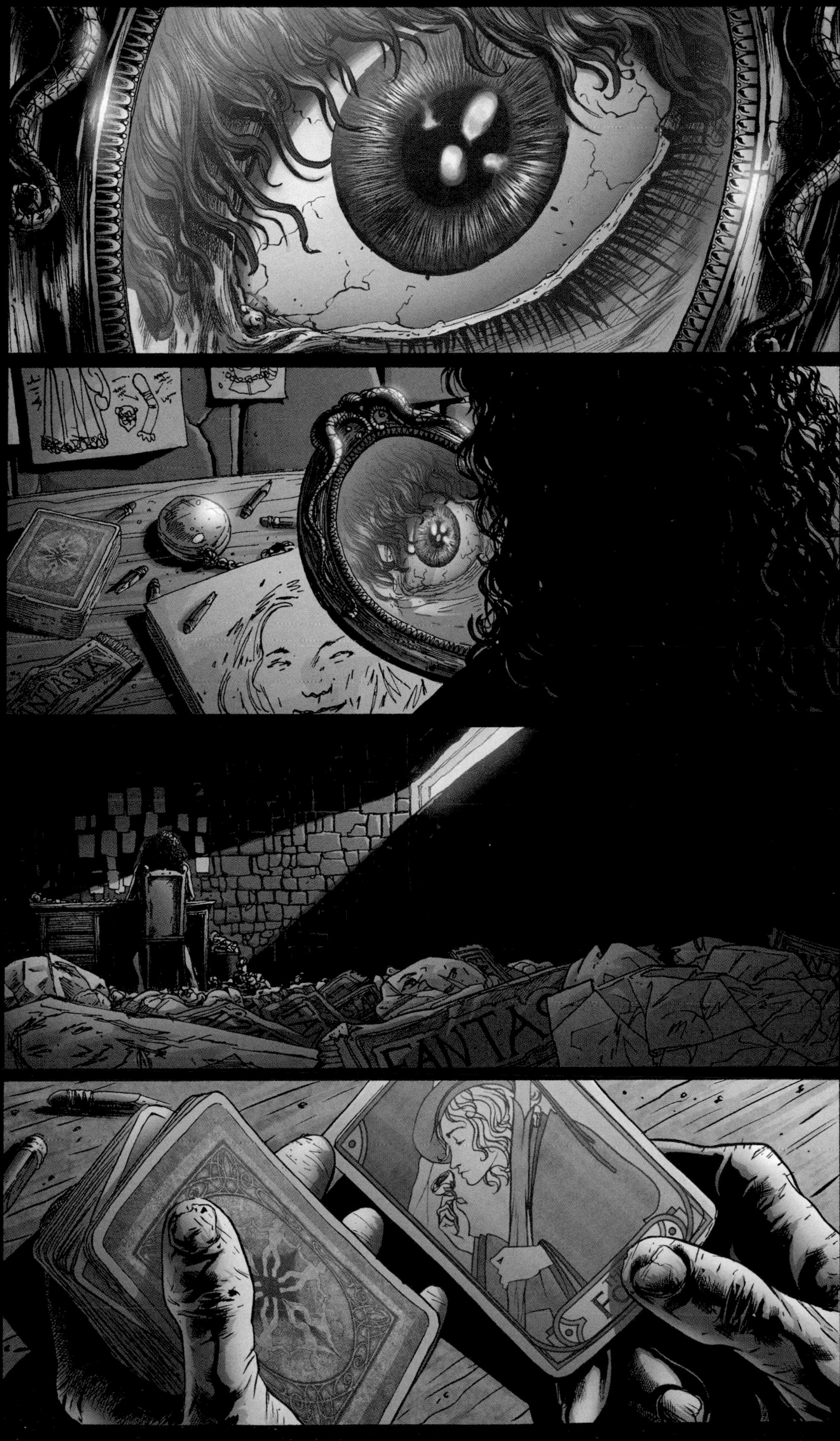

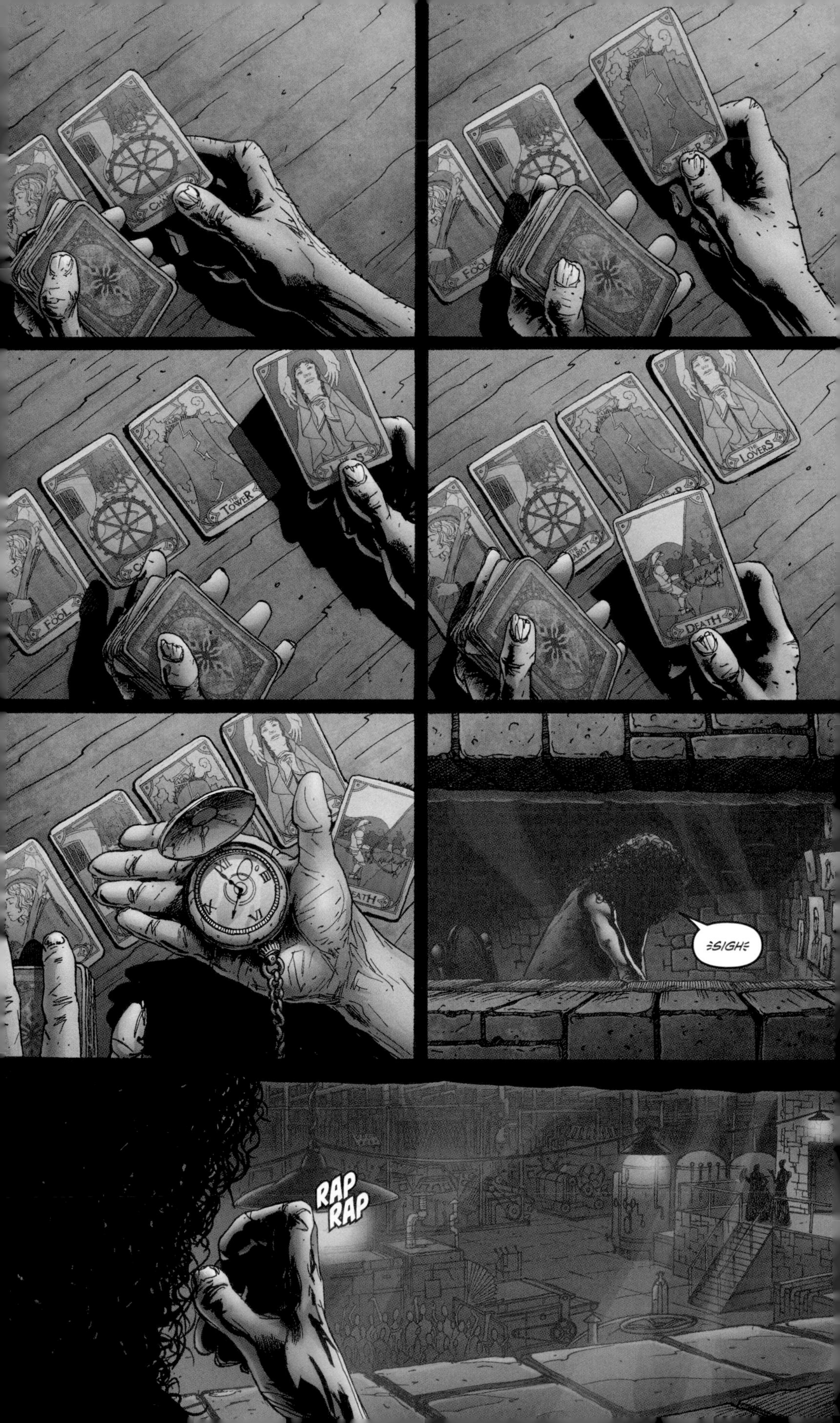
THE FOOL
THE TOWER
THE LOVERS
DEATH
SIGH
RAP RAP

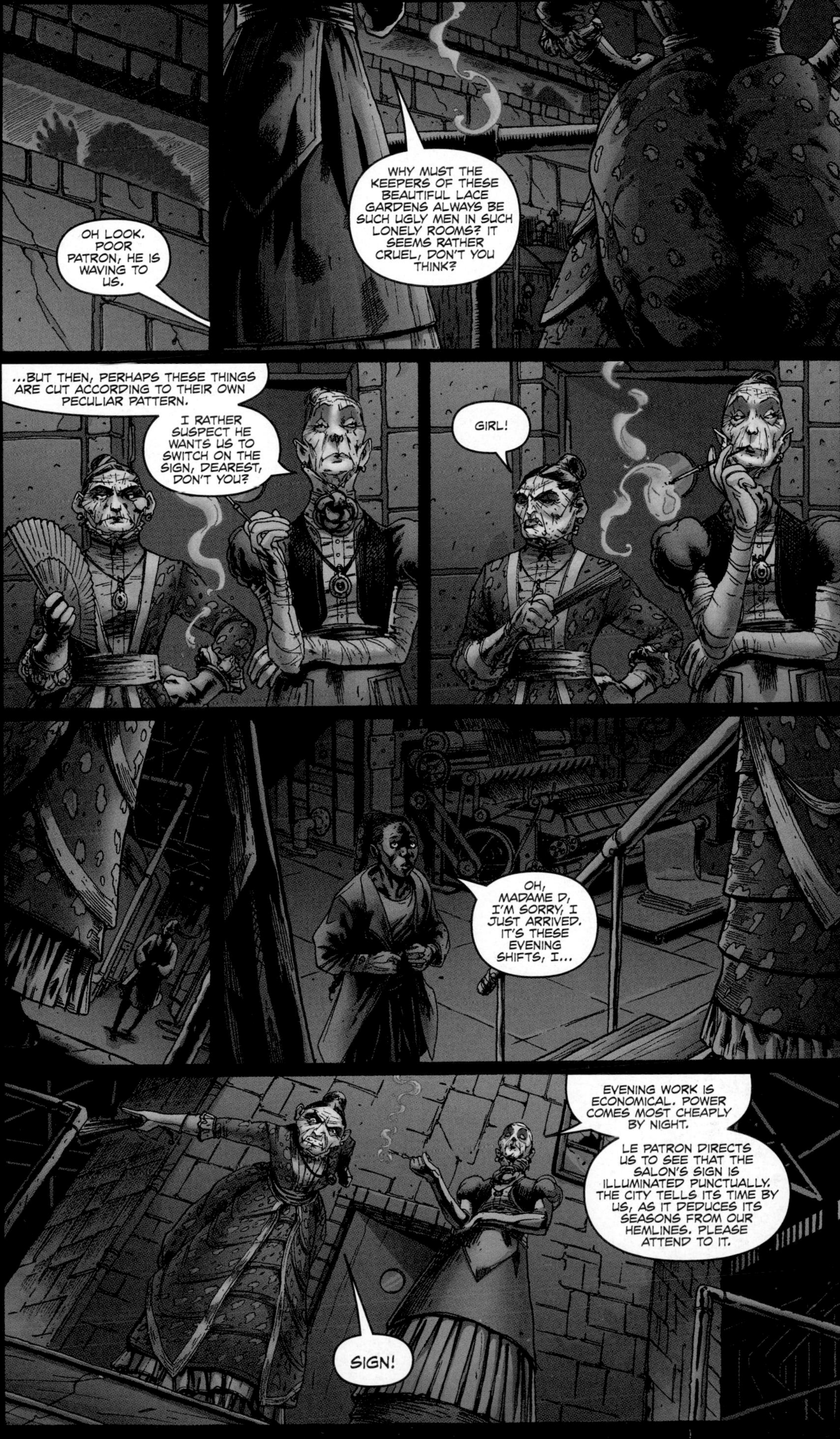
OH LOOK. POOR PATRON, HE IS WAVING TO US.
WHY MUST THE KEEPERS OF THESE BEAUTIFUL LACE GARDENS ALWAYS BE SUCH UGLY MEN IN SUCH LONELY ROOMS? IT SEEMS RATHER CRUEL, DON'T YOU THINK?
...BUT THEN, PERHAPS THESE THINGS ARE CUT ACCORDING TO THEIR OWN PECULIAR PATTERN.
I RATHER SUSPECT HE WANTS US TO SWITCH ON THE SIGN, DEAREST, DON'T YOU?
GIRL!
OH, MADAME D, I'M SORRY, I JUST ARRIVED. IT'S THESE EVENING SHIFTS, I...
EVENING WORK IS ECONOMICAL. POWER COMES MOST CHEAPLY BY NIGHT.
LE PATRON DIRECTS US TO SEE THAT THE SALON'S SIGN IS ILLUMINATED PUNCTUALLY. THE CITY TELLS ITS TIME BY US, AS IT DEDUCES ITS SEASONS FROM OUR HEMLINES. PLEASE ATTEND TO IT.
SIGN!

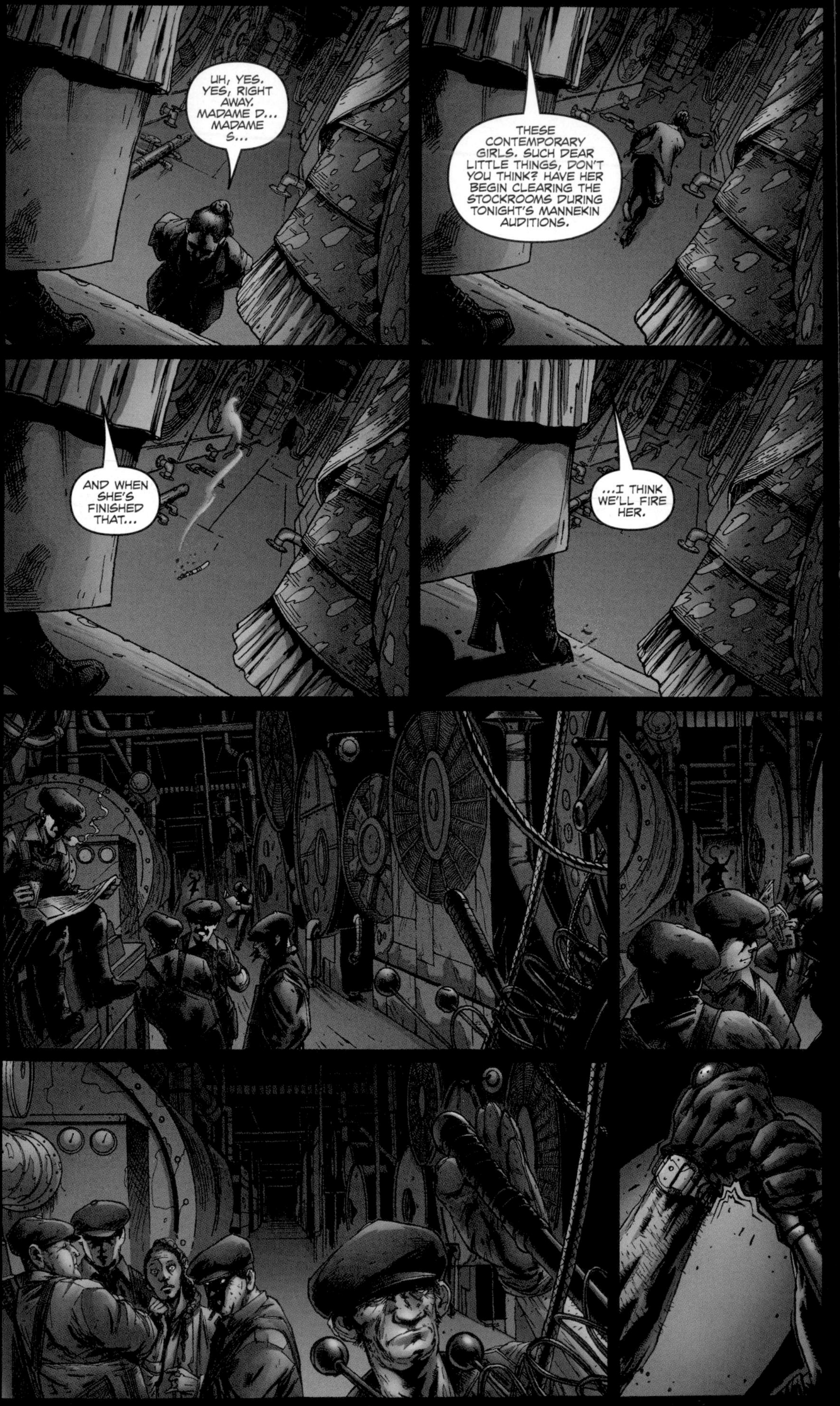

UH, YES. YES, RIGHT AWAY. MADAME D... MADAME S...
THESE CONTEMPORARY GIRLS. SUCH DEAR LITTLE THINGS, DON'T YOU THINK? HAVE HER BEGIN CLEARING THE STOCKROOMS DURING TONIGHT'S MANNEKIN AUDITIONS.
AND WHEN SHE'S FINISHED THAT...
...I THINK WE'LL FIRE HER.

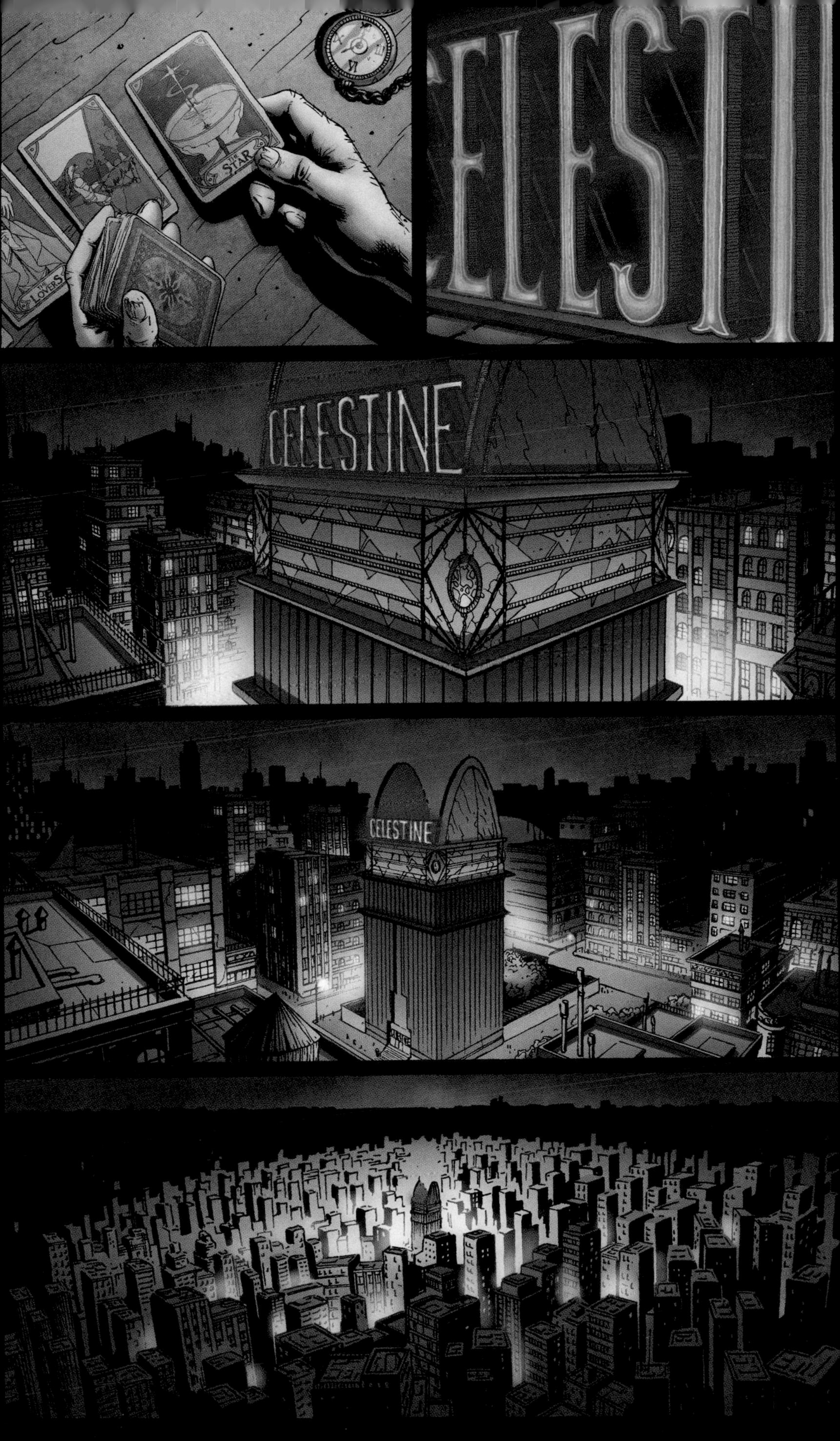
STAR
LOVERS
CELESTINE
CELESTINE

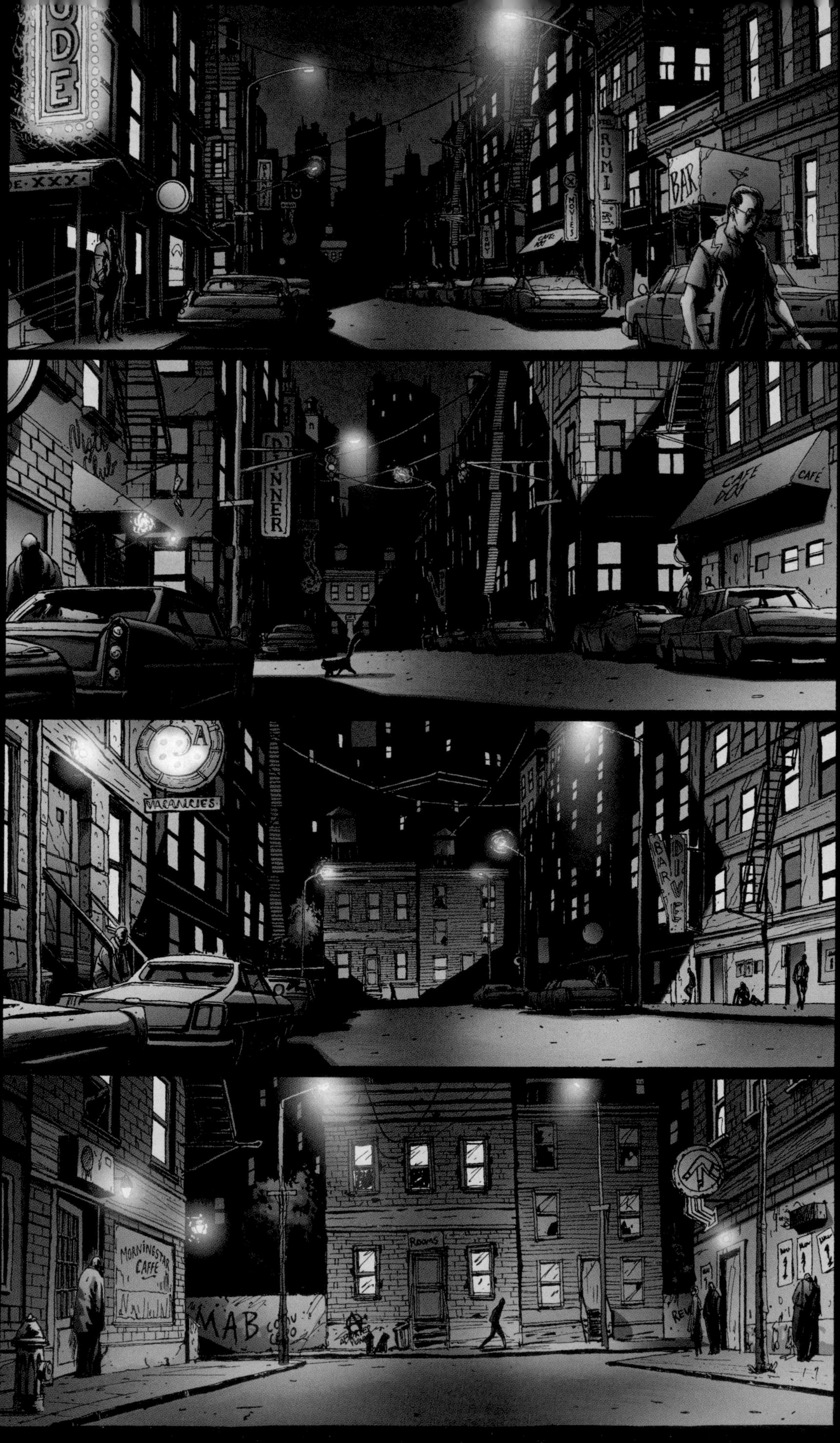
DE
DE·XXX
RUMI
MOVIES
BAR
DINNER
CAFÉ
VACANCIES
BAR
DIVE
MORNINGSTAR
CAFFE
Rooms
MAB

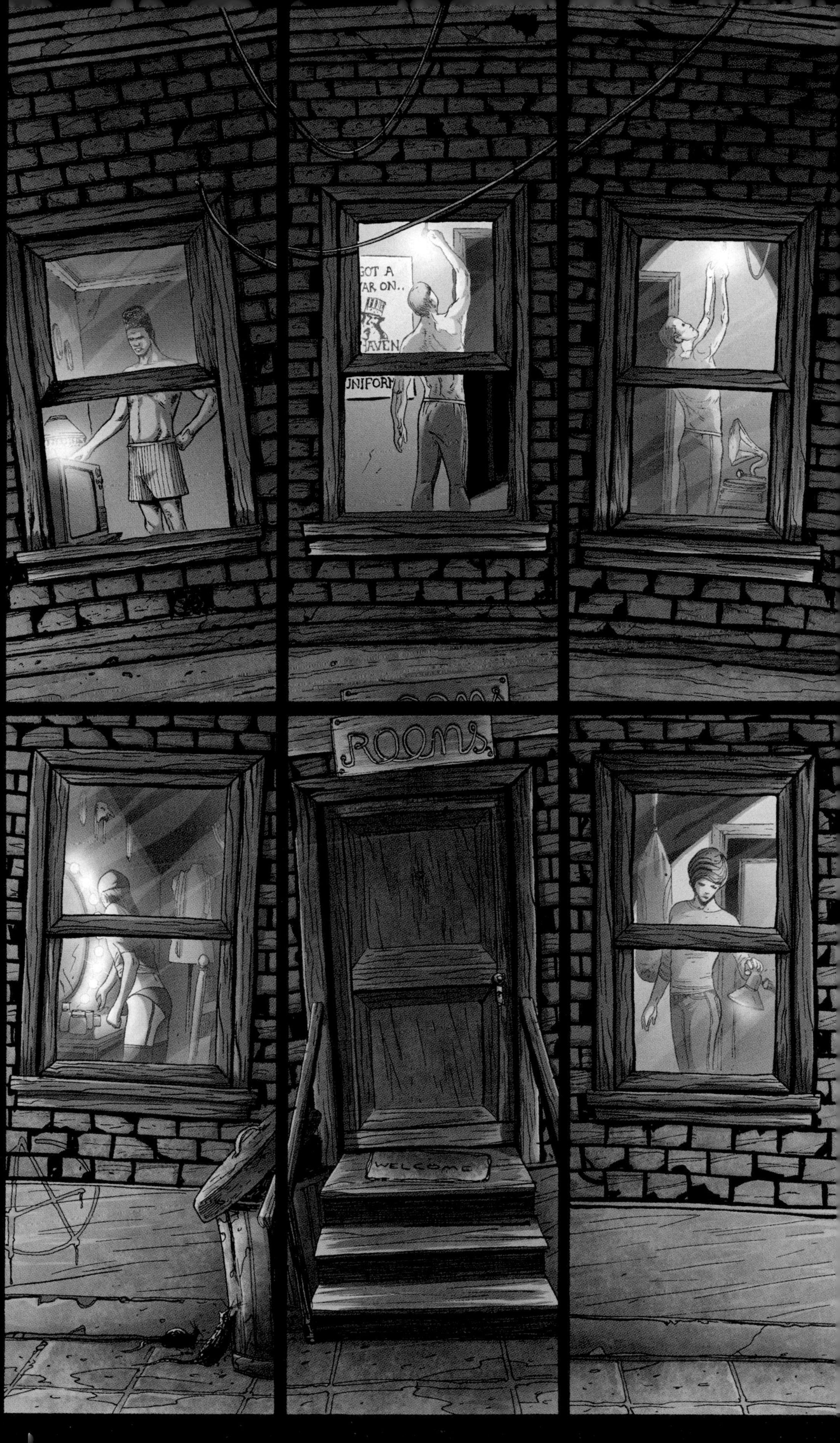
GOT A
ROOMS
WELCOME

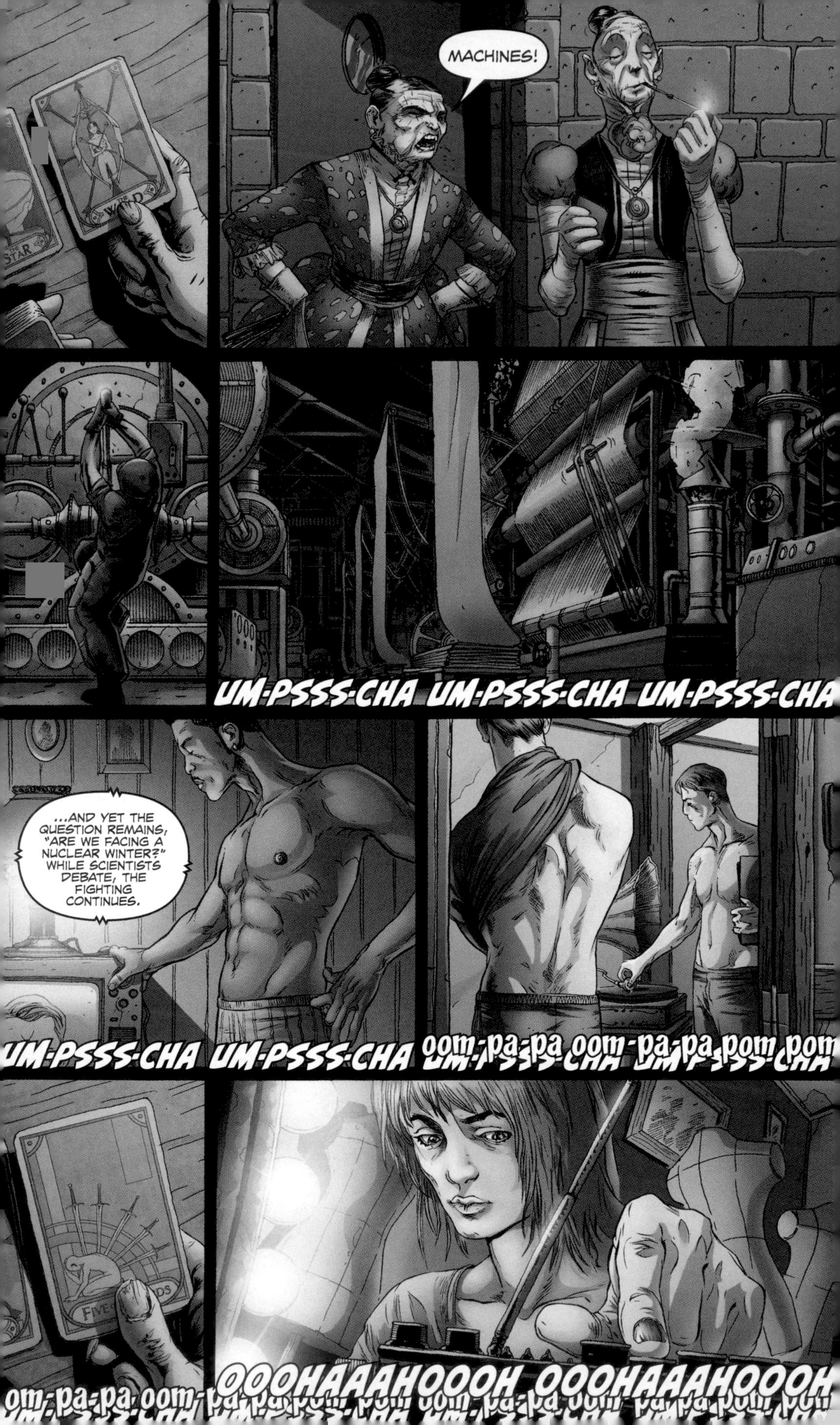
MACHINES!
UM-PSSS-CHA UM-PSSS-CHA UM-PSSS-CHA
...AND YET THE QUESTION REMAINS, "ARE WE FACING A NUCLEAR WINTER?" WHILE SCIENTISTS DEBATE, THE FIGHTING CONTINUES.
UM-PSSS-CHA UM-PSSS-CHA
oom-pa-pa oom-pa-pa pom pom
OOOHAAAHOOOH OOOHAAAHOOOH
om-pa-pa oom-

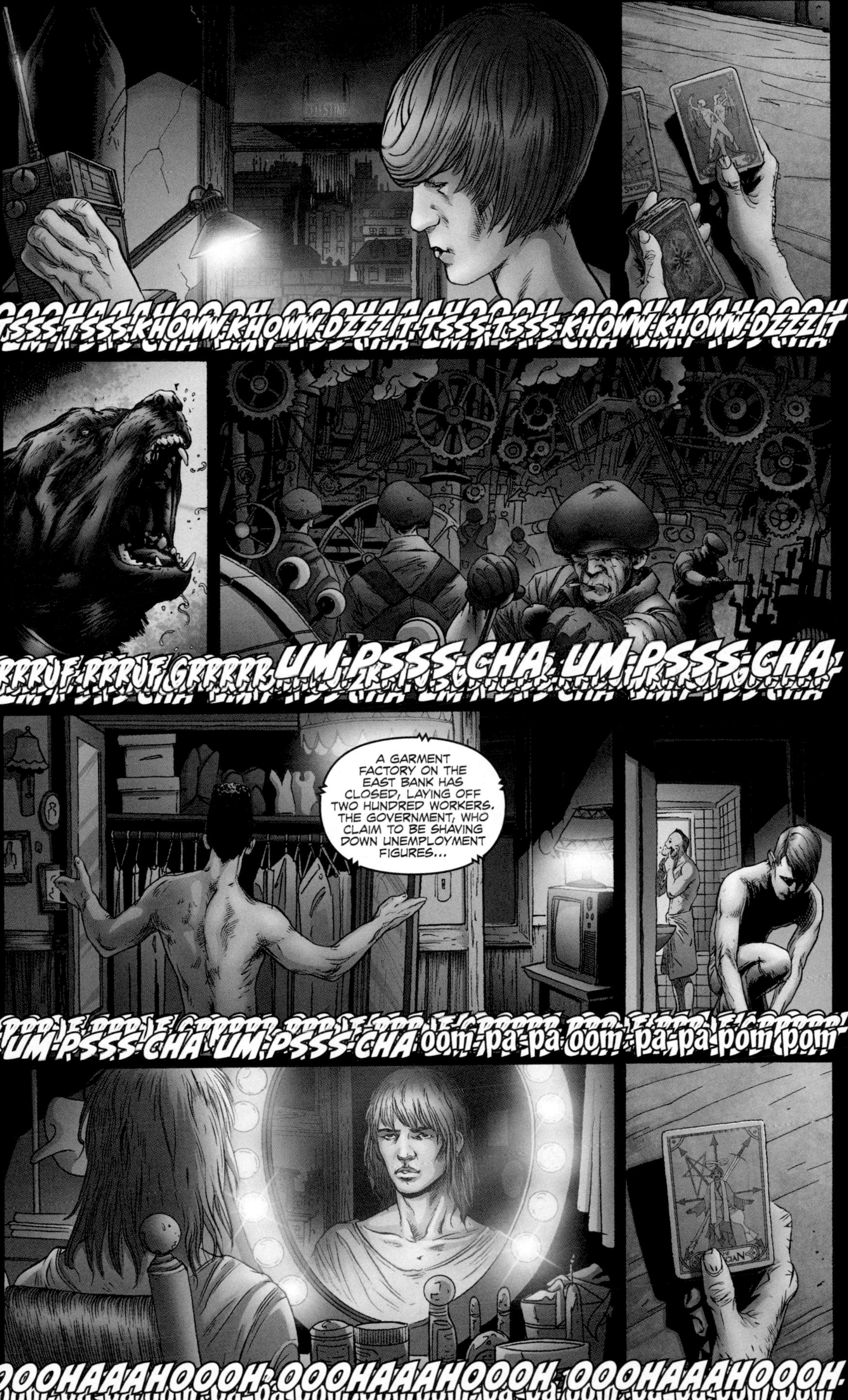
TSSS TSSS KHOWW KHOWW DZZZIT TSSS TSSS KHOWW KHOWW DZZZIT
RRRUF RRRUF GRRRRR
UM PSSS CHA UM PSSS CHA
A GARMENT FACTORY ON THE EAST BANK HAS CLOSED, LAYING OFF TWO HUNDRED WORKERS. THE GOVERNMENT, WHO CLAIM TO BE SHAVING DOWN UNEMPLOYMENT FIGURES...
UM PSSS CHA UM PSSS CHA oom pa pa oom pa pa pom pom
OOOHAAAHOOOH OOOHAAAHOOOH OOOHAAAHOOOH

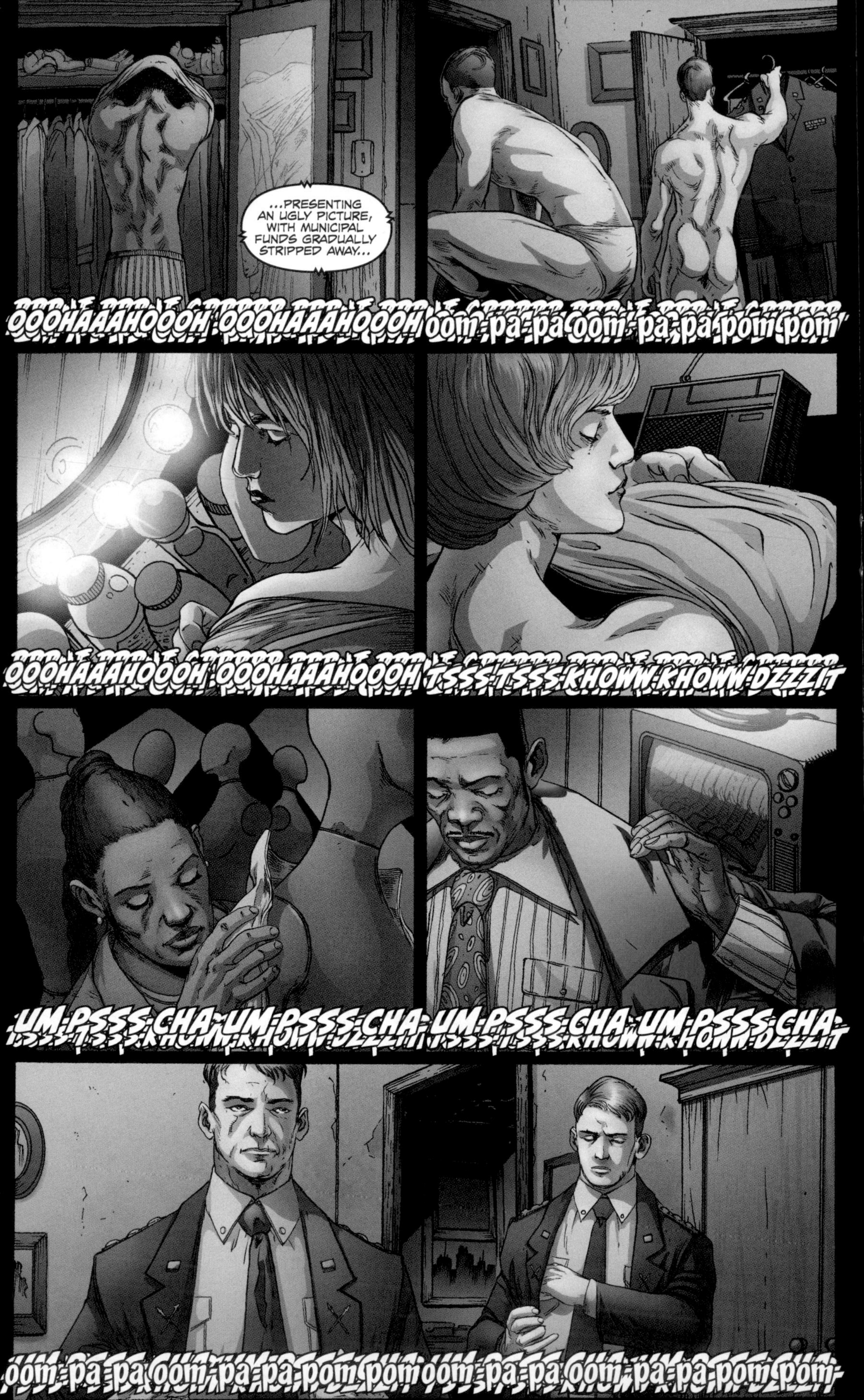
...PRESENTING AN UGLY PICTURE, WITH MUNICIPAL FUNDS GRADUALLY STRIPPED AWAY...
OOOHAAAHOOOH OOOHAAAHOOOH oom-pa-pa oom-pa-pa pom pom
OOOHAAAHOOOH OOOHAAAHOOOH TSSS TSSS KHOWW KHOWW DZZZIT
UM PSSS CHA UM PSSS CHA UM PSSS CHA UM PSSS CHA
oom-pa-pa oom-pa-pa pom pom oom-pa-pa oom-pa-pa pom pom

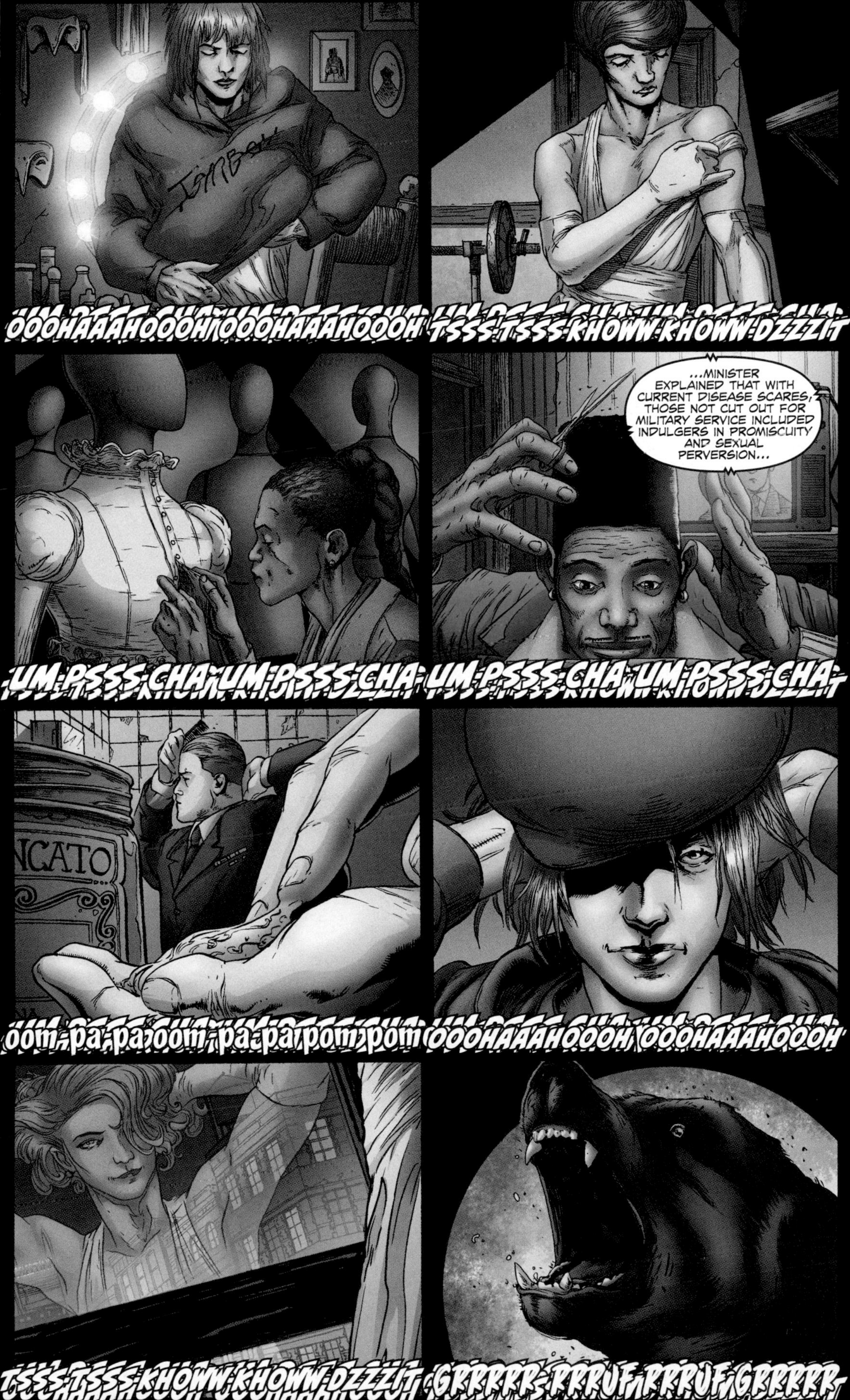
OOOHAAAAHOOOH OOOHAAAAHOOOH
TSSS TSSS KHOWW KHOWW DZZZIT
UM PSSS CHA UM PSSS CHA
...MINISTER EXPLAINED THAT WITH CURRENT DISEASE SCARES, THOSE NOT CUT OUT FOR MILITARY SERVICE INCLUDED INDULGERS IN PROMISCUITY AND SEXUAL PERVERSION...
UM PSSS CHA UM PSSS CHA
NCATO
oom pa pa oom pa pa pom pom
OOOHAAAAHOOOH OOOHAAAAHOOOH
TSSS TSSS KHOWW KHOWW DZZZIT
GRRRRR RRRUF RRRUF GRRRRR

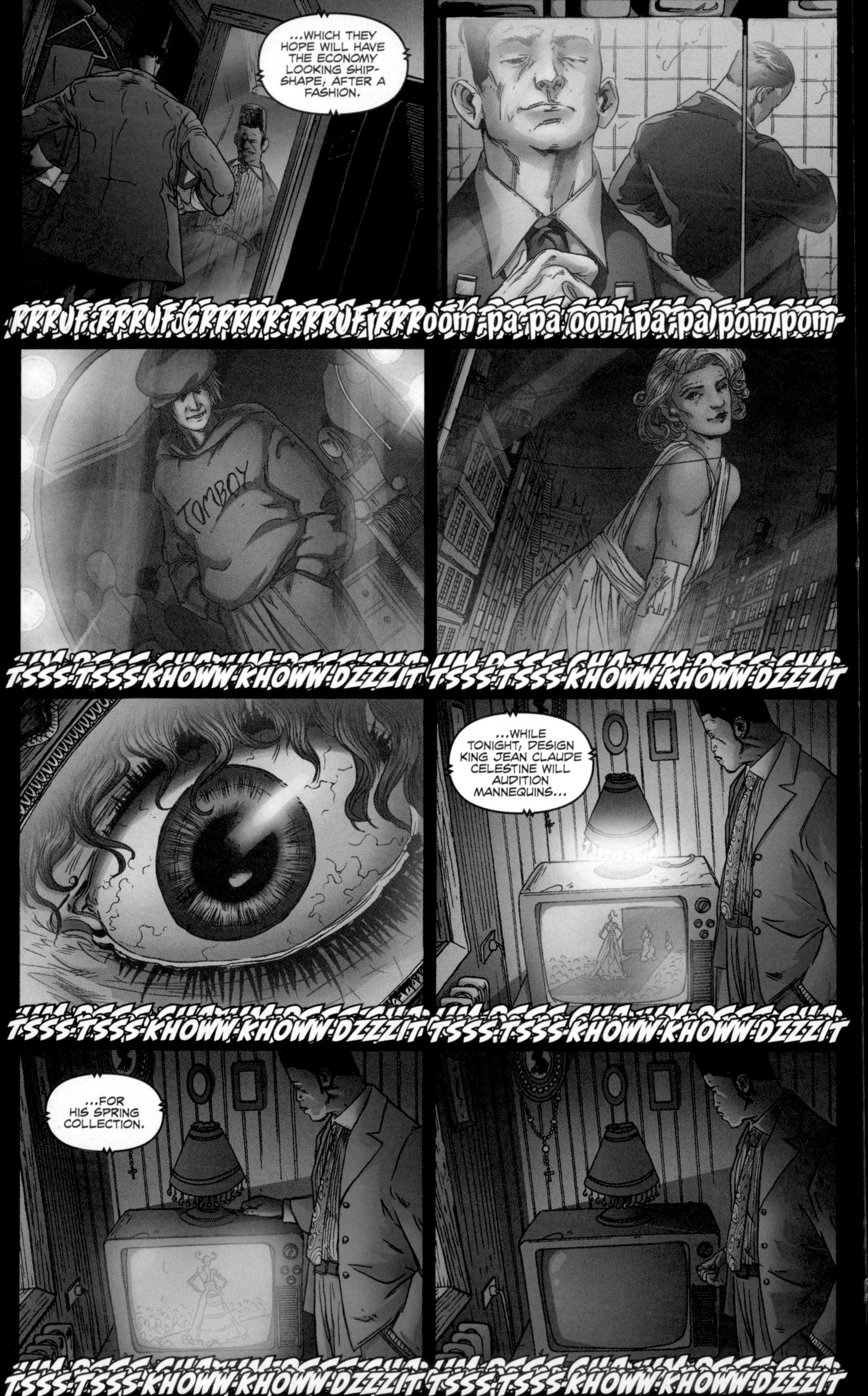
...WHICH THEY HOPE WILL HAVE THE ECONOMY LOOKING SHIP-SHAPE, AFTER A FASHION.
RRRUF RRRUF GRRRRR RRRUF RRRoom-pa-pa oom-pa-pa pom pom
TOMBOY
TSSS TSSS KHOWW KHOWW DZZZIT TSSS TSSS KHOWW KHOWW DZZZIT
...WHILE TONIGHT, DESIGN KING JEAN CLAUDE CELESTINE WILL AUDITION MANNEQUINS...
TSSS TSSS KHOWW KHOWW DZZZIT TSSS TSSS KHOWW KHOWW DZZZIT
...FOR HIS SPRING COLLECTION.
TSSS TSSS KHOWW KHOWW DZZZIT TSSS TSSS KHOWW KHOWW DZZZIT

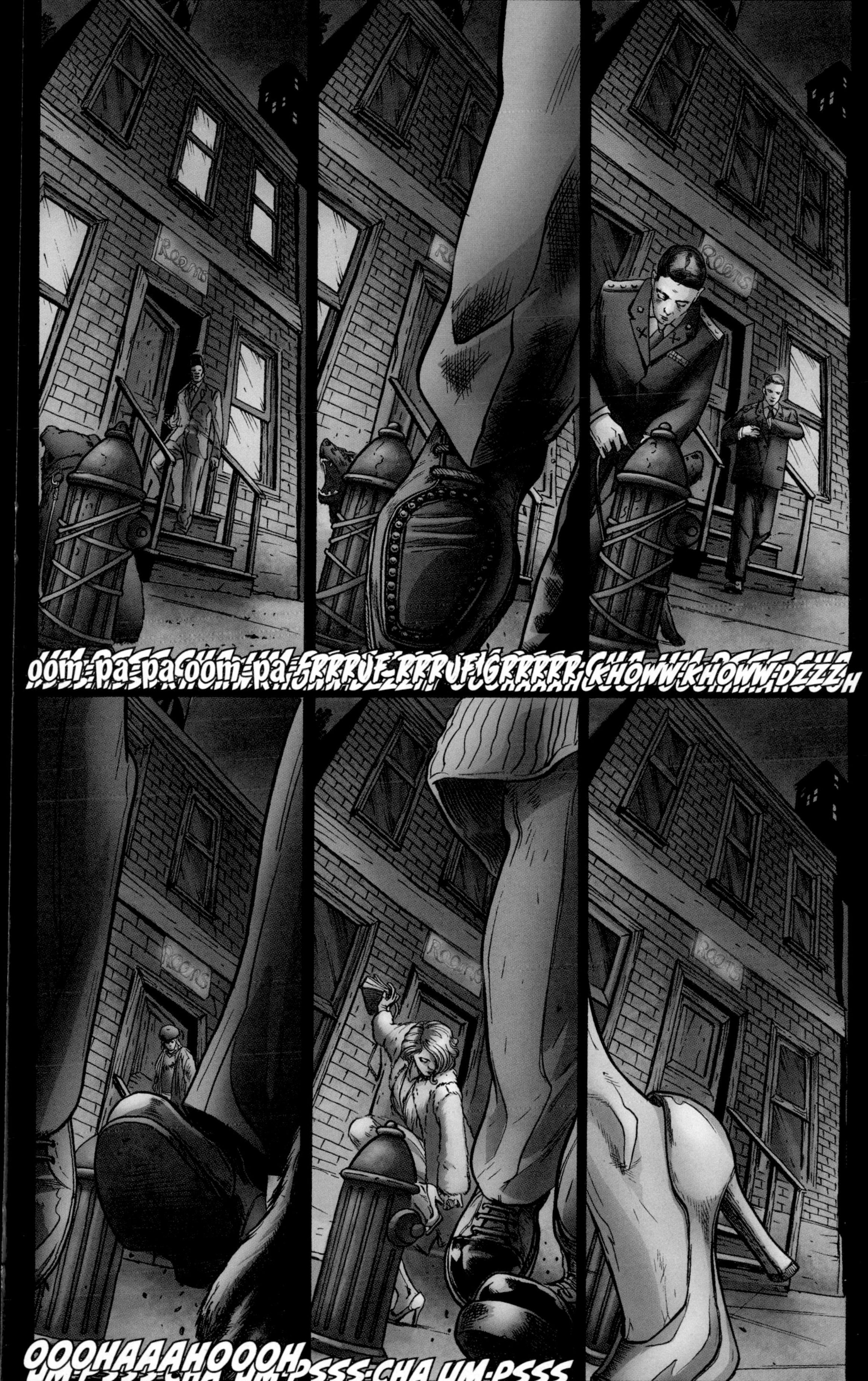
oom-pa-pa oom-pa-
FRRRUF-RRRUF
GRRRRR
KHOWW-KHOWW
DZZZH
OOOHAAAHOOOH
PSSS-CHA UM-PSSS

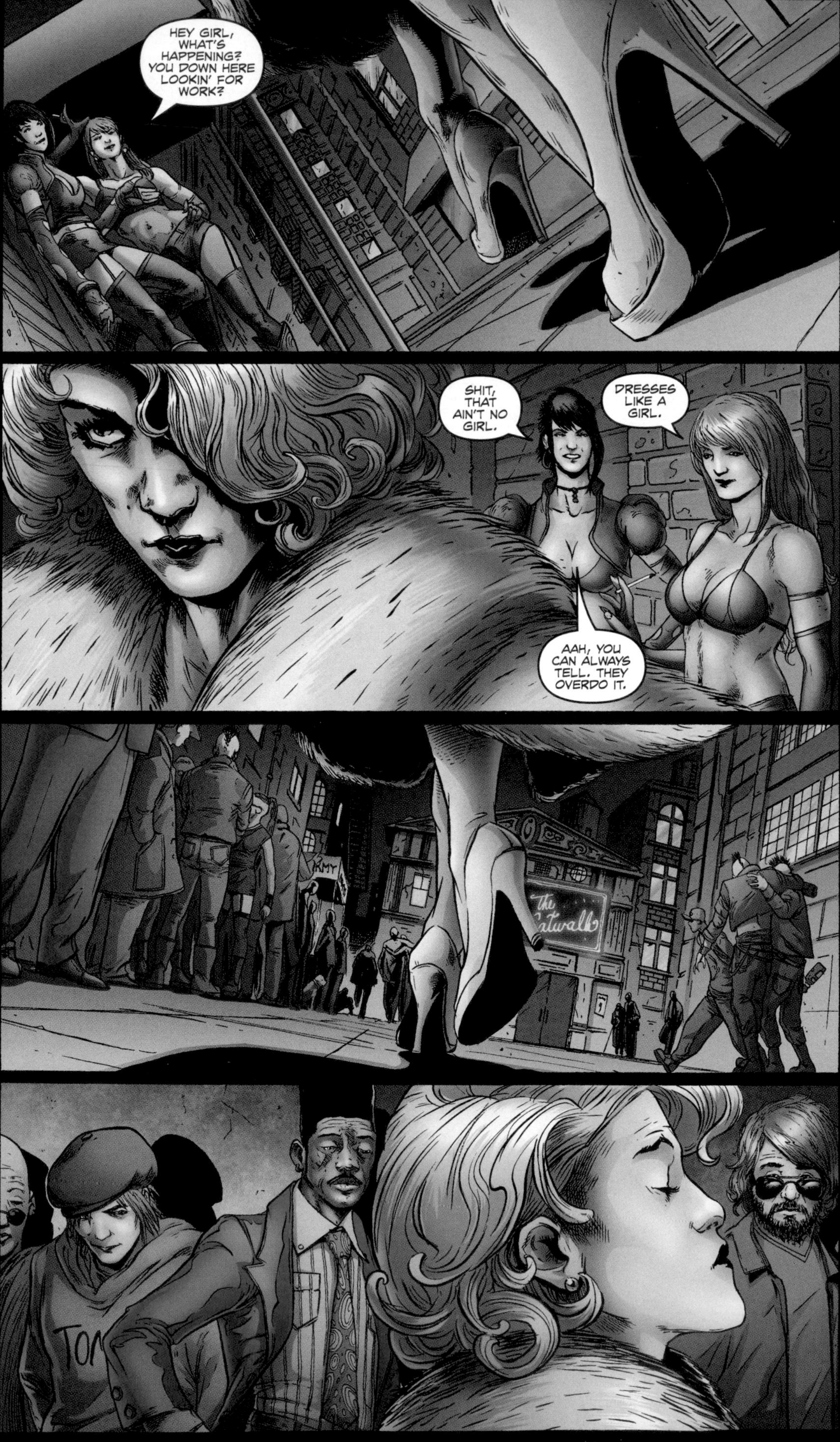
HEY GIRL, WHAT'S HAPPENING? YOU DOWN HERE LOOKIN' FOR WORK?
SHIT, THAT AIN'T NO GIRL.
DRESSES LIKE A GIRL.
AAH, YOU CAN ALWAYS TELL. THEY OVERDO IT.

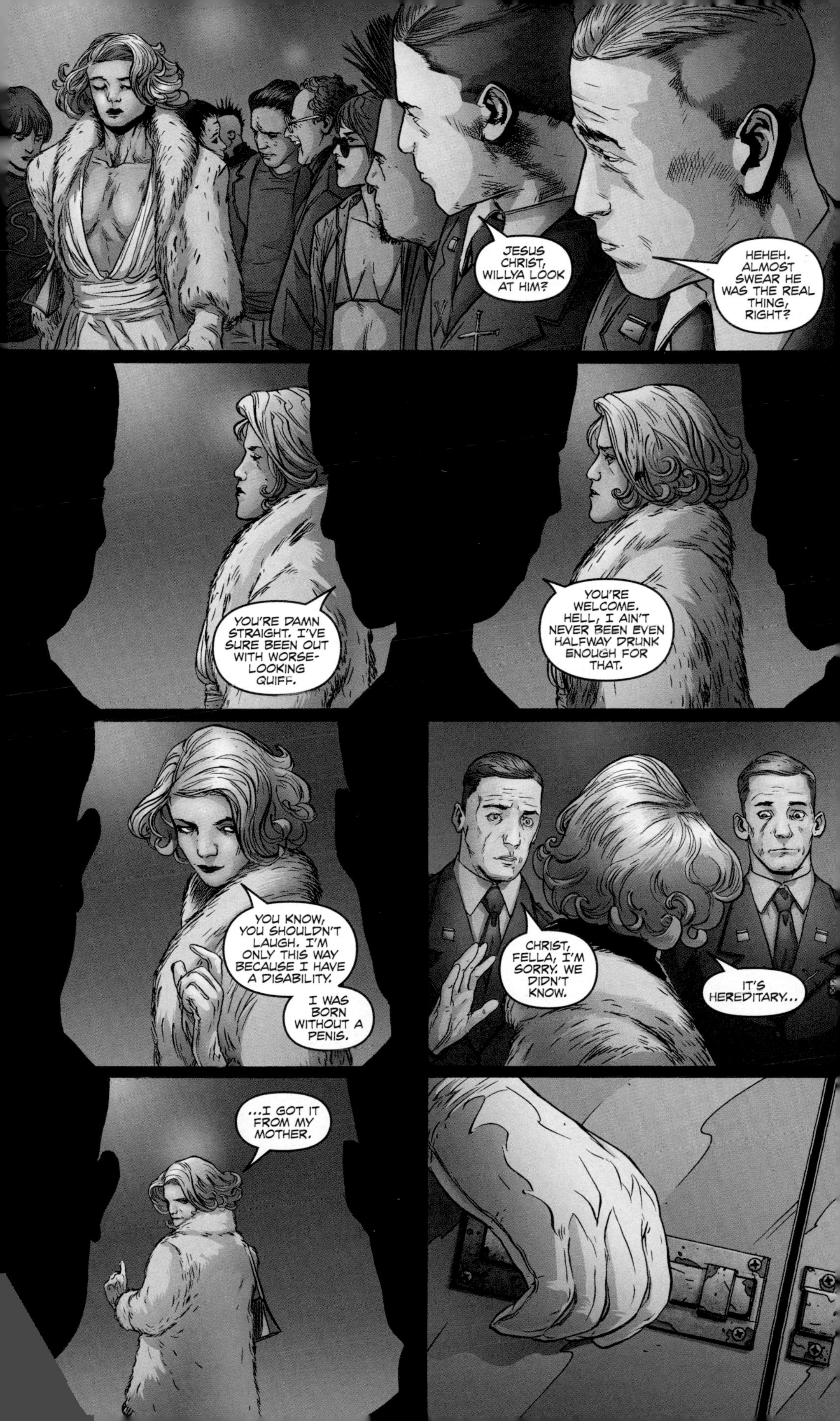
JESUS CHRIST, WILLYA LOOK AT HIM?
HEHEH. ALMOST SWEAR HE WAS THE REAL THING, RIGHT?
YOU'RE DAMN STRAIGHT. I'VE SURE BEEN OUT WITH WORSE-LOOKING QUIFF.
YOU'RE WELCOME. HELL, I AIN'T NEVER BEEN EVEN HALFWAY DRUNK ENOUGH FOR THAT.
YOU KNOW, YOU SHOULDN'T LAUGH. I'M ONLY THIS WAY BECAUSE I HAVE A DISABILITY.
I WAS BORN WITHOUT A PENIS.
CHRIST, FELLA, I'M SORRY. WE DIDN'T KNOW.
IT'S HEREDITARY...
...I GOT IT FROM MY MOTHER.

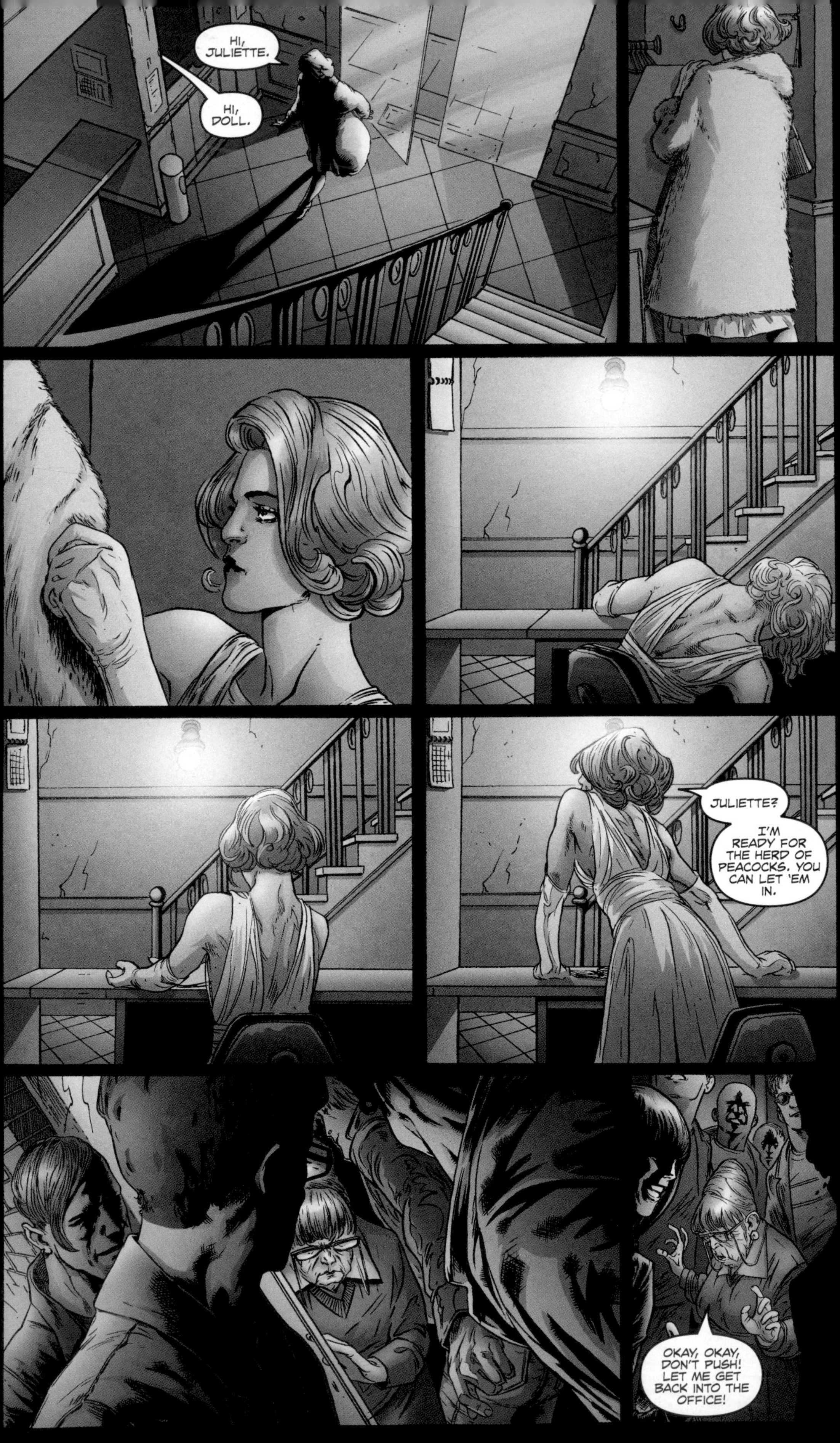
HI, JULIETTE.
HI, DOLL.
JULIETTE?
I'M READY FOR THE HERD OF PEACOCKS. YOU CAN LET 'EM IN.
OKAY, OKAY, DON'T PUSH! LET ME GET BACK INTO THE OFFICE!

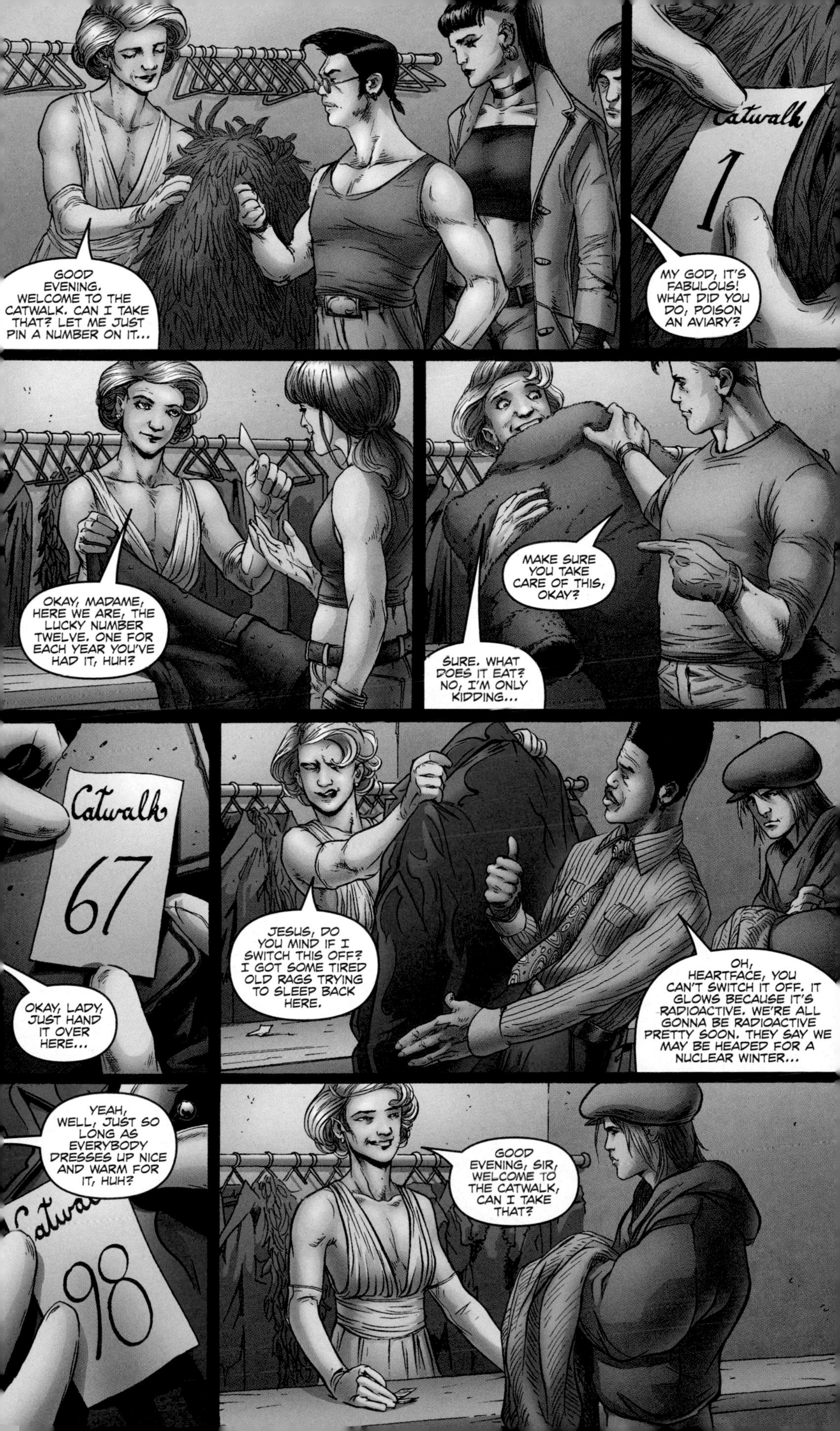
GOOD EVENING. WELCOME TO THE CATWALK. CAN I TAKE THAT? LET ME JUST PIN A NUMBER ON IT...
Catwalk
1
MY GOD, IT'S FABULOUS! WHAT DID YOU DO, POISON AN AVIARY?
OKAY, MADAME, HERE WE ARE, THE LUCKY NUMBER TWELVE. ONE FOR EACH YEAR YOU'VE HAD IT, HUH?
MAKE SURE YOU TAKE CARE OF THIS, OKAY?
SURE. WHAT DOES IT EAT? NO, I'M ONLY KIDDING...
Catwalk
67
OKAY, LADY, JUST HAND IT OVER HERE...
JESUS, DO YOU MIND IF I SWITCH THIS OFF? I GOT SOME TIRED OLD RAGS TRYING TO SLEEP BACK HERE.
OH, HEARTFACE, YOU CAN'T SWITCH IT OFF. IT GLOWS BECAUSE IT'S RADIOACTIVE. WE'RE ALL GONNA BE RADIOACTIVE PRETTY SOON. THEY SAY WE MAY BE HEADED FOR A NUCLEAR WINTER...
YEAH, WELL, JUST SO LONG AS EVERYBODY DRESSES UP NICE AND WARM FOR IT, HUH?
98
GOOD EVENING, SIR, WELCOME TO THE CATWALK, CAN I TAKE THAT?

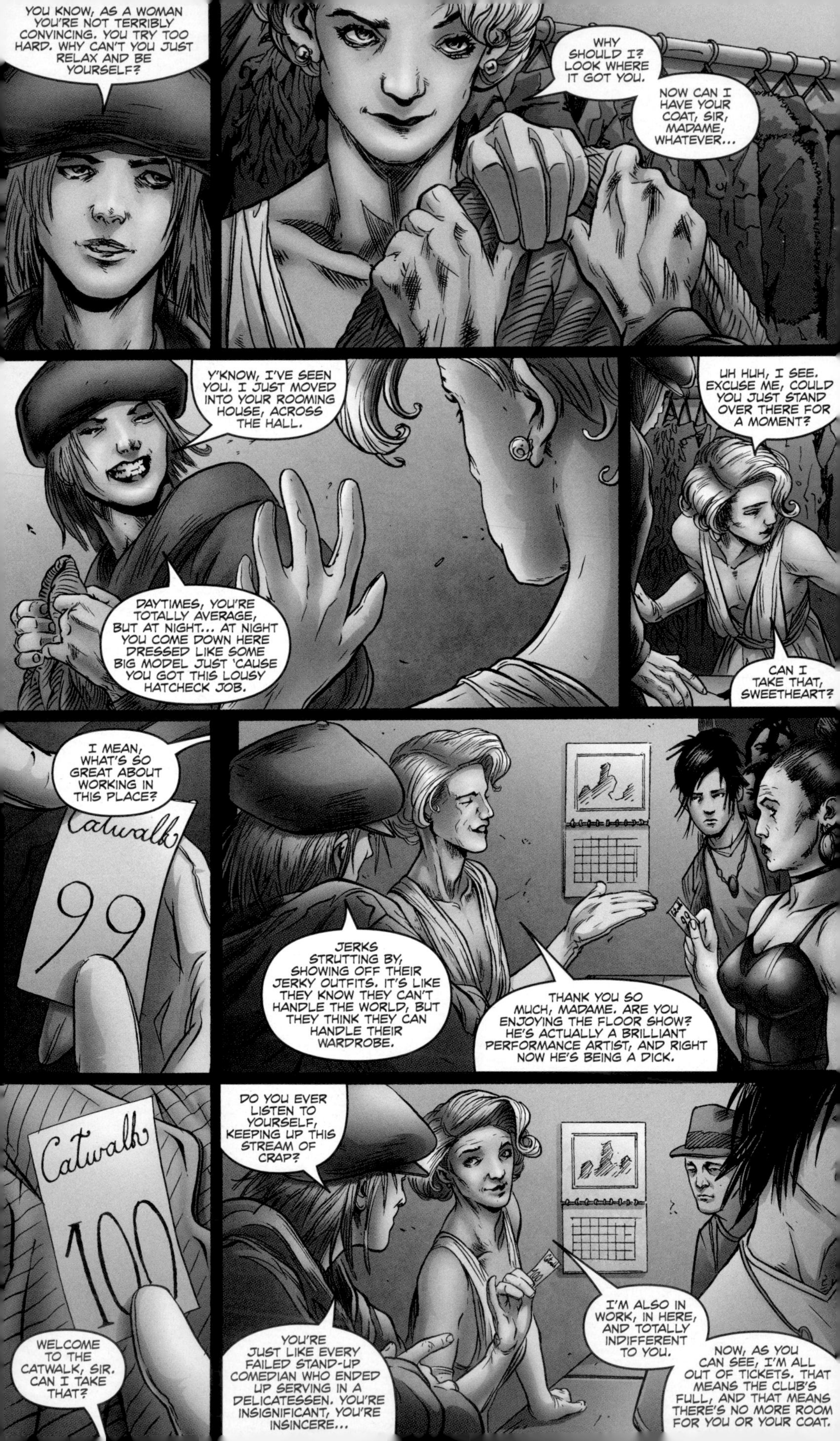
YOU KNOW, AS A WOMAN YOU'RE NOT TERRIBLY CONVINCING. YOU TRY TOO HARD. WHY CAN'T YOU JUST RELAX AND BE YOURSELF?
WHY SHOULD I? LOOK WHERE IT GOT YOU.
NOW CAN I HAVE YOUR COAT, SIR, MADAME, WHATEVER...
Y'KNOW, I'VE SEEN YOU. I JUST MOVED INTO YOUR ROOMING HOUSE, ACROSS THE HALL.
DAYTIMES, YOU'RE TOTALLY AVERAGE, BUT AT NIGHT... AT NIGHT YOU COME DOWN HERE DRESSED LIKE SOME BIG MODEL JUST 'CAUSE YOU GOT THIS LOUSY HATCHECK JOB.
UH HUH, I SEE. EXCUSE ME, COULD YOU JUST STAND OVER THERE FOR A MOMENT?
CAN I TAKE THAT, SWEETHEART?
I MEAN, WHAT'S SO GREAT ABOUT WORKING IN THIS PLACE?
Catwalk
99
JERKS STRUTTING BY, SHOWING OFF THEIR JERKY OUTFITS. IT'S LIKE THEY KNOW THEY CAN'T HANDLE THE WORLD, BUT THEY THINK THEY CAN HANDLE THEIR WARDROBE.
THANK YOU SO MUCH, MADAME. ARE YOU ENJOYING THE FLOOR SHOW? HE'S ACTUALLY A BRILLIANT PERFORMANCE ARTIST, AND RIGHT NOW HE'S BEING A DICK.
Catwalk
100
WELCOME TO THE CATWALK, SIR. CAN I TAKE THAT?
DO YOU EVER LISTEN TO YOURSELF, KEEPING UP THIS STREAM OF CRAP?
YOU'RE JUST LIKE EVERY FAILED STAND-UP COMEDIAN WHO ENDED UP SERVING IN A DELICATESSEN. YOU'RE INSIGNIFICANT, YOU'RE INSINCERE...
I'M ALSO IN WORK, IN HERE, AND TOTALLY INDIFFERENT TO YOU.
NOW, AS YOU CAN SEE, I'M ALL OUT OF TICKETS. THAT MEANS THE CLUB'S FULL, AND THAT MEANS THERE'S NO MORE ROOM FOR YOU OR YOUR COAT.

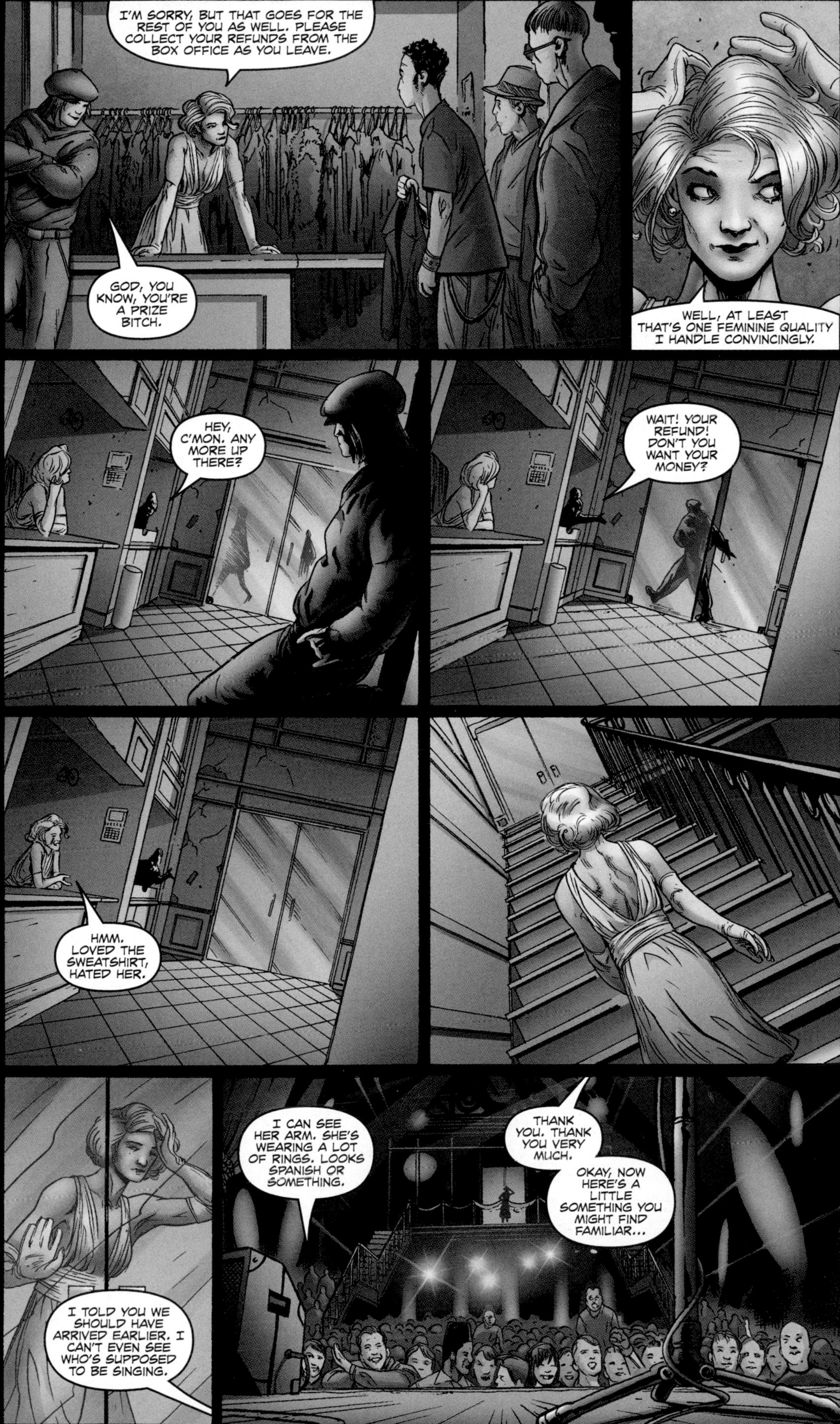
I'M SORRY; BUT THAT GOES FOR THE REST OF YOU AS WELL. PLEASE COLLECT YOUR REFUNDS FROM THE BOX OFFICE AS YOU LEAVE.
GOD, YOU KNOW, YOU'RE A PRIZE BITCH.
WELL, AT LEAST THAT'S ONE FEMININE QUALITY I HANDLE CONVINCINGLY.
HEY, C'MON. ANY MORE UP THERE?
WAIT! YOUR REFUND! DON'T YOU WANT YOUR MONEY?
HMM. LOVED THE SWEATSHIRT, HATED HER.
I TOLD YOU WE SHOULD HAVE ARRIVED EARLIER. I CAN'T EVEN SEE WHO'S SUPPOSED TO BE SINGING.
I CAN SEE HER ARM. SHE'S WEARING A LOT OF RINGS. LOOKS SPANISH OR SOMETHING.
THANK YOU. THANK YOU VERY MUCH.
OKAY, NOW HERE'S A LITTLE SOMETHING YOU MIGHT FIND FAMILIAR...

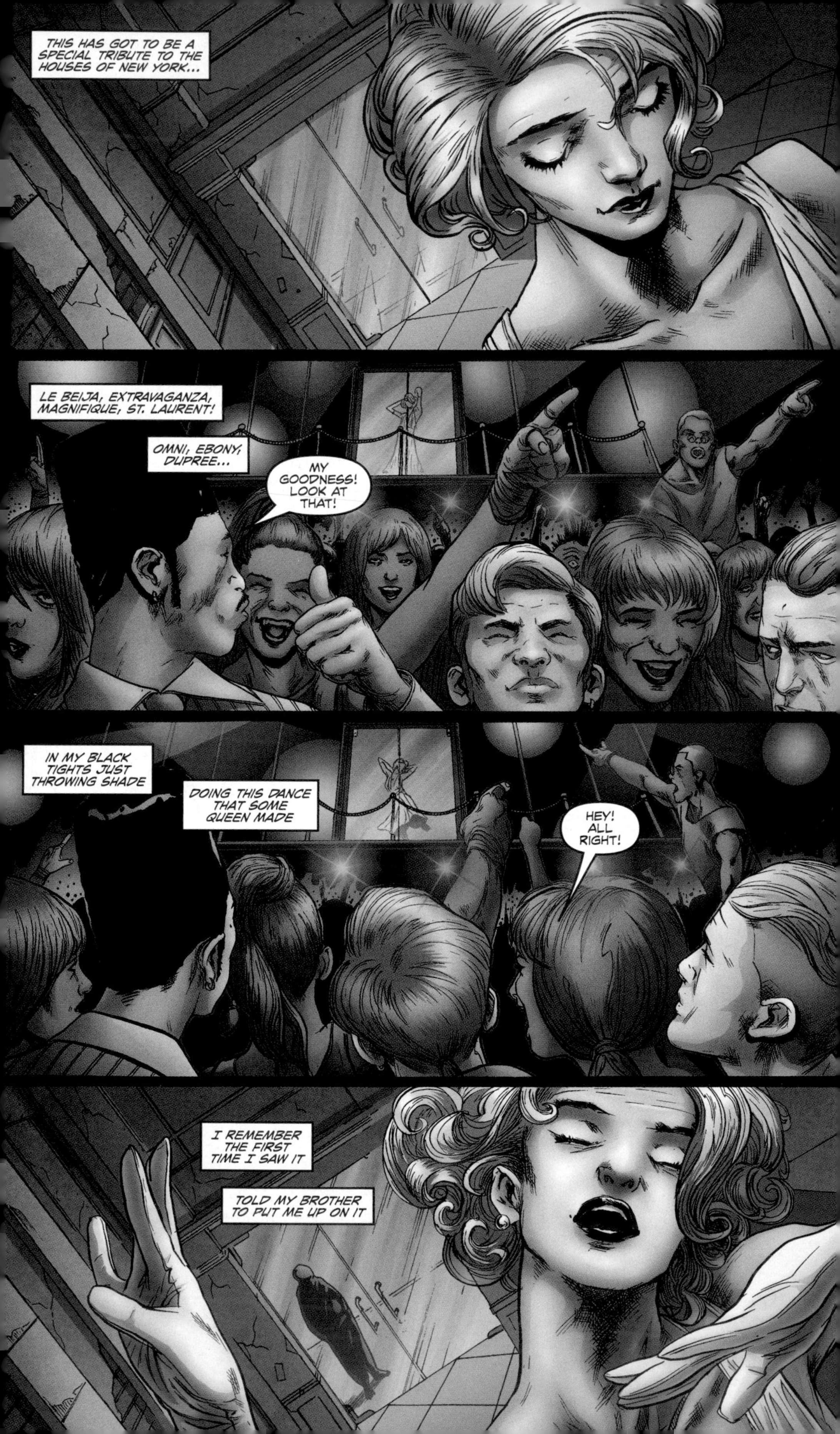
THIS HAS GOT TO BE A SPECIAL TRIBUTE TO THE HOUSES OF NEW YORK...
LE BEIJA, EXTRAVAGANZA, MAGNIFIQUE, ST. LAURENT!
OMNI, EBONY, DUPREE...
MY GOODNESS! LOOK AT THAT!
IN MY BLACK TIGHTS JUST THROWING SHADE
DOING THIS DANCE THAT SOME QUEEN MADE
HEY! ALL RIGHT!
I REMEMBER THE FIRST TIME I SAW IT
TOLD MY BROTHER TO PUT ME UP ON IT

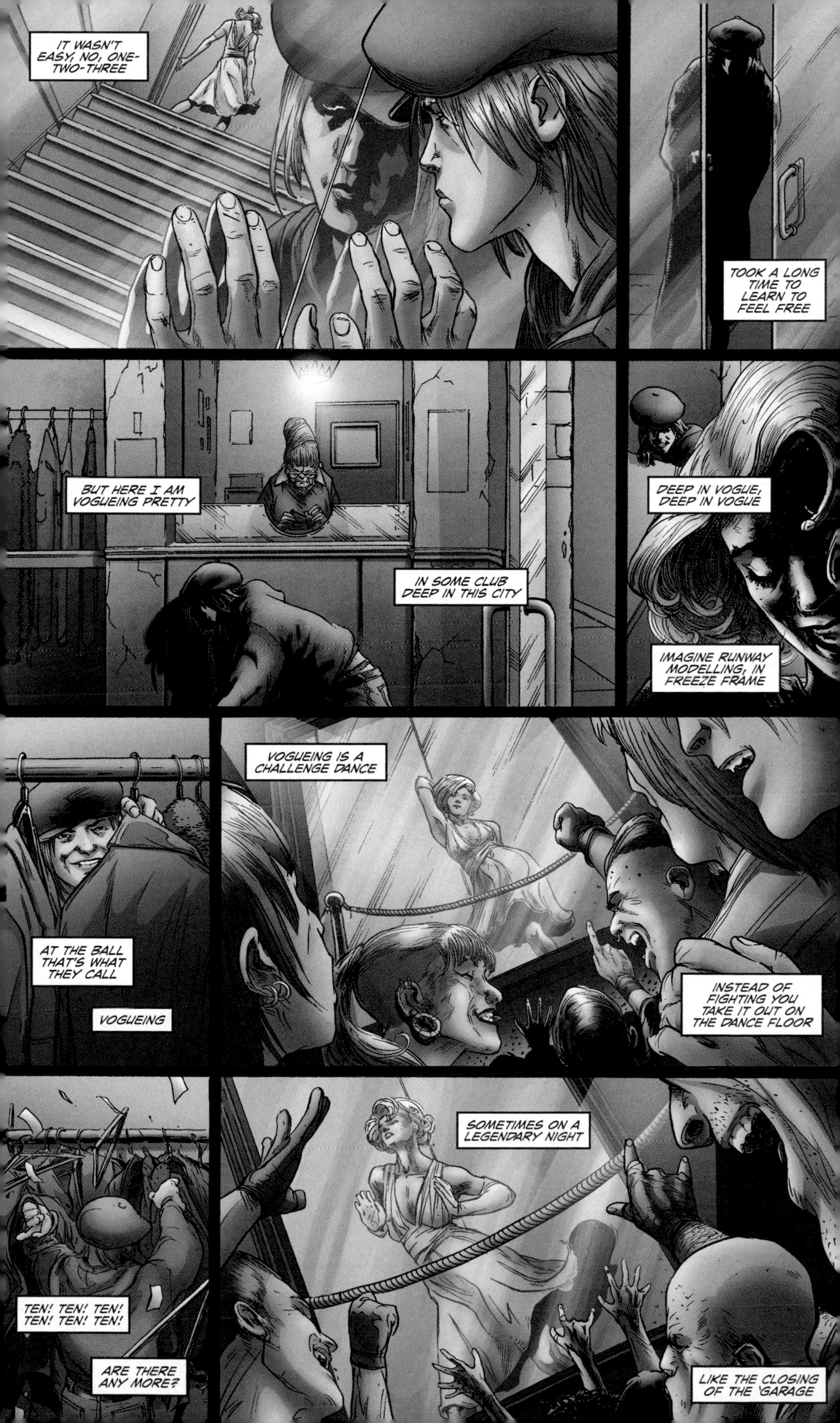
IT WASN'T EASY, NO, ONE-TWO-THREE
TOOK A LONG TIME TO LEARN TO FEEL FREE
BUT HERE I AM VOGUEING PRETTY
IN SOME CLUB DEEP IN THIS CITY
DEEP IN VOGUE, DEEP IN VOGUE
IMAGINE RUNWAY MODELLING, IN FREEZE FRAME
VOGUEING IS A CHALLENGE DANCE
AT THE BALL THAT'S WHAT THEY CALL
VOGUEING
INSTEAD OF FIGHTING YOU TAKE IT OUT ON THE DANCE FLOOR
TEN! TEN! TEN! TEN! TEN! TEN!
ARE THERE ANY MORE?
SOMETIMES ON A LEGENDARY NIGHT
LIKE THE CLOSING OF THE 'GARAGE

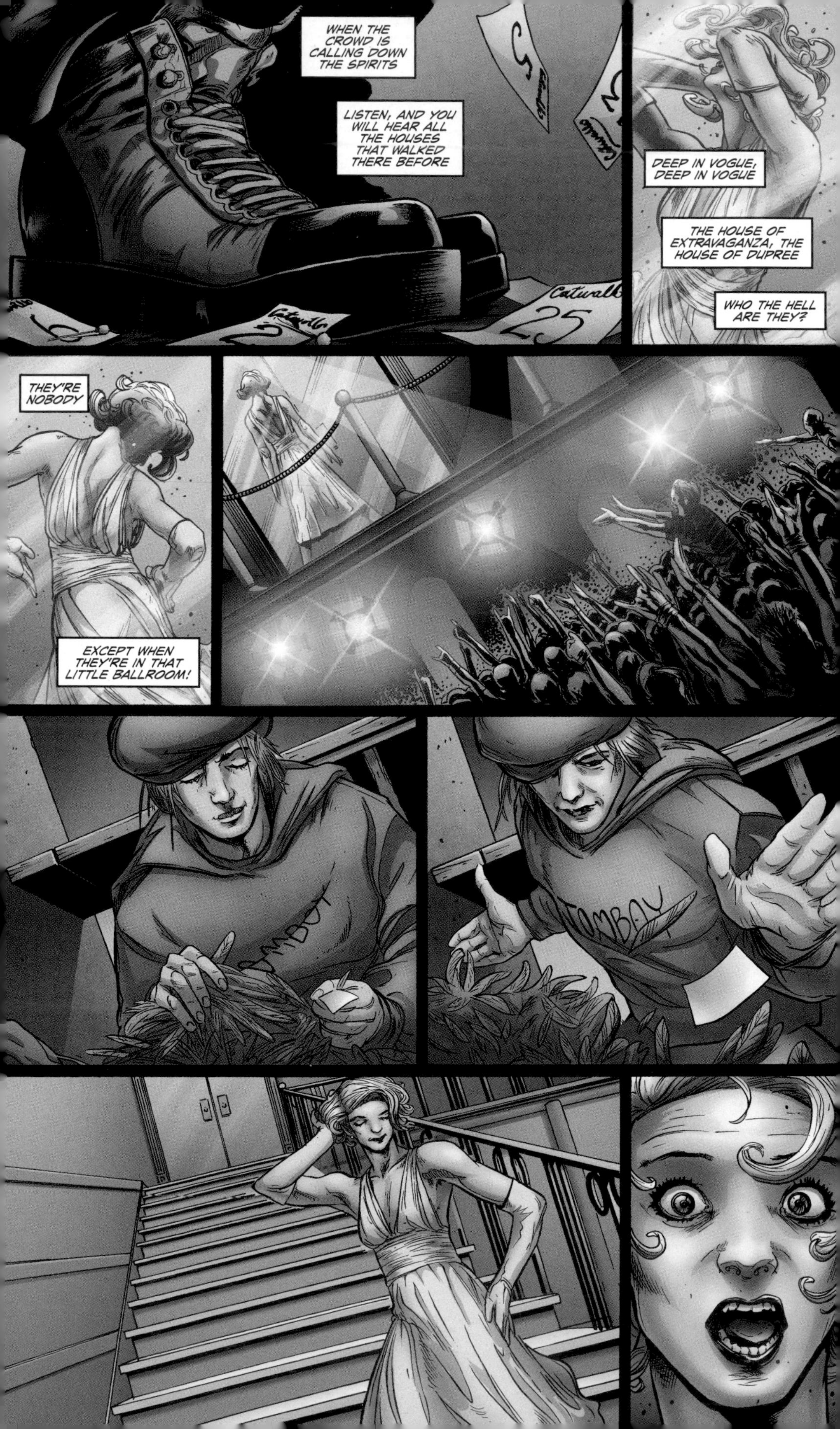
WHEN THE CROWD IS CALLING DOWN THE SPIRITS
LISTEN, AND YOU WILL HEAR ALL THE HOUSES THAT WALKED THERE BEFORE
Catwalk
25
DEEP IN VOGUE, DEEP IN VOGUE
THE HOUSE OF EXTRAVAGANZA, THE HOUSE OF DUPREE
WHO THE HELL ARE THEY?
THEY'RE NOBODY
EXCEPT WHEN THEY'RE IN THAT LITTLE BALLROOM!
TOMBOY

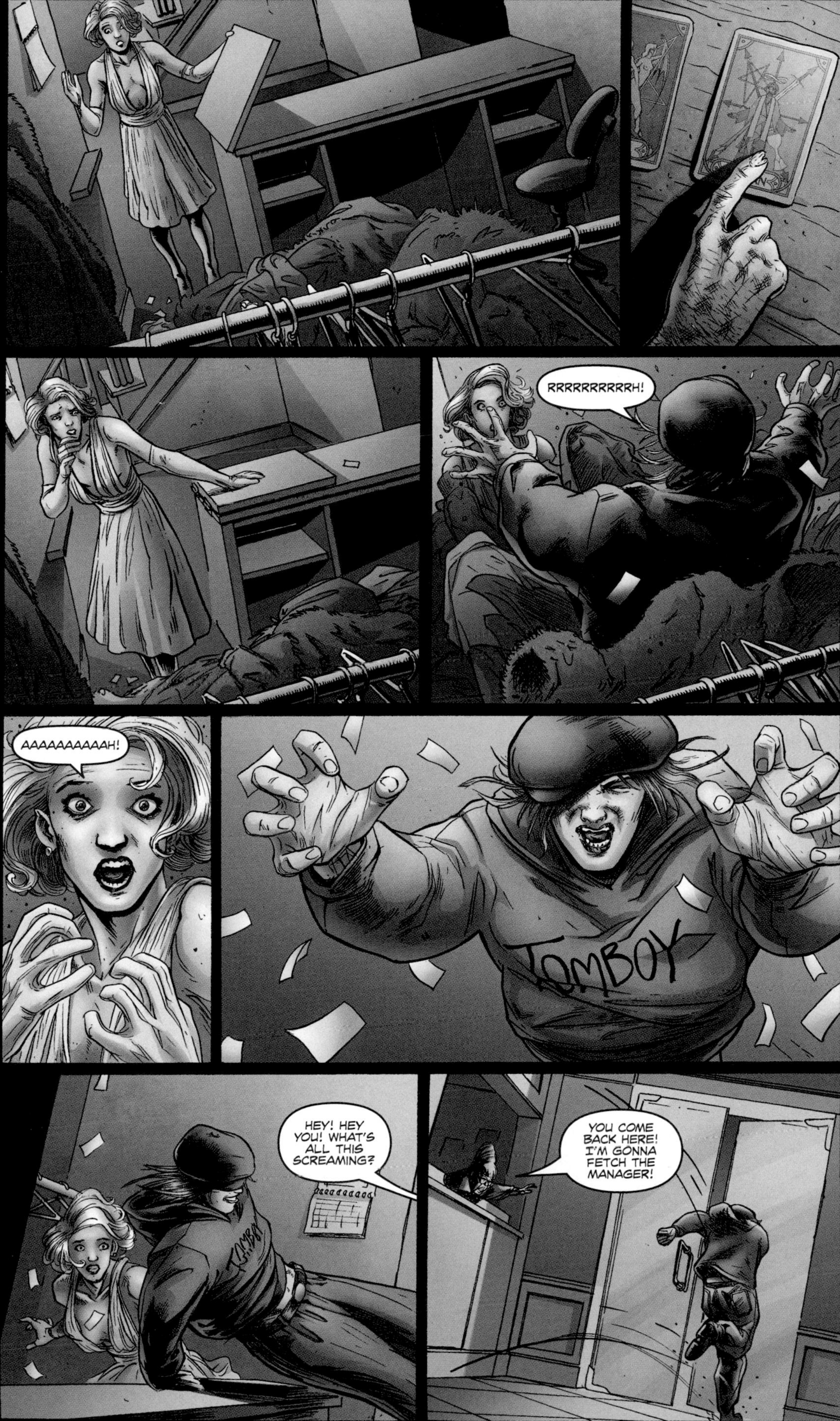
RRRRRRRRRRH!
AAAAAAAAAAAH!
TOMBOY
HEY! HEY YOU! WHAT'S ALL THIS SCREAMING?
YOU COME BACK HERE! I'M GONNA FETCH THE MANAGER!

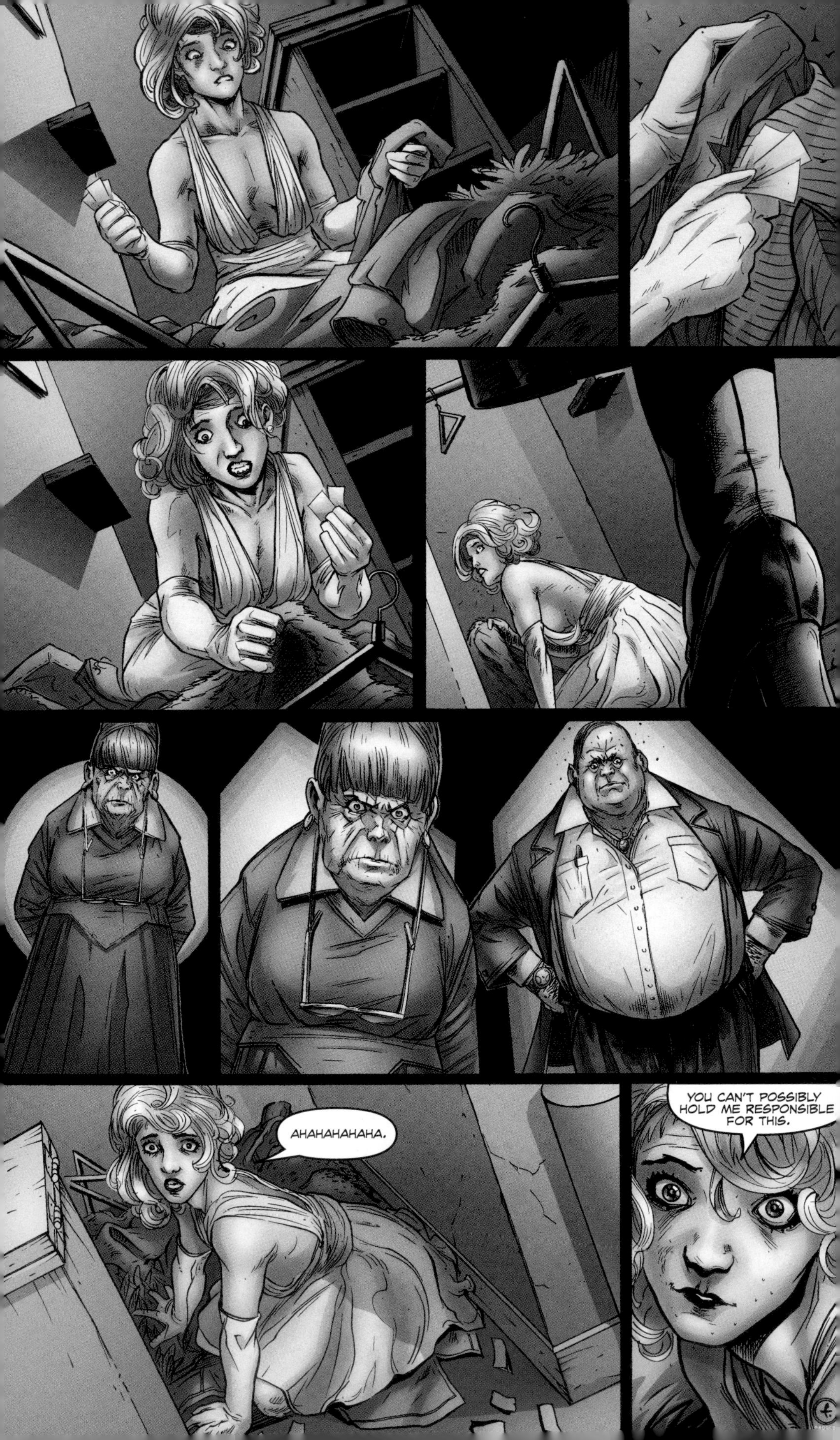
AHAHAHAHAHA.
YOU CAN'T POSSIBLY HOLD ME RESPONSIBLE FOR THIS.

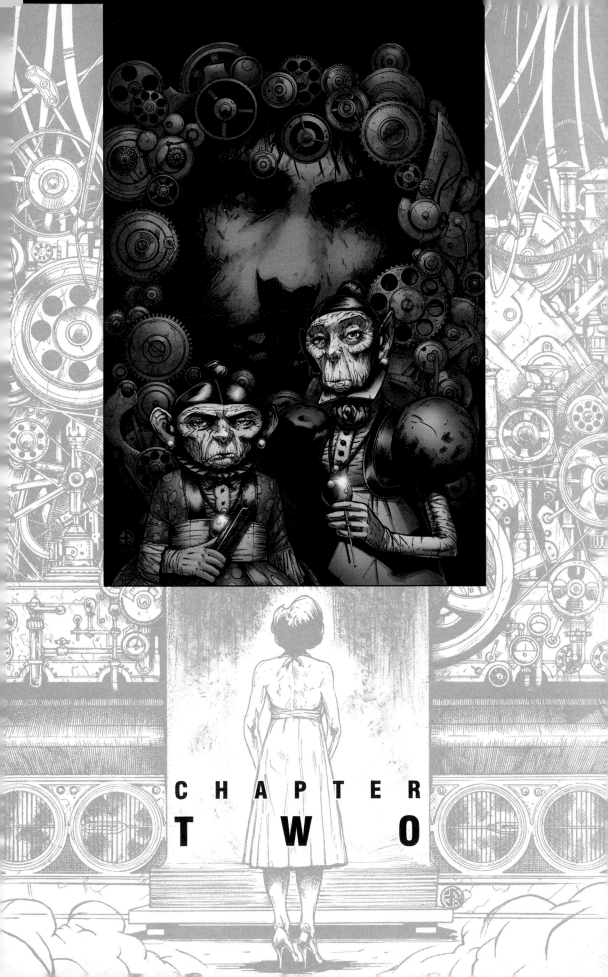

CHAPTER
TWO

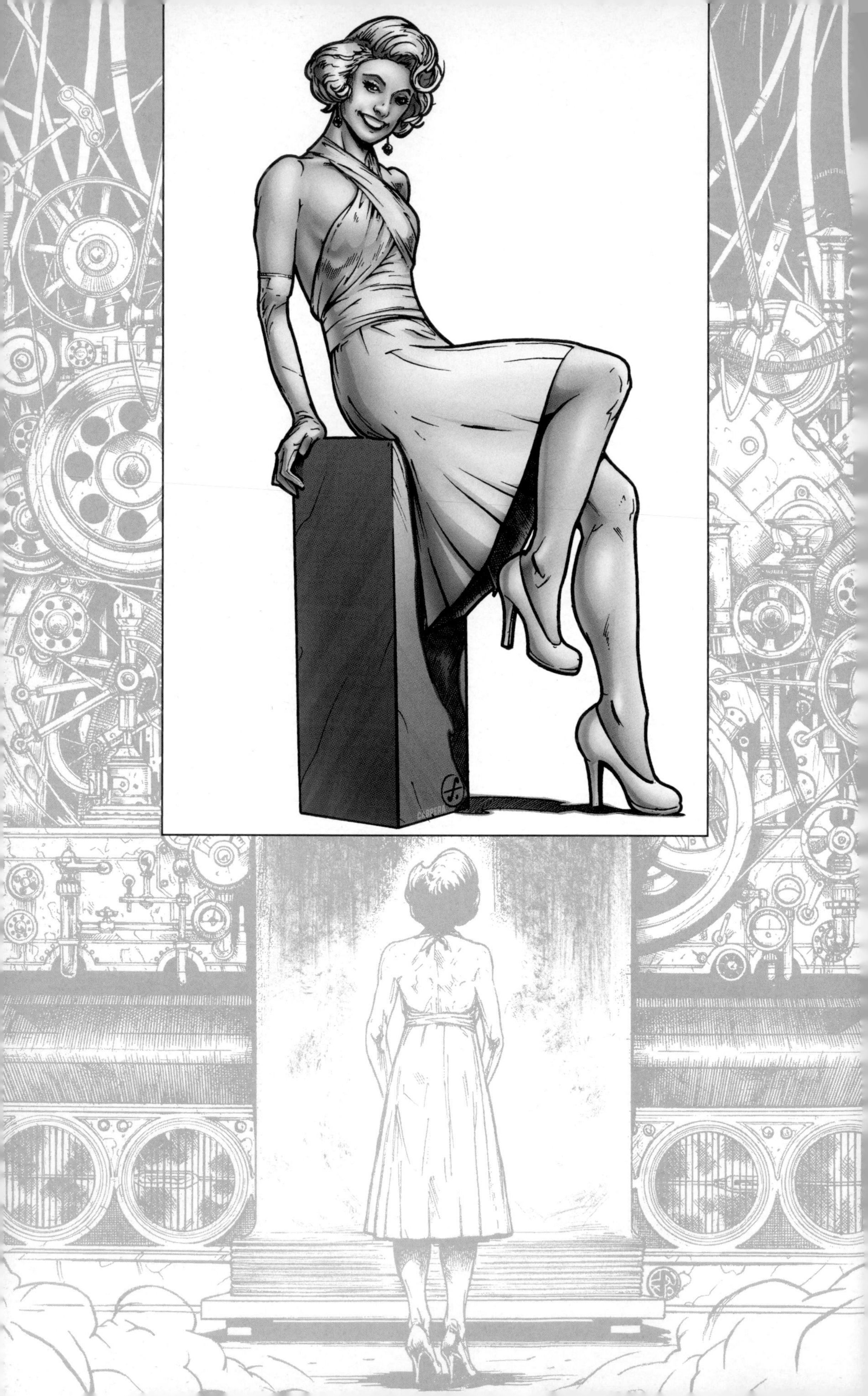

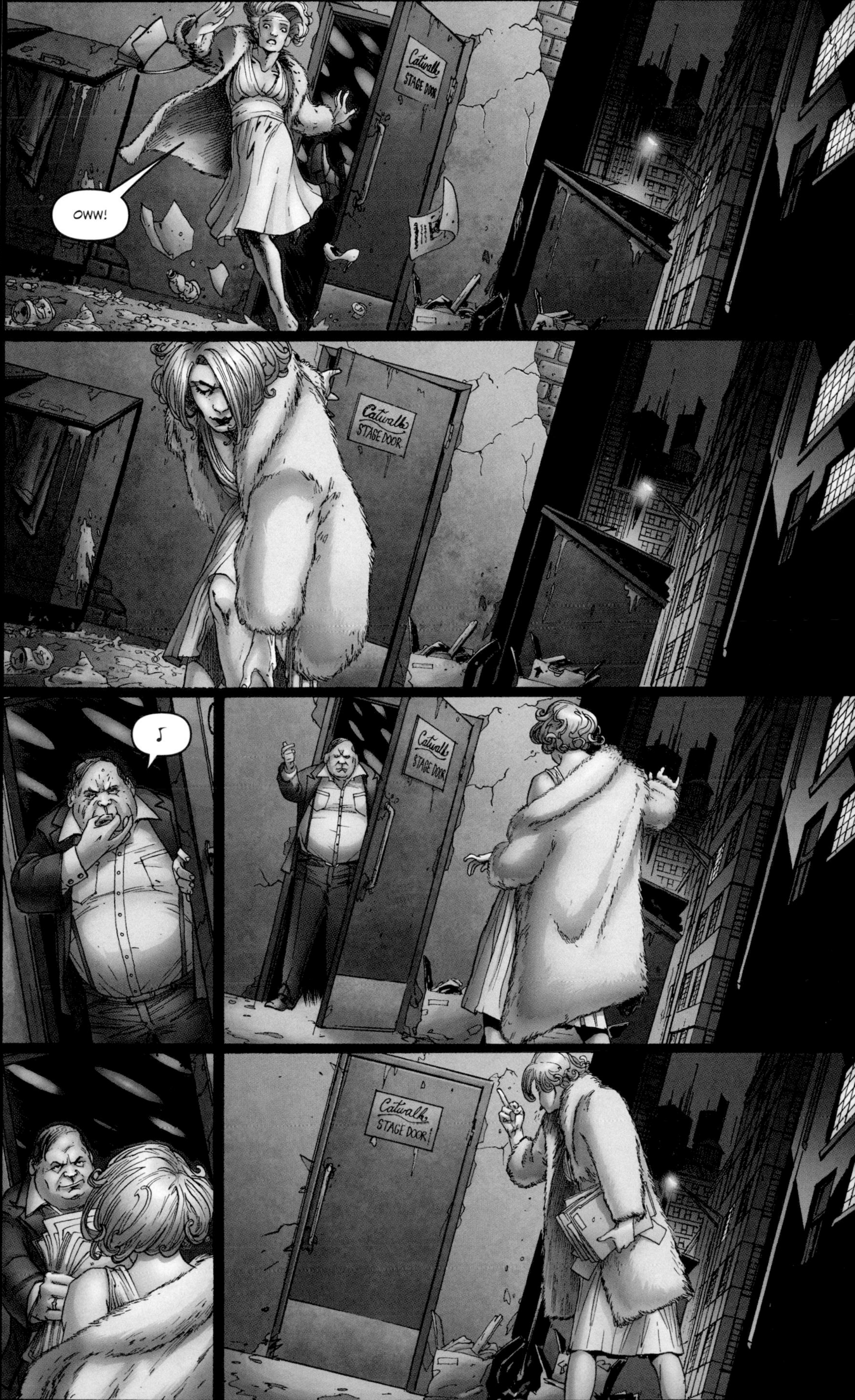
OWW!
♪
Catwalk
STAGE DOOR

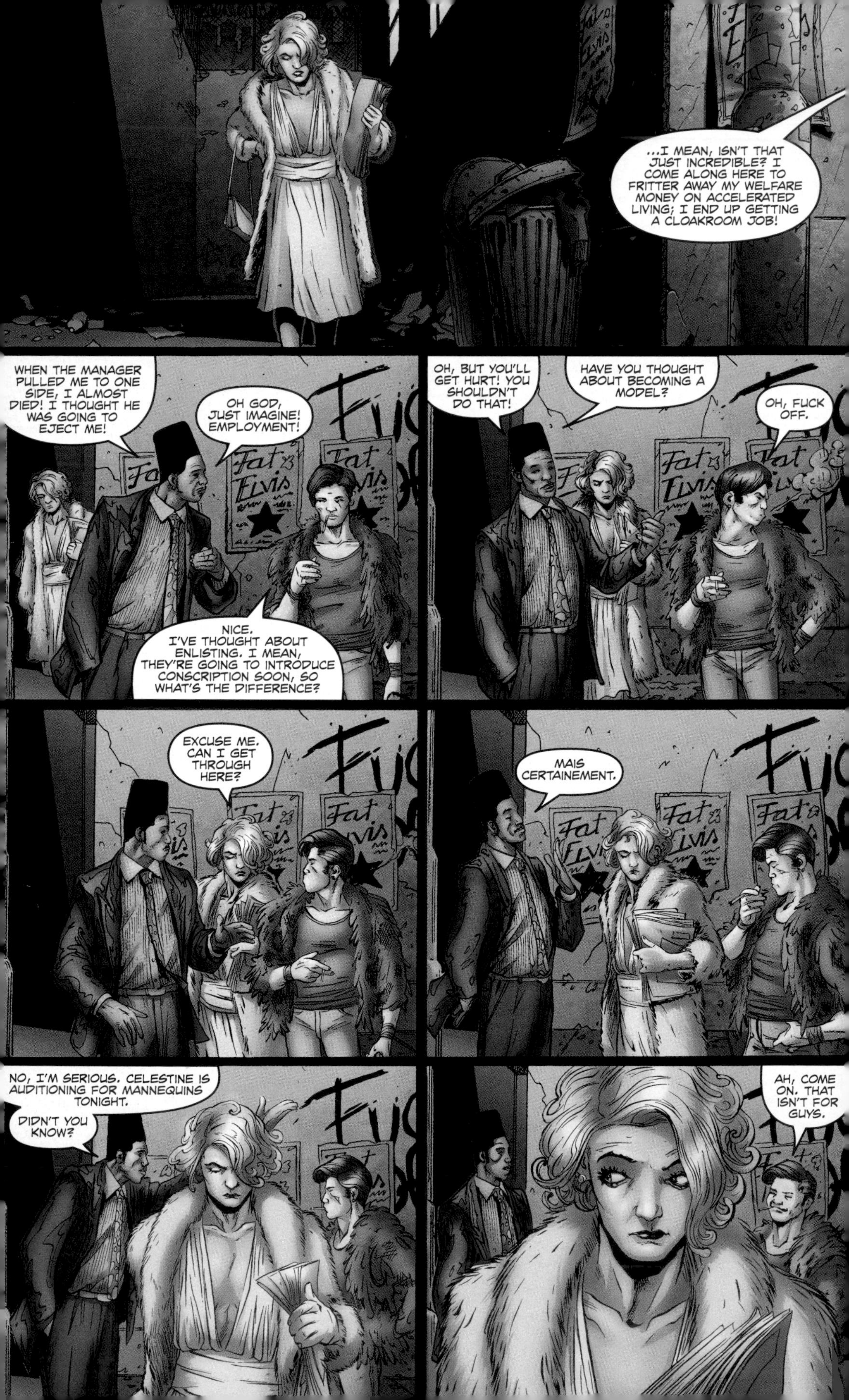
...I MEAN, ISN'T THAT JUST INCREDIBLE? I COME ALONG HERE TO FRITTER AWAY MY WELFARE MONEY ON ACCELERATED LIVING; I END UP GETTING A CLOAKROOM JOB!
WHEN THE MANAGER PULLED ME TO ONE SIDE, I ALMOST DIED! I THOUGHT HE WAS GOING TO EJECT ME!
OH GOD, JUST IMAGINE! EMPLOYMENT!
NICE. I'VE THOUGHT ABOUT ENLISTING. I MEAN, THEY'RE GOING TO INTRODUCE CONSCRIPTION SOON, SO WHAT'S THE DIFFERENCE?
OH, BUT YOU'LL GET HURT! YOU SHOULDN'T DO THAT!
HAVE YOU THOUGHT ABOUT BECOMING A MODEL?
OH, FUCK OFF.
EXCUSE ME. CAN I GET THROUGH HERE?
MAIS CERTAINEMENT.
NO, I'M SERIOUS. CELESTINE IS AUDITIONING FOR MANNEQUINS TONIGHT.
DIDN'T YOU KNOW?
AH, COME ON. THAT ISN'T FOR GUYS.

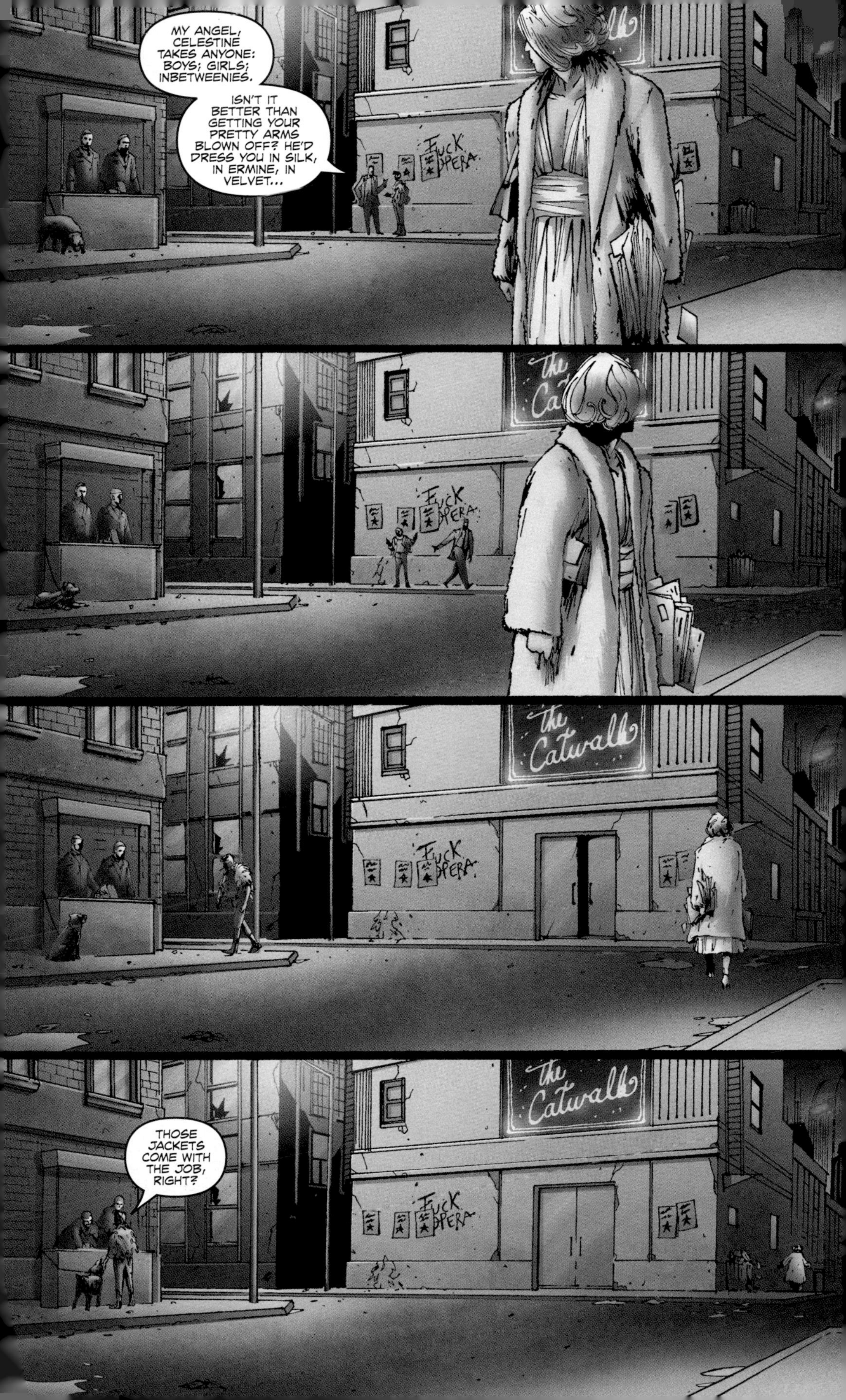
MY ANGEL, CELESTINE TAKES ANYONE: BOYS; GIRLS; INBETWEENIES.
ISN'T IT BETTER THAN GETTING YOUR PRETTY ARMS BLOWN OFF? HE'D DRESS YOU IN SILK, IN ERMINE, IN VELVET...
FUCK OPERA
the Catwalk
FUCK OPERA
the Catwalk
FUCK OPERA
THOSE JACKETS COME WITH THE JOB, RIGHT?
the Catwalk
FUCK OPERA

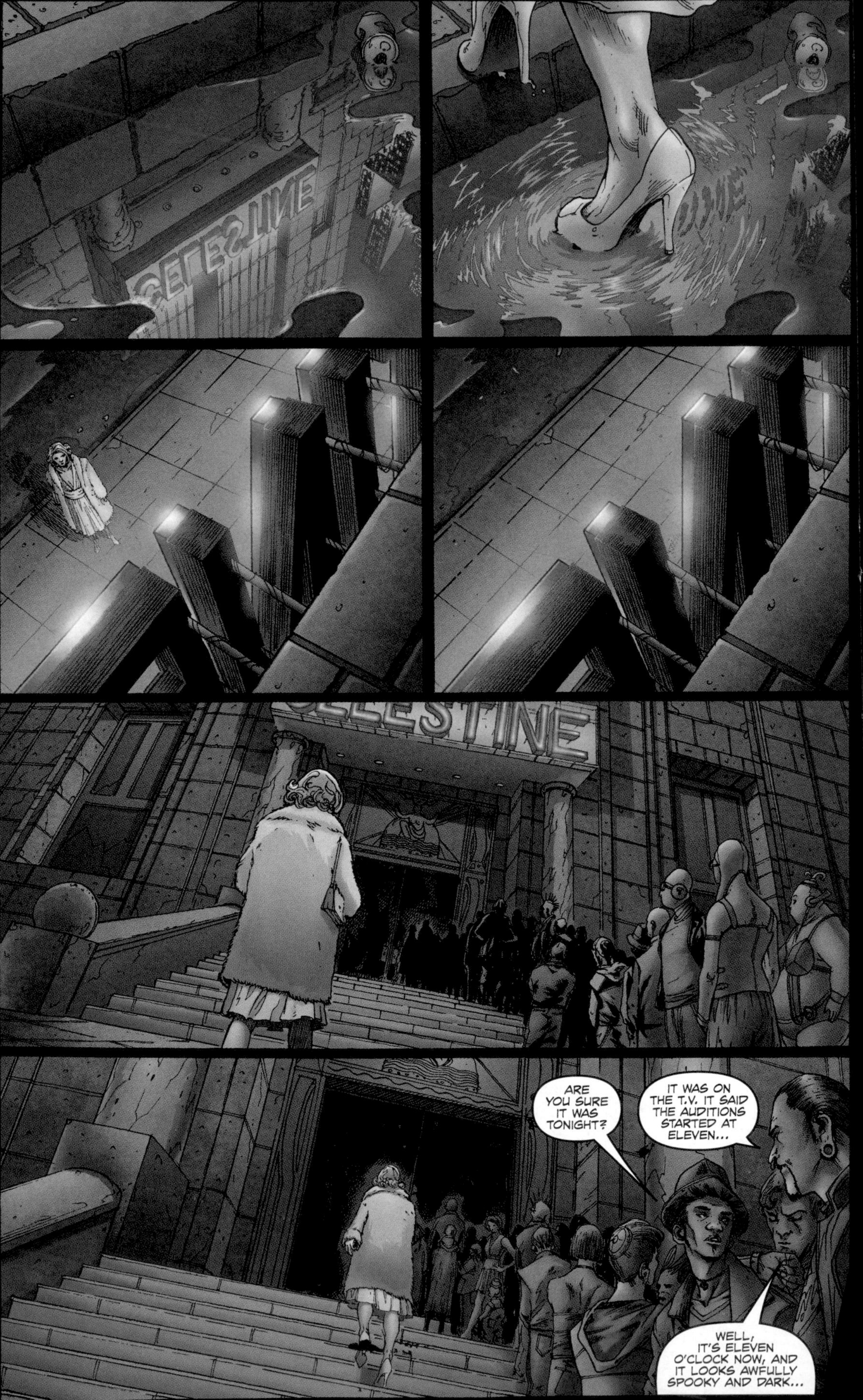
ARE YOU SURE IT WAS TONIGHT?
IT WAS ON THE T.V. IT SAID THE AUDITIONS STARTED AT ELEVEN...
WELL, IT'S ELEVEN O'CLOCK NOW, AND IT LOOKS AWFULLY SPOOKY AND DARK...

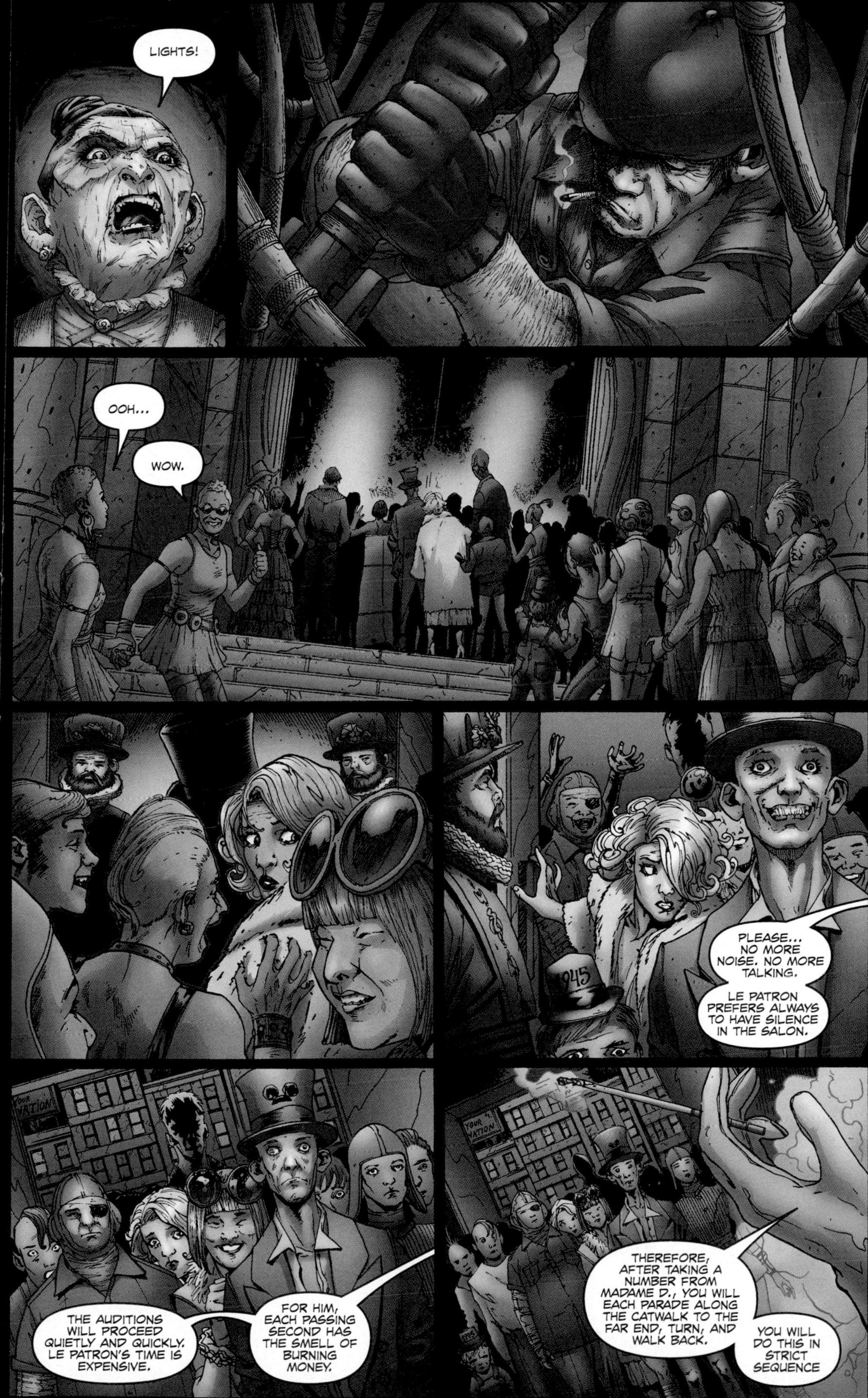
LIGHTS!
OOH...
WOW.
PLEASE... NO MORE NOISE. NO MORE TALKING.
LE PATRON PREFERS ALWAYS TO HAVE SILENCE IN THE SALON.
THE AUDITIONS WILL PROCEED QUIETLY AND QUICKLY. LE PATRON'S TIME IS EXPENSIVE.
FOR HIM, EACH PASSING SECOND HAS THE SMELL OF BURNING MONEY.
THEREFORE, AFTER TAKING A NUMBER FROM MADAME D., YOU WILL EACH PARADE ALONG THE CATWALK TO THE FAR END, TURN, AND WALK BACK.
YOU WILL DO THIS IN STRICT SEQUENCE

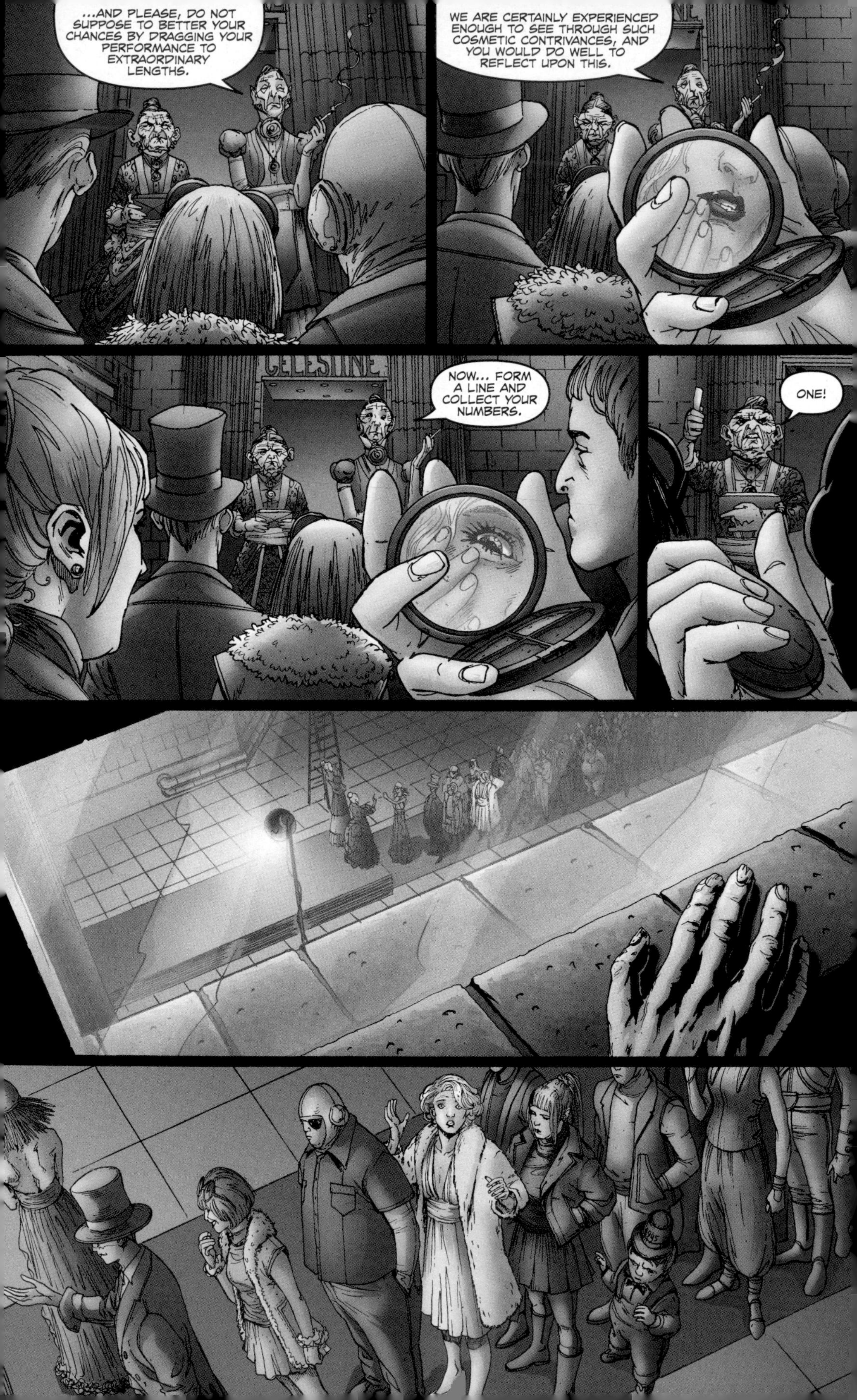
...AND PLEASE, DO NOT SUPPOSE TO BETTER YOUR CHANCES BY DRAGGING YOUR PERFORMANCE TO EXTRAORDINARY LENGTHS.
WE ARE CERTAINLY EXPERIENCED ENOUGH TO SEE THROUGH SUCH COSMETIC CONTRIVANCES, AND YOU WOULD DO WELL TO REFLECT UPON THIS.
CELESTINE
NOW... FORM A LINE AND COLLECT YOUR NUMBERS.
ONE!

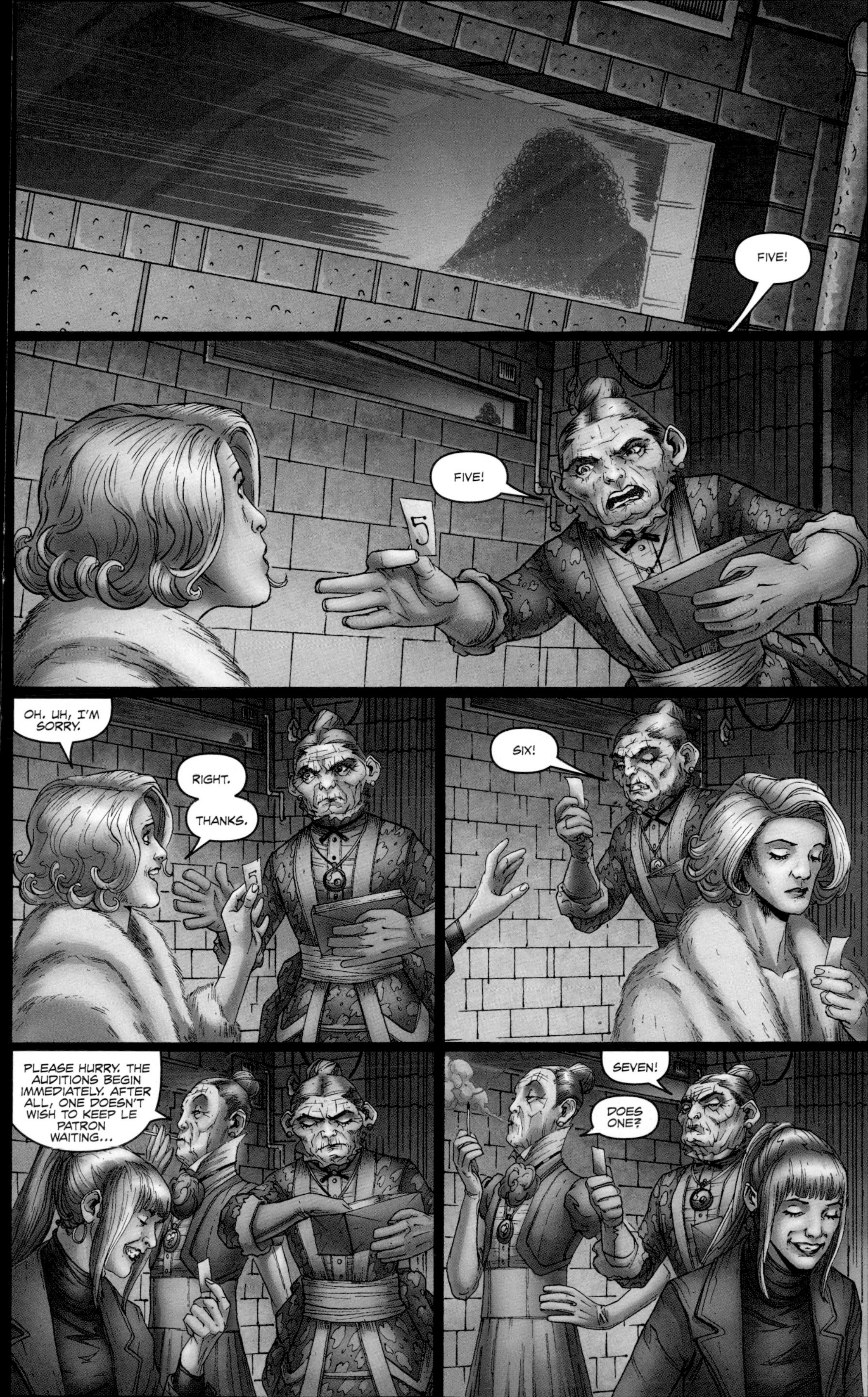
FIVE!
FIVE!
OH. UH, I'M SORRY.
RIGHT.
THANKS.
SIX!
PLEASE HURRY. THE AUDITIONS BEGIN IMMEDIATELY. AFTER ALL, ONE DOESN'T WISH TO KEEP LE PATRON WAITING...
SEVEN!
DOES ONE?

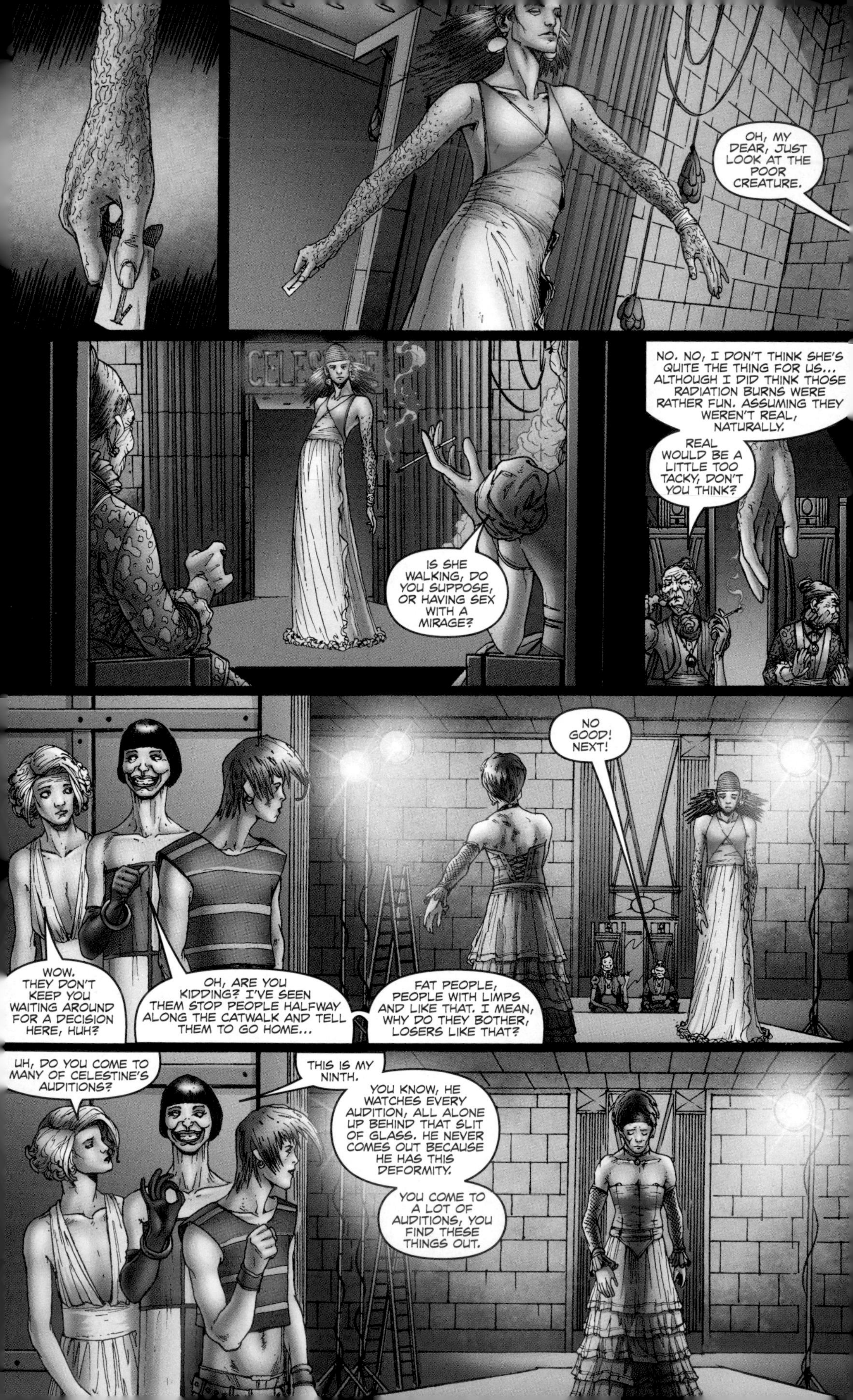
OH, MY DEAR, JUST LOOK AT THE POOR CREATURE.
CELESTINE
IS SHE WALKING, DO YOU SUPPOSE, OR HAVING SEX WITH A MIRAGE?
NO. NO, I DON'T THINK SHE'S QUITE THE THING FOR US... ALTHOUGH I DID THINK THOSE RADIATION BURNS WERE RATHER FUN. ASSUMING THEY WEREN'T REAL, NATURALLY.
REAL WOULD BE A LITTLE TOO TACKY, DON'T YOU THINK?
WOW. THEY DON'T KEEP YOU WAITING AROUND FOR A DECISION HERE, HUH?
OH, ARE YOU KIDDING? I'VE SEEN THEM STOP PEOPLE HALFWAY ALONG THE CATWALK AND TELL THEM TO GO HOME...
FAT PEOPLE, PEOPLE WITH LIMPS AND LIKE THAT. I MEAN, WHY DO THEY BOTHER, LOSERS LIKE THAT?
NO GOOD! NEXT!
UH, DO YOU COME TO MANY OF CELESTINE'S AUDITIONS?
THIS IS MY NINTH.
YOU KNOW, HE WATCHES EVERY AUDITION, ALL ALONE UP BEHIND THAT SLIT OF GLASS. HE NEVER COMES OUT BECAUSE HE HAS THIS DEFORMITY.
YOU COME TO A LOT OF AUDITIONS, YOU FIND THESE THINGS OUT.

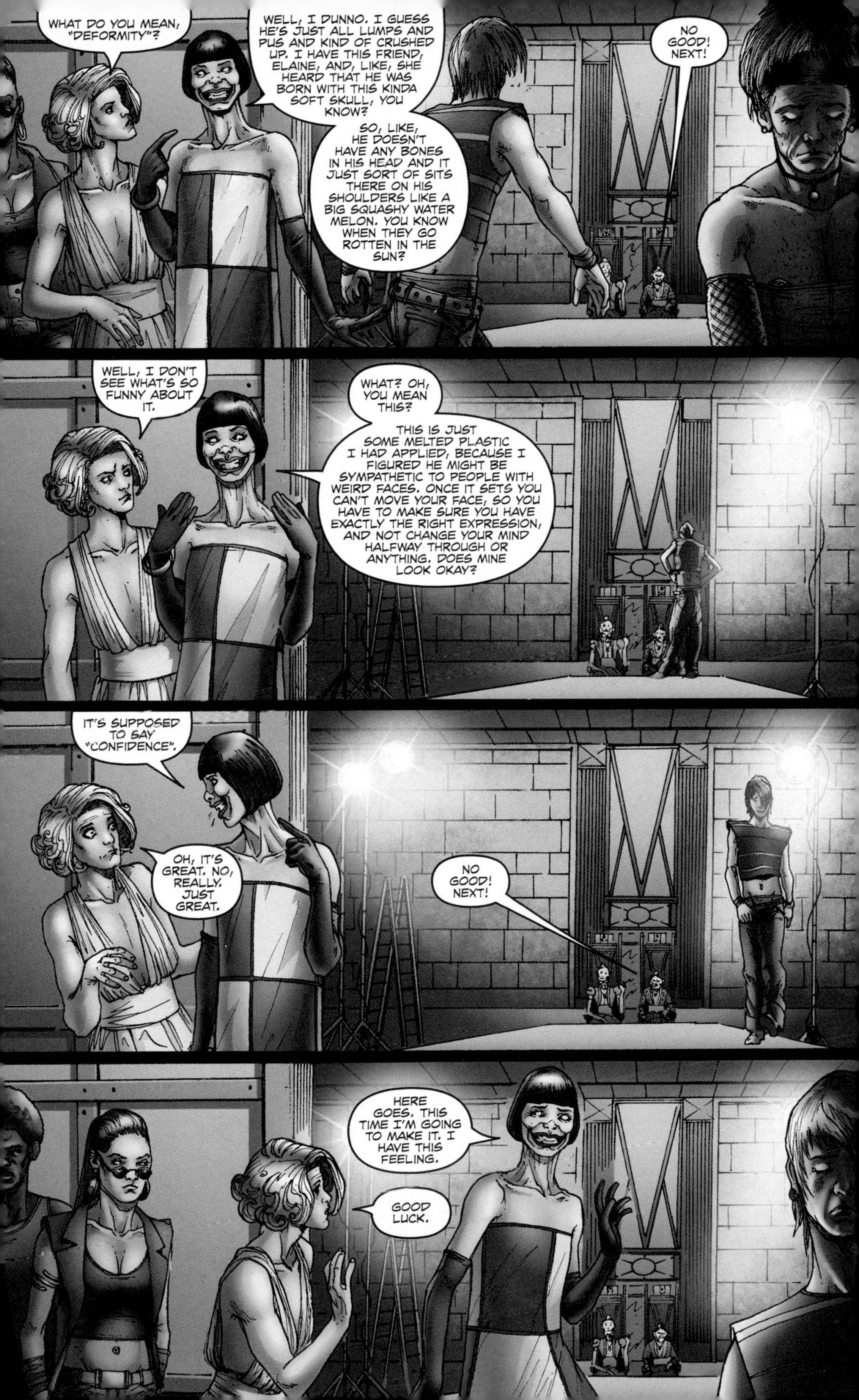
WHAT DO YOU MEAN, "DEFORMITY"?
WELL, I DUNNO. I GUESS HE'S JUST ALL LUMPS AND PUS AND KIND OF CRUSHED UP. I HAVE THIS FRIEND, ELAINE, AND, LIKE, SHE HEARD THAT HE WAS BORN WITH THIS KINDA SOFT SKULL, YOU KNOW?
SO, LIKE, HE DOESN'T HAVE ANY BONES IN HIS HEAD AND IT JUST SORT OF SITS THERE ON HIS SHOULDERS LIKE A BIG SQUASHY WATER MELON. YOU KNOW WHEN THEY GO ROTTEN IN THE SUN?
NO GOOD! NEXT!
WELL, I DON'T SEE WHAT'S SO FUNNY ABOUT IT.
WHAT? OH, YOU MEAN THIS?
THIS IS JUST SOME MELTED PLASTIC I HAD APPLIED, BECAUSE I FIGURED HE MIGHT BE SYMPATHETIC TO PEOPLE WITH WEIRD FACES. ONCE IT SETS YOU CAN'T MOVE YOUR FACE, SO YOU HAVE TO MAKE SURE YOU HAVE EXACTLY THE RIGHT EXPRESSION, AND NOT CHANGE YOUR MIND HALFWAY THROUGH OR ANYTHING. DOES MINE LOOK OKAY?
IT'S SUPPOSED TO SAY "CONFIDENCE".
OH, IT'S GREAT. NO, REALLY. JUST GREAT.
NO GOOD! NEXT!
HERE GOES. THIS TIME I'M GOING TO MAKE IT. I HAVE THIS FEELING.
GOOD LUCK.

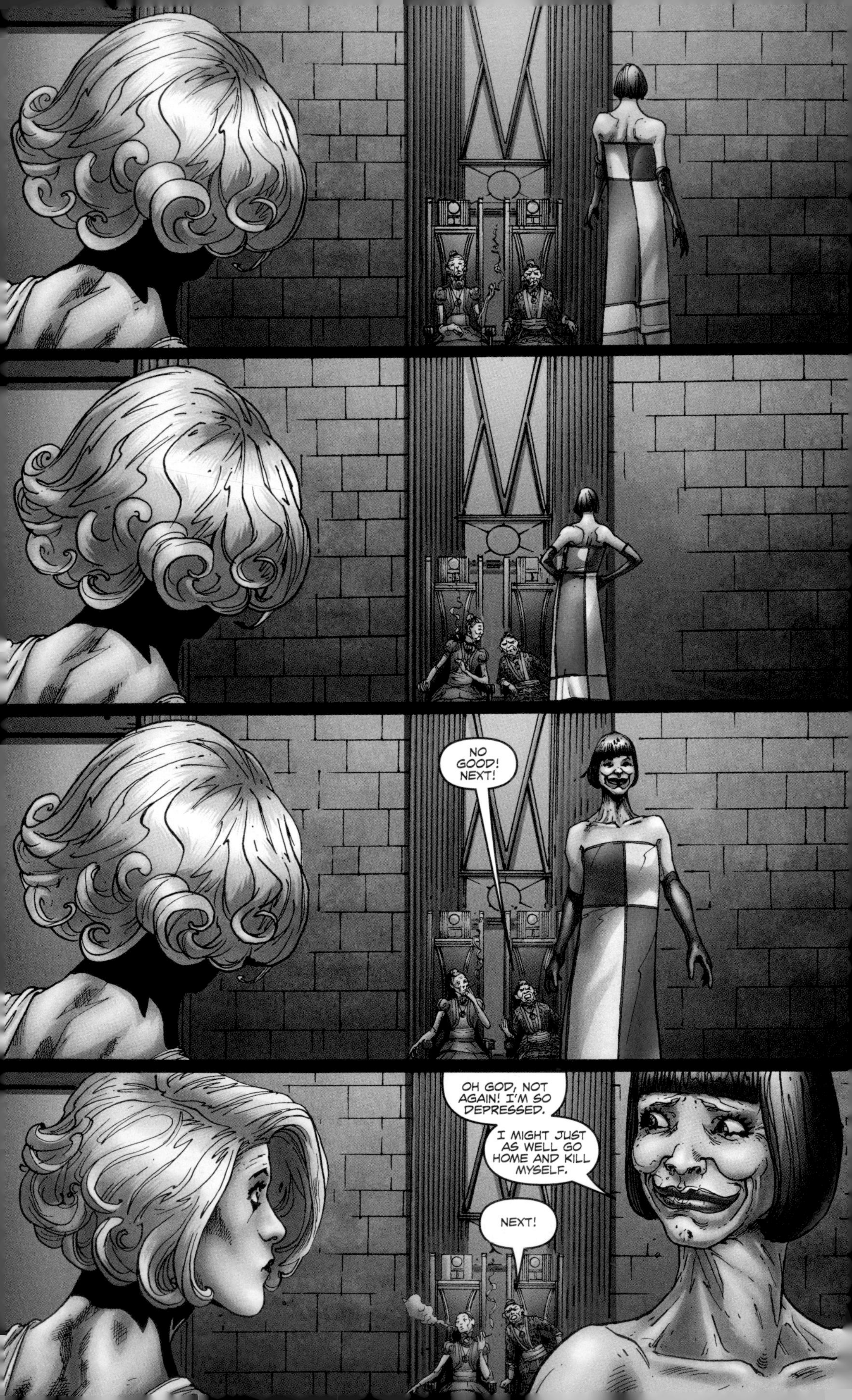
NO GOOD! NEXT!
OH GOD, NOT AGAIN! I'M SO DEPRESSED.
I MIGHT JUST AS WELL GO HOME AND KILL MYSELF.
NEXT!

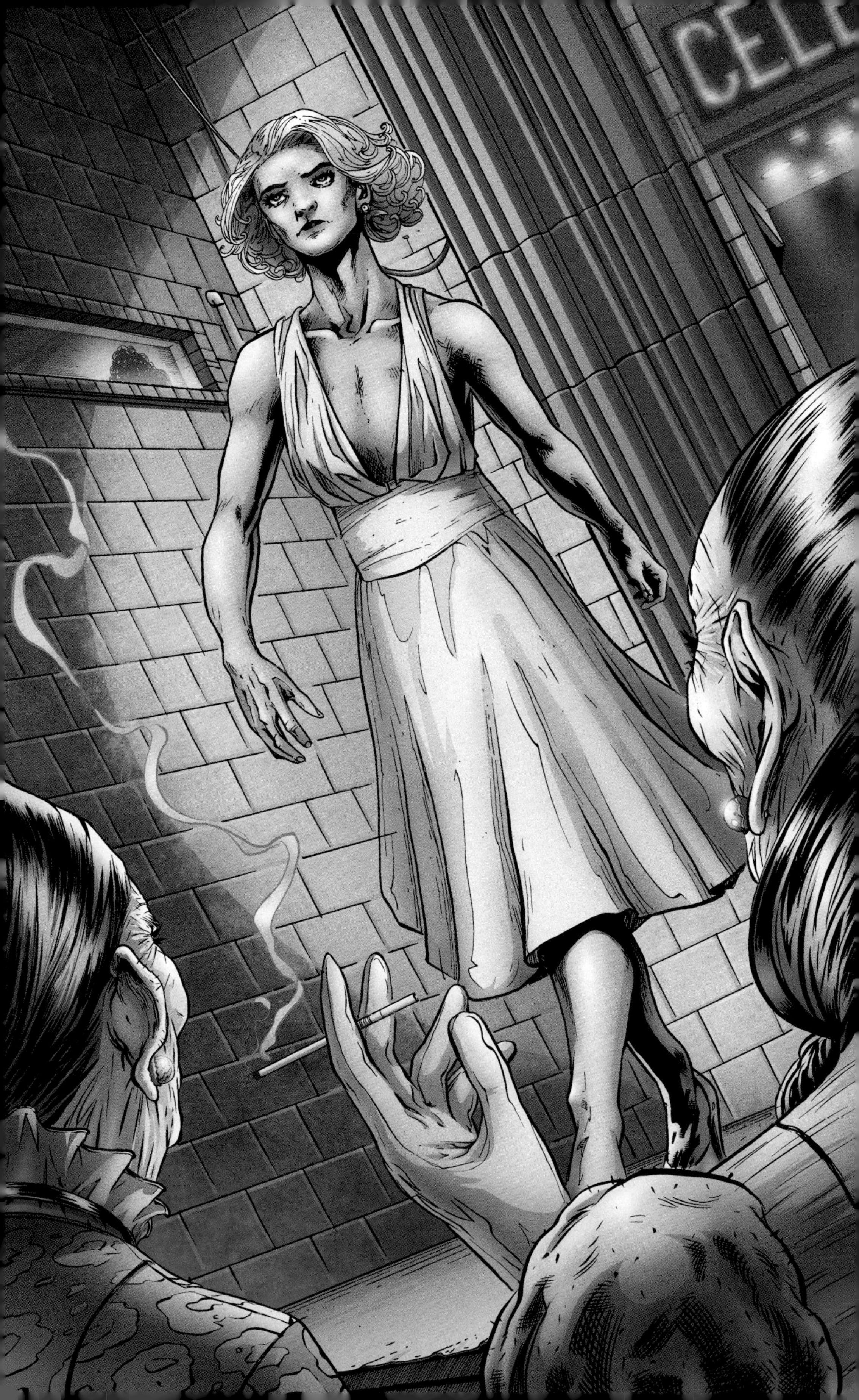

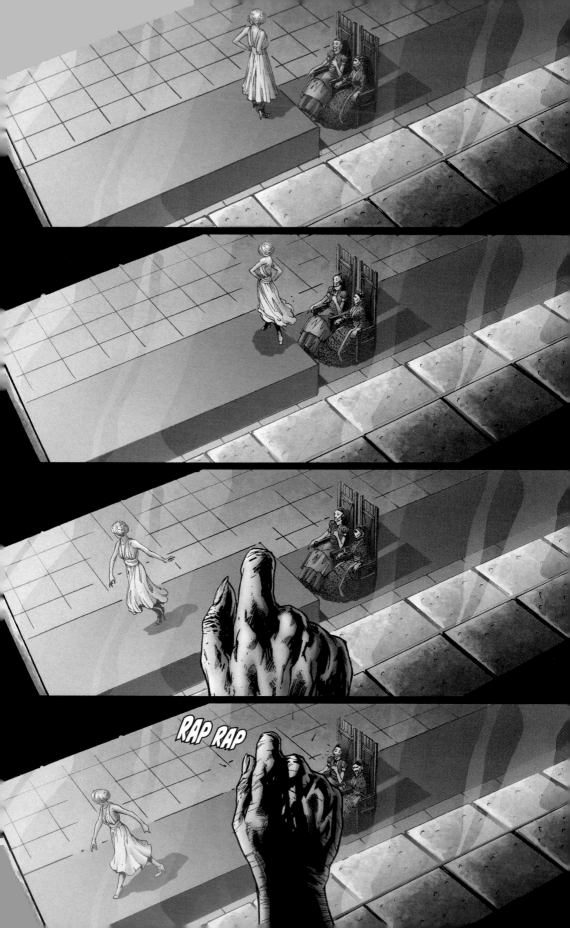

RAP RAP

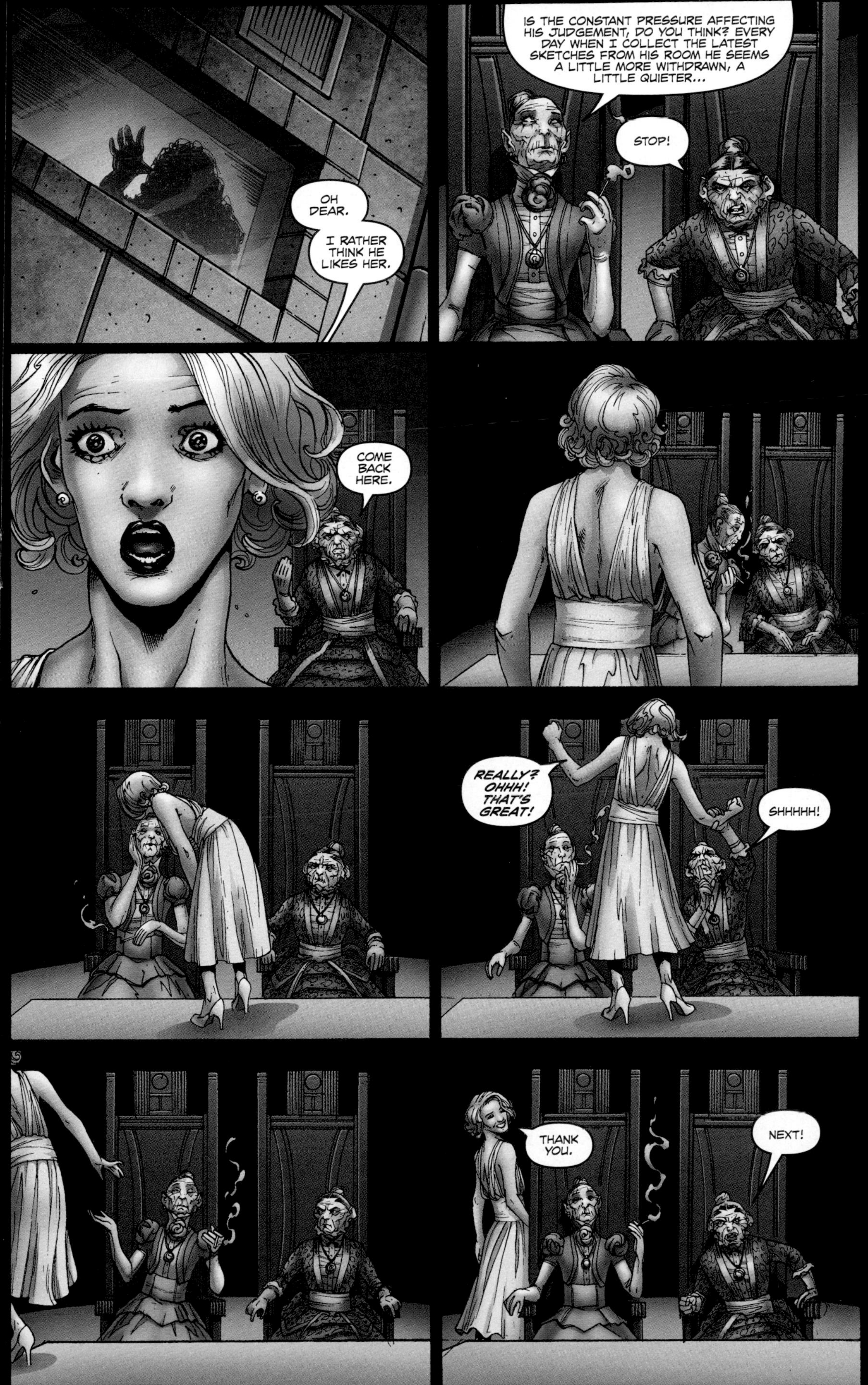
OH DEAR.
I RATHER THINK HE LIKES HER.
IS THE CONSTANT PRESSURE AFFECTING HIS JUDGEMENT, DO YOU THINK? EVERY DAY WHEN I COLLECT THE LATEST SKETCHES FROM HIS ROOM HE SEEMS A LITTLE MORE WITHDRAWN, A LITTLE QUIETER...
STOP!
COME BACK HERE.
REALLY? OHHH! THAT'S GREAT!
SHHHHH!
THANK YOU.
NEXT!

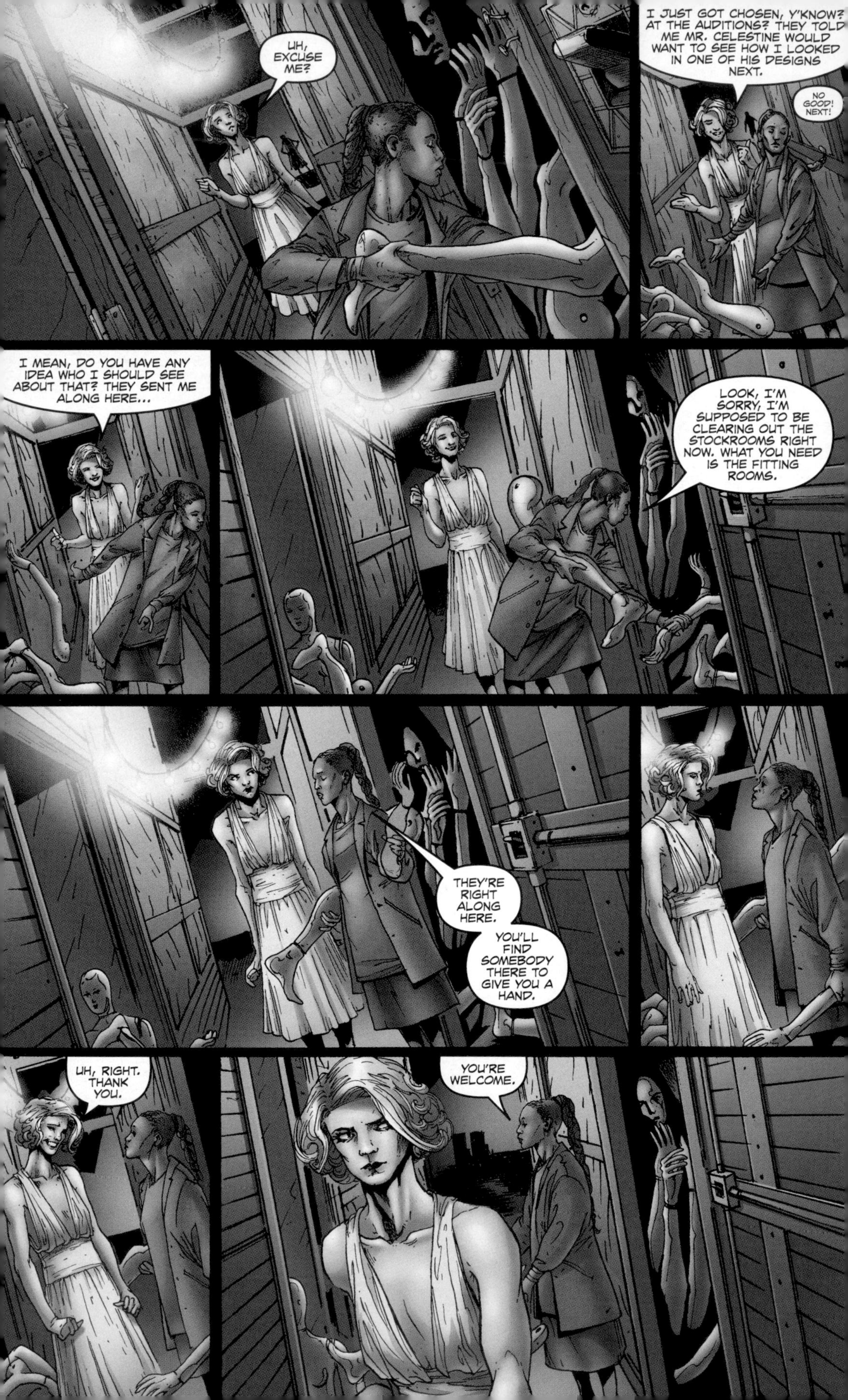
UH, EXCUSE ME?
I JUST GOT CHOSEN, Y'KNOW? AT THE AUDITIONS? THEY TOLD ME MR. CELESTINE WOULD WANT TO SEE HOW I LOOKED IN ONE OF HIS DESIGNS NEXT.
NO GOOD! NEXT!
I MEAN, DO YOU HAVE ANY IDEA WHO I SHOULD SEE ABOUT THAT? THEY SENT ME ALONG HERE...
LOOK, I'M SORRY, I'M SUPPOSED TO BE CLEARING OUT THE STOCKROOMS RIGHT NOW. WHAT YOU NEED IS THE FITTING ROOMS.
THEY'RE RIGHT ALONG HERE.
YOU'LL FIND SOMEBODY THERE TO GIVE YOU A HAND.
UH, RIGHT. THANK YOU.
YOU'RE WELCOME.

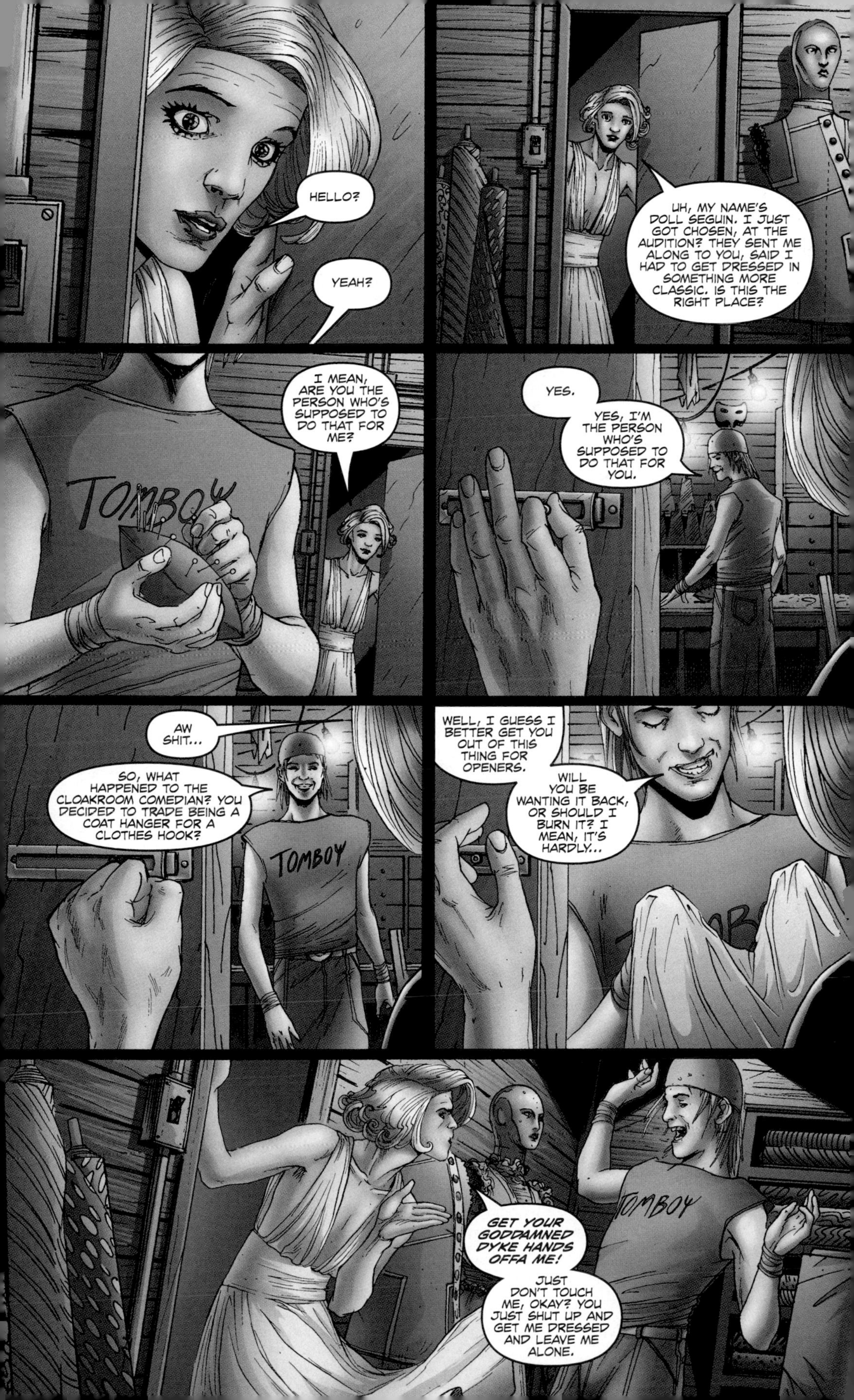
HELLO?
YEAH?
UH, MY NAME'S DOLL SEGUIN. I JUST GOT CHOSEN, AT THE AUDITION? THEY SENT ME ALONG TO YOU, SAID I HAD TO GET DRESSED IN SOMETHING MORE CLASSIC. IS THIS THE RIGHT PLACE?
TOMBOY
I MEAN, ARE YOU THE PERSON WHO'S SUPPOSED TO DO THAT FOR ME?
YES.
YES, I'M THE PERSON WHO'S SUPPOSED TO DO THAT FOR YOU.
AW SHIT...
SO, WHAT HAPPENED TO THE CLOAKROOM COMEDIAN? YOU DECIDED TO TRADE BEING A COAT HANGER FOR A CLOTHES HOOK?
TOMBOY
WELL, I GUESS I BETTER GET YOU OUT OF THIS THING FOR OPENERS.
WILL YOU BE WANTING IT BACK, OR SHOULD I BURN IT? I MEAN, IT'S HARDLY...
TOMBOY
GET YOUR GODDAMNED DYKE HANDS OFFA ME!
JUST DON'T TOUCH ME, OKAY? YOU JUST SHUT UP AND GET ME DRESSED AND LEAVE ME ALONE.

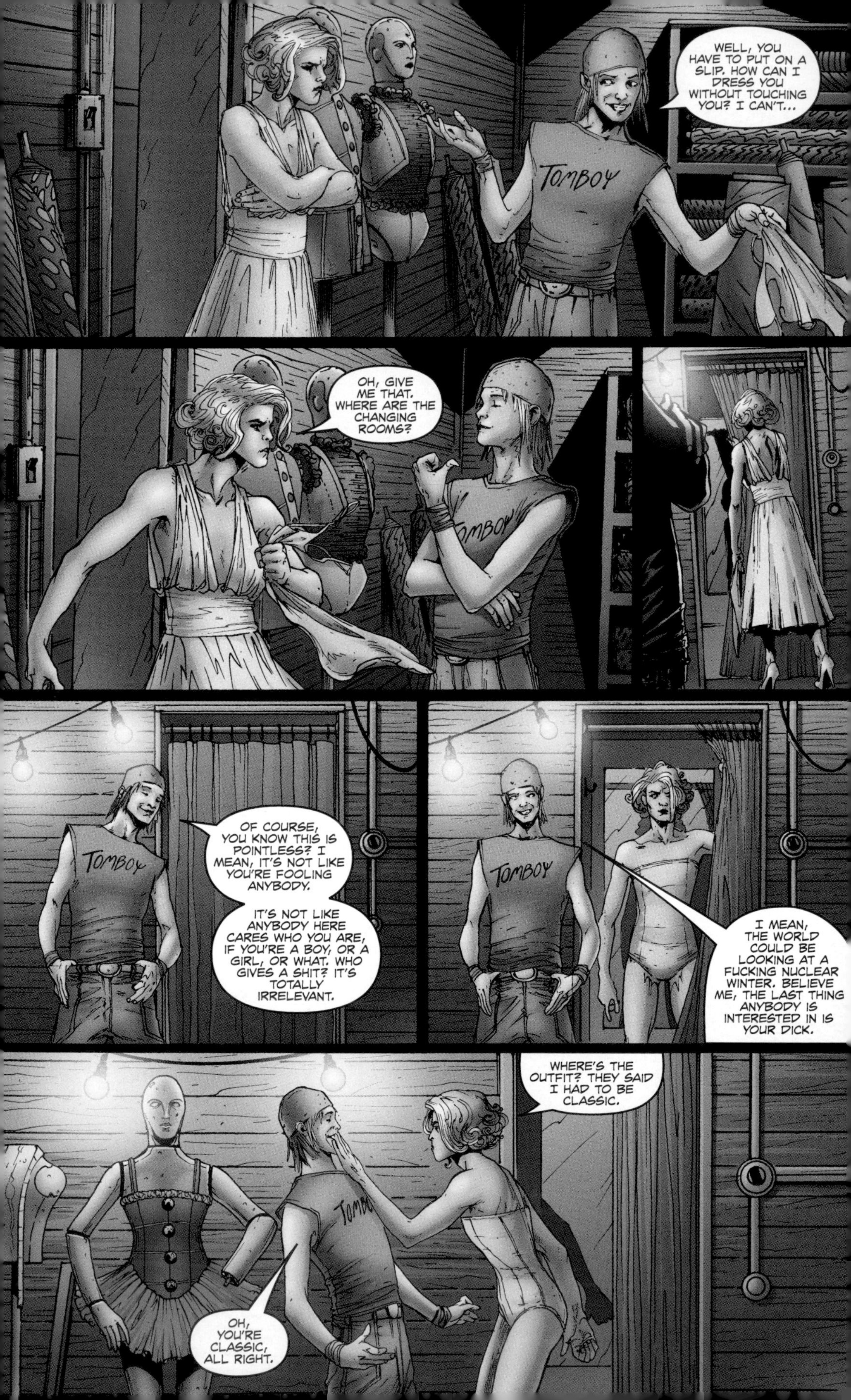

WELL, YOU HAVE TO PUT ON A SLIP. HOW CAN I DRESS YOU WITHOUT TOUCHING YOU? I CAN'T...
TOMBOY
OH, GIVE ME THAT. WHERE ARE THE CHANGING ROOMS?
OF COURSE, YOU KNOW THIS IS POINTLESS? I MEAN, IT'S NOT LIKE YOU'RE FOOLING ANYBODY.
IT'S NOT LIKE ANYBODY HERE CARES WHO YOU ARE, IF YOU'RE A BOY, OR A GIRL, OR WHAT. WHO GIVES A SHIT? IT'S TOTALLY IRRELEVANT.
I MEAN, THE WORLD COULD BE LOOKING AT A FUCKING NUCLEAR WINTER. BELIEVE ME, THE LAST THING ANYBODY IS INTERESTED IN IS YOUR DICK.
WHERE'S THE OUTFIT? THEY SAID I HAD TO BE CLASSIC.
OH, YOU'RE CLASSIC, ALL RIGHT.

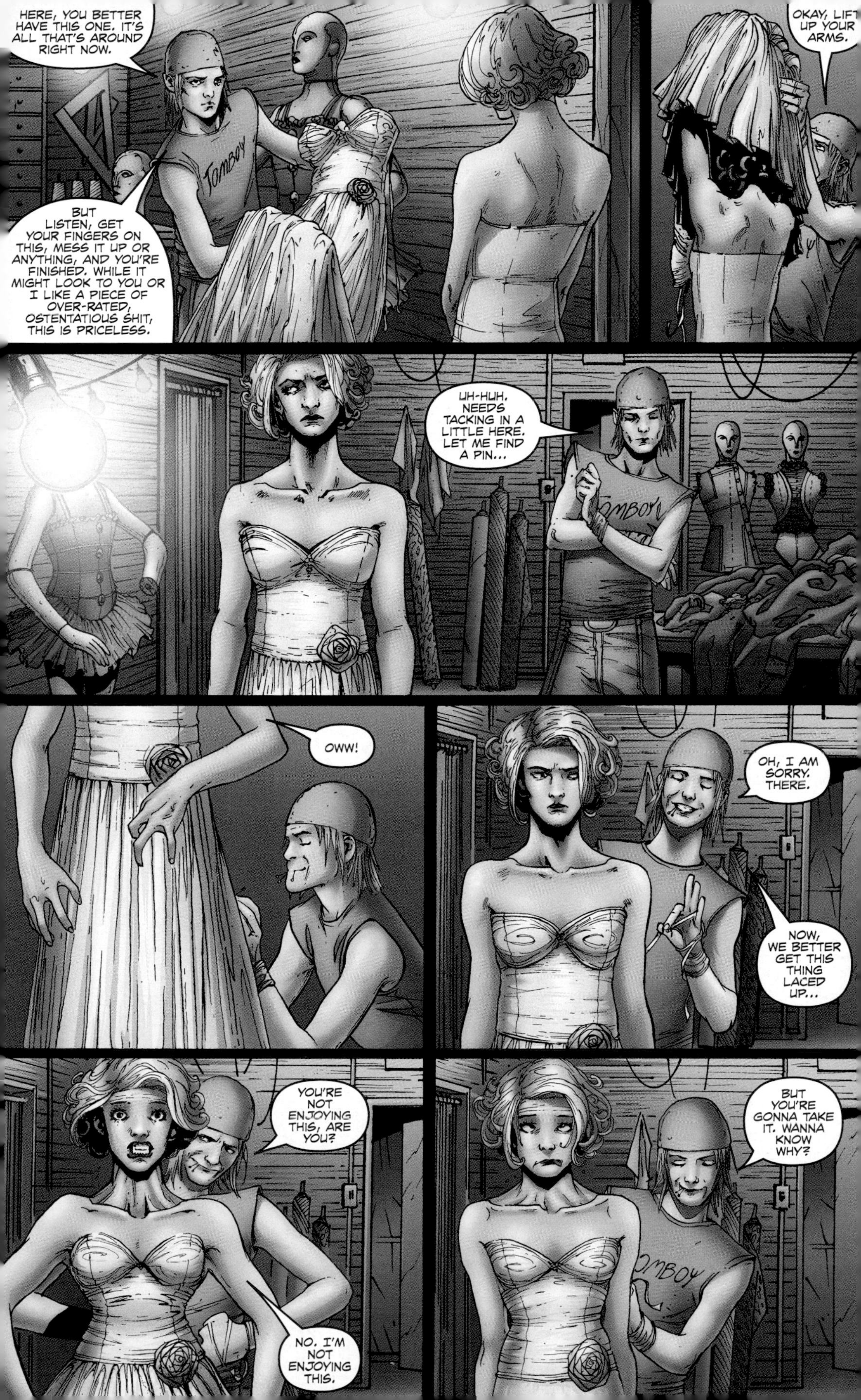
HERE, YOU BETTER HAVE THIS ONE. IT'S ALL THAT'S AROUND RIGHT NOW.
BUT LISTEN, GET YOUR FINGERS ON THIS, MESS IT UP OR ANYTHING, AND YOU'RE FINISHED. WHILE IT MIGHT LOOK TO YOU OR I LIKE A PIECE OF OVER-RATED, OSTENTATIOUS SHIT, THIS IS PRICELESS.
TOMBOY
OKAY, LIFT UP YOUR ARMS.
UH-HUH. NEEDS TACKING IN A LITTLE HERE. LET ME FIND A PIN...
TOMBOY
OWW!
OH, I AM SORRY. THERE.
NOW, WE BETTER GET THIS THING LACED UP...
YOU'RE NOT ENJOYING THIS, ARE YOU?
NO. I'M NOT ENJOYING THIS.
BUT YOU'RE GONNA TAKE IT. WANNA KNOW WHY?
TOMBOY

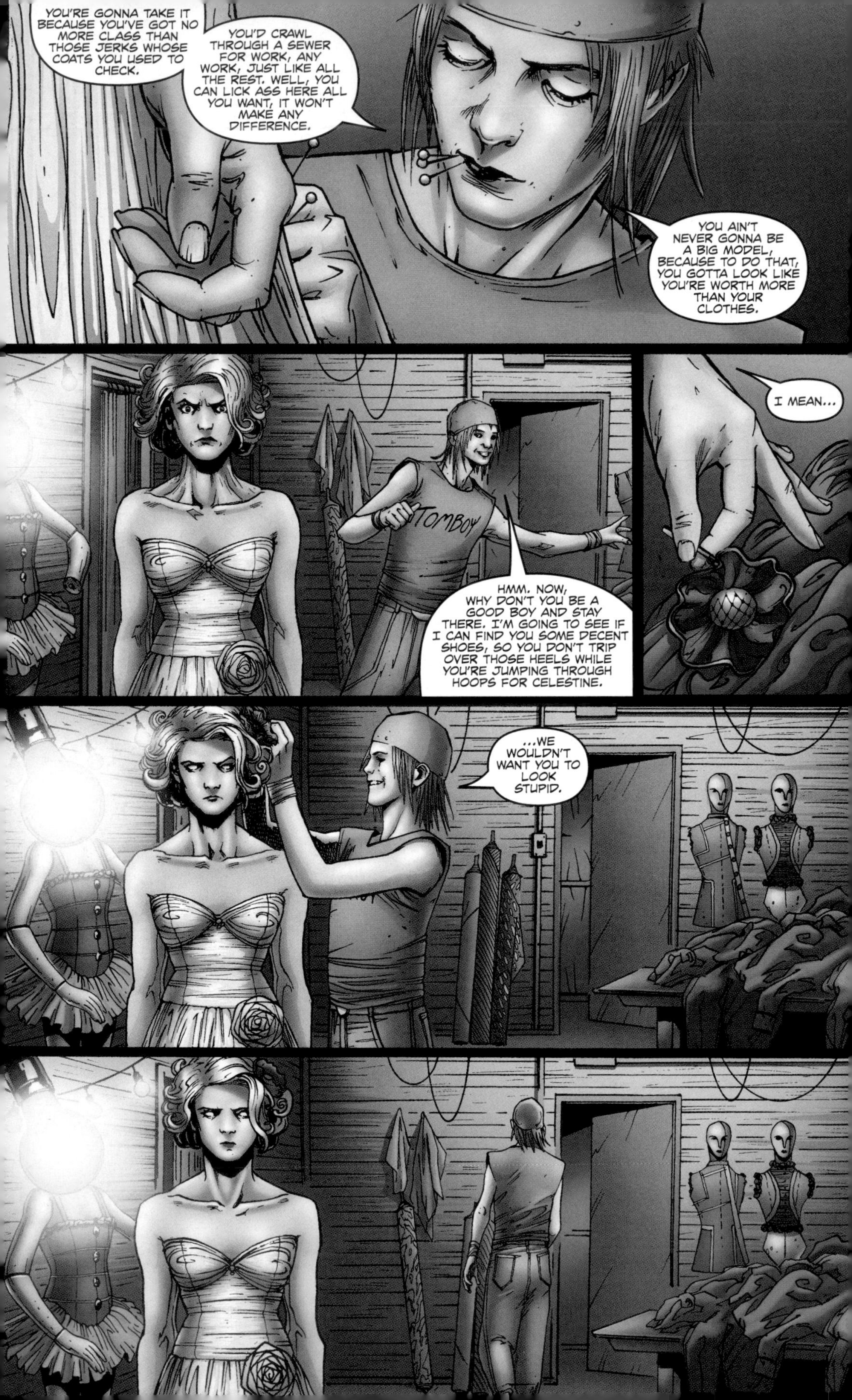
YOU'RE GONNA TAKE IT BECAUSE YOU'VE GOT NO MORE CLASS THAN THOSE JERKS WHOSE COATS YOU USED TO CHECK.
YOU'D CRAWL THROUGH A SEWER FOR WORK, ANY WORK, JUST LIKE ALL THE REST. WELL, YOU CAN LICK ASS HERE ALL YOU WANT, IT WON'T MAKE ANY DIFFERENCE.
YOU AIN'T NEVER GONNA BE A BIG MODEL, BECAUSE TO DO THAT, YOU GOTTA LOOK LIKE YOU'RE WORTH MORE THAN YOUR CLOTHES.
TOMBOY
HMM. NOW, WHY DON'T YOU BE A GOOD BOY AND STAY THERE. I'M GOING TO SEE IF I CAN FIND YOU SOME DECENT SHOES, SO YOU DON'T TRIP OVER THOSE HEELS WHILE YOU'RE JUMPING THROUGH HOOPS FOR CELESTINE.
I MEAN...
...WE WOULDN'T WANT YOU TO LOOK STUPID.

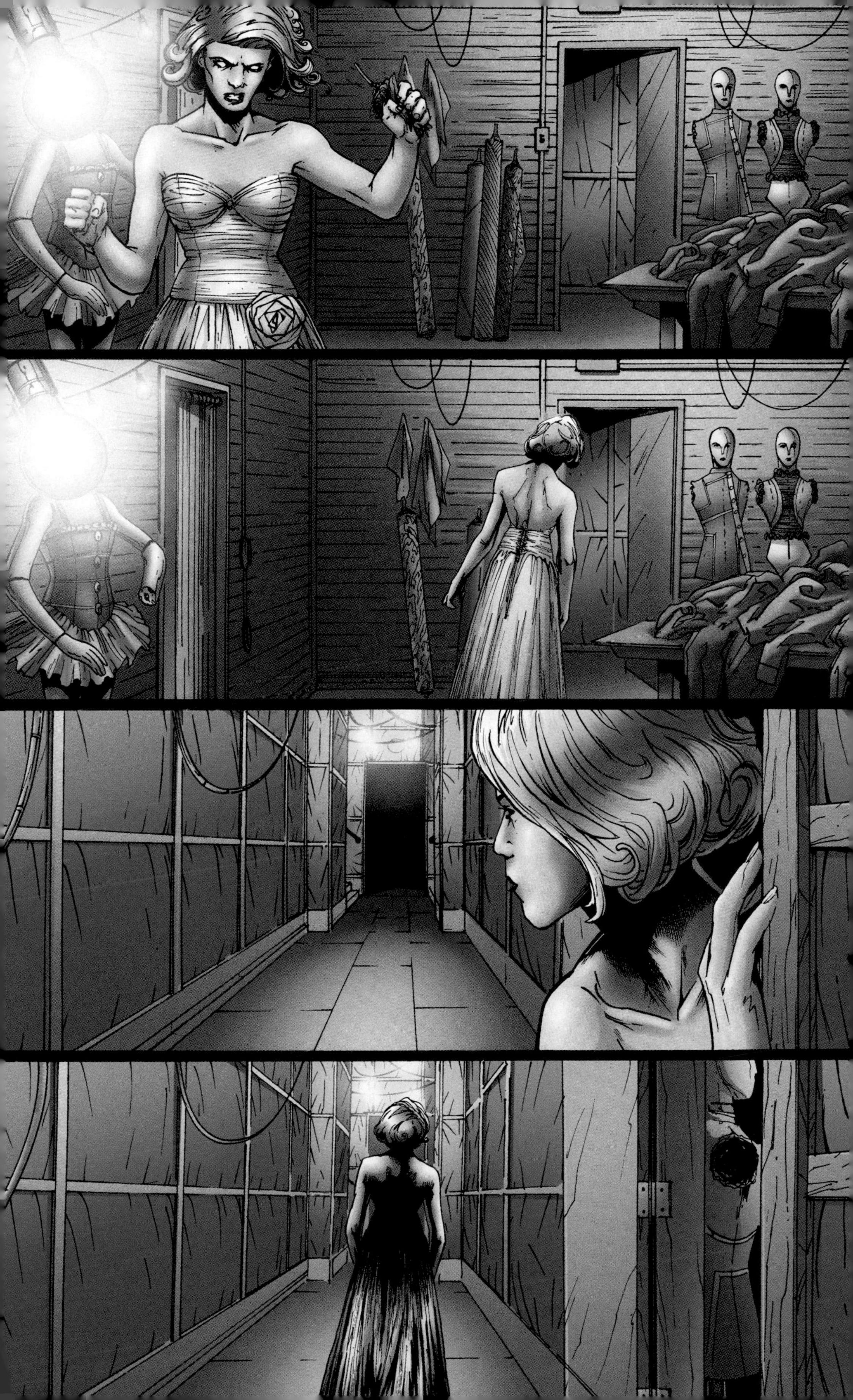

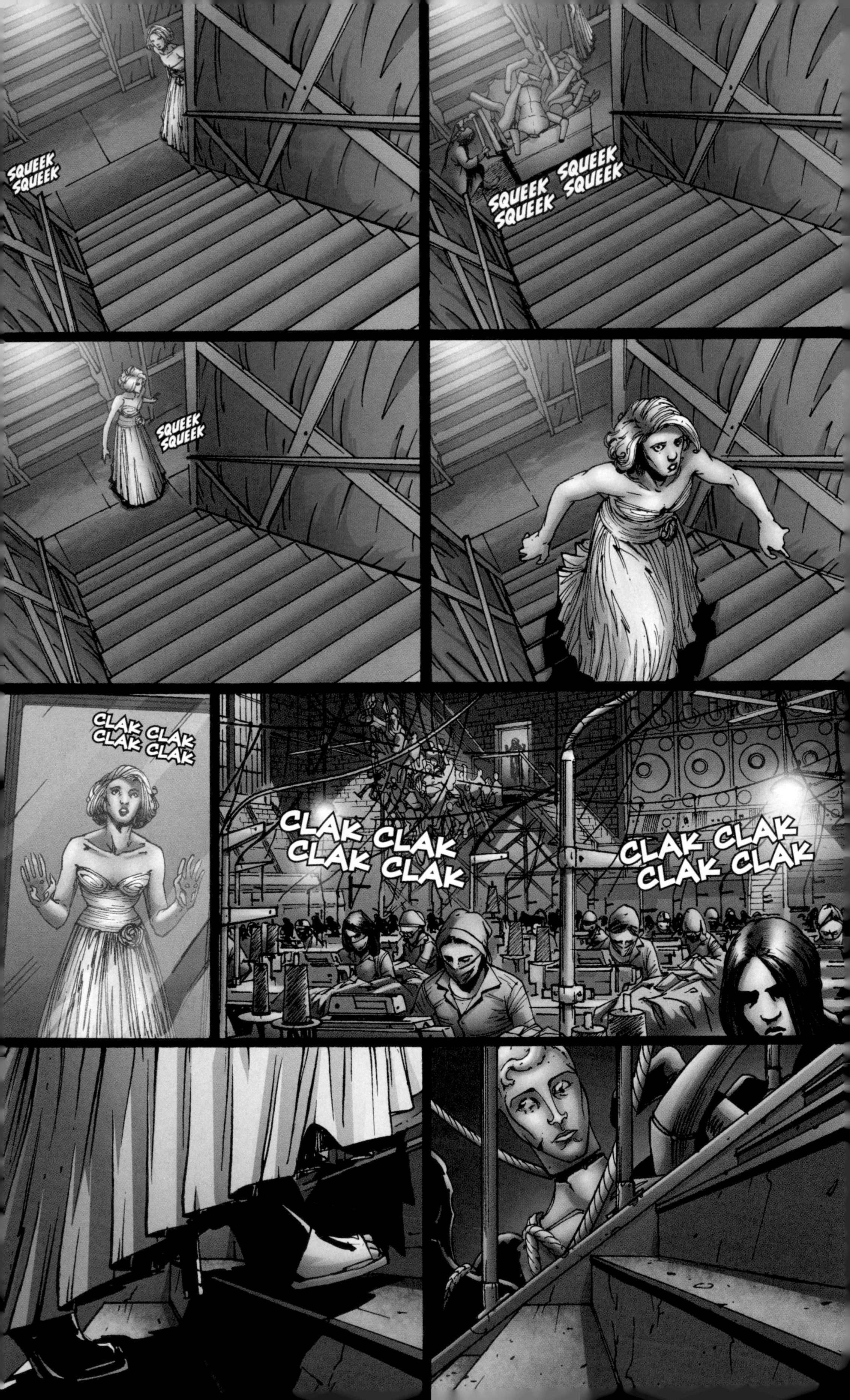
SQUEEK SQUEEK
SQUEEK SQUEEK
SQUEEK SQUEEK
SQUEEK SQUEEK
CLAK CLAK CLAK CLAK
CLAK CLAK CLAK CLAK
CLAK CLAK CLAK CLAK

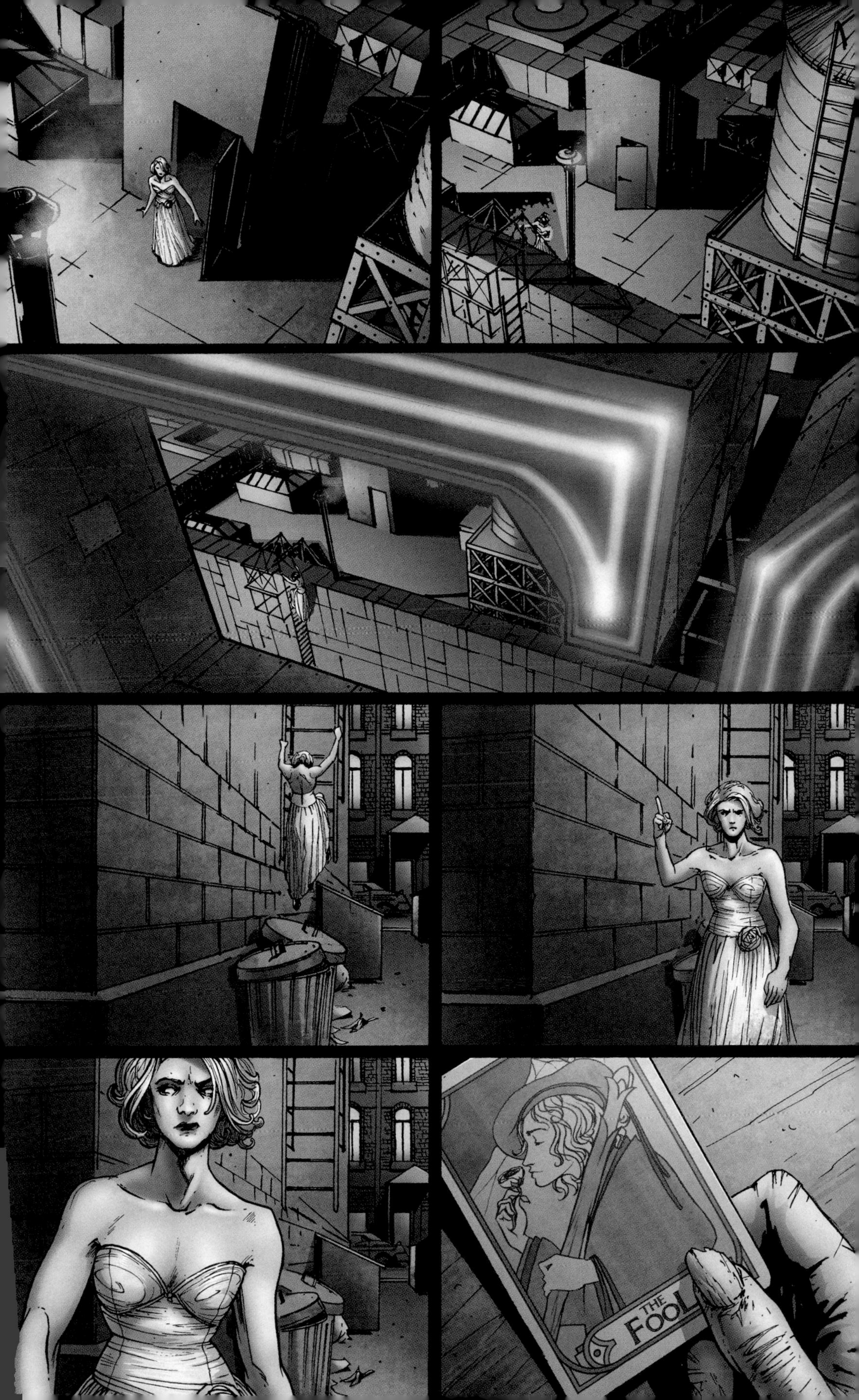
THE FOOL

CHAPTER THREE

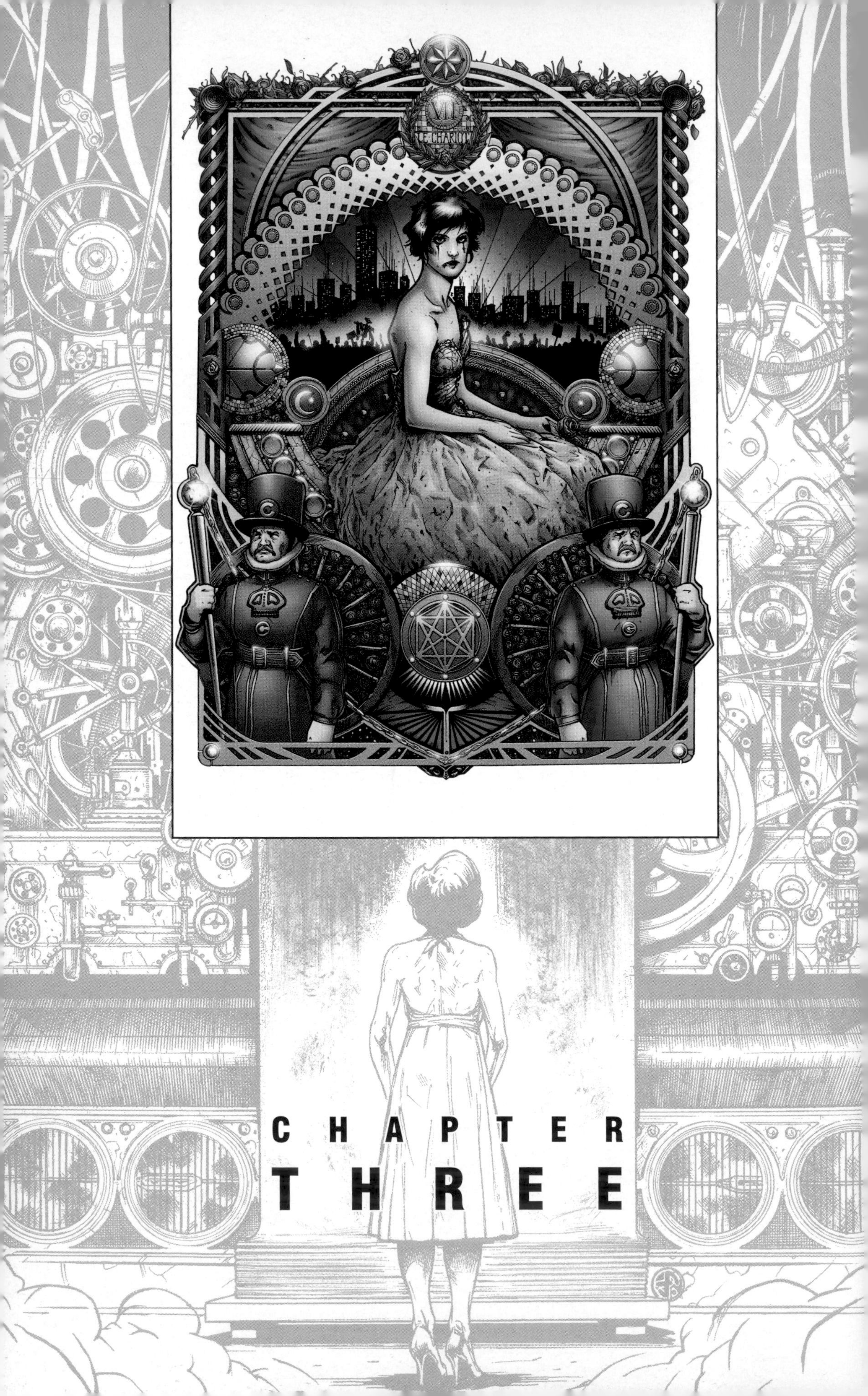
VII
LE CHARIOT

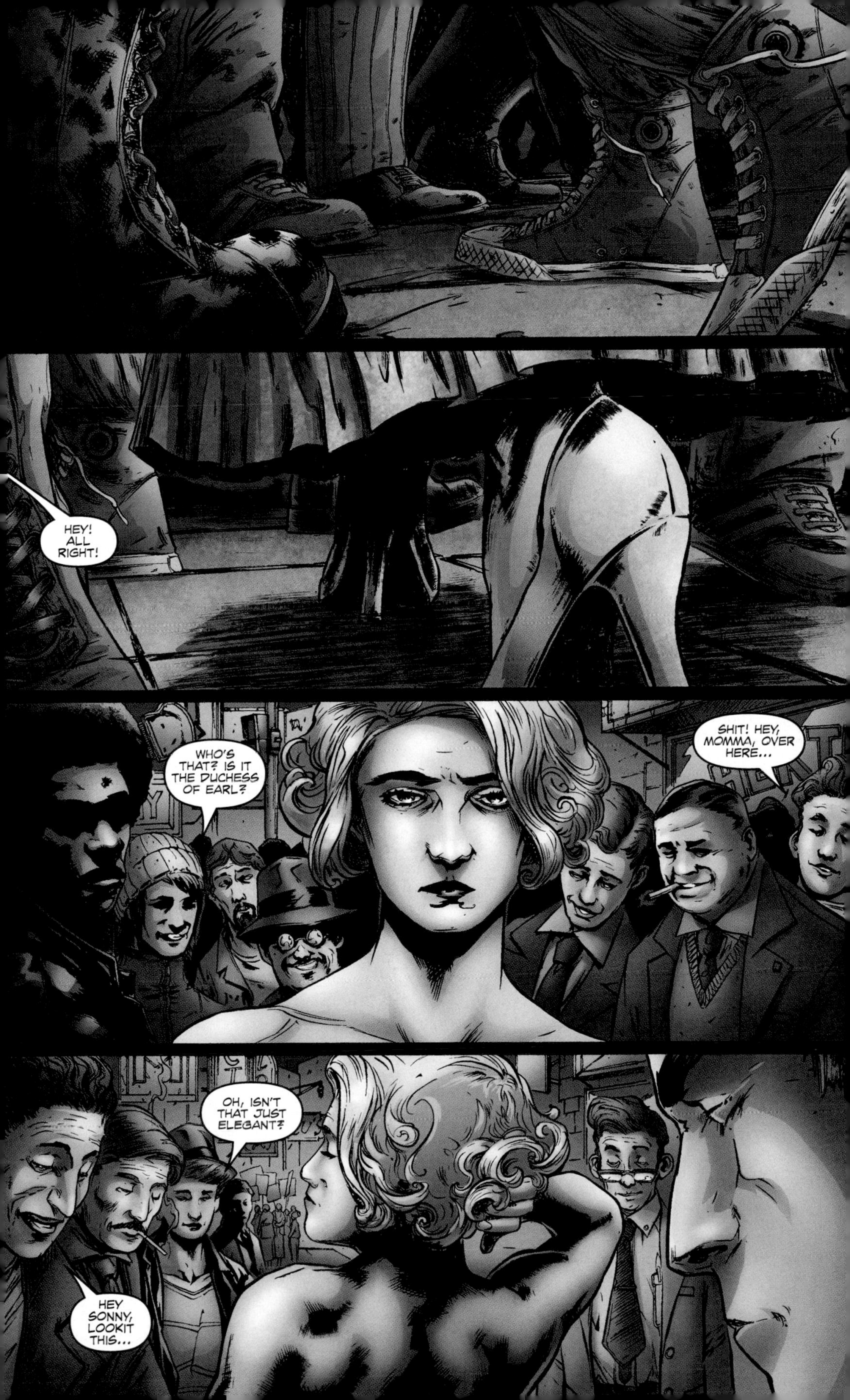
HEY! ALL RIGHT!
WHO'S THAT? IS IT THE DUCHESS OF EARL?
SHIT! HEY, MOMMA, OVER HERE...
OH, ISN'T THAT JUST ELEGANT?
HEY SONNY, LOOKIT THIS...

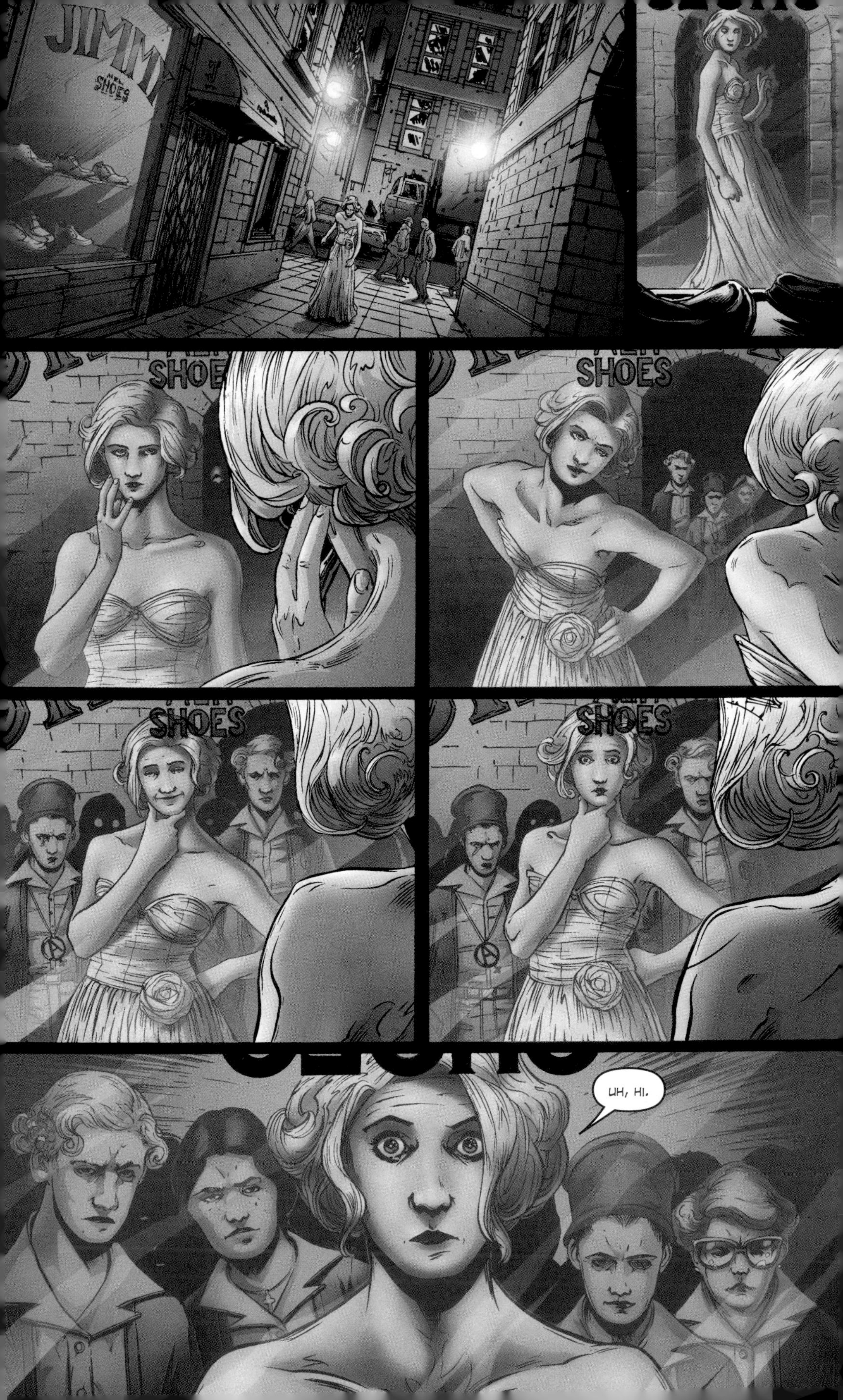
JIMMY
SHOES
UH, HI.

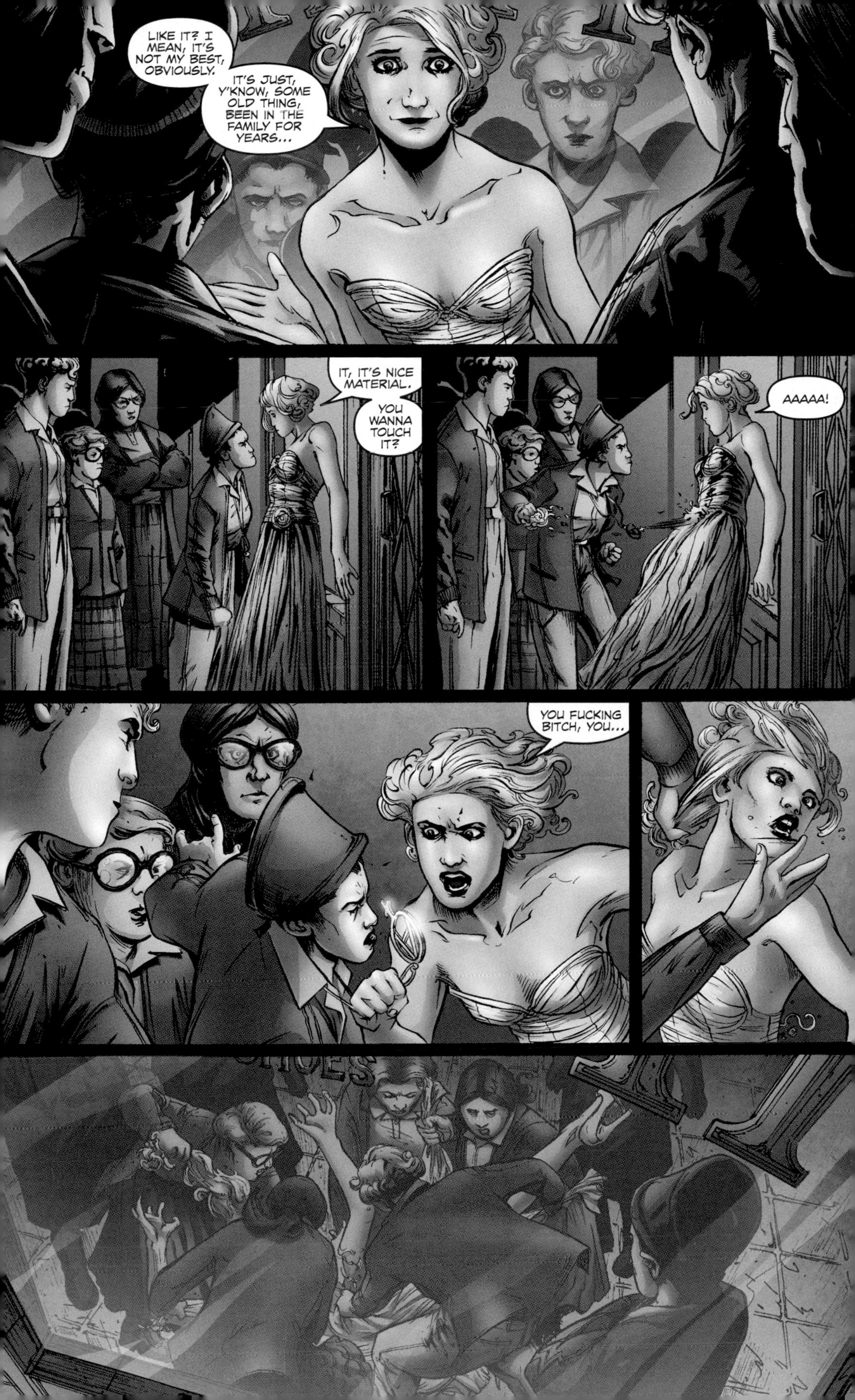
LIKE IT? I MEAN, IT'S NOT MY BEST, OBVIOUSLY.
IT'S JUST, Y'KNOW, SOME OLD THING, BEEN IN THE FAMILY FOR YEARS...
IT, IT'S NICE MATERIAL.
YOU WANNA TOUCH IT?
AAAAA!
YOU FUCKING BITCH, YOU...
SHOES

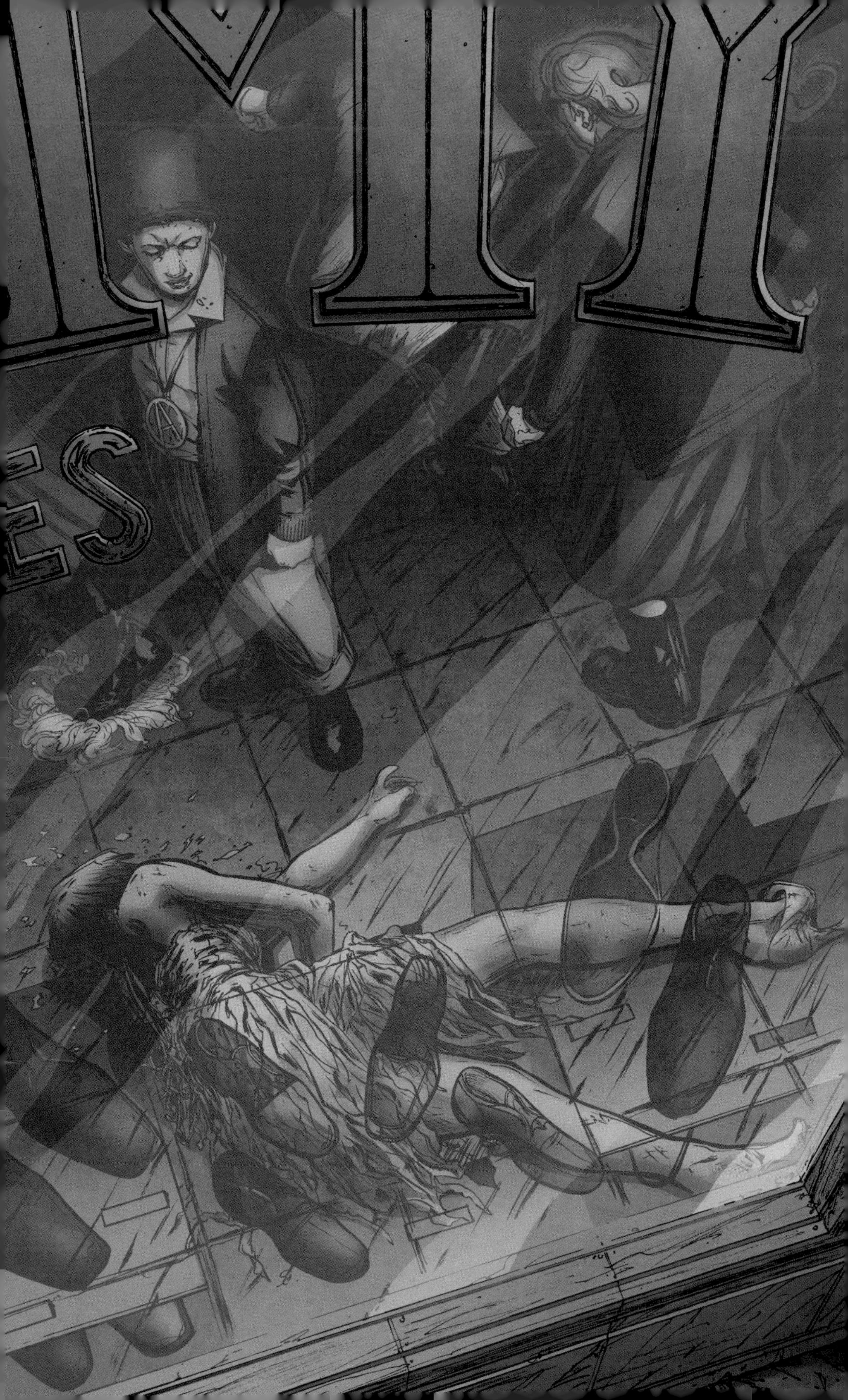

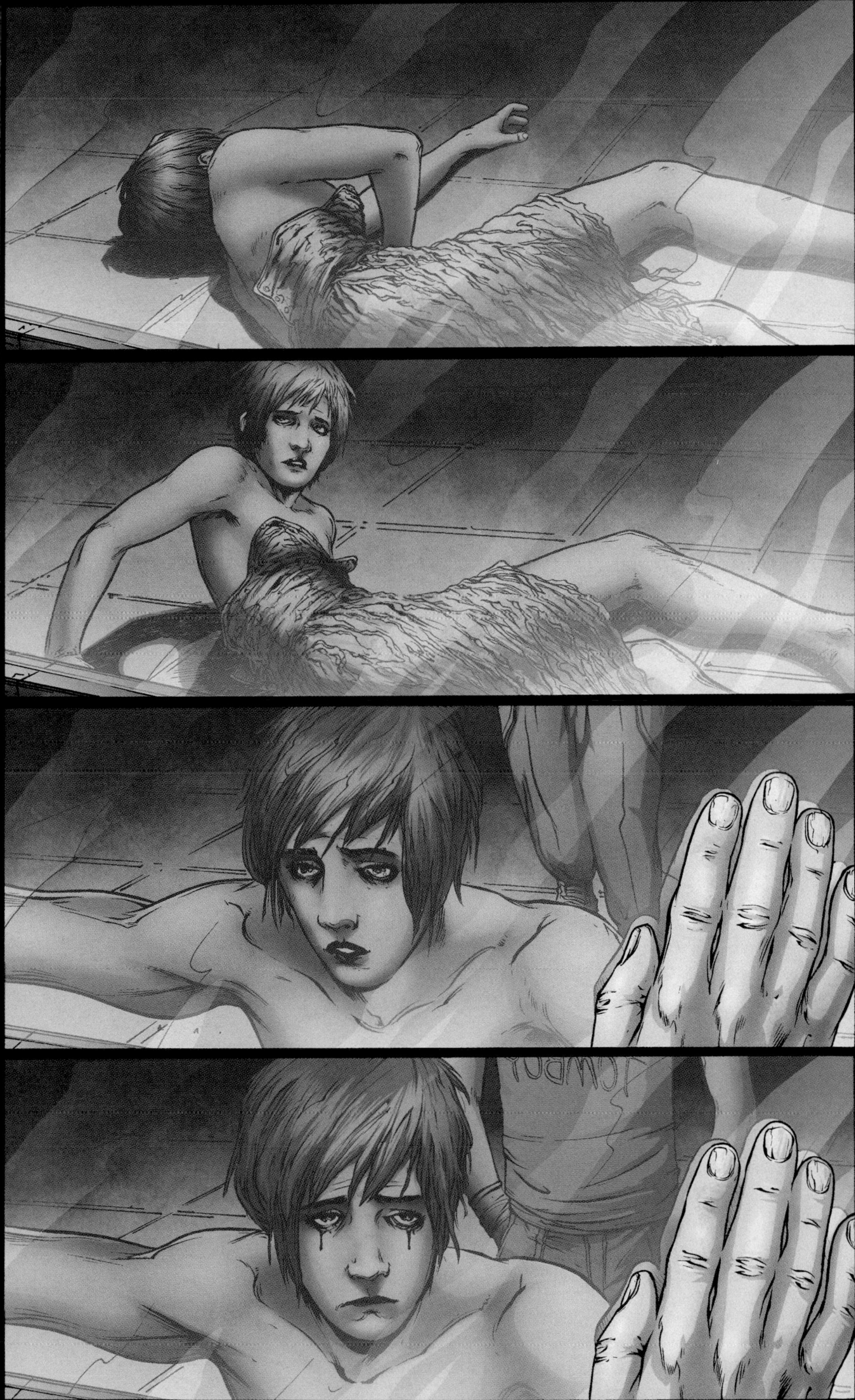

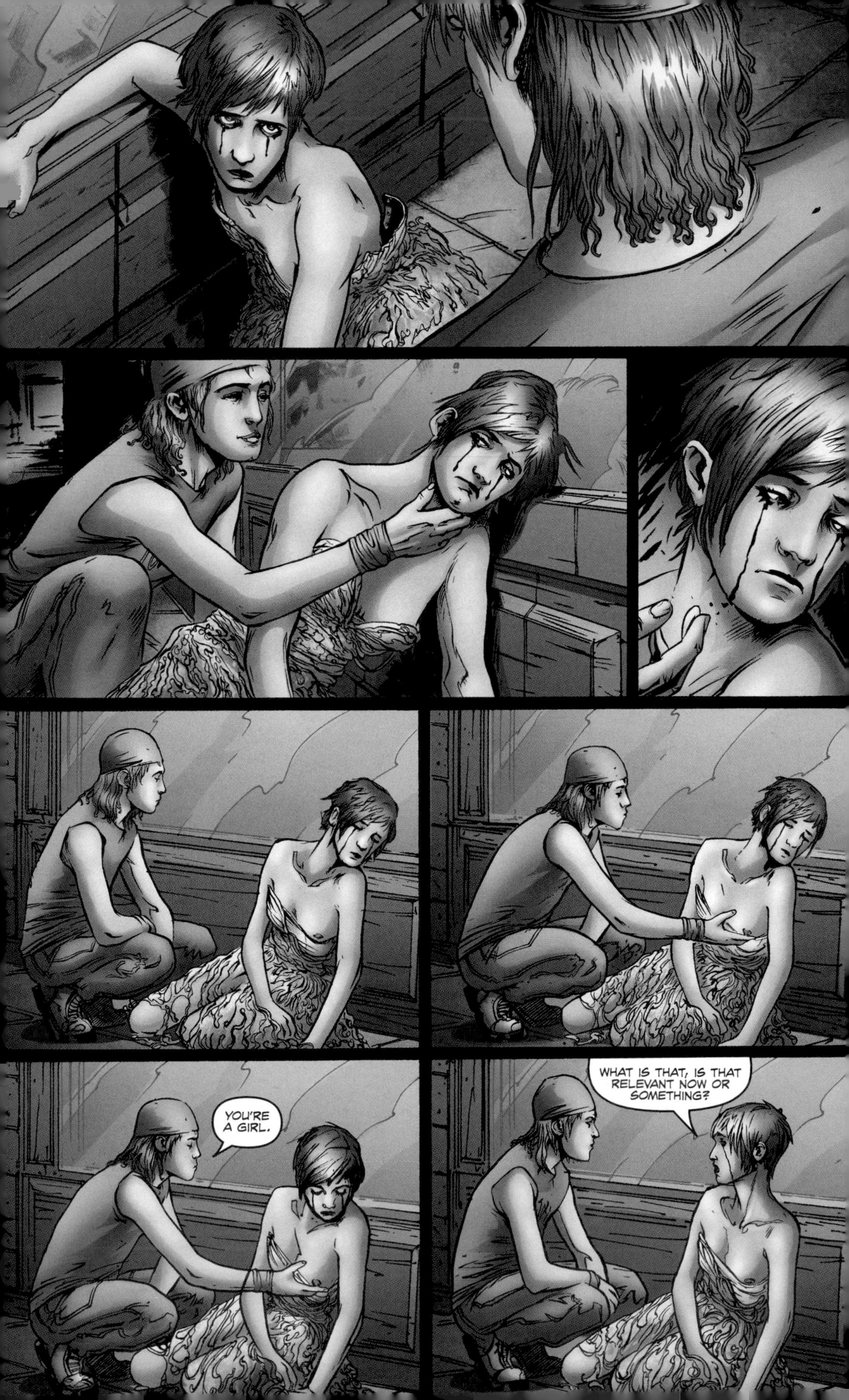
YOU'RE A GIRL.
WHAT IS THAT, IS THAT RELEVANT NOW OR SOMETHING?

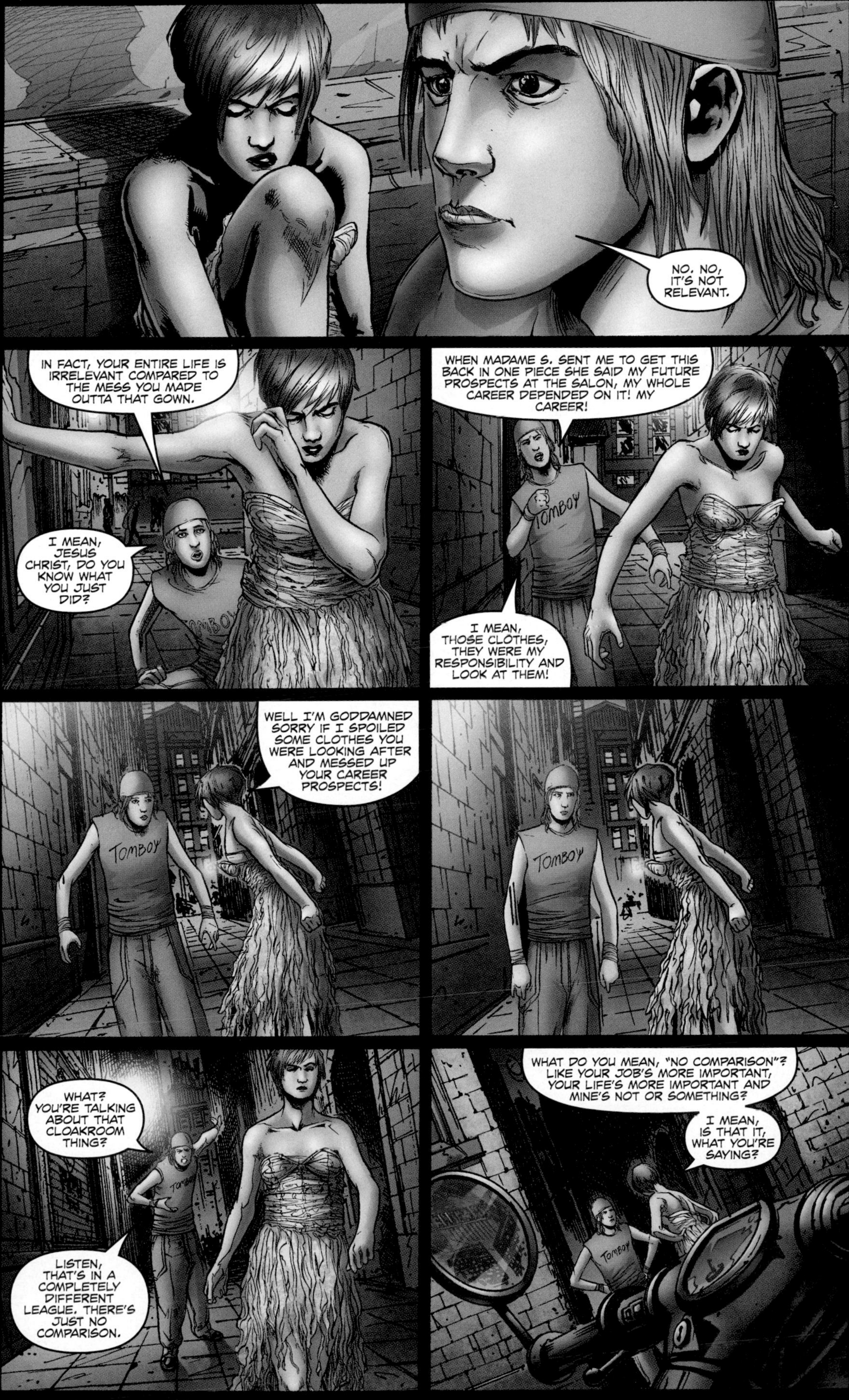
NO. NO, IT'S NOT RELEVANT.
IN FACT, YOUR ENTIRE LIFE IS IRRELEVANT COMPARED TO THE MESS YOU MADE OUTTA THAT GOWN.
I MEAN, JESUS CHRIST, DO YOU KNOW WHAT YOU JUST DID?
TOMBOY
WHEN MADAME S. SENT ME TO GET THIS BACK IN ONE PIECE SHE SAID MY FUTURE PROSPECTS AT THE SALON, MY WHOLE CAREER DEPENDED ON IT! MY CAREER!
TOMBOY
I MEAN, THOSE CLOTHES, THEY WERE MY RESPONSIBILITY AND LOOK AT THEM!
WELL I'M GODDAMNED SORRY IF I SPOILED SOME CLOTHES YOU WERE LOOKING AFTER AND MESSED UP YOUR CAREER PROSPECTS!
TOMBOY
TOMBOY
WHAT? YOU'RE TALKING ABOUT THAT CLOAKROOM THING?
LISTEN, THAT'S IN A COMPLETELY DIFFERENT LEAGUE. THERE'S JUST NO COMPARISON.
WHAT DO YOU MEAN, "NO COMPARISON"? LIKE YOUR JOB'S MORE IMPORTANT, YOUR LIFE'S MORE IMPORTANT AND MINE'S NOT OR SOMETHING?
I MEAN, IS THAT IT, WHAT YOU'RE SAYING?
TOMBOY

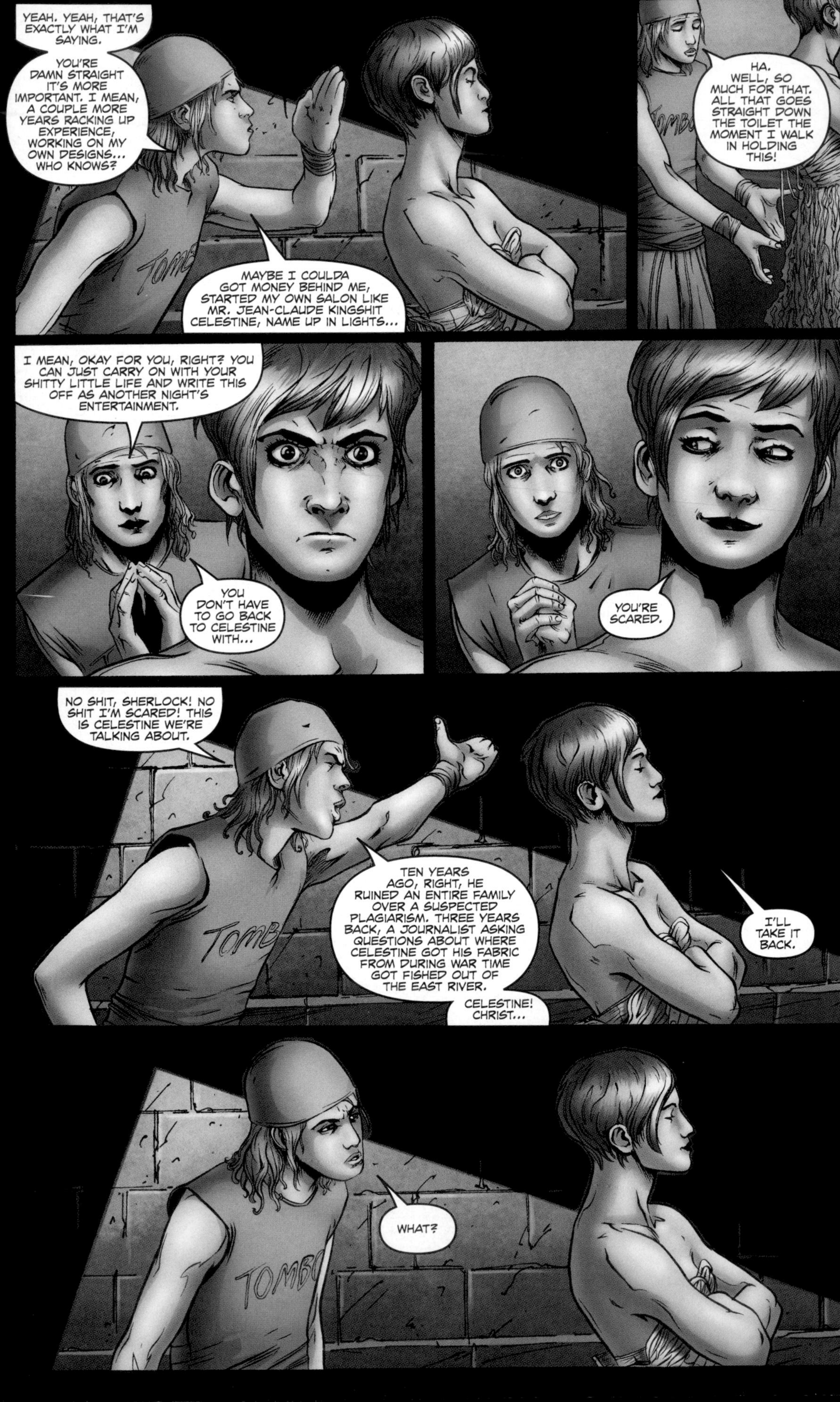
YEAH. YEAH, THAT'S EXACTLY WHAT I'M SAYING.
YOU'RE DAMN STRAIGHT IT'S MORE IMPORTANT. I MEAN, A COUPLE MORE YEARS RACKING UP EXPERIENCE, WORKING ON MY OWN DESIGNS... WHO KNOWS?
MAYBE I COULDA GOT MONEY BEHIND ME, STARTED MY OWN SALON LIKE MR. JEAN-CLAUDE KINGSHIT CELESTINE, NAME UP IN LIGHTS...
HA. WELL, SO MUCH FOR THAT. ALL THAT GOES STRAIGHT DOWN THE TOILET THE MOMENT I WALK IN HOLDING THIS!
I MEAN, OKAY FOR YOU, RIGHT? YOU CAN JUST CARRY ON WITH YOUR SHITTY LITTLE LIFE AND WRITE THIS OFF AS ANOTHER NIGHT'S ENTERTAINMENT.
YOU DON'T HAVE TO GO BACK TO CELESTINE WITH...
YOU'RE SCARED.
NO SHIT, SHERLOCK! NO SHIT I'M SCARED! THIS IS CELESTINE WE'RE TALKING ABOUT.
TEN YEARS AGO, RIGHT, HE RUINED AN ENTIRE FAMILY OVER A SUSPECTED PLAGIARISM. THREE YEARS BACK, A JOURNALIST ASKING QUESTIONS ABOUT WHERE CELESTINE GOT HIS FABRIC FROM DURING WAR TIME GOT FISHED OUT OF THE EAST RIVER.
CELESTINE! CHRIST...
I'LL TAKE IT BACK.
WHAT?

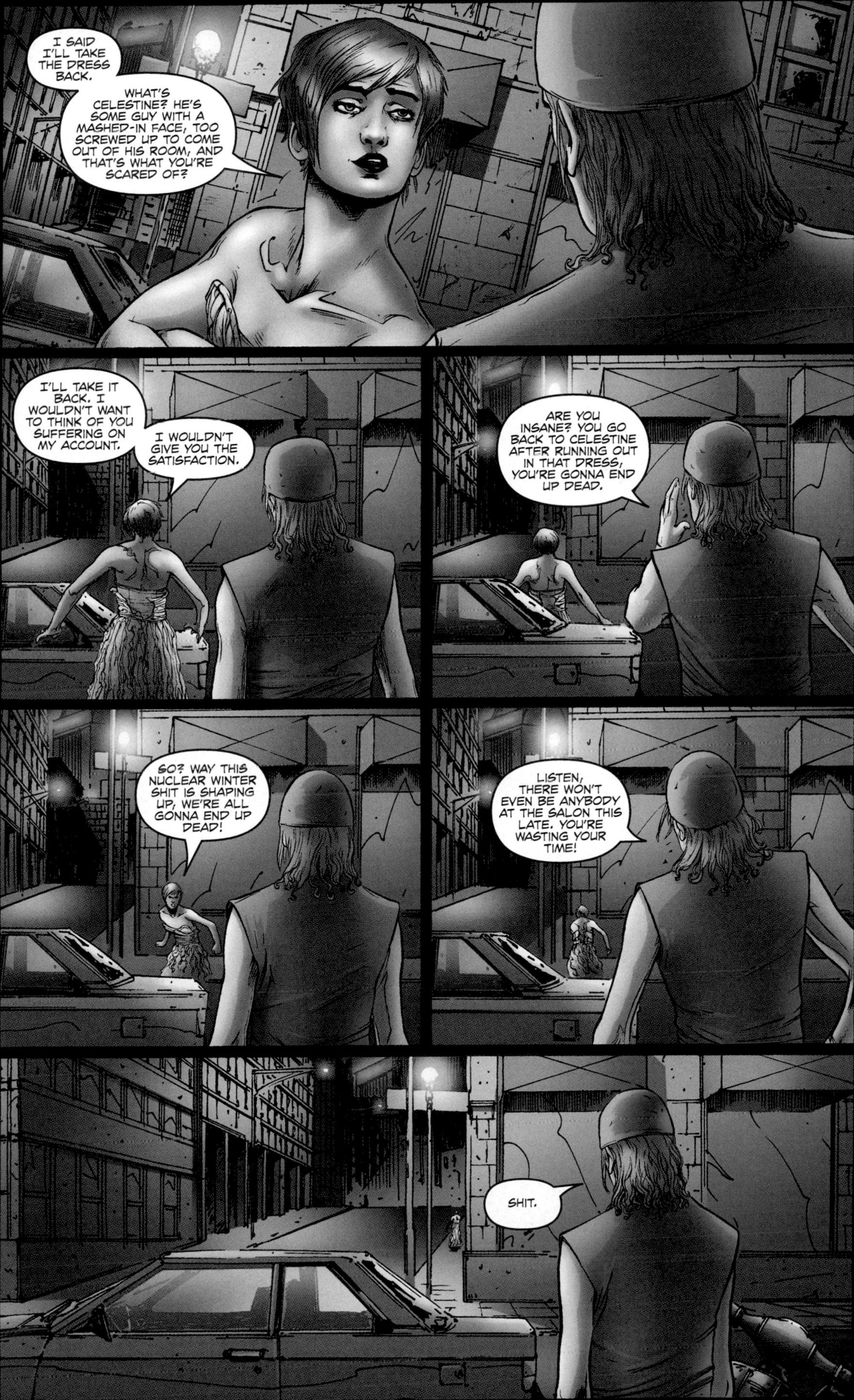
I SAID I'LL TAKE THE DRESS BACK.
WHAT'S CELESTINE? HE'S SOME GUY WITH A MASHED-IN FACE, TOO SCREWED UP TO COME OUT OF HIS ROOM, AND THAT'S WHAT YOU'RE SCARED OF?
I'LL TAKE IT BACK. I WOULDN'T WANT TO THINK OF YOU SUFFERING ON MY ACCOUNT.
I WOULDN'T GIVE YOU THE SATISFACTION.
ARE YOU INSANE? YOU GO BACK TO CELESTINE AFTER RUNNING OUT IN THAT DRESS, YOU'RE GONNA END UP DEAD.
SO? WAY THIS NUCLEAR WINTER SHIT IS SHAPING UP, WE'RE ALL GONNA END UP DEAD!
LISTEN, THERE WON'T EVEN BE ANYBODY AT THE SALON THIS LATE. YOU'RE WASTING YOUR TIME!
SHIT.

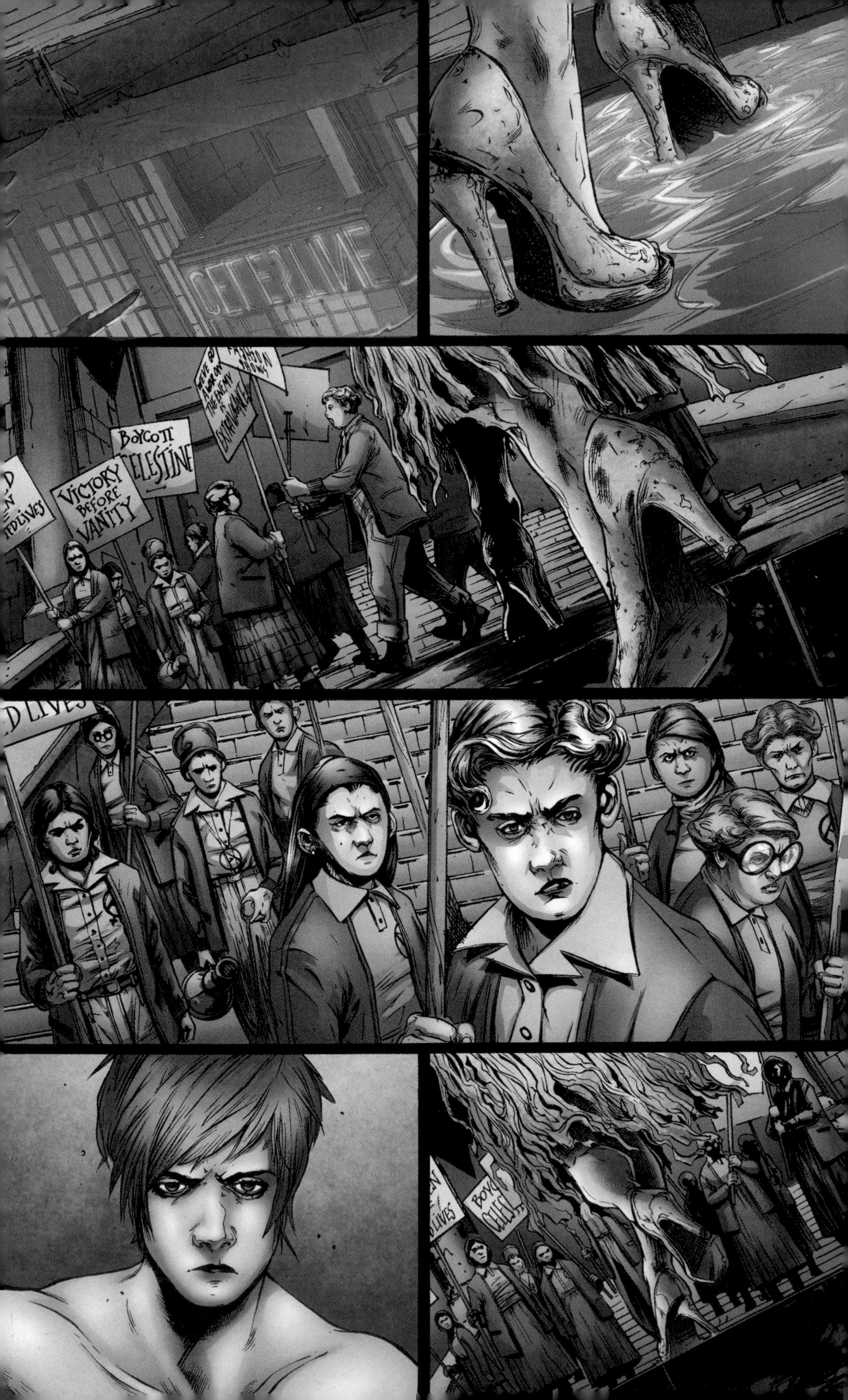
BOYCOTT CELESTINE
VICTORY BEFORE VANITY
THE ENEMY IS EXTRAVAGANCE

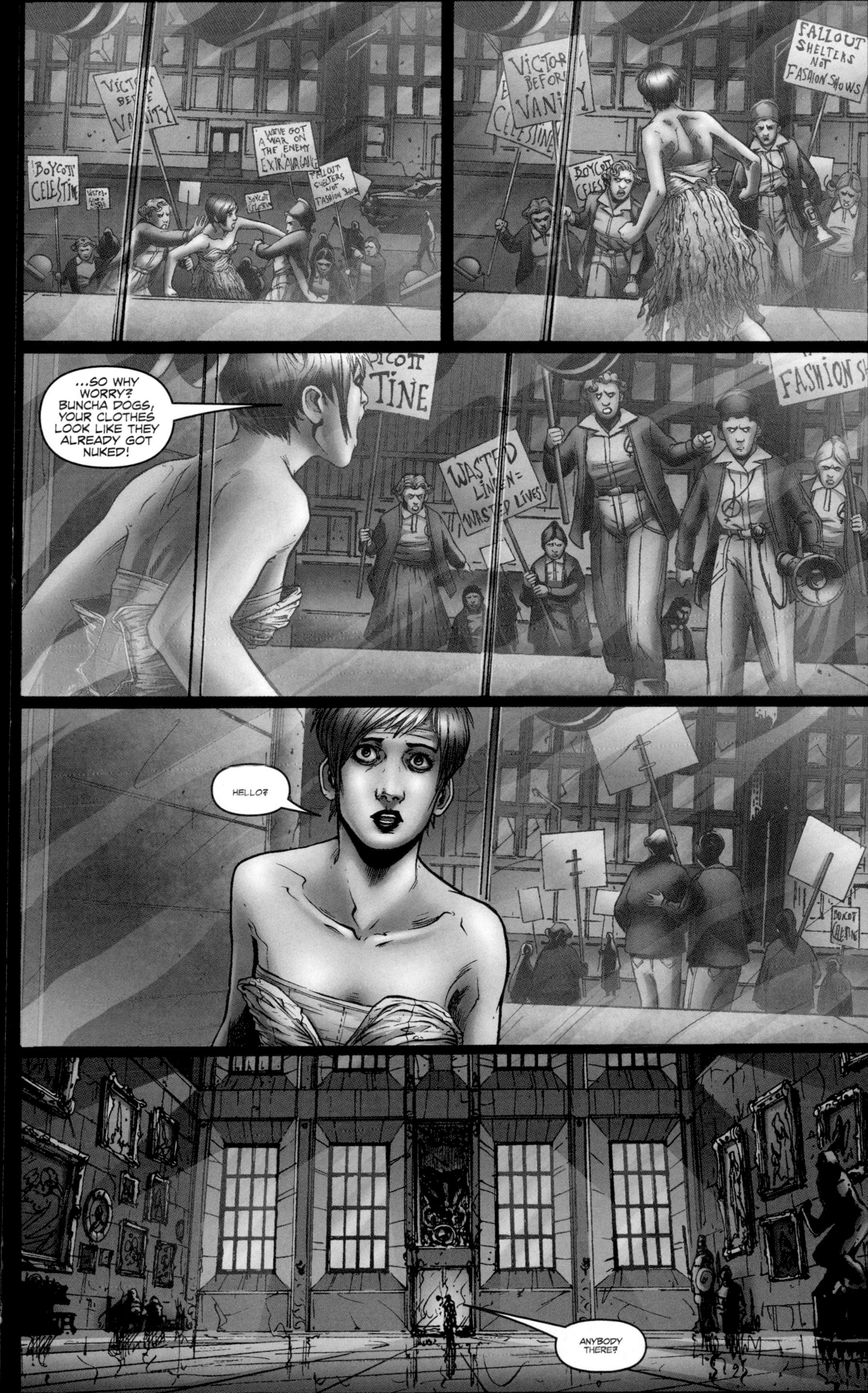
BOYCOTT CELESTINE
FALLOUT SHELTERS NOT FASHION SHOWS
...SO WHY WORRY? BUNCHA DOGS, YOUR CLOTHES LOOK LIKE THEY ALREADY GOT NUKED!
WASTED LINEN = WASTED LIVES
HELLO?
ANYBODY THERE?

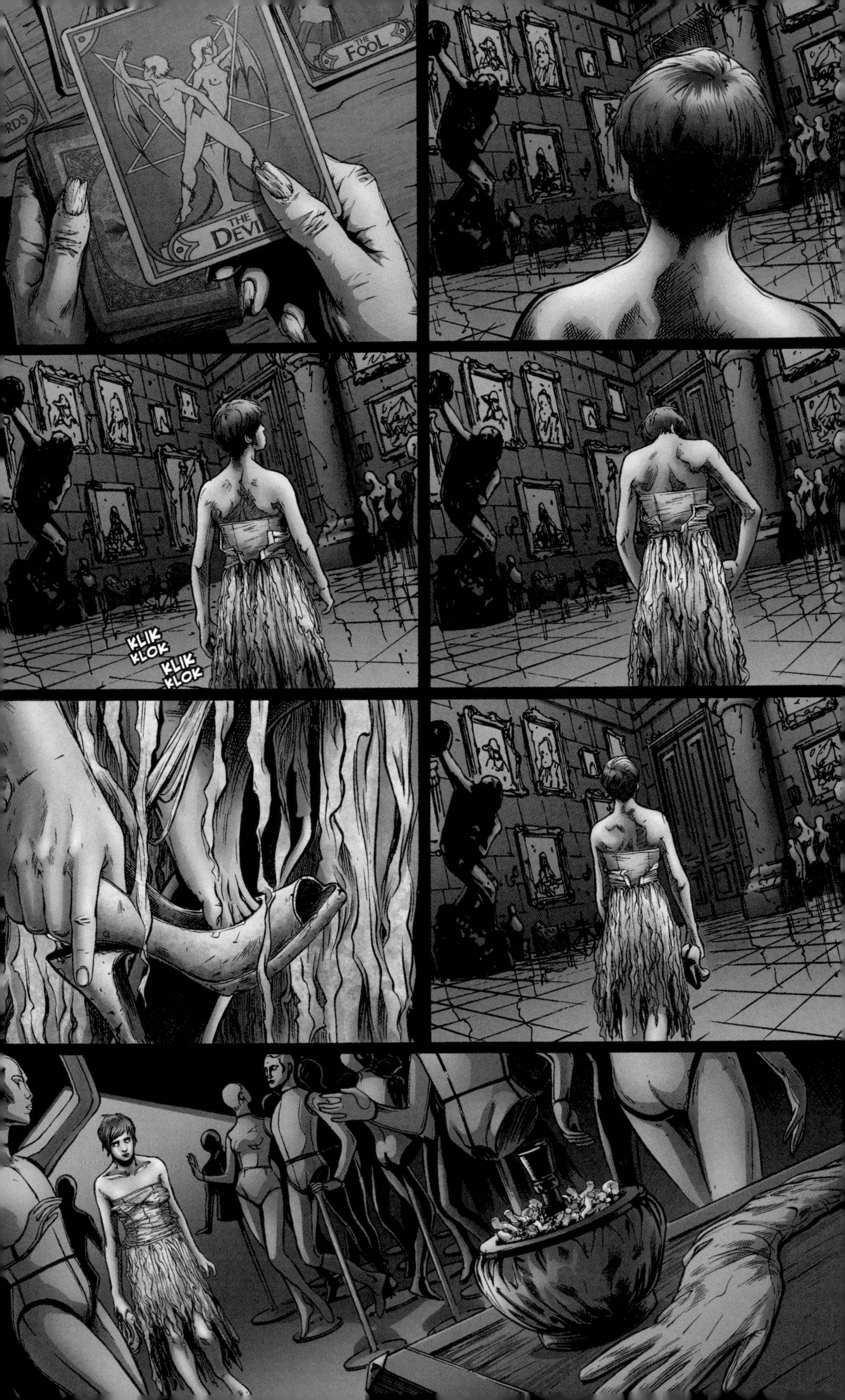

THE FOOL
THE DEVIL
KLIK
KLOK
KLIK
KLOK

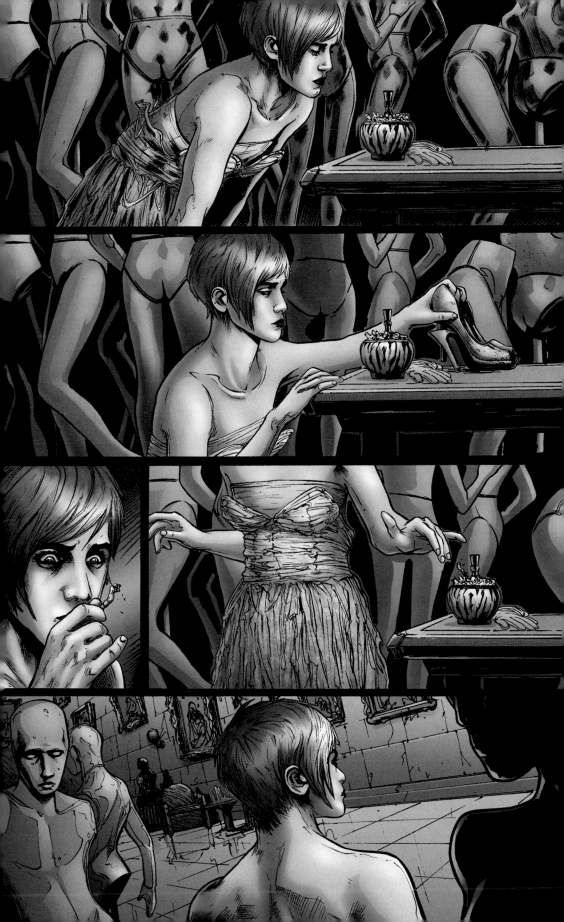

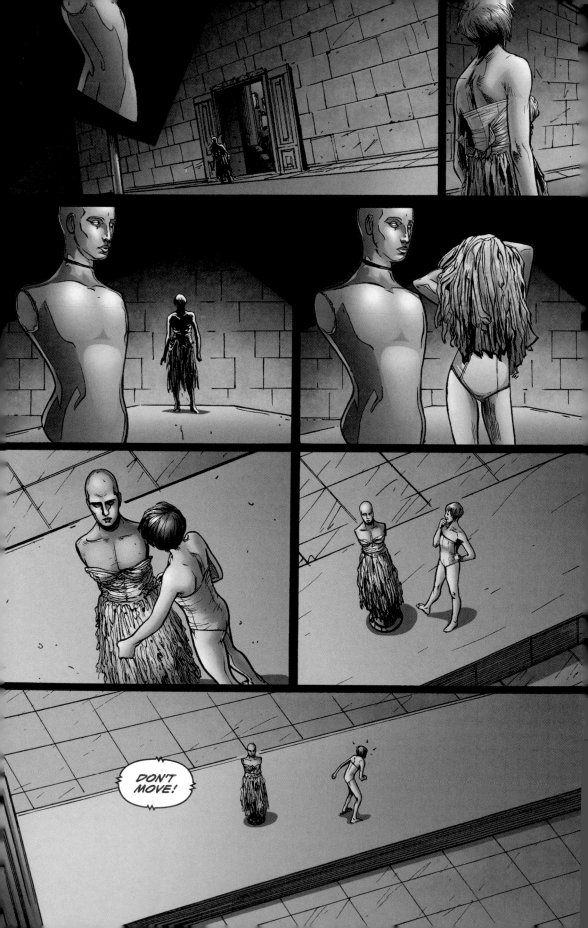

DON'T MOVE!

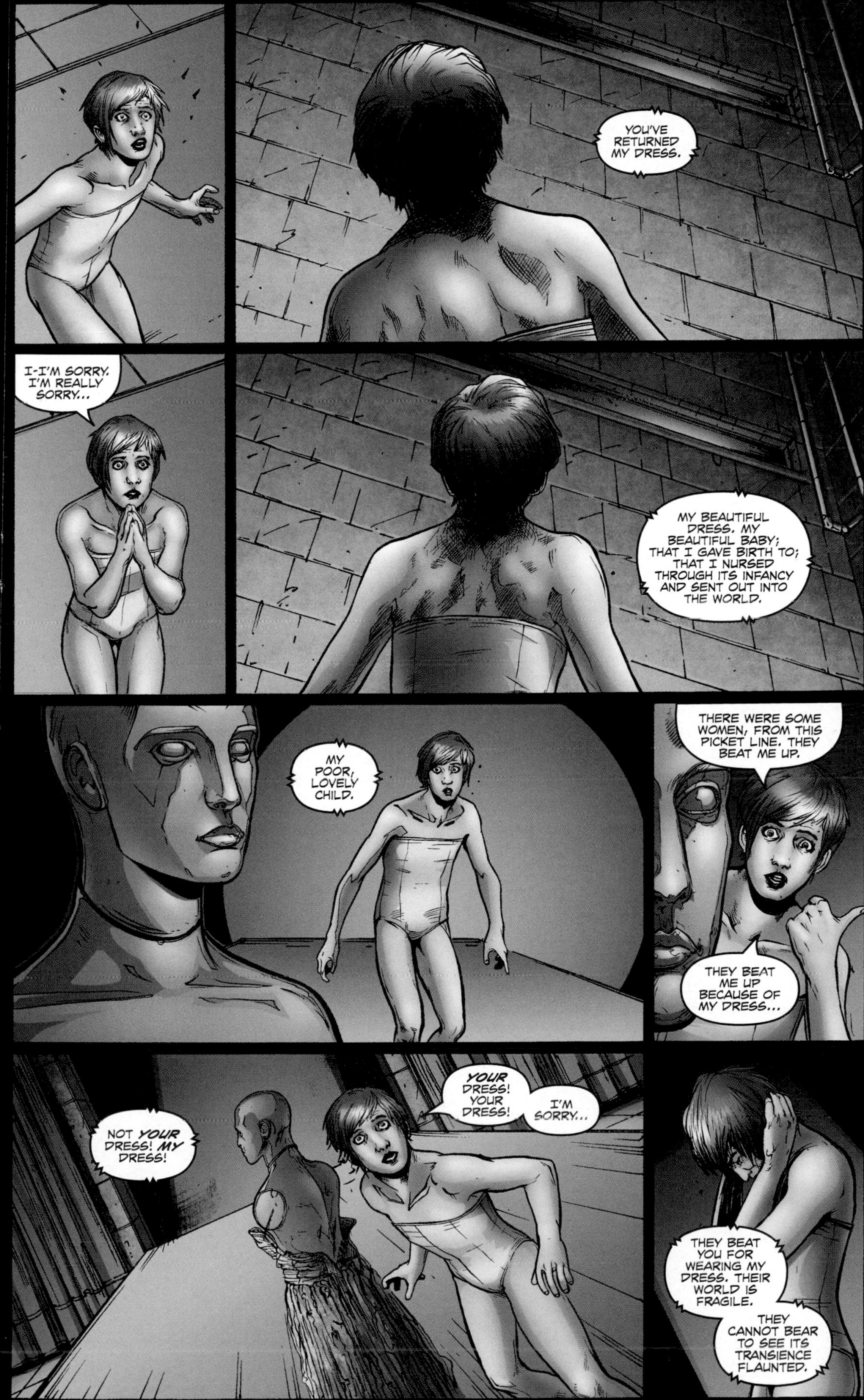
YOU'VE RETURNED MY DRESS.
I-I'M SORRY. I'M REALLY SORRY...
MY BEAUTIFUL DRESS. MY BEAUTIFUL BABY; THAT I GAVE BIRTH TO; THAT I NURSED THROUGH ITS INFANCY AND SENT OUT INTO THE WORLD.
MY POOR, LOVELY CHILD.
THERE WERE SOME WOMEN, FROM THIS PICKET LINE. THEY BEAT ME UP.
THEY BEAT ME UP BECAUSE OF MY DRESS...
YOUR DRESS! YOUR DRESS!
I'M SORRY...
NOT *YOUR* DRESS! *MY* DRESS!
THEY BEAT YOU FOR WEARING MY DRESS. THEIR WORLD IS FRAGILE.
THEY CANNOT BEAR TO SEE ITS TRANSIENCE FLAUNTED.

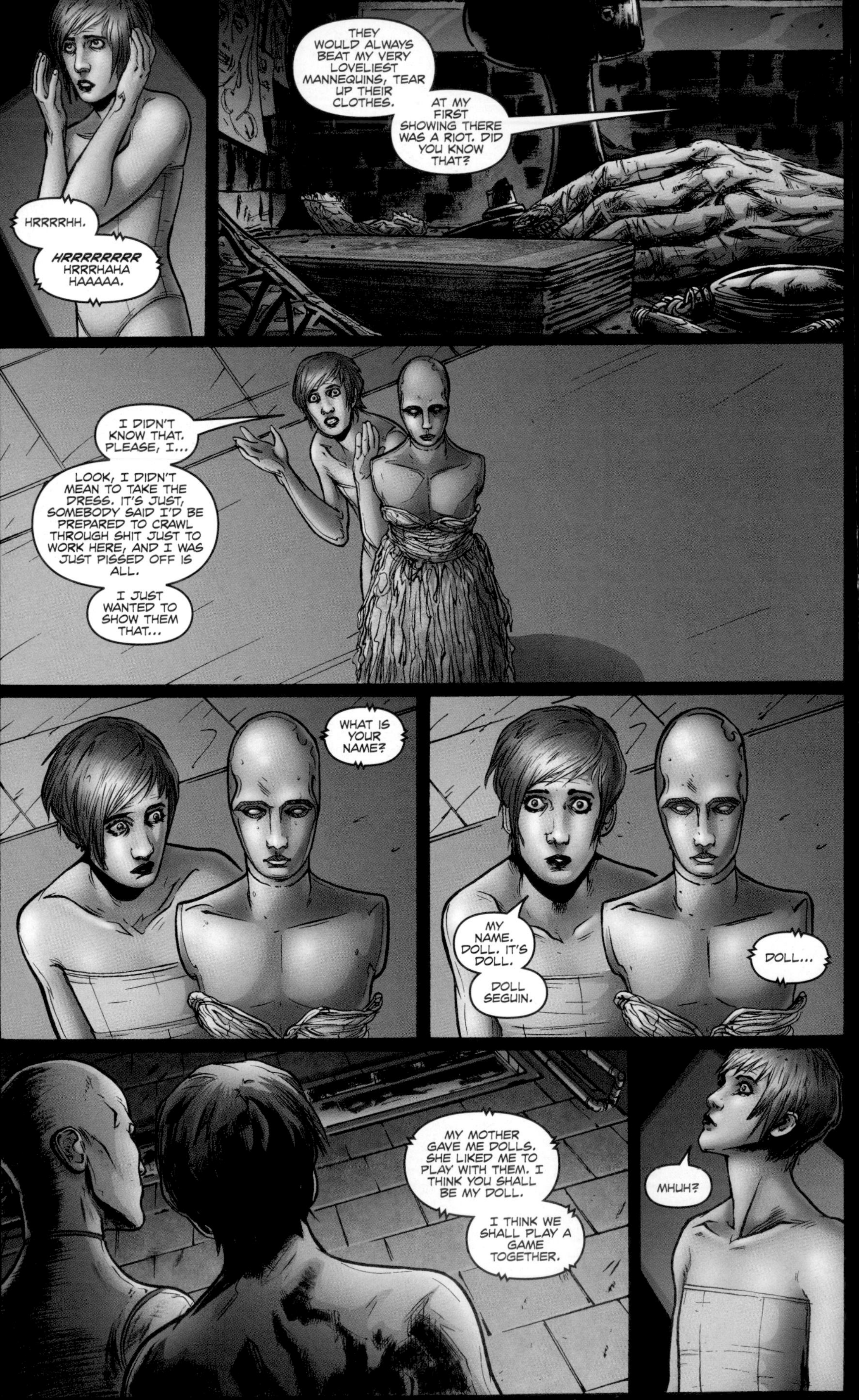
HRRRRHH.
HRRRRRRRR HRRRHAHA HAAAAA.
THEY WOULD ALWAYS BEAT MY VERY LOVELIEST MANNEQUINS, TEAR UP THEIR CLOTHES.
AT MY FIRST SHOWING THERE WAS A RIOT. DID YOU KNOW THAT?
I DIDN'T KNOW THAT. PLEASE, I...
LOOK, I DIDN'T MEAN TO TAKE THE DRESS. IT'S JUST, SOMEBODY SAID I'D BE PREPARED TO CRAWL THROUGH SHIT JUST TO WORK HERE, AND I WAS JUST PISSED OFF IS ALL.
I JUST WANTED TO SHOW THEM THAT...
WHAT IS YOUR NAME?
MY NAME. DOLL. IT'S DOLL.
DOLL SEGUIN.
DOLL...
MY MOTHER GAVE ME DOLLS. SHE LIKED ME TO PLAY WITH THEM. I THINK YOU SHALL BE MY DOLL.
I THINK WE SHALL PLAY A GAME TOGETHER.
MHUH?

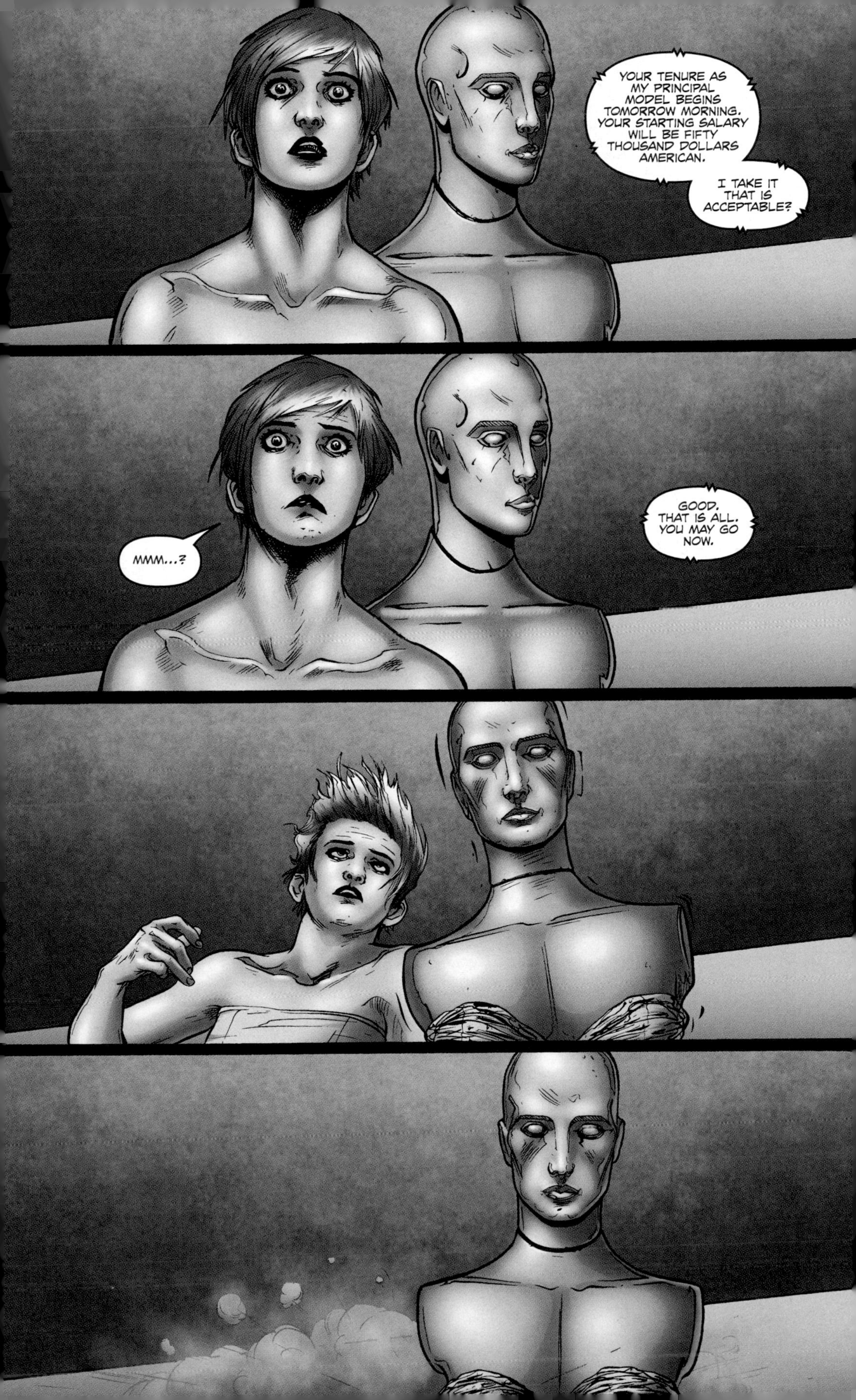
YOUR TENURE AS MY PRINCIPAL MODEL BEGINS TOMORROW MORNING. YOUR STARTING SALARY WILL BE FIFTY THOUSAND DOLLARS AMERICAN.
I TAKE IT THAT IS ACCEPTABLE?
MMM...?
GOOD. THAT IS ALL. YOU MAY GO NOW.

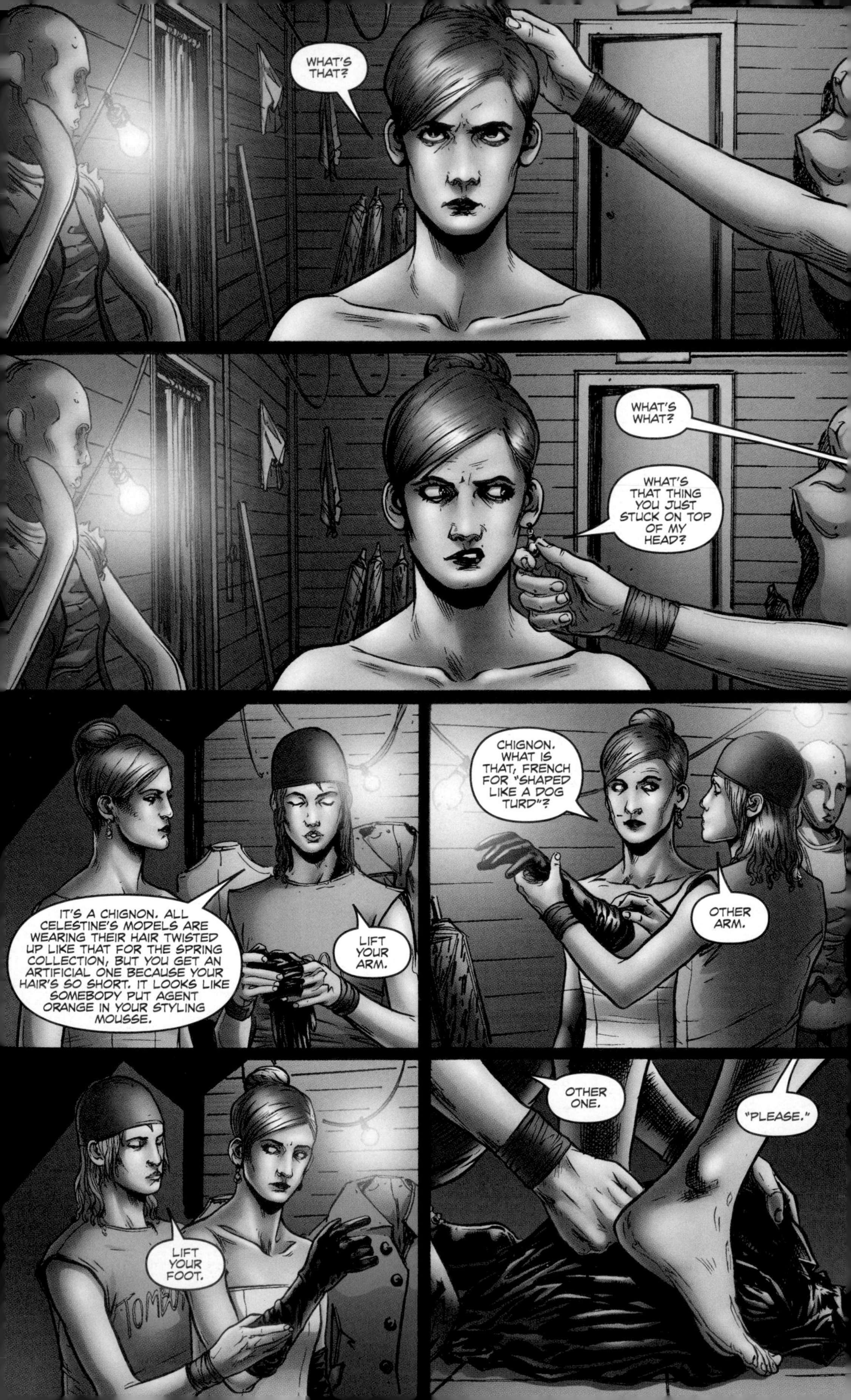
WHAT'S THAT?
WHAT'S WHAT?
WHAT'S THAT THING YOU JUST STUCK ON TOP OF MY HEAD?
IT'S A CHIGNON. ALL CELESTINE'S MODELS ARE WEARING THEIR HAIR TWISTED UP LIKE THAT FOR THE SPRING COLLECTION, BUT YOU GET AN ARTIFICIAL ONE BECAUSE YOUR HAIR'S SO SHORT. IT LOOKS LIKE SOMEBODY PUT AGENT ORANGE IN YOUR STYLING MOUSSE.
LIFT YOUR ARM.
CHIGNON. WHAT IS THAT, FRENCH FOR "SHAPED LIKE A DOG TURD"?
OTHER ARM.
LIFT YOUR FOOT.
OTHER ONE.
"PLEASE."

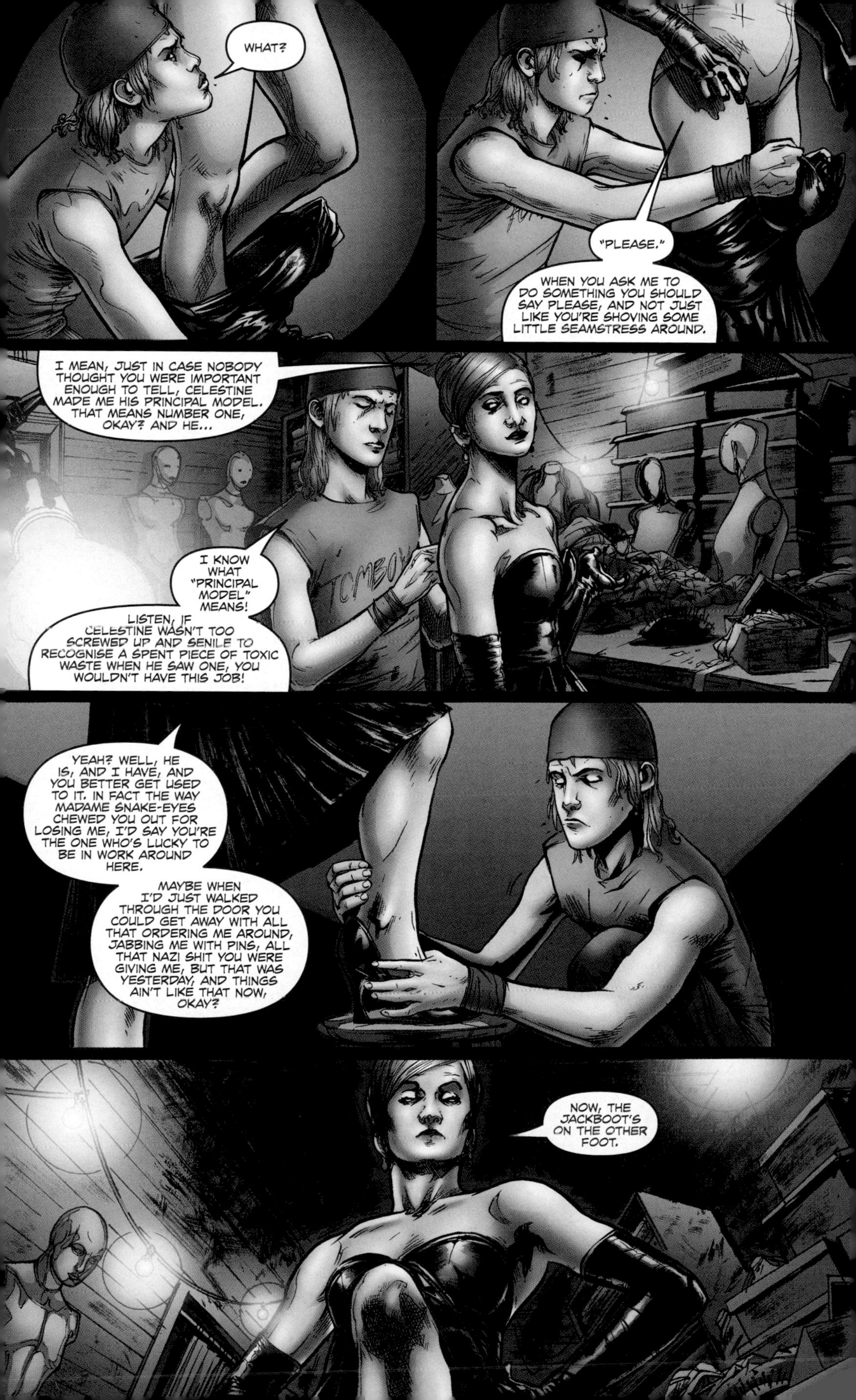
WHAT?
"PLEASE."
WHEN YOU ASK ME TO DO SOMETHING YOU SHOULD SAY PLEASE, AND NOT JUST LIKE YOU'RE SHOVING SOME LITTLE SEAMSTRESS AROUND.
I MEAN, JUST IN CASE NOBODY THOUGHT YOU WERE IMPORTANT ENOUGH TO TELL, CELESTINE MADE ME HIS PRINCIPAL MODEL. THAT MEANS NUMBER ONE, OKAY? AND HE...
I KNOW WHAT "PRINCIPAL MODEL" MEANS!
LISTEN, IF CELESTINE WASN'T TOO SCREWED UP AND SENILE TO RECOGNISE A SPENT PIECE OF TOXIC WASTE WHEN HE SAW ONE, YOU WOULDN'T HAVE THIS JOB!
TOMBOY
YEAH? WELL, HE IS, AND I HAVE, AND YOU BETTER GET USED TO IT. IN FACT THE WAY MADAME SNAKE-EYES CHEWED YOU OUT FOR LOSING ME, I'D SAY YOU'RE THE ONE WHO'S LUCKY TO BE IN WORK AROUND HERE.
MAYBE WHEN I'D JUST WALKED THROUGH THE DOOR YOU COULD GET AWAY WITH ALL THAT ORDERING ME AROUND, JABBING ME WITH PINS, ALL THAT NAZI SHIT YOU WERE GIVING ME, BUT THAT WAS YESTERDAY, AND THINGS AIN'T LIKE THAT NOW, OKAY?
NOW, THE JACKBOOT'S ON THE OTHER FOOT.

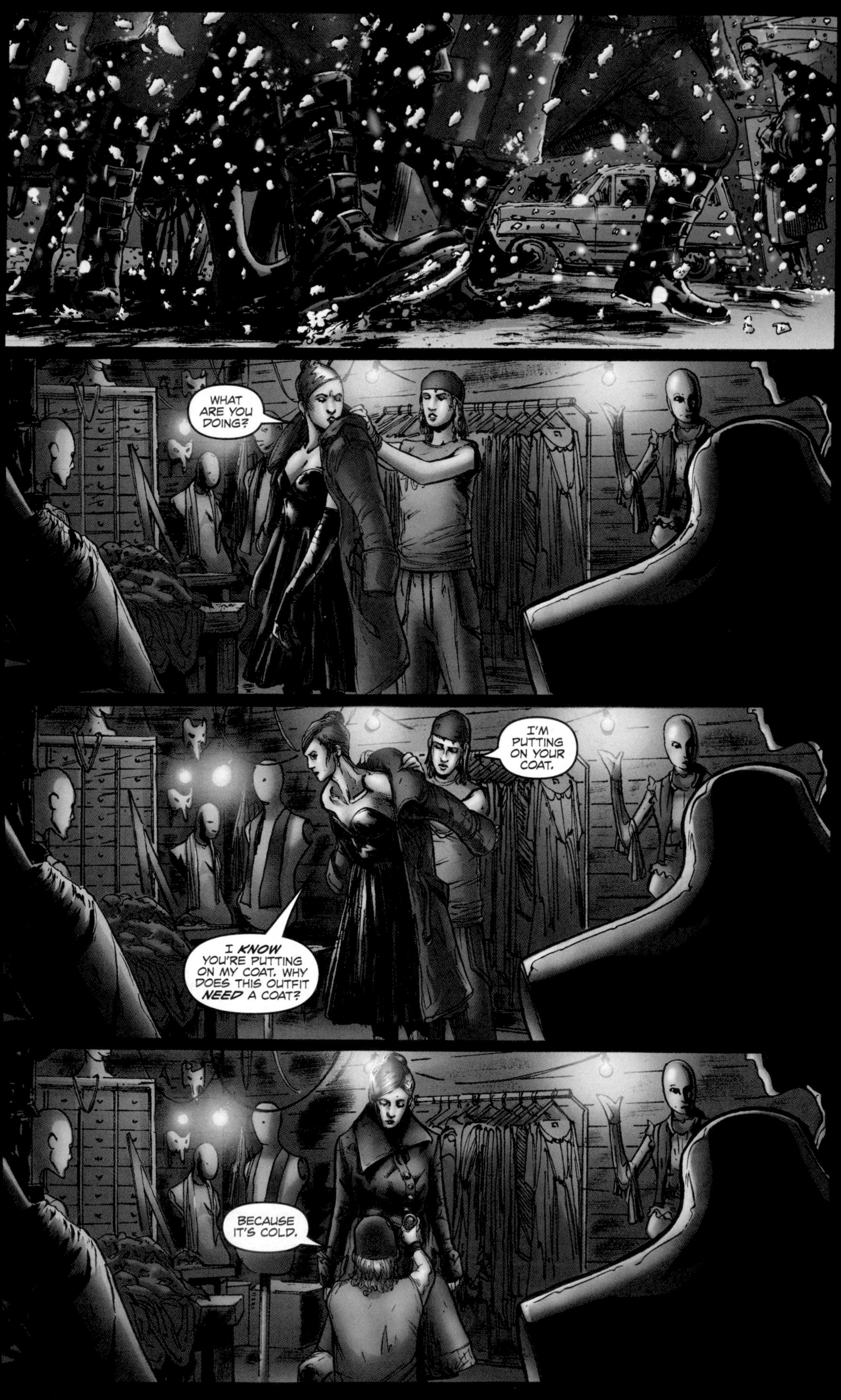
WHAT ARE YOU DOING?
I'M PUTTING ON YOUR COAT.
I *KNOW* YOU'RE PUTTING ON MY COAT. WHY DOES THIS OUTFIT *NEED* A COAT?
BECAUSE IT'S COLD.

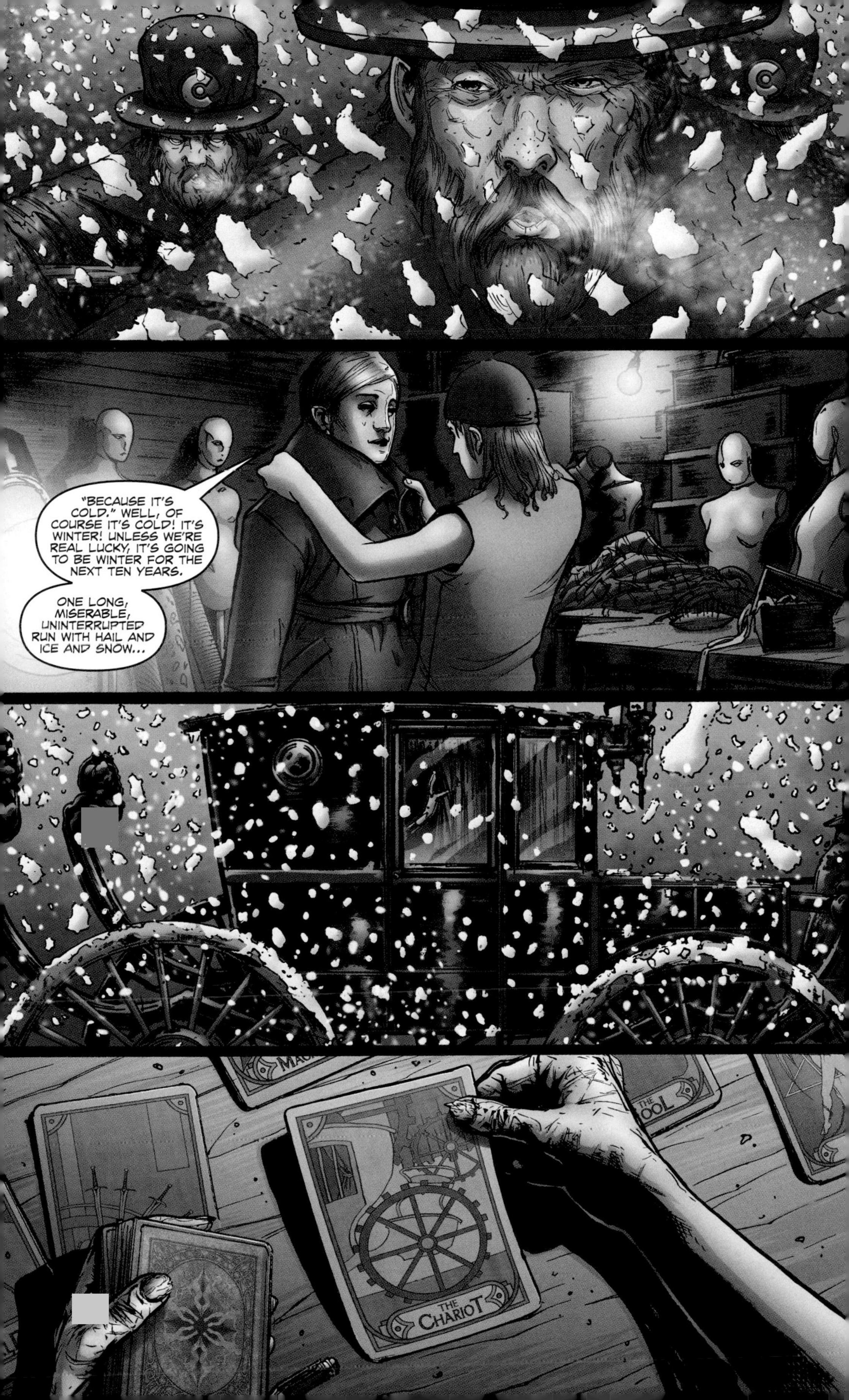

"BECAUSE IT'S COLD." WELL, OF COURSE IT'S COLD! IT'S WINTER! UNLESS WE'RE REAL LUCKY, IT'S GOING TO BE WINTER FOR THE NEXT TEN YEARS.
ONE LONG, MISERABLE, UNINTERRUPTED RUN WITH HAIL AND ICE AND SNOW...
THE CHARIOT

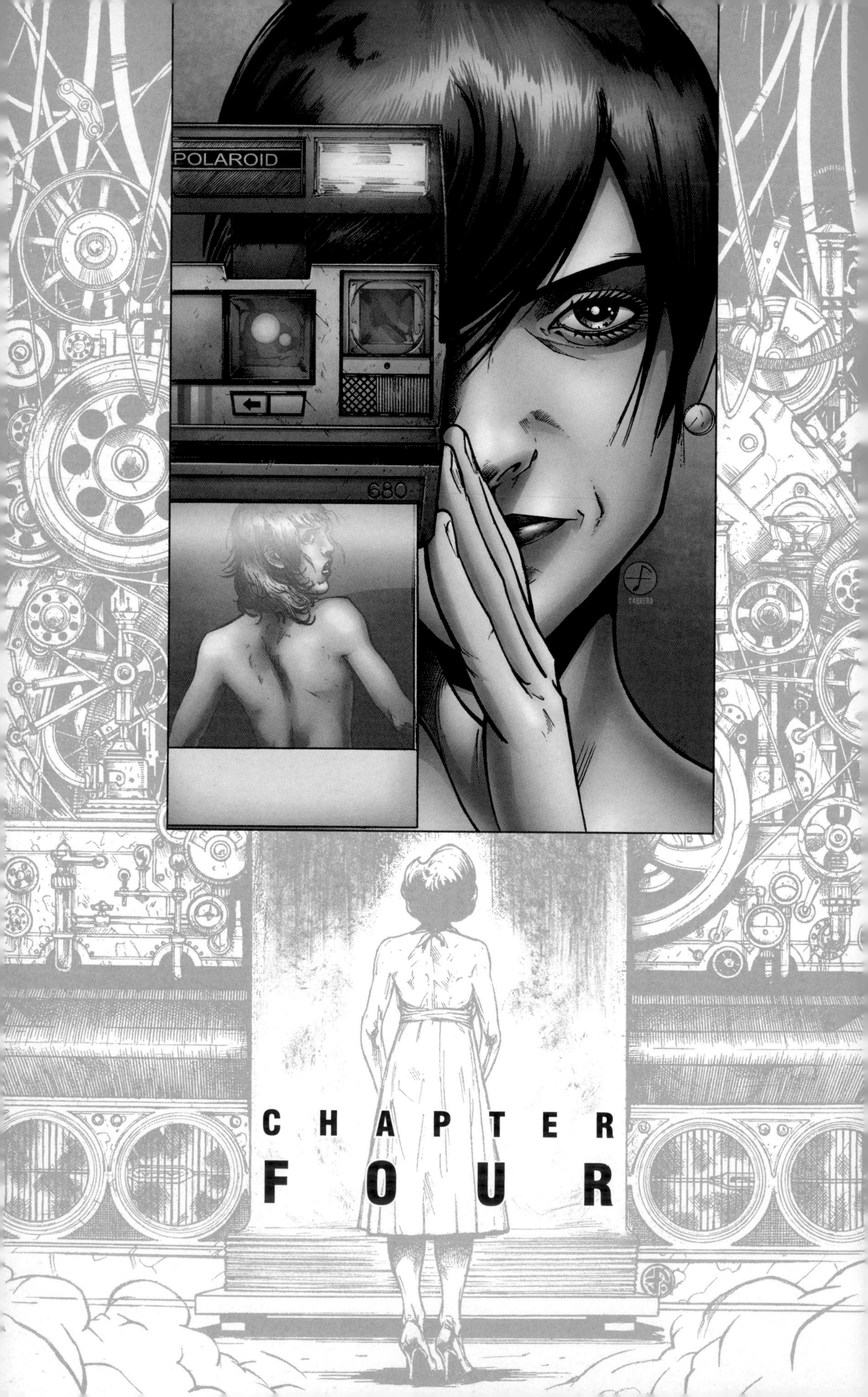
POLAROID
680
CABRERA

CHAPTER FOUR

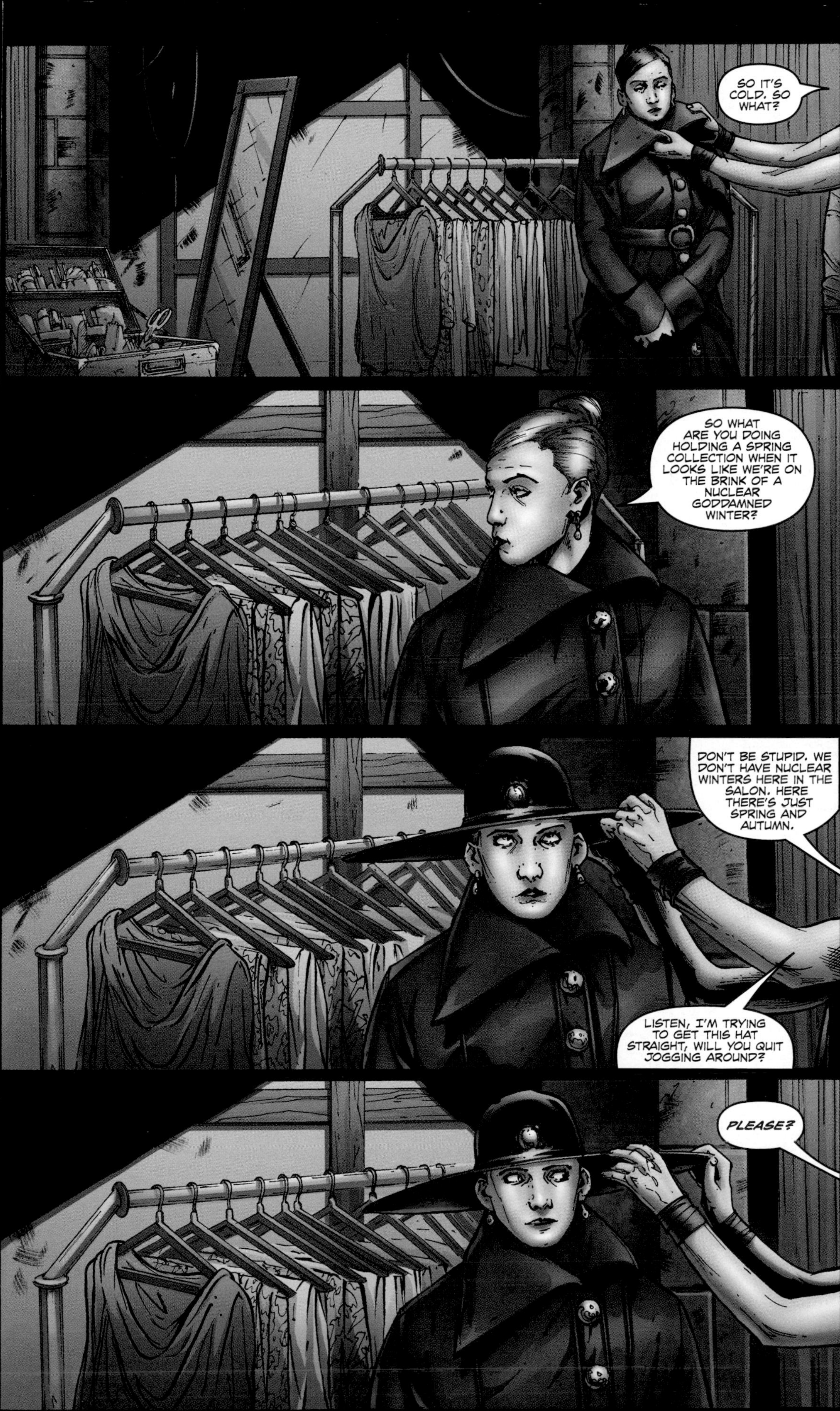
SO IT'S COLD. SO WHAT?
SO WHAT ARE YOU DOING HOLDING A SPRING COLLECTION WHEN IT LOOKS LIKE WE'RE ON THE BRINK OF A NUCLEAR GODDAMNED WINTER?
DON'T BE STUPID. WE DON'T HAVE NUCLEAR WINTERS HERE IN THE SALON. HERE THERE'S JUST SPRING AND AUTUMN.
LISTEN, I'M TRYING TO GET THIS HAT STRAIGHT, WILL YOU QUIT JOGGING AROUND?
PLEASE?

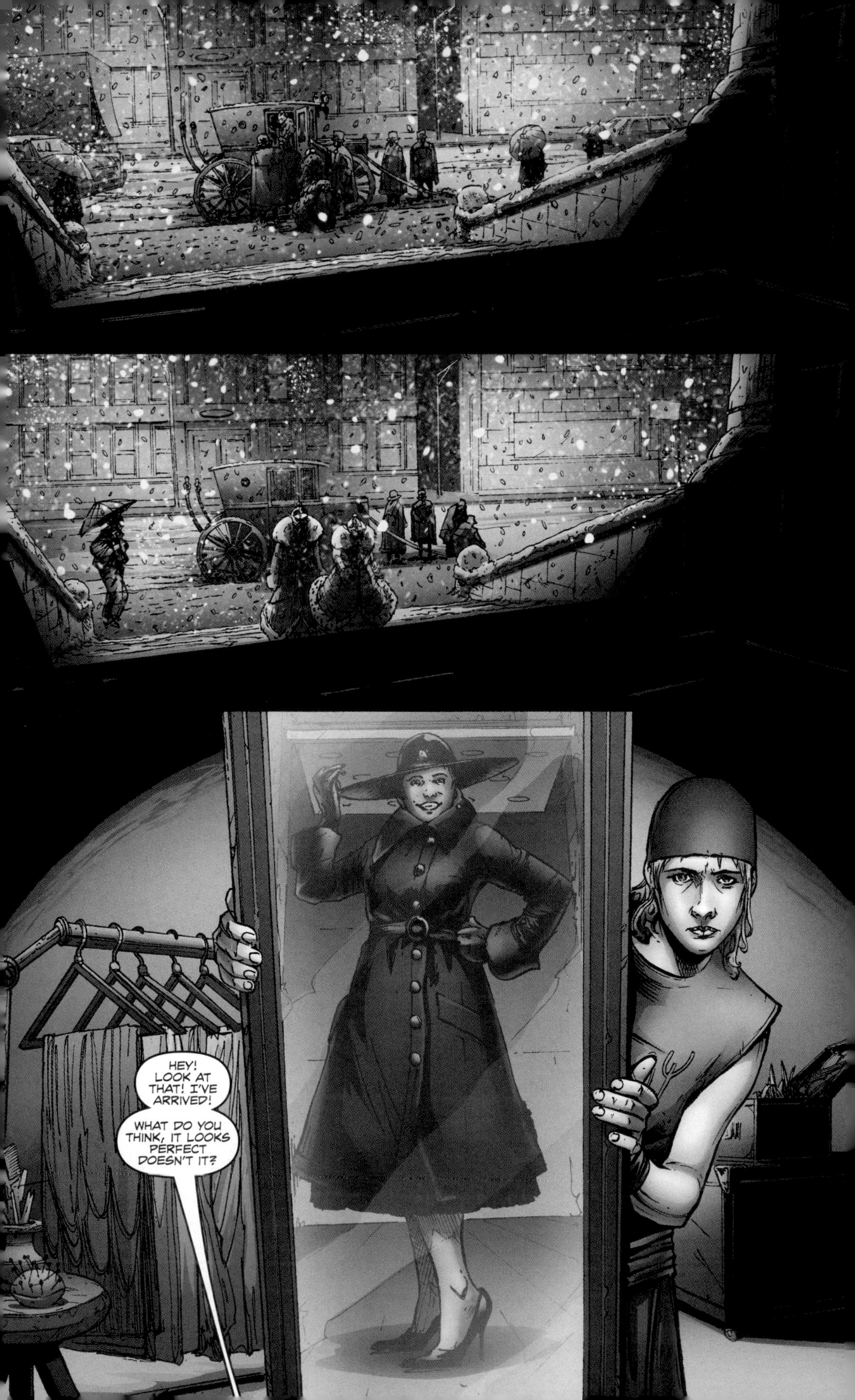
HEY! LOOK AT THAT! I'VE ARRIVED!
WHAT DO YOU THINK, IT LOOKS PERFECT DOESN'T IT?

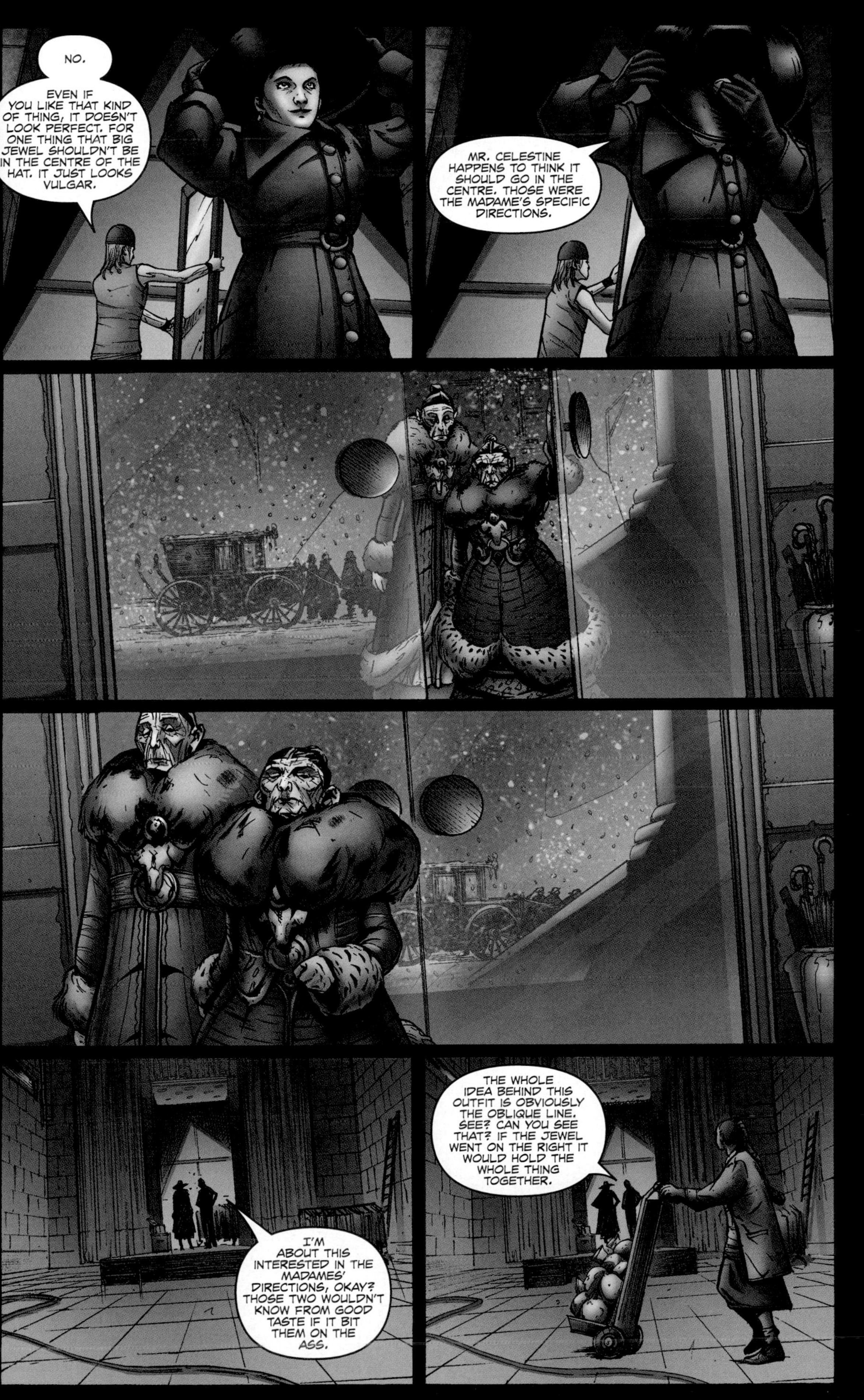
NO.
EVEN IF YOU LIKE THAT KIND OF THING, IT DOESN'T LOOK PERFECT. FOR ONE THING THAT BIG JEWEL SHOULDN'T BE IN THE CENTRE OF THE HAT. IT JUST LOOKS VULGAR.
MR. CELESTINE HAPPENS TO THINK IT SHOULD GO IN THE CENTRE. THOSE WERE THE MADAME'S SPECIFIC DIRECTIONS.
I'M ABOUT THIS INTERESTED IN THE MADAMES' DIRECTIONS, OKAY? THOSE TWO WOULDN'T KNOW FROM GOOD TASTE IF IT BIT THEM ON THE ASS.
THE WHOLE IDEA BEHIND THIS OUTFIT IS OBVIOUSLY THE OBLIQUE LINE. SEE? CAN YOU SEE THAT? IF THE JEWEL WENT ON THE RIGHT IT WOULD HOLD THE WHOLE THING TOGETHER.

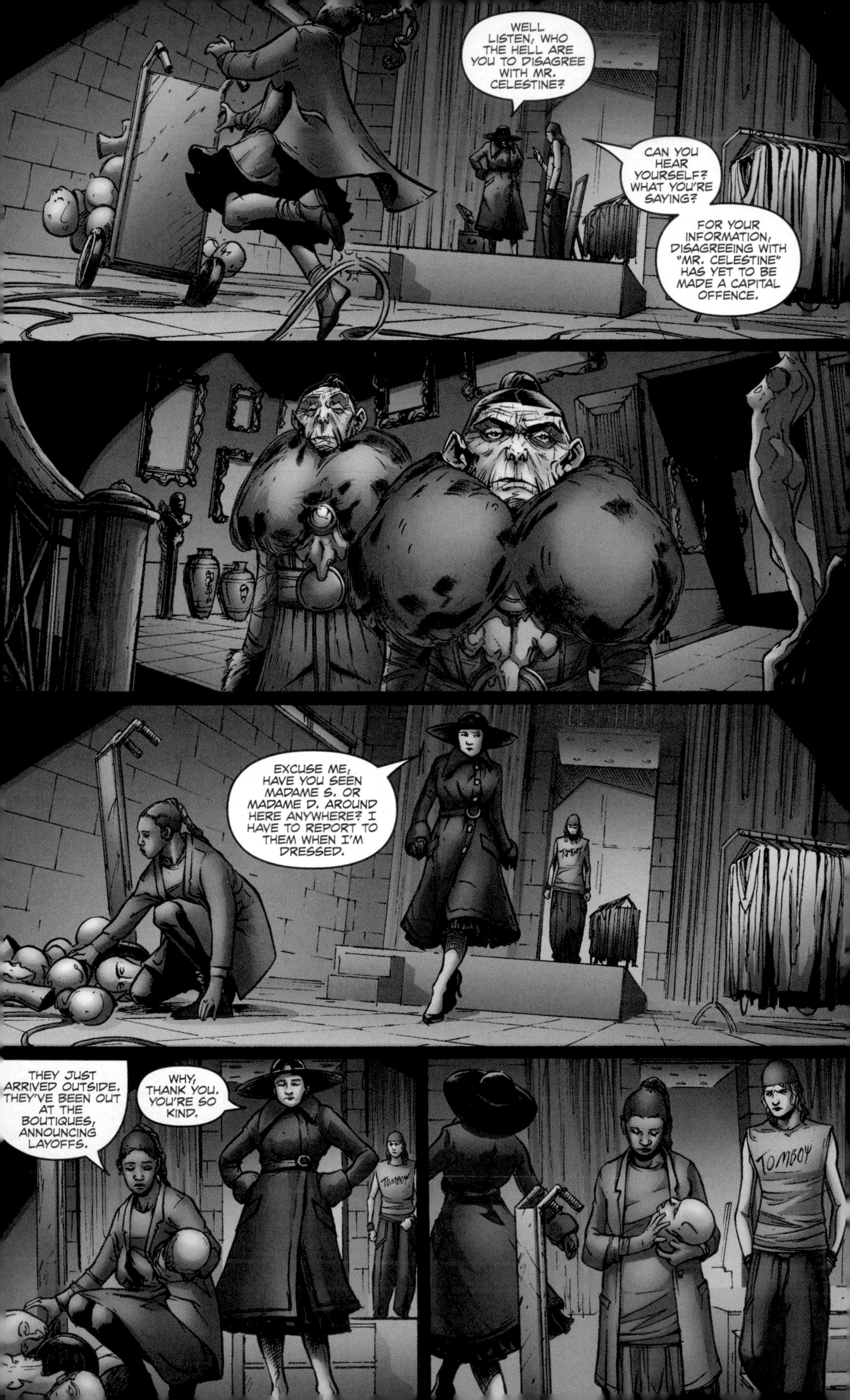
WELL LISTEN, WHO THE HELL ARE YOU TO DISAGREE WITH MR. CELESTINE?
CAN YOU HEAR YOURSELF? WHAT YOU'RE SAYING?
FOR YOUR INFORMATION, DISAGREEING WITH "MR. CELESTINE" HAS YET TO BE MADE A CAPITAL OFFENCE.
EXCUSE ME, HAVE YOU SEEN MADAME S. OR MADAME D. AROUND HERE ANYWHERE? I HAVE TO REPORT TO THEM WHEN I'M DRESSED.
TOMBOY
THEY JUST ARRIVED OUTSIDE. THEY'VE BEEN OUT AT THE BOUTIQUES, ANNOUNCING LAYOFFS.
WHY, THANK YOU. YOU'RE SO KIND.
TOMBOY
TOMBOY

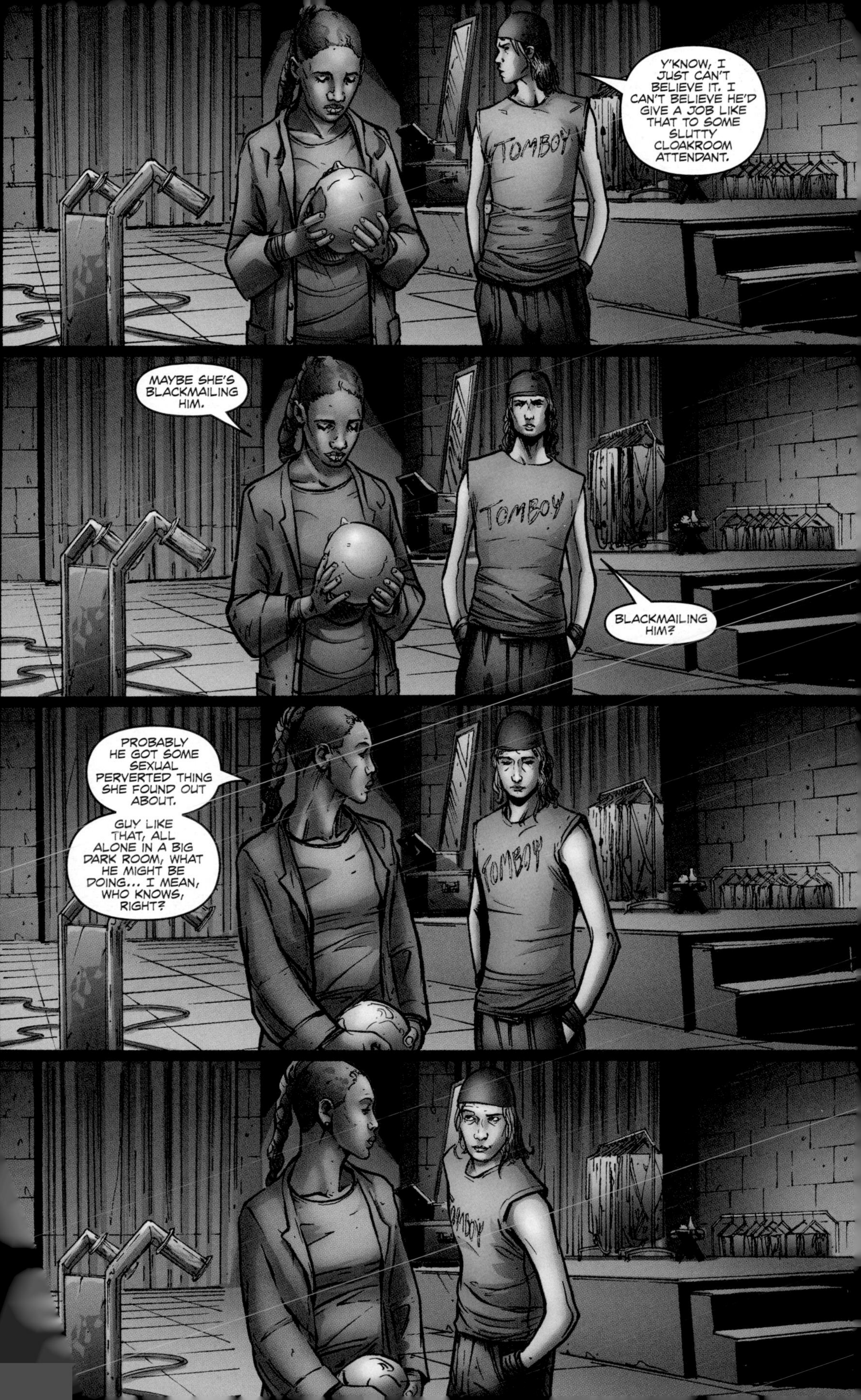
Y'KNOW, I JUST CAN'T BELIEVE IT. I CAN'T BELIEVE HE'D GIVE A JOB LIKE THAT TO SOME SLUTTY CLOAKROOM ATTENDANT.
TOMBOY
MAYBE SHE'S BLACKMAILING HIM.
TOMBOY
BLACKMAILING HIM?
PROBABLY HE GOT SOME SEXUAL PERVERTED THING SHE FOUND OUT ABOUT.
GUY LIKE THAT, ALL ALONE IN A BIG DARK ROOM, WHAT HE MIGHT BE DOING... I MEAN, WHO KNOWS, RIGHT?
TOMBOY
TOMBOY

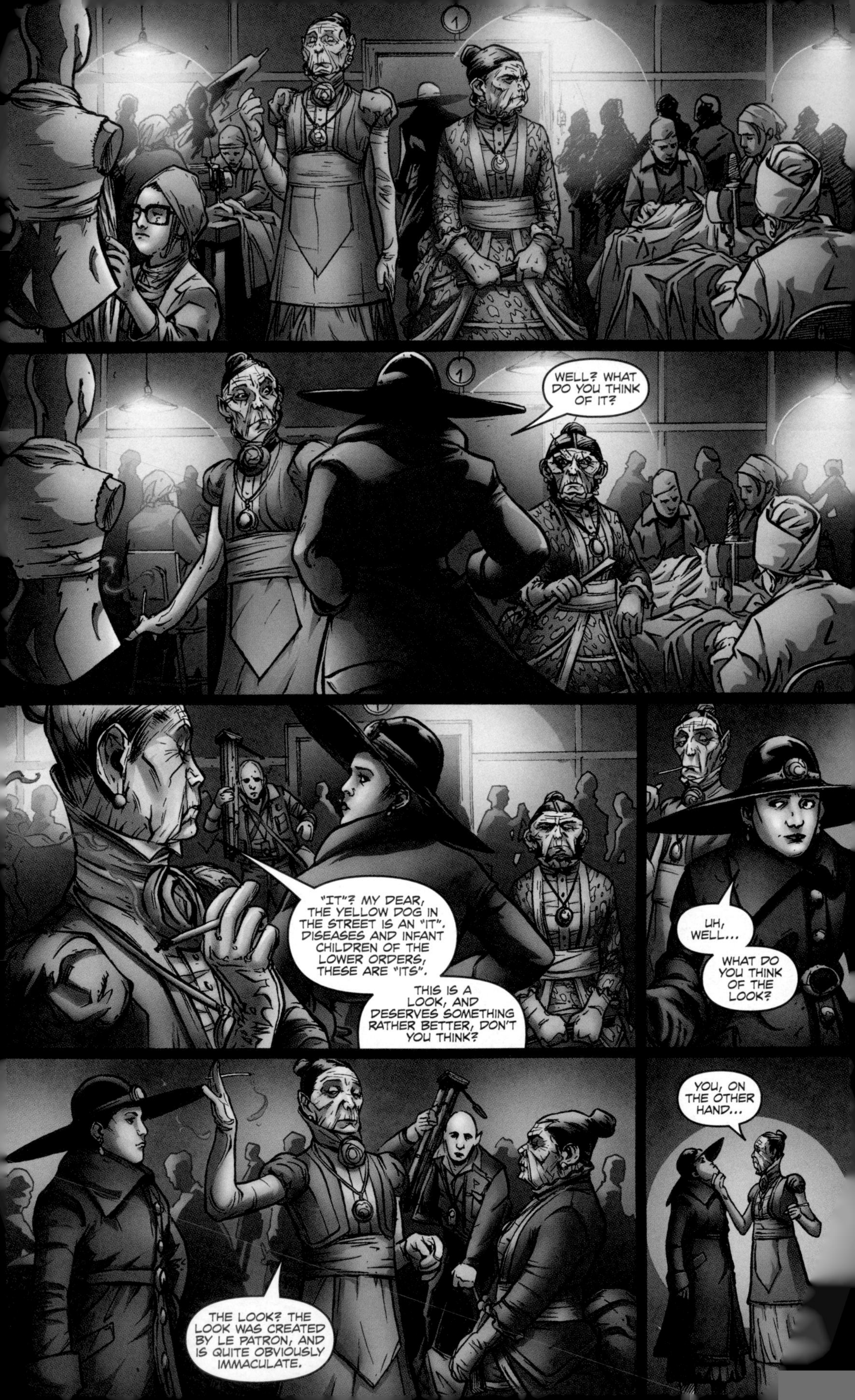
WELL? WHAT DO YOU THINK OF IT?
"IT"? MY DEAR, THE YELLOW DOG IN THE STREET IS AN "IT". DISEASES AND INFANT CHILDREN OF THE LOWER ORDERS, THESE ARE "ITS".
THIS IS A LOOK, AND DESERVES SOMETHING RATHER BETTER, DON'T YOU THINK?
UH, WELL...
WHAT DO YOU THINK OF THE LOOK?
THE LOOK? THE LOOK WAS CREATED BY LE PATRON, AND IS QUITE OBVIOUSLY IMMACULATE.
YOU, ON THE OTHER HAND...

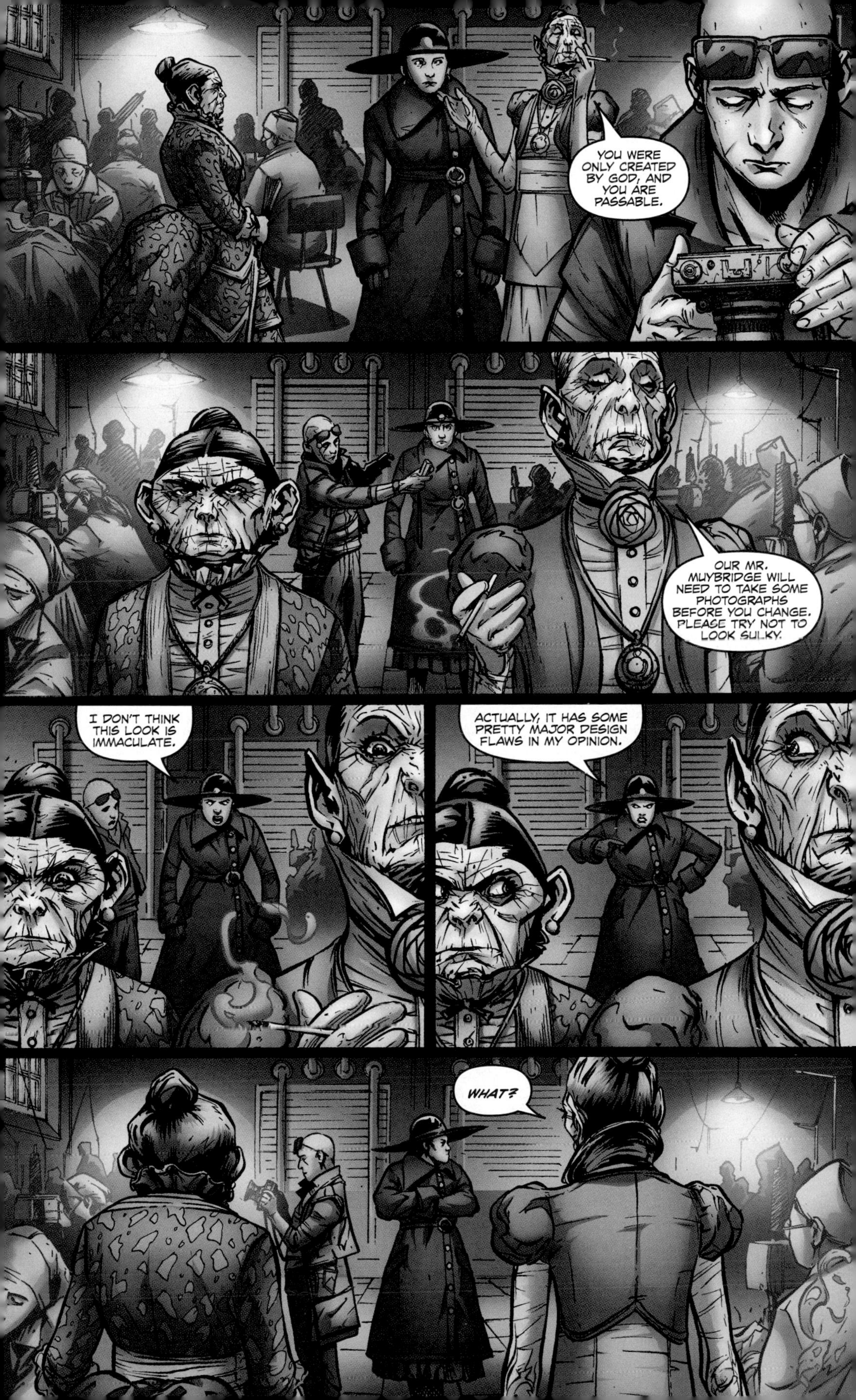
YOU WERE ONLY CREATED BY GOD, AND YOU ARE PASSABLE.
OUR MR. MUYBRIDGE WILL NEED TO TAKE SOME PHOTOGRAPHS BEFORE YOU CHANGE. PLEASE TRY NOT TO LOOK SULKY.
I DON'T THINK THIS LOOK IS IMMACULATE.
ACTUALLY, IT HAS SOME PRETTY MAJOR DESIGN FLAWS IN MY OPINION.
WHAT?

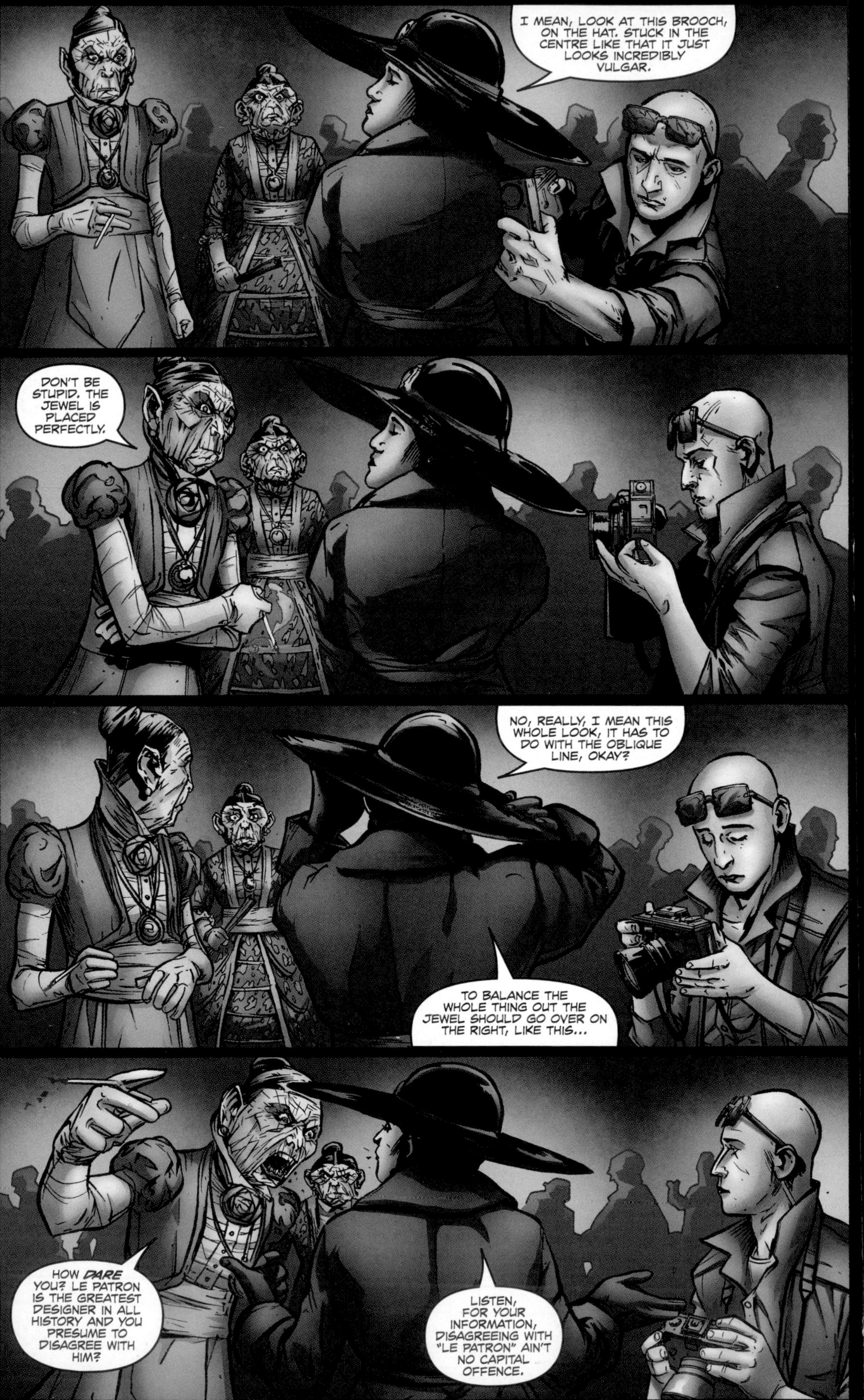
I MEAN, LOOK AT THIS BROOCH, ON THE HAT. STUCK IN THE CENTRE LIKE THAT IT JUST LOOKS INCREDIBLY VULGAR.
DON'T BE STUPID. THE JEWEL IS PLACED PERFECTLY.
NO, REALLY, I MEAN THIS WHOLE LOOK, IT HAS TO DO WITH THE OBLIQUE LINE, OKAY?
TO BALANCE THE WHOLE THING OUT THE JEWEL SHOULD GO OVER ON THE RIGHT, LIKE THIS...
HOW DARE YOU? LE PATRON IS THE GREATEST DESIGNER IN ALL HISTORY AND YOU PRESUME TO DISAGREE WITH HIM?
LISTEN, FOR YOUR INFORMATION, DISAGREEING WITH "LE PATRON" AIN'T NO CAPITAL OFFENCE.

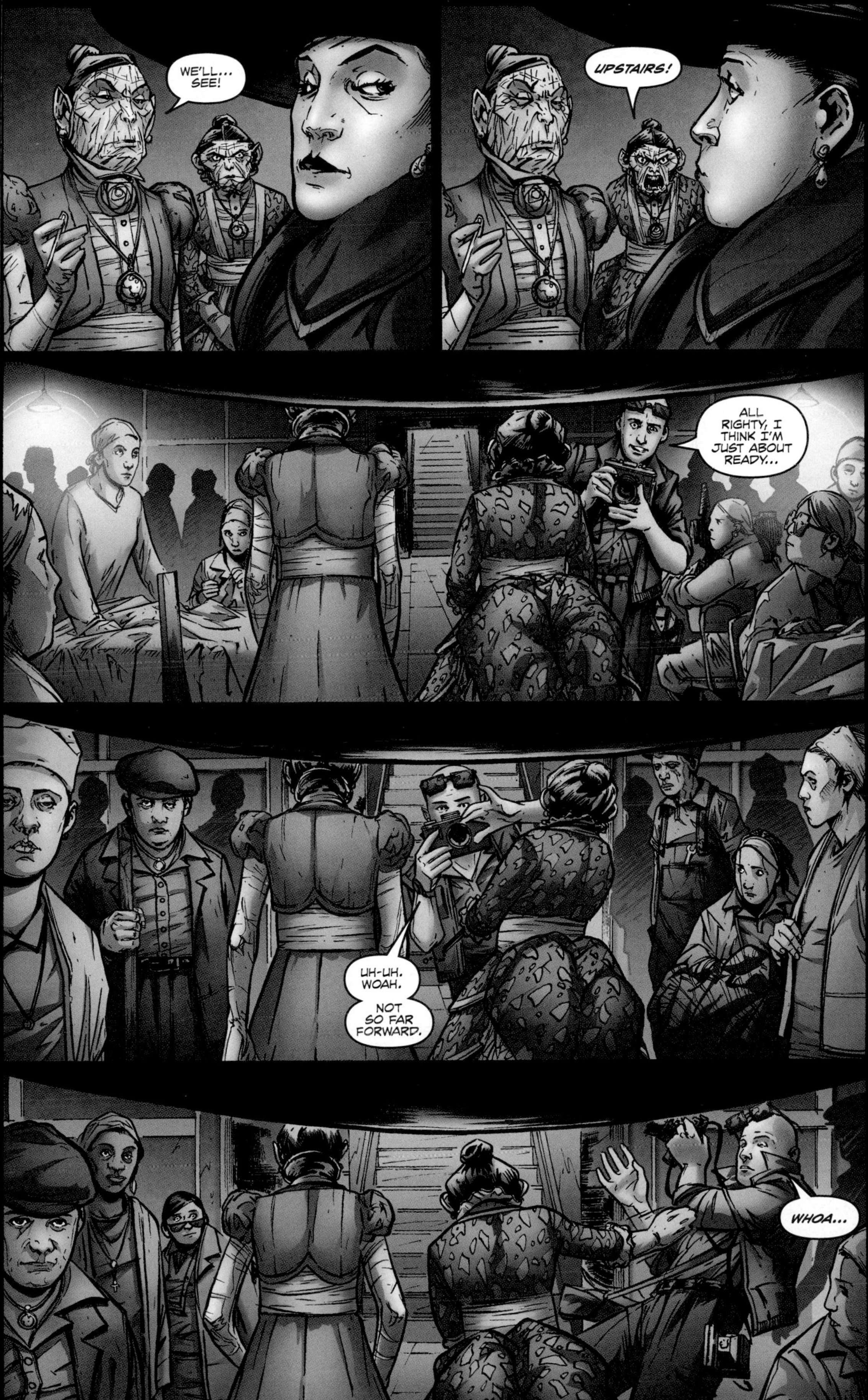
WE'LL... SEE!
UPSTAIRS!
ALL RIGHTY, I THINK I'M JUST ABOUT READY...
UH-UH. WOAH.
NOT SO FAR FORWARD.
WHOA...

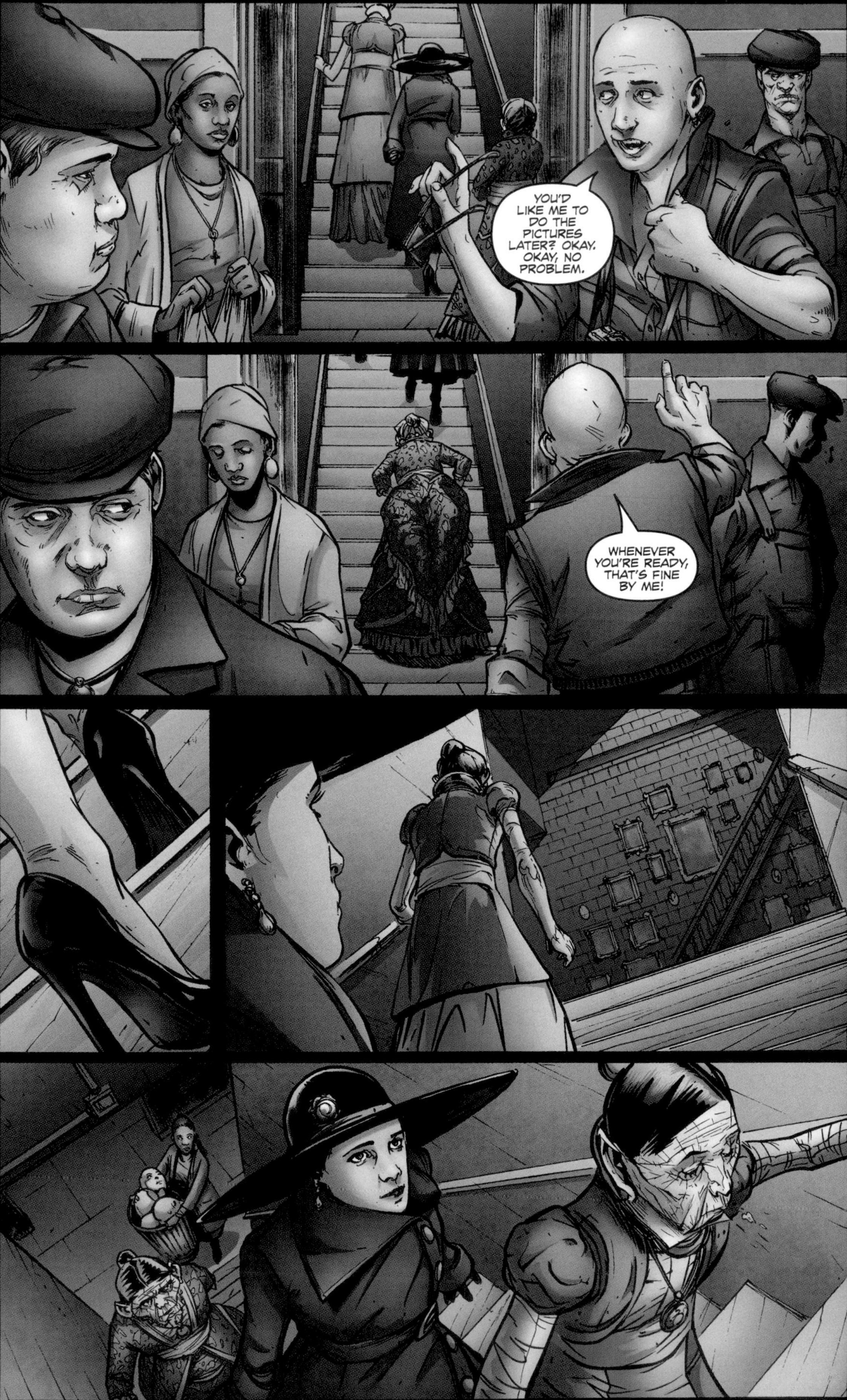
YOU'D LIKE ME TO DO THE PICTURES LATER? OKAY. OKAY, NO PROBLEM.
WHENEVER YOU'RE READY, THAT'S FINE BY ME!

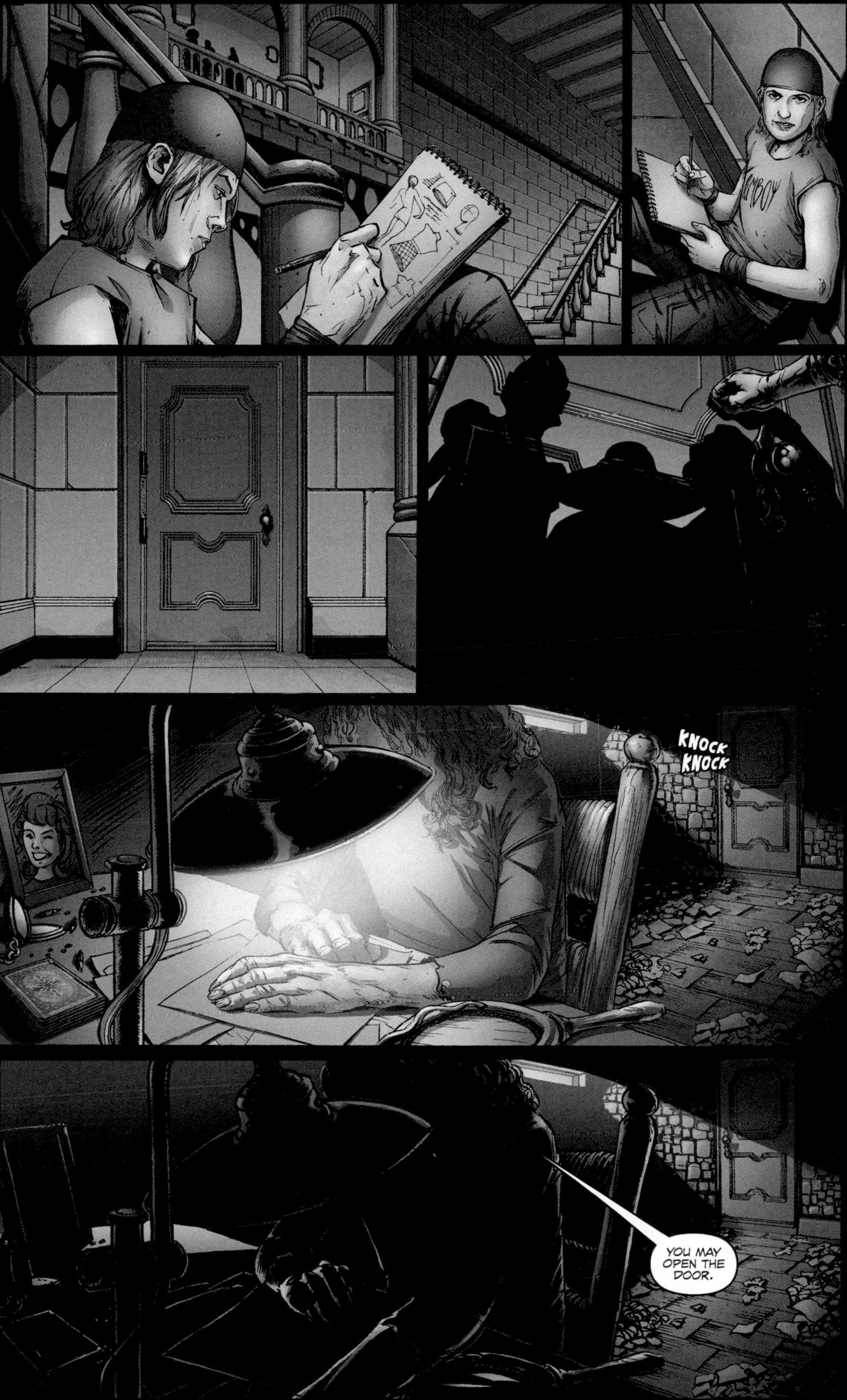
KNOCK
KNOCK
YOU MAY OPEN THE DOOR.

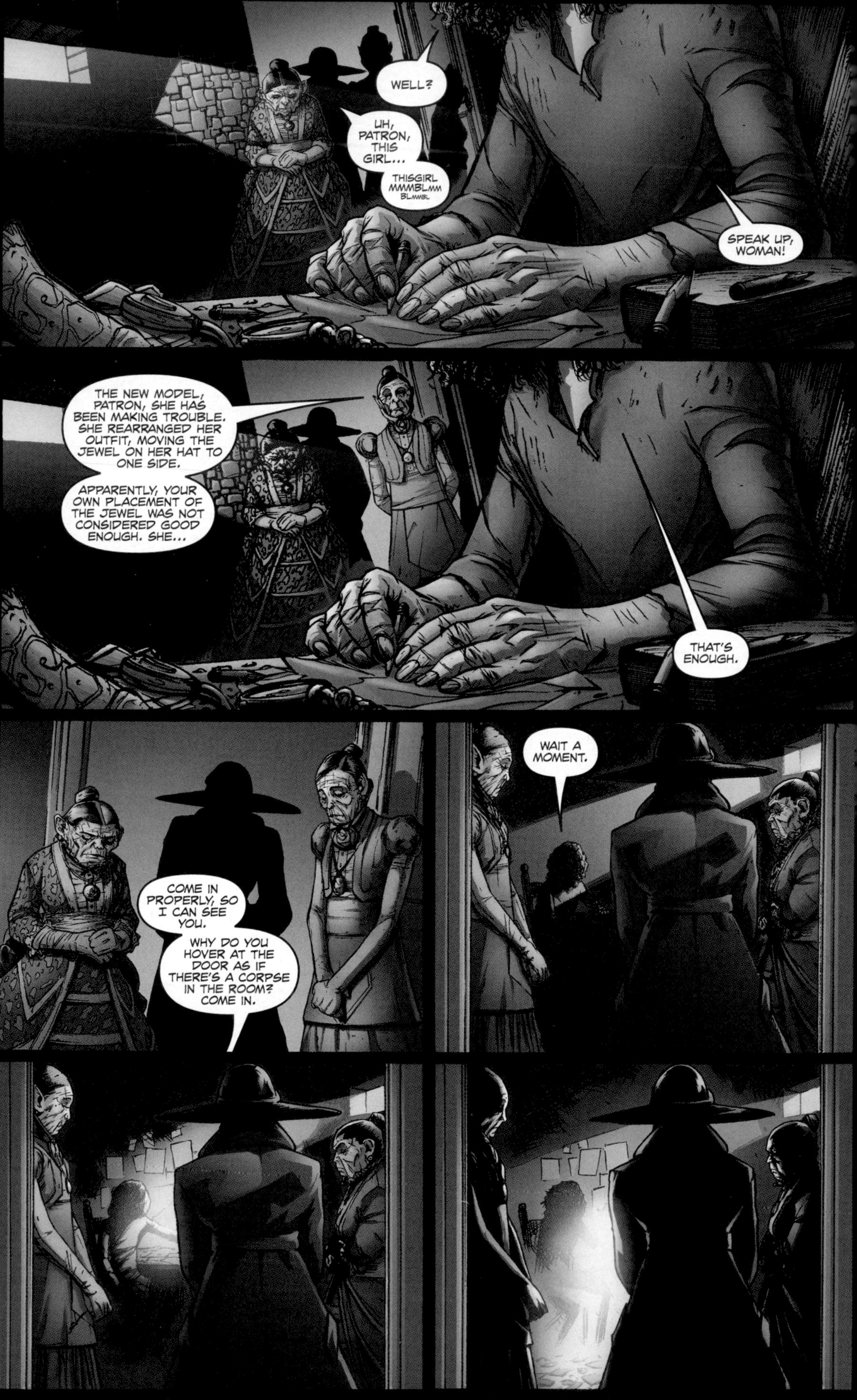
WELL?
UH, PATRON, THIS GIRL...
THISGIRL MMMBLMM BLMMBL
SPEAK UP, WOMAN!
THE NEW MODEL, PATRON, SHE HAS BEEN MAKING TROUBLE. SHE REARRANGED HER OUTFIT, MOVING THE JEWEL ON HER HAT TO ONE SIDE.
APPARENTLY, YOUR OWN PLACEMENT OF THE JEWEL WAS NOT CONSIDERED GOOD ENOUGH. SHE...
THAT'S ENOUGH.
COME IN PROPERLY, SO I CAN SEE YOU.
WHY DO YOU HOVER AT THE DOOR AS IF THERE'S A CORPSE IN THE ROOM? COME IN.
WAIT A MOMENT.

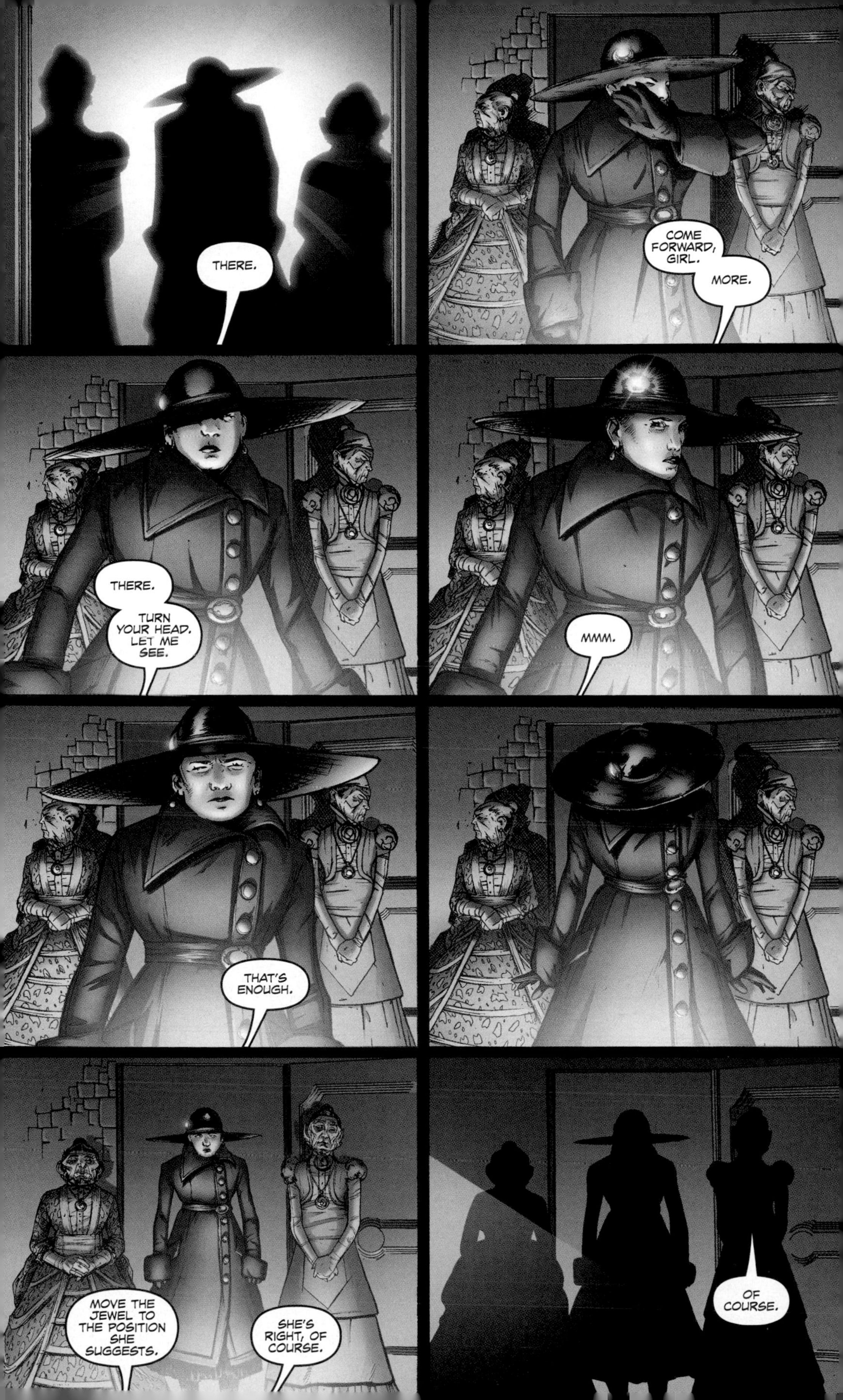
THERE.
COME FORWARD, GIRL.
MORE.
THERE.
TURN YOUR HEAD. LET ME SEE.
MMM.
THAT'S ENOUGH.
MOVE THE JEWEL TO THE POSITION SHE SUGGESTS.
SHE'S RIGHT, OF COURSE.
OF COURSE.

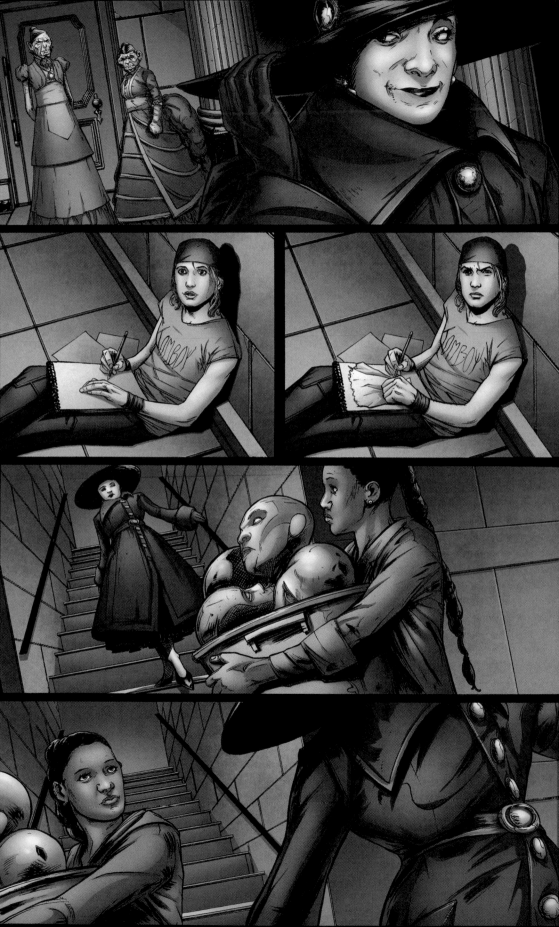

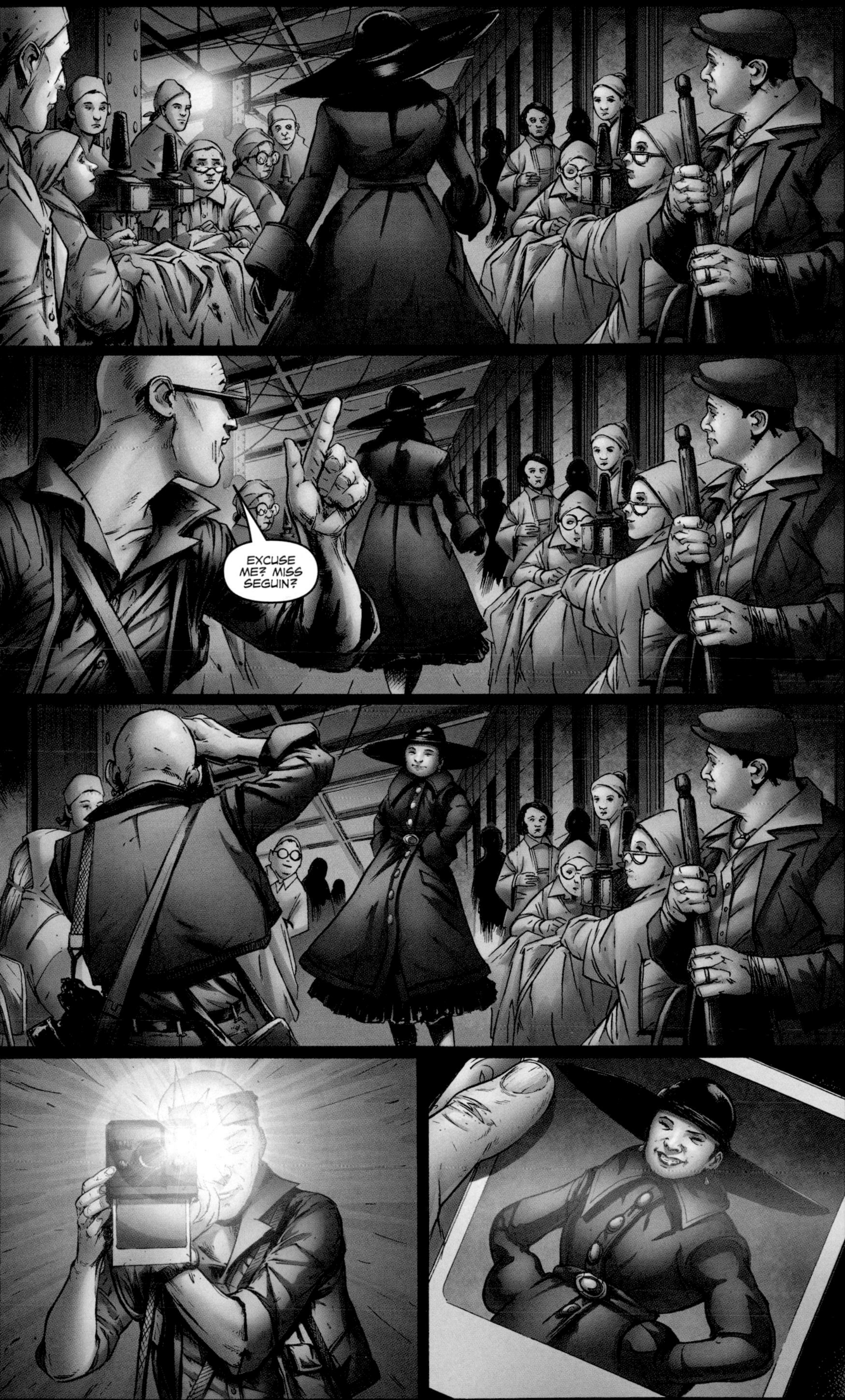
EXCUSE ME? MISS SEGUIN?

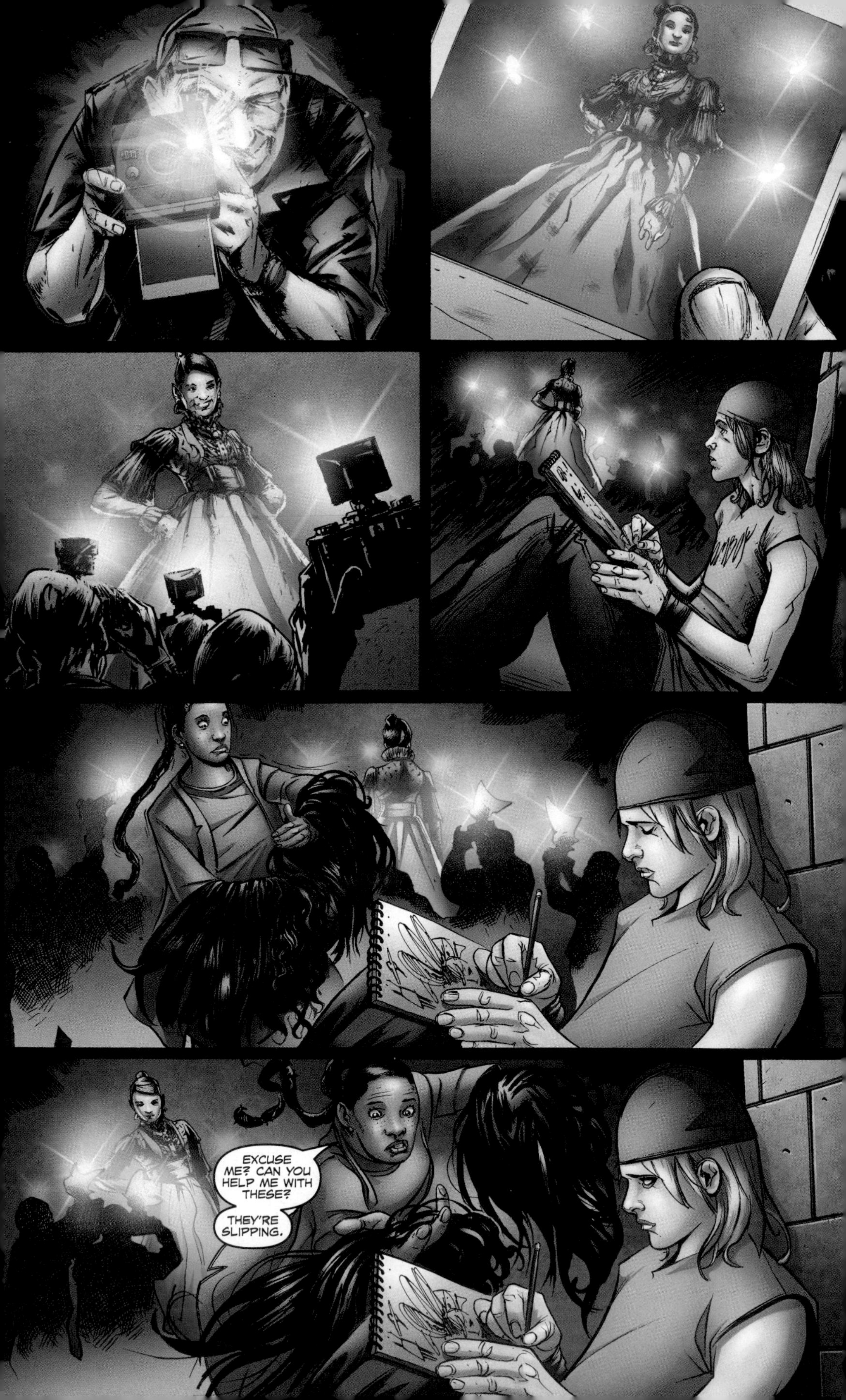
EXCUSE ME? CAN YOU HELP ME WITH THESE?
THEY'RE SLIPPING.

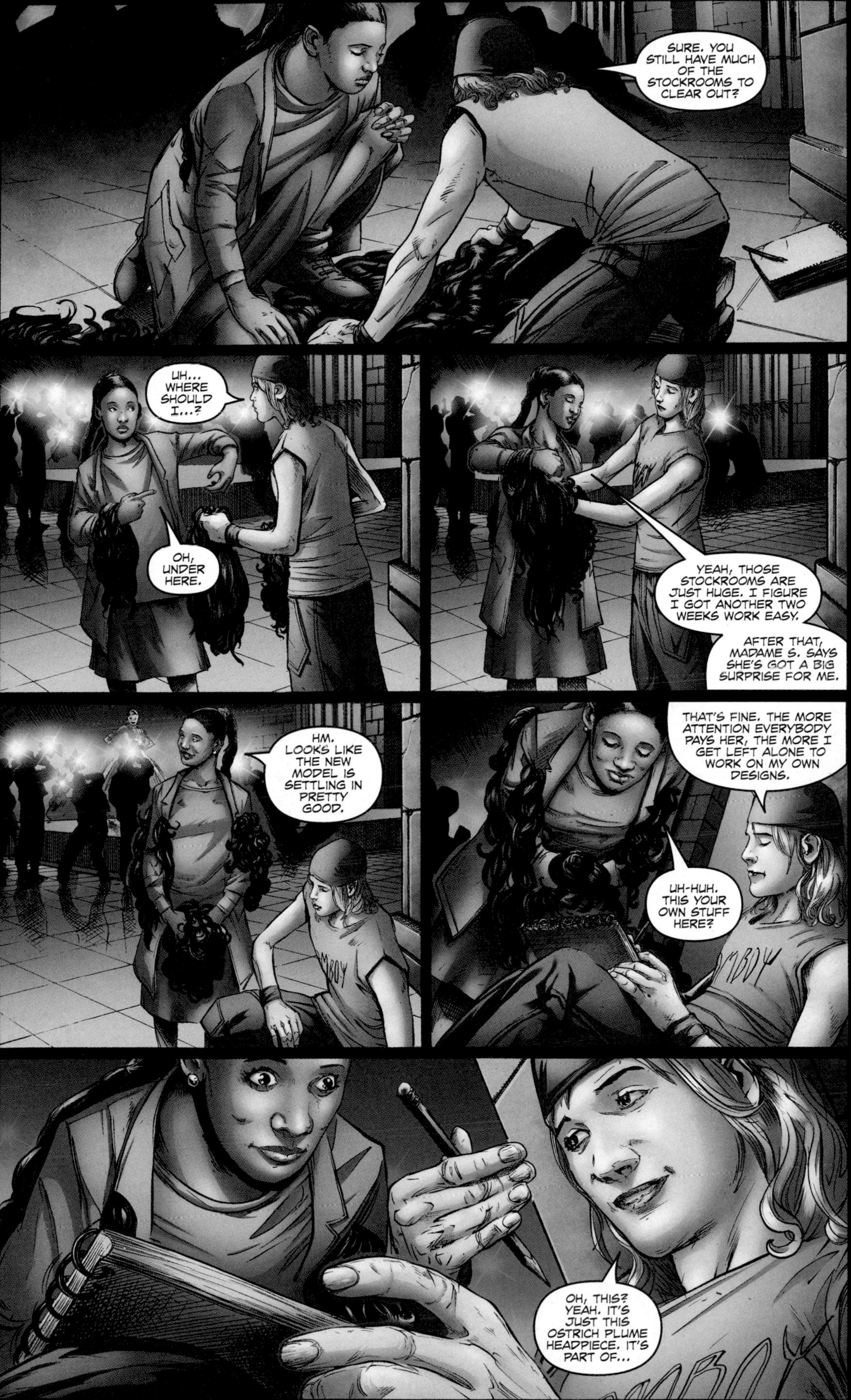
SURE. YOU STILL HAVE MUCH OF THE STOCKROOMS TO CLEAR OUT?
UH... WHERE SHOULD I...?
OH, UNDER HERE.
YEAH, THOSE STOCKROOMS ARE JUST HUGE. I FIGURE I GOT ANOTHER TWO WEEKS WORK EASY.
AFTER THAT, MADAME S. SAYS SHE'S GOT A BIG SURPRISE FOR ME.
HM. LOOKS LIKE THE NEW MODEL IS SETTLING IN PRETTY GOOD.
THAT'S FINE. THE MORE ATTENTION EVERYBODY PAYS HER, THE MORE I GET LEFT ALONE TO WORK ON MY OWN DESIGNS.
UH-HUH. THIS YOUR OWN STUFF HERE?
OH, THIS? YEAH. IT'S JUST THIS OSTRICH PLUME HEADPIECE. IT'S PART OF...

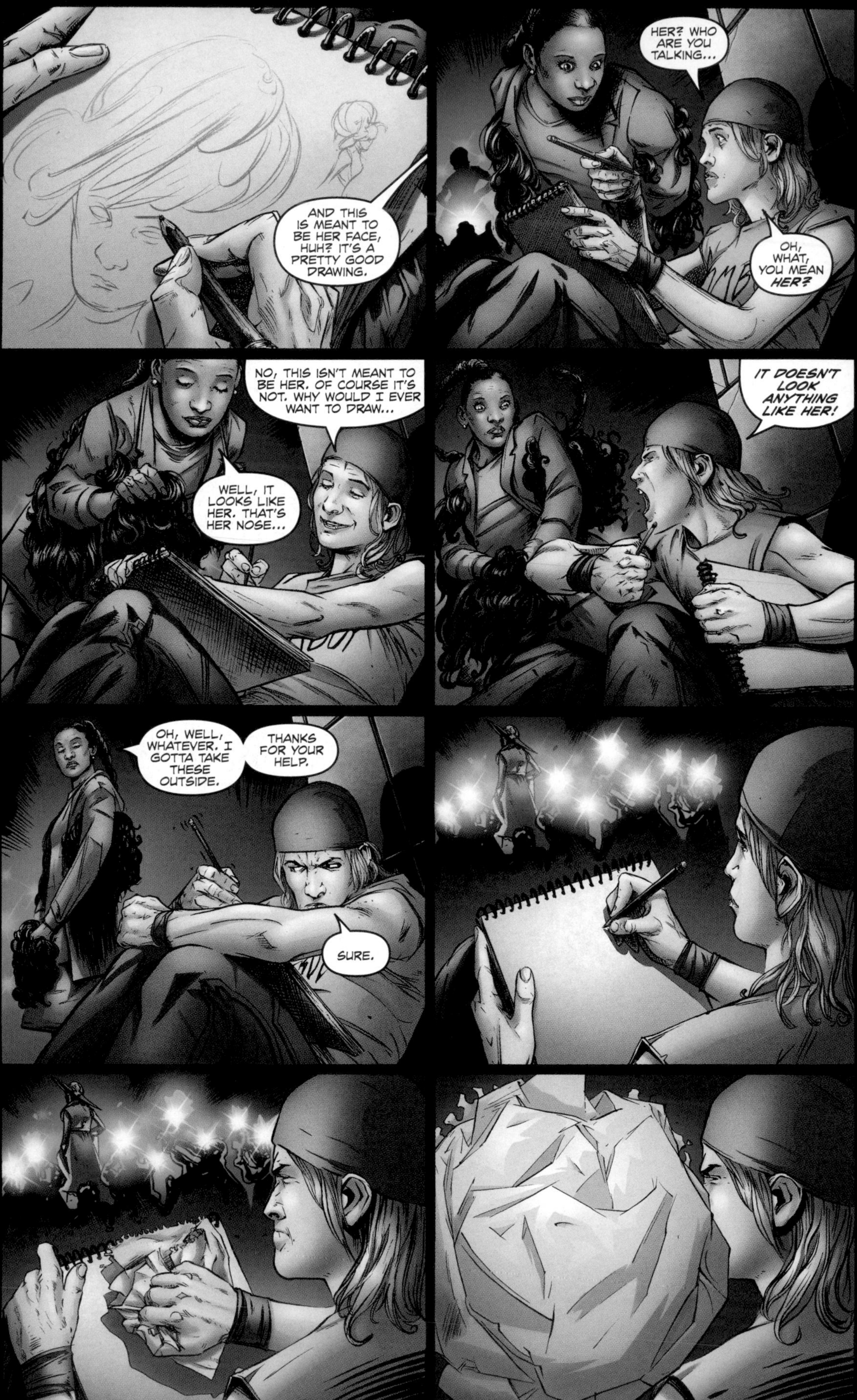
AND THIS IS MEANT TO BE HER FACE, HUH? IT'S A PRETTY GOOD DRAWING.
HER? WHO ARE YOU TALKING...
OH, WHAT, YOU MEAN HER?
NO, THIS ISN'T MEANT TO BE HER. OF COURSE IT'S NOT. WHY WOULD I EVER WANT TO DRAW...
WELL, IT LOOKS LIKE HER. THAT'S HER NOSE...
IT DOESN'T LOOK ANYTHING LIKE HER!
OH, WELL, WHATEVER. I GOTTA TAKE THESE OUTSIDE.
THANKS FOR YOUR HELP.
SURE.

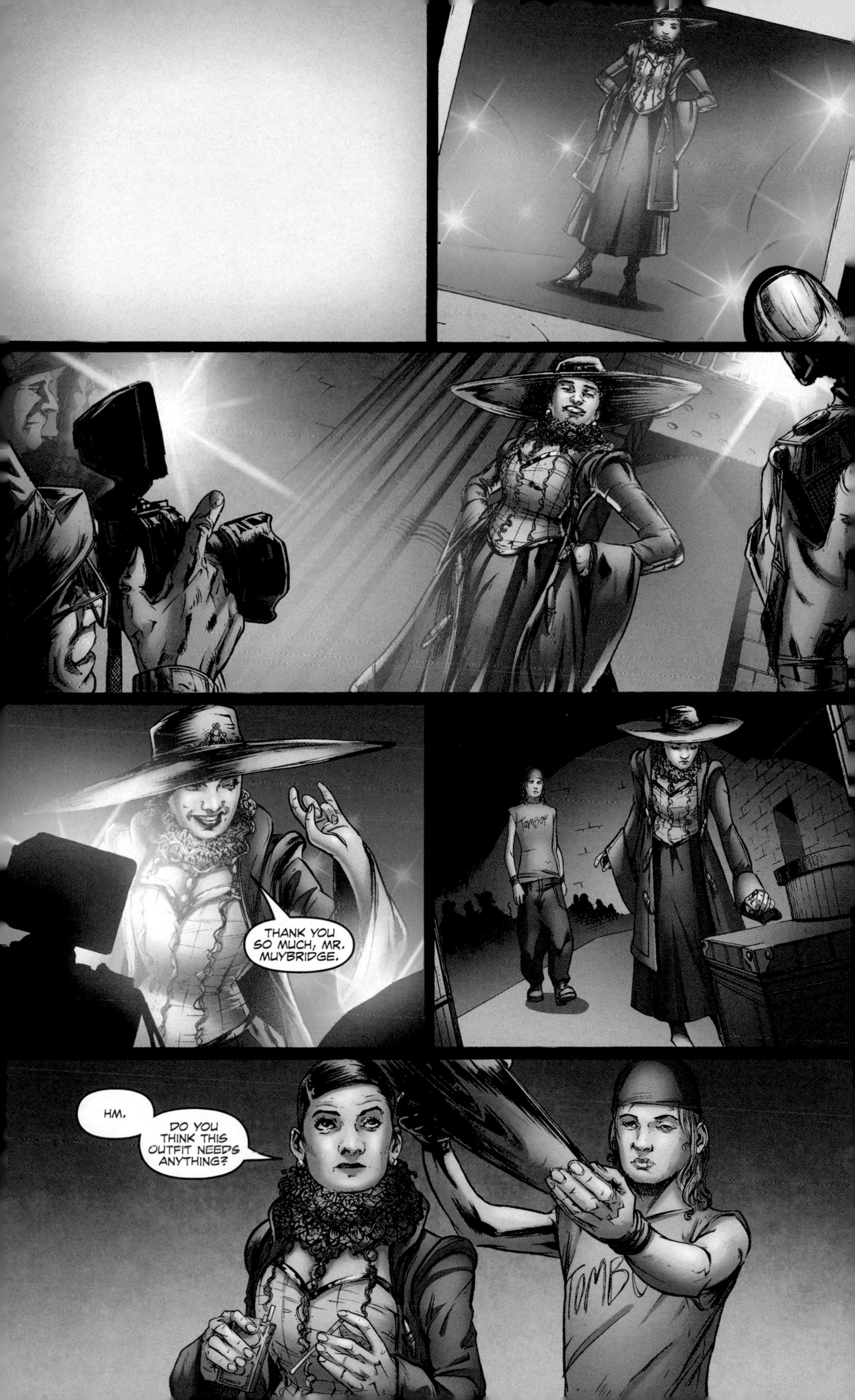
THANK YOU SO MUCH, MR. MUYBRIDGE.
TOMBOY
HM.
DO YOU THINK THIS OUTFIT NEEDS ANYTHING?
TOMB

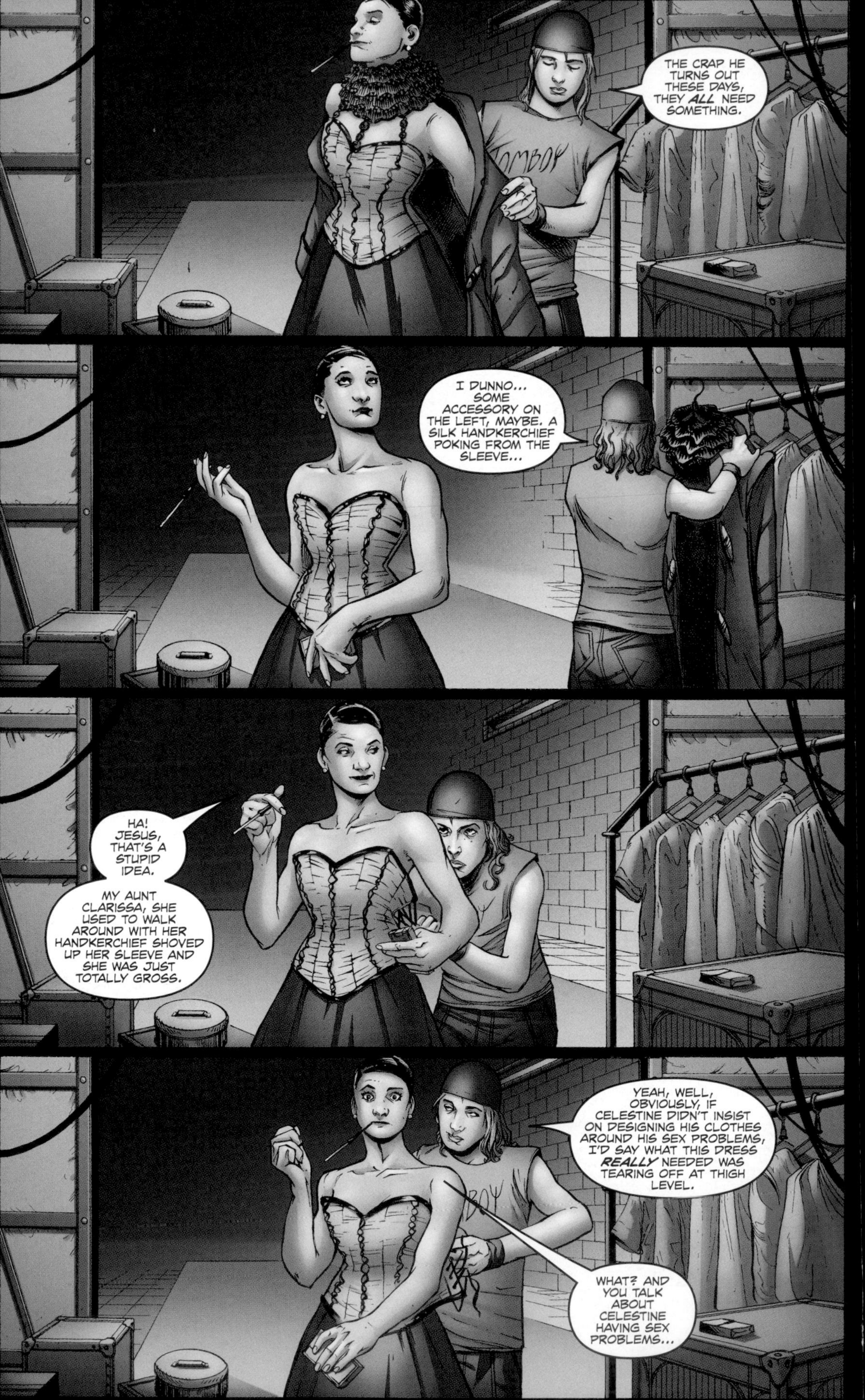
THE CRAP HE TURNS OUT THESE DAYS, THEY *ALL* NEED SOMETHING.
TOMBOY
I DUNNO... SOME ACCESSORY ON THE LEFT, MAYBE. A SILK HANDKERCHIEF POKING FROM THE SLEEVE...
HA! JESUS, THAT'S A STUPID IDEA.
MY AUNT CLARISSA, SHE USED TO WALK AROUND WITH HER HANDKERCHIEF SHOVED UP HER SLEEVE AND SHE WAS JUST TOTALLY GROSS.
YEAH, WELL, OBVIOUSLY, IF CELESTINE DIDN'T INSIST ON DESIGNING HIS CLOTHES AROUND HIS SEX PROBLEMS, I'D SAY WHAT THIS DRESS *REALLY* NEEDED WAS TEARING OFF AT THIGH LEVEL.
WHAT? AND YOU TALK ABOUT CELESTINE HAVING SEX PROBLEMS...

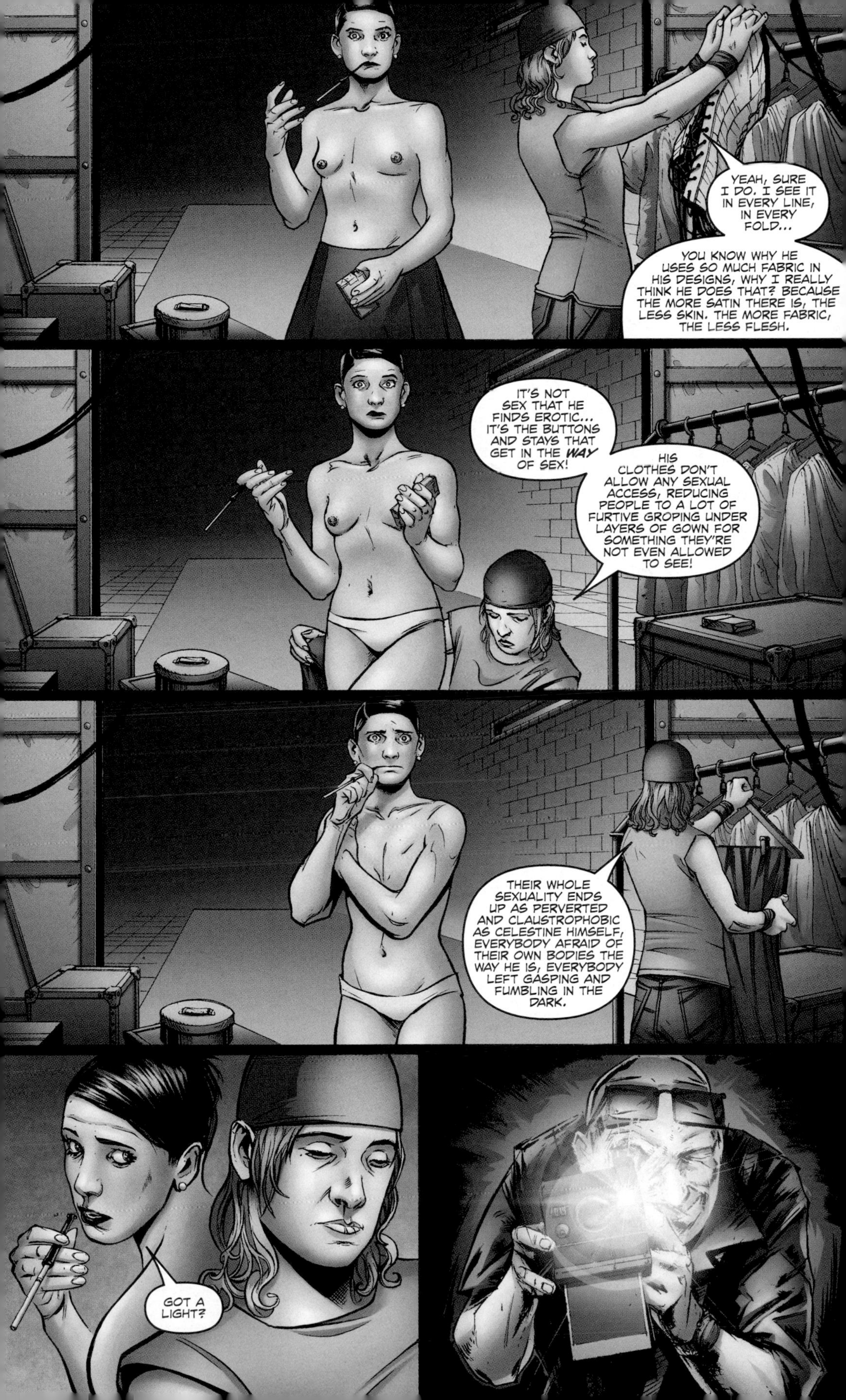
YEAH, SURE I DO. I SEE IT IN EVERY LINE, IN EVERY FOLD...
YOU KNOW WHY HE USES SO MUCH FABRIC IN HIS DESIGNS, WHY I REALLY THINK HE DOES THAT? BECAUSE THE MORE SATIN THERE IS, THE LESS SKIN. THE MORE FABRIC, THE LESS FLESH.
IT'S NOT SEX THAT HE FINDS EROTIC... IT'S THE BUTTONS AND STAYS THAT GET IN THE *WAY* OF SEX!
HIS CLOTHES DON'T ALLOW ANY SEXUAL ACCESS, REDUCING PEOPLE TO A LOT OF FURTIVE GROPING UNDER LAYERS OF GOWN FOR SOMETHING THEY'RE NOT EVEN ALLOWED TO SEE!
THEIR WHOLE SEXUALITY ENDS UP AS PERVERTED AND CLAUSTROPHOBIC AS CELESTINE HIMSELF, EVERYBODY AFRAID OF THEIR OWN BODIES THE WAY HE IS, EVERYBODY LEFT GASPING AND FUMBLING IN THE DARK.
GOT A LIGHT?

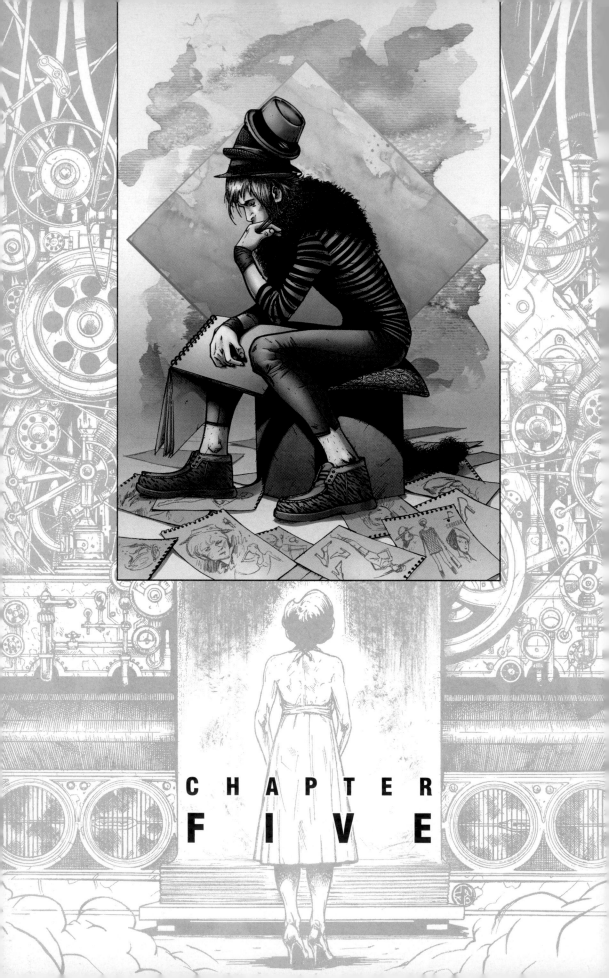

CHAPTER FIVE

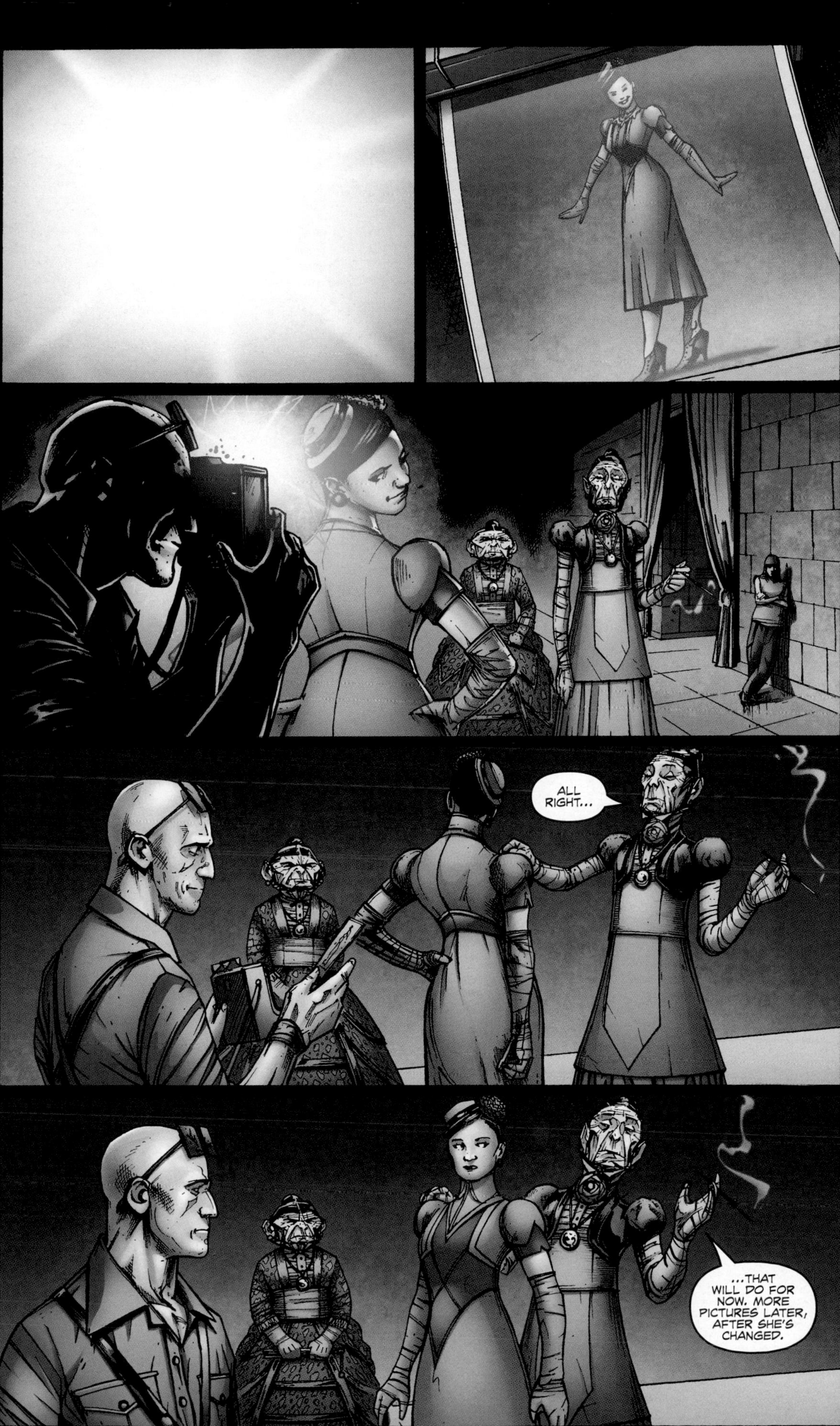
ALL RIGHT...
...THAT WILL DO FOR NOW. MORE PICTURES LATER, AFTER SHE'S CHANGED.

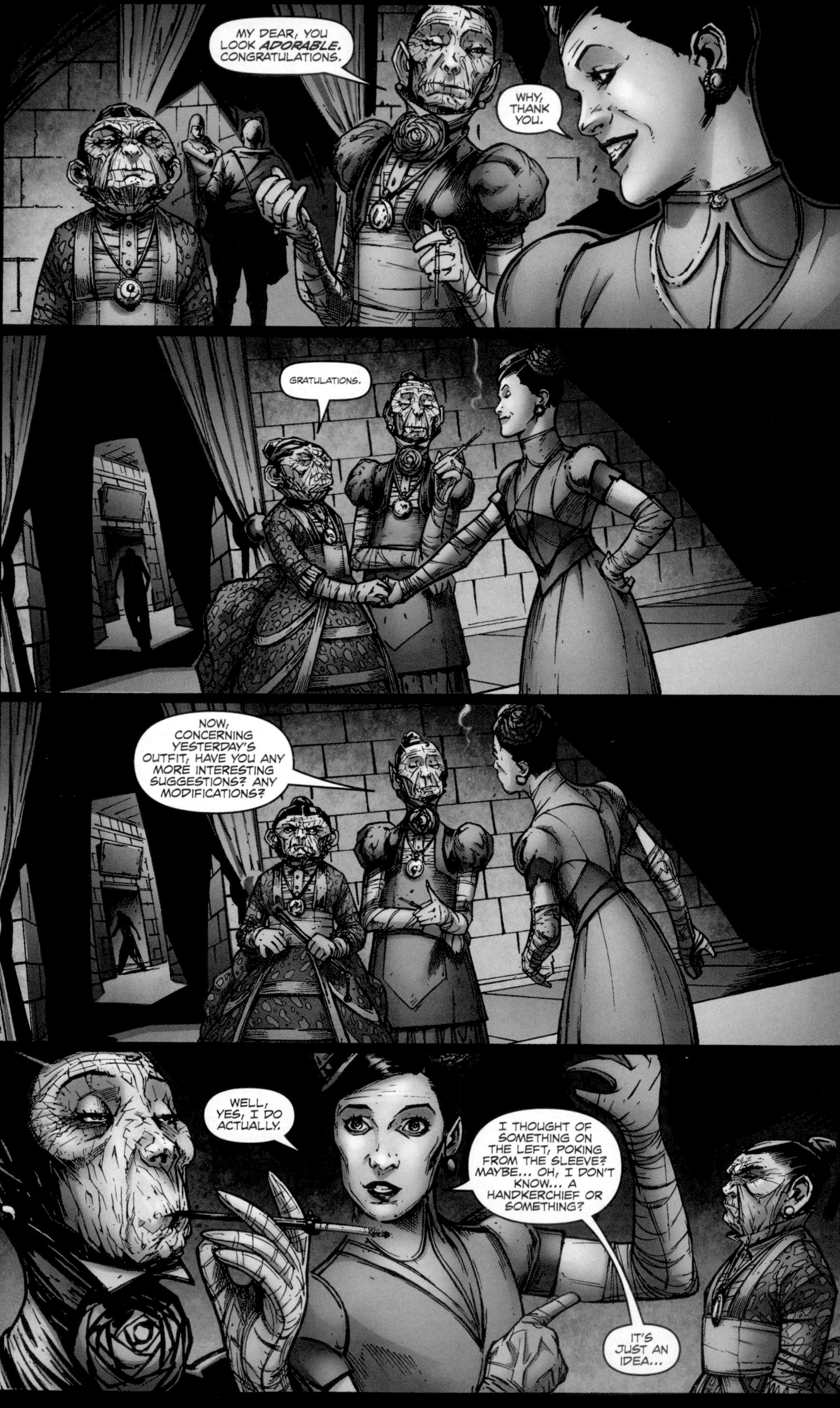
MY DEAR, YOU LOOK *ADORABLE.* CONGRATULATIONS.
WHY, THANK YOU.
GRATULATIONS.
NOW, CONCERNING YESTERDAY'S OUTFIT, HAVE YOU ANY MORE INTERESTING SUGGESTIONS? ANY MODIFICATIONS?
WELL, YES, I DO ACTUALLY.
I THOUGHT OF SOMETHING ON THE LEFT, POKING FROM THE SLEEVE? MAYBE... OH, I DON'T KNOW... A HANDKERCHIEF OR SOMETHING?
IT'S JUST AN IDEA...

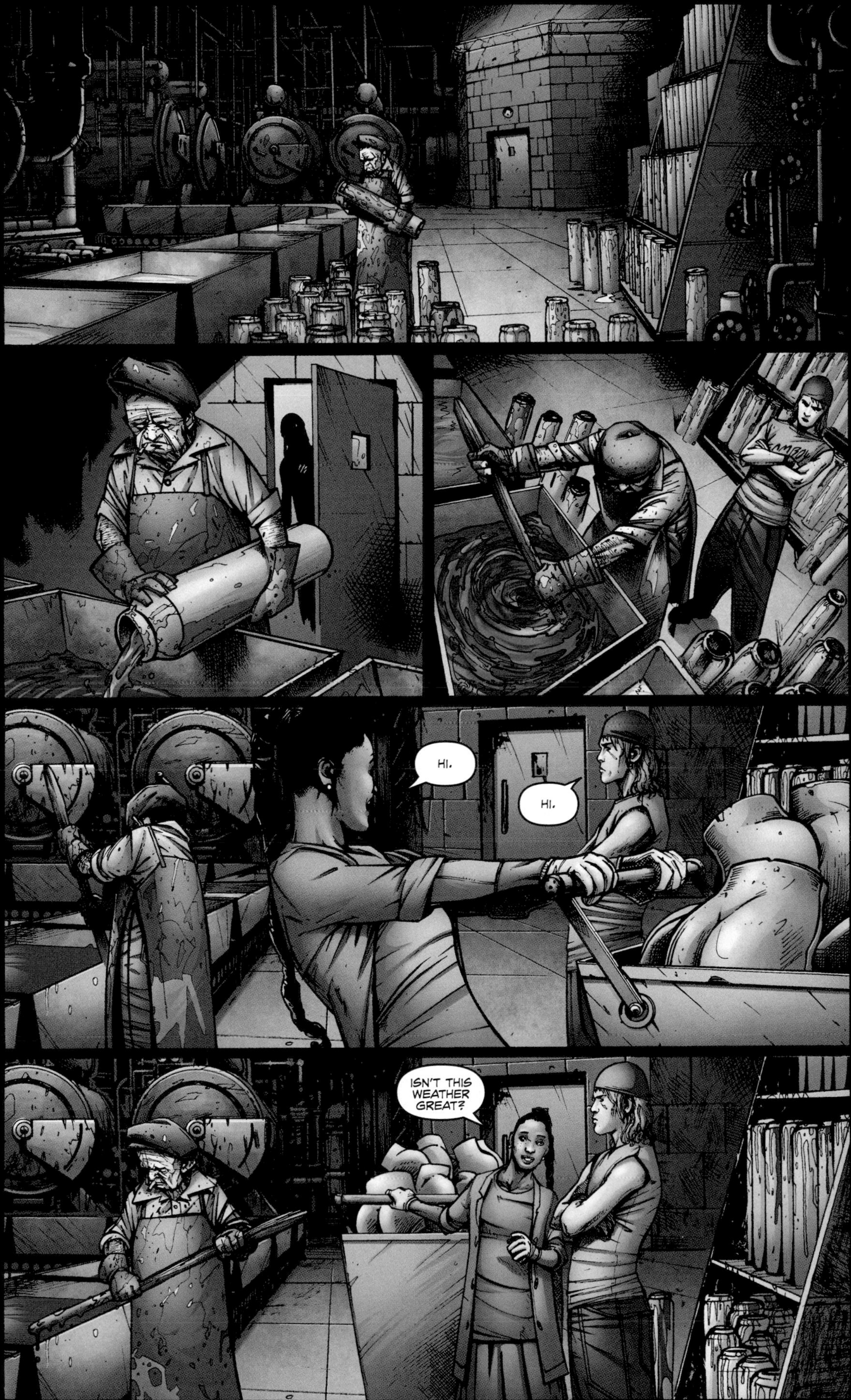
HI.
HI.
ISN'T THIS WEATHER GREAT?

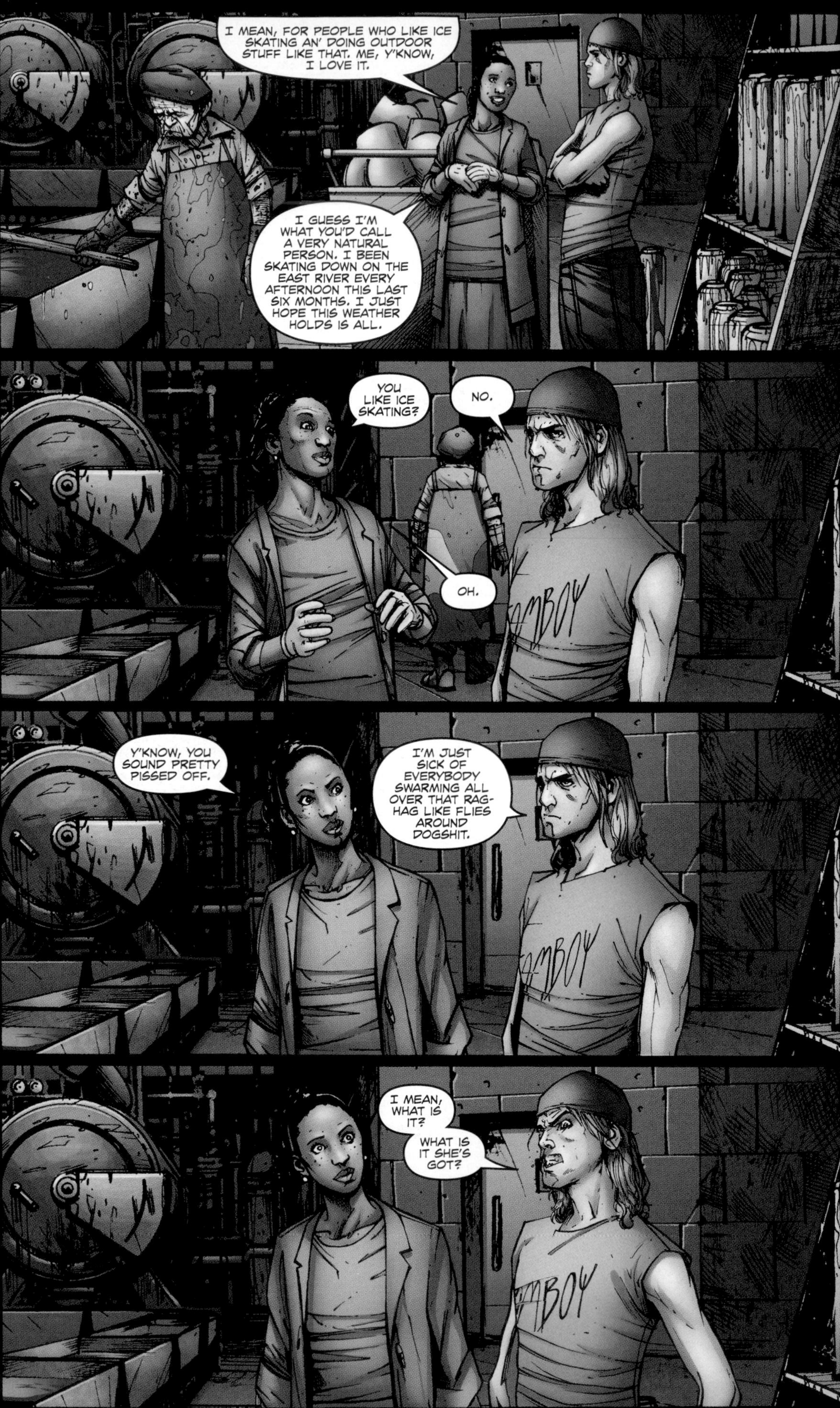
I MEAN, FOR PEOPLE WHO LIKE ICE SKATING AN' DOING OUTDOOR STUFF LIKE THAT. ME, Y'KNOW, I LOVE IT.
I GUESS I'M WHAT YOU'D CALL A VERY NATURAL PERSON. I BEEN SKATING DOWN ON THE EAST RIVER EVERY AFTERNOON THIS LAST SIX MONTHS. I JUST HOPE THIS WEATHER HOLDS IS ALL.
YOU LIKE ICE SKATING?
NO.
OH.
Y'KNOW, YOU SOUND PRETTY PISSED OFF.
I'M JUST SICK OF EVERYBODY SWARMING ALL OVER THAT RAG-HAG LIKE FLIES AROUND DOGSHIT.
I MEAN, WHAT IS IT?
WHAT IS IT SHE'S GOT?

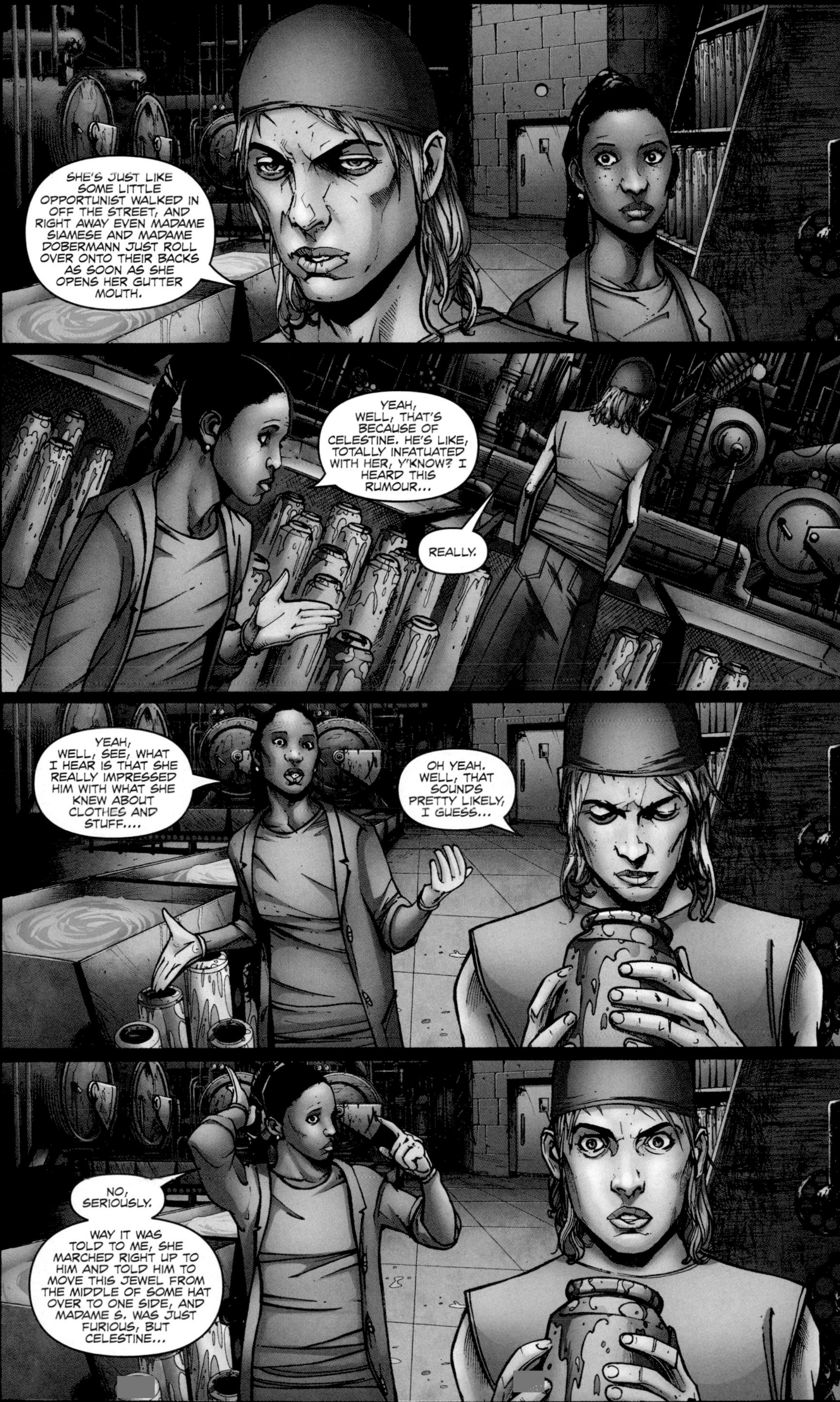
SHE'S JUST LIKE SOME LITTLE OPPORTUNIST WALKED IN OFF THE STREET, AND RIGHT AWAY EVEN MADAME SIAMESE AND MADAME DOBERMANN JUST ROLL OVER ONTO THEIR BACKS AS SOON AS SHE OPENS HER GUTTER MOUTH.
YEAH, WELL, THAT'S BECAUSE OF CELESTINE. HE'S LIKE, TOTALLY INFATUATED WITH HER, Y'KNOW? I HEARD THIS RUMOUR...
REALLY.
YEAH, WELL, SEE, WHAT I HEAR IS THAT SHE REALLY IMPRESSED HIM WITH WHAT SHE KNEW ABOUT CLOTHES AND STUFF....
OH YEAH. WELL, THAT SOUNDS PRETTY LIKELY, I GUESS...
NO, SERIOUSLY.
WAY IT WAS TOLD TO ME, SHE MARCHED RIGHT UP TO HIM AND TOLD HIM TO MOVE THIS JEWEL FROM THE MIDDLE OF SOME HAT OVER TO ONE SIDE, AND MADAME S. WAS JUST FURIOUS, BUT CELESTINE...

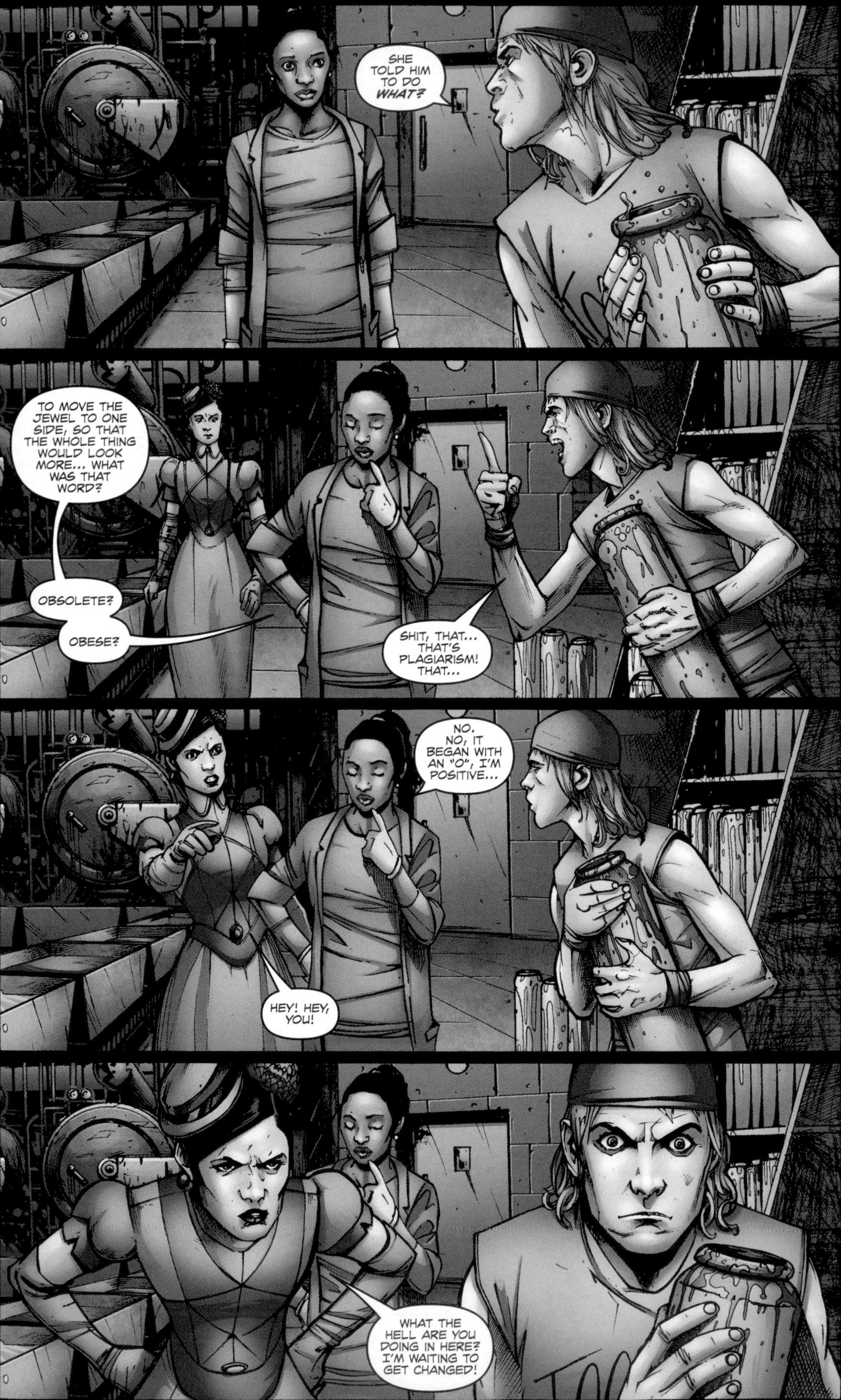
SHE TOLD HIM TO DO *WHAT?*
TO MOVE THE JEWEL TO ONE SIDE, SO THAT THE WHOLE THING WOULD LOOK MORE... WHAT WAS THAT WORD?
OBSOLETE?
OBESE?
SHIT, THAT... THAT'S PLAGIARISM! THAT...
NO. NO, IT BEGAN WITH AN "O", I'M POSITIVE...
HEY! HEY, YOU!
WHAT THE HELL ARE YOU DOING IN HERE? I'M WAITING TO GET CHANGED!

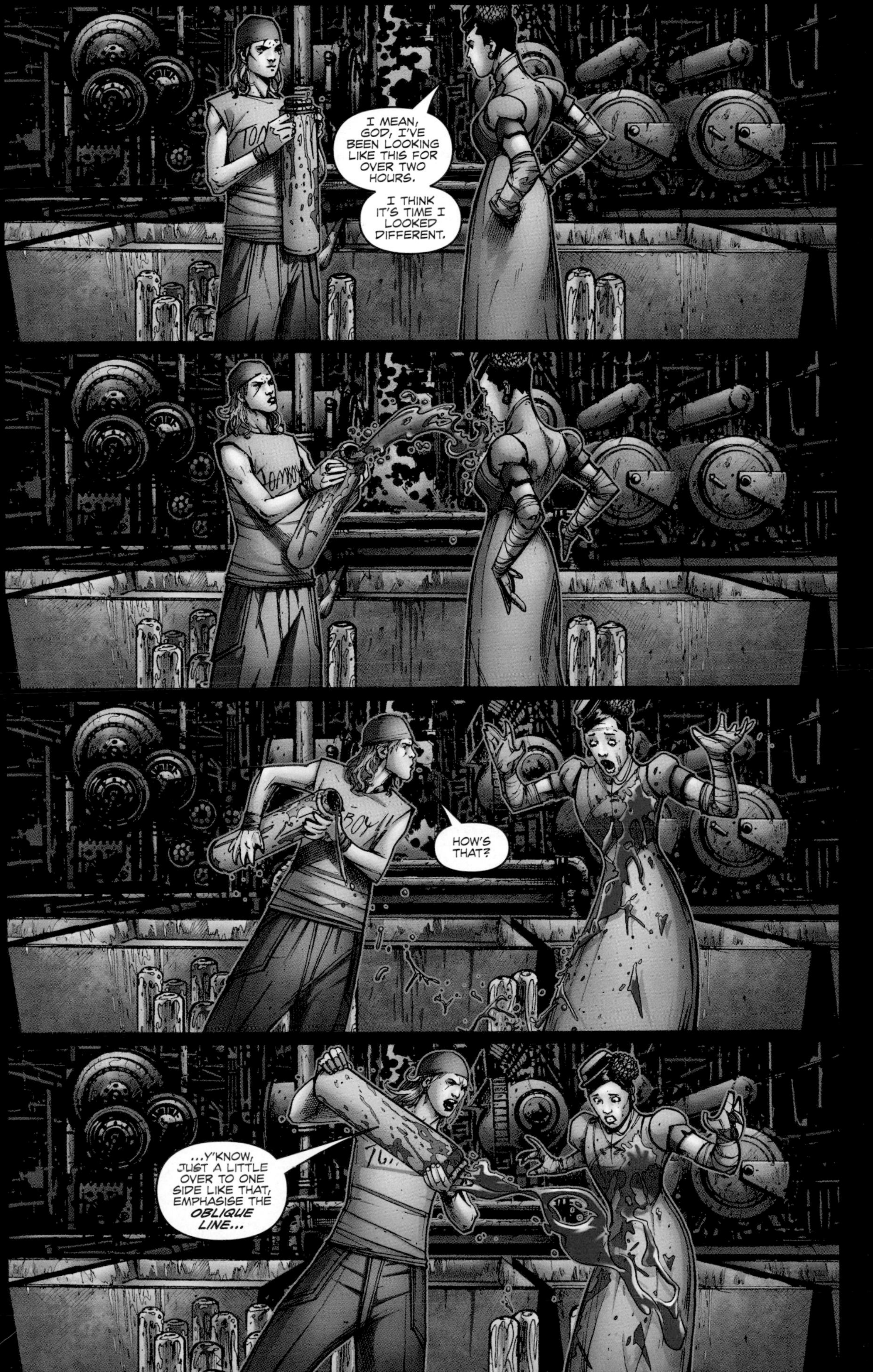

I MEAN, GOD, I'VE BEEN LOOKING LIKE THIS FOR OVER TWO HOURS.
I THINK IT'S TIME I LOOKED DIFFERENT.
HOW'S THAT?
...Y'KNOW, JUST A LITTLE OVER TO ONE SIDE LIKE THAT, EMPHASISE THE *OBLIQUE LINE*...

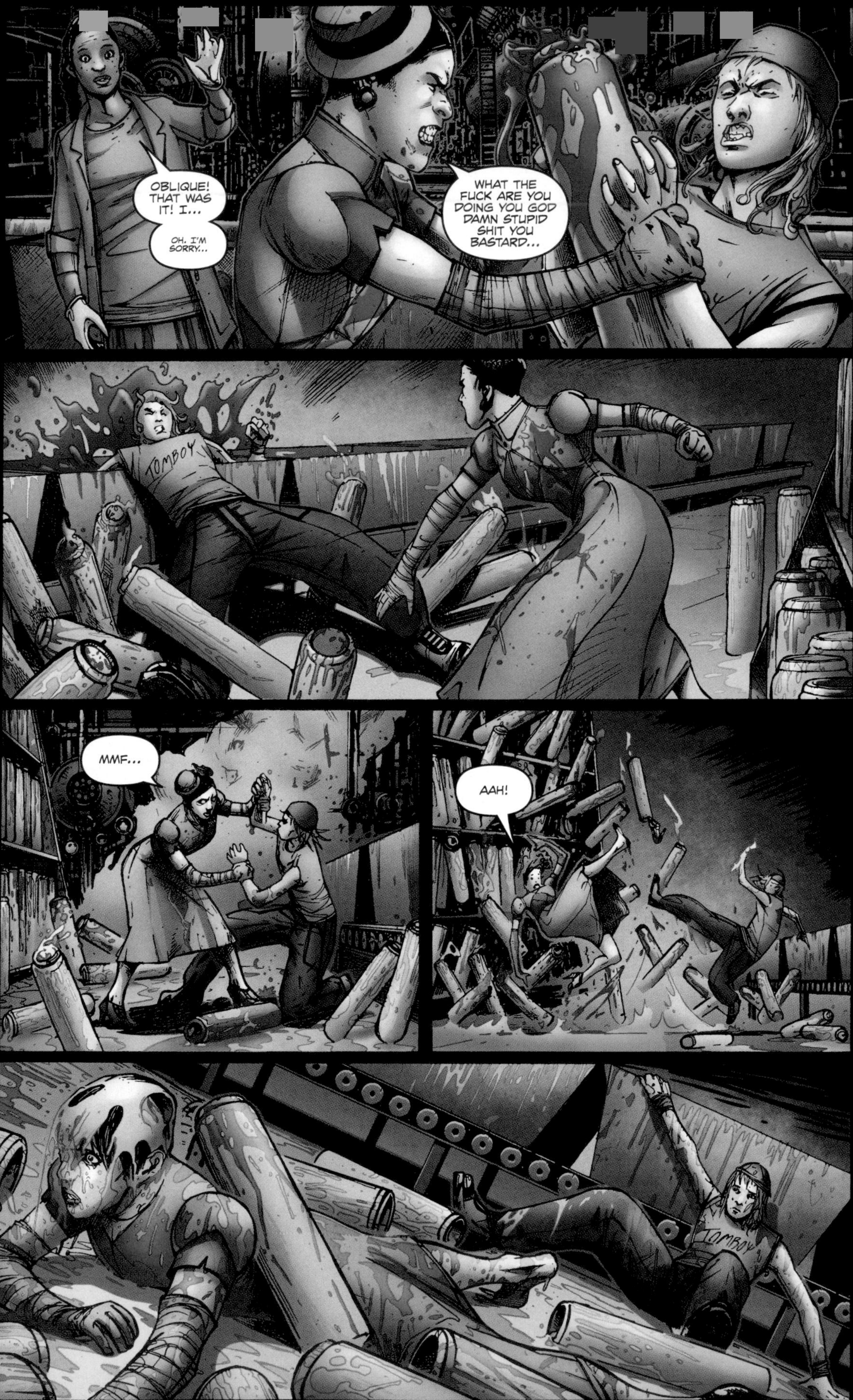
OBLIQUE! THAT WAS IT! I...
OH. I'M SORRY...
WHAT THE FUCK ARE YOU DOING YOU GOD DAMN STUPID SHIT YOU BASTARD...
TOMBOY
MMF...
AAH!
TOMBOY

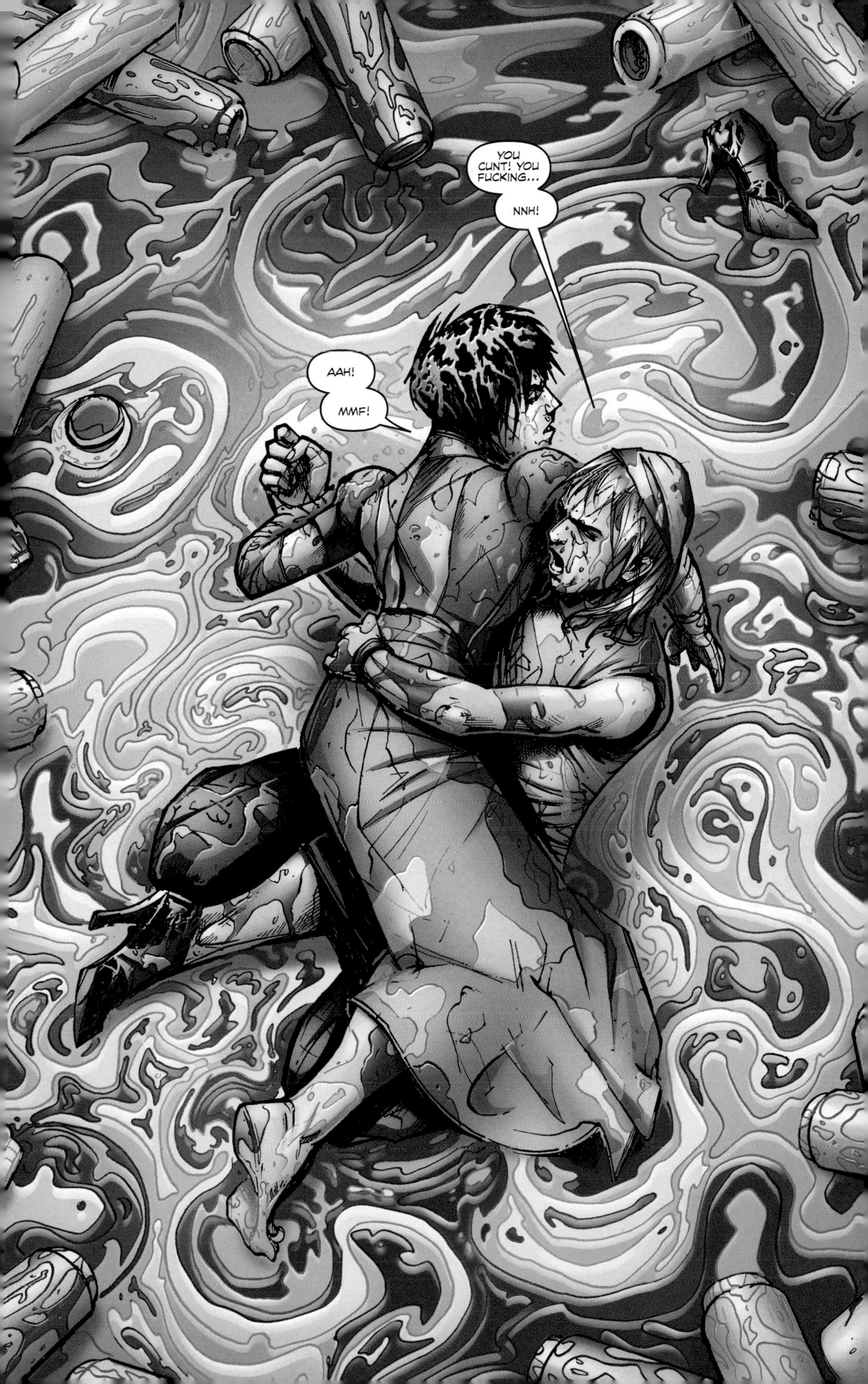
YOU CUNT! YOU FUCKING...
NNH!
AAH!
MMF!

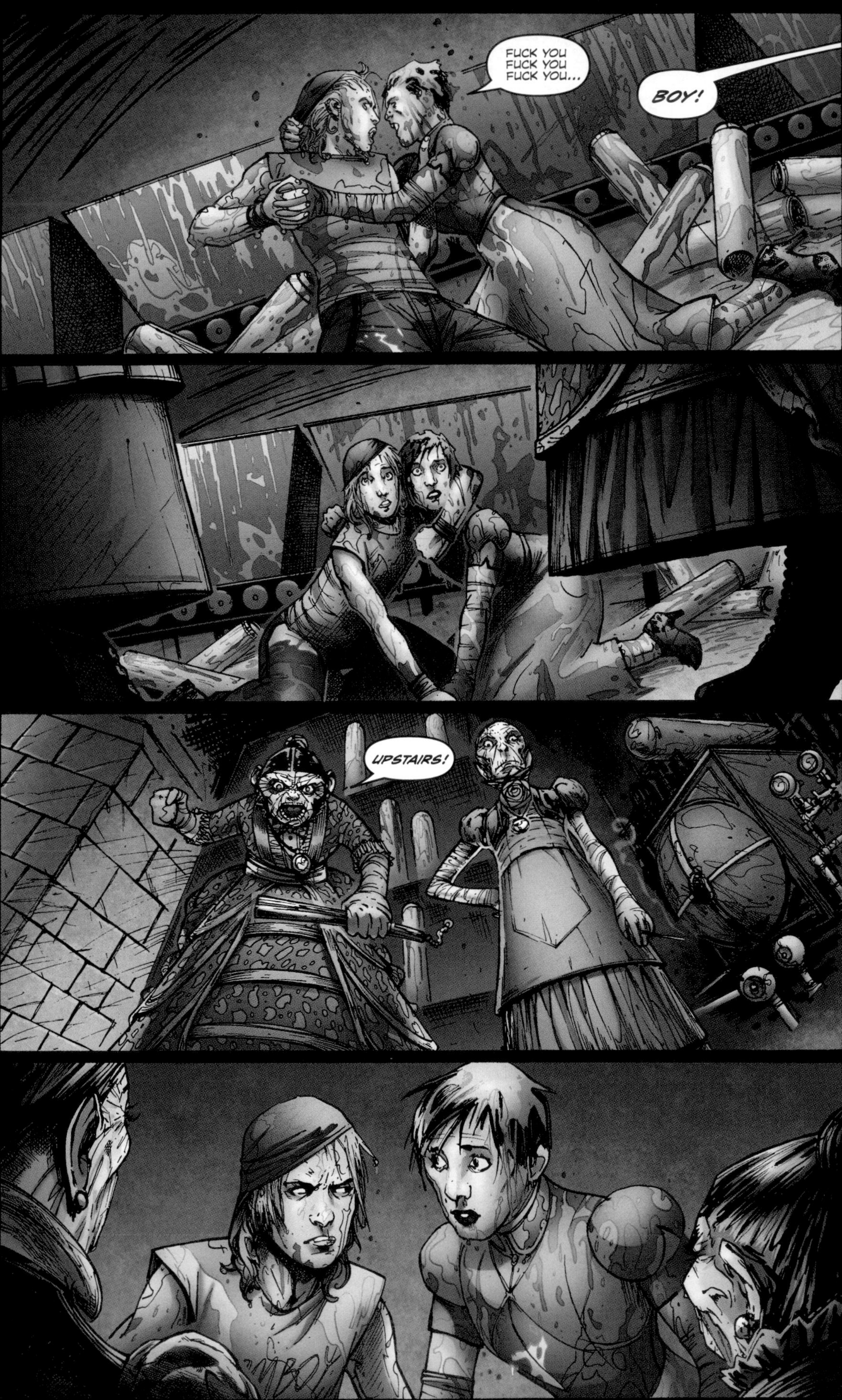
FUCK YOU
FUCK YOU
FUCK YOU...
BOY!
UPSTAIRS!

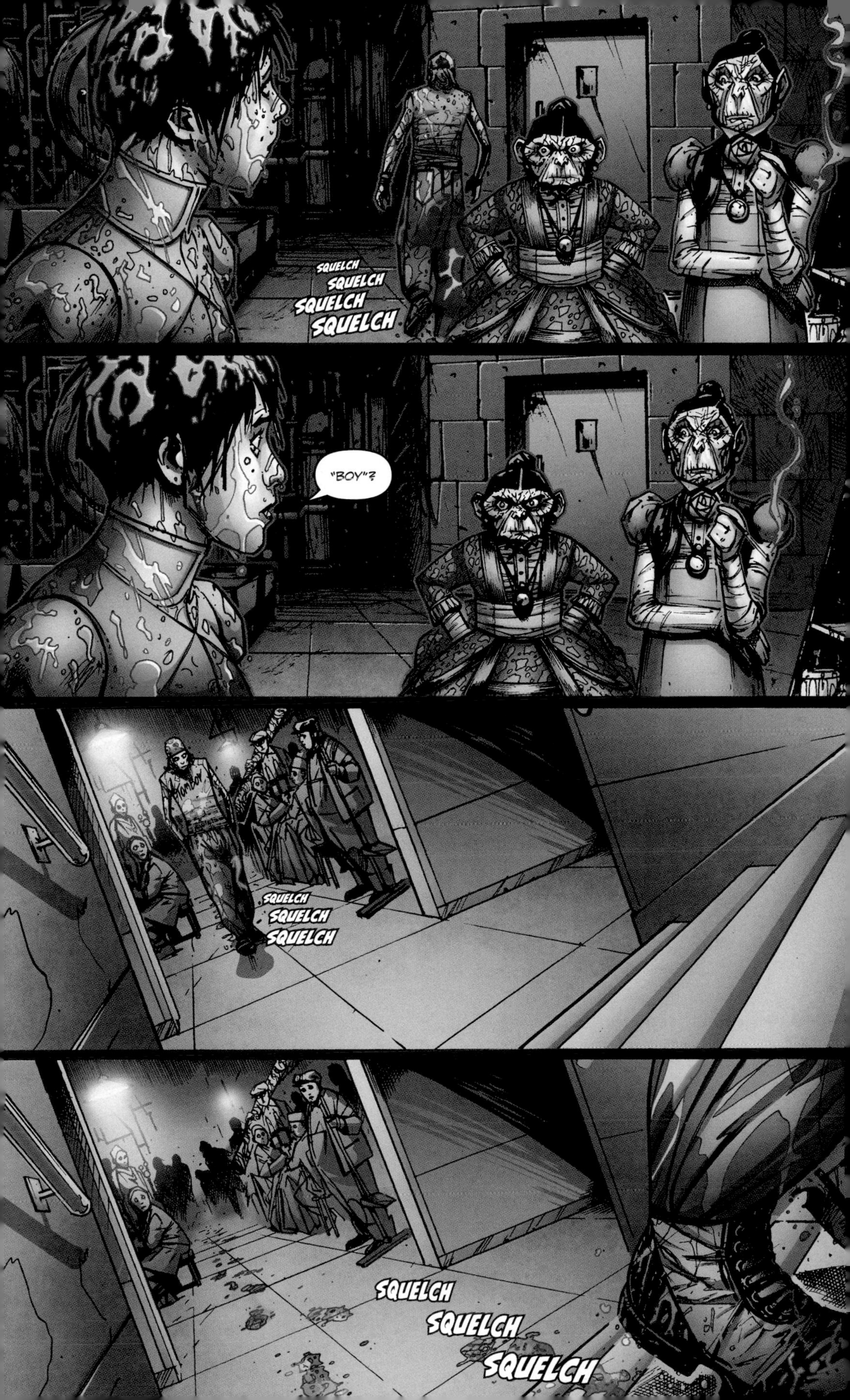
SQUELCH
SQUELCH
SQUELCH
SQUELCH
"BOY"?
SQUELCH
SQUELCH
SQUELCH
SQUELCH
SQUELCH
SQUELCH

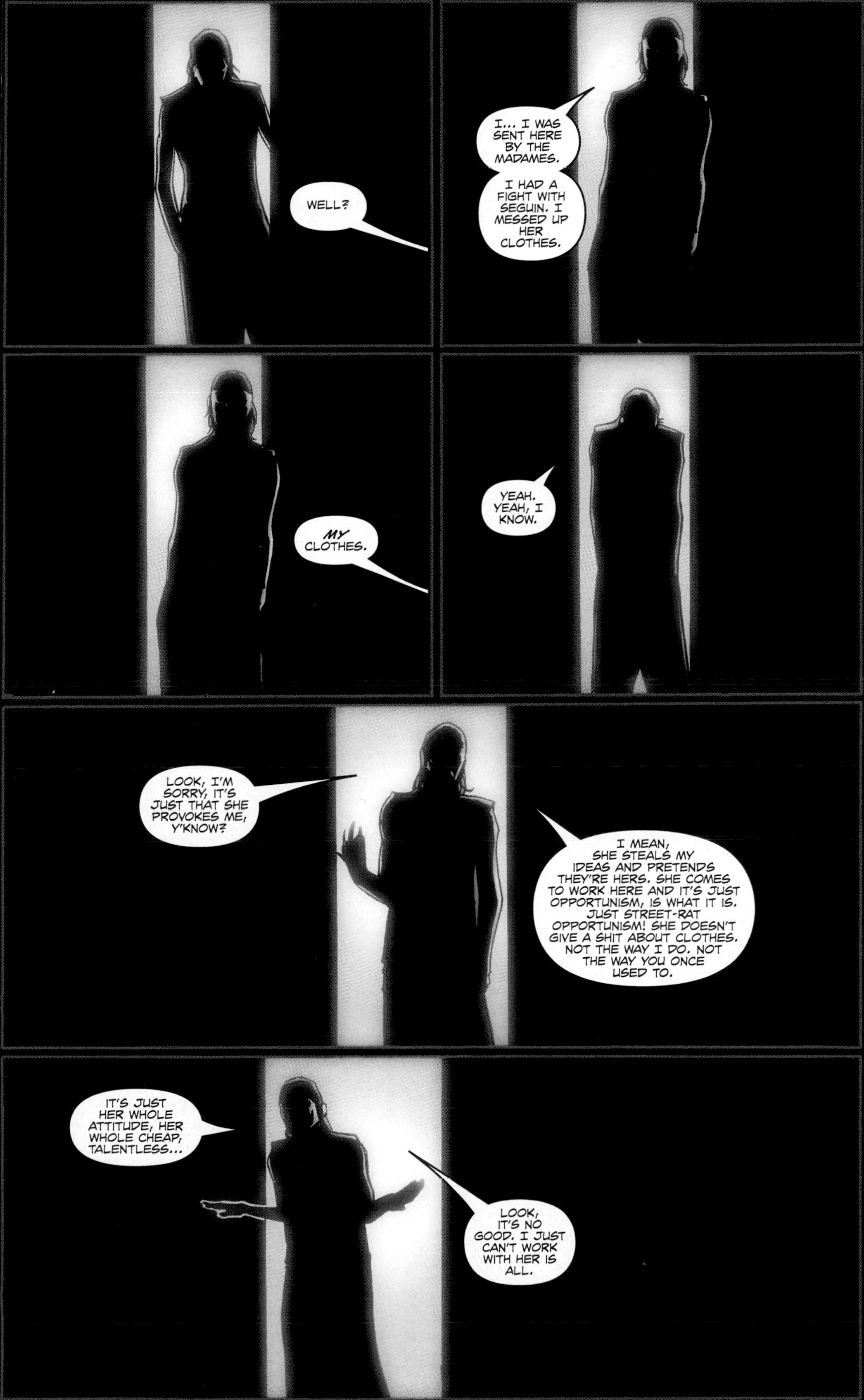
WELL?
I... I WAS SENT HERE BY THE MADAMES.
I HAD A FIGHT WITH SEGUIN. I MESSED UP HER CLOTHES.
MY CLOTHES.
YEAH. YEAH, I KNOW.
LOOK, I'M SORRY, IT'S JUST THAT SHE PROVOKES ME, Y'KNOW?
I MEAN, SHE STEALS MY IDEAS AND PRETENDS THEY'RE HERS. SHE COMES TO WORK HERE AND IT'S JUST OPPORTUNISM, IS WHAT IT IS. JUST STREET-RAT OPPORTUNISM! SHE DOESN'T GIVE A SHIT ABOUT CLOTHES. NOT THE WAY I DO. NOT THE WAY YOU ONCE USED TO.
IT'S JUST HER WHOLE ATTITUDE, HER WHOLE CHEAP, TALENTLESS...
LOOK, IT'S NO GOOD. I JUST CAN'T WORK WITH HER IS ALL.

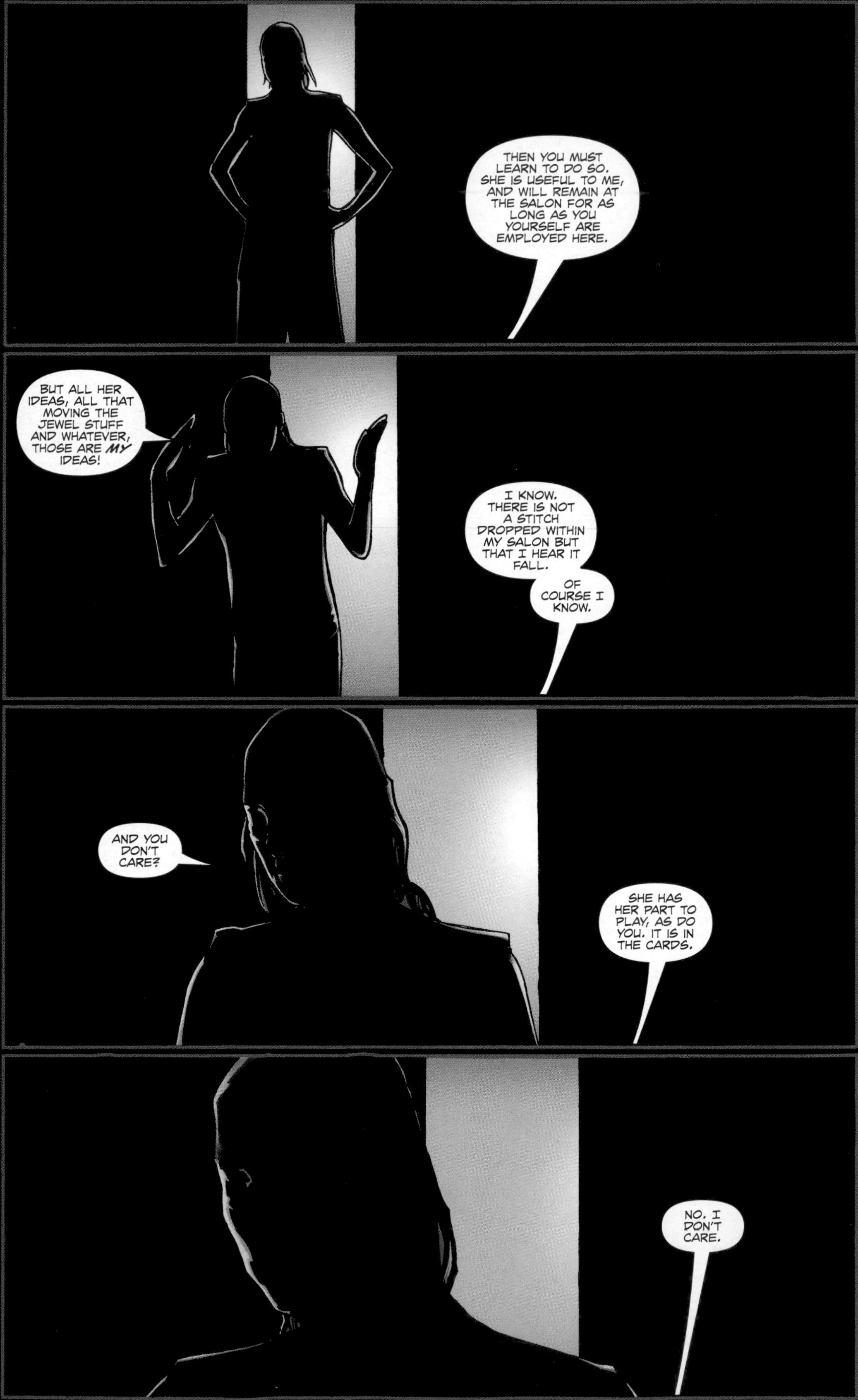
THEN YOU MUST LEARN TO DO SO. SHE IS USEFUL TO ME, AND WILL REMAIN AT THE SALON FOR AS LONG AS YOU YOURSELF ARE EMPLOYED HERE.
BUT ALL HER IDEAS, ALL THAT MOVING THE JEWEL STUFF AND WHATEVER, THOSE ARE *MY* IDEAS!
I KNOW. THERE IS NOT A STITCH DROPPED WITHIN MY SALON BUT THAT I HEAR IT FALL.
OF COURSE I KNOW.
AND YOU DON'T CARE?
SHE HAS HER PART TO PLAY, AS DO YOU. IT IS IN THE CARDS.
NO. I DON'T CARE.

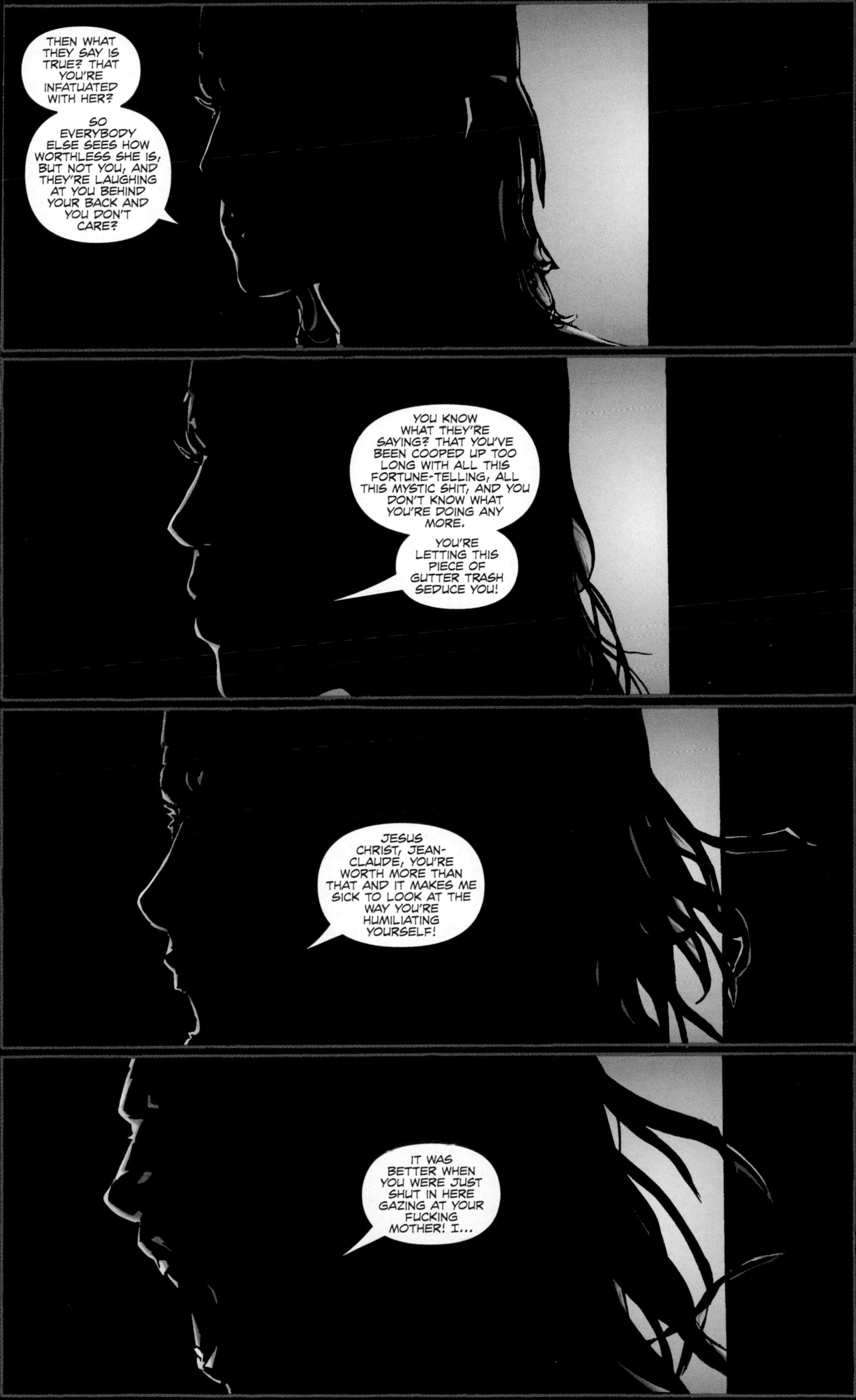
THEN WHAT THEY SAY IS TRUE? THAT YOU'RE INFATUATED WITH HER?
SO EVERYBODY ELSE SEES HOW WORTHLESS SHE IS, BUT NOT YOU, AND THEY'RE LAUGHING AT YOU BEHIND YOUR BACK AND YOU DON'T CARE?
YOU KNOW WHAT THEY'RE SAYING? THAT YOU'VE BEEN COOPED UP TOO LONG WITH ALL THIS FORTUNE-TELLING, ALL THIS MYSTIC SHIT, AND YOU DON'T KNOW WHAT YOU'RE DOING ANY MORE.
YOU'RE LETTING THIS PIECE OF GUTTER TRASH SEDUCE YOU!
JESUS CHRIST, JEAN-CLAUDE, YOU'RE WORTH MORE THAN THAT AND IT MAKES ME SICK TO LOOK AT THE WAY YOU'RE HUMILIATING YOURSELF!
IT WAS BETTER WHEN YOU WERE JUST SHUT IN HERE GAZING AT YOUR FUCKING MOTHER! I...

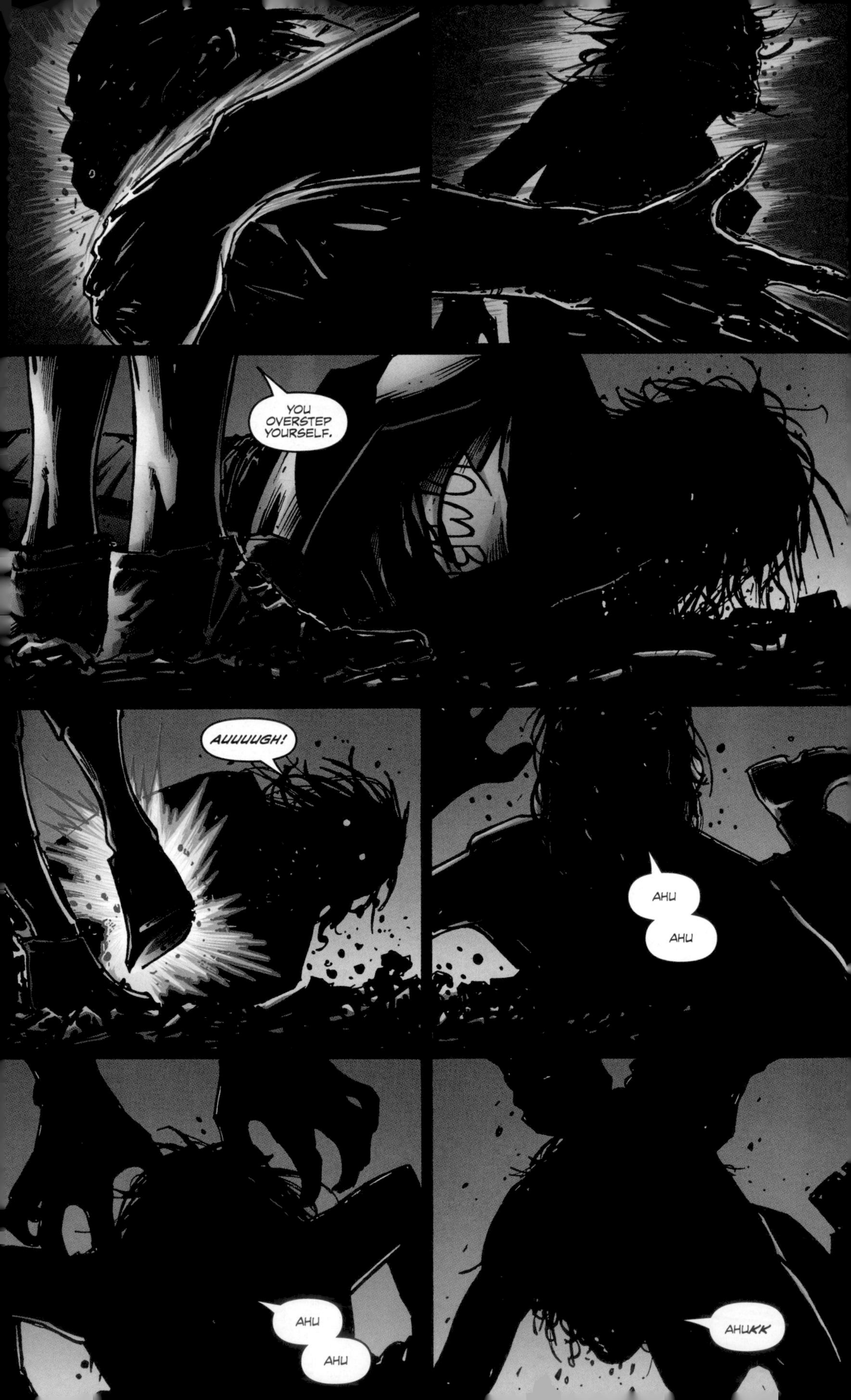
YOU OVERSTEP YOURSELF.
AUUUUGH!
AHU
AHU
AHU
AHU
AHUKK

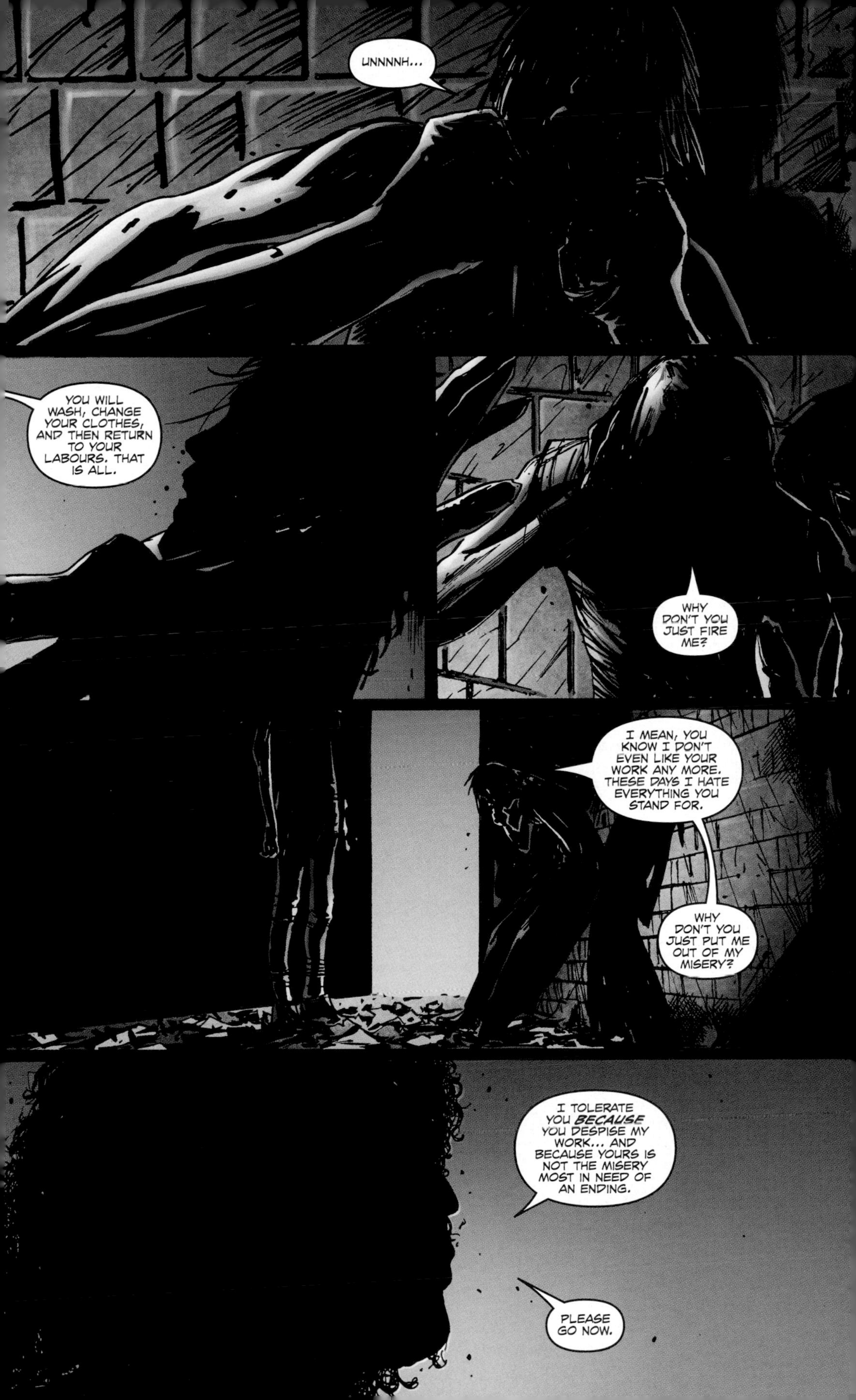
UNNNNH...
YOU WILL WASH, CHANGE YOUR CLOTHES, AND THEN RETURN TO YOUR LABOURS. THAT IS ALL.
WHY DON'T YOU JUST FIRE ME?
I MEAN, YOU KNOW I DON'T EVEN LIKE YOUR WORK ANY MORE. THESE DAYS I HATE EVERYTHING YOU STAND FOR.
WHY DON'T YOU JUST PUT ME OUT OF MY MISERY?
I TOLERATE YOU *BECAUSE* YOU DESPISE MY WORK... AND BECAUSE YOURS IS NOT THE MISERY MOST IN NEED OF AN ENDING.
PLEASE GO NOW.

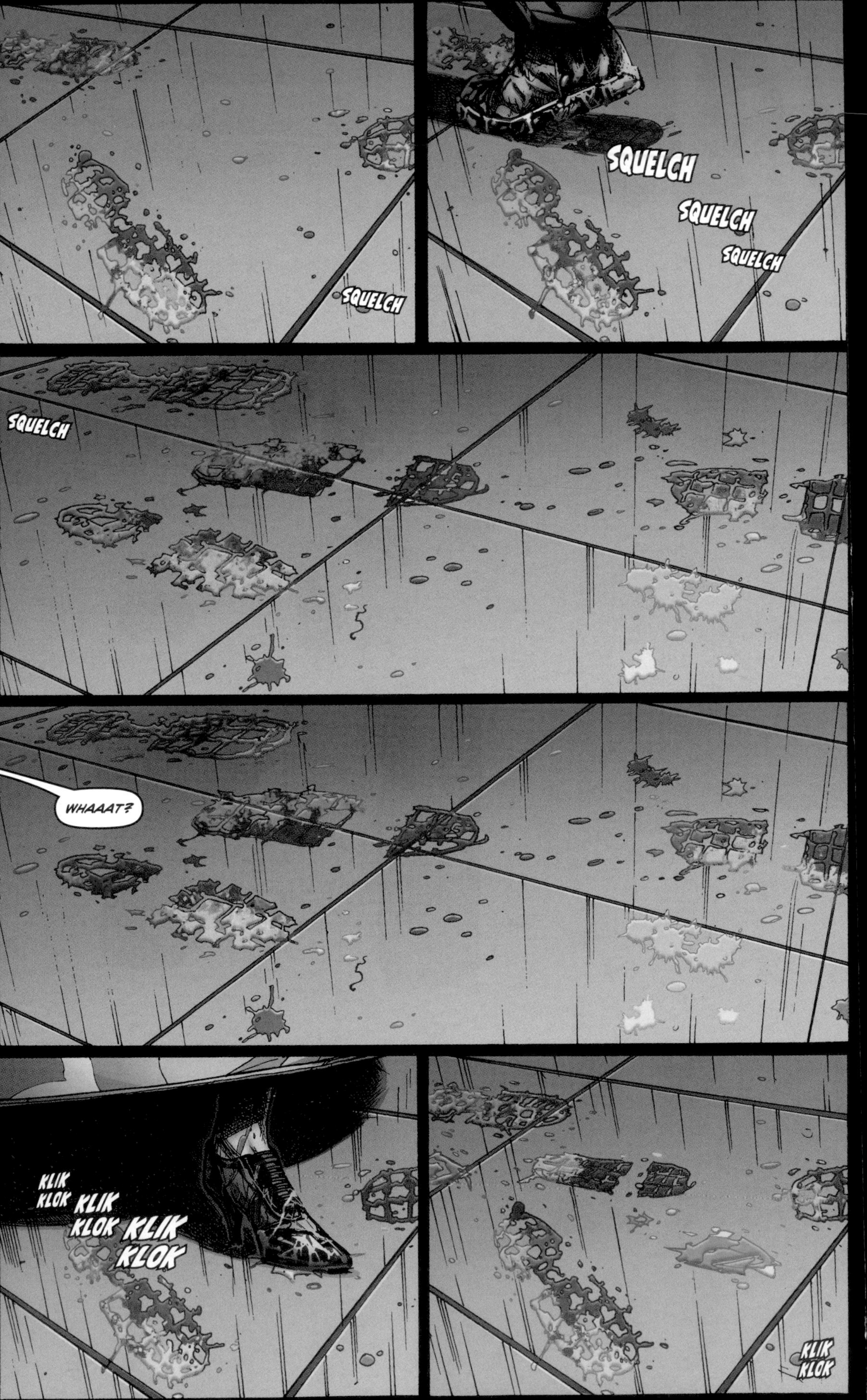
SQUELCH
SQUELCH
SQUELCH
SQUELCH
SQUELCH
WHAAAT?
KLIK
KLOK
KLIK
KLOK
KLIK
KLOK
KLIK
KLOK

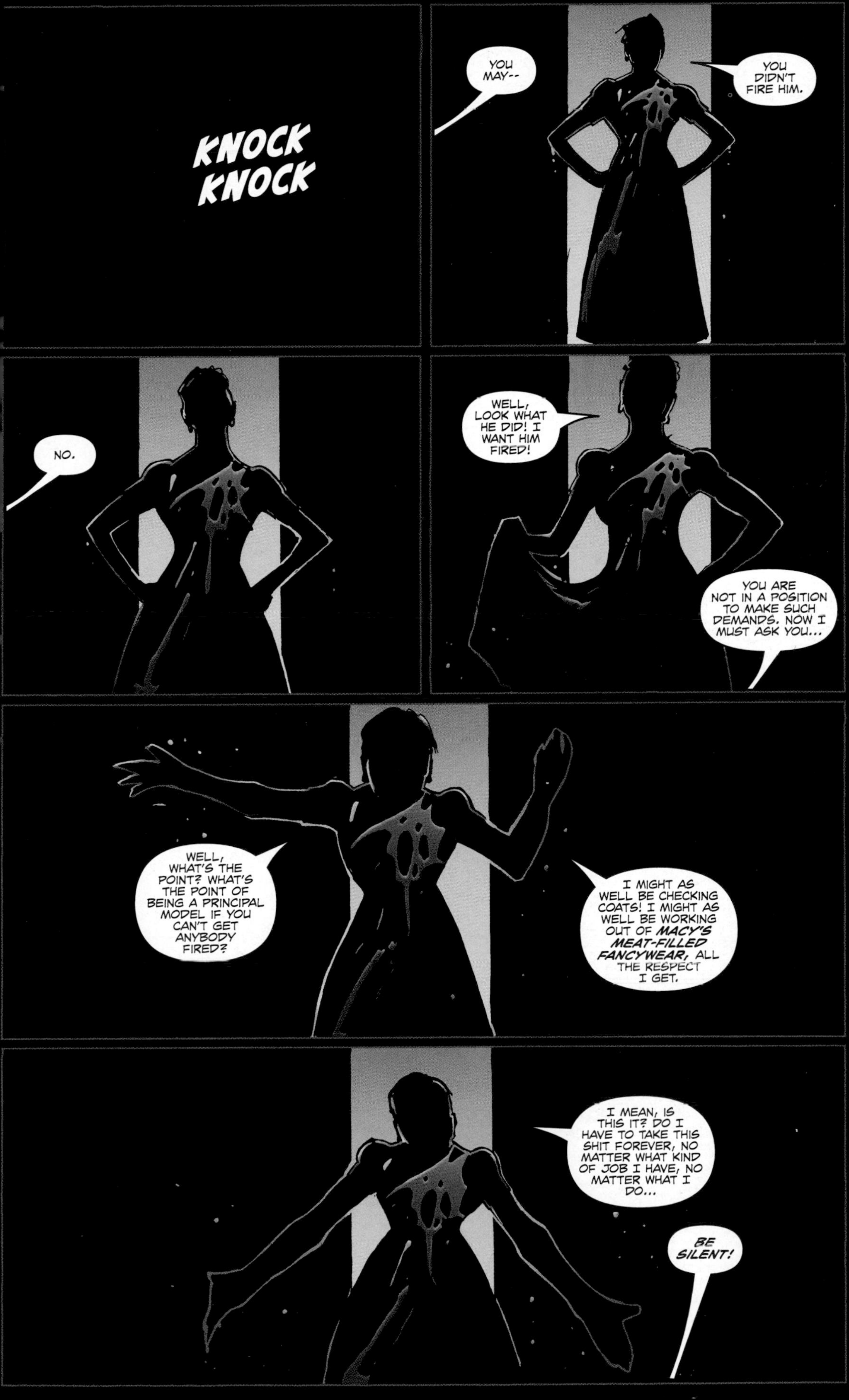
KNOCK KNOCK
YOU MAY--
YOU DIDN'T FIRE HIM.
NO.
WELL, LOOK WHAT HE DID! I WANT HIM FIRED!
YOU ARE NOT IN A POSITION TO MAKE SUCH DEMANDS. NOW I MUST ASK YOU...
WELL, WHAT'S THE POINT? WHAT'S THE POINT OF BEING A PRINCIPAL MODEL IF YOU CAN'T GET ANYBODY FIRED?
I MIGHT AS WELL BE CHECKING COATS! I MIGHT AS WELL BE WORKING OUT OF MACY'S MEAT-FILLED FANCYWEAR, ALL THE RESPECT I GET.
I MEAN, IS THIS IT? DO I HAVE TO TAKE THIS SHIT FOREVER, NO MATTER WHAT KIND OF JOB I HAVE, NO MATTER WHAT I DO...
BE SILENT!

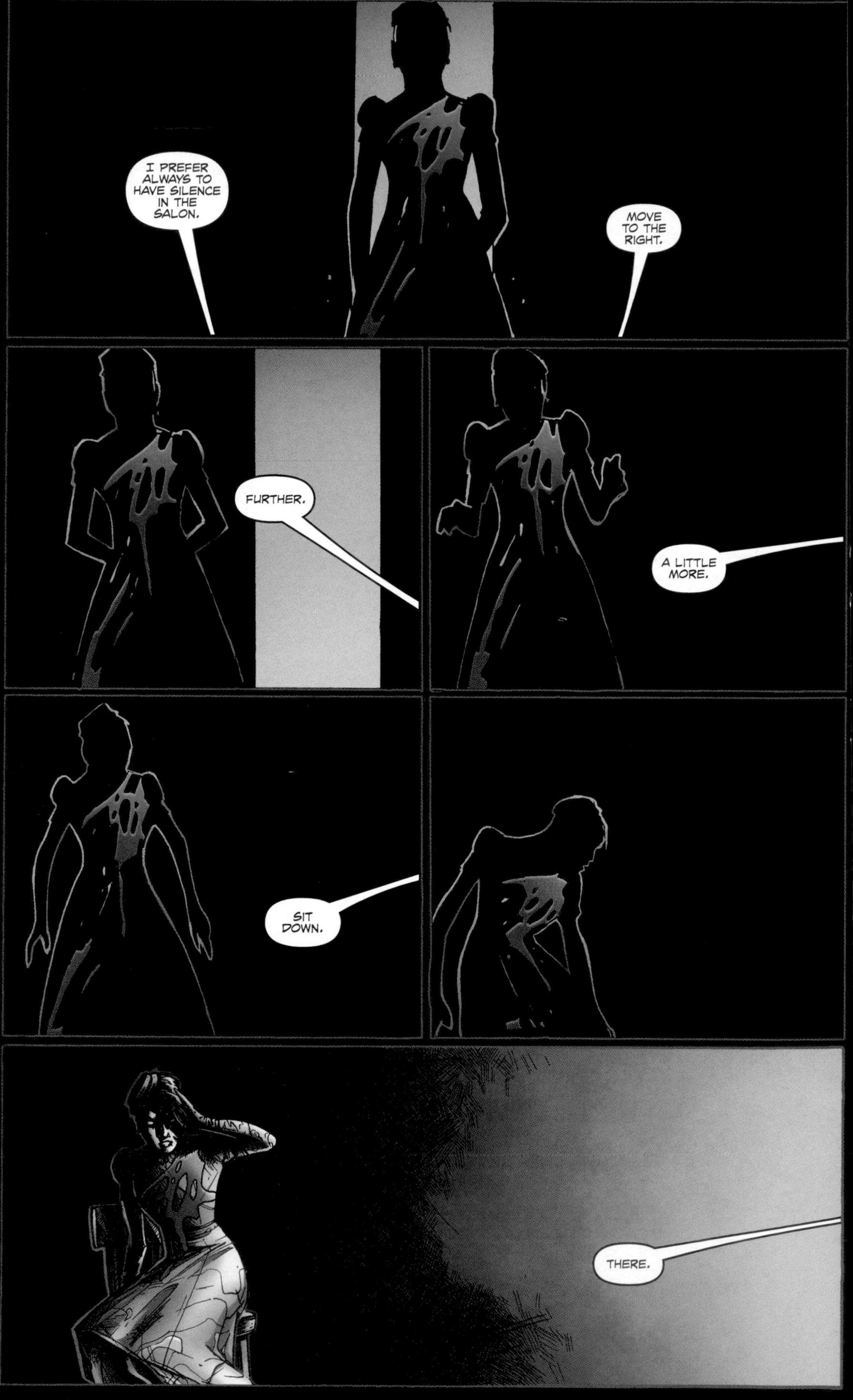
I PREFER ALWAYS TO HAVE SILENCE IN THE SALON.
MOVE TO THE RIGHT.
FURTHER.
A LITTLE MORE.
SIT DOWN.
THERE.

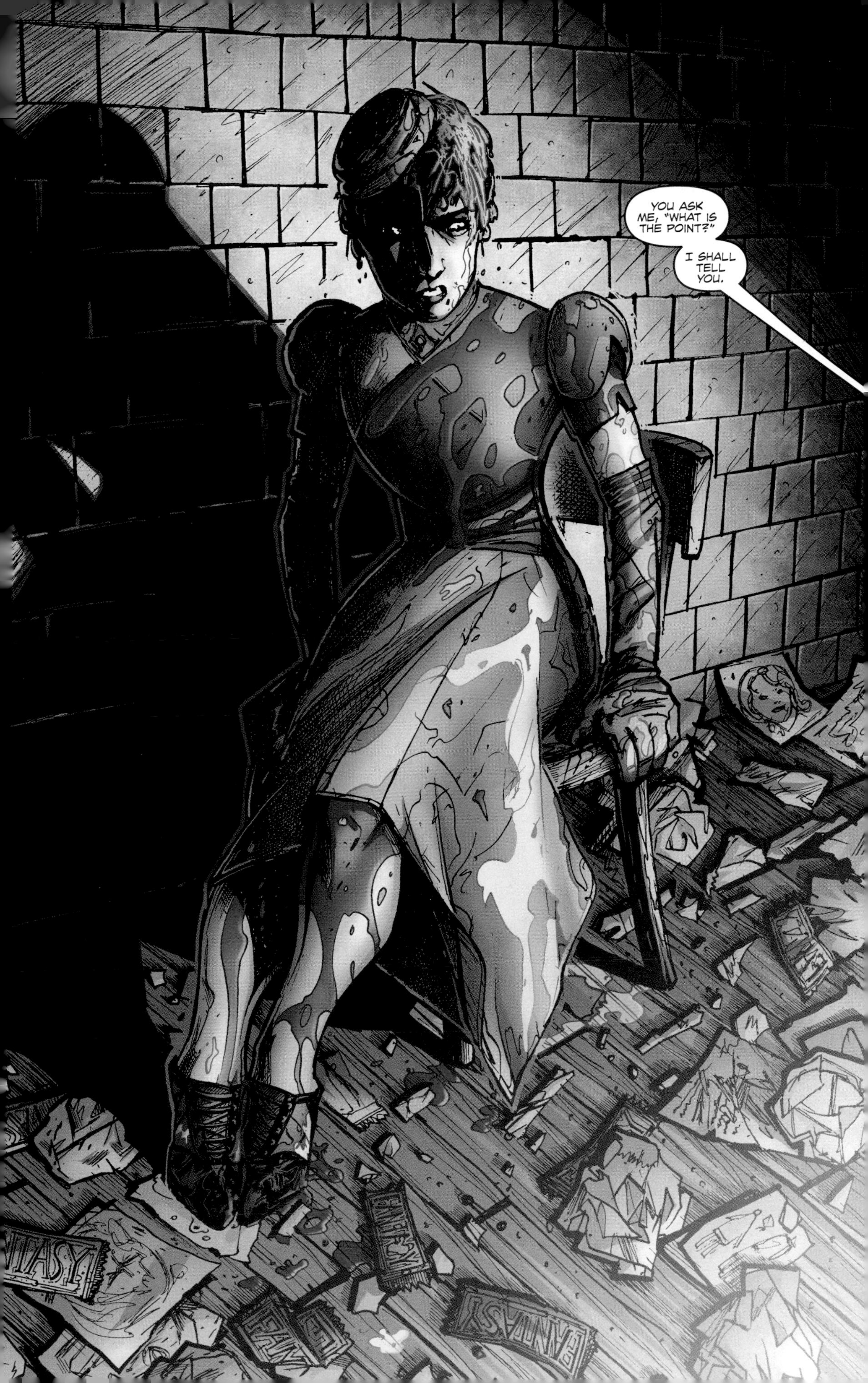
YOU ASK ME, "WHAT IS THE POINT?"
I SHALL TELL YOU.

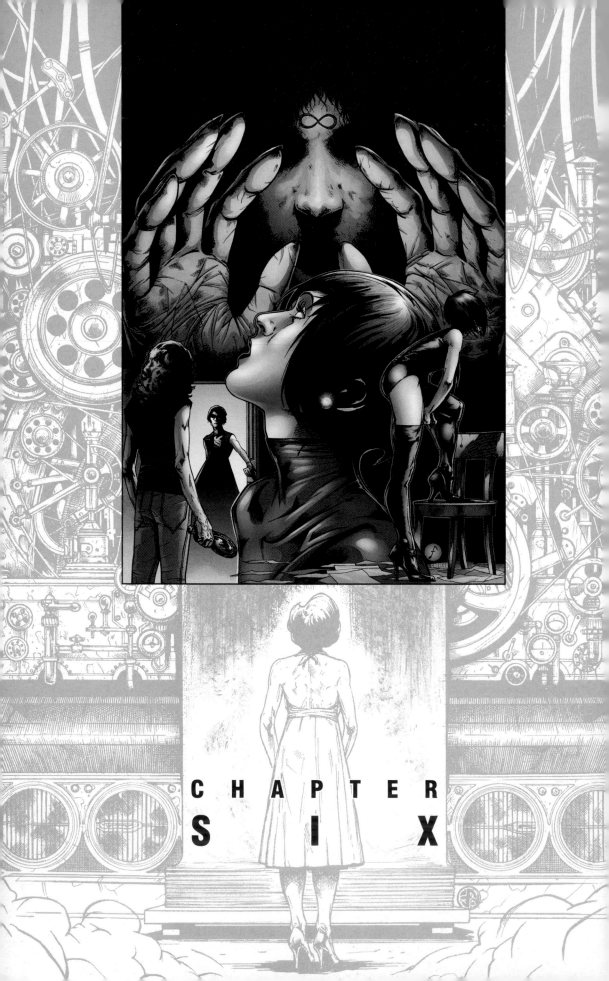

CHAPTER
SIX

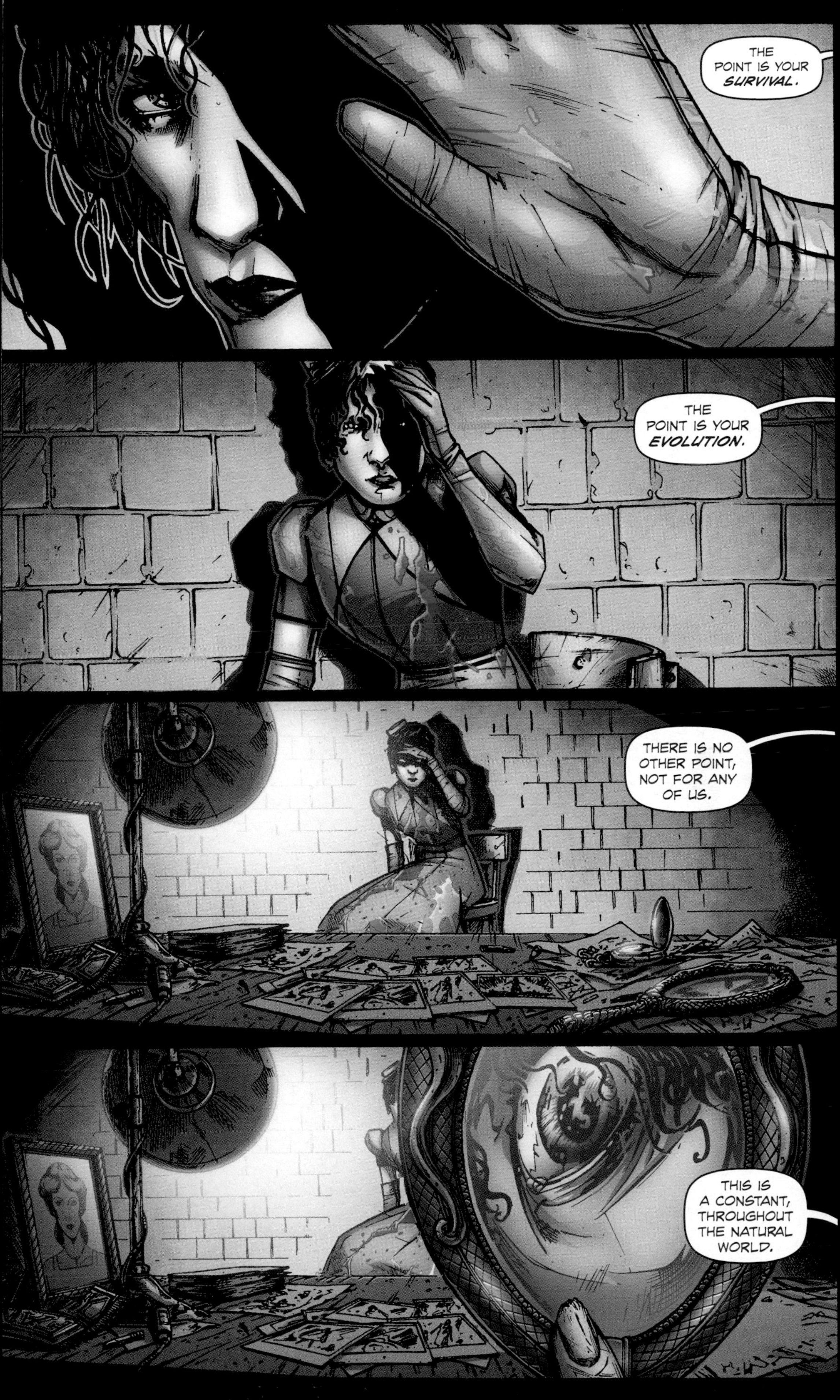
THE POINT IS YOUR SURVIVAL.
THE POINT IS YOUR EVOLUTION.
THERE IS NO OTHER POINT, NOT FOR ANY OF US.
THIS IS A CONSTANT, THROUGHOUT THE NATURAL WORLD.

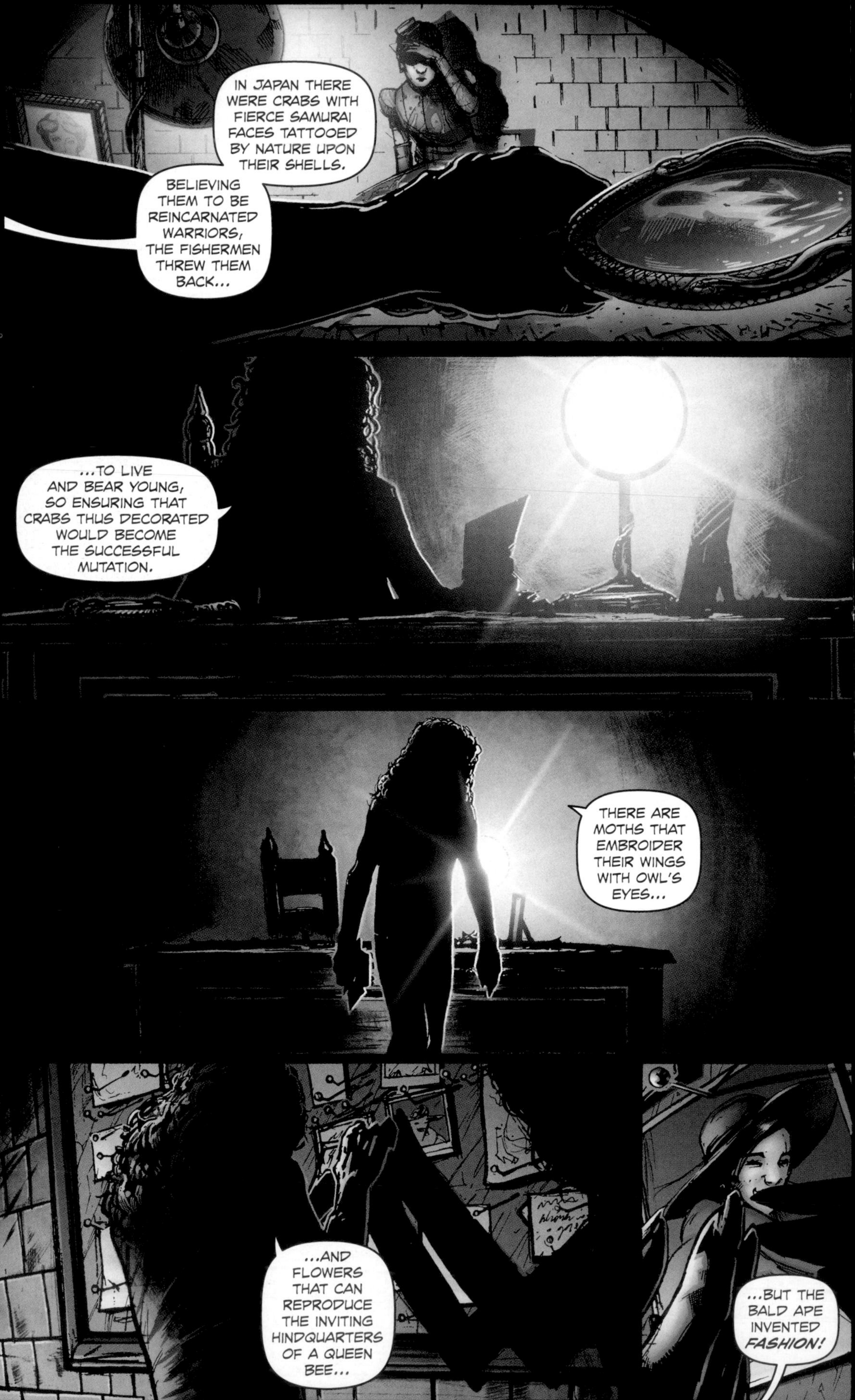
IN JAPAN THERE WERE CRABS WITH FIERCE SAMURAI FACES TATTOOED BY NATURE UPON THEIR SHELLS.
BELIEVING THEM TO BE REINCARNATED WARRIORS, THE FISHERMEN THREW THEM BACK...
...TO LIVE AND BEAR YOUNG, SO ENSURING THAT CRABS THUS DECORATED WOULD BECOME THE SUCCESSFUL MUTATION.
THERE ARE MOTHS THAT EMBROIDER THEIR WINGS WITH OWL'S EYES...
...AND FLOWERS THAT CAN REPRODUCE THE INVITING HINDQUARTERS OF A QUEEN BEE...
...BUT THE BALD APE INVENTED *FASHION!*

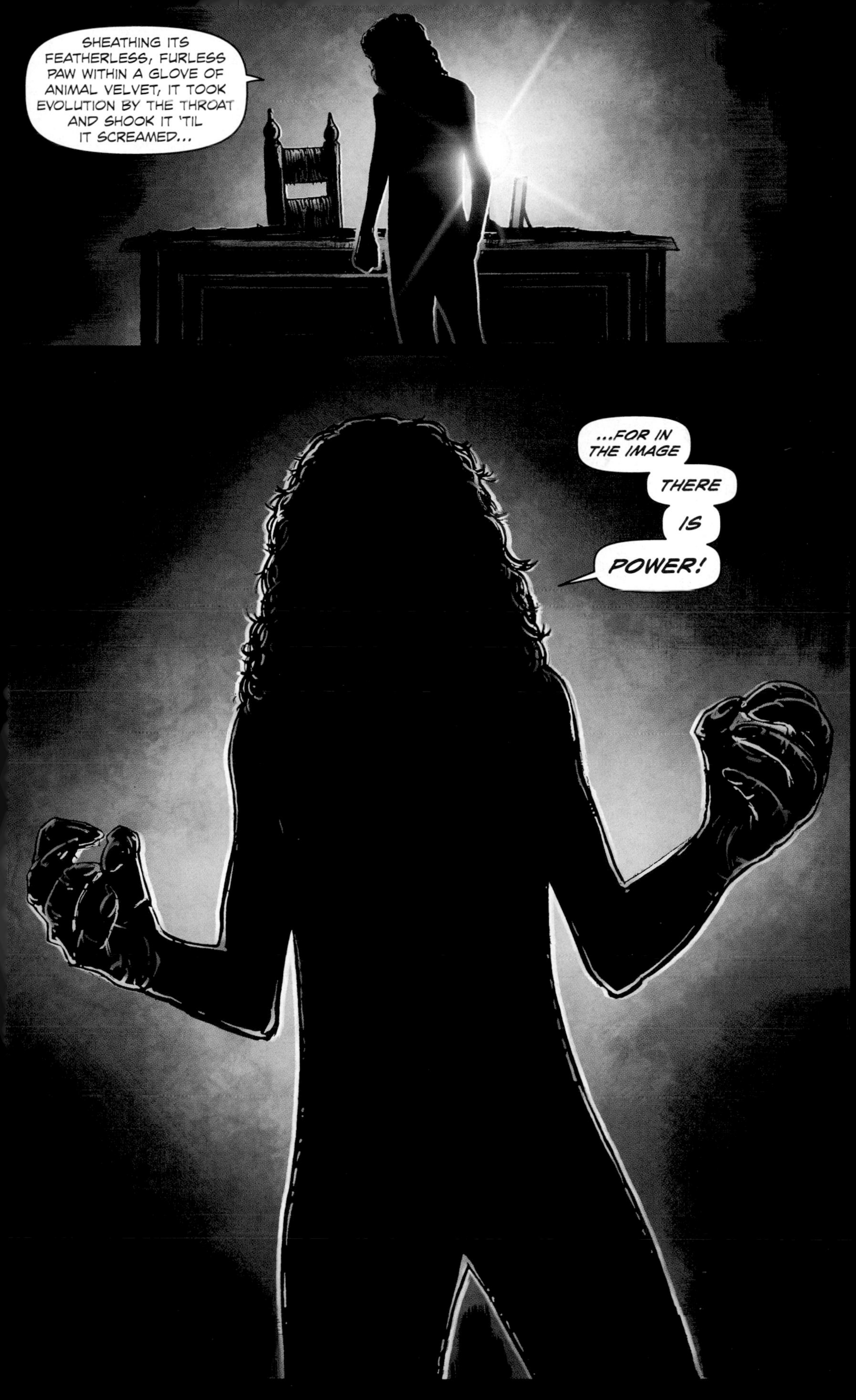
SHEATHING ITS FEATHERLESS, FURLESS PAW WITHIN A GLOVE OF ANIMAL VELVET, IT TOOK EVOLUTION BY THE THROAT AND SHOOK IT 'TIL IT SCREAMED...
...FOR IN THE IMAGE THERE IS POWER!

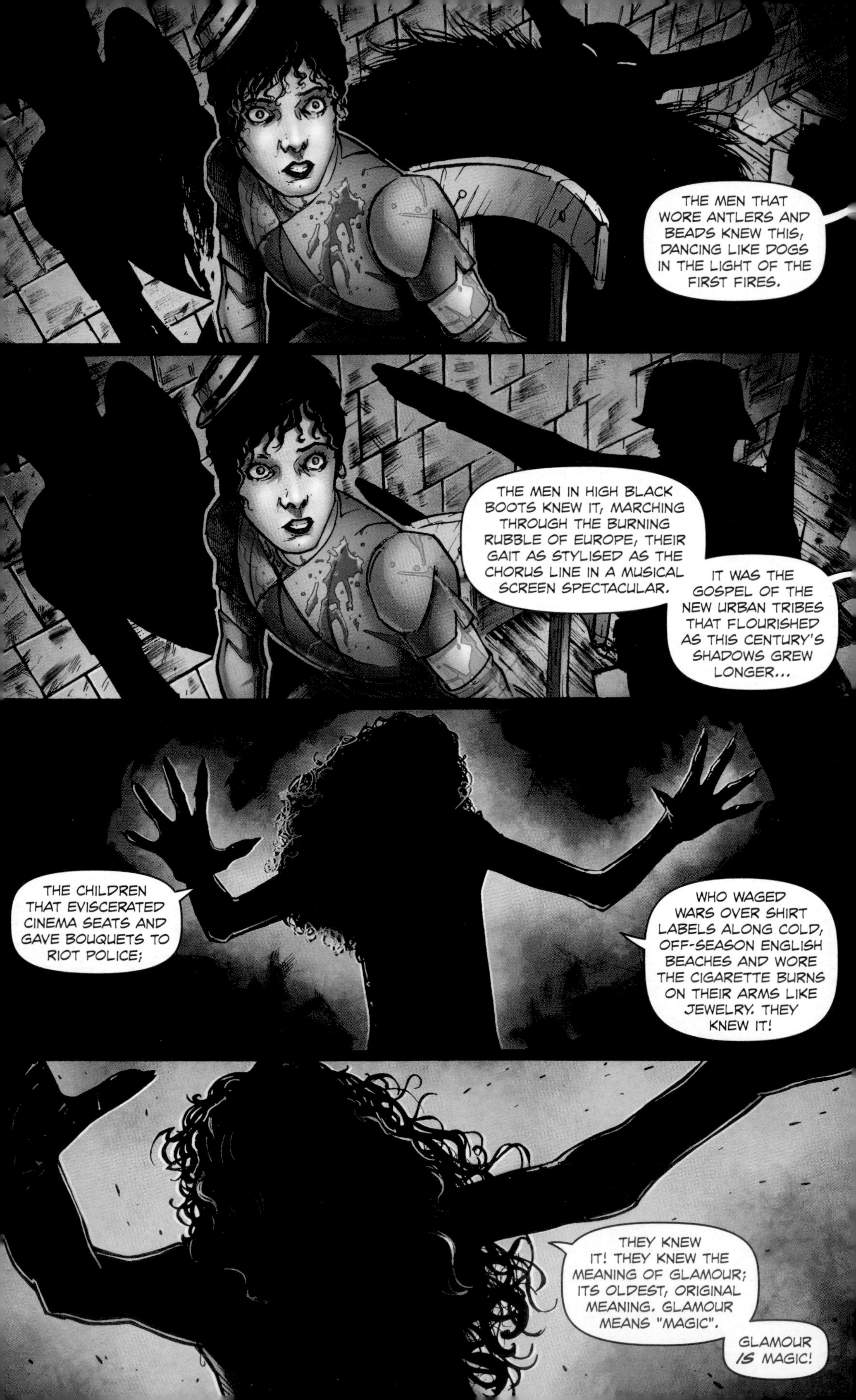
THE MEN THAT WORE ANTLERS AND BEADS KNEW THIS, DANCING LIKE DOGS IN THE LIGHT OF THE FIRST FIRES.
THE MEN IN HIGH BLACK BOOTS KNEW IT, MARCHING THROUGH THE BURNING RUBBLE OF EUROPE, THEIR GAIT AS STYLISED AS THE CHORUS LINE IN A MUSICAL SCREEN SPECTACULAR.
IT WAS THE GOSPEL OF THE NEW URBAN TRIBES THAT FLOURISHED AS THIS CENTURY'S SHADOWS GREW LONGER...
THE CHILDREN THAT EVISCERATED CINEMA SEATS AND GAVE BOUQUETS TO RIOT POLICE;
WHO WAGED WARS OVER SHIRT LABELS ALONG COLD, OFF-SEASON ENGLISH BEACHES AND WORE THE CIGARETTE BURNS ON THEIR ARMS LIKE JEWELRY. THEY KNEW IT!
THEY KNEW IT! THEY KNEW THE MEANING OF GLAMOUR; ITS OLDEST, ORIGINAL MEANING. GLAMOUR MEANS "MAGIC".
GLAMOUR *IS* MAGIC!

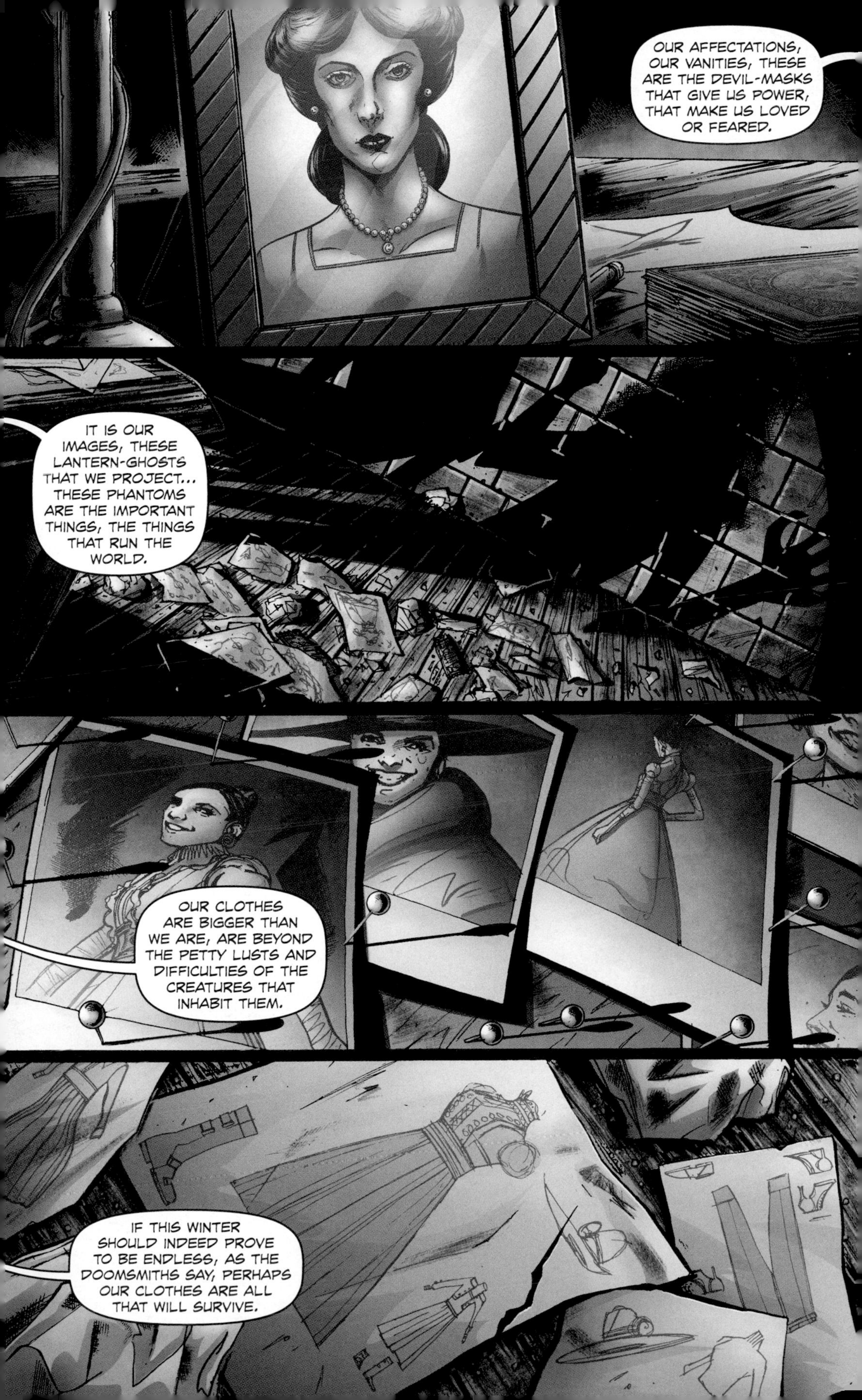
OUR AFFECTATIONS, OUR VANITIES, THESE ARE THE DEVIL-MASKS THAT GIVE US POWER, THAT MAKE US LOVED OR FEARED.
IT IS OUR IMAGES, THESE LANTERN-GHOSTS THAT WE PROJECT... THESE PHANTOMS ARE THE IMPORTANT THINGS, THE THINGS THAT RUN THE WORLD.
OUR CLOTHES ARE BIGGER THAN WE ARE, ARE BEYOND THE PETTY LUSTS AND DIFFICULTIES OF THE CREATURES THAT INHABIT THEM.
IF THIS WINTER SHOULD INDEED PROVE TO BE ENDLESS, AS THE DOOMSMITHS SAY, PERHAPS OUR CLOTHES ARE ALL THAT WILL SURVIVE.

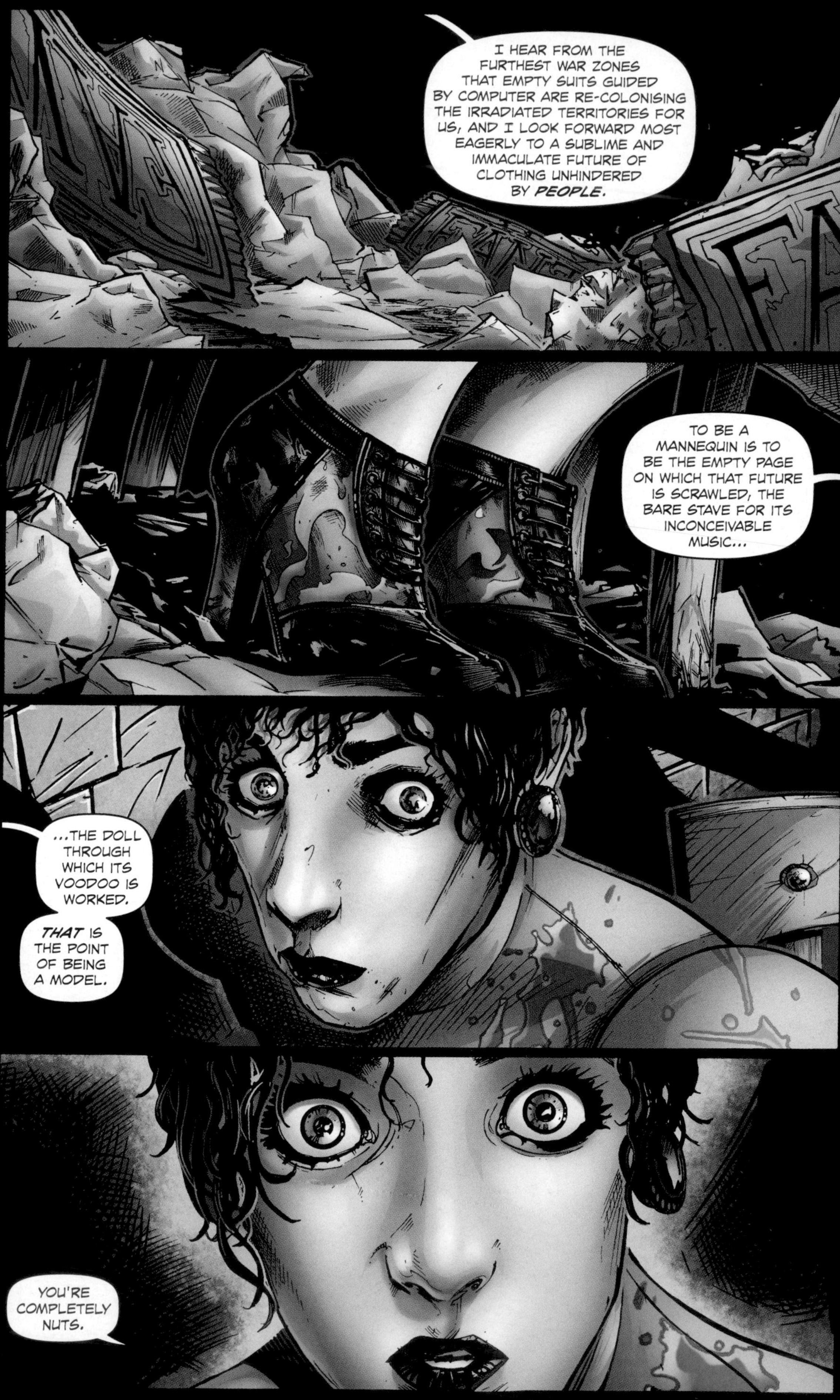
I HEAR FROM THE FURTHEST WAR ZONES THAT EMPTY SUITS GUIDED BY COMPUTER ARE RE-COLONISING THE IRRADIATED TERRITORIES FOR US, AND I LOOK FORWARD MOST EAGERLY TO A SUBLIME AND IMMACULATE FUTURE OF CLOTHING UNHINDERED BY *PEOPLE*.
TO BE A MANNEQUIN IS TO BE THE EMPTY PAGE ON WHICH THAT FUTURE IS SCRAWLED, THE BARE STAVE FOR ITS INCONCEIVABLE MUSIC...
...THE DOLL THROUGH WHICH ITS VOODOO IS WORKED.
THAT IS THE POINT OF BEING A MODEL.
YOU'RE COMPLETELY NUTS.

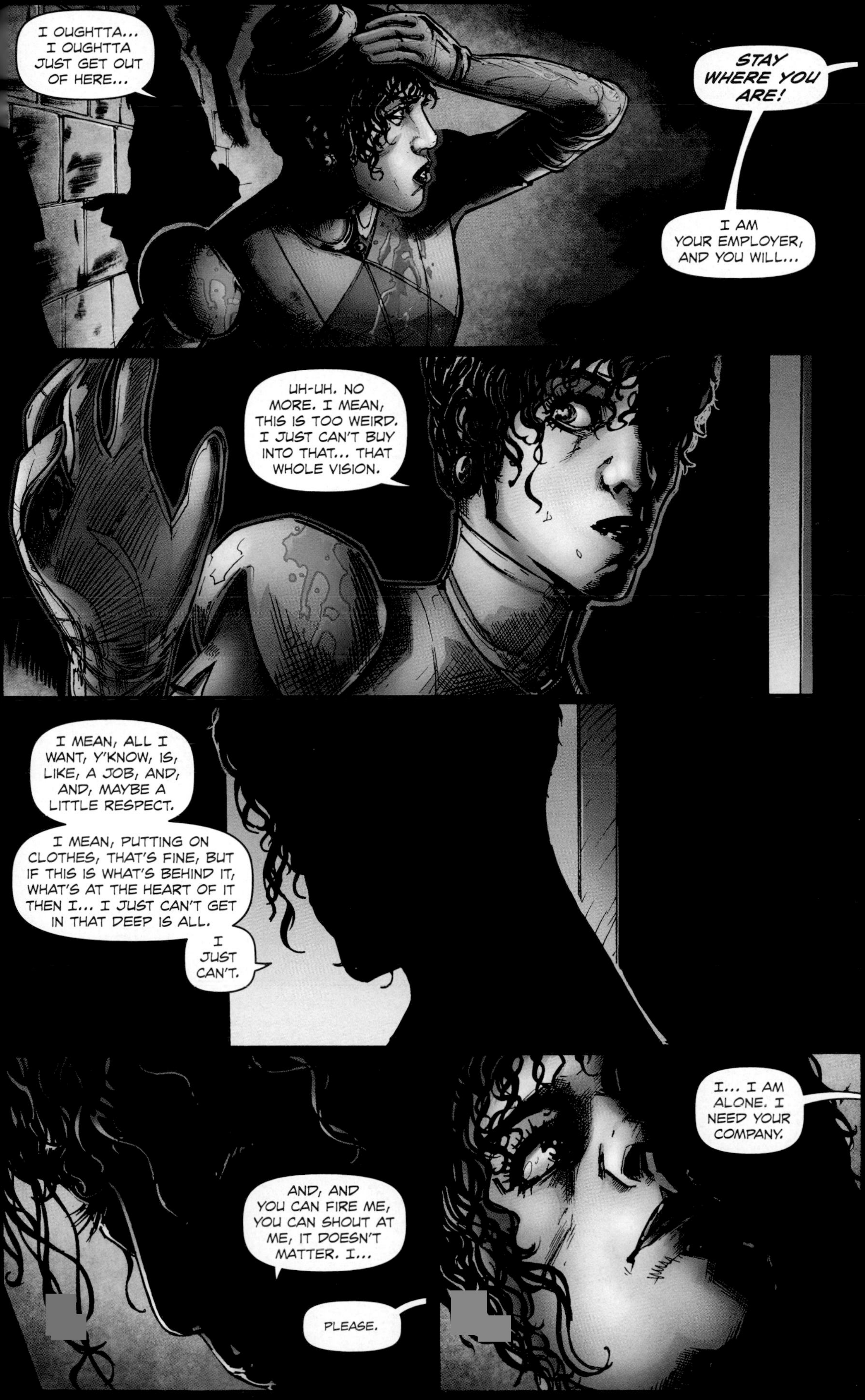

I OUGHTTA... I OUGHTTA JUST GET OUT OF HERE...
STAY WHERE YOU ARE!
I AM YOUR EMPLOYER, AND YOU WILL...
UH-UH. NO MORE. I MEAN, THIS IS TOO WEIRD. I JUST CAN'T BUY INTO THAT... THAT WHOLE VISION.
I MEAN, ALL I WANT, Y'KNOW, IS, LIKE, A JOB, AND, AND, MAYBE A LITTLE RESPECT.
I MEAN, PUTTING ON CLOTHES, THAT'S FINE, BUT IF THIS IS WHAT'S BEHIND IT, WHAT'S AT THE HEART OF IT THEN I... I JUST CAN'T GET IN THAT DEEP IS ALL.
I JUST CAN'T.
AND, AND YOU CAN FIRE ME, YOU CAN SHOUT AT ME, IT DOESN'T MATTER. I...
PLEASE.
I... I AM ALONE. I NEED YOUR COMPANY.

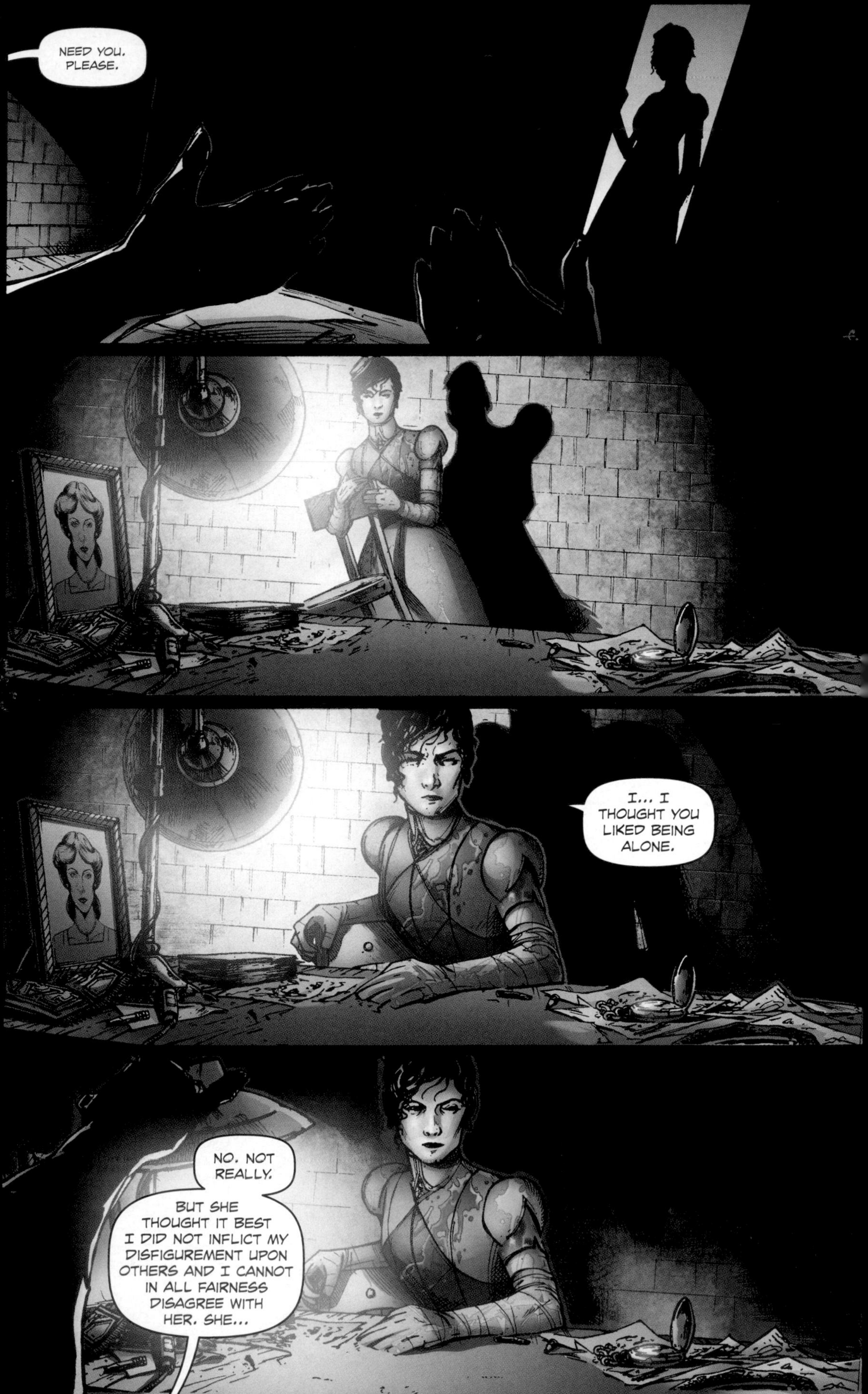
NEED YOU. PLEASE.
I... I THOUGHT YOU LIKED BEING ALONE.
NO. NOT REALLY.
BUT SHE THOUGHT IT BEST I DID NOT INFLICT MY DISFIGUREMENT UPON OTHERS AND I CANNOT IN ALL FAIRNESS DISAGREE WITH HER. SHE...

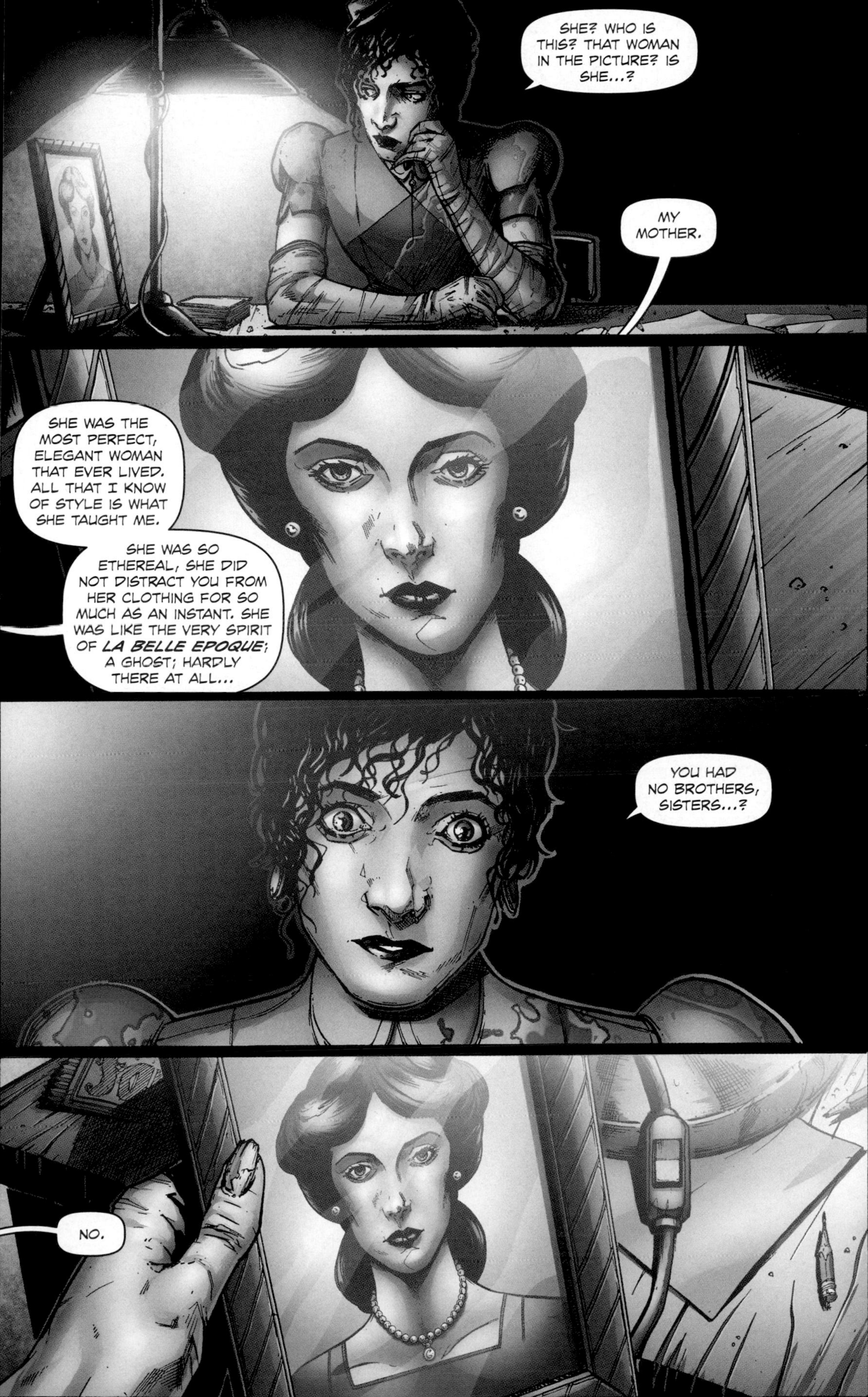
SHE? WHO IS THIS? THAT WOMAN IN THE PICTURE? IS SHE...?
MY MOTHER.
SHE WAS THE MOST PERFECT, ELEGANT WOMAN THAT EVER LIVED. ALL THAT I KNOW OF STYLE IS WHAT SHE TAUGHT ME.
SHE WAS SO ETHEREAL, SHE DID NOT DISTRACT YOU FROM HER CLOTHING FOR SO MUCH AS AN INSTANT. SHE WAS LIKE THE VERY SPIRIT OF *LA BELLE EPOQUE*; A GHOST; HARDLY THERE AT ALL...
YOU HAD NO BROTHERS, SISTERS...?
NO.

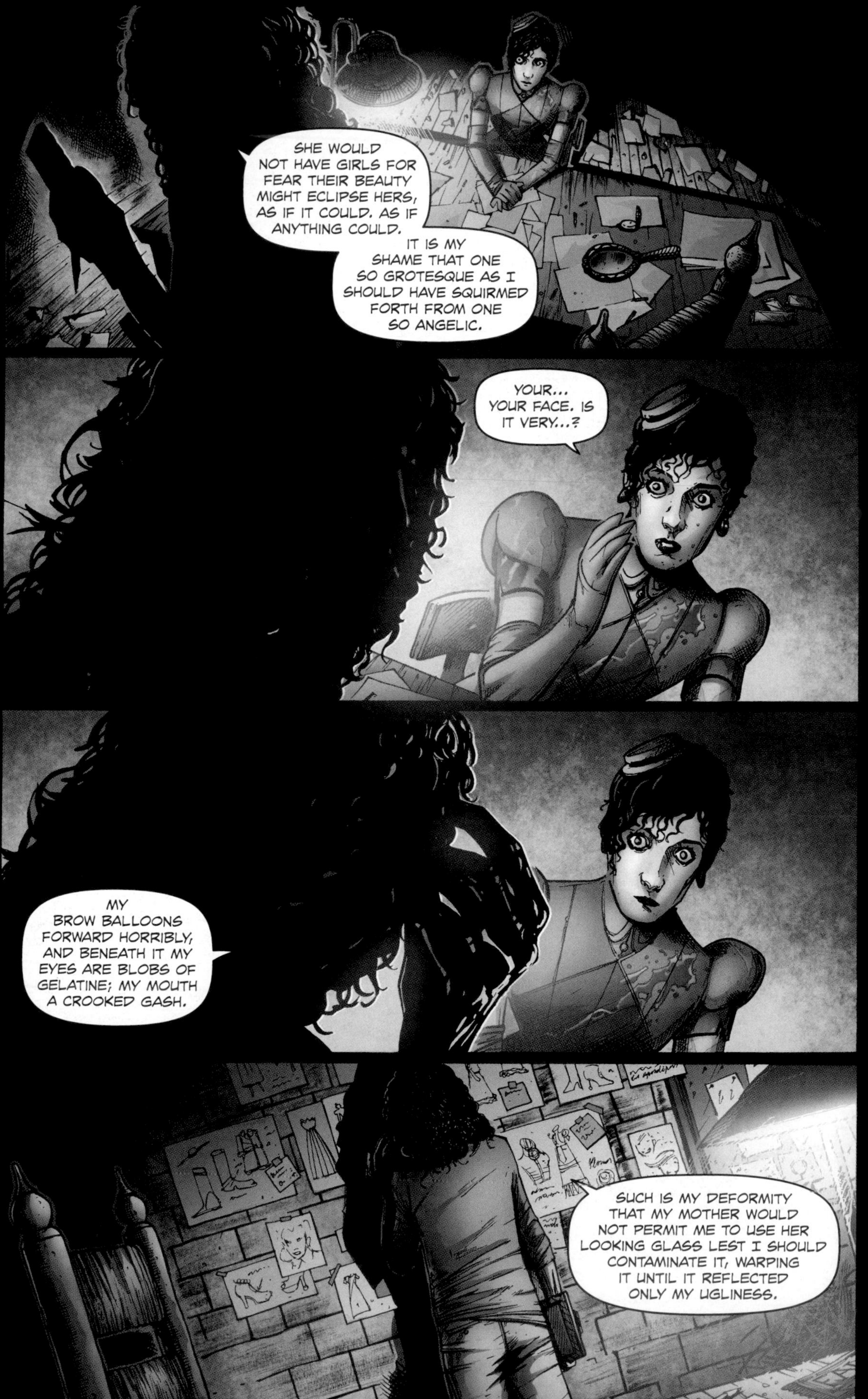
SHE WOULD NOT HAVE GIRLS FOR FEAR THEIR BEAUTY MIGHT ECLIPSE HERS, AS IF IT COULD. AS IF ANYTHING COULD.
IT IS MY SHAME THAT ONE SO GROTESQUE AS I SHOULD HAVE SQUIRMED FORTH FROM ONE SO ANGELIC.
YOUR... YOUR FACE. IS IT VERY...?
MY BROW BALLOONS FORWARD HORRIBLY, AND BENEATH IT MY EYES ARE BLOBS OF GELATINE; MY MOUTH A CROOKED GASH.
SUCH IS MY DEFORMITY THAT MY MOTHER WOULD NOT PERMIT ME TO USE HER LOOKING GLASS LEST I SHOULD CONTAMINATE IT, WARPING IT UNTIL IT REFLECTED ONLY MY UGLINESS.

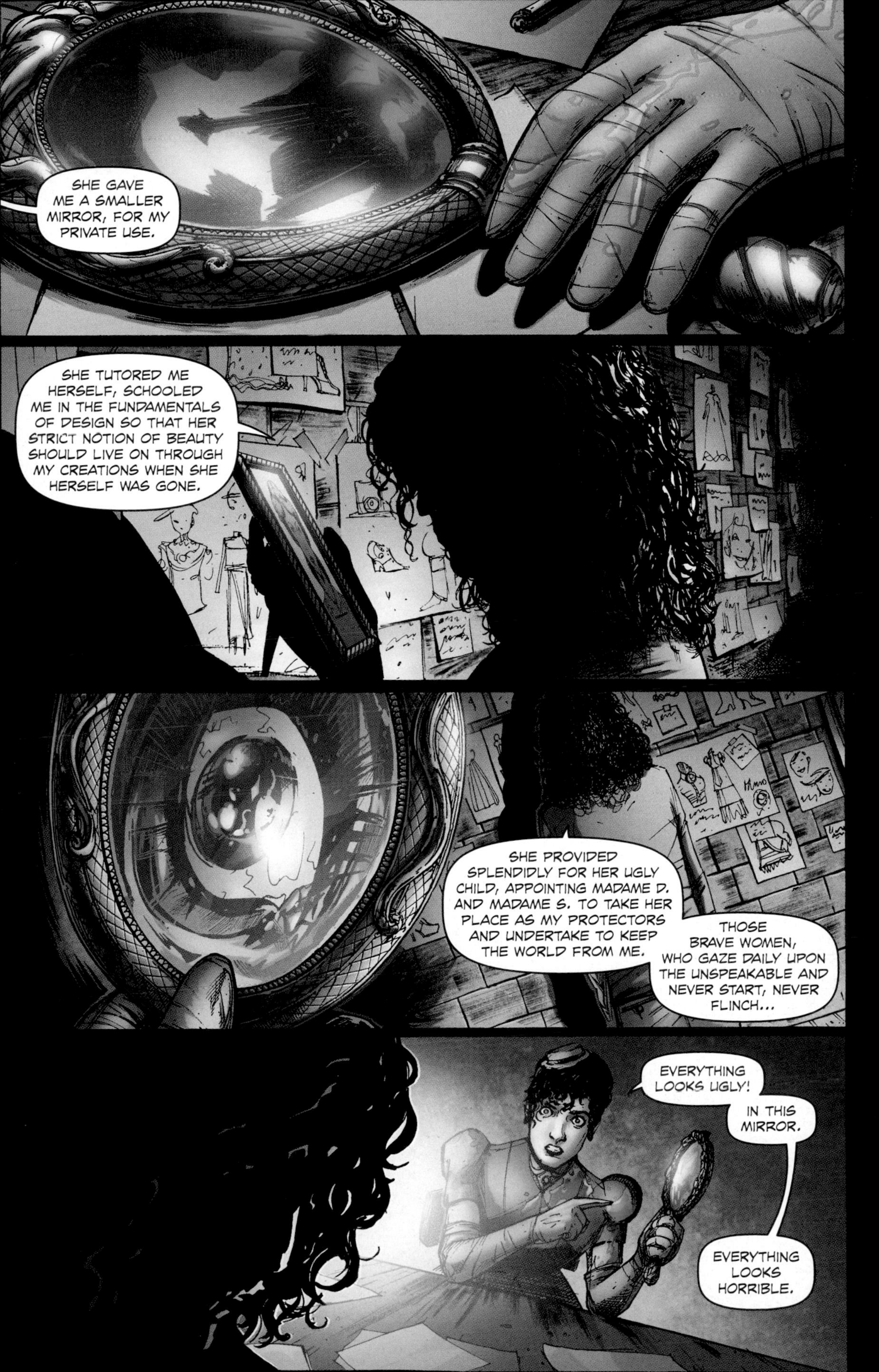
SHE GAVE ME A SMALLER MIRROR, FOR MY PRIVATE USE.
SHE TUTORED ME HERSELF, SCHOOLED ME IN THE FUNDAMENTALS OF DESIGN SO THAT HER STRICT NOTION OF BEAUTY SHOULD LIVE ON THROUGH MY CREATIONS WHEN SHE HERSELF WAS GONE.
SHE PROVIDED SPLENDIDLY FOR HER UGLY CHILD, APPOINTING MADAME D. AND MADAME S. TO TAKE HER PLACE AS MY PROTECTORS AND UNDERTAKE TO KEEP THE WORLD FROM ME.
THOSE BRAVE WOMEN, WHO GAZE DAILY UPON THE UNSPEAKABLE AND NEVER START, NEVER FLINCH...
EVERYTHING LOOKS UGLY!
IN THIS MIRROR.
EVERYTHING LOOKS HORRIBLE.

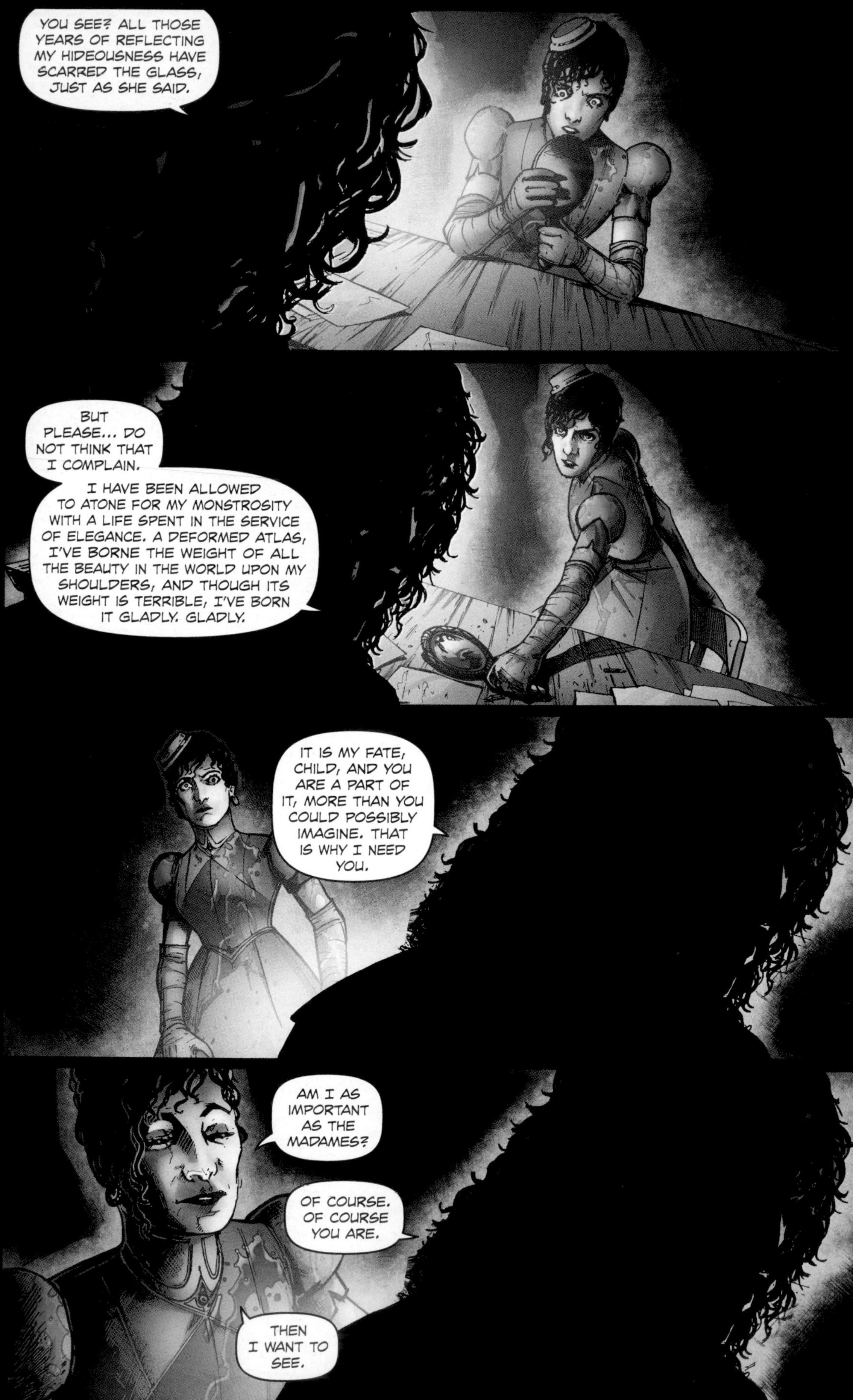
YOU SEE? ALL THOSE YEARS OF REFLECTING MY HIDEOUSNESS HAVE SCARRED THE GLASS, JUST AS SHE SAID.
BUT PLEASE... DO NOT THINK THAT I COMPLAIN.
I HAVE BEEN ALLOWED TO ATONE FOR MY MONSTROSITY WITH A LIFE SPENT IN THE SERVICE OF ELEGANCE. A DEFORMED ATLAS, I'VE BORNE THE WEIGHT OF ALL THE BEAUTY IN THE WORLD UPON MY SHOULDERS, AND THOUGH ITS WEIGHT IS TERRIBLE, I'VE BORN IT GLADLY. GLADLY.
IT IS MY FATE, CHILD, AND YOU ARE A PART OF IT, MORE THAN YOU COULD POSSIBLY IMAGINE. THAT IS WHY I NEED YOU.
AM I AS IMPORTANT AS THE MADAMES?
OF COURSE. OF COURSE YOU ARE.
THEN I WANT TO SEE.

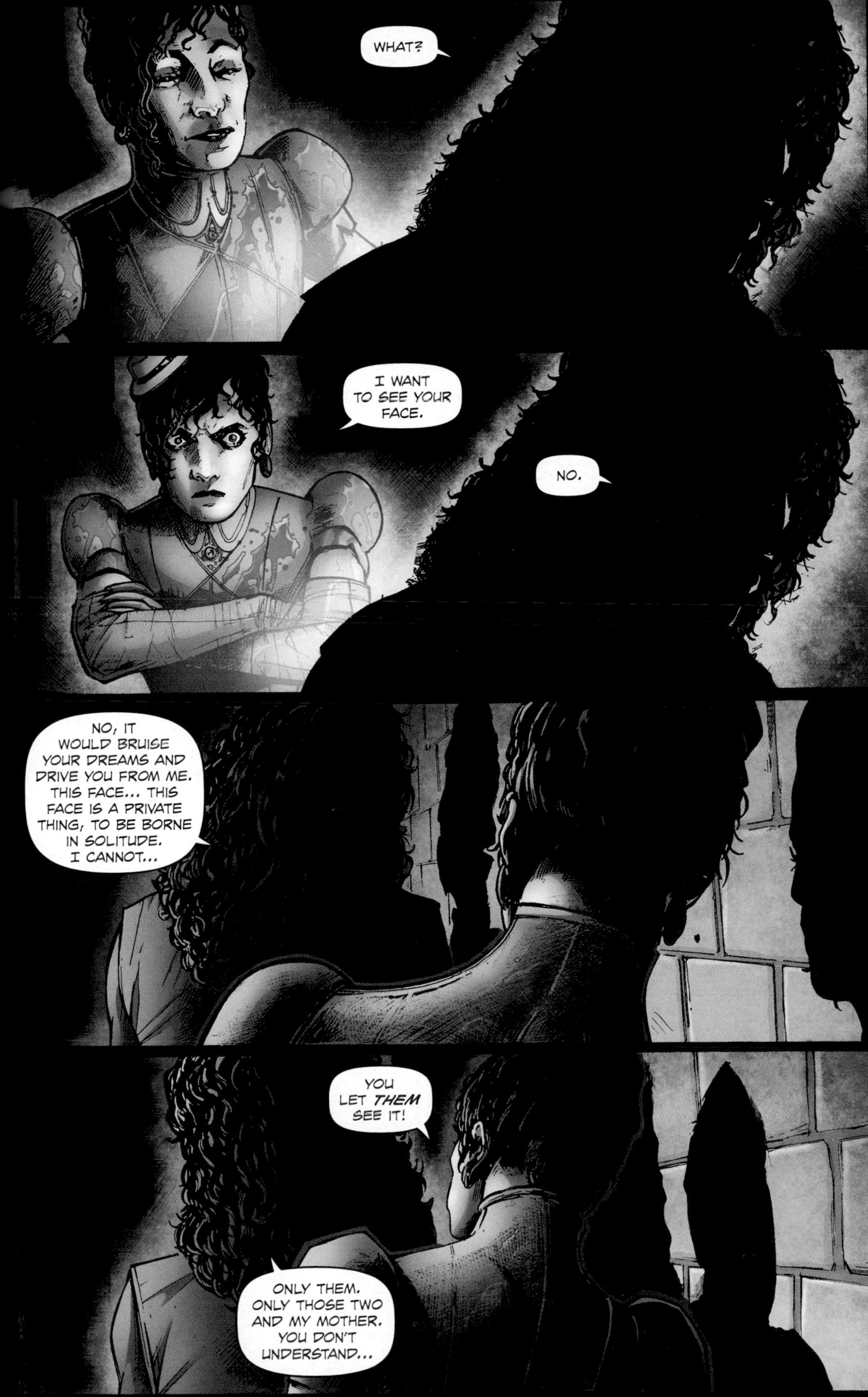
WHAT?
I WANT TO SEE YOUR FACE.
NO.
NO, IT WOULD BRUISE YOUR DREAMS AND DRIVE YOU FROM ME. THIS FACE... THIS FACE IS A PRIVATE THING, TO BE BORNE IN SOLITUDE. I CANNOT...
YOU LET *THEM* SEE IT!
ONLY THEM. ONLY THOSE TWO AND MY MOTHER. YOU DON'T UNDERSTAND...

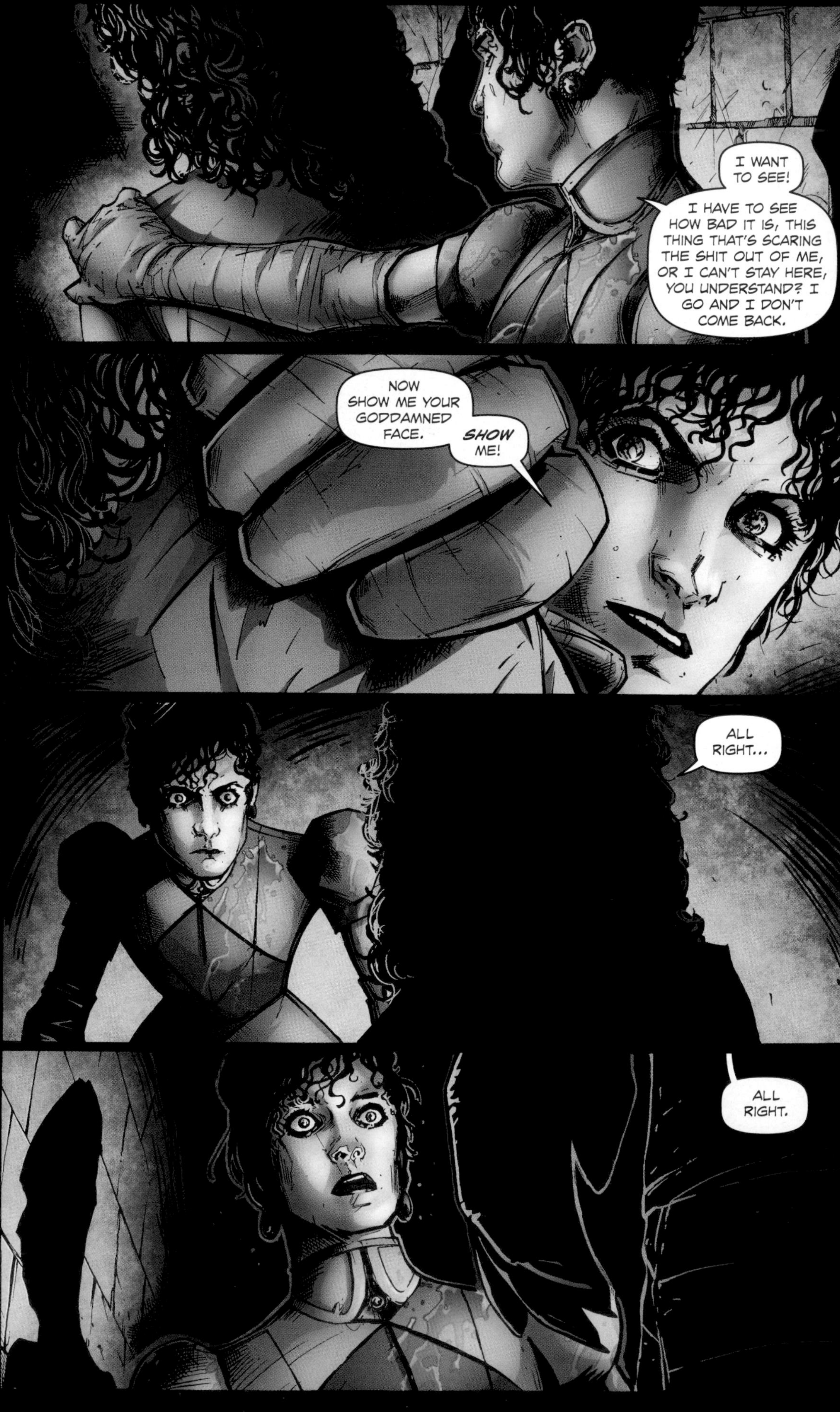
I WANT TO SEE!
I HAVE TO SEE HOW BAD IT IS, THIS THING THAT'S SCARING THE SHIT OUT OF ME, OR I CAN'T STAY HERE, YOU UNDERSTAND? I GO AND I DON'T COME BACK.
NOW SHOW ME YOUR GODDAMNED FACE.
SHOW ME!
ALL RIGHT...
ALL RIGHT.

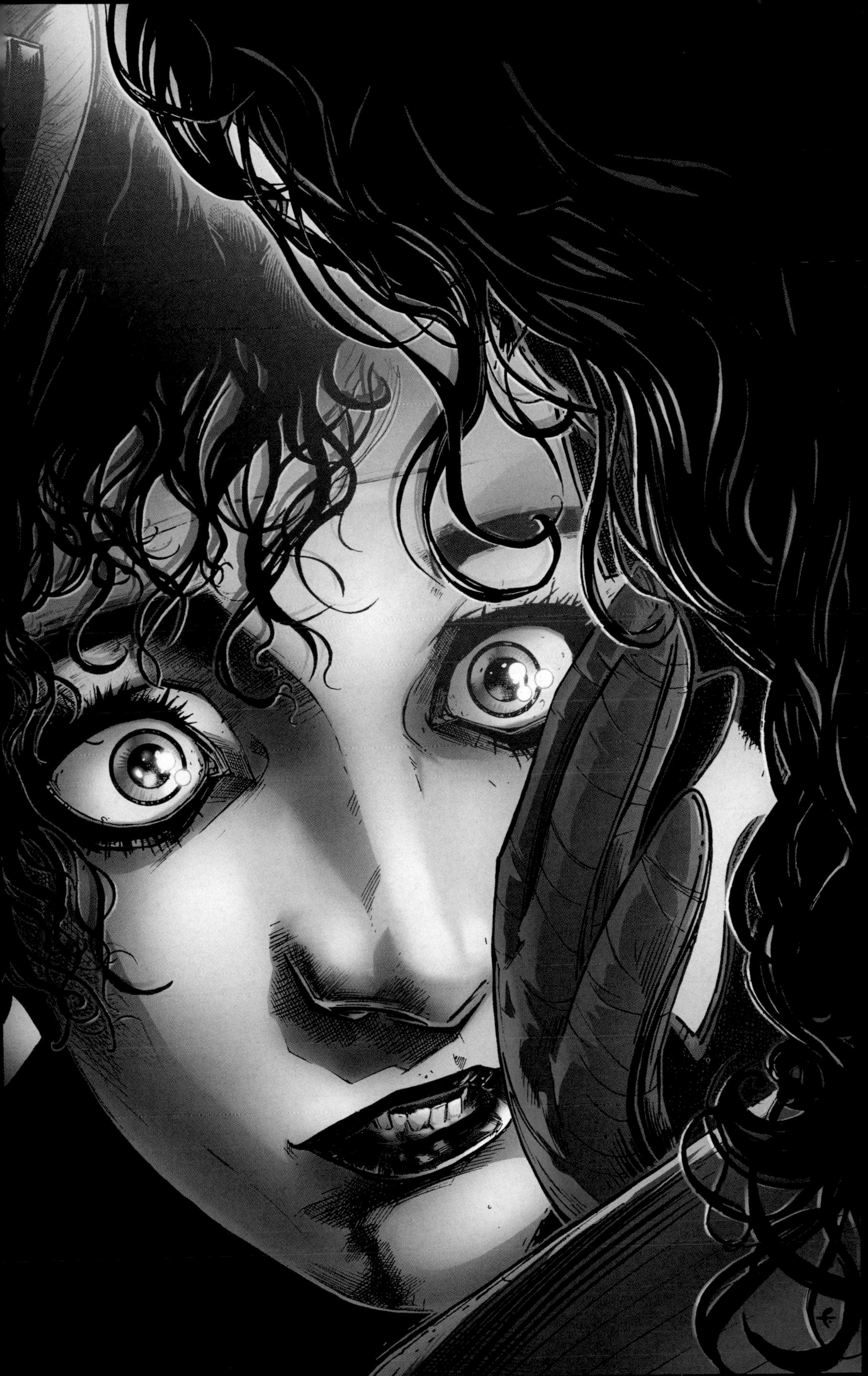

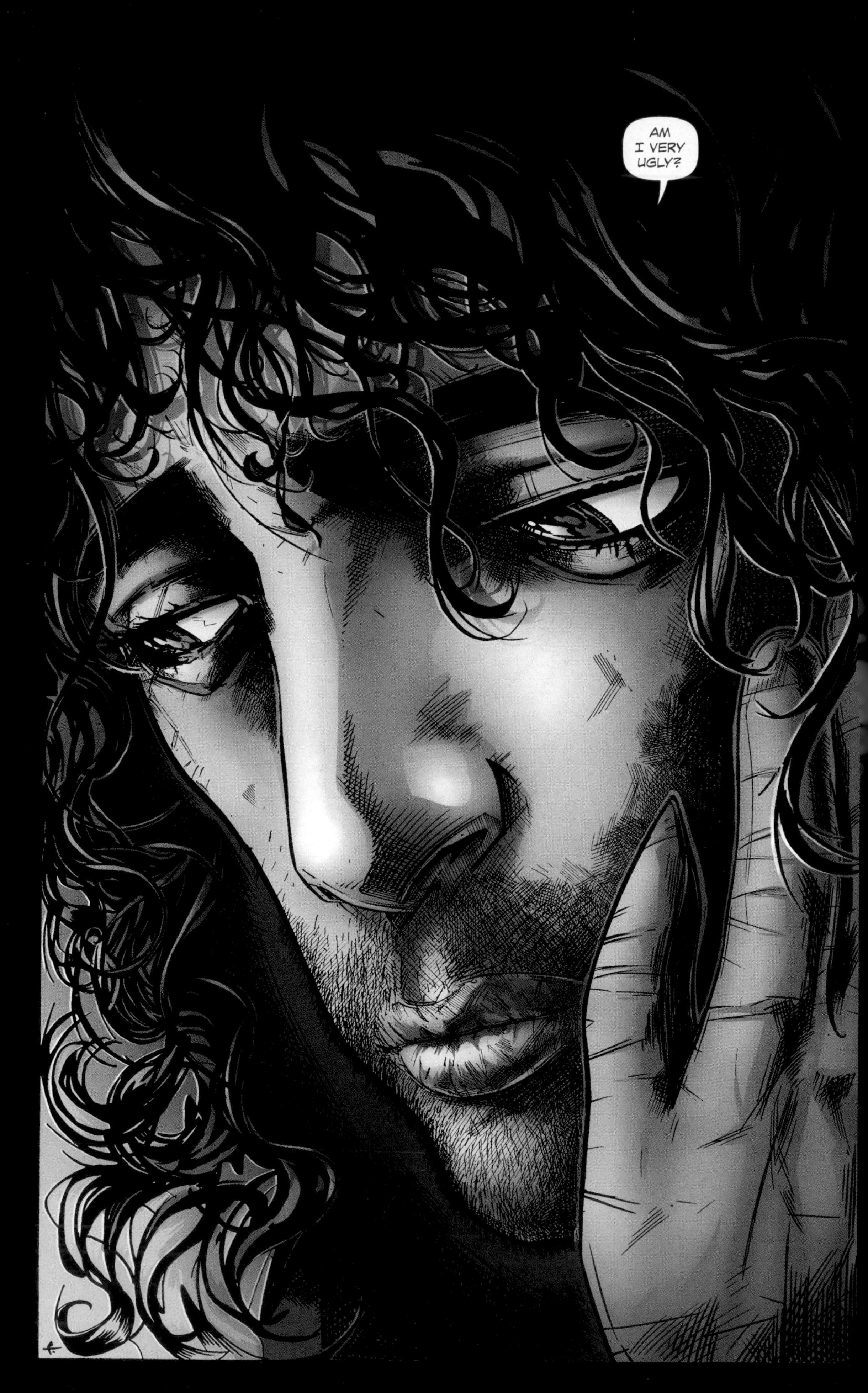
AM I VERY UGLY?

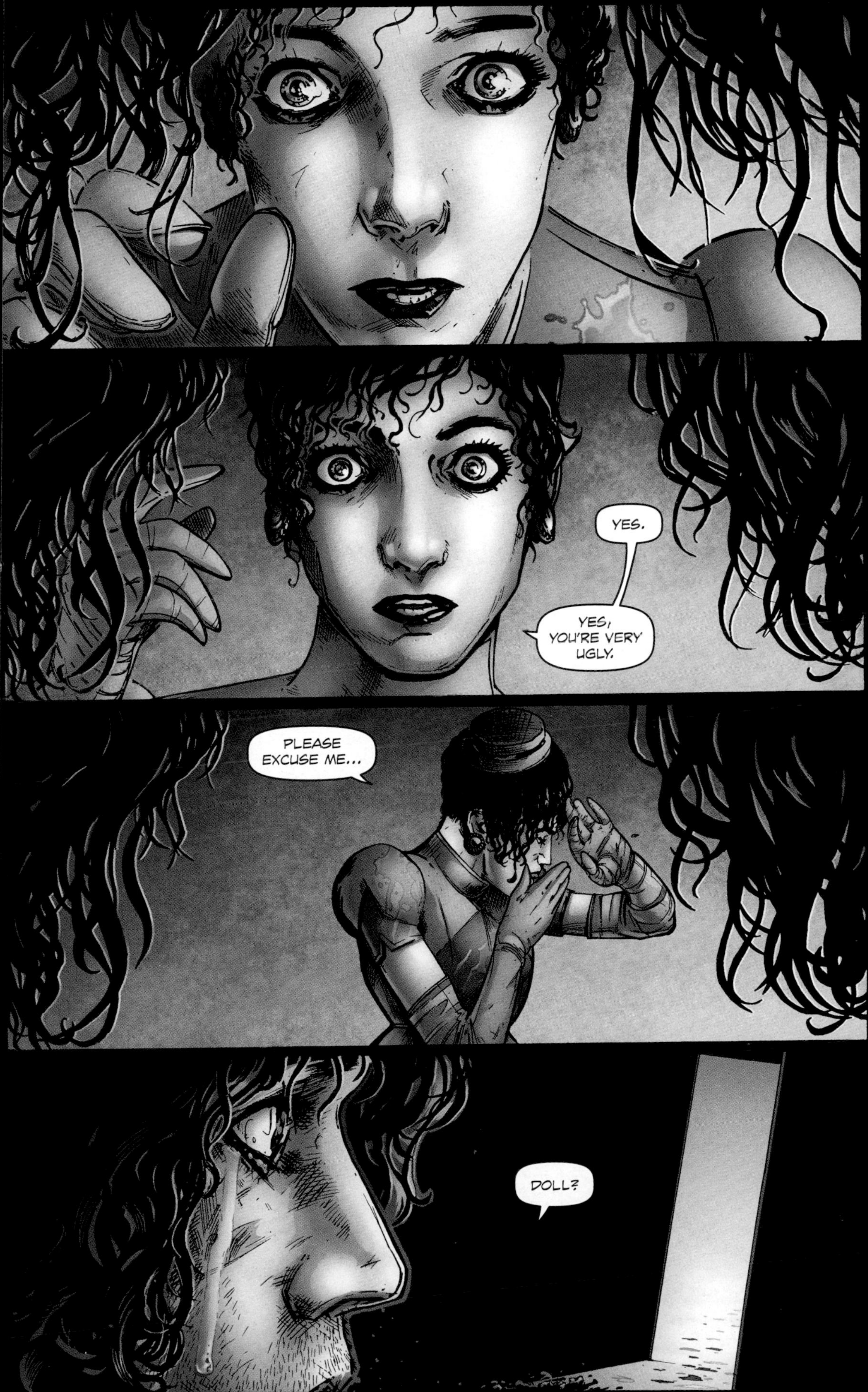
YES.
YES, YOU'RE VERY UGLY.
PLEASE EXCUSE ME...
DOLL?

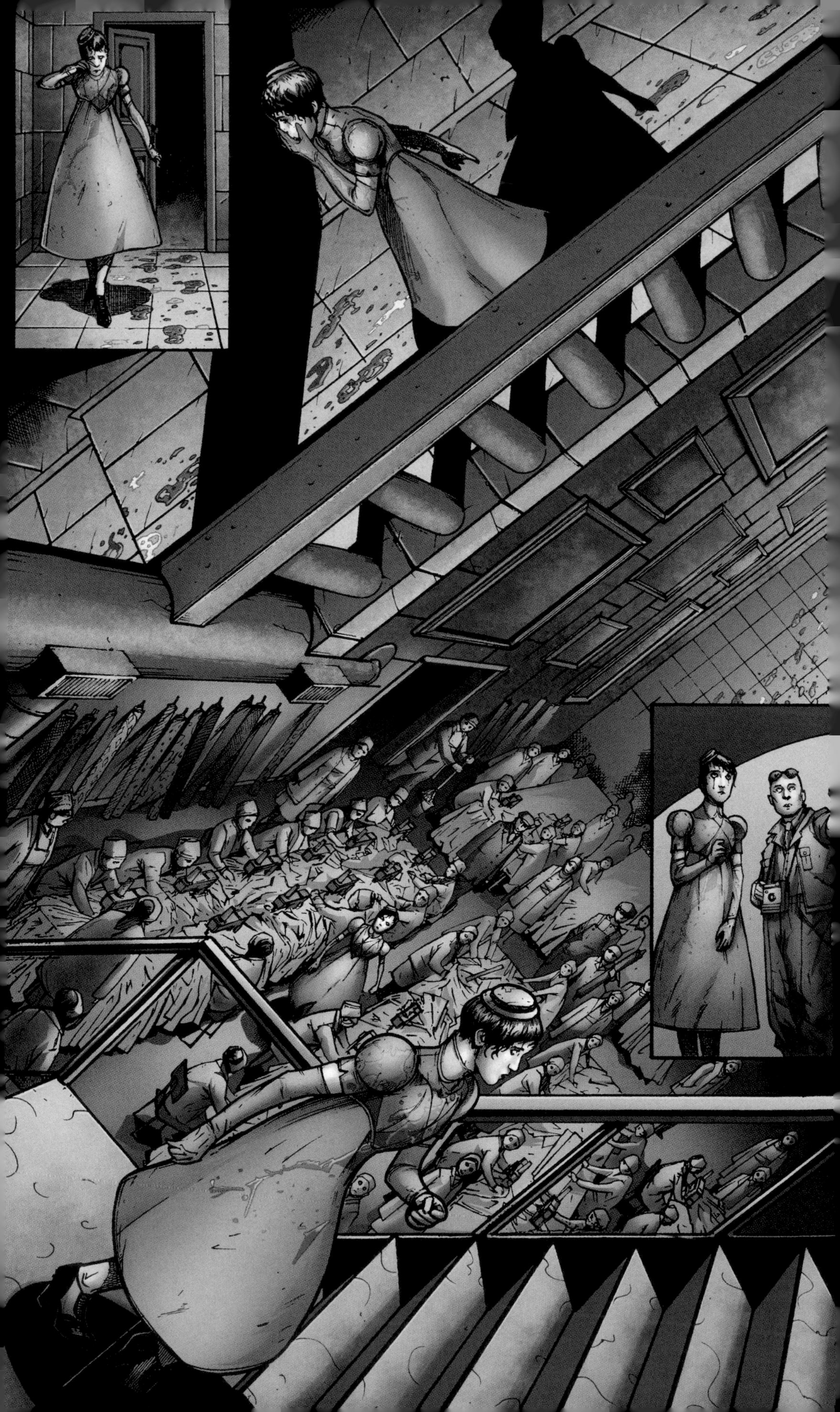

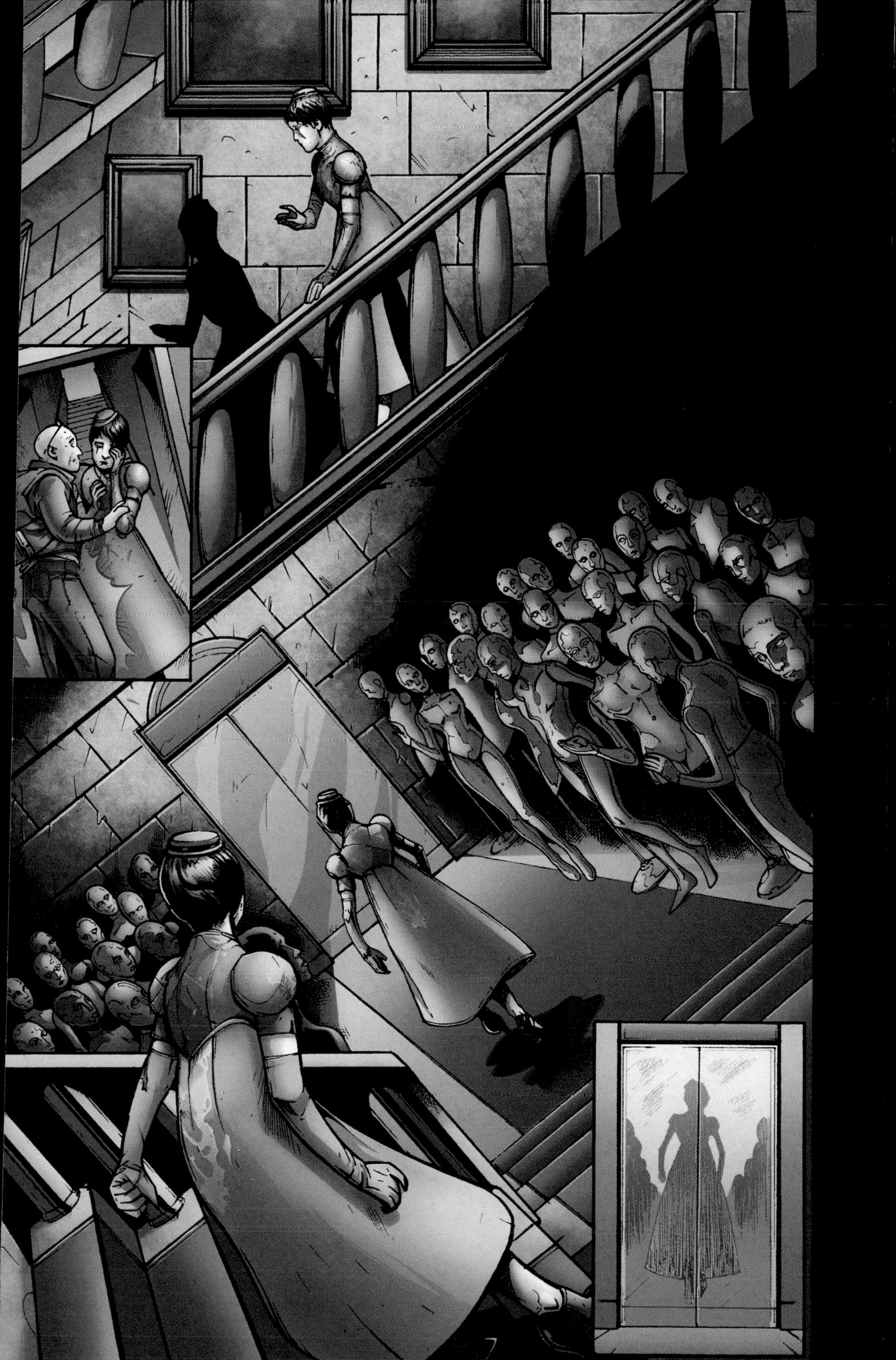

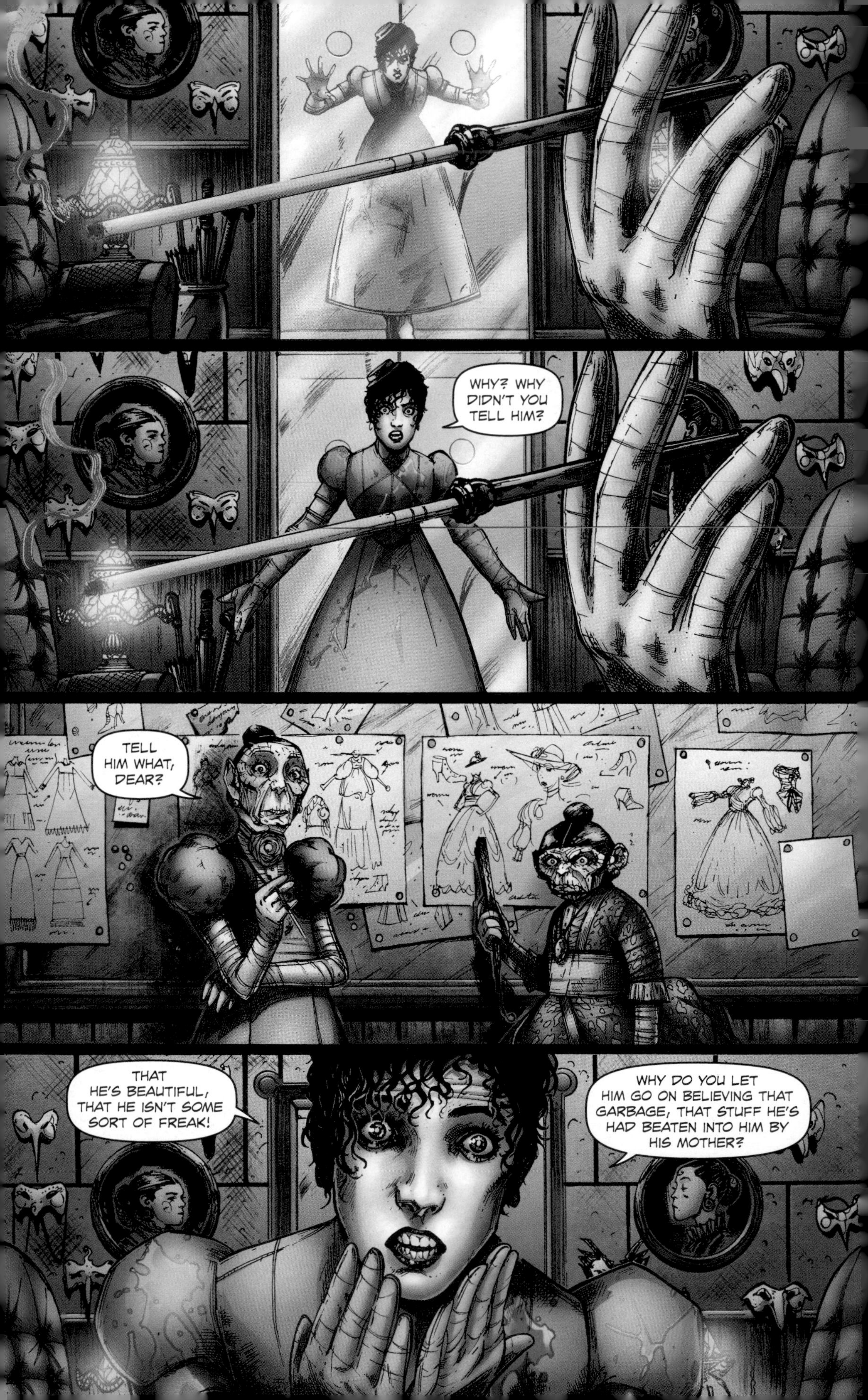
WHY? WHY DIDN'T YOU TELL HIM?
TELL HIM WHAT, DEAR?
THAT HE'S BEAUTIFUL, THAT HE ISN'T SOME SORT OF FREAK!
WHY DO YOU LET HIM GO ON BELIEVING THAT GARBAGE, THAT STUFF HE'S HAD BEATEN INTO HIM BY HIS MOTHER?

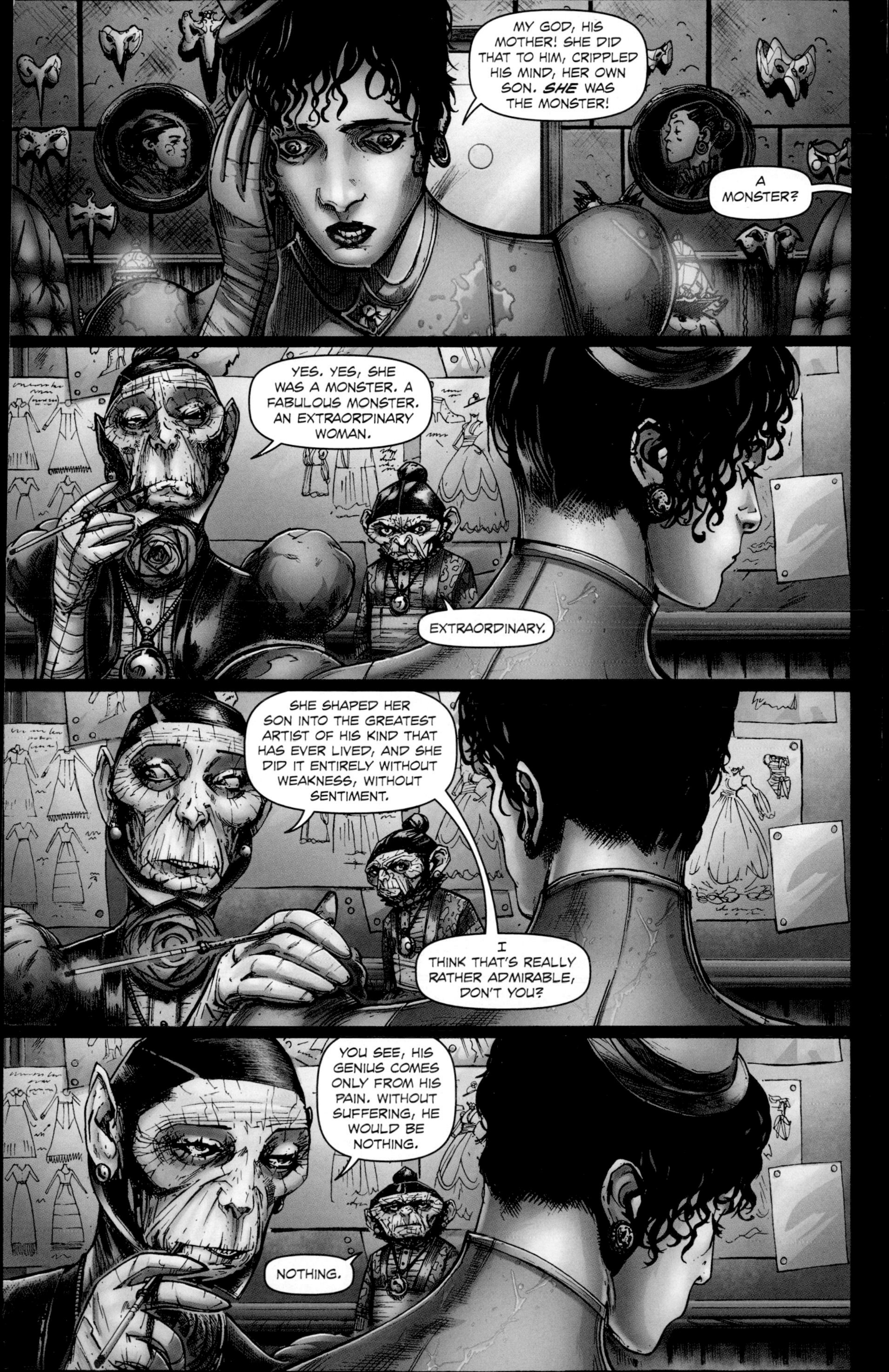
MY GOD, HIS MOTHER! SHE DID THAT TO HIM, CRIPPLED HIS MIND, HER OWN SON. *SHE* WAS THE MONSTER!
A MONSTER?
YES. YES, SHE WAS A MONSTER. A FABULOUS MONSTER. AN EXTRAORDINARY WOMAN.
EXTRAORDINARY.
SHE SHAPED HER SON INTO THE GREATEST ARTIST OF HIS KIND THAT HAS EVER LIVED, AND SHE DID IT ENTIRELY WITHOUT WEAKNESS, WITHOUT SENTIMENT.
I THINK THAT'S REALLY RATHER ADMIRABLE, DON'T YOU?
YOU SEE, HIS GENIUS COMES ONLY FROM HIS PAIN. WITHOUT SUFFERING, HE WOULD BE NOTHING.
NOTHING.

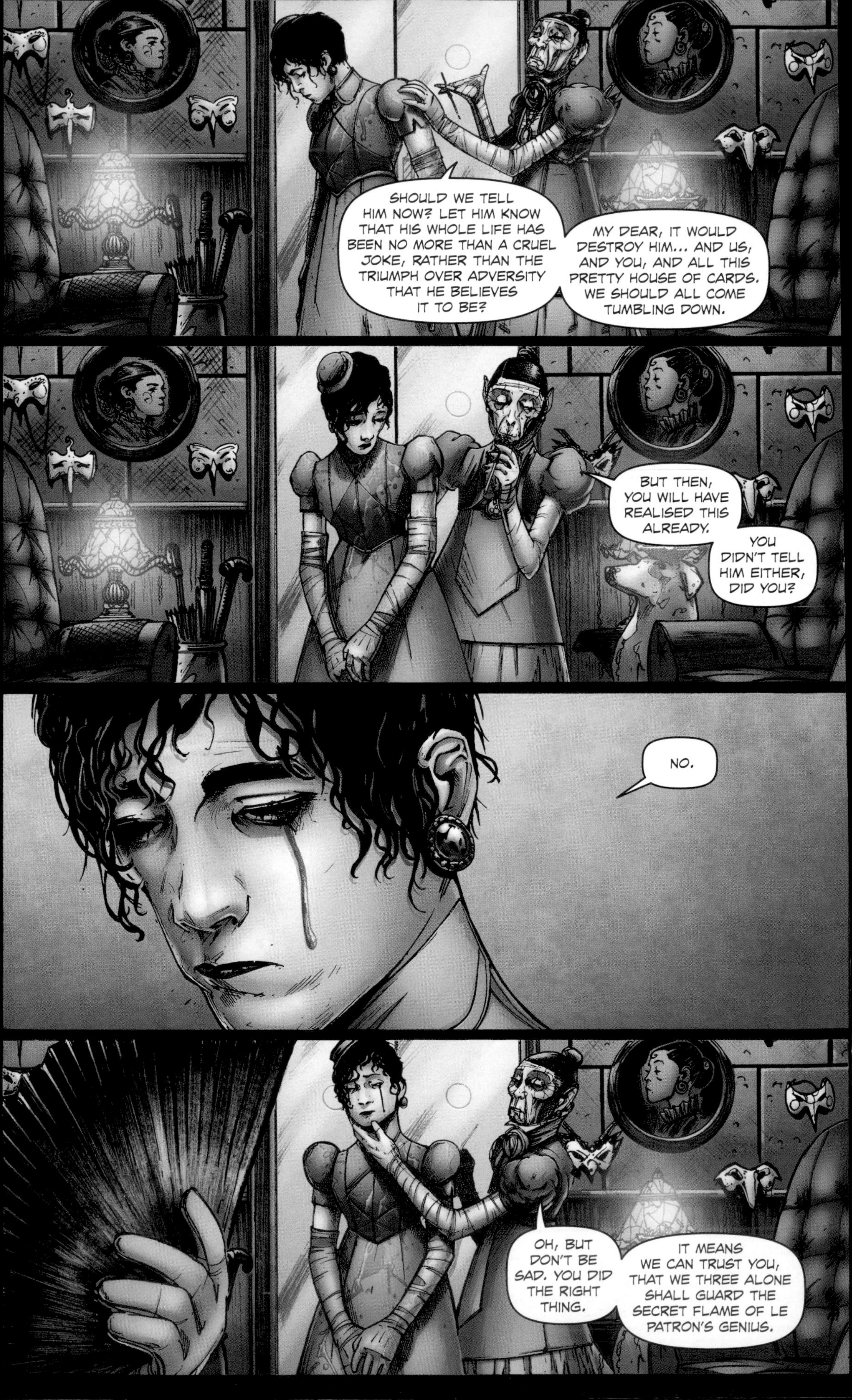
SHOULD WE TELL HIM NOW? LET HIM KNOW THAT HIS WHOLE LIFE HAS BEEN NO MORE THAN A CRUEL JOKE, RATHER THAN THE TRIUMPH OVER ADVERSITY THAT HE BELIEVES IT TO BE?
MY DEAR, IT WOULD DESTROY HIM... AND US, AND YOU, AND ALL THIS PRETTY HOUSE OF CARDS. WE SHOULD ALL COME TUMBLING DOWN.
BUT THEN, YOU WILL HAVE REALISED THIS ALREADY.
YOU DIDN'T TELL HIM EITHER, DID YOU?
NO.
OH, BUT DON'T BE SAD. YOU DID THE RIGHT THING.
IT MEANS WE CAN TRUST YOU, THAT WE THREE ALONE SHALL GUARD THE SECRET FLAME OF LE PATRON'S GENIUS.

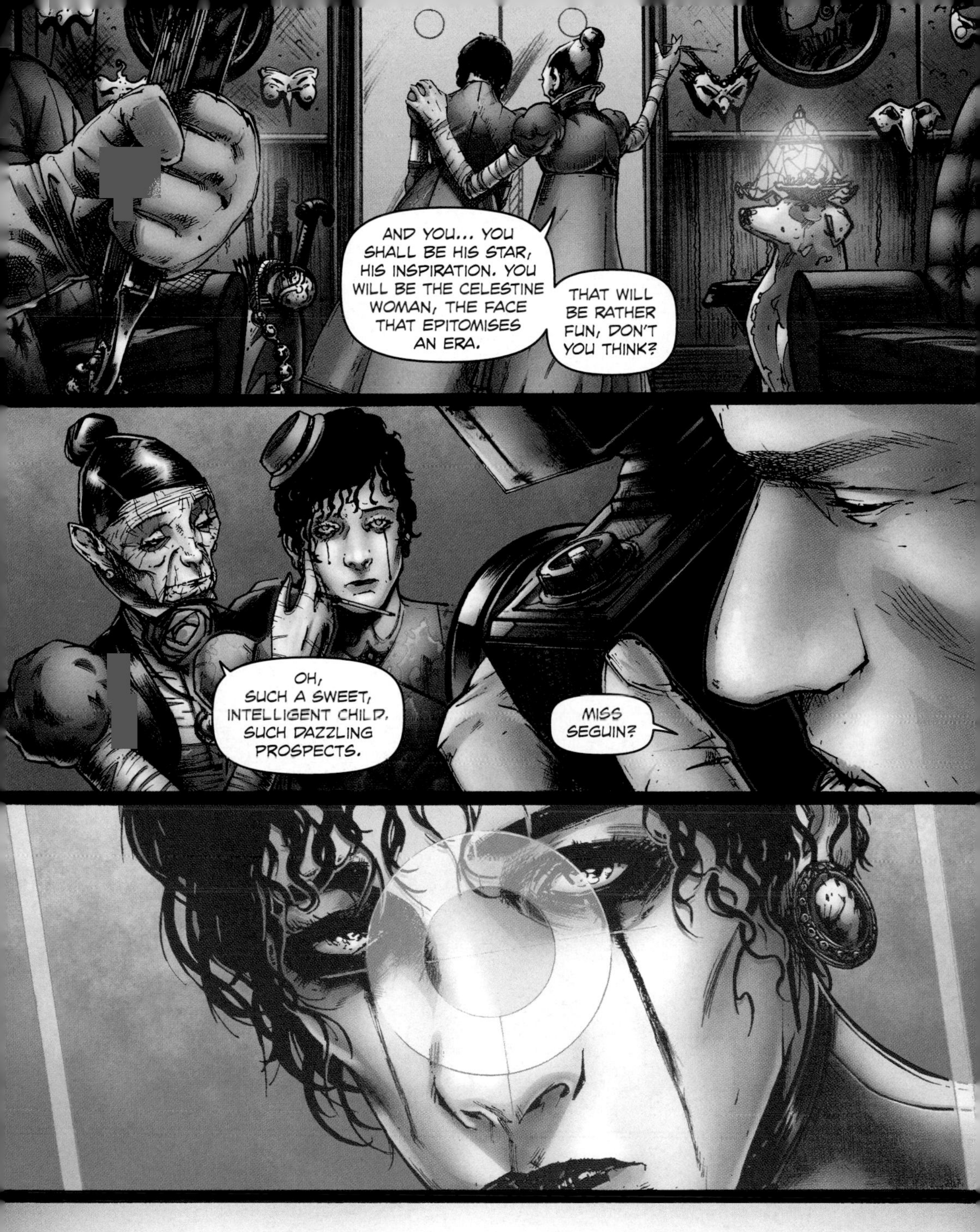
AND YOU... YOU SHALL BE HIS STAR, HIS INSPIRATION. YOU WILL BE THE CELESTINE WOMAN, THE FACE THAT EPITOMISES AN ERA.
THAT WILL BE RATHER FUN, DON'T YOU THINK?
OH, SUCH A SWEET, INTELLIGENT CHILD. SUCH DAZZLING PROSPECTS.
MISS SEGUIN?

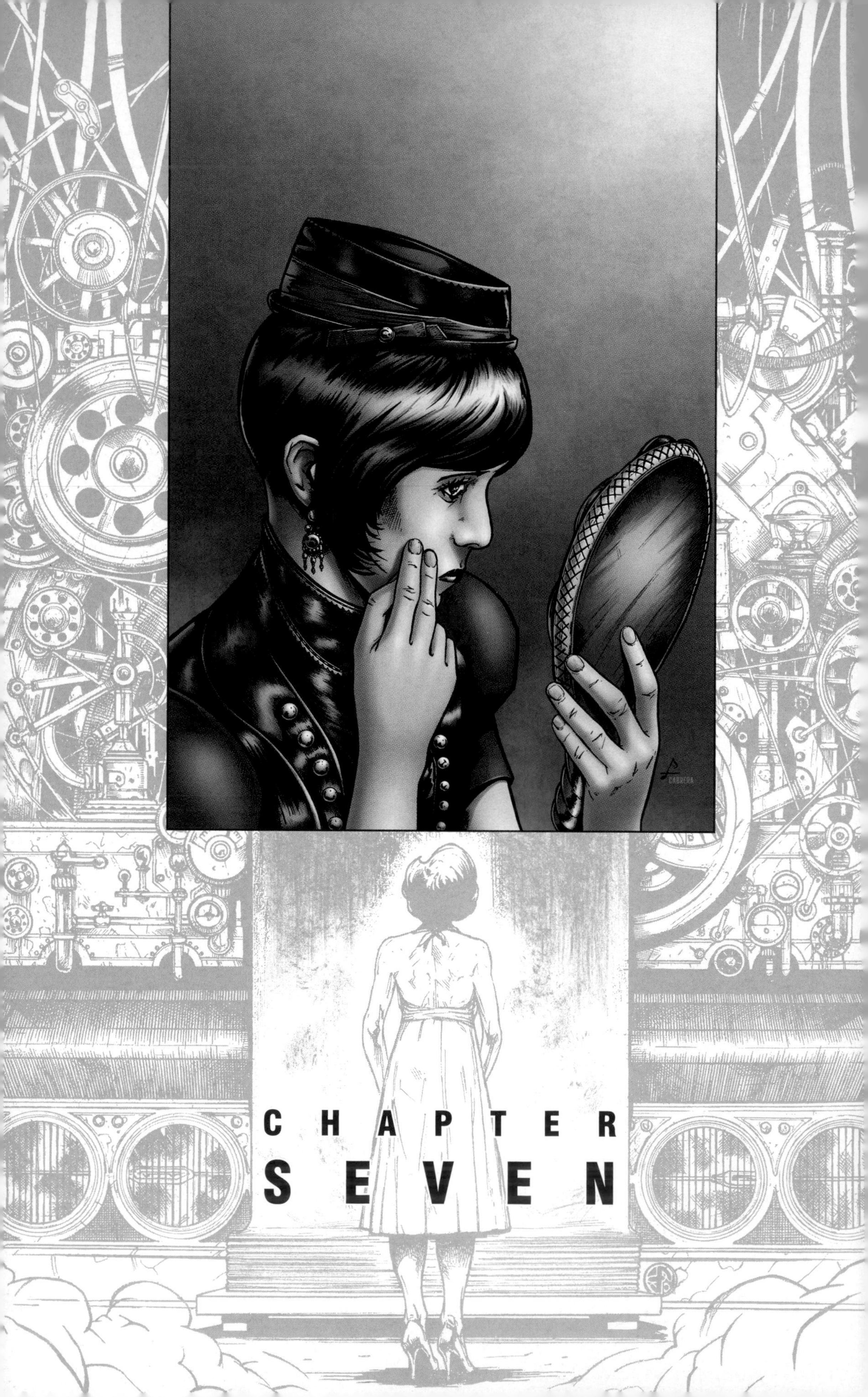

CHAPTER SEVEN

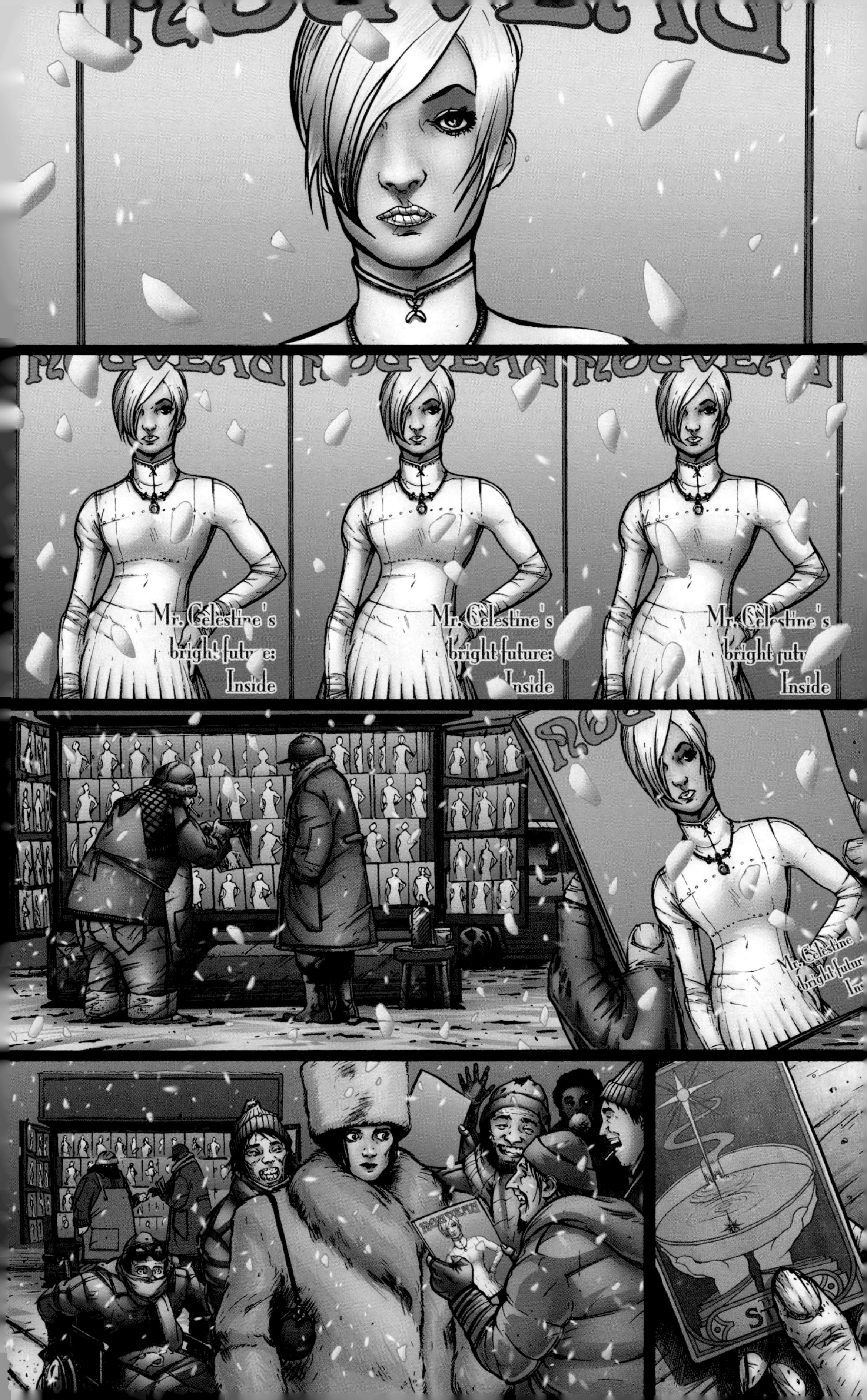
Mr. Celestine's
bright future:
Inside

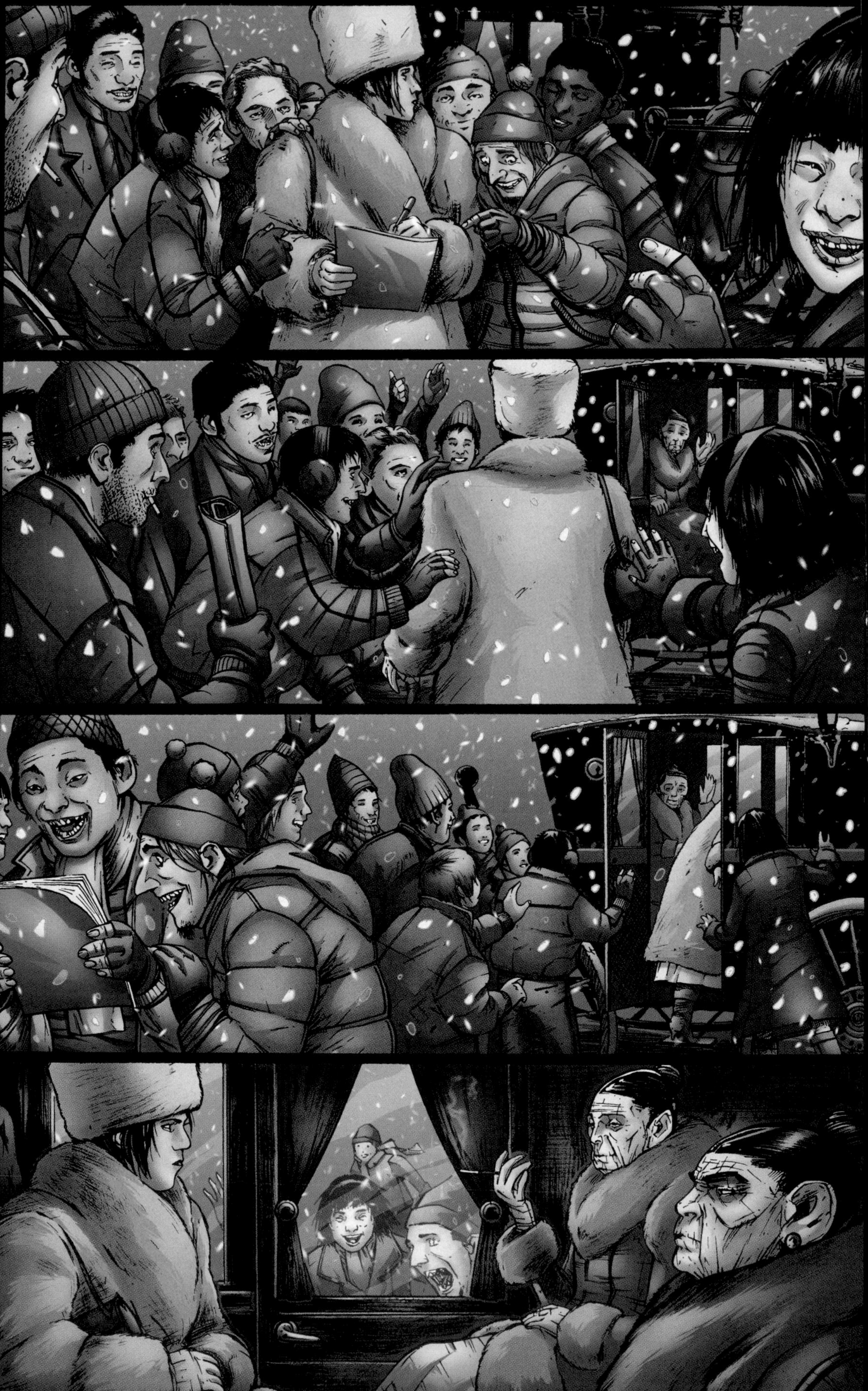

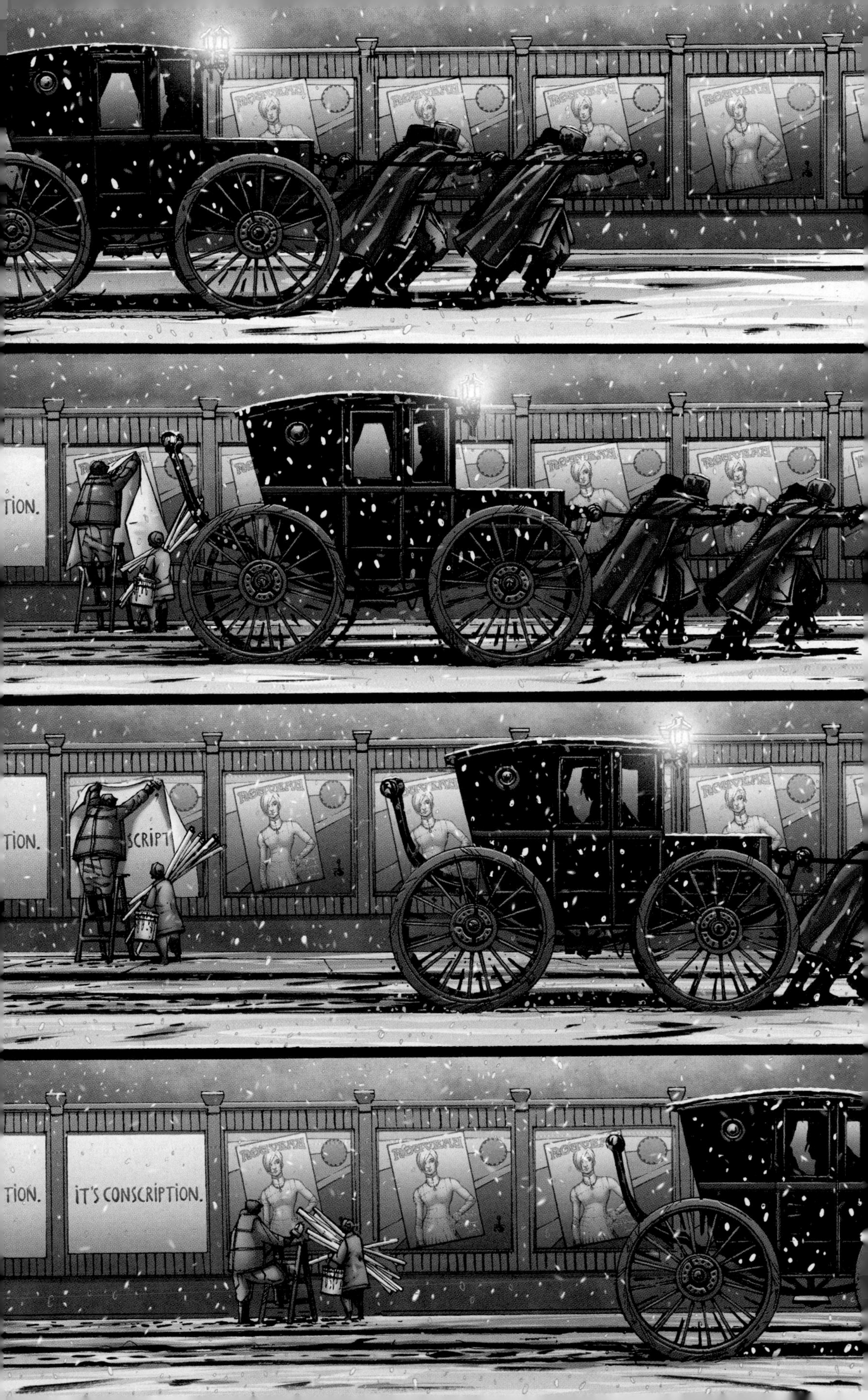
TION.
TION.
SCRIPT
TION.
IT'S CONSCRIPTION.

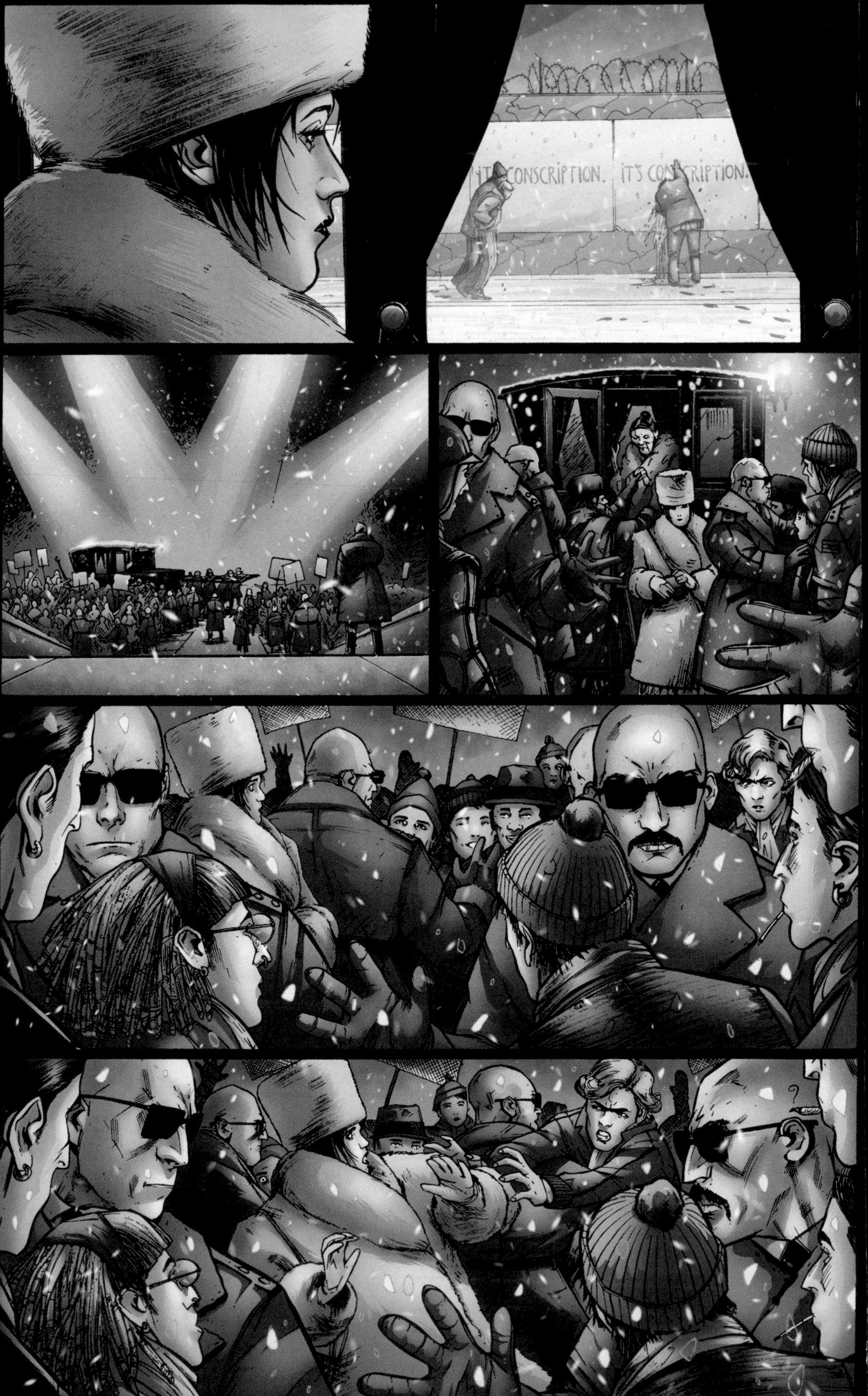
IT'S CONSCRIPTION.
IT'S CONSCRIPTION.

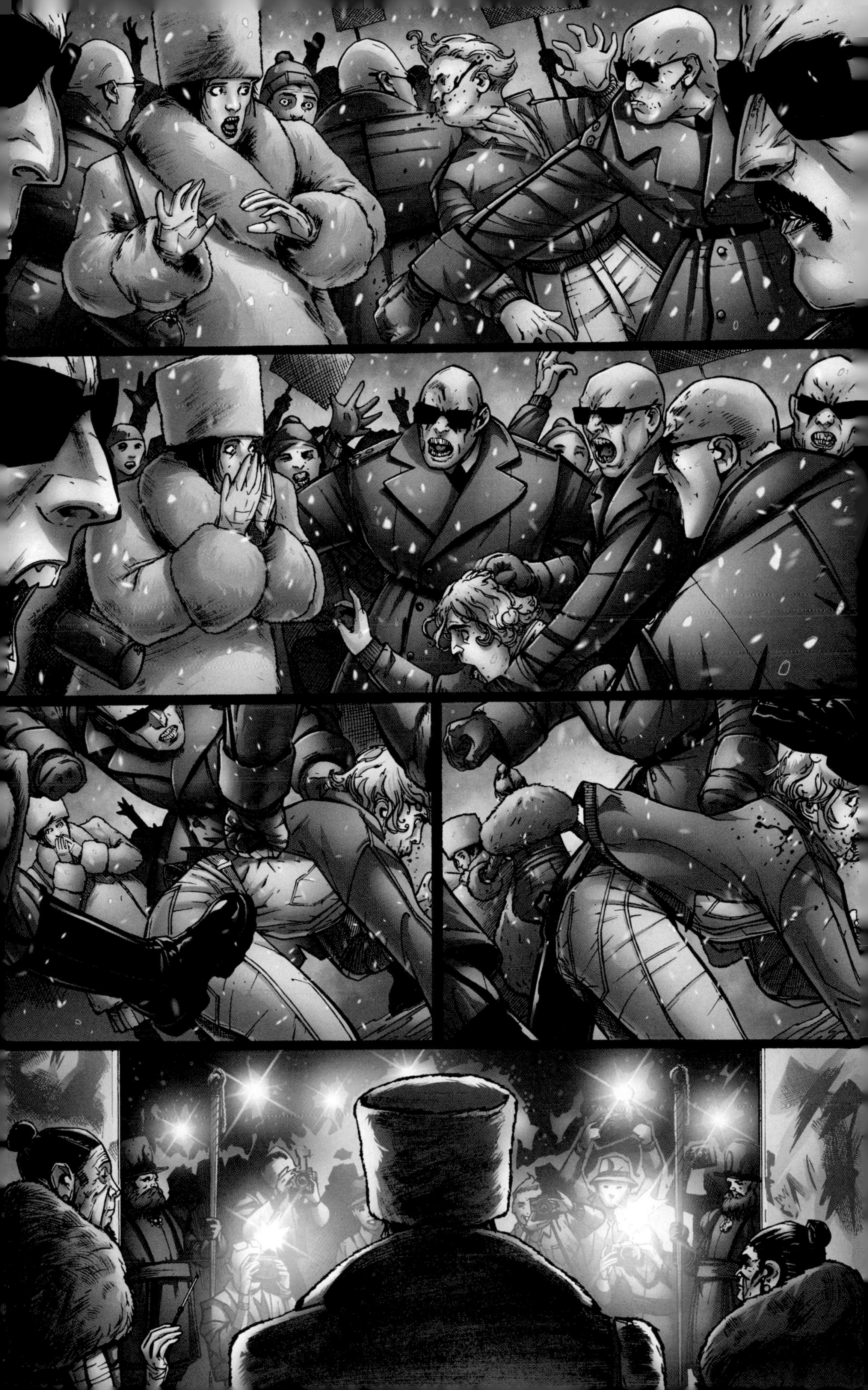

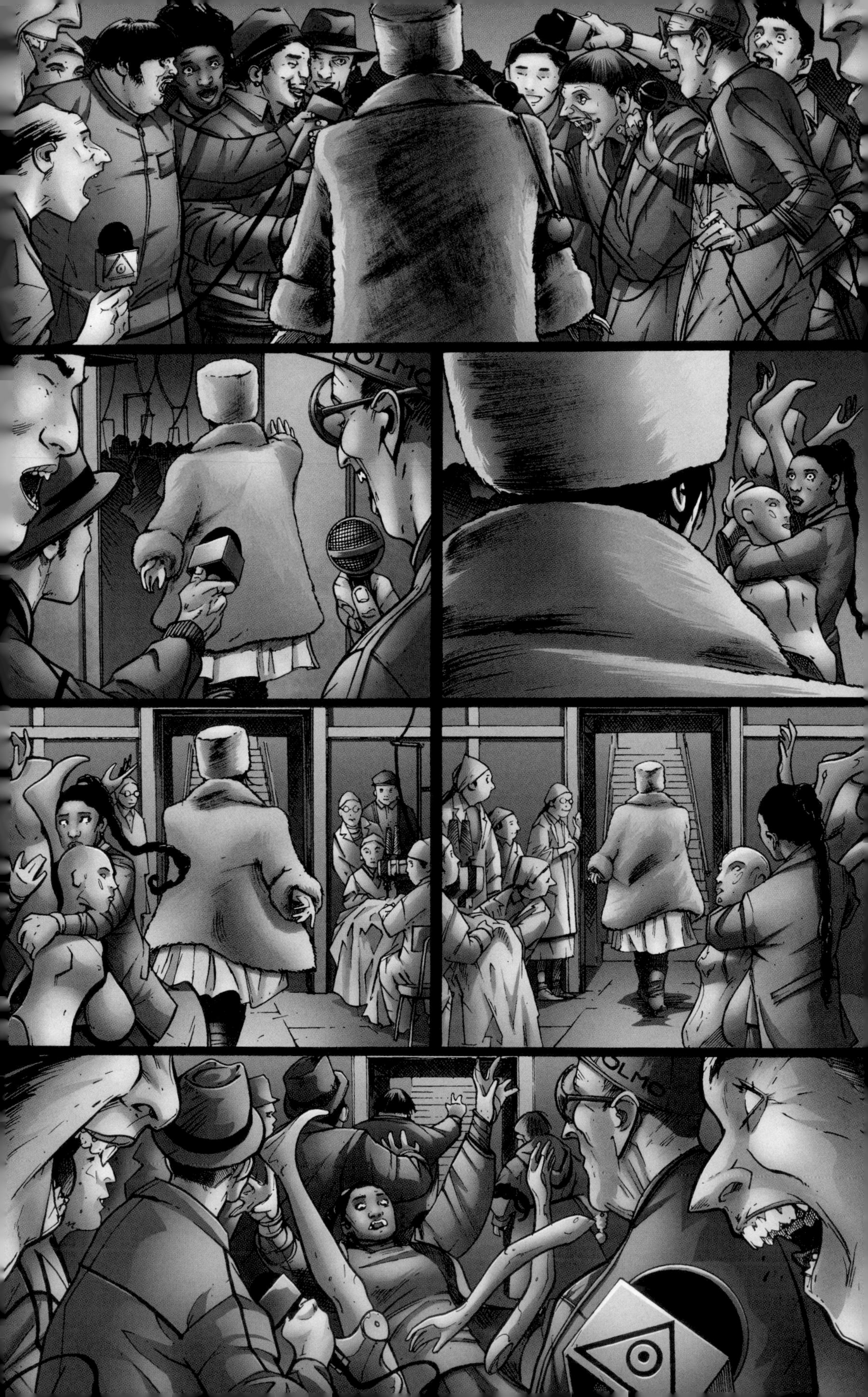
OLMO

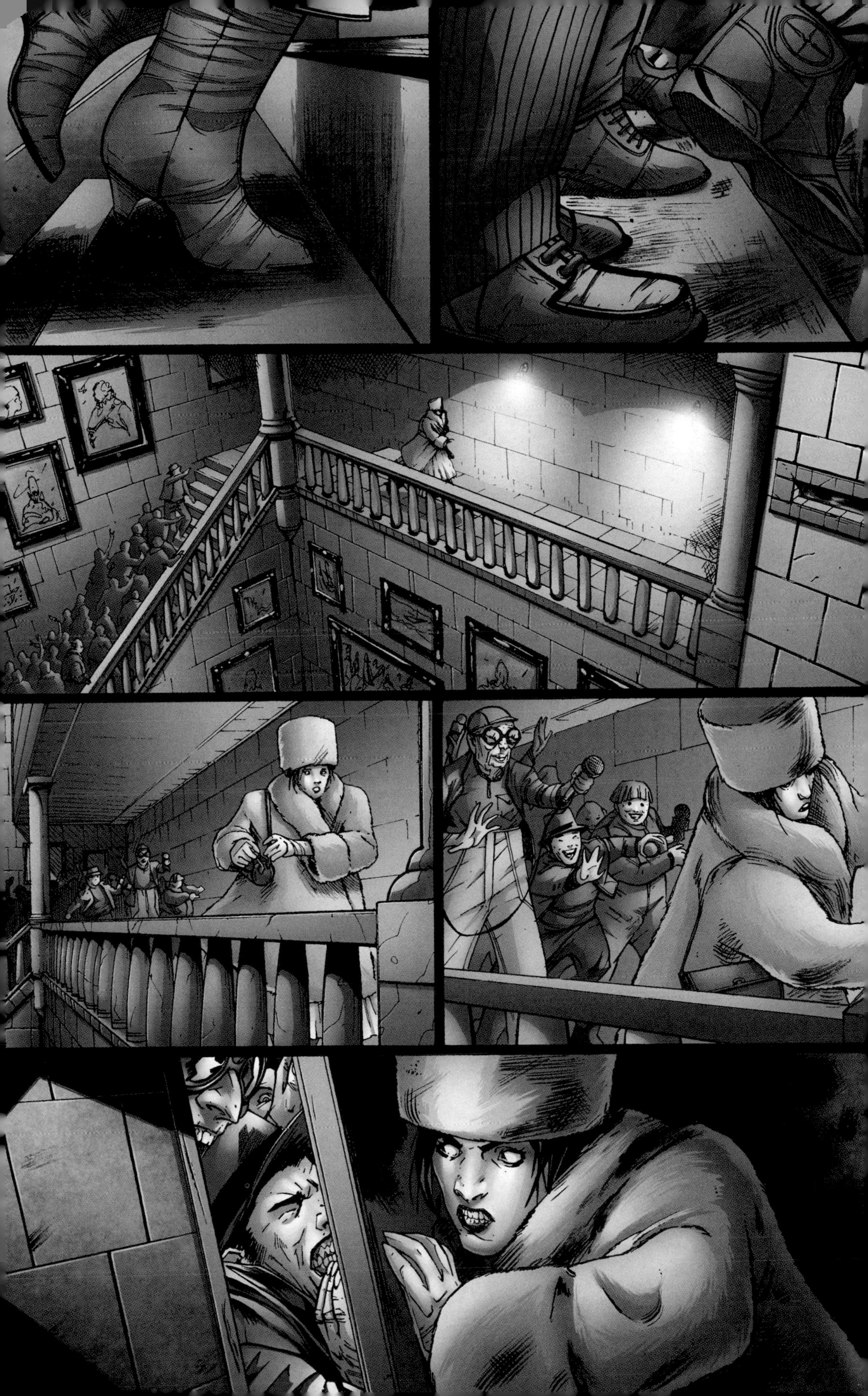

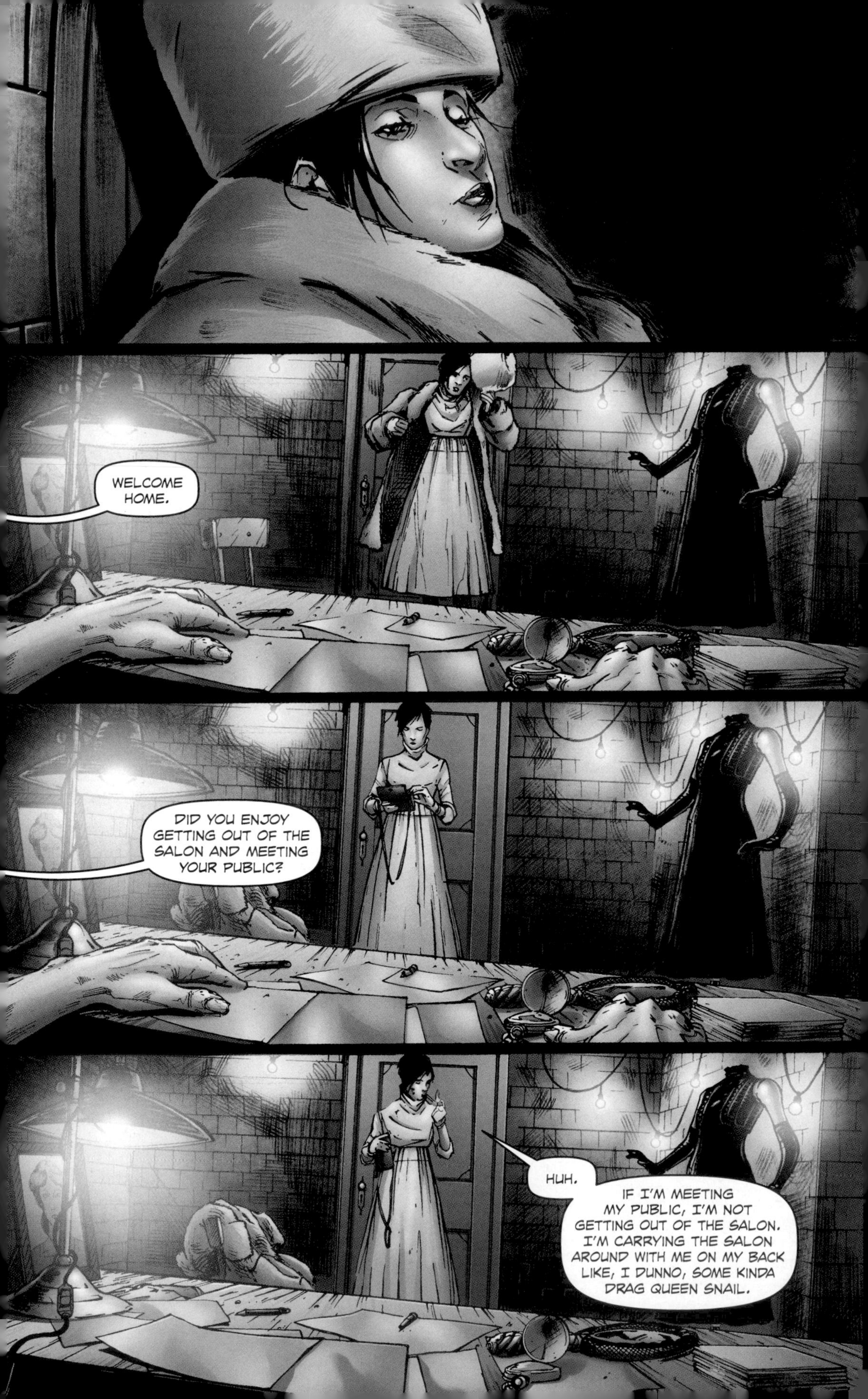
WELCOME HOME.
DID YOU ENJOY GETTING OUT OF THE SALON AND MEETING YOUR PUBLIC?
HUH.
IF I'M MEETING MY PUBLIC, I'M NOT GETTING OUT OF THE SALON. I'M CARRYING THE SALON AROUND WITH ME ON MY BACK LIKE, I DUNNO, SOME KINDA DRAG QUEEN SNAIL.

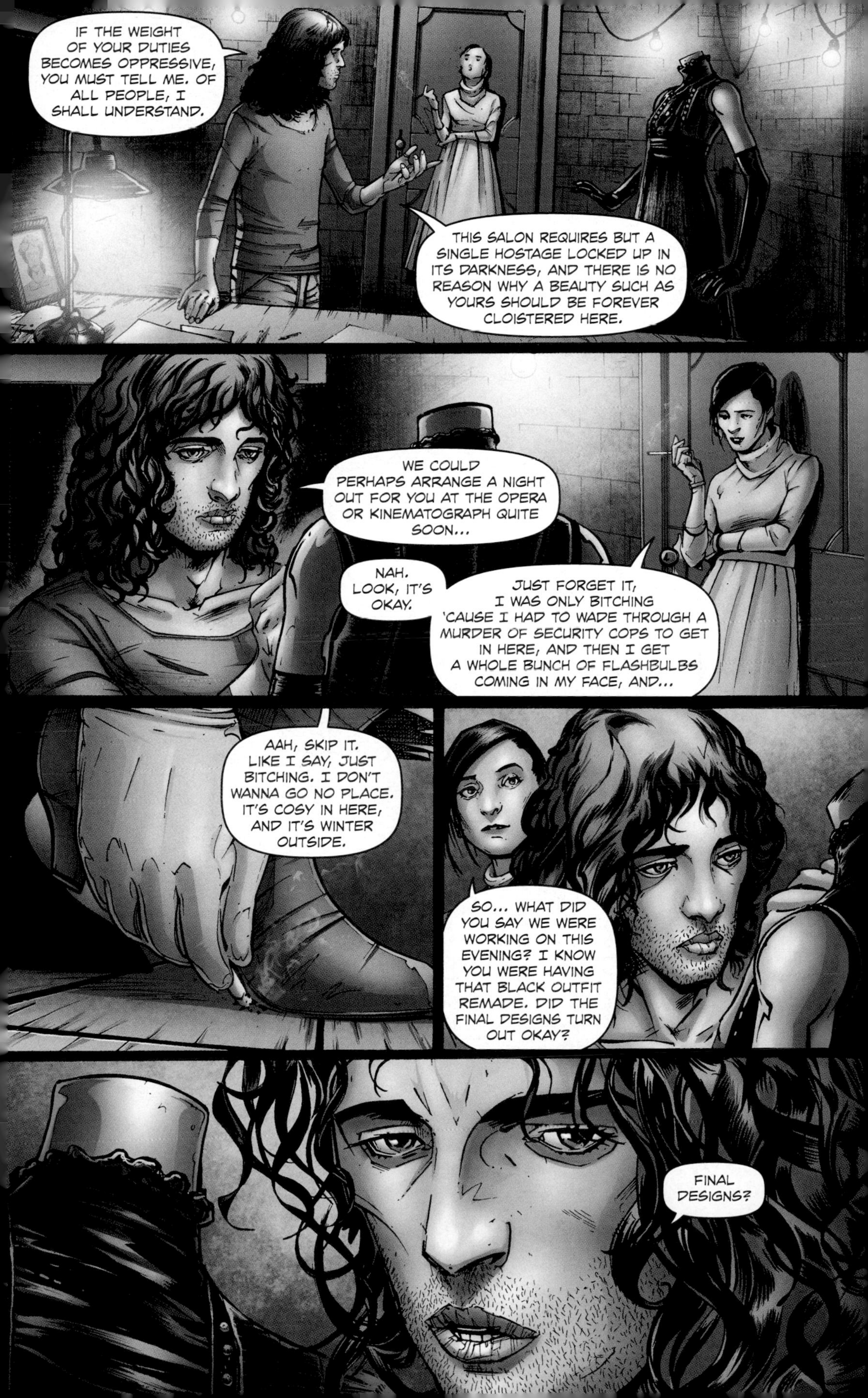

IF THE WEIGHT OF YOUR DUTIES BECOMES OPPRESSIVE, YOU MUST TELL ME. OF ALL PEOPLE, I SHALL UNDERSTAND.
THIS SALON REQUIRES BUT A SINGLE HOSTAGE LOCKED UP IN ITS DARKNESS, AND THERE IS NO REASON WHY A BEAUTY SUCH AS YOURS SHOULD BE FOREVER CLOISTERED HERE.
WE COULD PERHAPS ARRANGE A NIGHT OUT FOR YOU AT THE OPERA OR KINEMATOGRAPH QUITE SOON...
NAH. LOOK, IT'S OKAY.
JUST FORGET IT, I WAS ONLY BITCHING 'CAUSE I HAD TO WADE THROUGH A MURDER OF SECURITY COPS TO GET IN HERE, AND THEN I GET A WHOLE BUNCH OF FLASHBULBS COMING IN MY FACE, AND...
AAH, SKIP IT. LIKE I SAY, JUST BITCHING. I DON'T WANNA GO NO PLACE. IT'S COSY IN HERE, AND IT'S WINTER OUTSIDE.
SO... WHAT DID YOU SAY WE WERE WORKING ON THIS EVENING? I KNOW YOU WERE HAVING THAT BLACK OUTFIT REMADE. DID THE FINAL DESIGNS TURN OUT OKAY?
FINAL DESIGNS?

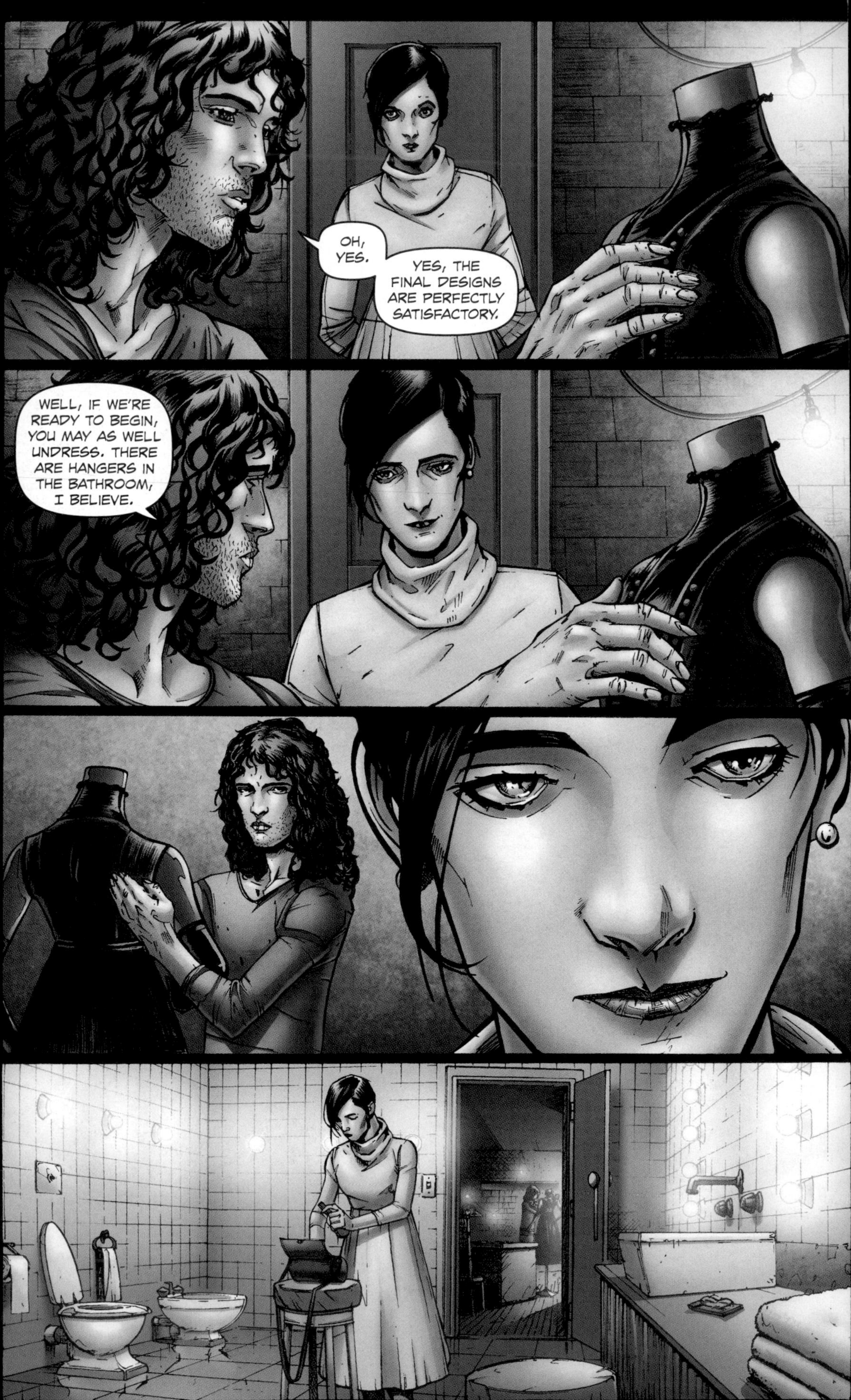
OH, YES.
YES, THE FINAL DESIGNS ARE PERFECTLY SATISFACTORY.
WELL, IF WE'RE READY TO BEGIN, YOU MAY AS WELL UNDRESS. THERE ARE HANGERS IN THE BATHROOM, I BELIEVE.

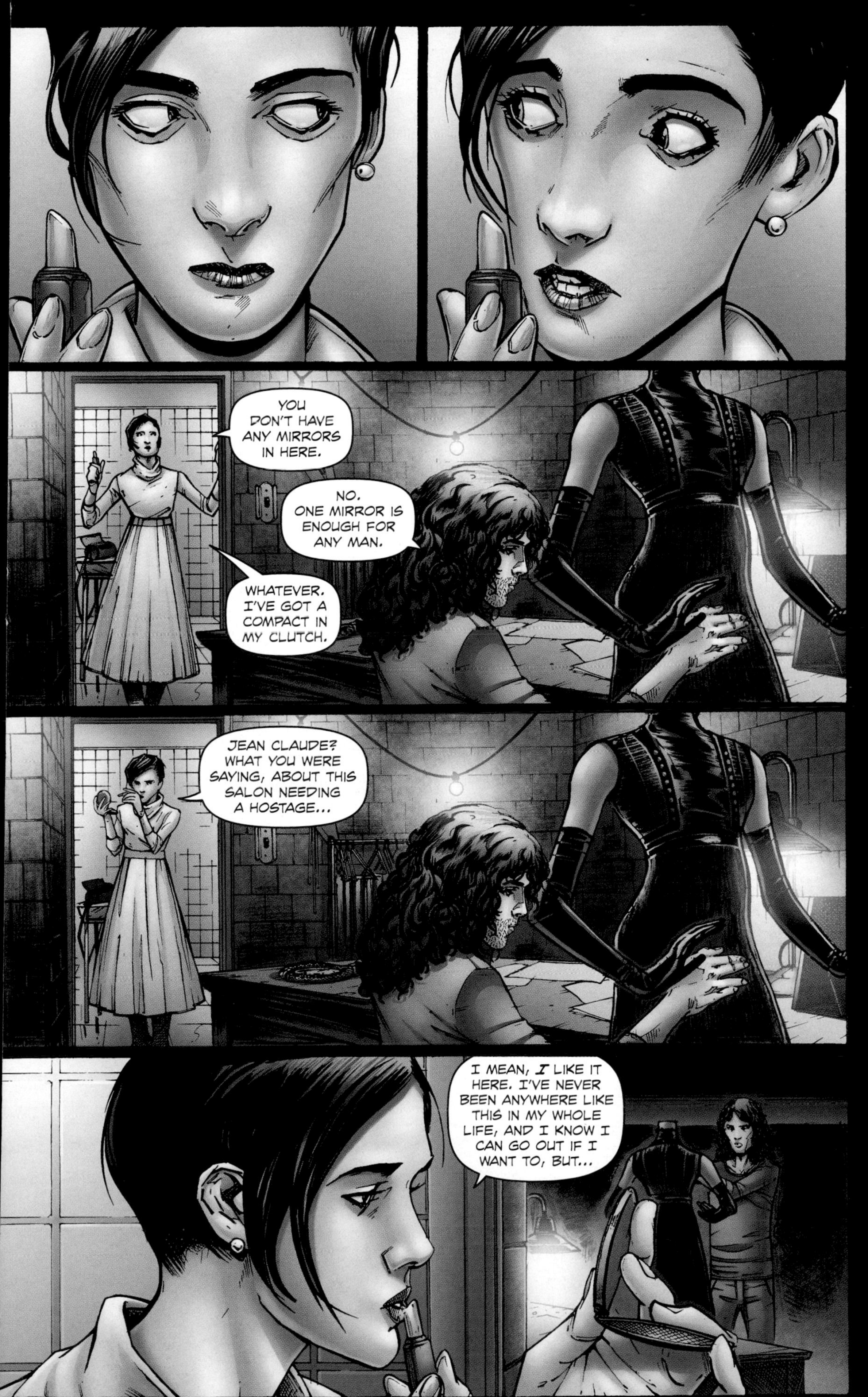
YOU DON'T HAVE ANY MIRRORS IN HERE.
NO. ONE MIRROR IS ENOUGH FOR ANY MAN.
WHATEVER. I'VE GOT A COMPACT IN MY CLUTCH.
JEAN CLAUDE? WHAT YOU WERE SAYING, ABOUT THIS SALON NEEDING A HOSTAGE...
I MEAN, I LIKE IT HERE. I'VE NEVER BEEN ANYWHERE LIKE THIS IN MY WHOLE LIFE, AND I KNOW I CAN GO OUT IF I WANT TO, BUT...

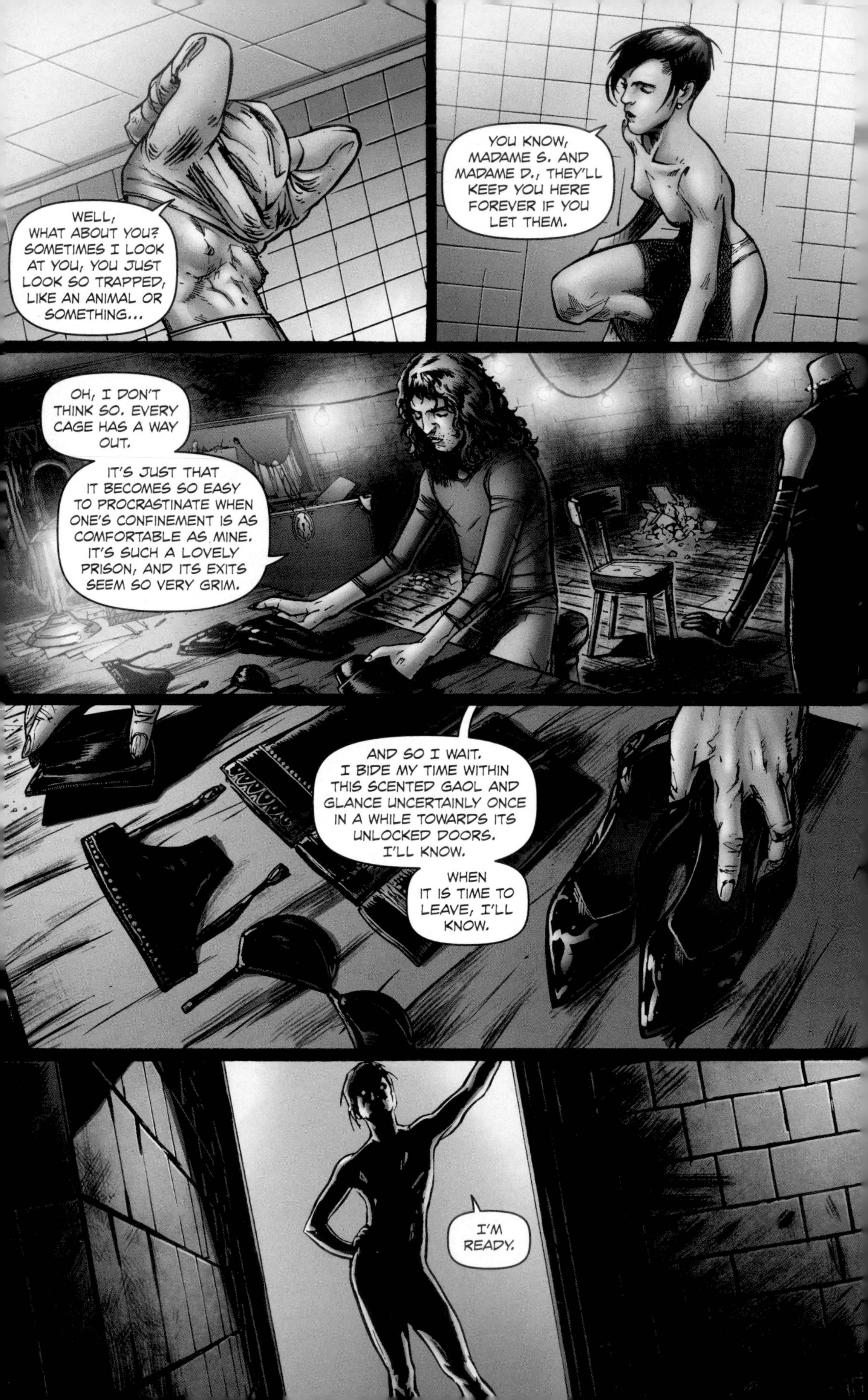
WELL, WHAT ABOUT YOU? SOMETIMES I LOOK AT YOU, YOU JUST LOOK SO TRAPPED, LIKE AN ANIMAL OR SOMETHING...
YOU KNOW, MADAME S. AND MADAME D., THEY'LL KEEP YOU HERE FOREVER IF YOU LET THEM.
OH, I DON'T THINK SO. EVERY CAGE HAS A WAY OUT.
IT'S JUST THAT IT BECOMES SO EASY TO PROCRASTINATE WHEN ONE'S CONFINEMENT IS AS COMFORTABLE AS MINE. IT'S SUCH A LOVELY PRISON, AND ITS EXITS SEEM SO VERY GRIM.
AND SO I WAIT. I BIDE MY TIME WITHIN THIS SCENTED GAOL AND GLANCE UNCERTAINLY ONCE IN A WHILE TOWARDS ITS UNLOCKED DOORS. I'LL KNOW.
WHEN IT IS TIME TO LEAVE, I'LL KNOW.
I'M READY.

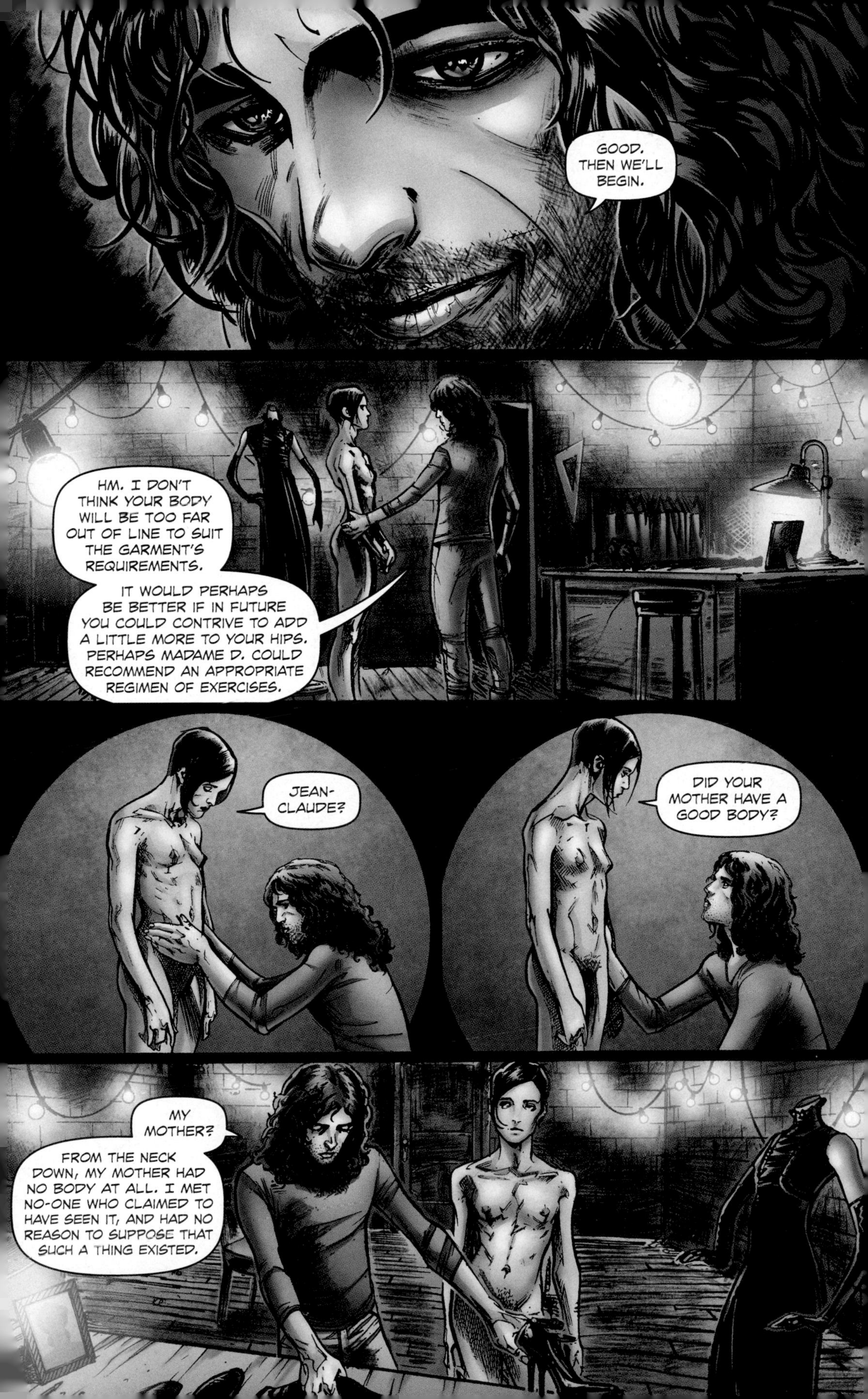
GOOD. THEN WE'LL BEGIN.
HM. I DON'T THINK YOUR BODY WILL BE TOO FAR OUT OF LINE TO SUIT THE GARMENT'S REQUIREMENTS.
IT WOULD PERHAPS BE BETTER IF IN FUTURE YOU COULD CONTRIVE TO ADD A LITTLE MORE TO YOUR HIPS. PERHAPS MADAME D. COULD RECOMMEND AN APPROPRIATE REGIMEN OF EXERCISES.
JEAN-CLAUDE?
DID YOUR MOTHER HAVE A GOOD BODY?
MY MOTHER?
FROM THE NECK DOWN, MY MOTHER HAD NO BODY AT ALL. I MET NO-ONE WHO CLAIMED TO HAVE SEEN IT, AND HAD NO REASON TO SUPPOSE THAT SUCH A THING EXISTED.

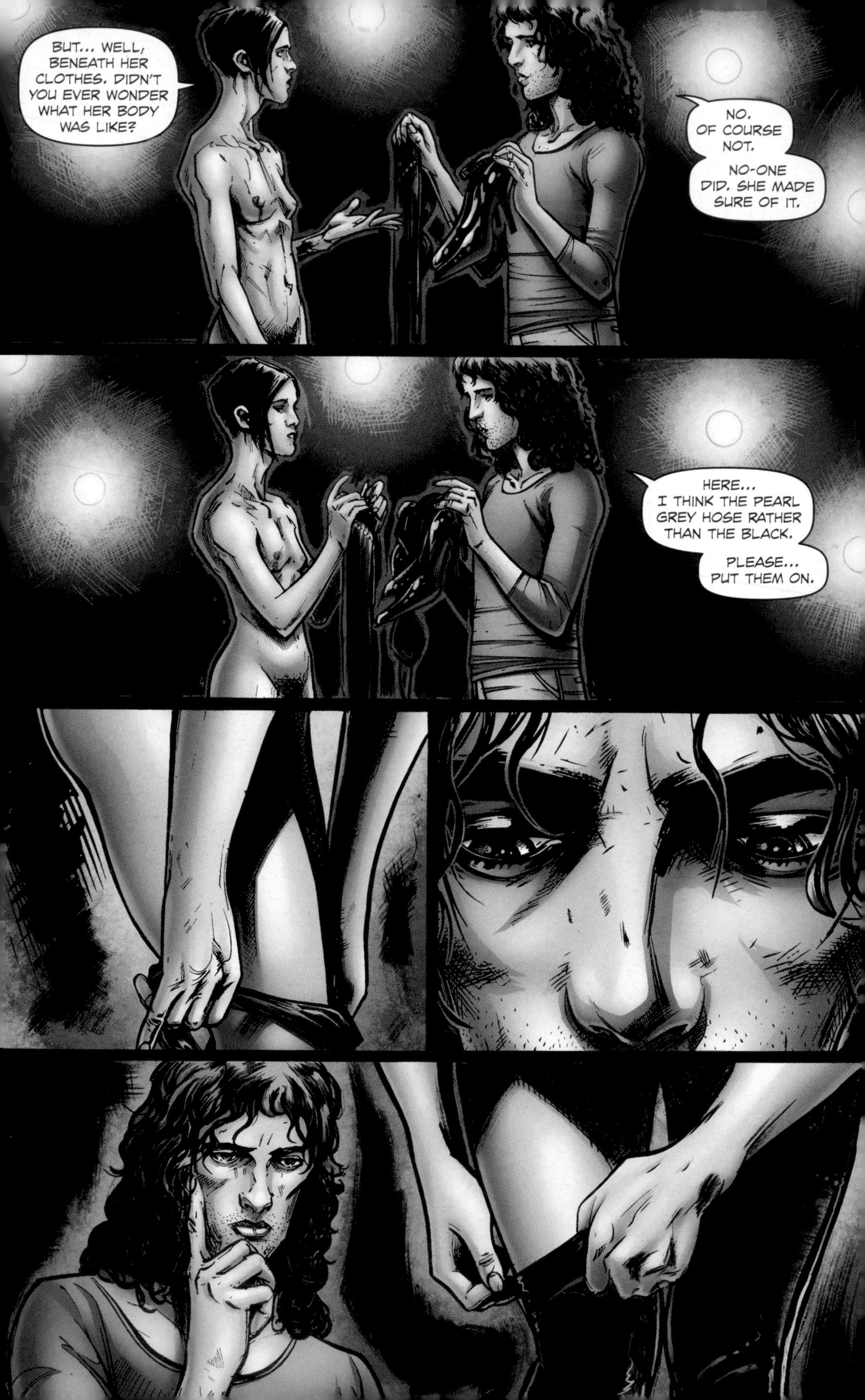
BUT... WELL, BENEATH HER CLOTHES. DIDN'T YOU EVER WONDER WHAT HER BODY WAS LIKE?
NO. OF COURSE NOT.
NO-ONE DID. SHE MADE SURE OF IT.
HERE... I THINK THE PEARL GREY HOSE RATHER THAN THE BLACK.
PLEASE... PUT THEM ON.

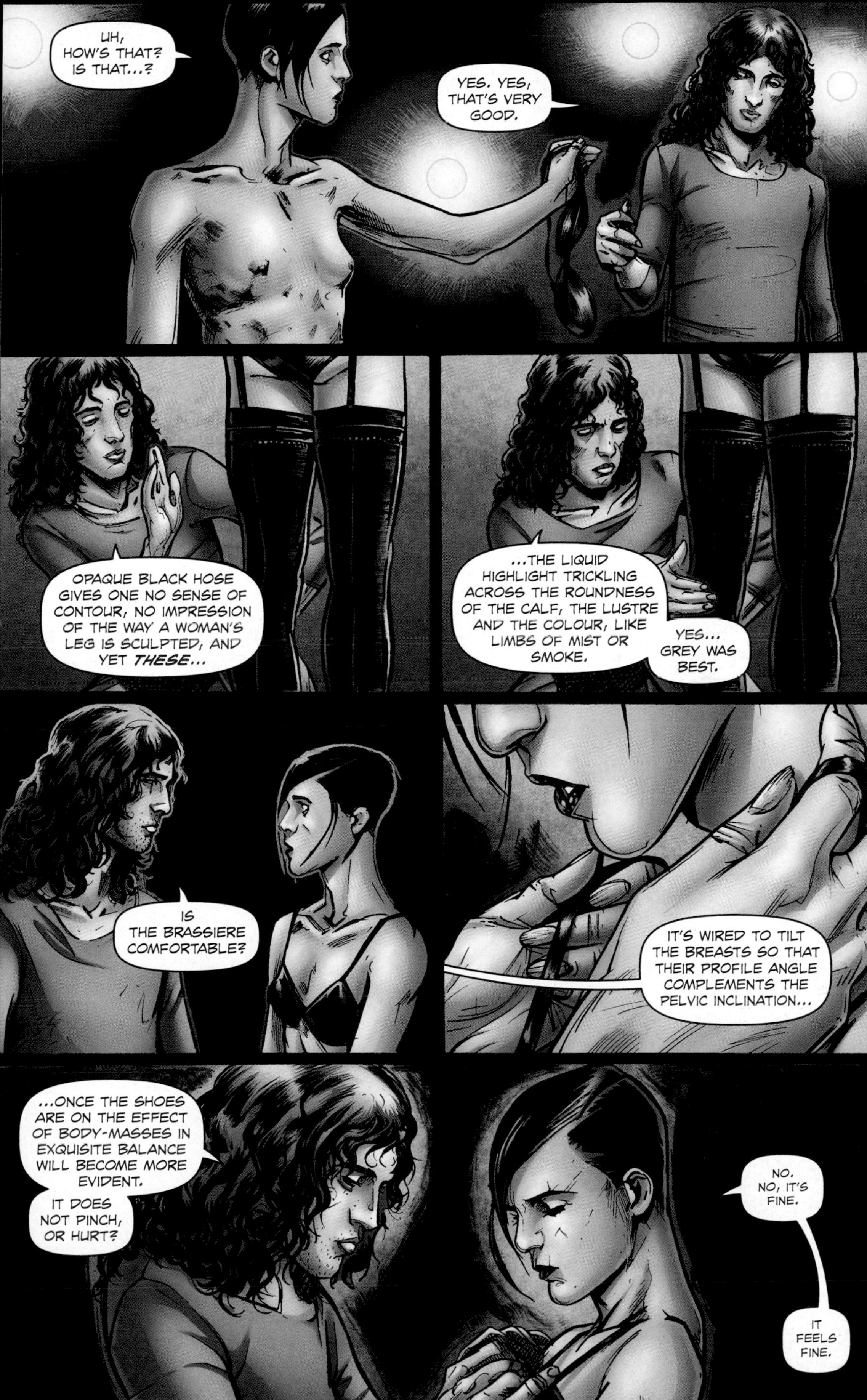
UH, HOW'S THAT? IS THAT...?
YES. YES, THAT'S VERY GOOD.
OPAQUE BLACK HOSE GIVES ONE NO SENSE OF CONTOUR, NO IMPRESSION OF THE WAY A WOMAN'S LEG IS SCULPTED, AND YET *THESE*...
...THE LIQUID HIGHLIGHT TRICKLING ACROSS THE ROUNDNESS OF THE CALF, THE LUSTRE AND THE COLOUR, LIKE LIMBS OF MIST OR SMOKE.
YES... GREY WAS BEST.
IS THE BRASSIERE COMFORTABLE?
IT'S WIRED TO TILT THE BREASTS SO THAT THEIR PROFILE ANGLE COMPLEMENTS THE PELVIC INCLINATION...
...ONCE THE SHOES ARE ON THE EFFECT OF BODY-MASSES IN EXQUISITE BALANCE WILL BECOME MORE EVIDENT.
IT DOES NOT PINCH, OR HURT?
NO. NO, IT'S FINE.
IT FEELS FINE.

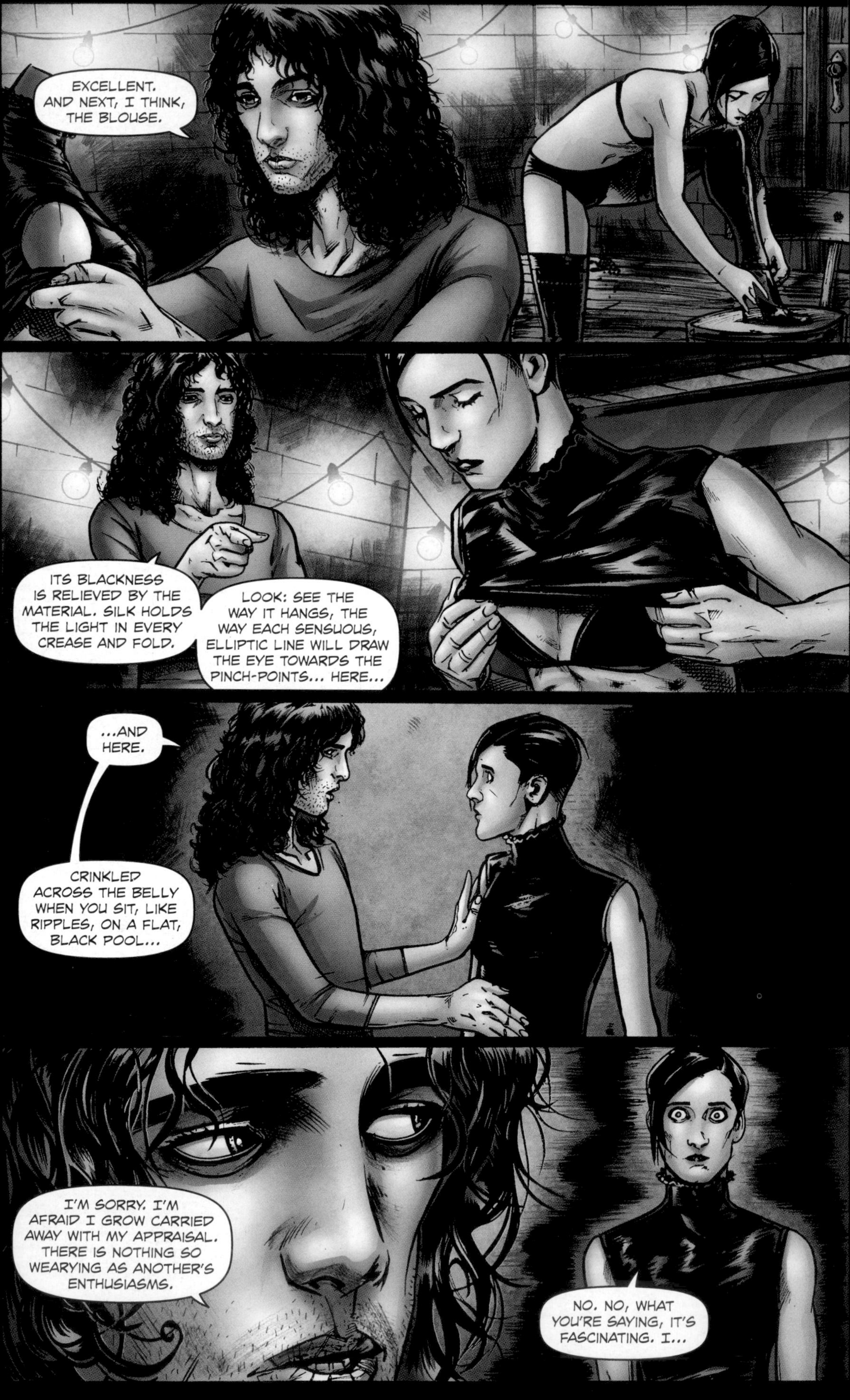
EXCELLENT. AND NEXT, I THINK, THE BLOUSE.
ITS BLACKNESS IS RELIEVED BY THE MATERIAL. SILK HOLDS THE LIGHT IN EVERY CREASE AND FOLD.
LOOK: SEE THE WAY IT HANGS, THE WAY EACH SENSUOUS, ELLIPTIC LINE WILL DRAW THE EYE TOWARDS THE PINCH-POINTS... HERE...
...AND HERE.
CRINKLED ACROSS THE BELLY WHEN YOU SIT, LIKE RIPPLES, ON A FLAT, BLACK POOL...
I'M SORRY. I'M AFRAID I GROW CARRIED AWAY WITH MY APPRAISAL. THERE IS NOTHING SO WEARYING AS ANOTHER'S ENTHUSIASMS.
NO. NO, WHAT YOU'RE SAYING, IT'S FASCINATING. I...

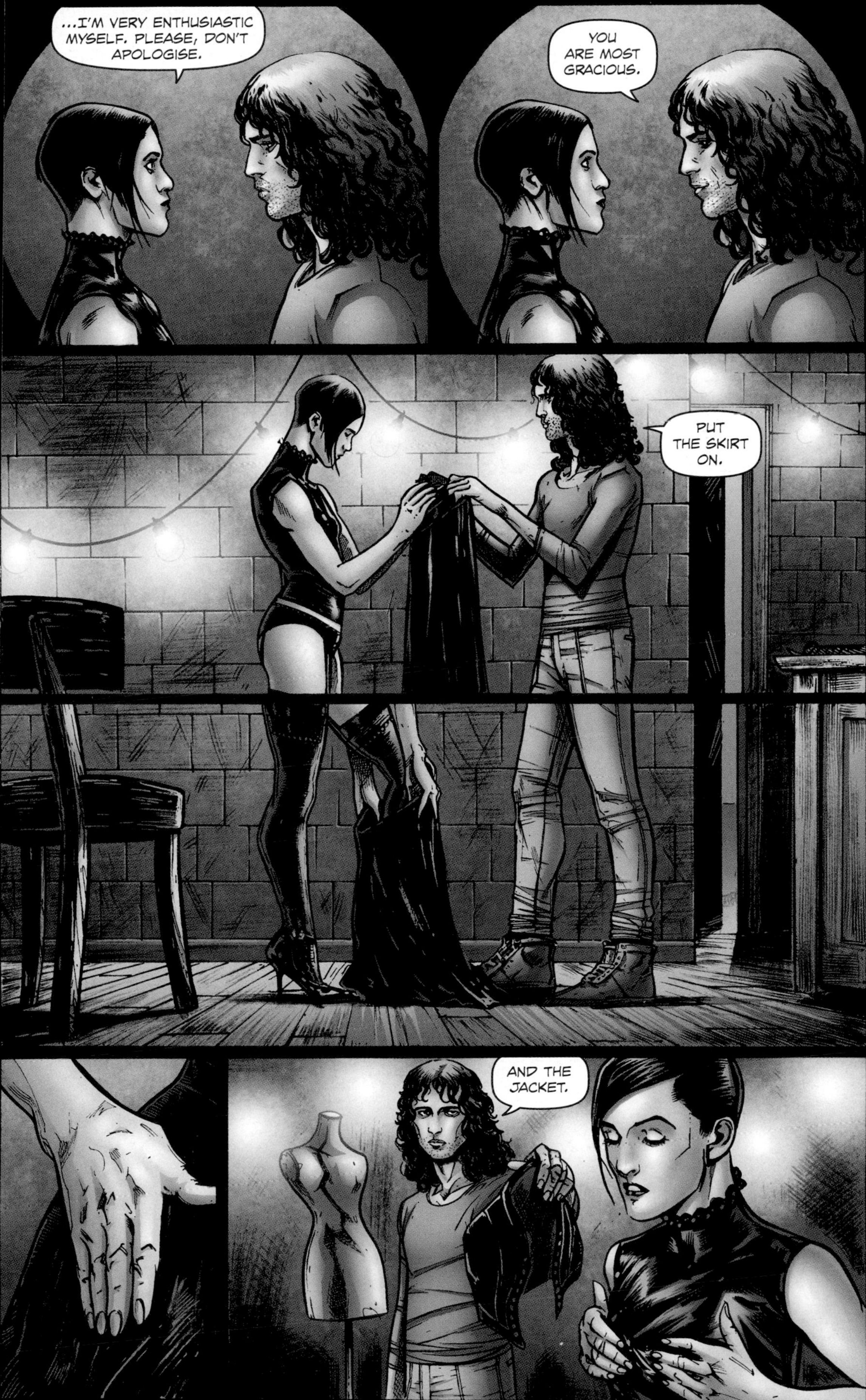
...I'M VERY ENTHUSIASTIC MYSELF. PLEASE, DON'T APOLOGISE.
YOU ARE MOST GRACIOUS.
PUT THE SKIRT ON.
AND THE JACKET.

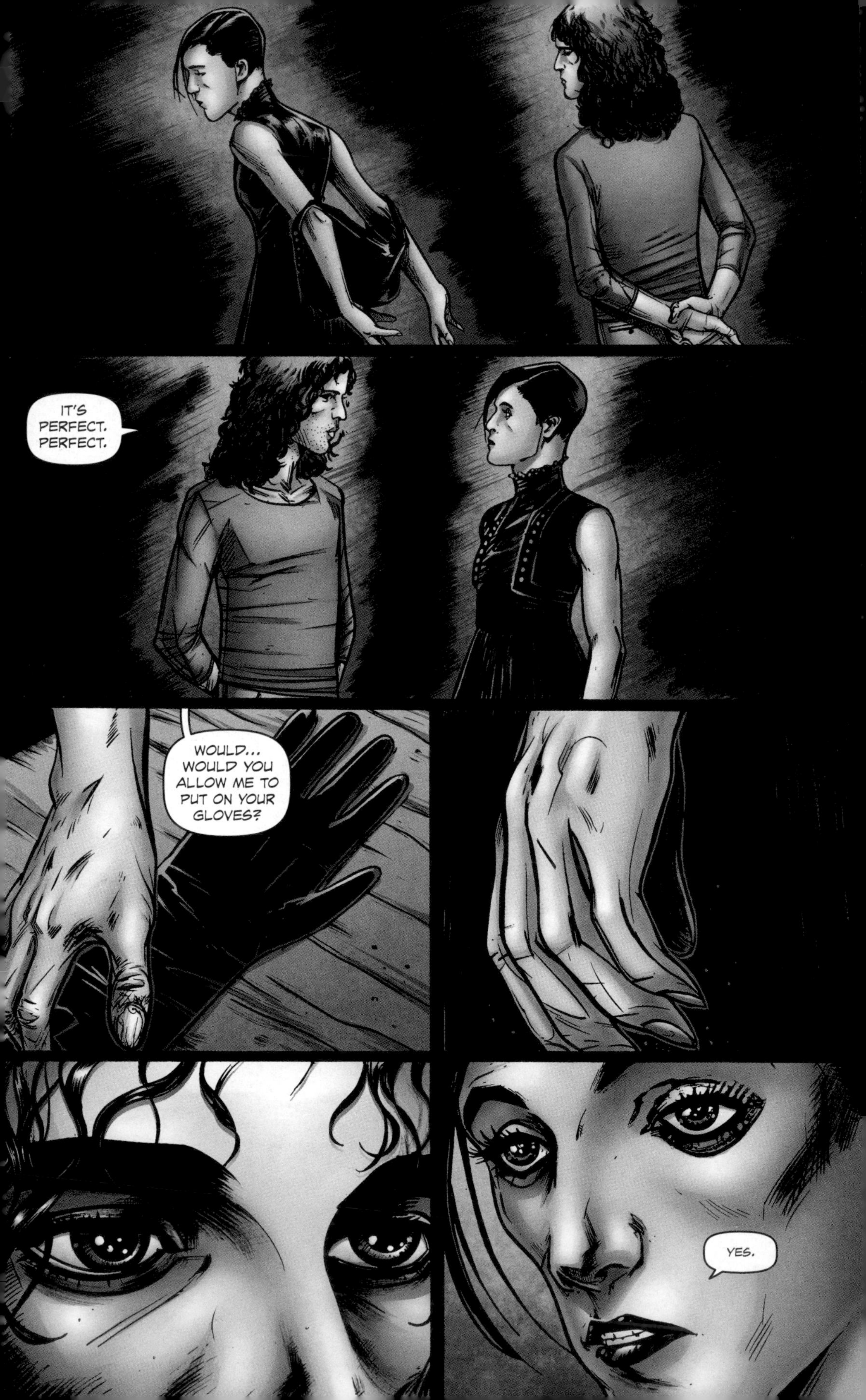
IT'S PERFECT. PERFECT.
WOULD... WOULD YOU ALLOW ME TO PUT ON YOUR GLOVES?
YES.

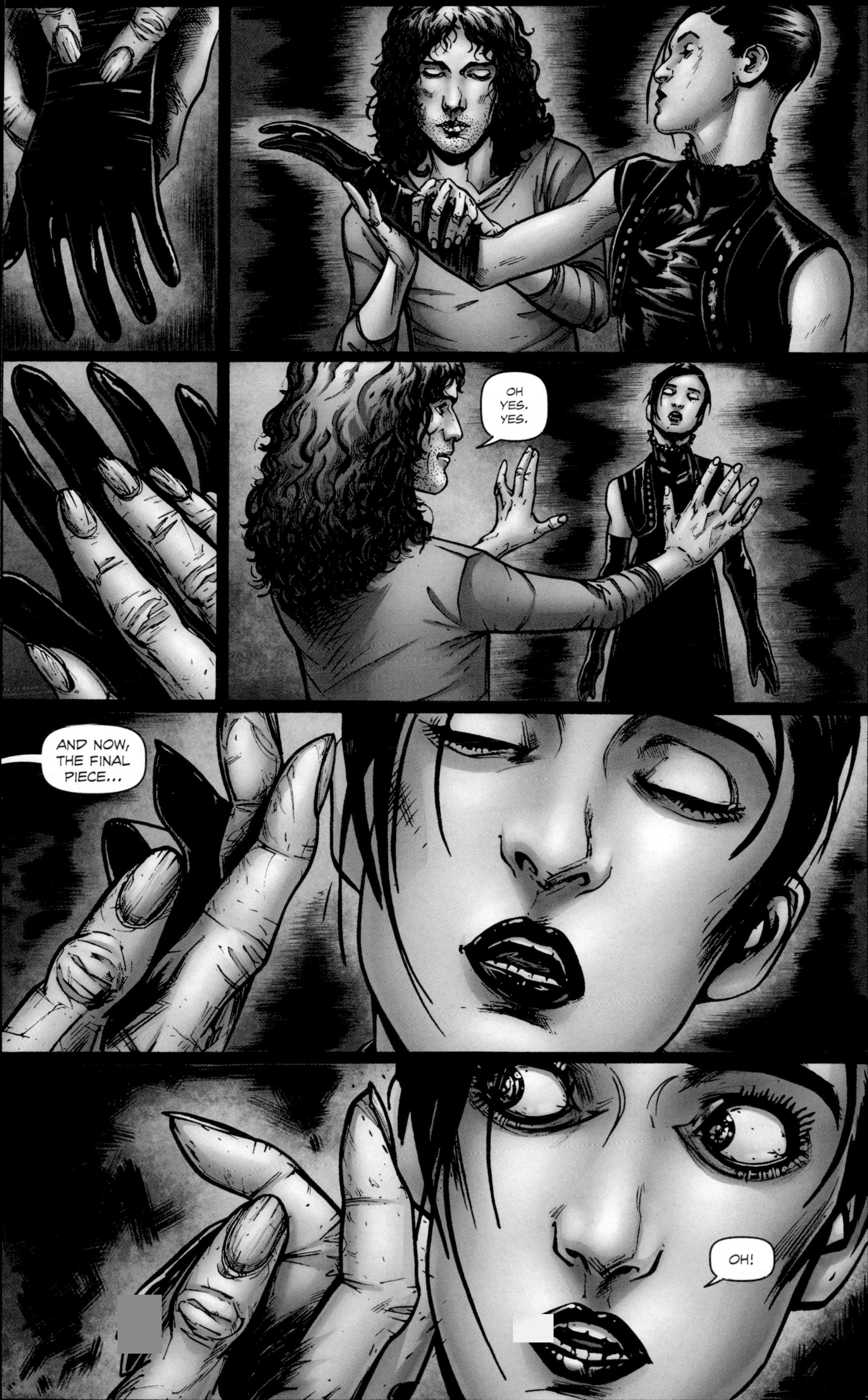
OH YES. YES.
AND NOW, THE FINAL PIECE...
OH!

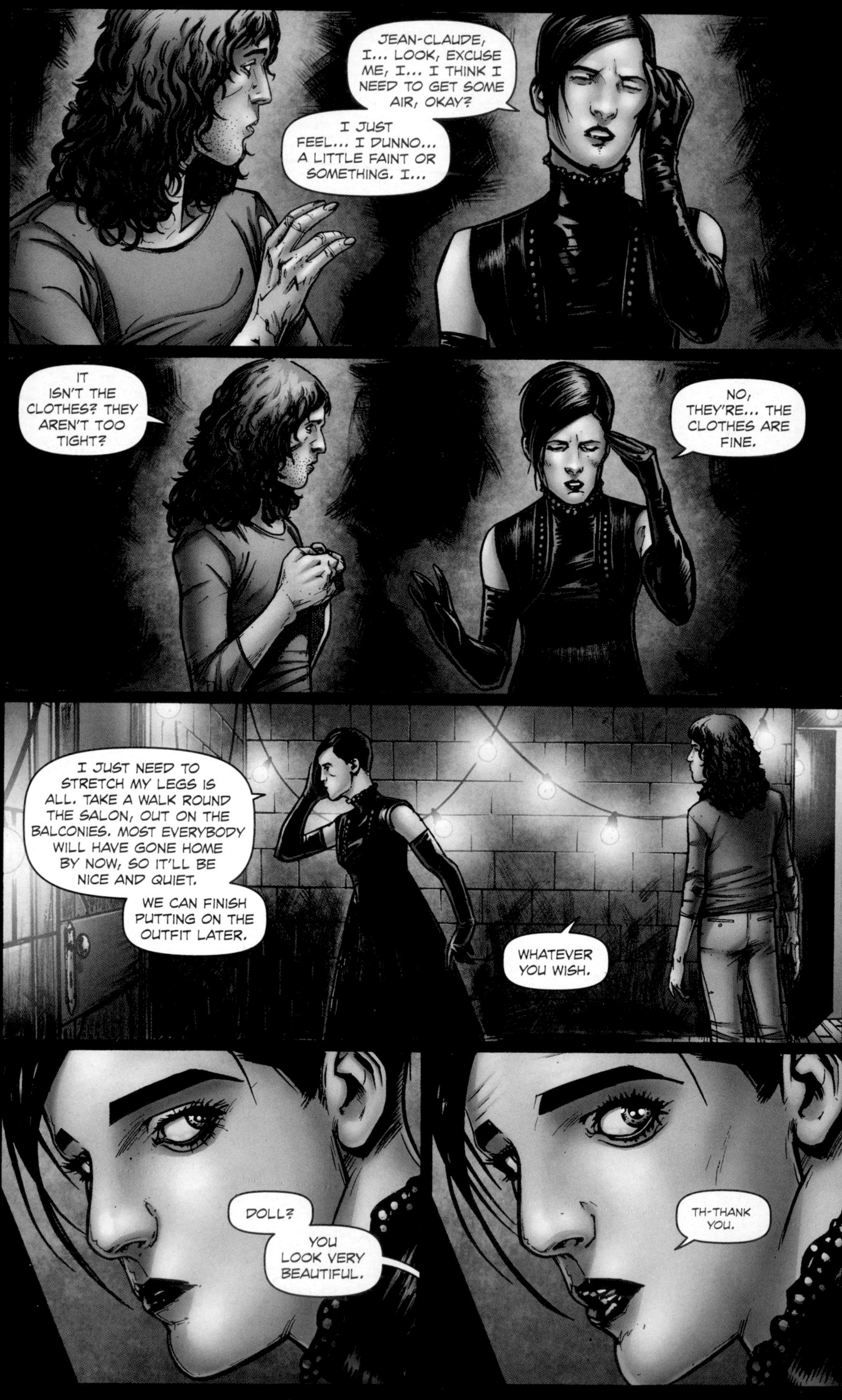
JEAN-CLAUDE, I... LOOK, EXCUSE ME, I... I THINK I NEED TO GET SOME AIR, OKAY?
I JUST FEEL... I DUNNO... A LITTLE FAINT OR SOMETHING. I...
IT ISN'T THE CLOTHES? THEY AREN'T TOO TIGHT?
NO, THEY'RE... THE CLOTHES ARE FINE.
I JUST NEED TO STRETCH MY LEGS IS ALL. TAKE A WALK ROUND THE SALON, OUT ON THE BALCONIES. MOST EVERYBODY WILL HAVE GONE HOME BY NOW, SO IT'LL BE NICE AND QUIET.
WE CAN FINISH PUTTING ON THE OUTFIT LATER.
WHATEVER YOU WISH.
DOLL?
YOU LOOK VERY BEAUTIFUL.
TH-THANK YOU.

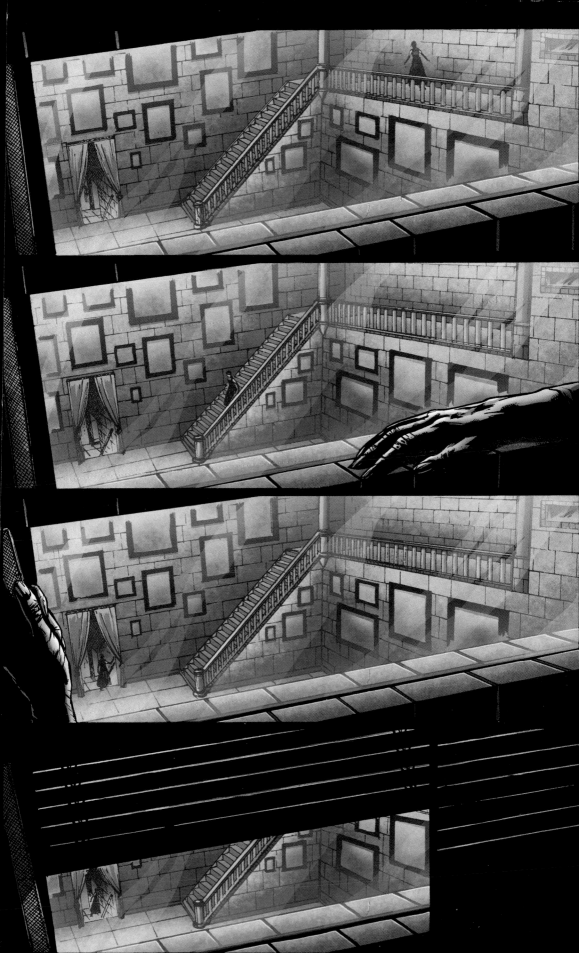

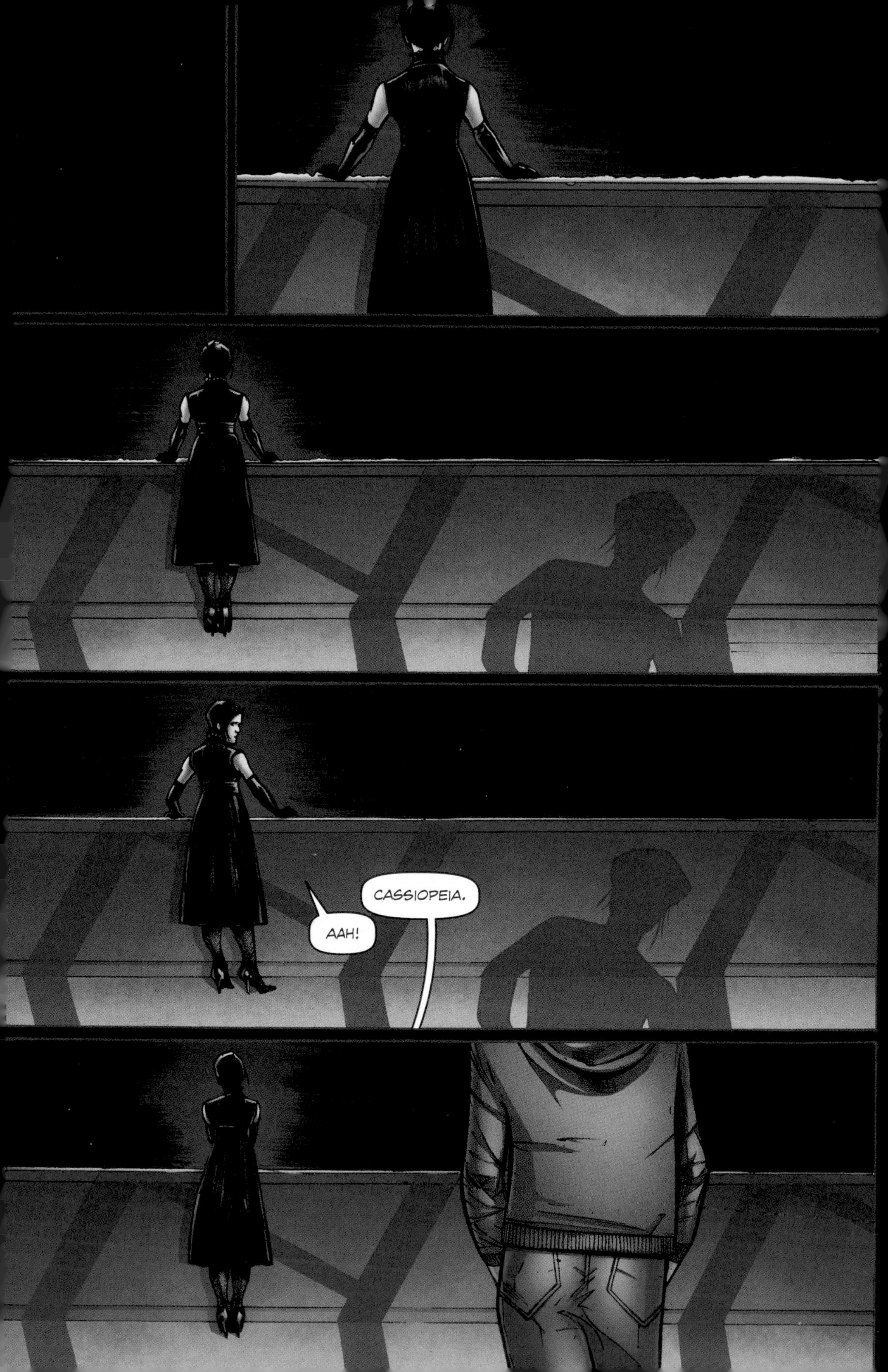
AAH!
CASSIOPEIA.

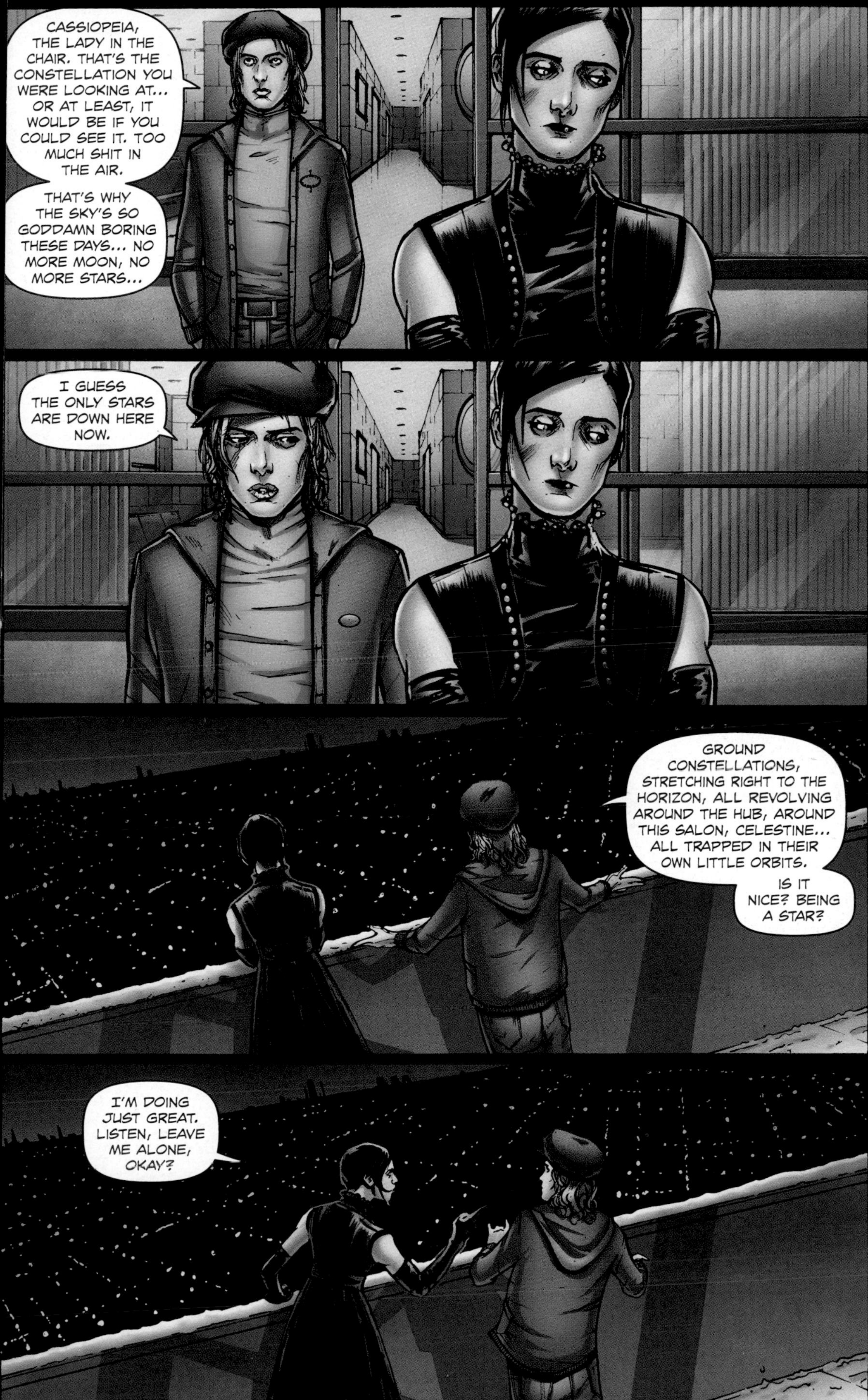
CASSIOPEIA, THE LADY IN THE CHAIR. THAT'S THE CONSTELLATION YOU WERE LOOKING AT... OR AT LEAST, IT WOULD BE IF YOU COULD SEE IT. TOO MUCH SHIT IN THE AIR.
THAT'S WHY THE SKY'S SO GODDAMN BORING THESE DAYS... NO MORE MOON, NO MORE STARS...
I GUESS THE ONLY STARS ARE DOWN HERE NOW.
GROUND CONSTELLATIONS, STRETCHING RIGHT TO THE HORIZON, ALL REVOLVING AROUND THE HUB, AROUND THIS SALON, CELESTINE... ALL TRAPPED IN THEIR OWN LITTLE ORBITS.
IS IT NICE? BEING A STAR?
I'M DOING JUST GREAT. LISTEN, LEAVE ME ALONE, OKAY?

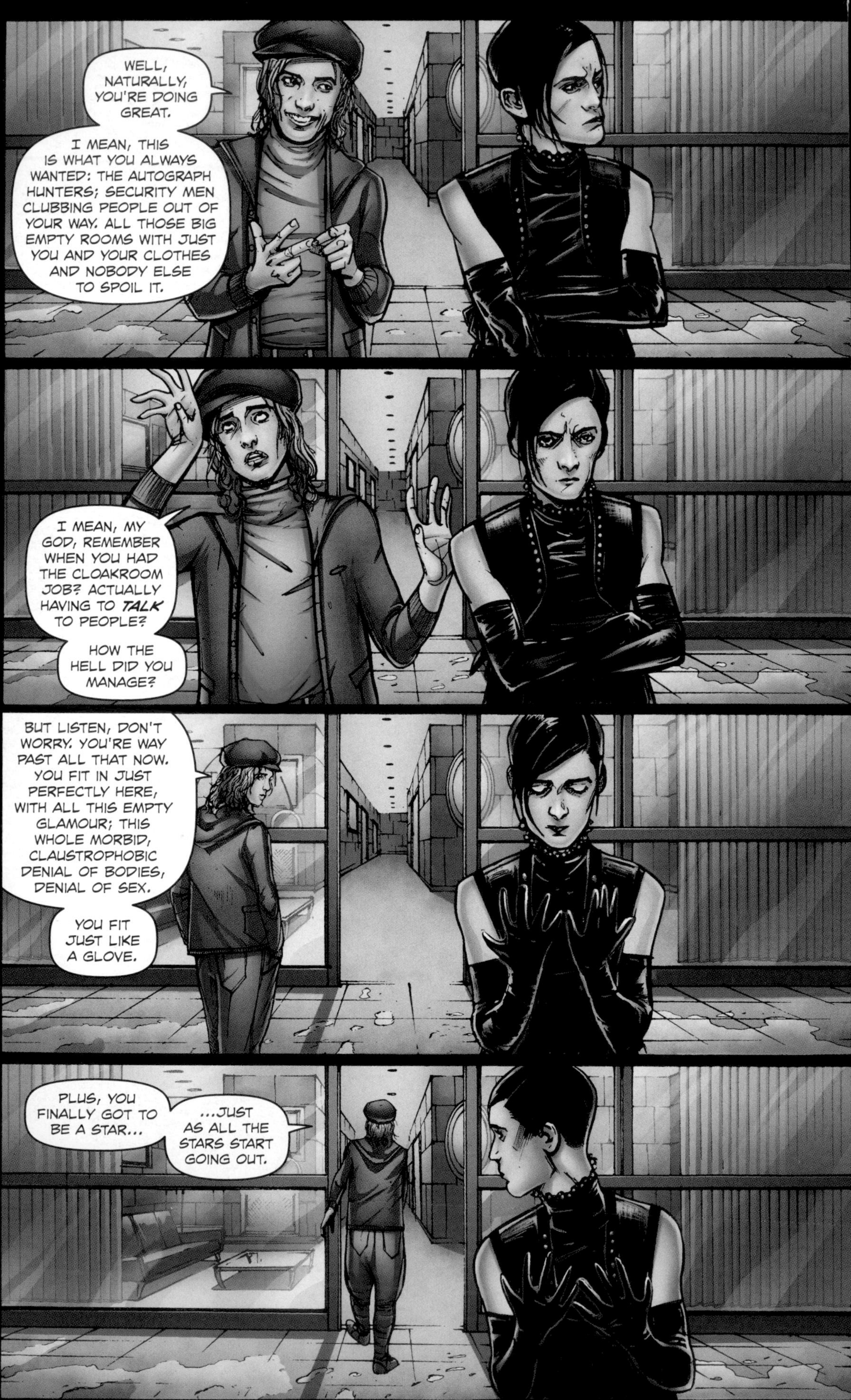
WELL, NATURALLY, YOU'RE DOING GREAT.
I MEAN, THIS IS WHAT YOU ALWAYS WANTED: THE AUTOGRAPH HUNTERS; SECURITY MEN CLUBBING PEOPLE OUT OF YOUR WAY. ALL THOSE BIG EMPTY ROOMS WITH JUST YOU AND YOUR CLOTHES AND NOBODY ELSE TO SPOIL IT.
I MEAN, MY GOD, REMEMBER WHEN YOU HAD THE CLOAKROOM JOB? ACTUALLY HAVING TO *TALK* TO PEOPLE?
HOW THE HELL DID YOU MANAGE?
BUT LISTEN, DON'T WORRY. YOU'RE WAY PAST ALL THAT NOW. YOU FIT IN JUST PERFECTLY HERE, WITH ALL THIS EMPTY GLAMOUR; THIS WHOLE MORBID, CLAUSTROPHOBIC DENIAL OF BODIES, DENIAL OF SEX.
YOU FIT JUST LIKE A GLOVE.
PLUS, YOU FINALLY GOT TO BE A STAR...
...JUST AS ALL THE STARS START GOING OUT.

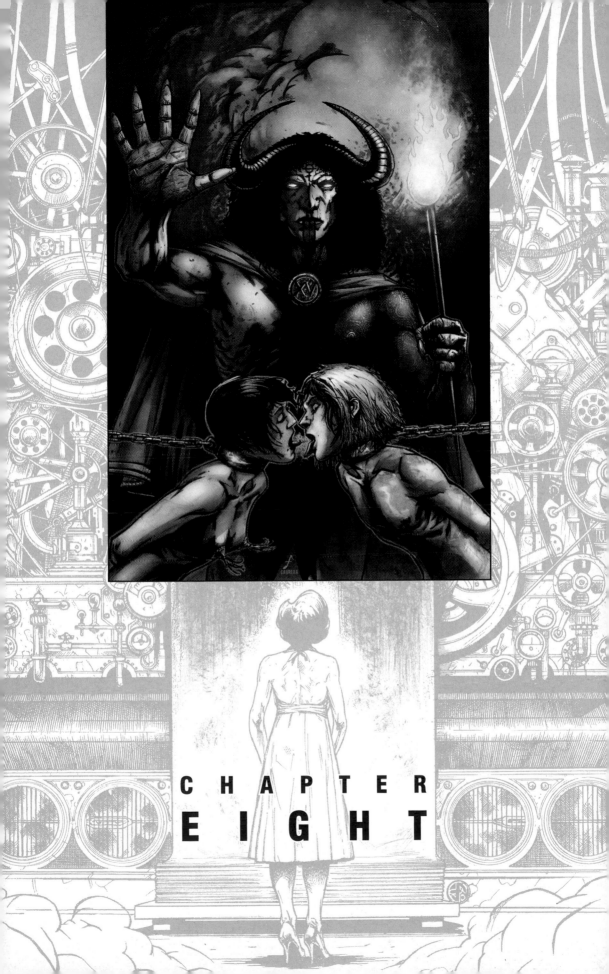

CHAPTER
EIGHT

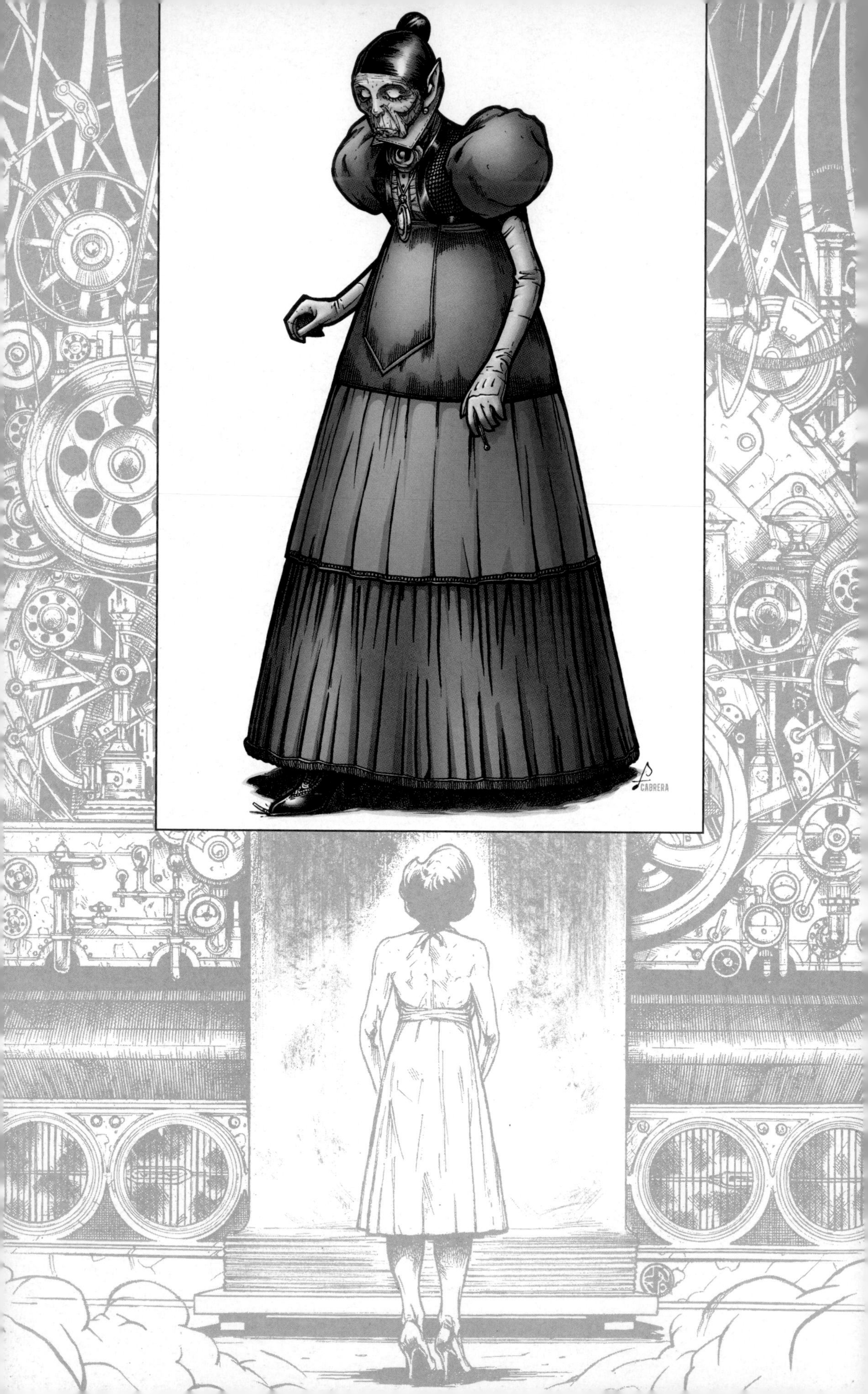
CABRERA

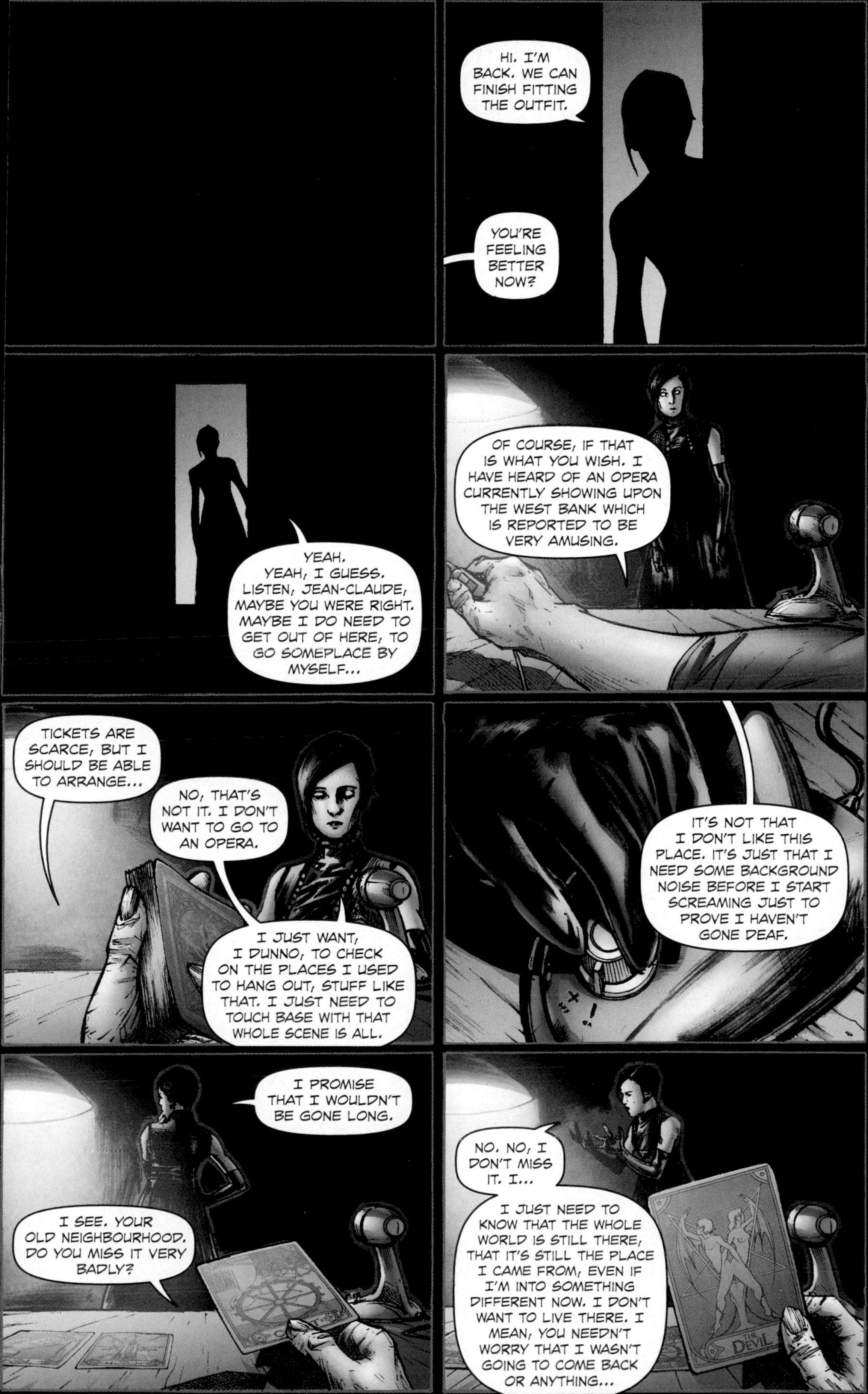
HI. I'M BACK. WE CAN FINISH FITTING THE OUTFIT.
YOU'RE FEELING BETTER NOW?
YEAH. YEAH, I GUESS. LISTEN, JEAN-CLAUDE, MAYBE YOU WERE RIGHT. MAYBE I DO NEED TO GET OUT OF HERE, TO GO SOMEPLACE BY MYSELF...
OF COURSE, IF THAT IS WHAT YOU WISH. I HAVE HEARD OF AN OPERA CURRENTLY SHOWING UPON THE WEST BANK WHICH IS REPORTED TO BE VERY AMUSING.
TICKETS ARE SCARCE, BUT I SHOULD BE ABLE TO ARRANGE...
NO, THAT'S NOT IT. I DON'T WANT TO GO TO AN OPERA.
I JUST WANT, I DUNNO, TO CHECK ON THE PLACES I USED TO HANG OUT, STUFF LIKE THAT. I JUST NEED TO TOUCH BASE WITH THAT WHOLE SCENE IS ALL.
IT'S NOT THAT I DON'T LIKE THIS PLACE. IT'S JUST THAT I NEED SOME BACKGROUND NOISE BEFORE I START SCREAMING JUST TO PROVE I HAVEN'T GONE DEAF.
I PROMISE THAT I WOULDN'T BE GONE LONG.
I SEE. YOUR OLD NEIGHBOURHOOD. DO YOU MISS IT VERY BADLY?
NO. NO, I DON'T MISS IT. I...
I JUST NEED TO KNOW THAT THE WHOLE WORLD IS STILL THERE, THAT IT'S STILL THE PLACE I CAME FROM, EVEN IF I'M INTO SOMETHING DIFFERENT NOW. I DON'T WANT TO LIVE THERE. I MEAN, YOU NEEDN'T WORRY THAT I WASN'T GOING TO COME BACK OR ANYTHING...
THE DEVIL

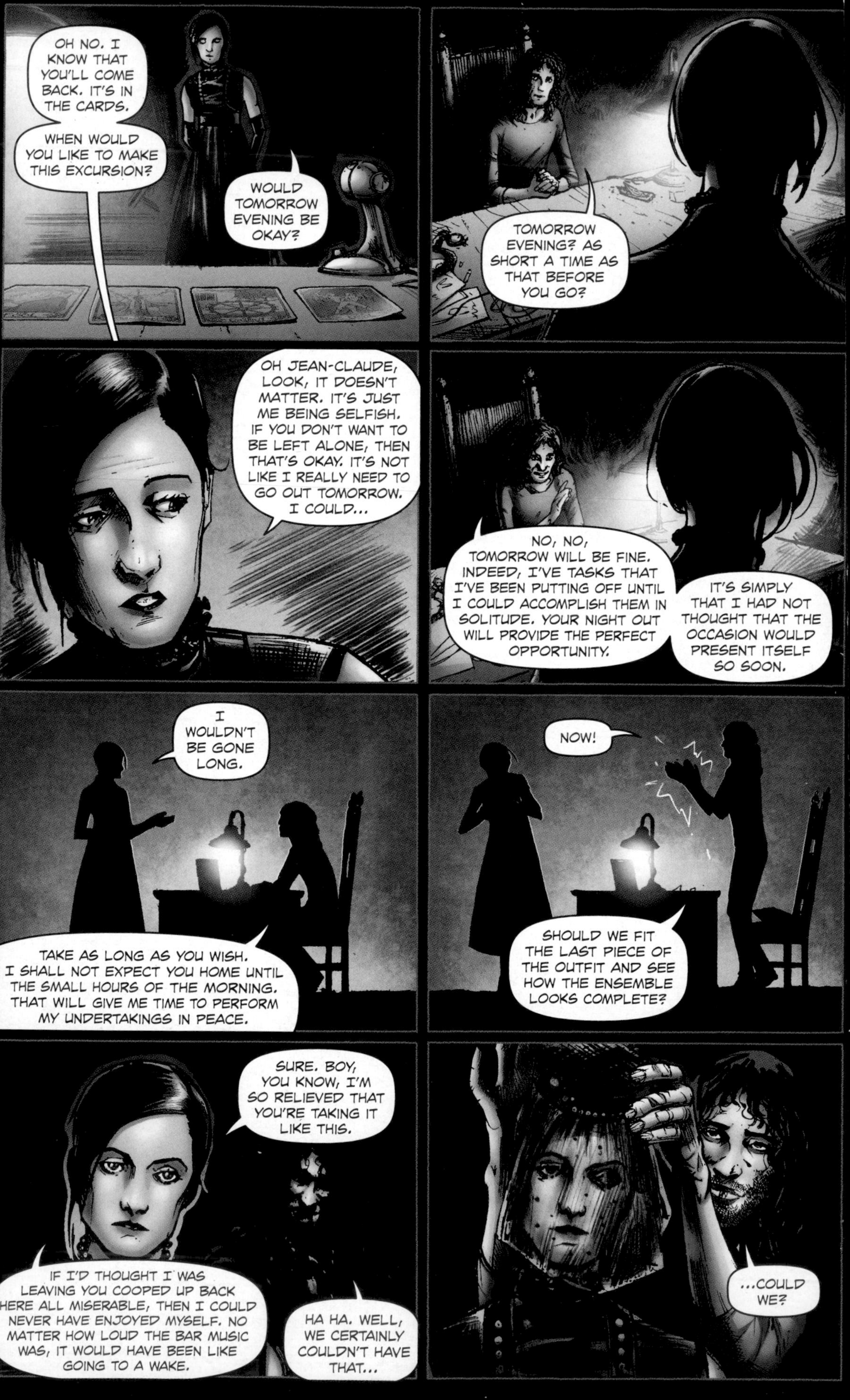
OH NO. I KNOW THAT YOU'LL COME BACK. IT'S IN THE CARDS.
WHEN WOULD YOU LIKE TO MAKE THIS EXCURSION?
WOULD TOMORROW EVENING BE OKAY?
TOMORROW EVENING? AS SHORT A TIME AS THAT BEFORE YOU GO?
OH JEAN-CLAUDE, LOOK, IT DOESN'T MATTER. IT'S JUST ME BEING SELFISH. IF YOU DON'T WANT TO BE LEFT ALONE, THEN THAT'S OKAY. IT'S NOT LIKE I REALLY NEED TO GO OUT TOMORROW. I COULD...
NO, NO, TOMORROW WILL BE FINE. INDEED, I'VE TASKS THAT I'VE BEEN PUTTING OFF UNTIL I COULD ACCOMPLISH THEM IN SOLITUDE. YOUR NIGHT OUT WILL PROVIDE THE PERFECT OPPORTUNITY.
IT'S SIMPLY THAT I HAD NOT THOUGHT THAT THE OCCASION WOULD PRESENT ITSELF SO SOON.
I WOULDN'T BE GONE LONG.
TAKE AS LONG AS YOU WISH. I SHALL NOT EXPECT YOU HOME UNTIL THE SMALL HOURS OF THE MORNING. THAT WILL GIVE ME TIME TO PERFORM MY UNDERTAKINGS IN PEACE.
NOW!
SHOULD WE FIT THE LAST PIECE OF THE OUTFIT AND SEE HOW THE ENSEMBLE LOOKS COMPLETE?
SURE. BOY, YOU KNOW, I'M SO RELIEVED THAT YOU'RE TAKING IT LIKE THIS.
IF I'D THOUGHT I WAS LEAVING YOU COOPED UP BACK HERE ALL MISERABLE, THEN I COULD NEVER HAVE ENJOYED MYSELF. NO MATTER HOW LOUD THE BAR MUSIC WAS, IT WOULD HAVE BEEN LIKE GOING TO A WAKE.
HA HA. WELL, WE CERTAINLY COULDN'T HAVE THAT...
...COULD WE?

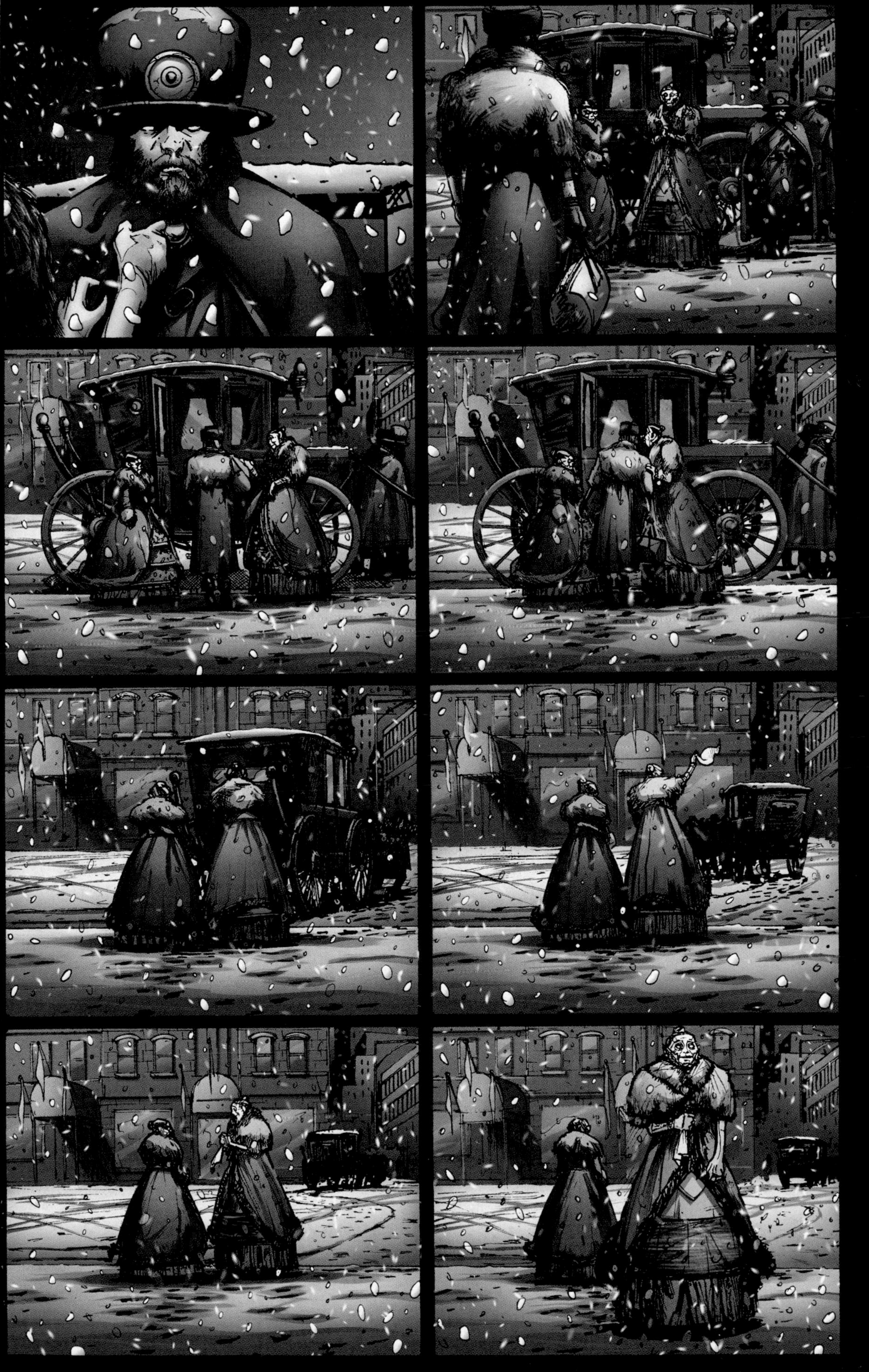

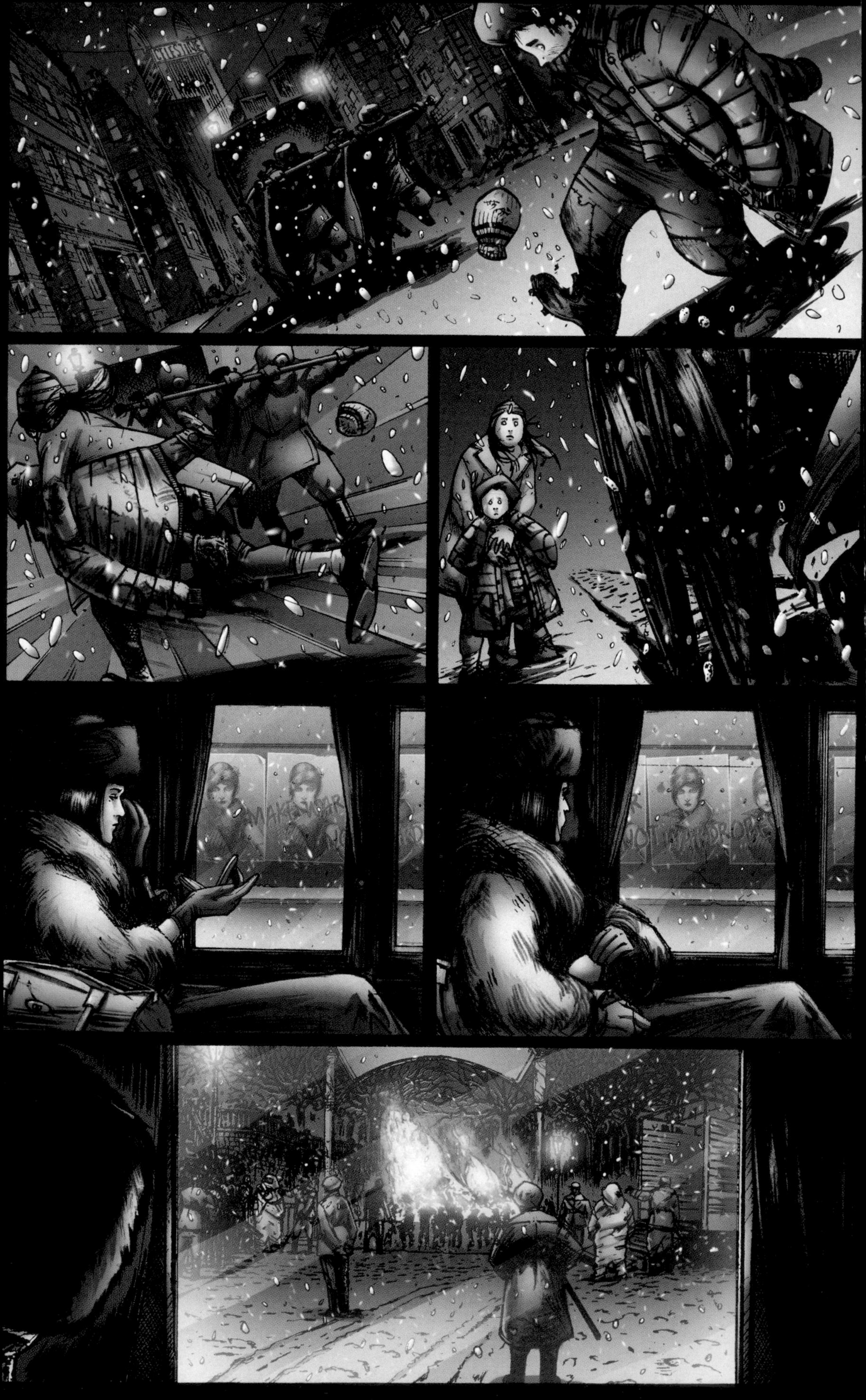
MAKE WAR

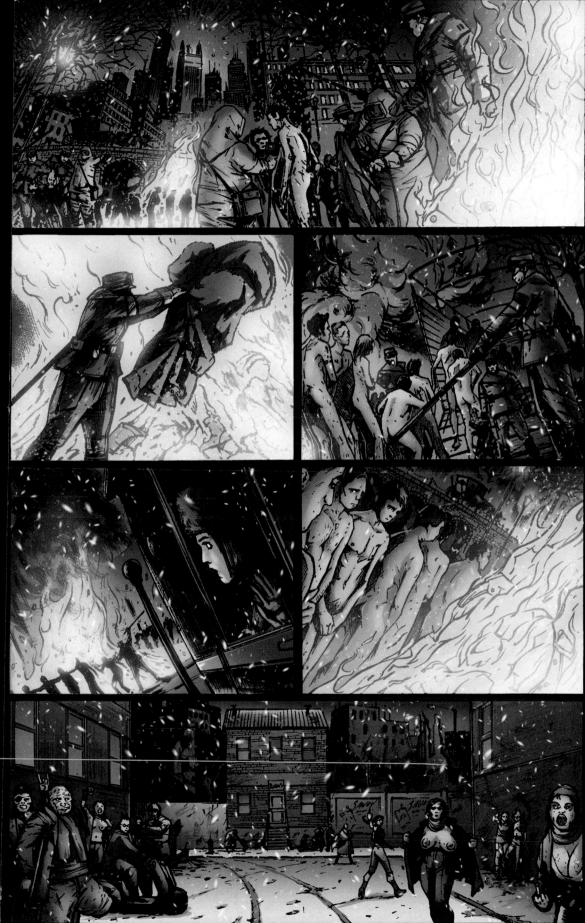

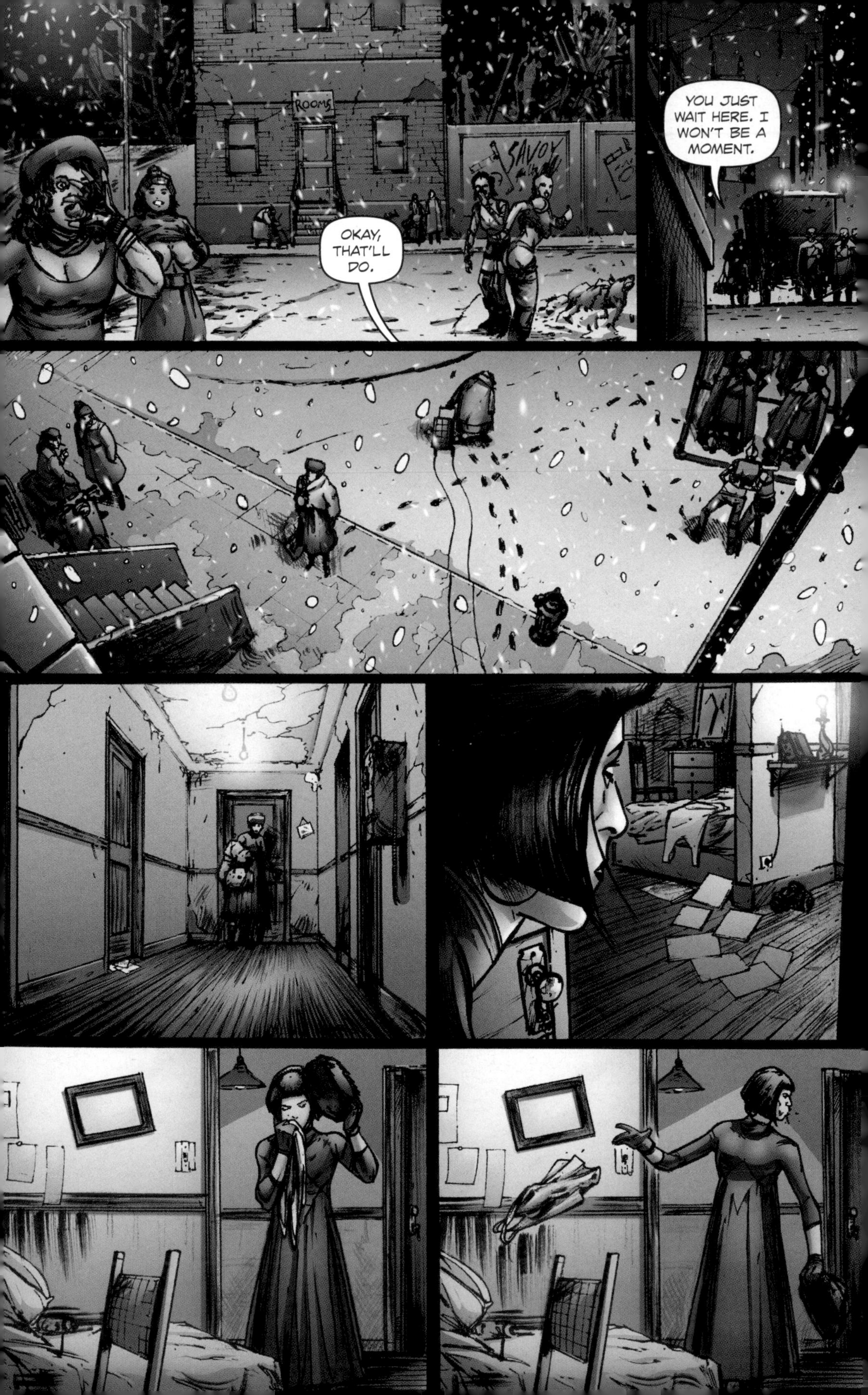
ROOMS
OKAY, THAT'LL DO.
YOU JUST WAIT HERE. I WON'T BE A MOMENT.

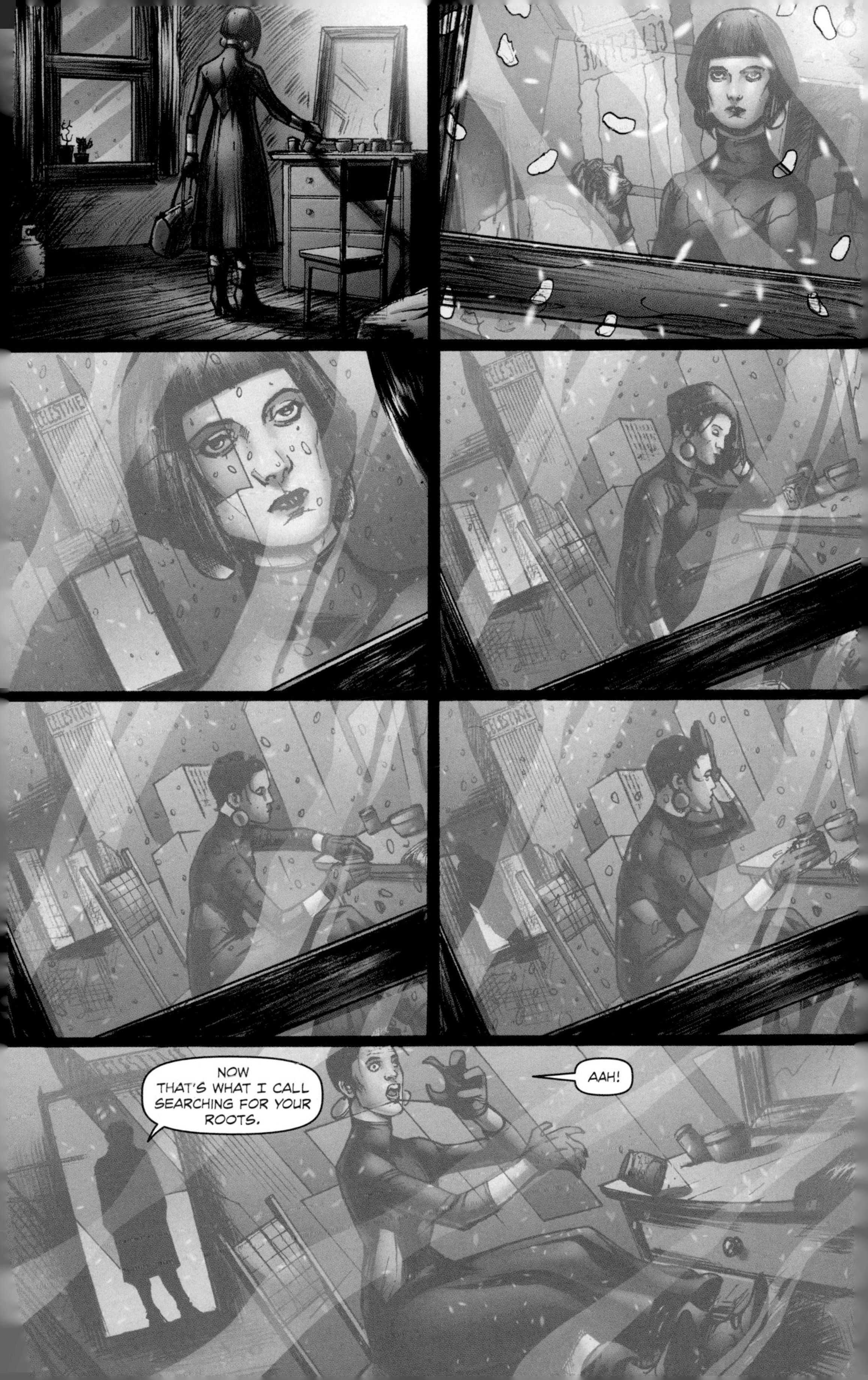
NOW THAT'S WHAT I CALL SEARCHING FOR YOUR ROOTS.
AAH!

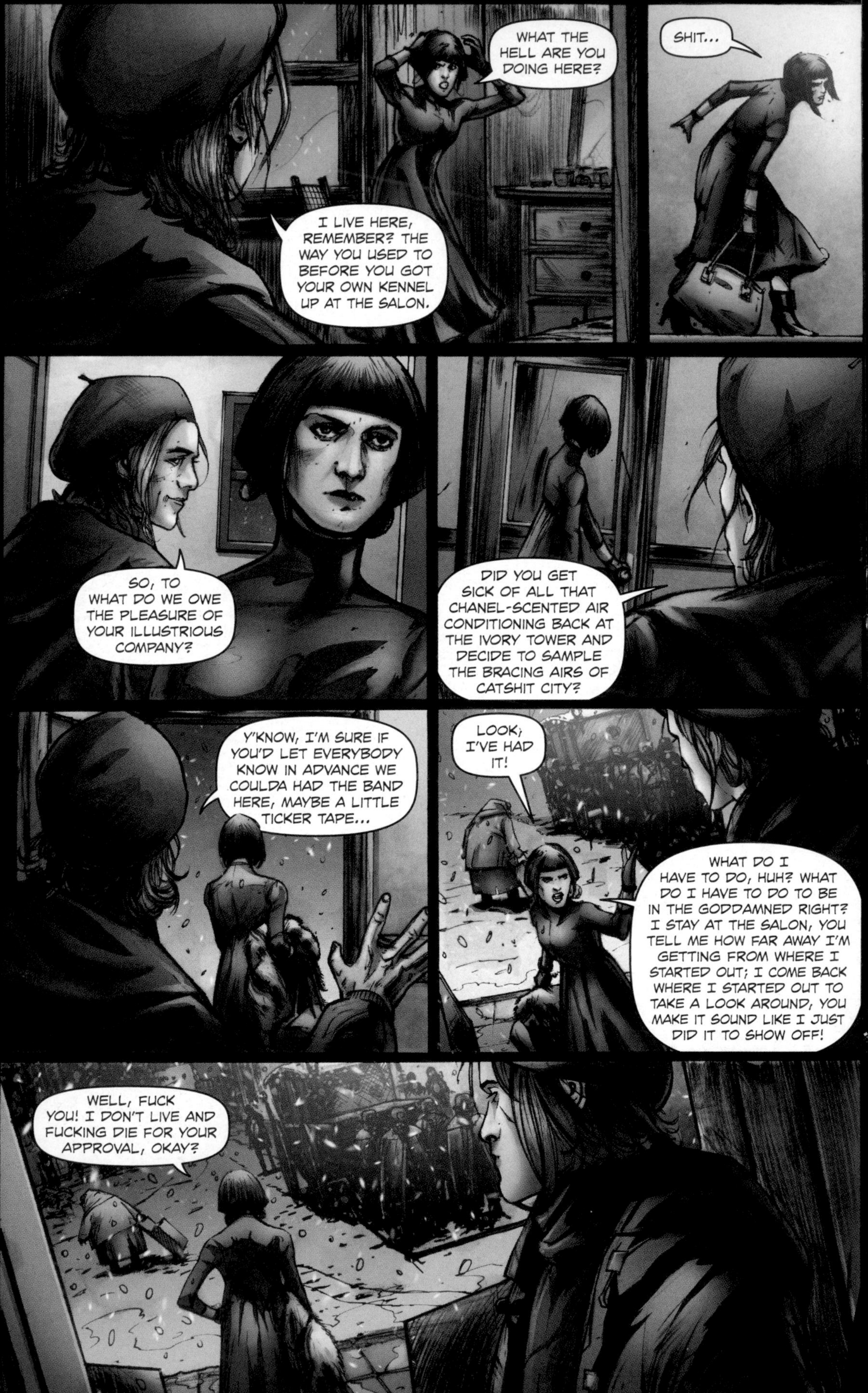
WHAT THE HELL ARE YOU DOING HERE?
I LIVE HERE, REMEMBER? THE WAY YOU USED TO BEFORE YOU GOT YOUR OWN KENNEL UP AT THE SALON.
SHIT...
SO, TO WHAT DO WE OWE THE PLEASURE OF YOUR ILLUSTRIOUS COMPANY?
DID YOU GET SICK OF ALL THAT CHANEL-SCENTED AIR CONDITIONING BACK AT THE IVORY TOWER AND DECIDE TO SAMPLE THE BRACING AIRS OF CATSHIT CITY?
Y'KNOW, I'M SURE IF YOU'D LET EVERYBODY KNOW IN ADVANCE WE COULDA HAD THE BAND HERE, MAYBE A LITTLE TICKER TAPE...
LOOK; I'VE HAD IT!
WHAT DO I HAVE TO DO, HUH? WHAT DO I HAVE TO DO TO BE IN THE GODDAMNED RIGHT? I STAY AT THE SALON, YOU TELL ME HOW FAR AWAY I'M GETTING FROM WHERE I STARTED OUT; I COME BACK WHERE I STARTED OUT TO TAKE A LOOK AROUND, YOU MAKE IT SOUND LIKE I JUST DID IT TO SHOW OFF!
WELL, FUCK YOU! I DON'T LIVE AND FUCKING DIE FOR YOUR APPROVAL, OKAY?

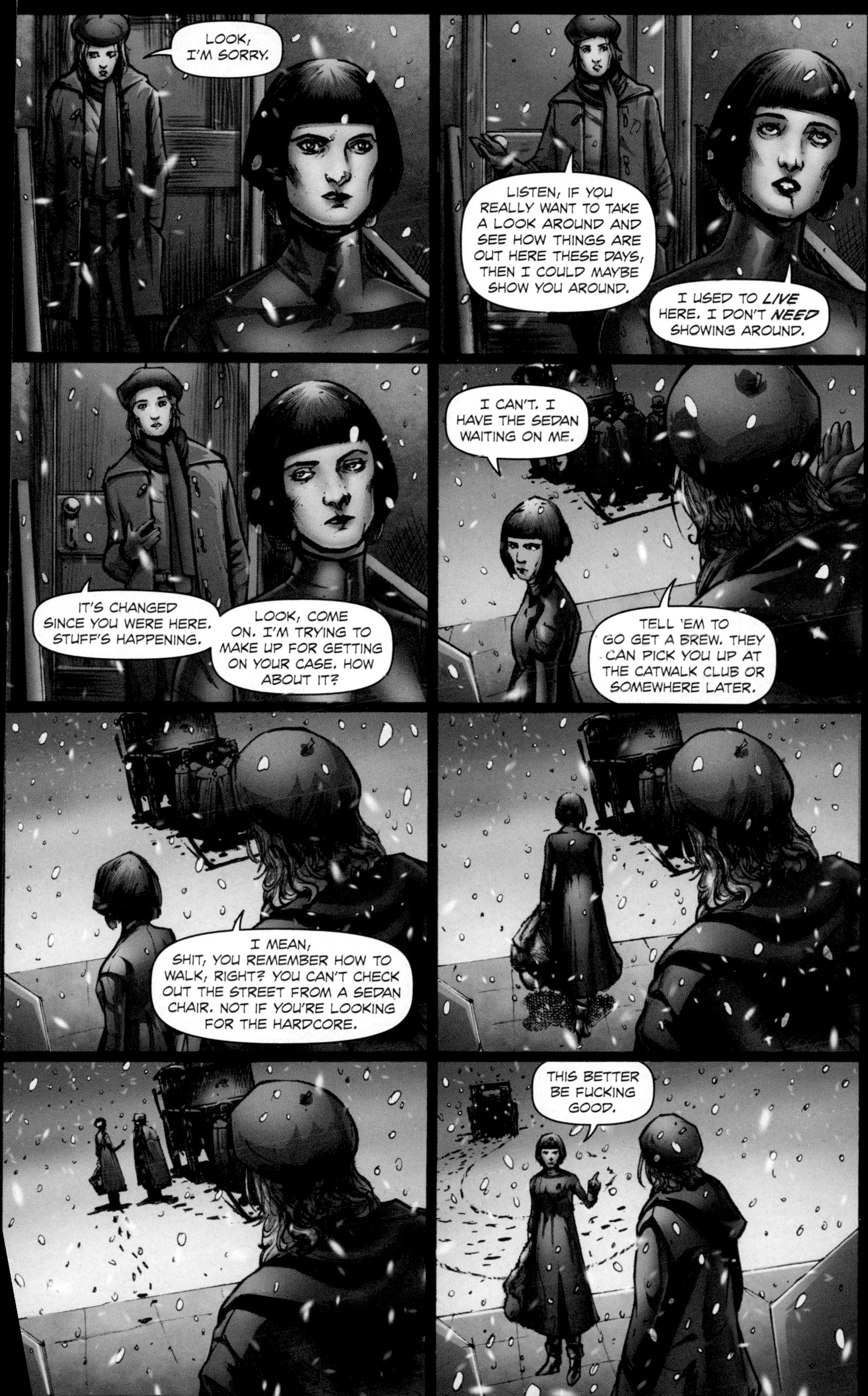
LOOK, I'M SORRY.
LISTEN, IF YOU REALLY WANT TO TAKE A LOOK AROUND AND SEE HOW THINGS ARE OUT HERE THESE DAYS, THEN I COULD MAYBE SHOW YOU AROUND.
I USED TO *LIVE* HERE. I DON'T *NEED* SHOWING AROUND.
IT'S CHANGED SINCE YOU WERE HERE. STUFF'S HAPPENING.
LOOK, COME ON. I'M TRYING TO MAKE UP FOR GETTING ON YOUR CASE. HOW ABOUT IT?
I CAN'T. I HAVE THE SEDAN WAITING ON ME.
TELL 'EM TO GO GET A BREW. THEY CAN PICK YOU UP AT THE CATWALK CLUB OR SOMEWHERE LATER.
I MEAN, SHIT, YOU REMEMBER HOW TO WALK, RIGHT? YOU CAN'T CHECK OUT THE STREET FROM A SEDAN CHAIR. NOT IF YOU'RE LOOKING FOR THE HARDCORE.
THIS BETTER BE FUCKING GOOD.

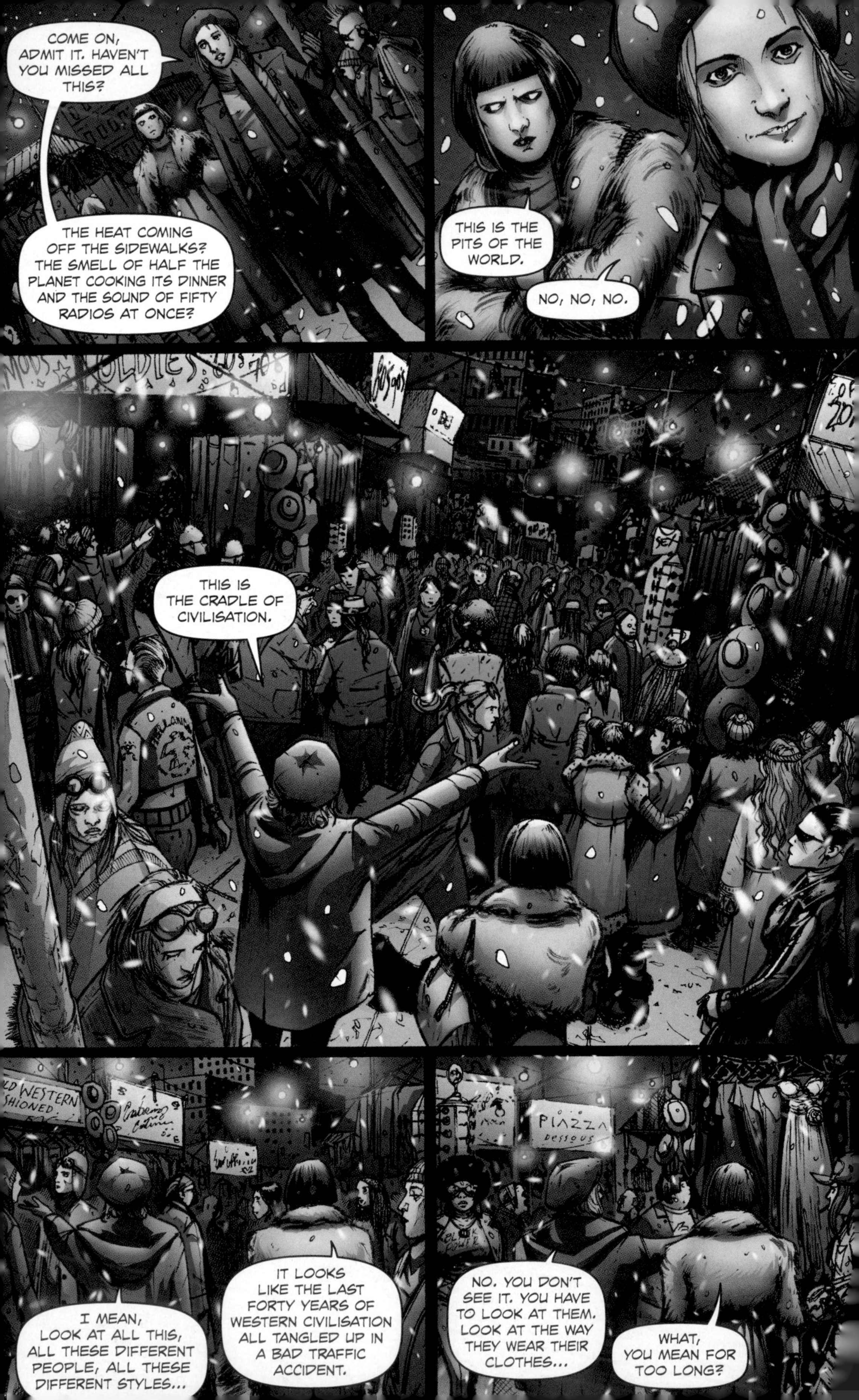
COME ON, ADMIT IT. HAVEN'T YOU MISSED ALL THIS?
THE HEAT COMING OFF THE SIDEWALKS? THE SMELL OF HALF THE PLANET COOKING ITS DINNER AND THE SOUND OF FIFTY RADIOS AT ONCE?
THIS IS THE PITS OF THE WORLD.
NO, NO, NO.
MODS
OLDIES
THIS IS THE CRADLE OF CIVILISATION.
WESTERN
PIAZZA
DESSOUS
I MEAN, LOOK AT ALL THIS, ALL THESE DIFFERENT PEOPLE, ALL THESE DIFFERENT STYLES...
IT LOOKS LIKE THE LAST FORTY YEARS OF WESTERN CIVILISATION ALL TANGLED UP IN A BAD TRAFFIC ACCIDENT.
NO. YOU DON'T SEE IT. YOU HAVE TO LOOK AT THEM. LOOK AT THE WAY THEY WEAR THEIR CLOTHES...
WHAT, YOU MEAN FOR TOO LONG?

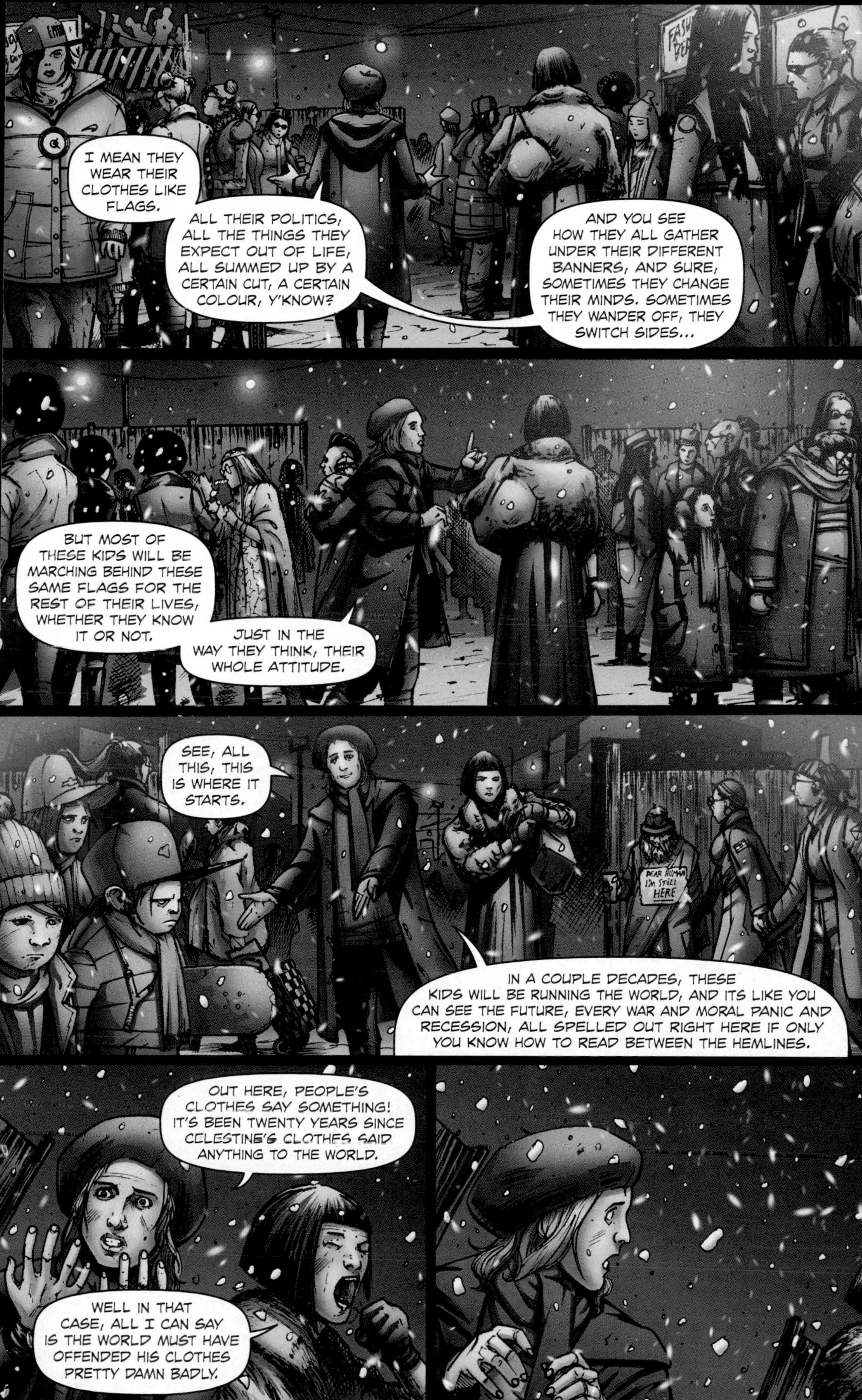
I MEAN THEY WEAR THEIR CLOTHES LIKE FLAGS.
ALL THEIR POLITICS, ALL THE THINGS THEY EXPECT OUT OF LIFE, ALL SUMMED UP BY A CERTAIN CUT, A CERTAIN COLOUR, Y'KNOW?
AND YOU SEE HOW THEY ALL GATHER UNDER THEIR DIFFERENT BANNERS, AND SURE, SOMETIMES THEY CHANGE THEIR MINDS. SOMETIMES THEY WANDER OFF, THEY SWITCH SIDES...
BUT MOST OF THESE KIDS WILL BE MARCHING BEHIND THESE SAME FLAGS FOR THE REST OF THEIR LIVES, WHETHER THEY KNOW IT OR NOT.
JUST IN THE WAY THEY THINK, THEIR WHOLE ATTITUDE.
SEE, ALL THIS, THIS IS WHERE IT STARTS.
DEAR HUMAN I'M STILL HERE
IN A COUPLE DECADES, THESE KIDS WILL BE RUNNING THE WORLD, AND ITS LIKE YOU CAN SEE THE FUTURE, EVERY WAR AND MORAL PANIC AND RECESSION, ALL SPELLED OUT RIGHT HERE IF ONLY YOU KNOW HOW TO READ BETWEEN THE HEMLINES.
OUT HERE, PEOPLE'S CLOTHES SAY SOMETHING! IT'S BEEN TWENTY YEARS SINCE CELESTINE'S CLOTHES SAID ANYTHING TO THE WORLD.
WELL IN THAT CASE, ALL I CAN SAY IS THE WORLD MUST HAVE OFFENDED HIS CLOTHES PRETTY DAMN BADLY.

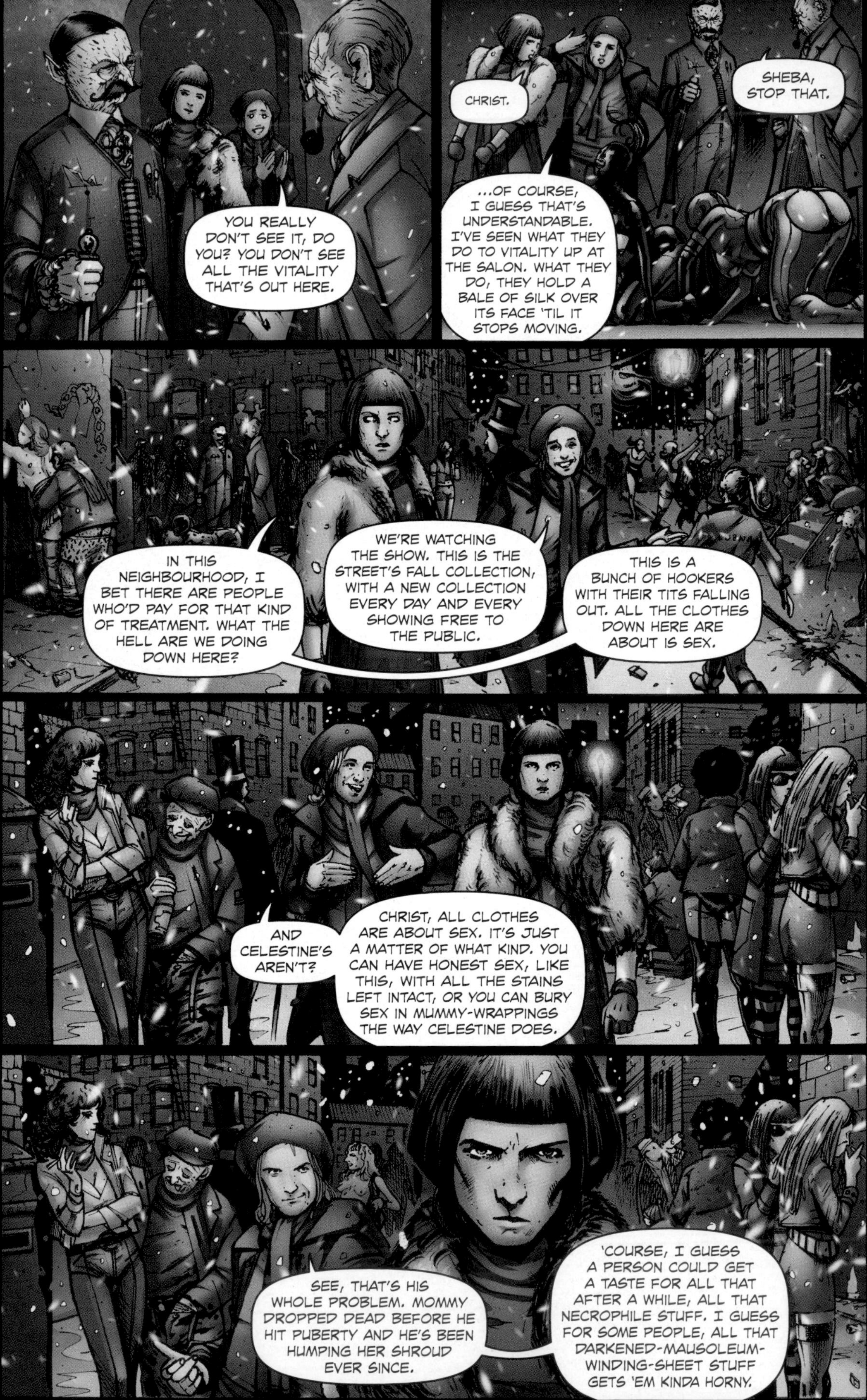
YOU REALLY DON'T SEE IT, DO YOU? YOU DON'T SEE ALL THE VITALITY THAT'S OUT HERE.
CHRIST.
...OF COURSE, I GUESS THAT'S UNDERSTANDABLE. I'VE SEEN WHAT THEY DO TO VITALITY UP AT THE SALON. WHAT THEY DO, THEY HOLD A BALE OF SILK OVER ITS FACE 'TIL IT STOPS MOVING.
SHEBA, STOP THAT.
IN THIS NEIGHBOURHOOD, I BET THERE ARE PEOPLE WHO'D PAY FOR THAT KIND OF TREATMENT. WHAT THE HELL ARE WE DOING DOWN HERE?
WE'RE WATCHING THE SHOW. THIS IS THE STREET'S FALL COLLECTION, WITH A NEW COLLECTION EVERY DAY AND EVERY SHOWING FREE TO THE PUBLIC.
THIS IS A BUNCH OF HOOKERS WITH THEIR TITS FALLING OUT. ALL THE CLOTHES DOWN HERE ARE ABOUT IS SEX.
AND CELESTINE'S AREN'T?
CHRIST, ALL CLOTHES ARE ABOUT SEX. IT'S JUST A MATTER OF WHAT KIND. YOU CAN HAVE HONEST SEX, LIKE THIS, WITH ALL THE STAINS LEFT INTACT, OR YOU CAN BURY SEX IN MUMMY-WRAPPINGS THE WAY CELESTINE DOES.
SEE, THAT'S HIS WHOLE PROBLEM. MOMMY DROPPED DEAD BEFORE HE HIT PUBERTY AND HE'S BEEN HUMPING HER SHROUD EVER SINCE.
'COURSE, I GUESS A PERSON COULD GET A TASTE FOR ALL THAT AFTER A WHILE, ALL THAT NECROPHILE STUFF. I GUESS FOR SOME PEOPLE, ALL THAT DARKENED-MAUSOLEUM-WINDING-SHEET STUFF GETS 'EM KINDA HORNY.

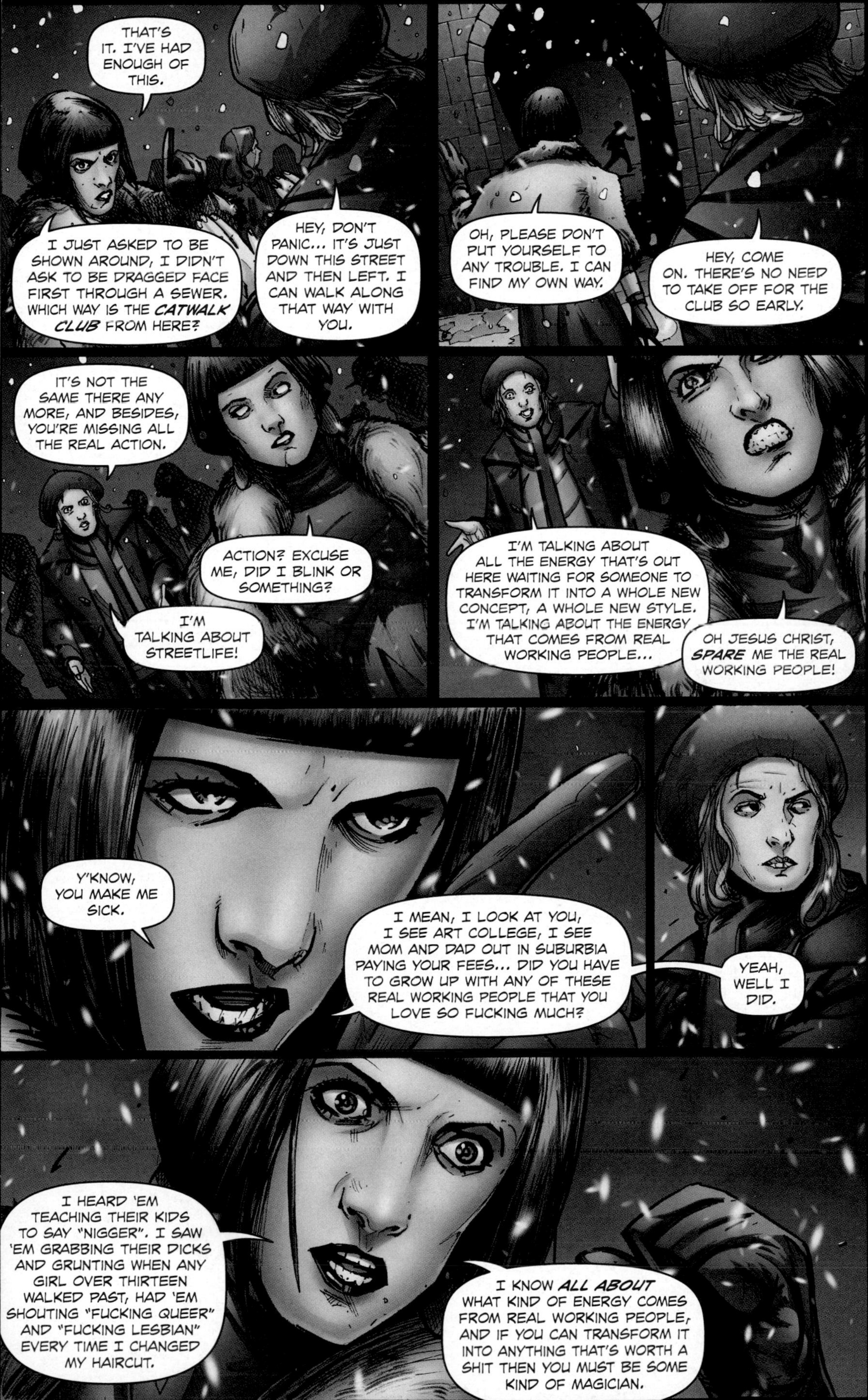
THAT'S IT. I'VE HAD ENOUGH OF THIS.
I JUST ASKED TO BE SHOWN AROUND, I DIDN'T ASK TO BE DRAGGED FACE FIRST THROUGH A SEWER. WHICH WAY IS THE *CATWALK CLUB* FROM HERE?
HEY, DON'T PANIC... IT'S JUST DOWN THIS STREET AND THEN LEFT. I CAN WALK ALONG THAT WAY WITH YOU.
OH, PLEASE DON'T PUT YOURSELF TO ANY TROUBLE. I CAN FIND MY OWN WAY.
HEY, COME ON. THERE'S NO NEED TO TAKE OFF FOR THE CLUB SO EARLY.
IT'S NOT THE SAME THERE ANY MORE, AND BESIDES, YOU'RE MISSING ALL THE REAL ACTION.
ACTION? EXCUSE ME, DID I BLINK OR SOMETHING?
I'M TALKING ABOUT STREETLIFE!
I'M TALKING ABOUT ALL THE ENERGY THAT'S OUT HERE WAITING FOR SOMEONE TO TRANSFORM IT INTO A WHOLE NEW CONCEPT, A WHOLE NEW STYLE. I'M TALKING ABOUT THE ENERGY THAT COMES FROM REAL WORKING PEOPLE...
OH JESUS CHRIST, *SPARE* ME THE REAL WORKING PEOPLE!
Y'KNOW, YOU MAKE ME SICK.
I MEAN, I LOOK AT YOU, I SEE ART COLLEGE, I SEE MOM AND DAD OUT IN SUBURBIA PAYING YOUR FEES... DID YOU HAVE TO GROW UP WITH ANY OF THESE REAL WORKING PEOPLE THAT YOU LOVE SO FUCKING MUCH?
YEAH, WELL I DID.
I HEARD 'EM TEACHING THEIR KIDS TO SAY "NIGGER". I SAW 'EM GRABBING THEIR DICKS AND GRUNTING WHEN ANY GIRL OVER THIRTEEN WALKED PAST, HAD 'EM SHOUTING "FUCKING QUEER" AND "FUCKING LESBIAN" EVERY TIME I CHANGED MY HAIRCUT.
I KNOW *ALL ABOUT* WHAT KIND OF ENERGY COMES FROM REAL WORKING PEOPLE, AND IF YOU CAN TRANSFORM IT INTO ANYTHING THAT'S WORTH A SHIT THEN YOU MUST BE SOME KIND OF MAGICIAN.

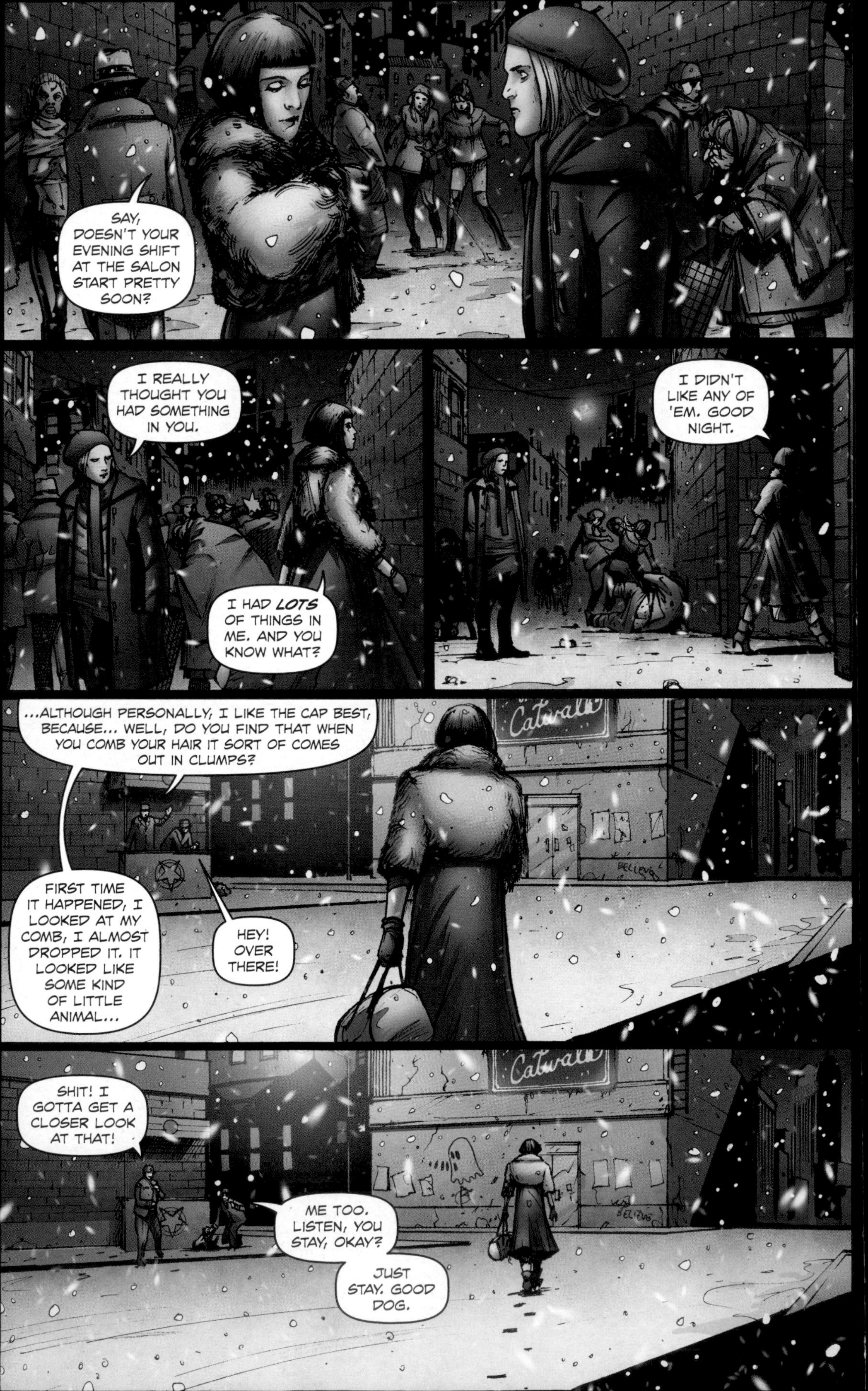
SAY, DOESN'T YOUR EVENING SHIFT AT THE SALON START PRETTY SOON?
I REALLY THOUGHT YOU HAD SOMETHING IN YOU.
I HAD LOTS OF THINGS IN ME. AND YOU KNOW WHAT?
I DIDN'T LIKE ANY OF 'EM. GOOD NIGHT.
...ALTHOUGH PERSONALLY, I LIKE THE CAP BEST, BECAUSE... WELL, DO YOU FIND THAT WHEN YOU COMB YOUR HAIR IT SORT OF COMES OUT IN CLUMPS?
FIRST TIME IT HAPPENED, I LOOKED AT MY COMB, I ALMOST DROPPED IT. IT LOOKED LIKE SOME KIND OF LITTLE ANIMAL...
HEY! OVER THERE!
Catwalk
SHIT! I GOTTA GET A CLOSER LOOK AT THAT!
ME TOO. LISTEN, YOU STAY, OKAY?
JUST STAY. GOOD DOG.

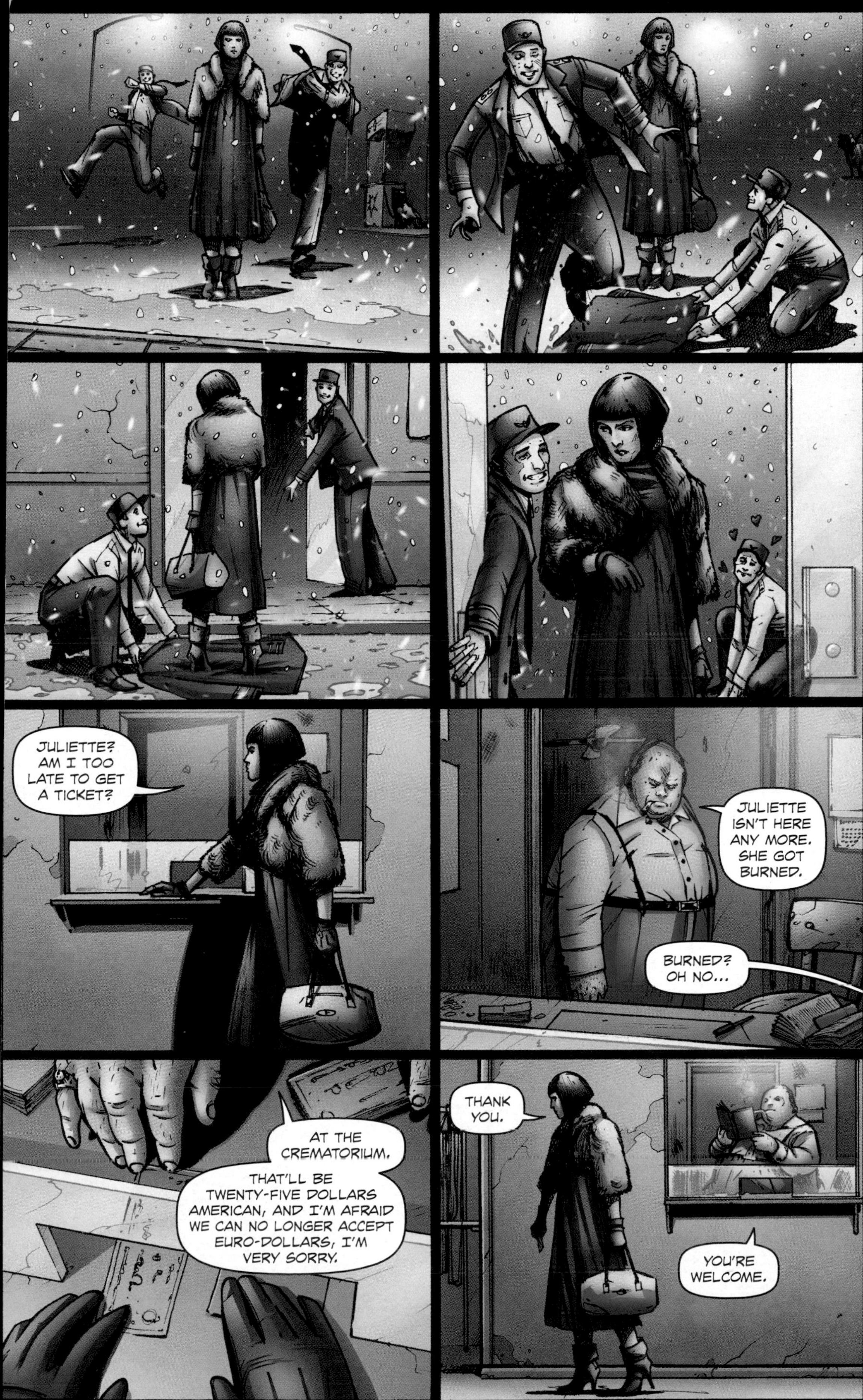
JULIETTE? AM I TOO LATE TO GET A TICKET?
JULIETTE ISN'T HERE ANY MORE. SHE GOT BURNED.
BURNED? OH NO...
AT THE CREMATORIUM.
THAT'LL BE TWENTY-FIVE DOLLARS AMERICAN, AND I'M AFRAID WE CAN NO LONGER ACCEPT EURO-DOLLARS, I'M VERY SORRY.
THANK YOU.
YOU'RE WELCOME.

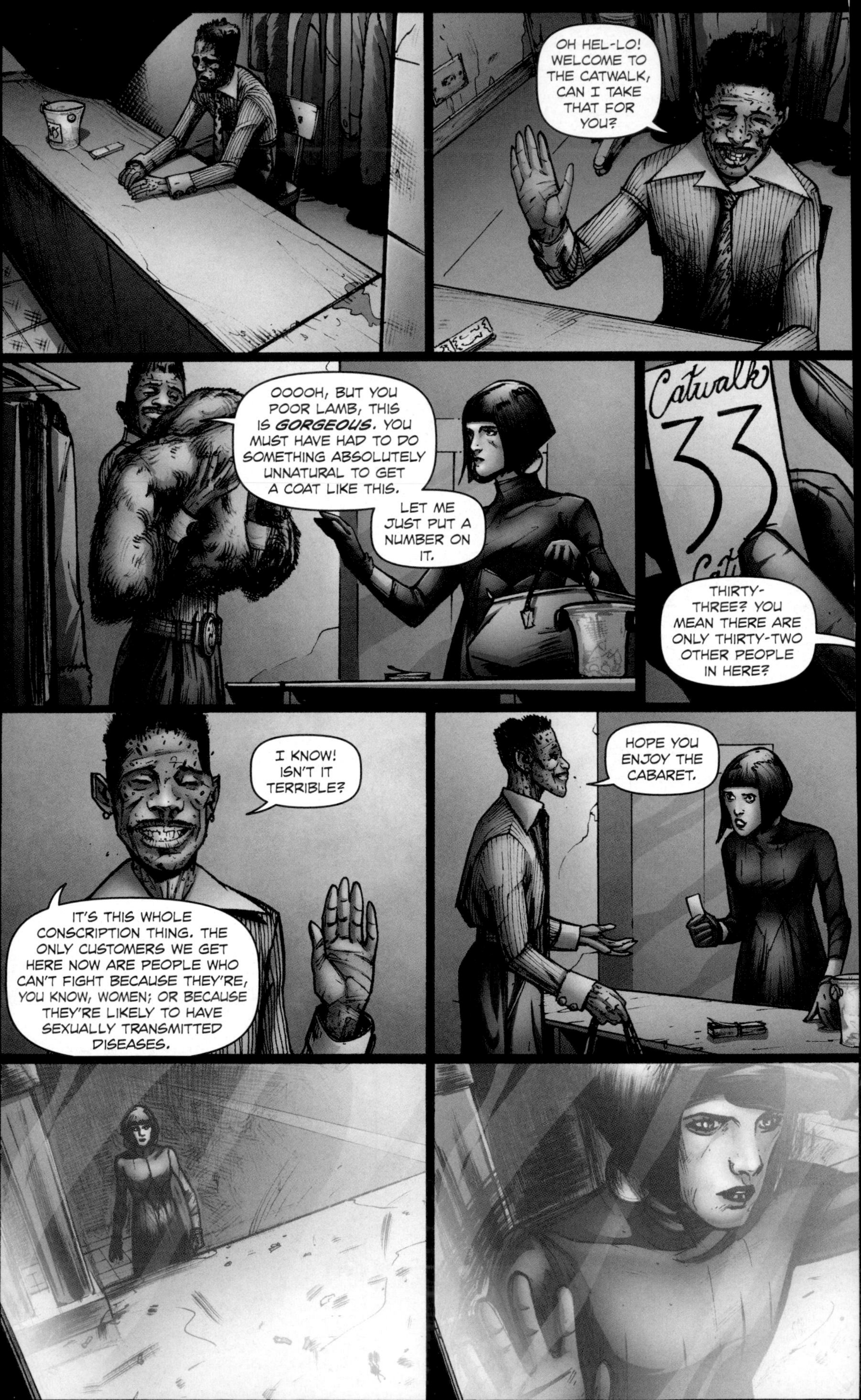
OH HEL-LO! WELCOME TO THE CATWALK, CAN I TAKE THAT FOR YOU?
OOOOH, BUT YOU POOR LAMB, THIS IS GORGEOUS. YOU MUST HAVE HAD TO DO SOMETHING ABSOLUTELY UNNATURAL TO GET A COAT LIKE THIS.
LET ME JUST PUT A NUMBER ON IT.
Catwalk 33
THIRTY-THREE? YOU MEAN THERE ARE ONLY THIRTY-TWO OTHER PEOPLE IN HERE?
I KNOW! ISN'T IT TERRIBLE?
IT'S THIS WHOLE CONSCRIPTION THING. THE ONLY CUSTOMERS WE GET HERE NOW ARE PEOPLE WHO CAN'T FIGHT BECAUSE THEY'RE, YOU KNOW, WOMEN; OR BECAUSE THEY'RE LIKELY TO HAVE SEXUALLY TRANSMITTED DISEASES.
HOPE YOU ENJOY THE CABARET.

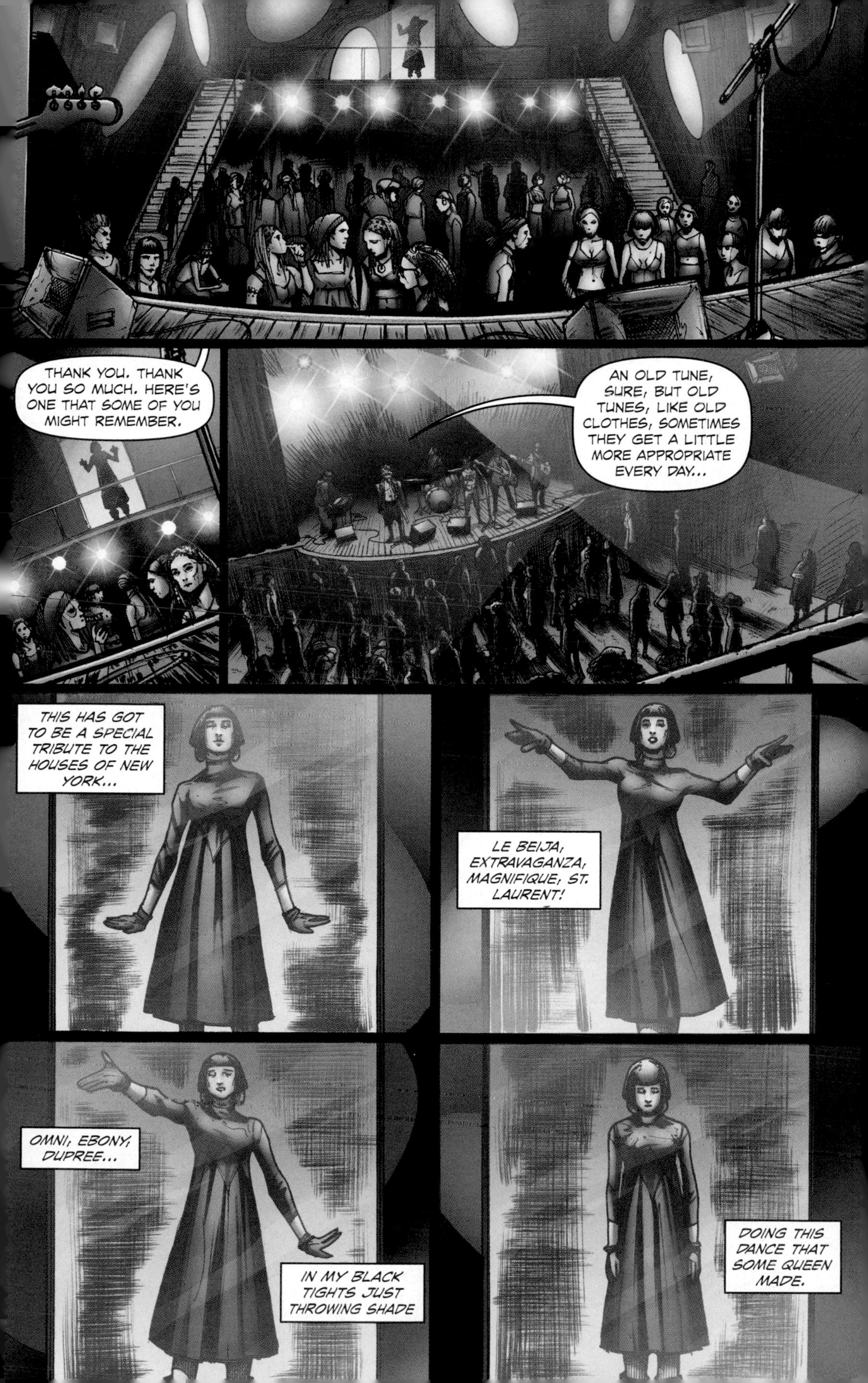
THANK YOU. THANK YOU SO MUCH. HERE'S ONE THAT SOME OF YOU MIGHT REMEMBER.
AN OLD TUNE, SURE, BUT OLD TUNES, LIKE OLD CLOTHES, SOMETIMES THEY GET A LITTLE MORE APPROPRIATE EVERY DAY...
THIS HAS GOT TO BE A SPECIAL TRIBUTE TO THE HOUSES OF NEW YORK...
LE BEIJA, EXTRAVAGANZA, MAGNIFIQUE, ST. LAURENT!
OMNI, EBONY, DUPREE...
IN MY BLACK TIGHTS JUST THROWING SHADE
DOING THIS DANCE THAT SOME QUEEN MADE.

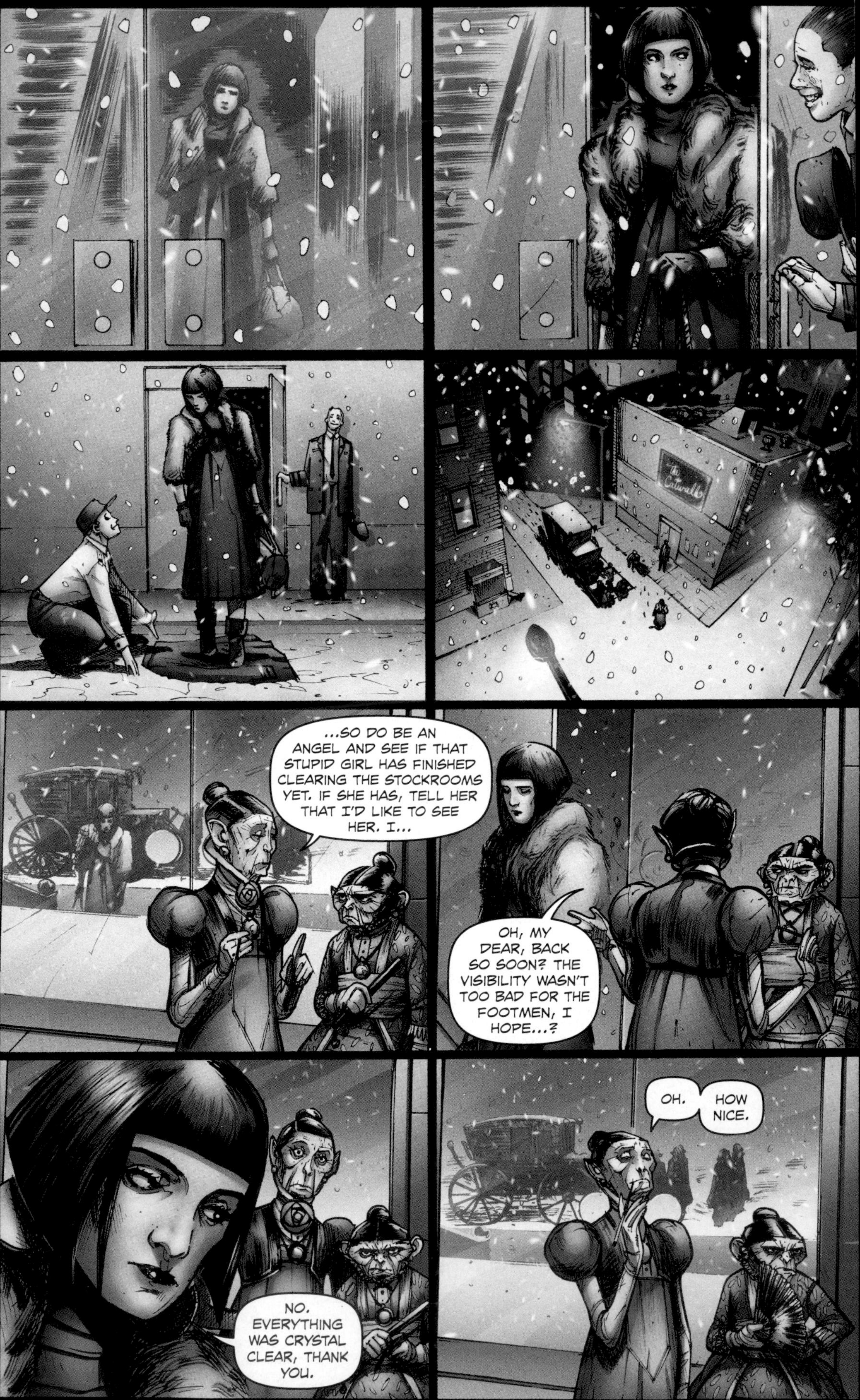
...SO DO BE AN ANGEL AND SEE IF THAT STUPID GIRL HAS FINISHED CLEARING THE STOCKROOMS YET. IF SHE HAS, TELL HER THAT I'D LIKE TO SEE HER. I...
OH, MY DEAR, BACK SO SOON? THE VISIBILITY WASN'T TOO BAD FOR THE FOOTMEN, I HOPE...?
NO. EVERYTHING WAS CRYSTAL CLEAR, THANK YOU.
OH.
HOW NICE.

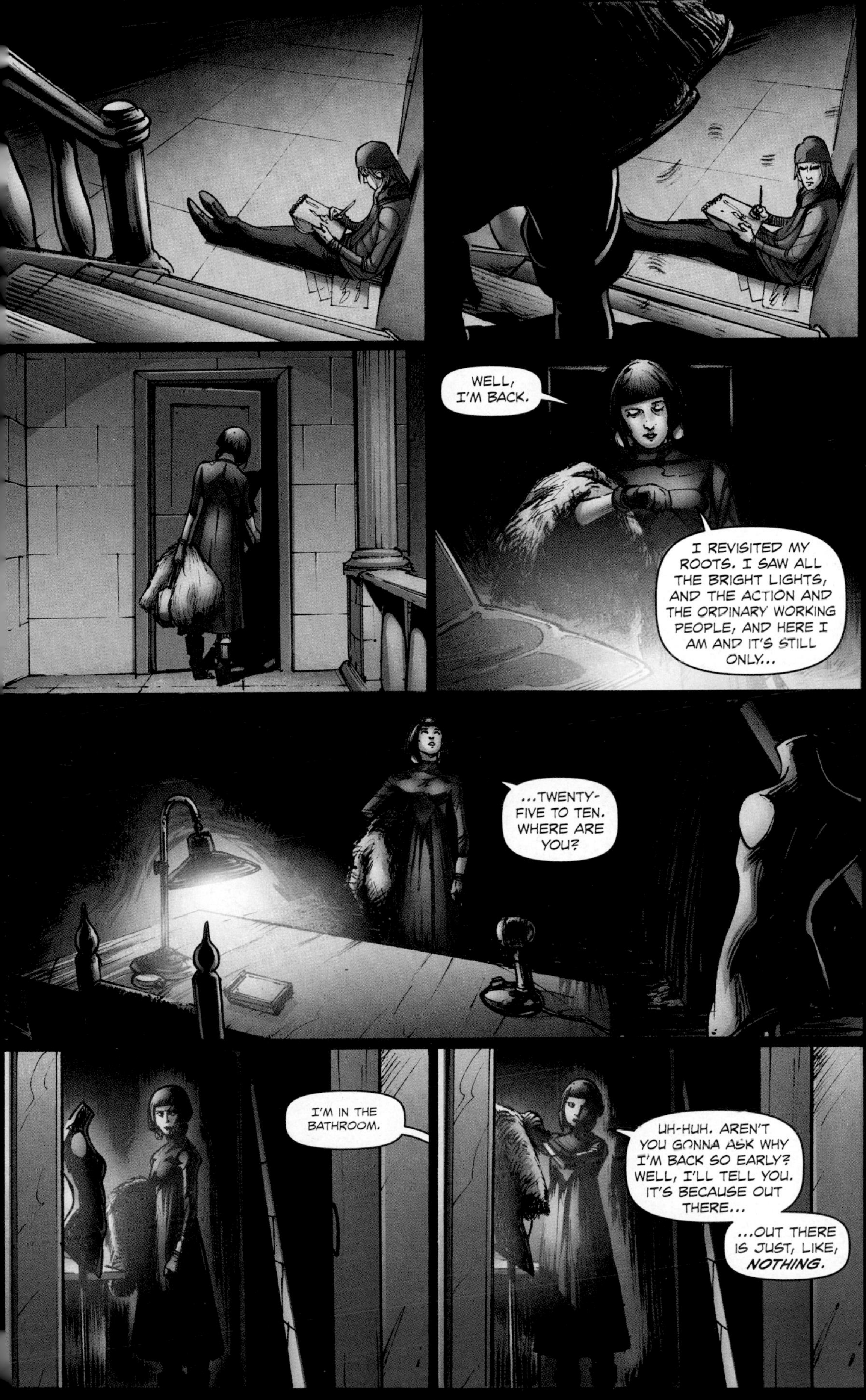
WELL, I'M BACK.
I REVISITED MY ROOTS. I SAW ALL THE BRIGHT LIGHTS, AND THE ACTION AND THE ORDINARY WORKING PEOPLE, AND HERE I AM AND IT'S STILL ONLY...
...TWENTY-FIVE TO TEN. WHERE ARE YOU?
I'M IN THE BATHROOM.
UH-HUH. AREN'T YOU GONNA ASK WHY I'M BACK SO EARLY? WELL, I'LL TELL YOU. IT'S BECAUSE OUT THERE...
...OUT THERE IS JUST, LIKE, *NOTHING*.

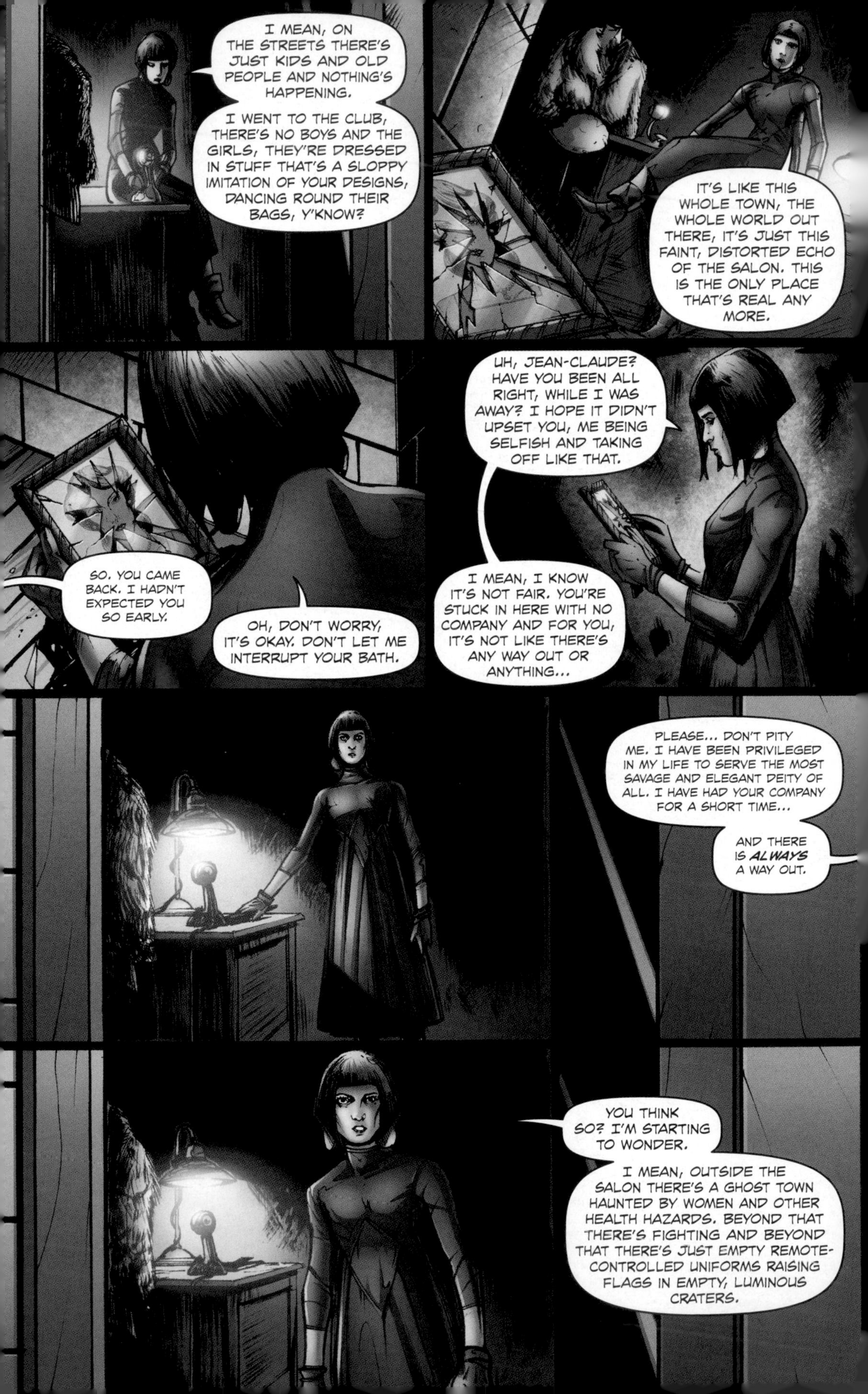
I MEAN, ON THE STREETS THERE'S JUST KIDS AND OLD PEOPLE AND NOTHING'S HAPPENING.
I WENT TO THE CLUB, THERE'S NO BOYS AND THE GIRLS, THEY'RE DRESSED IN STUFF THAT'S A SLOPPY IMITATION OF YOUR DESIGNS, DANCING ROUND THEIR BAGS, Y'KNOW?
IT'S LIKE THIS WHOLE TOWN, THE WHOLE WORLD OUT THERE, IT'S JUST THIS FAINT, DISTORTED ECHO OF THE SALON. THIS IS THE ONLY PLACE THAT'S REAL ANY MORE.
SO. YOU CAME BACK. I HADN'T EXPECTED YOU SO EARLY.
OH, DON'T WORRY, IT'S OKAY. DON'T LET ME INTERRUPT YOUR BATH.
UH, JEAN-CLAUDE? HAVE YOU BEEN ALL RIGHT, WHILE I WAS AWAY? I HOPE IT DIDN'T UPSET YOU, ME BEING SELFISH AND TAKING OFF LIKE THAT.
I MEAN, I KNOW IT'S NOT FAIR. YOU'RE STUCK IN HERE WITH NO COMPANY AND FOR YOU, IT'S NOT LIKE THERE'S ANY WAY OUT OR ANYTHING...
PLEASE... DON'T PITY ME. I HAVE BEEN PRIVILEGED IN MY LIFE TO SERVE THE MOST SAVAGE AND ELEGANT DEITY OF ALL. I HAVE HAD YOUR COMPANY FOR A SHORT TIME...
AND THERE IS ***ALWAYS*** A WAY OUT.
YOU THINK SO? I'M STARTING TO WONDER.
I MEAN, OUTSIDE THE SALON THERE'S A GHOST TOWN HAUNTED BY WOMEN AND OTHER HEALTH HAZARDS. BEYOND THAT THERE'S FIGHTING AND BEYOND THAT THERE'S JUST EMPTY REMOTE-CONTROLLED UNIFORMS RAISING FLAGS IN EMPTY, LUMINOUS CRATERS.

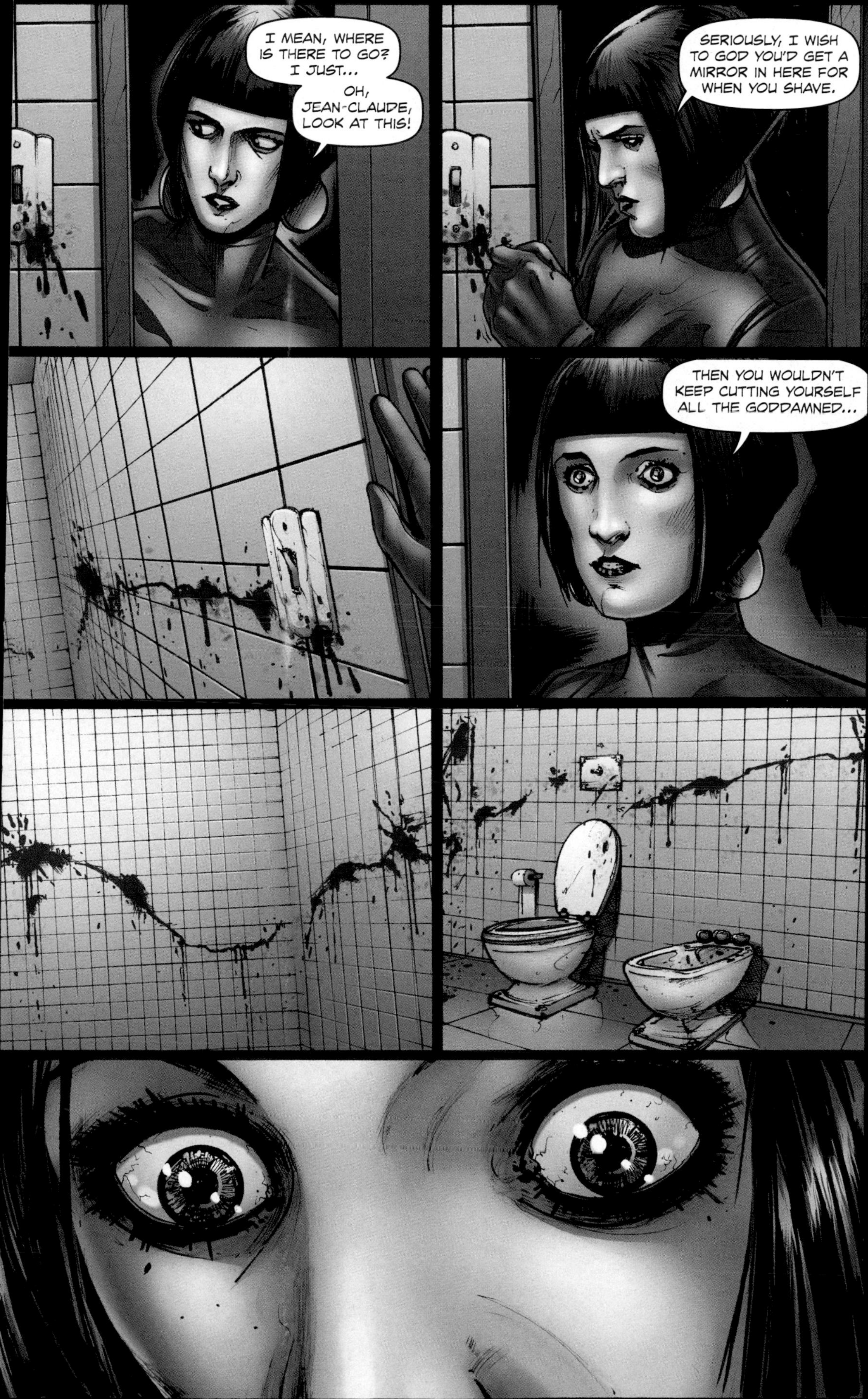
I MEAN, WHERE IS THERE TO GO? I JUST...
OH, JEAN-CLAUDE, LOOK AT THIS!
SERIOUSLY, I WISH TO GOD YOU'D GET A MIRROR IN HERE FOR WHEN YOU SHAVE.
THEN YOU WOULDN'T KEEP CUTTING YOURSELF ALL THE GODDAMNED...

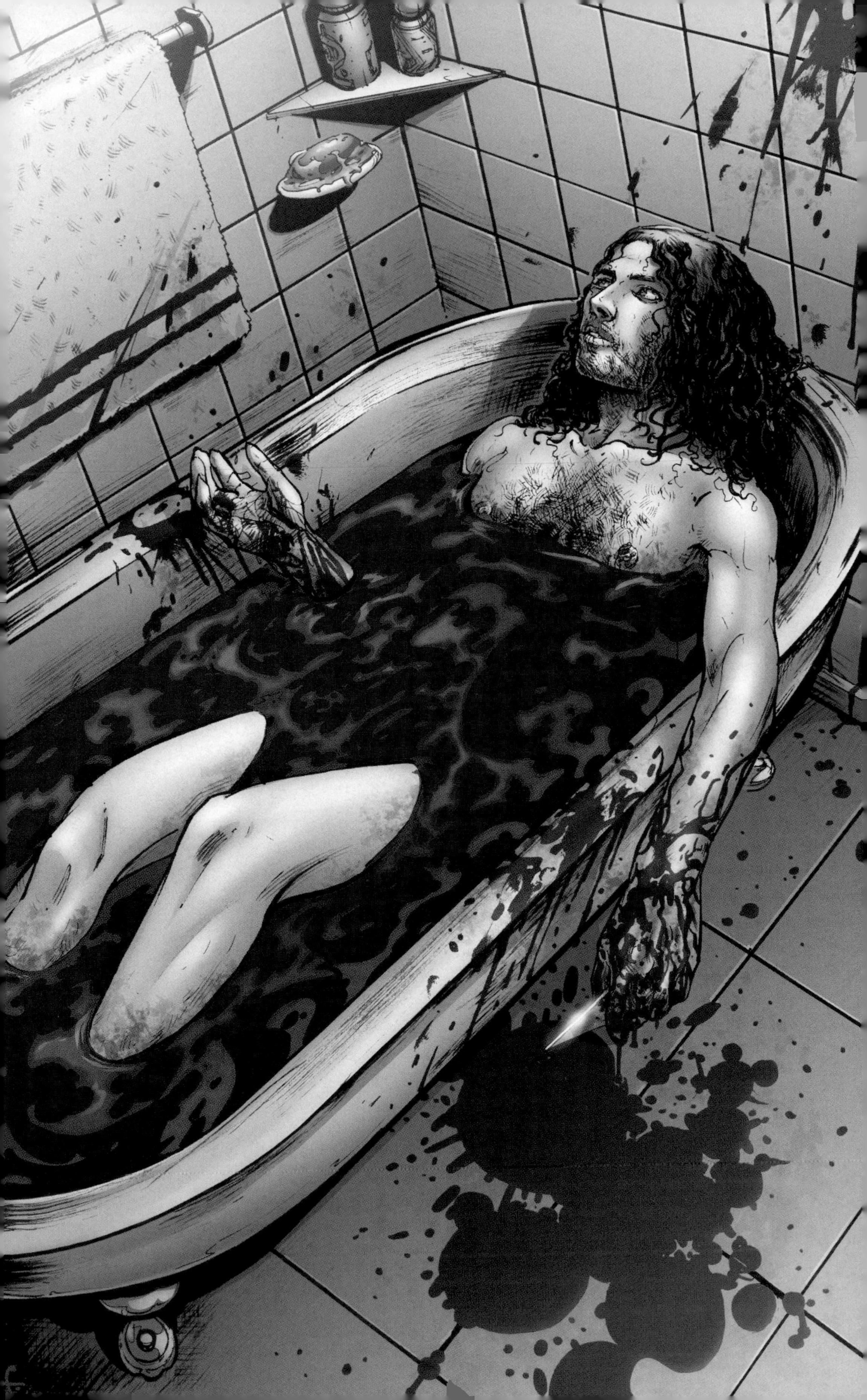

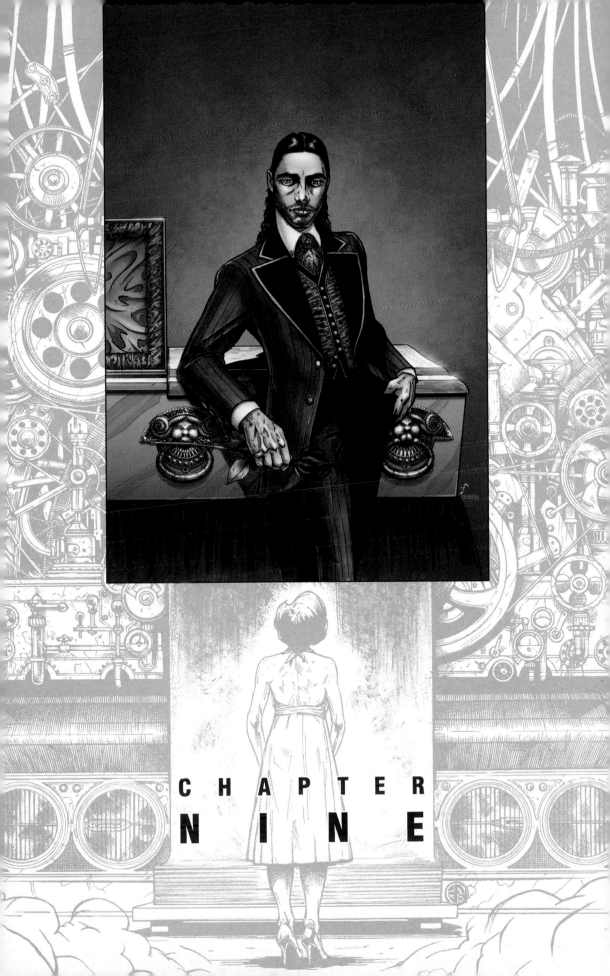

CHAPTER
NINE

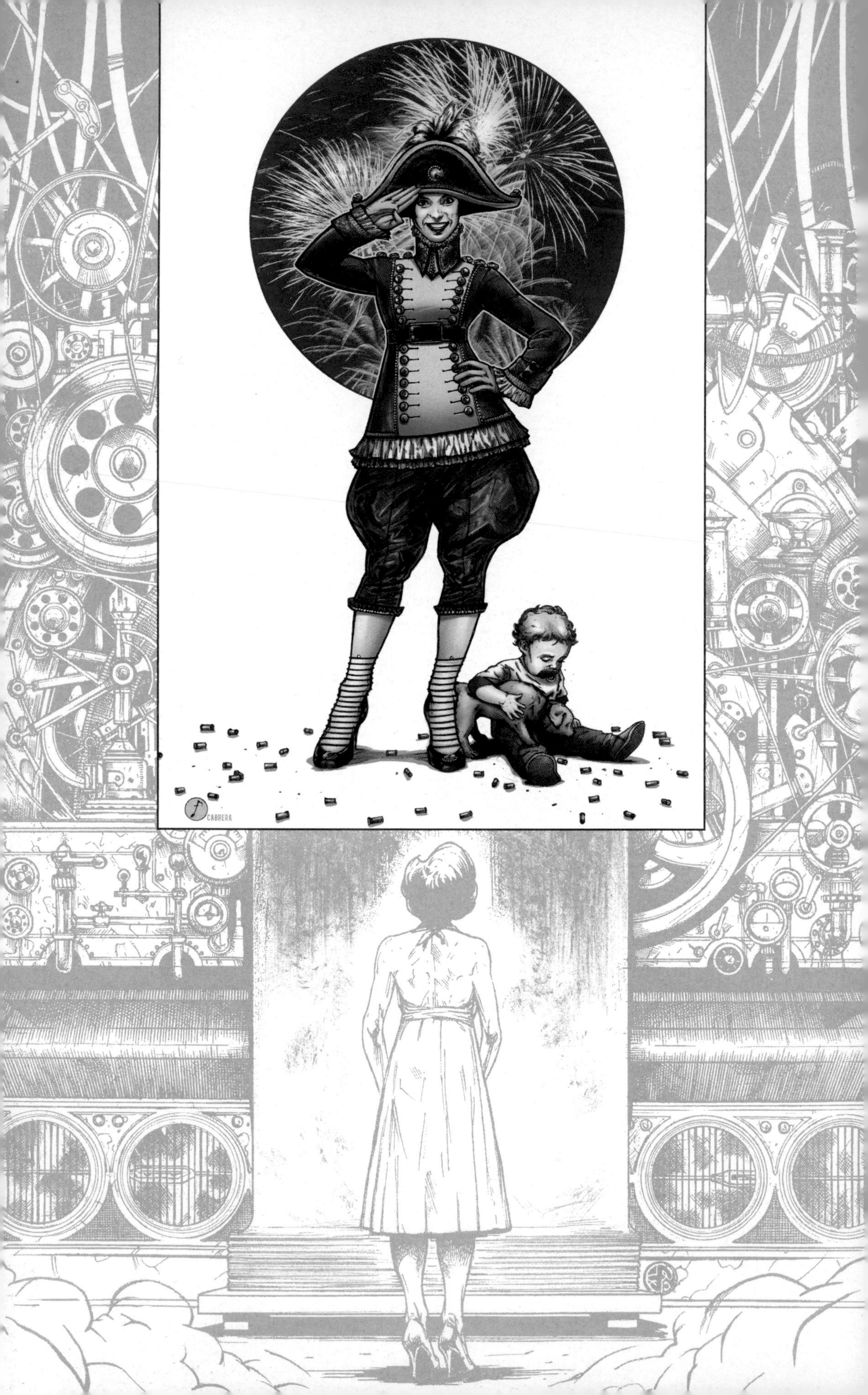
CABRERA

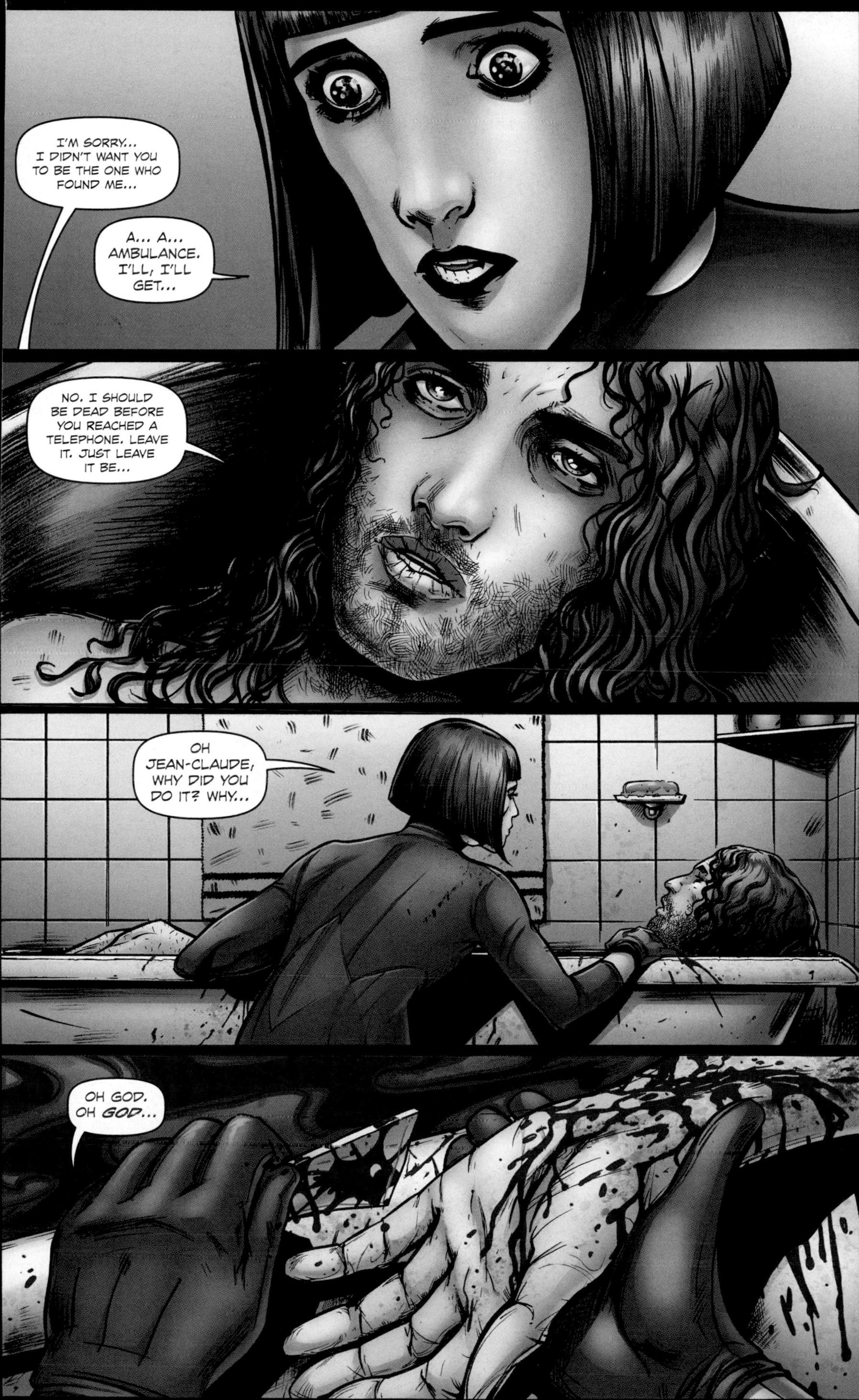
I'M SORRY... I DIDN'T WANT YOU TO BE THE ONE WHO FOUND ME...
A... A... AMBULANCE. I'LL, I'LL GET...
NO. I SHOULD BE DEAD BEFORE YOU REACHED A TELEPHONE. LEAVE IT. JUST LEAVE IT BE...
OH JEAN-CLAUDE, WHY DID YOU DO IT? WHY...
OH GOD. OH GOD...

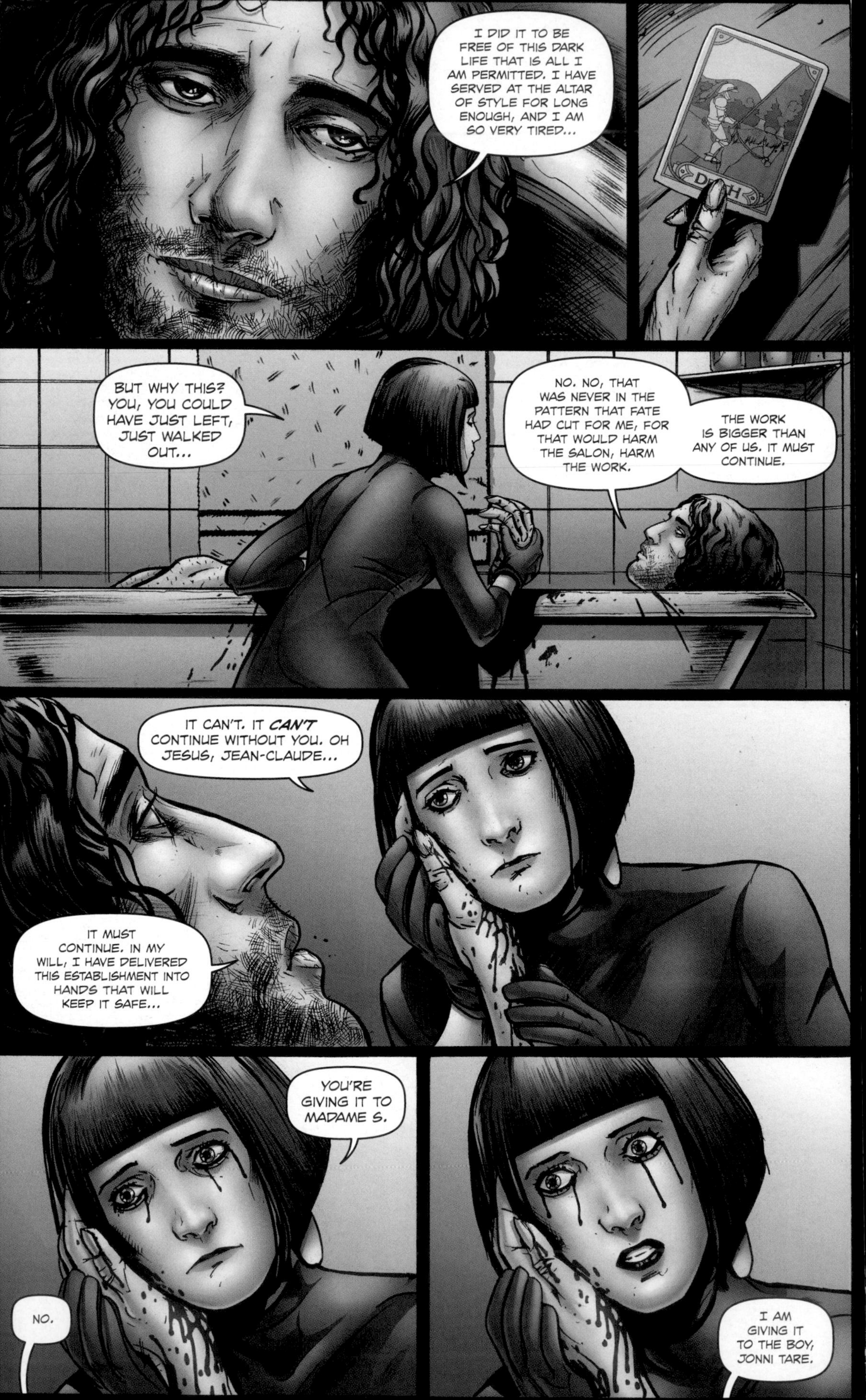
I DID IT TO BE FREE OF THIS DARK LIFE THAT IS ALL I AM PERMITTED. I HAVE SERVED AT THE ALTAR OF STYLE FOR LONG ENOUGH, AND I AM SO VERY TIRED...
BUT WHY THIS? YOU, YOU COULD HAVE JUST LEFT, JUST WALKED OUT...
NO. NO, THAT WAS NEVER IN THE PATTERN THAT FATE HAD CUT FOR ME, FOR THAT WOULD HARM THE SALON, HARM THE WORK.
THE WORK IS BIGGER THAN ANY OF US. IT MUST CONTINUE.
IT CAN'T. IT *CAN'T* CONTINUE WITHOUT YOU. OH JESUS, JEAN-CLAUDE...
IT MUST CONTINUE. IN MY WILL, I HAVE DELIVERED THIS ESTABLISHMENT INTO HANDS THAT WILL KEEP IT SAFE...
YOU'RE GIVING IT TO MADAME S.
NO.
I AM GIVING IT TO THE BOY, JONNI TARE.

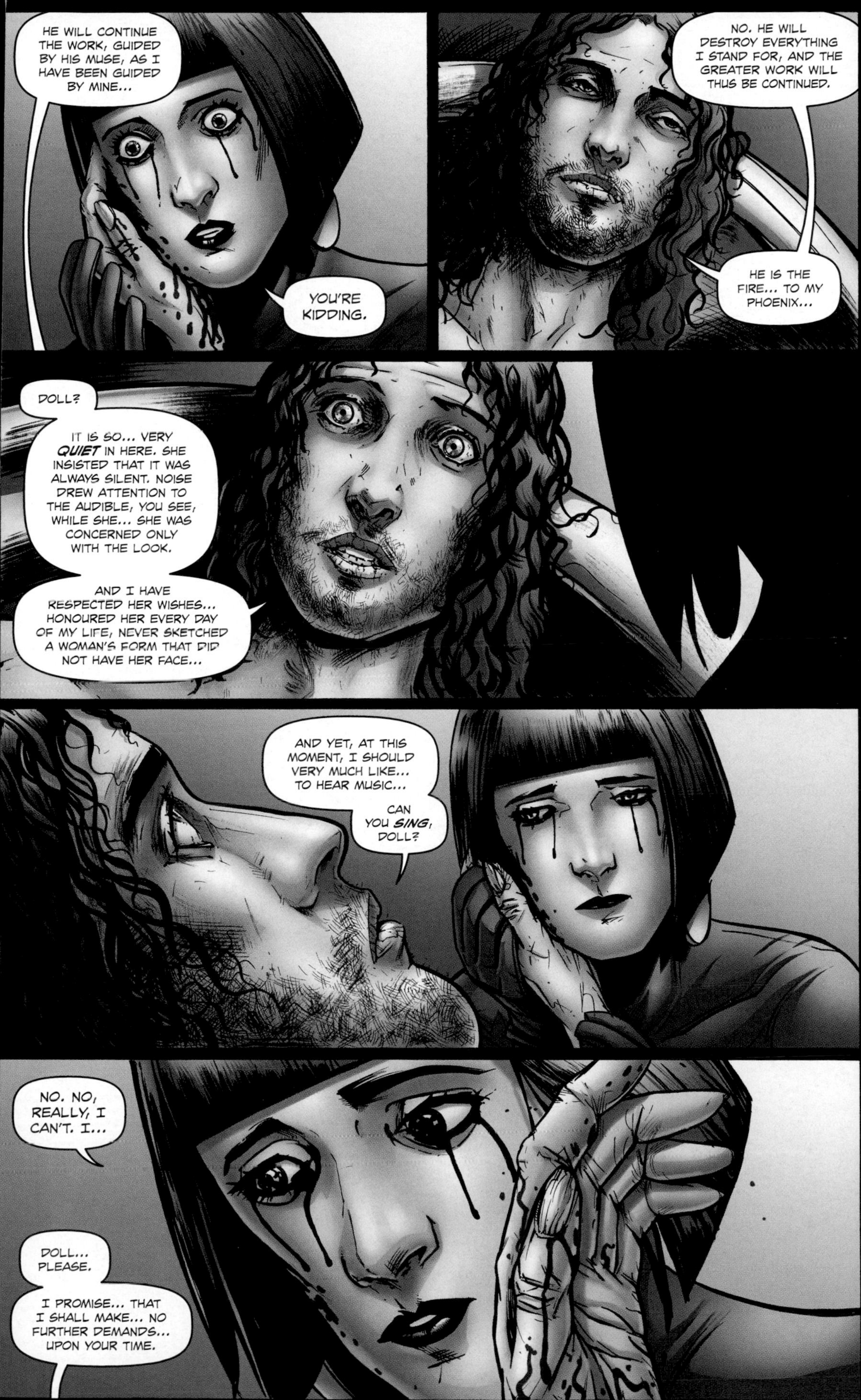
HE WILL CONTINUE THE WORK, GUIDED BY HIS MUSE, AS I HAVE BEEN GUIDED BY MINE...
YOU'RE KIDDING.
NO. HE WILL DESTROY EVERYTHING I STAND FOR, AND THE GREATER WORK WILL THUS BE CONTINUED.
HE IS THE FIRE... TO MY PHOENIX...
DOLL?
IT IS SO... VERY QUIET IN HERE. SHE INSISTED THAT IT WAS ALWAYS SILENT. NOISE DREW ATTENTION TO THE AUDIBLE, YOU SEE, WHILE SHE... SHE WAS CONCERNED ONLY WITH THE LOOK.
AND I HAVE RESPECTED HER WISHES... HONOURED HER EVERY DAY OF MY LIFE, NEVER SKETCHED A WOMAN'S FORM THAT DID NOT HAVE HER FACE...
AND YET, AT THIS MOMENT, I SHOULD VERY MUCH LIKE... TO HEAR MUSIC...
CAN YOU SING, DOLL?
NO. NO, REALLY, I CAN'T. I...
DOLL... PLEASE.
I PROMISE... THAT I SHALL MAKE... NO FURTHER DEMANDS... UPON YOUR TIME.

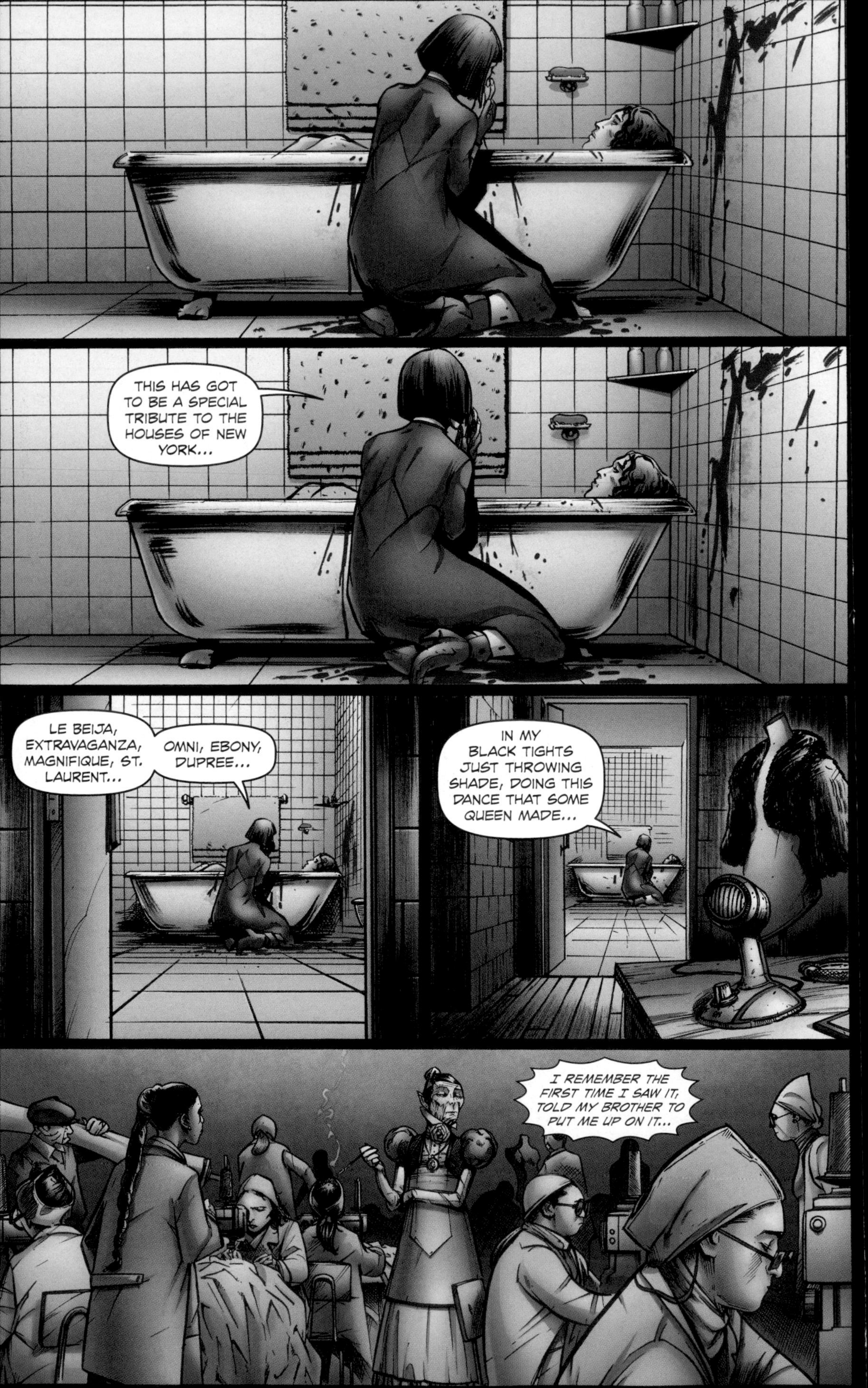
THIS HAS GOT TO BE A SPECIAL TRIBUTE TO THE HOUSES OF NEW YORK...
LE BEIJA, EXTRAVAGANZA, MAGNIFIQUE, ST. LAURENT...
OMNI, EBONY, DUPREE...
IN MY BLACK TIGHTS JUST THROWING SHADE, DOING THIS DANCE THAT SOME QUEEN MADE...
I REMEMBER THE FIRST TIME I SAW IT, TOLD MY BROTHER TO PUT ME UP ON IT...

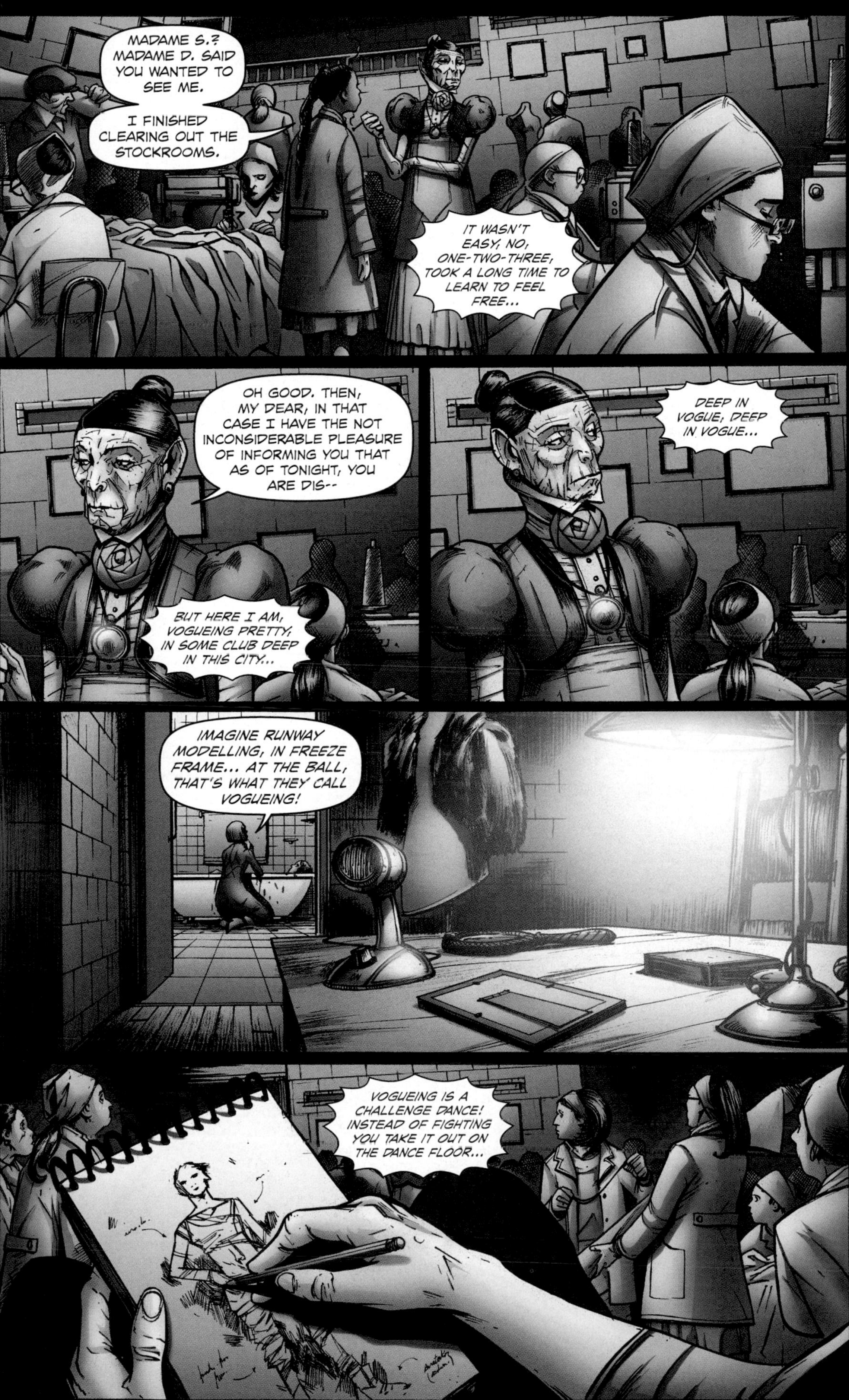
MADAME S.? MADAME D. SAID YOU WANTED TO SEE ME.
I FINISHED CLEARING OUT THE STOCKROOMS.
IT WASN'T EASY, NO, ONE-TWO-THREE, TOOK A LONG TIME TO LEARN TO FEEL FREE...
OH GOOD. THEN, MY DEAR, IN THAT CASE I HAVE THE NOT INCONSIDERABLE PLEASURE OF INFORMING YOU THAT AS OF TONIGHT, YOU ARE DIS--
BUT HERE I AM, VOGUEING PRETTY, IN SOME CLUB DEEP IN THIS CITY...
DEEP IN VOGUE, DEEP IN VOGUE...
IMAGINE RUNWAY MODELLING, IN FREEZE FRAME... AT THE BALL, THAT'S WHAT THEY CALL VOGUEING!
VOGUEING IS A CHALLENGE DANCE! INSTEAD OF FIGHTING YOU TAKE IT OUT ON THE DANCE FLOOR...

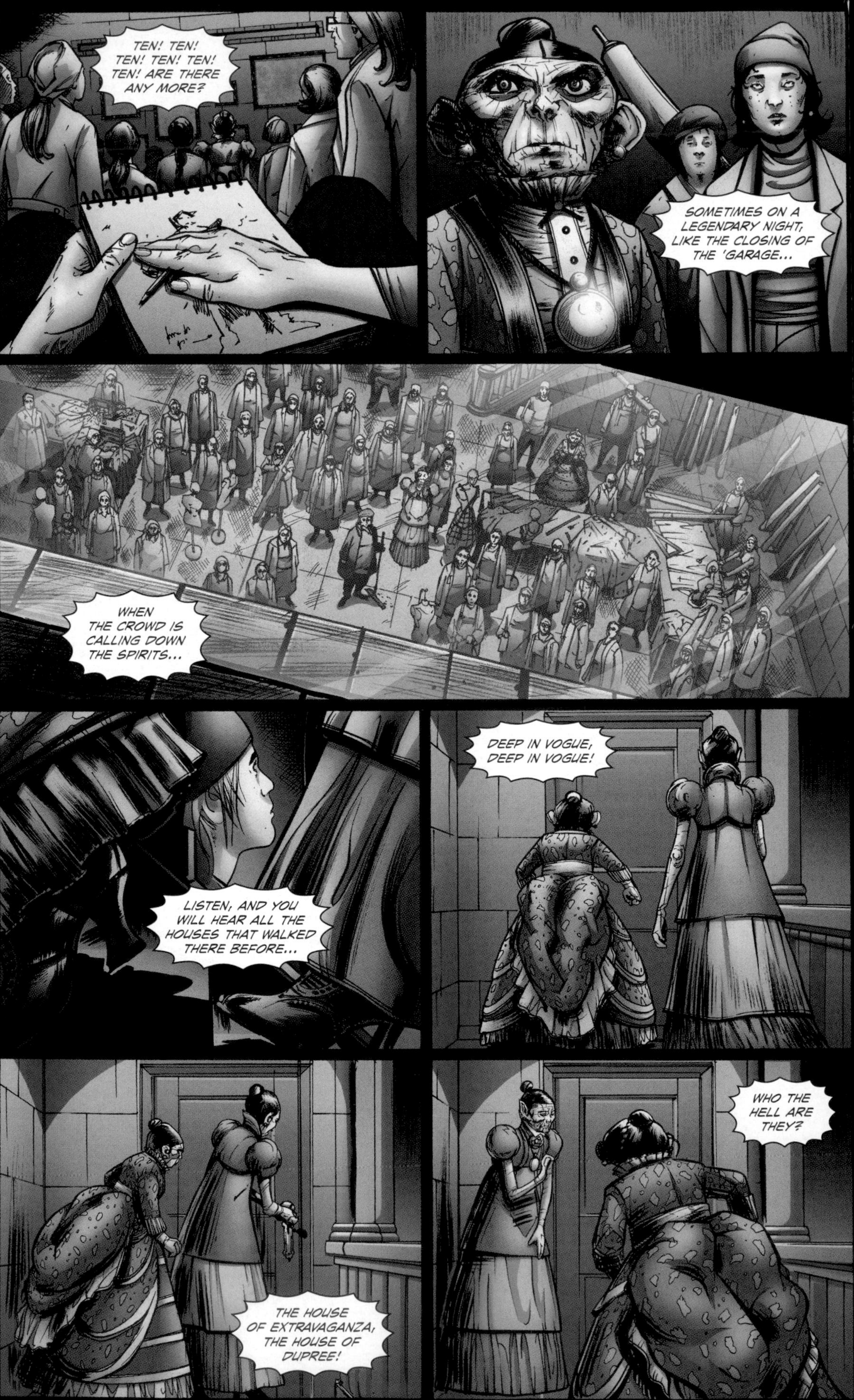
TEN! TEN! TEN! TEN! TEN! TEN! ARE THERE ANY MORE?
SOMETIMES ON A LEGENDARY NIGHT, LIKE THE CLOSING OF THE 'GARAGE...
WHEN THE CROWD IS CALLING DOWN THE SPIRITS...
LISTEN, AND YOU WILL HEAR ALL THE HOUSES THAT WALKED THERE BEFORE...
DEEP IN VOGUE, DEEP IN VOGUE!
THE HOUSE OF EXTRAVAGANZA, THE HOUSE OF DUPREE!
WHO THE HELL ARE THEY?

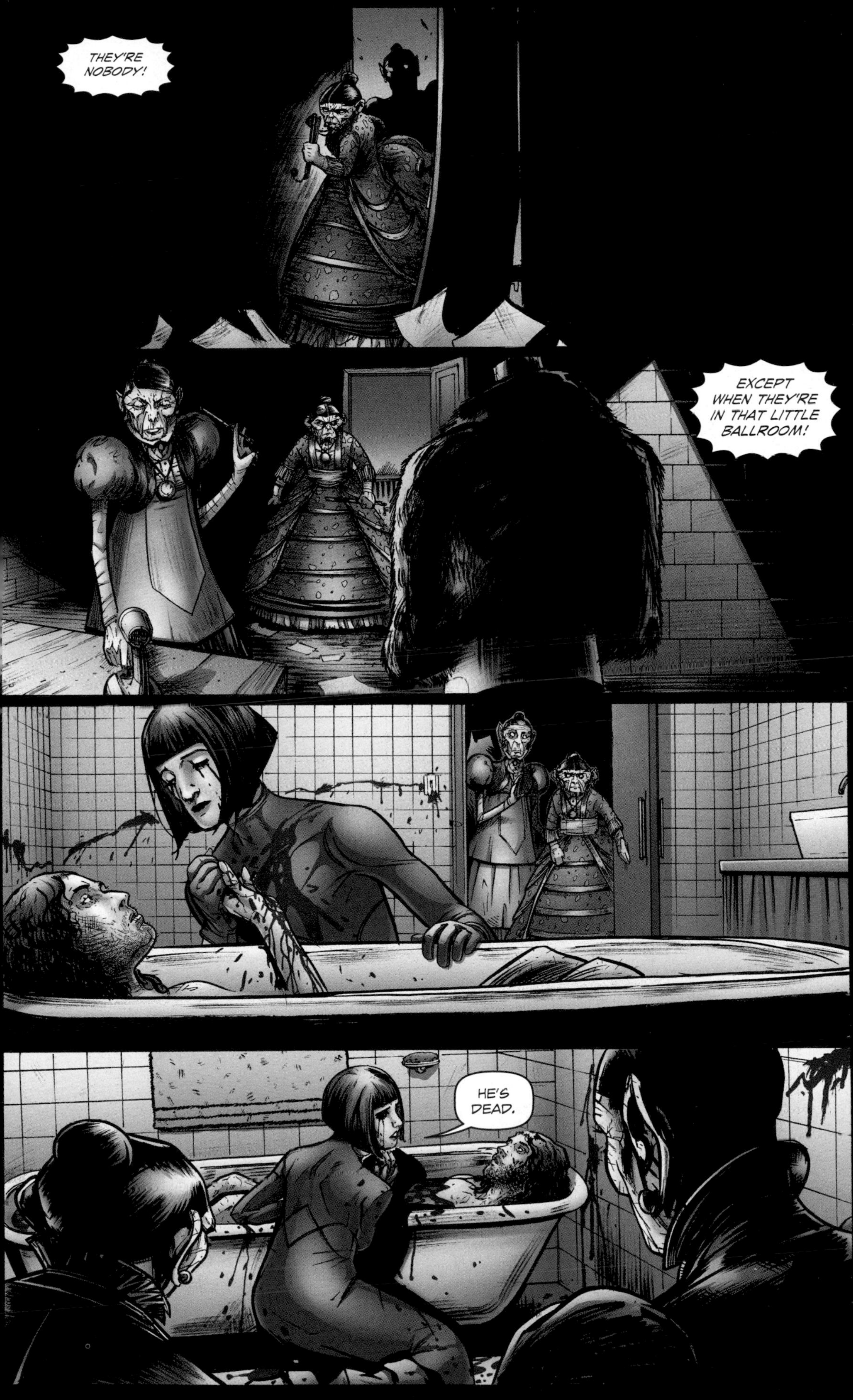
THEY'RE NOBODY!
EXCEPT WHEN THEY'RE IN THAT LITTLE BALLROOM!
HE'S DEAD.

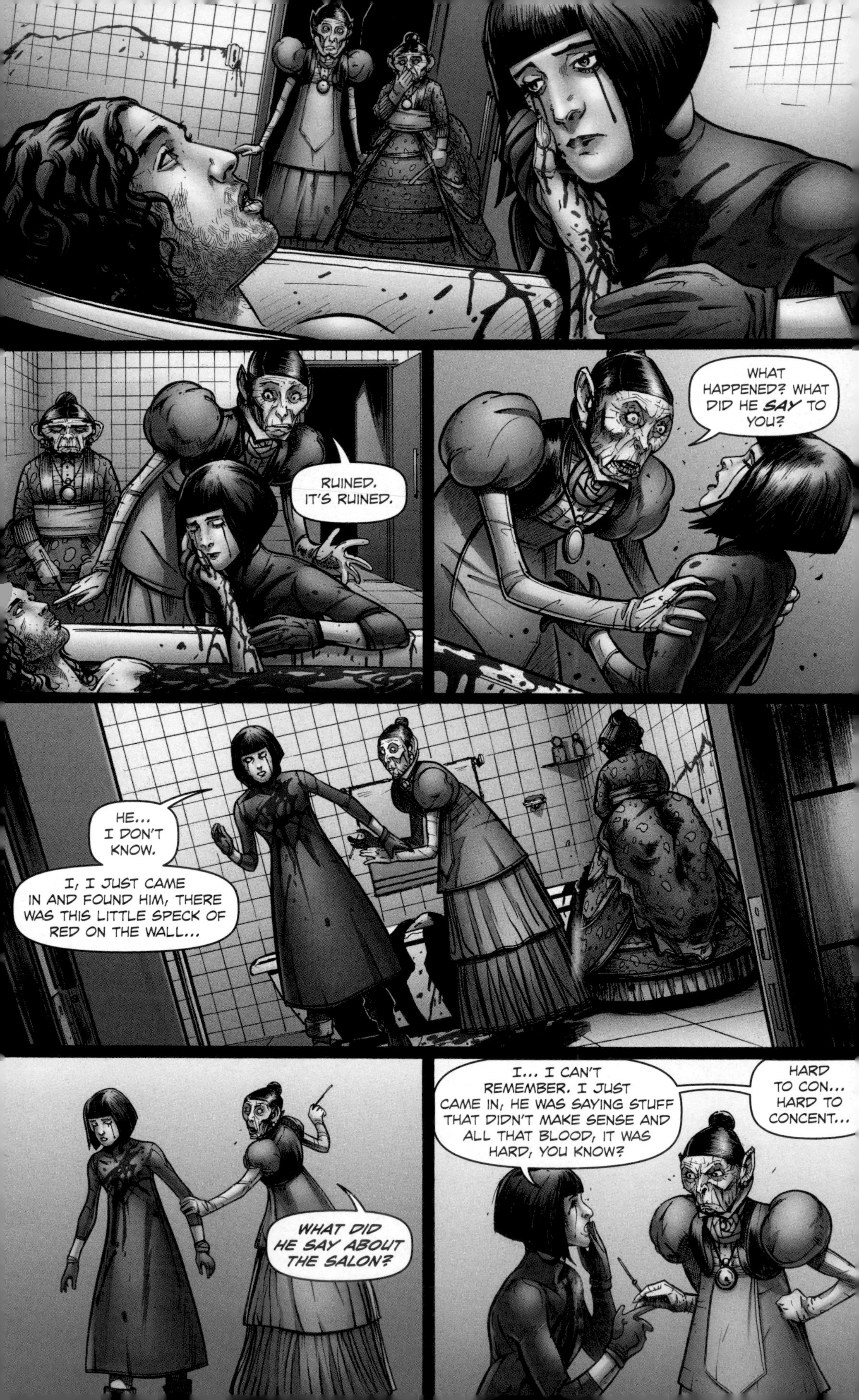
RUINED. IT'S RUINED.
WHAT HAPPENED? WHAT DID HE *SAY* TO YOU?
HE... I DON'T KNOW.
I, I JUST CAME IN AND FOUND HIM, THERE WAS THIS LITTLE SPECK OF RED ON THE WALL...
WHAT DID HE SAY ABOUT THE SALON?
I... I CAN'T REMEMBER. I JUST CAME IN, HE WAS SAYING STUFF THAT DIDN'T MAKE SENSE AND ALL THAT BLOOD, IT WAS HARD, YOU KNOW?
HARD TO CON... HARD TO CONCENT...

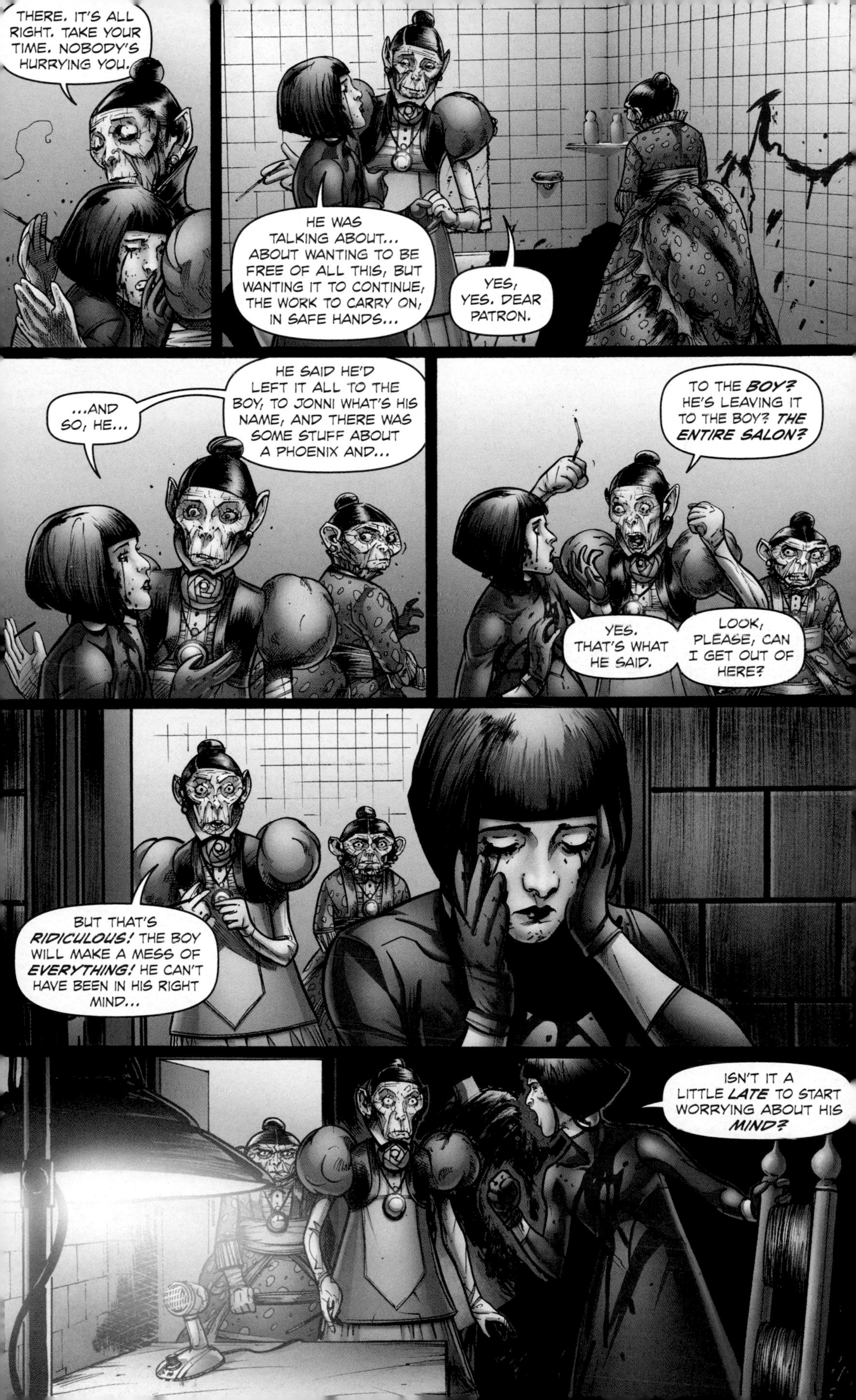
THERE. IT'S ALL RIGHT. TAKE YOUR TIME. NOBODY'S HURRYING YOU.
HE WAS TALKING ABOUT... ABOUT WANTING TO BE FREE OF ALL THIS, BUT WANTING IT TO CONTINUE, THE WORK TO CARRY ON, IN SAFE HANDS...
YES, YES. DEAR PATRON.
...AND SO, HE...
HE SAID HE'D LEFT IT ALL TO THE BOY, TO JONNI WHAT'S HIS NAME, AND THERE WAS SOME STUFF ABOUT A PHOENIX AND...
TO THE *BOY?* HE'S LEAVING IT TO THE BOY? *THE ENTIRE SALON?*
YES. THAT'S WHAT HE SAID.
LOOK, PLEASE, CAN I GET OUT OF HERE?
BUT THAT'S *RIDICULOUS!* THE BOY WILL MAKE A MESS OF *EVERYTHING!* HE CAN'T HAVE BEEN IN HIS RIGHT MIND...
ISN'T IT A LITTLE *LATE* TO START WORRYING ABOUT HIS *MIND?*

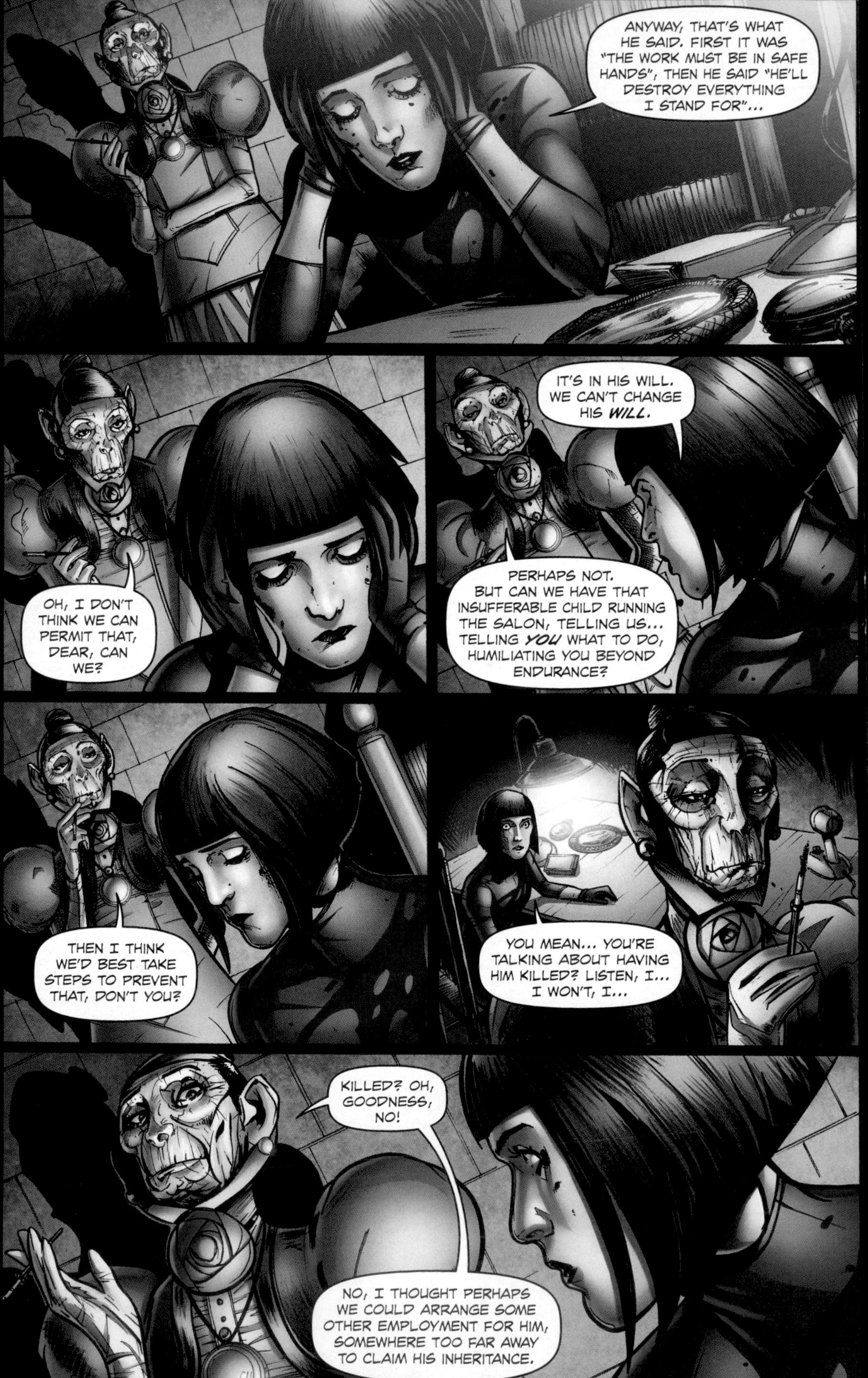
ANYWAY, THAT'S WHAT HE SAID. FIRST IT WAS "THE WORK MUST BE IN SAFE HANDS", THEN HE SAID "HE'LL DESTROY EVERYTHING I STAND FOR"...
OH, I DON'T THINK WE CAN PERMIT THAT, DEAR, CAN WE?
IT'S IN HIS WILL. WE CAN'T CHANGE HIS *WILL*.
PERHAPS NOT. BUT CAN WE HAVE THAT INSUFFERABLE CHILD RUNNING THE SALON, TELLING US... TELLING *YOU* WHAT TO DO, HUMILIATING YOU BEYOND ENDURANCE?
THEN I THINK WE'D BEST TAKE STEPS TO PREVENT THAT, DON'T YOU?
YOU MEAN... YOU'RE TALKING ABOUT HAVING HIM KILLED? LISTEN, I... I WON'T, I...
KILLED? OH, GOODNESS, NO!
NO, I THOUGHT PERHAPS WE COULD ARRANGE SOME OTHER EMPLOYMENT FOR HIM, SOMEWHERE TOO FAR AWAY TO CLAIM HIS INHERITANCE.

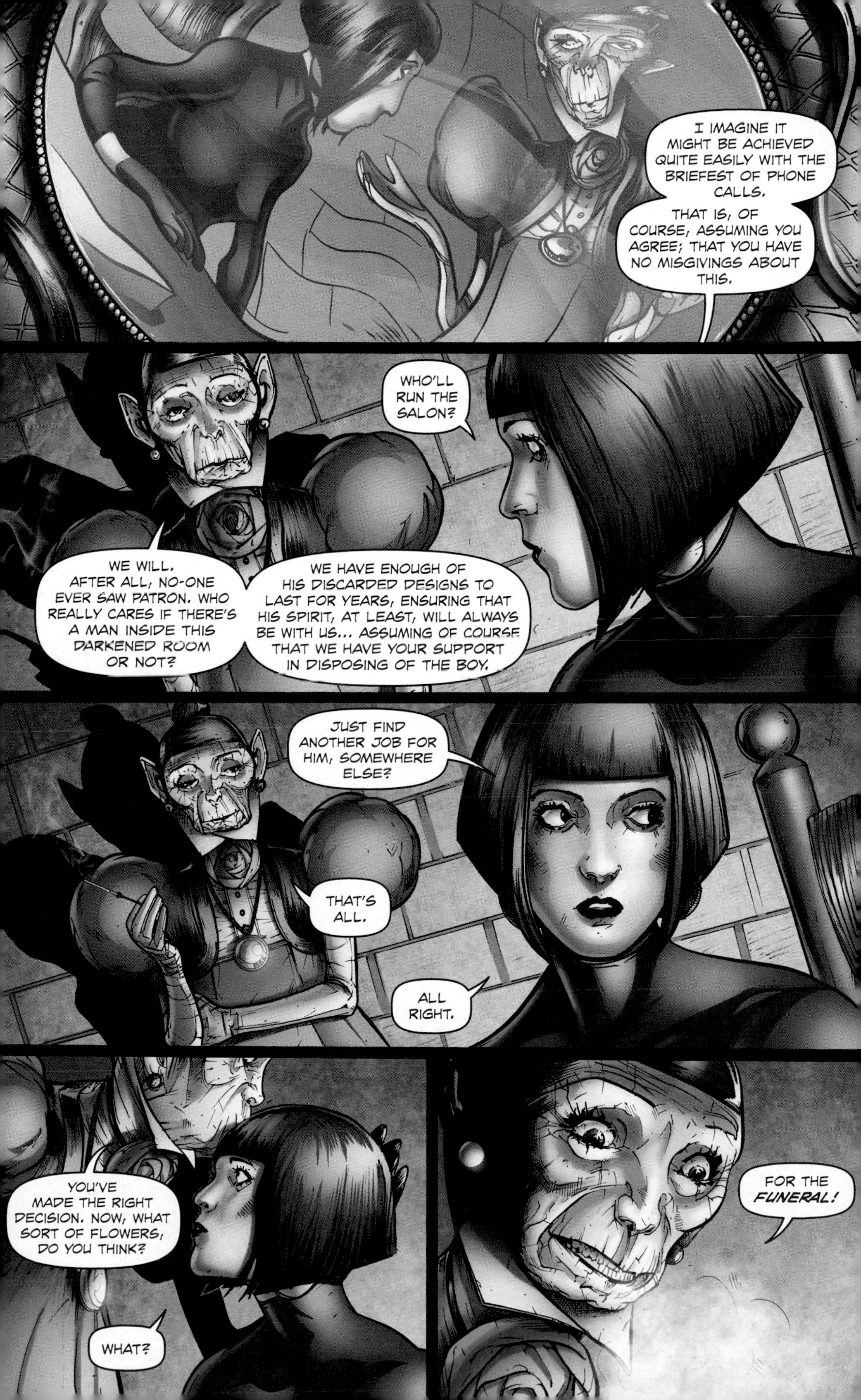
I IMAGINE IT MIGHT BE ACHIEVED QUITE EASILY WITH THE BRIEFEST OF PHONE CALLS.
THAT IS, OF COURSE, ASSUMING YOU AGREE; THAT YOU HAVE NO MISGIVINGS ABOUT THIS.
WHO'LL RUN THE SALON?
WE WILL. AFTER ALL, NO-ONE EVER SAW PATRON. WHO REALLY CARES IF THERE'S A MAN INSIDE THIS DARKENED ROOM OR NOT?
WE HAVE ENOUGH OF HIS DISCARDED DESIGNS TO LAST FOR YEARS, ENSURING THAT HIS SPIRIT, AT LEAST, WILL ALWAYS BE WITH US... ASSUMING OF COURSE THAT WE HAVE YOUR SUPPORT IN DISPOSING OF THE BOY.
JUST FIND ANOTHER JOB FOR HIM, SOMEWHERE ELSE?
THAT'S ALL.
ALL RIGHT.
YOU'VE MADE THE RIGHT DECISION. NOW, WHAT SORT OF FLOWERS, DO YOU THINK?
WHAT?
FOR THE *FUNERAL!*

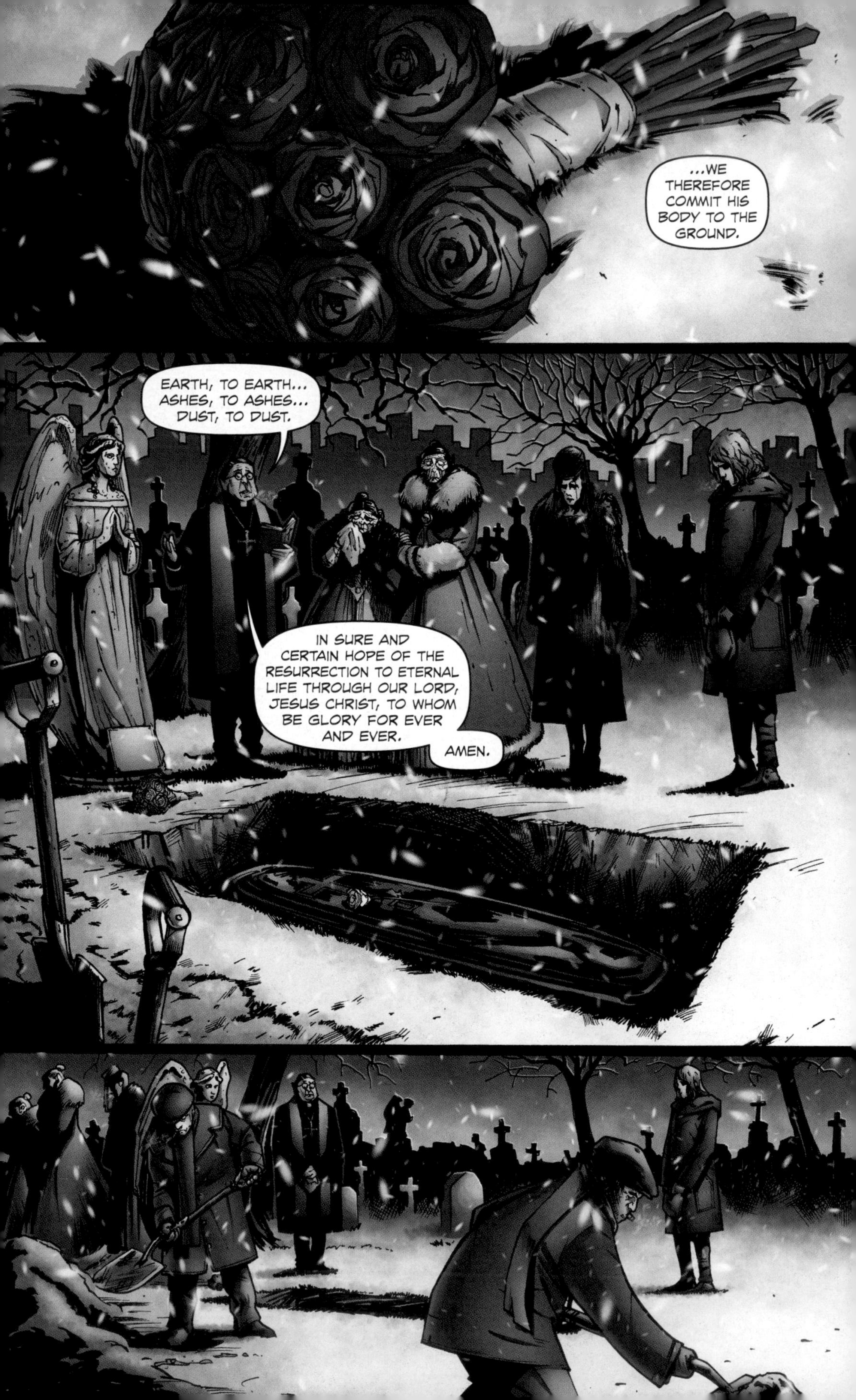
...WE THEREFORE COMMIT HIS BODY TO THE GROUND.
EARTH, TO EARTH... ASHES, TO ASHES... DUST, TO DUST.
IN SURE AND CERTAIN HOPE OF THE RESURRECTION TO ETERNAL LIFE THROUGH OUR LORD, JESUS CHRIST, TO WHOM BE GLORY FOR EVER AND EVER.
AMEN.

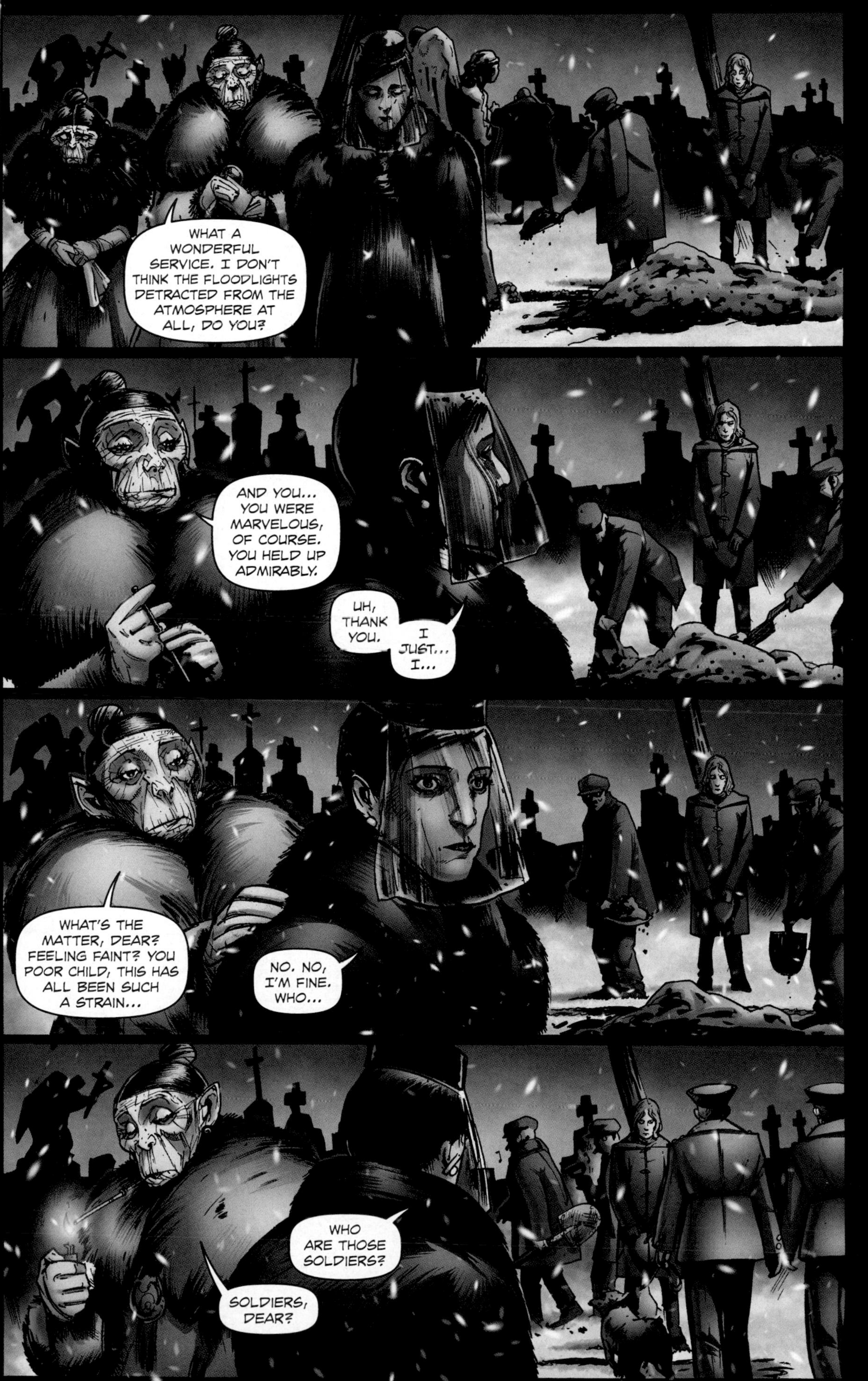
WHAT A WONDERFUL SERVICE. I DON'T THINK THE FLOODLIGHTS DETRACTED FROM THE ATMOSPHERE AT ALL, DO YOU?
AND YOU... YOU WERE MARVELOUS, OF COURSE. YOU HELD UP ADMIRABLY.
UH, THANK YOU.
I JUST... I...
WHAT'S THE MATTER, DEAR? FEELING FAINT? YOU POOR CHILD, THIS HAS ALL BEEN SUCH A STRAIN...
NO. NO, I'M FINE. WHO...
WHO ARE THOSE SOLDIERS?
SOLDIERS, DEAR?

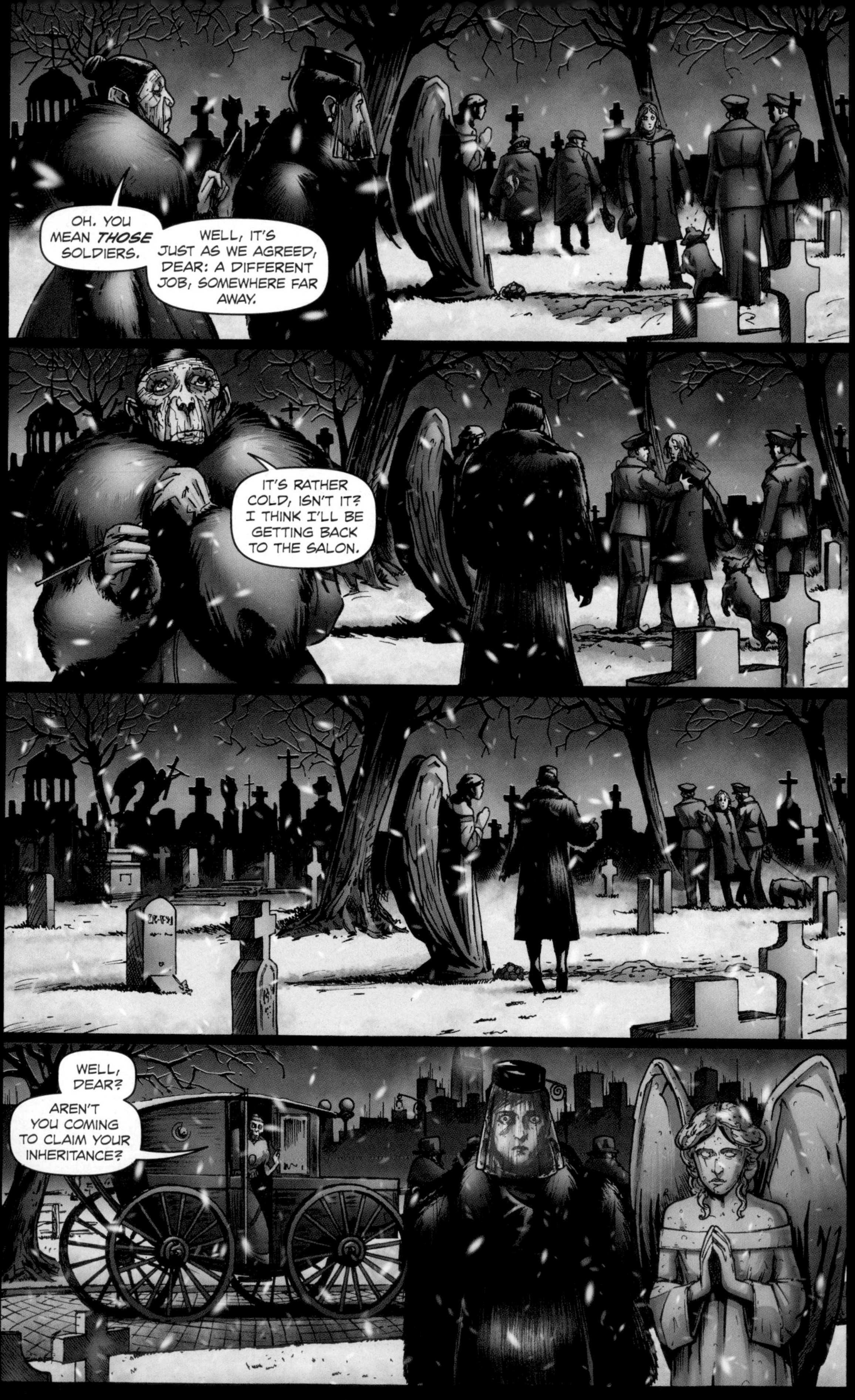
OH. YOU MEAN *THOSE* SOLDIERS.
WELL, IT'S JUST AS WE AGREED, DEAR: A DIFFERENT JOB, SOMEWHERE FAR AWAY.
IT'S RATHER COLD, ISN'T IT? I THINK I'LL BE GETTING BACK TO THE SALON.
WELL, DEAR?
AREN'T YOU COMING TO CLAIM YOUR INHERITANCE?

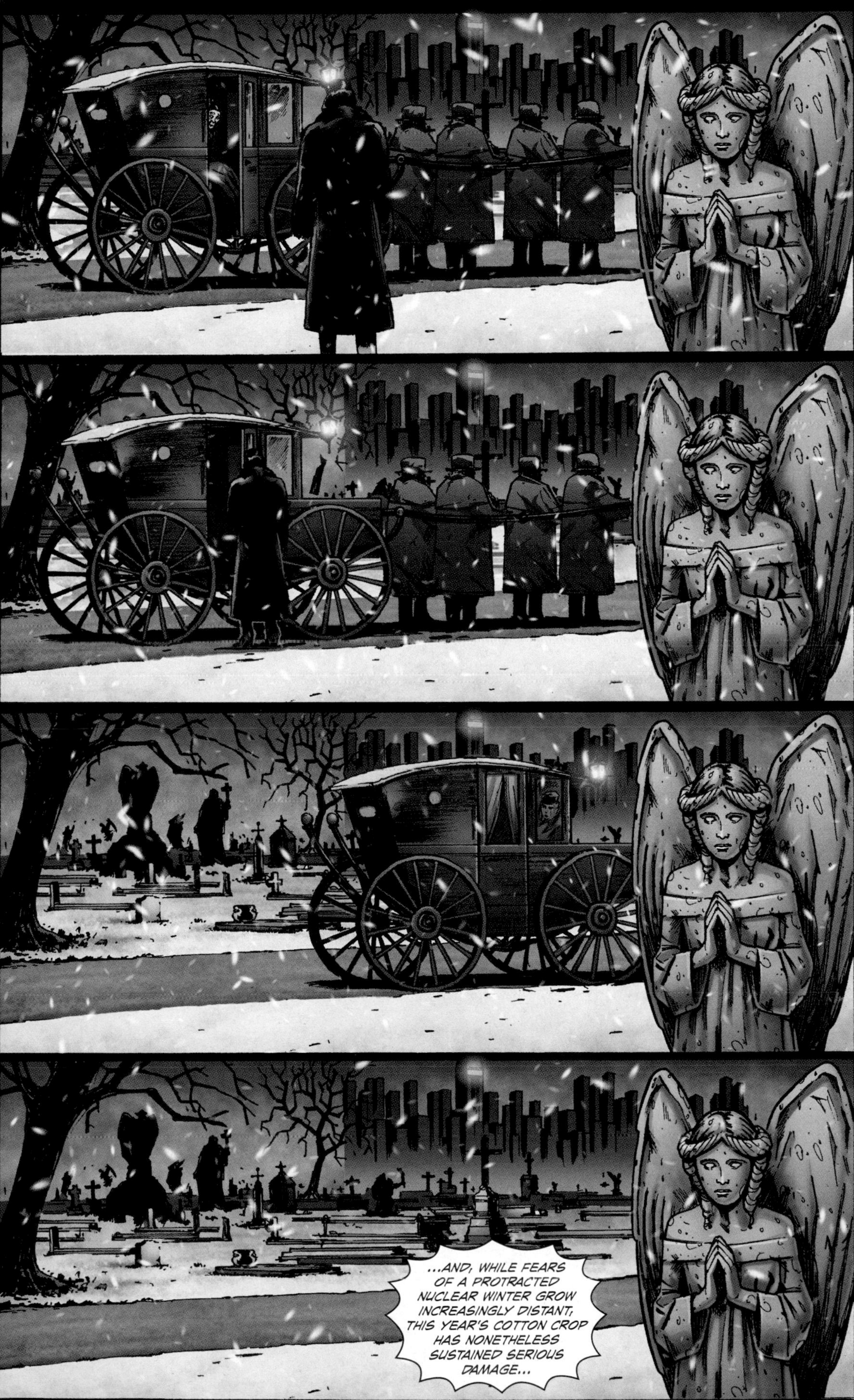
...AND, WHILE FEARS OF A PROTRACTED NUCLEAR WINTER GROW INCREASINGLY DISTANT, THIS YEAR'S COTTON CROP HAS NONETHELESS SUSTAINED SERIOUS DAMAGE...

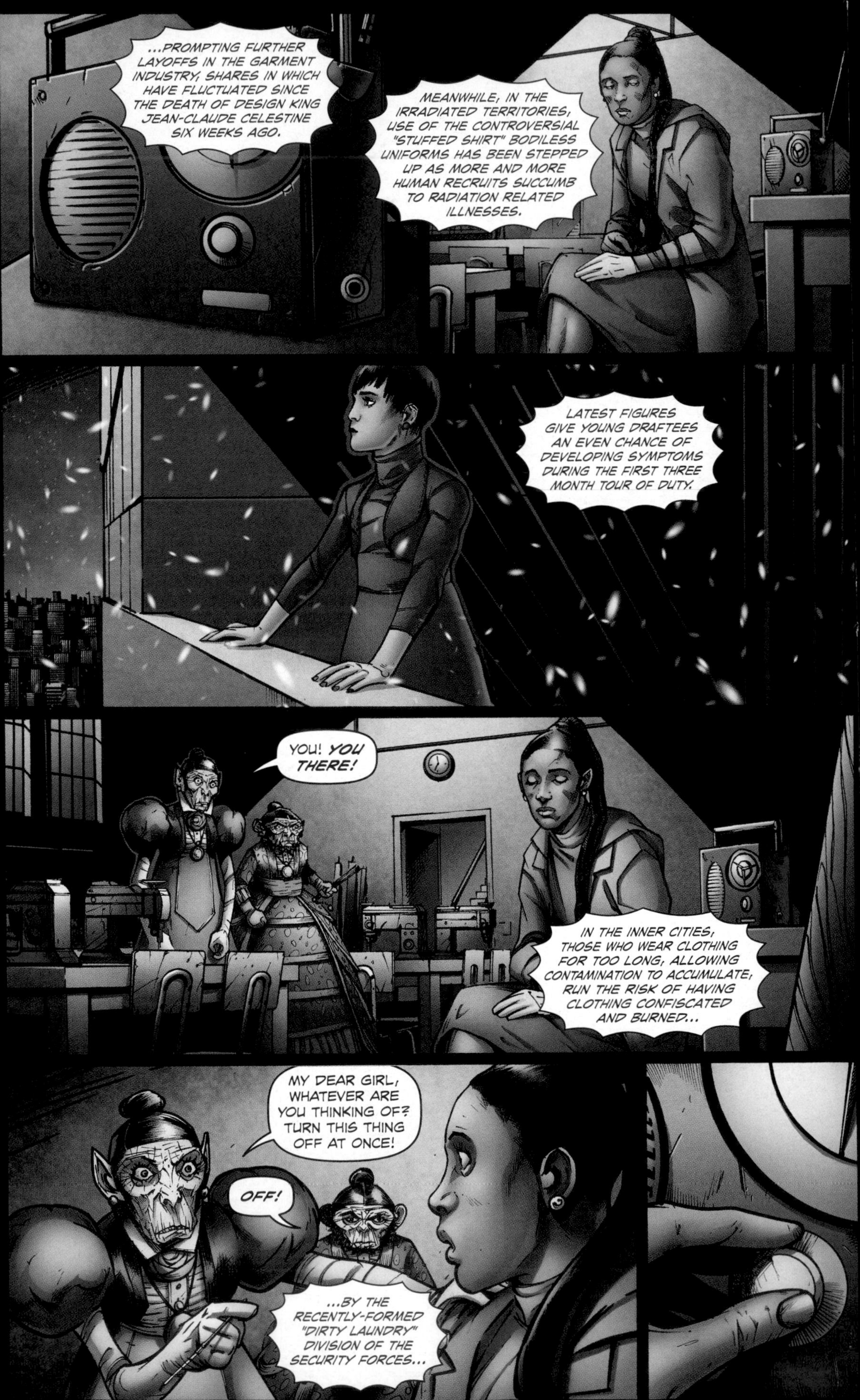
...PROMPTING FURTHER LAYOFFS IN THE GARMENT INDUSTRY, SHARES IN WHICH HAVE FLUCTUATED SINCE THE DEATH OF DESIGN KING JEAN-CLAUDE CELESTINE SIX WEEKS AGO.
MEANWHILE, IN THE IRRADIATED TERRITORIES, USE OF THE CONTROVERSIAL "STUFFED SHIRT" BODILESS UNIFORMS HAS BEEN STEPPED UP AS MORE AND MORE HUMAN RECRUITS SUCCUMB TO RADIATION RELATED ILLNESSES.
LATEST FIGURES GIVE YOUNG DRAFTEES AN EVEN CHANCE OF DEVELOPING SYMPTOMS DURING THE FIRST THREE MONTH TOUR OF DUTY.
YOU! YOU THERE!
IN THE INNER CITIES, THOSE WHO WEAR CLOTHING FOR TOO LONG, ALLOWING CONTAMINATION TO ACCUMULATE, RUN THE RISK OF HAVING CLOTHING CONFISCATED AND BURNED...
MY DEAR GIRL, WHATEVER ARE YOU THINKING OF? TURN THIS THING OFF AT ONCE!
OFF!
...BY THE RECENTLY-FORMED "DIRTY LAUNDRY" DIVISION OF THE SECURITY FORCES...

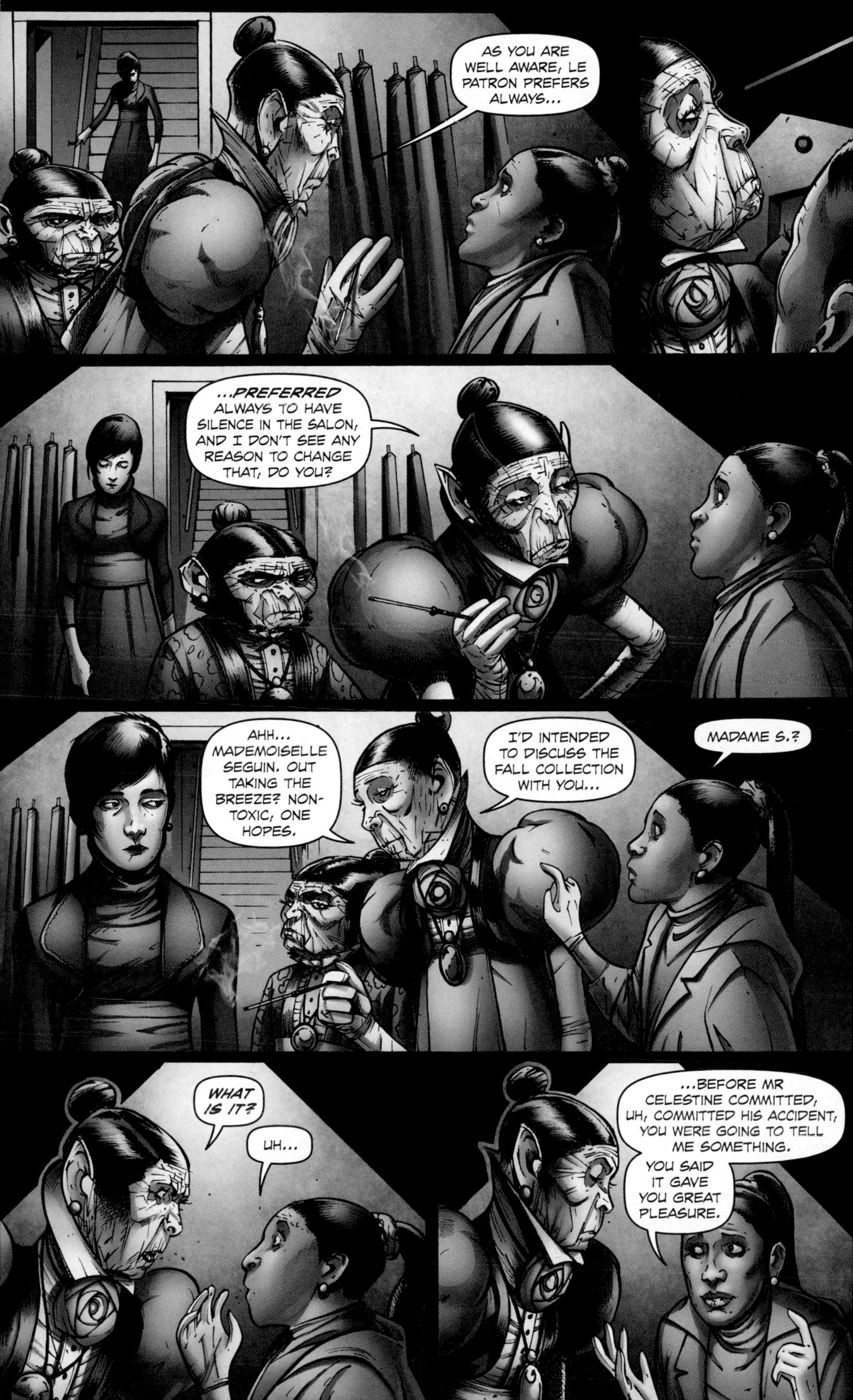
AS YOU ARE WELL AWARE, LE PATRON PREFERS ALWAYS...
...PREFERRED ALWAYS TO HAVE SILENCE IN THE SALON, AND I DON'T SEE ANY REASON TO CHANGE THAT, DO YOU?
AHH... MADEMOISELLE SEGUIN. OUT TAKING THE BREEZE? NON-TOXIC, ONE HOPES.
I'D INTENDED TO DISCUSS THE FALL COLLECTION WITH YOU...
MADAME S.?
WHAT IS IT?
UH...
...BEFORE MR CELESTINE COMMITTED, UH, COMMITTED HIS ACCIDENT, YOU WERE GOING TO TELL ME SOMETHING.
YOU SAID IT GAVE YOU GREAT PLEASURE.

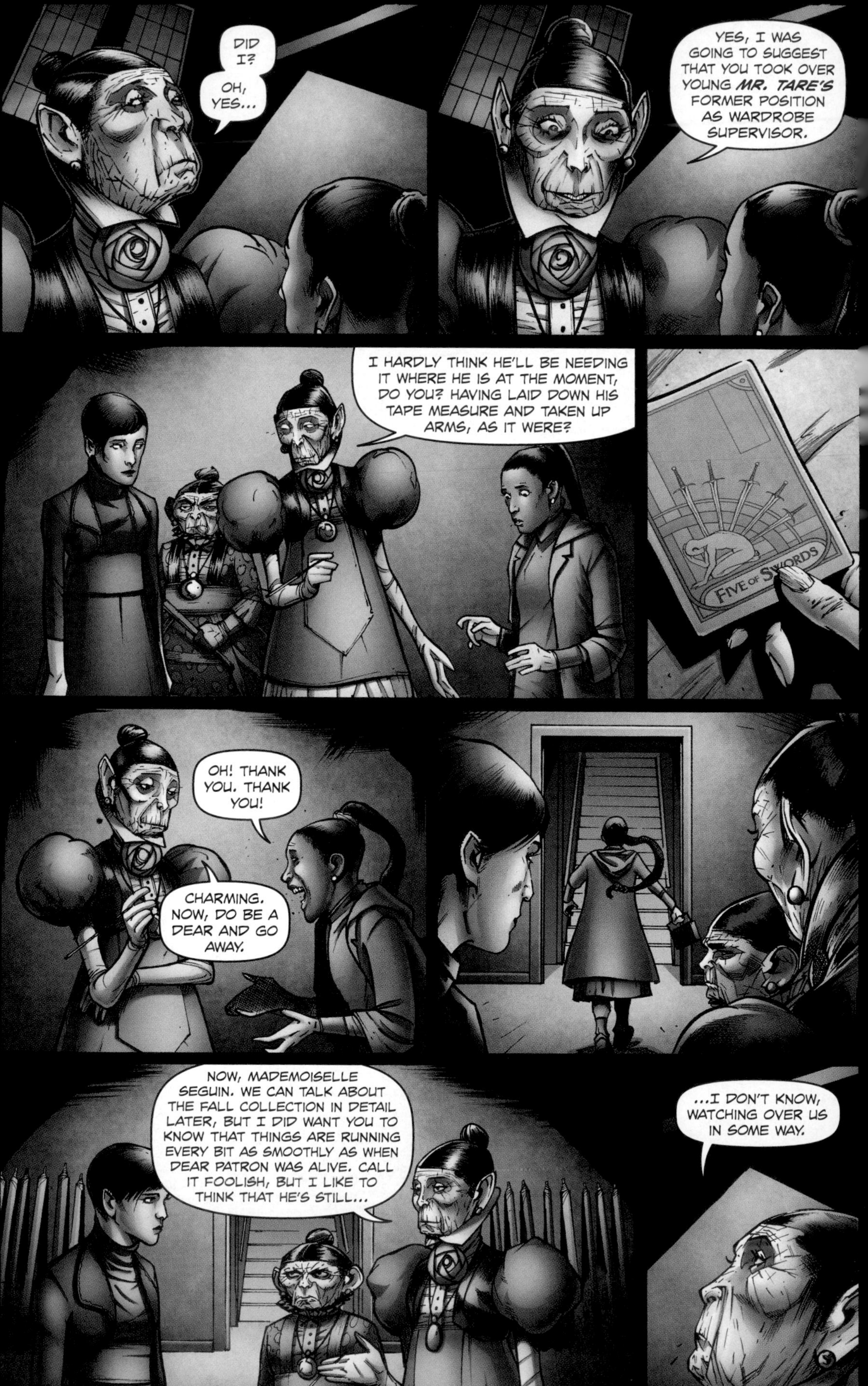
DID I?
OH, YES...
YES, I WAS GOING TO SUGGEST THAT YOU TOOK OVER YOUNG MR. TARE'S FORMER POSITION AS WARDROBE SUPERVISOR.
I HARDLY THINK HE'LL BE NEEDING IT WHERE HE IS AT THE MOMENT, DO YOU? HAVING LAID DOWN HIS TAPE MEASURE AND TAKEN UP ARMS, AS IT WERE?
FIVE OF SWORDS
OH! THANK YOU. THANK YOU!
CHARMING. NOW, DO BE A DEAR AND GO AWAY.
NOW, MADEMOISELLE SEGUIN. WE CAN TALK ABOUT THE FALL COLLECTION IN DETAIL LATER, BUT I DID WANT YOU TO KNOW THAT THINGS ARE RUNNING EVERY BIT AS SMOOTHLY AS WHEN DEAR PATRON WAS ALIVE. CALL IT FOOLISH, BUT I LIKE TO THINK THAT HE'S STILL...
...I DON'T KNOW, WATCHING OVER US IN SOME WAY.

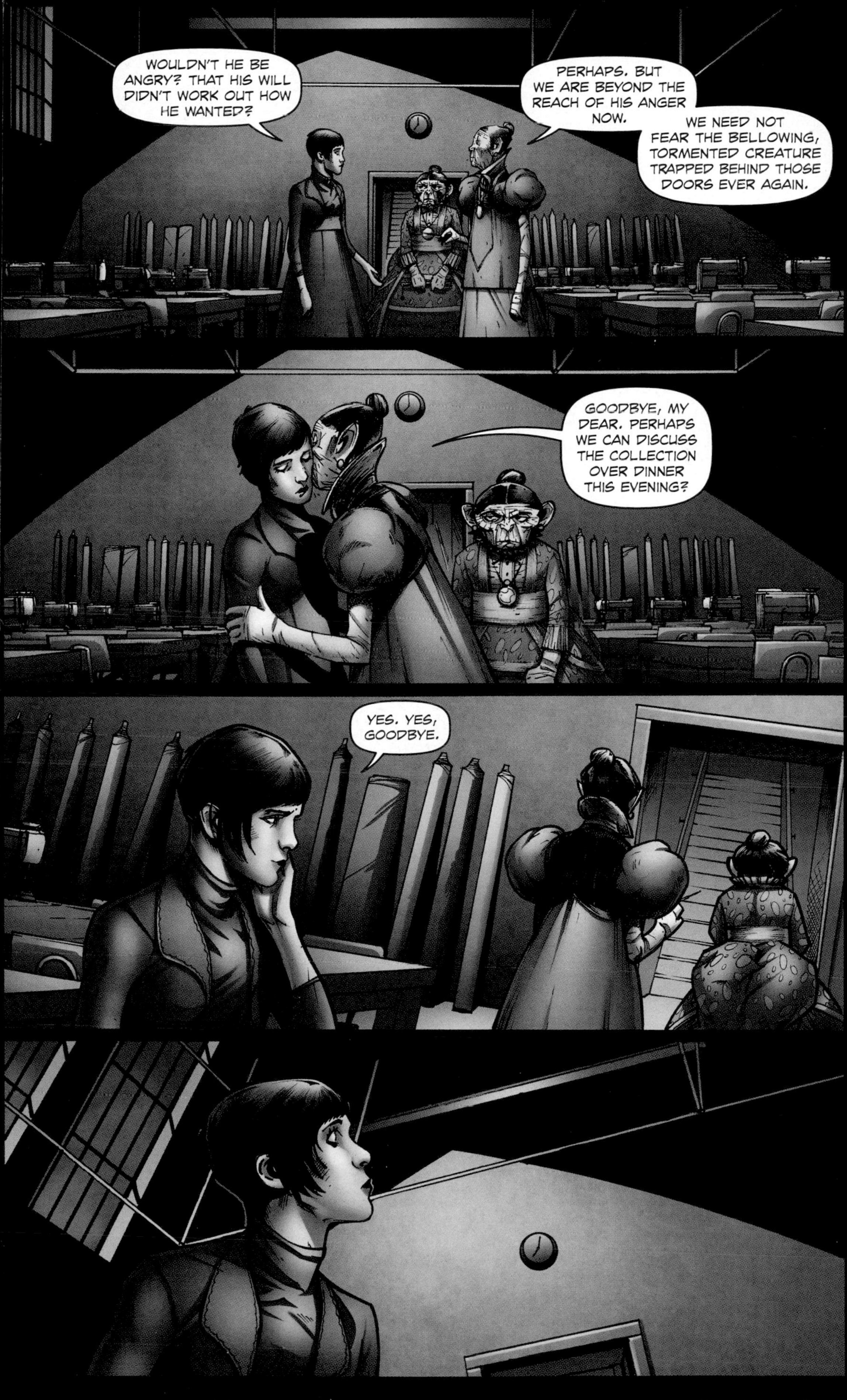
WOULDN'T HE BE ANGRY? THAT HIS WILL DIDN'T WORK OUT HOW HE WANTED?
PERHAPS. BUT WE ARE BEYOND THE REACH OF HIS ANGER NOW.
WE NEED NOT FEAR THE BELLOWING, TORMENTED CREATURE TRAPPED BEHIND THOSE DOORS EVER AGAIN.
GOODBYE, MY DEAR. PERHAPS WE CAN DISCUSS THE COLLECTION OVER DINNER THIS EVENING?
YES. YES, GOODBYE.

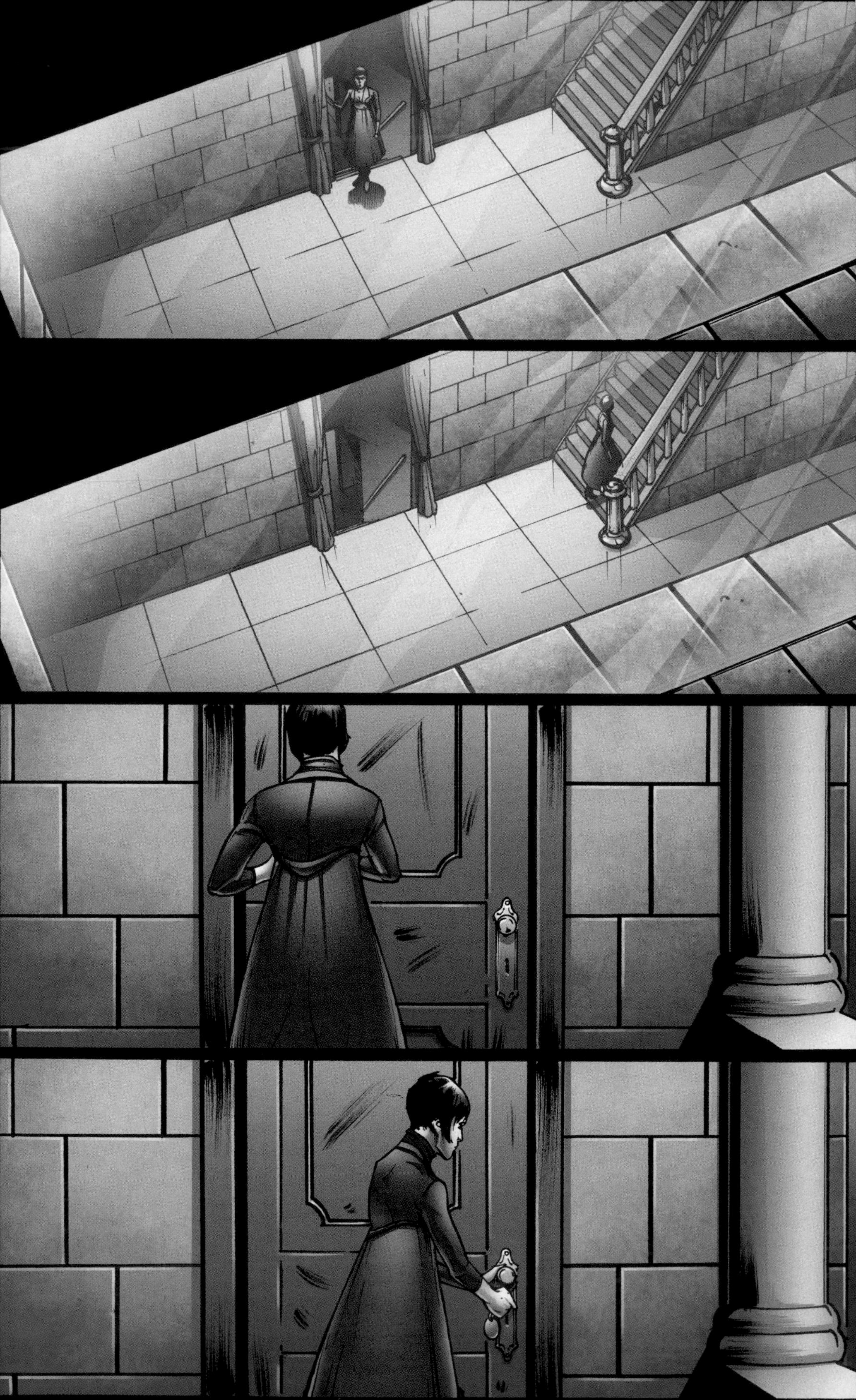

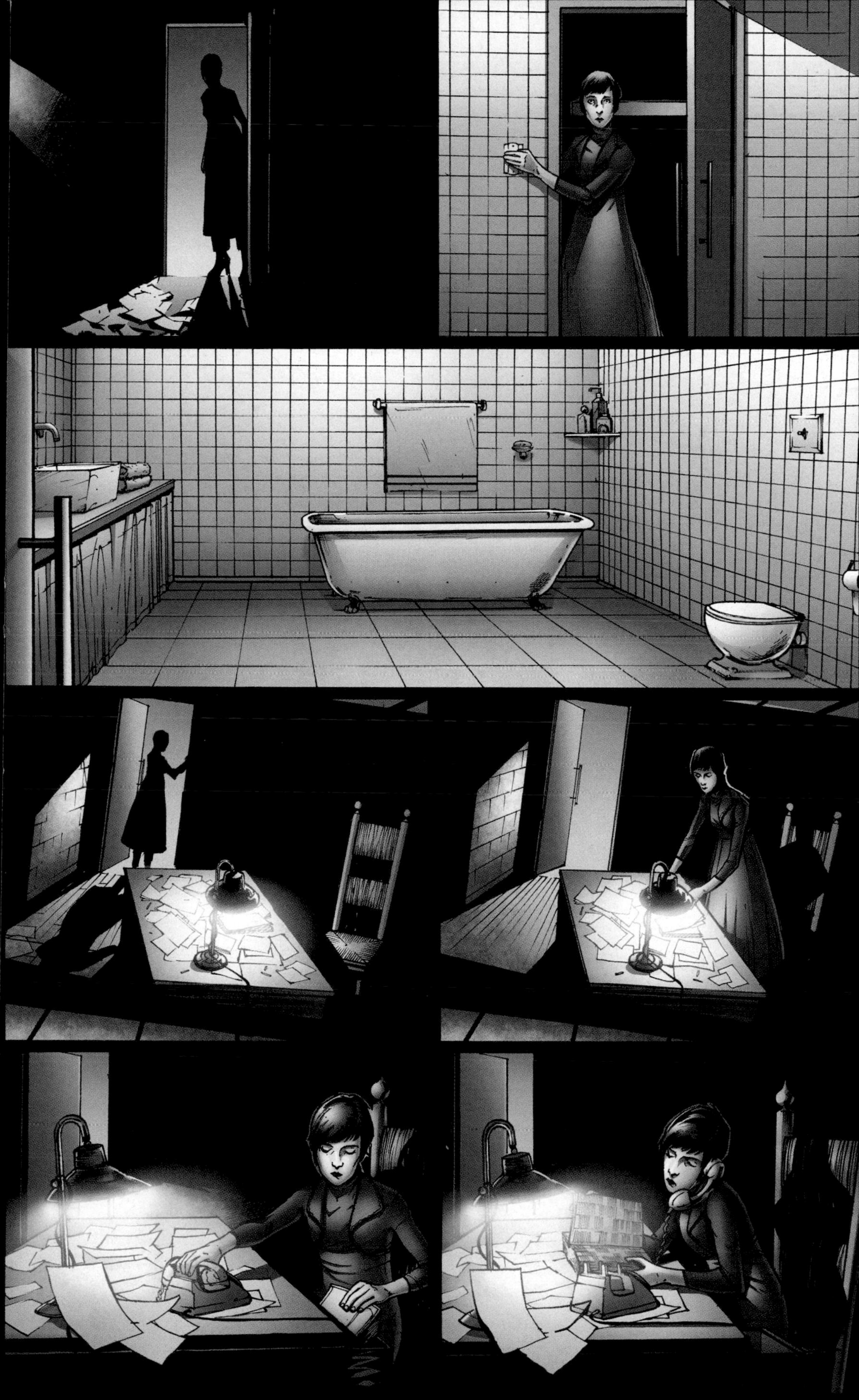

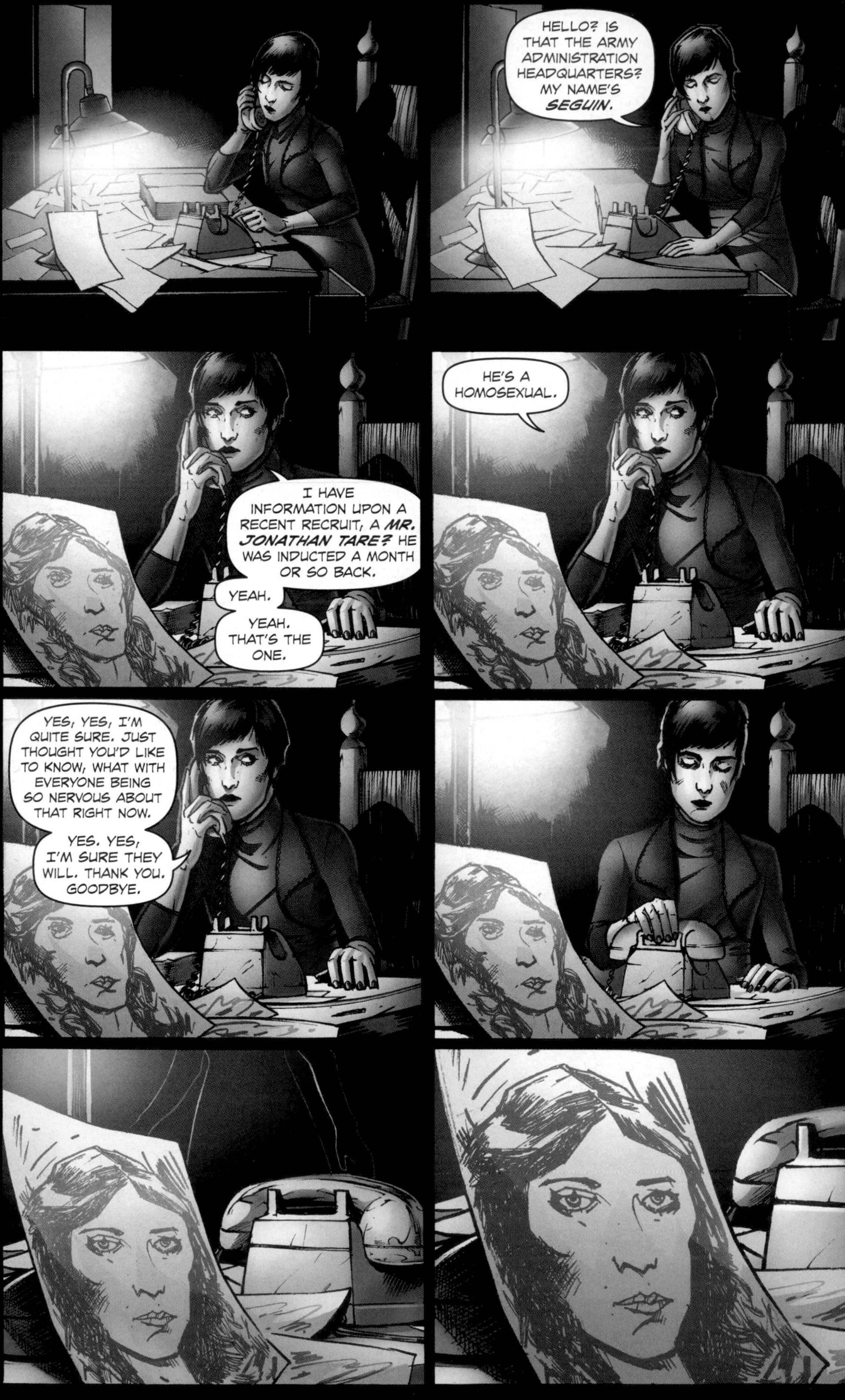
HELLO? IS THAT THE ARMY ADMINISTRATION HEADQUARTERS? MY NAME'S SEGUIN.
I HAVE INFORMATION UPON A RECENT RECRUIT, A MR. JONATHAN TARE? HE WAS INDUCTED A MONTH OR SO BACK.
YEAH.
YEAH. THAT'S THE ONE.
HE'S A HOMOSEXUAL.
YES, YES, I'M QUITE SURE. JUST THOUGHT YOU'D LIKE TO KNOW, WHAT WITH EVERYONE BEING SO NERVOUS ABOUT THAT RIGHT NOW.
YES. YES, I'M SURE THEY WILL. THANK YOU. GOODBYE.

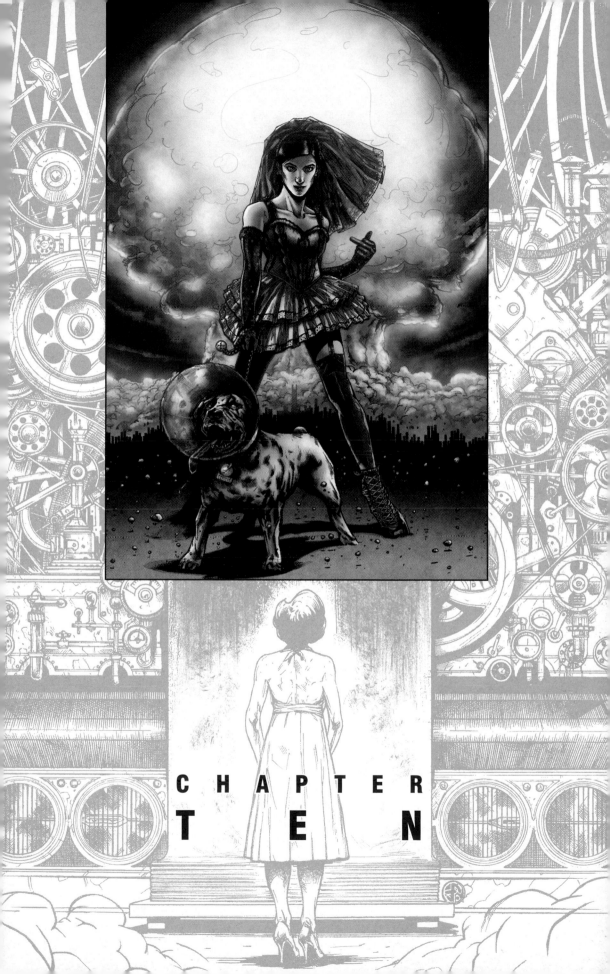

CHAPTER
TEN

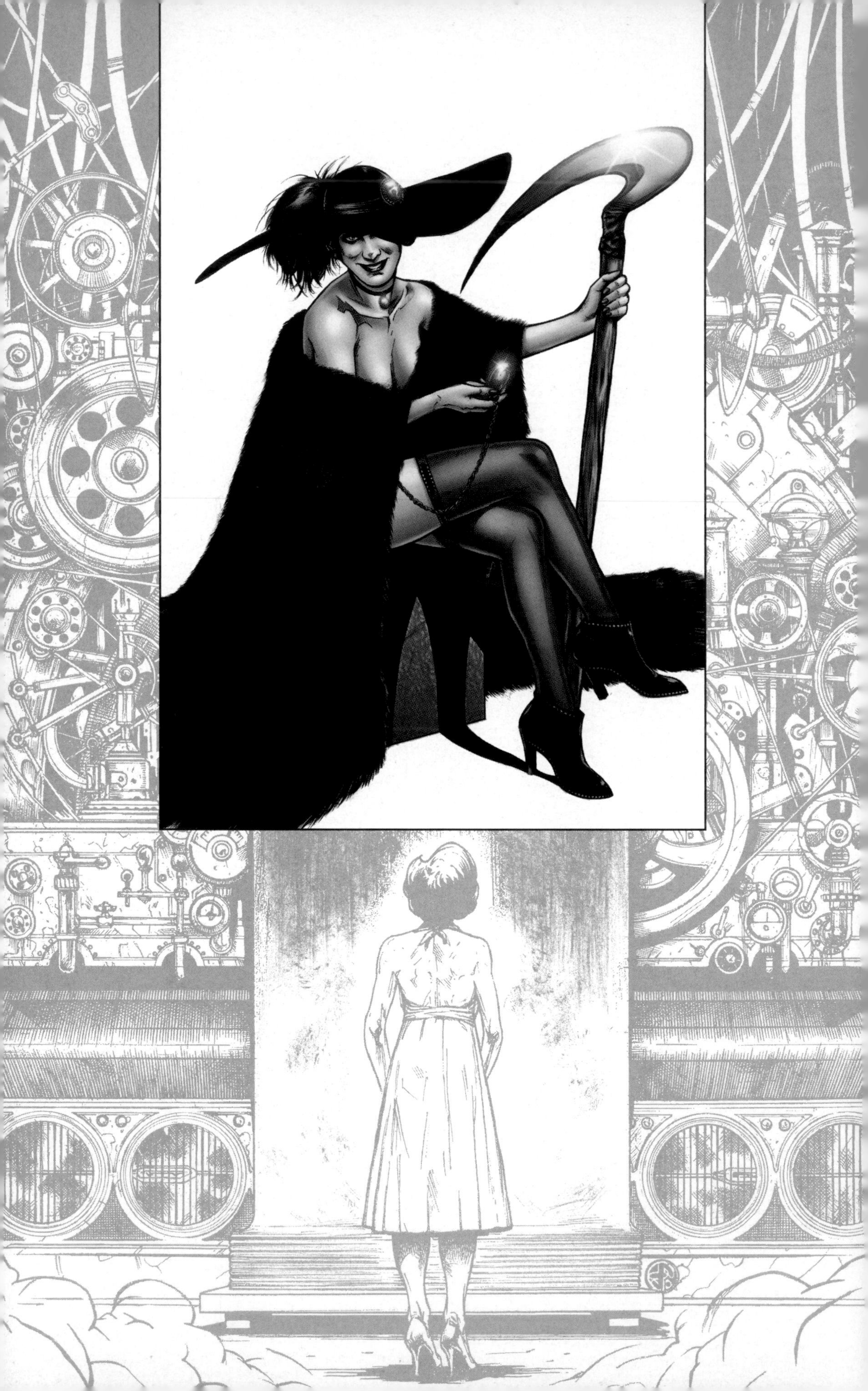

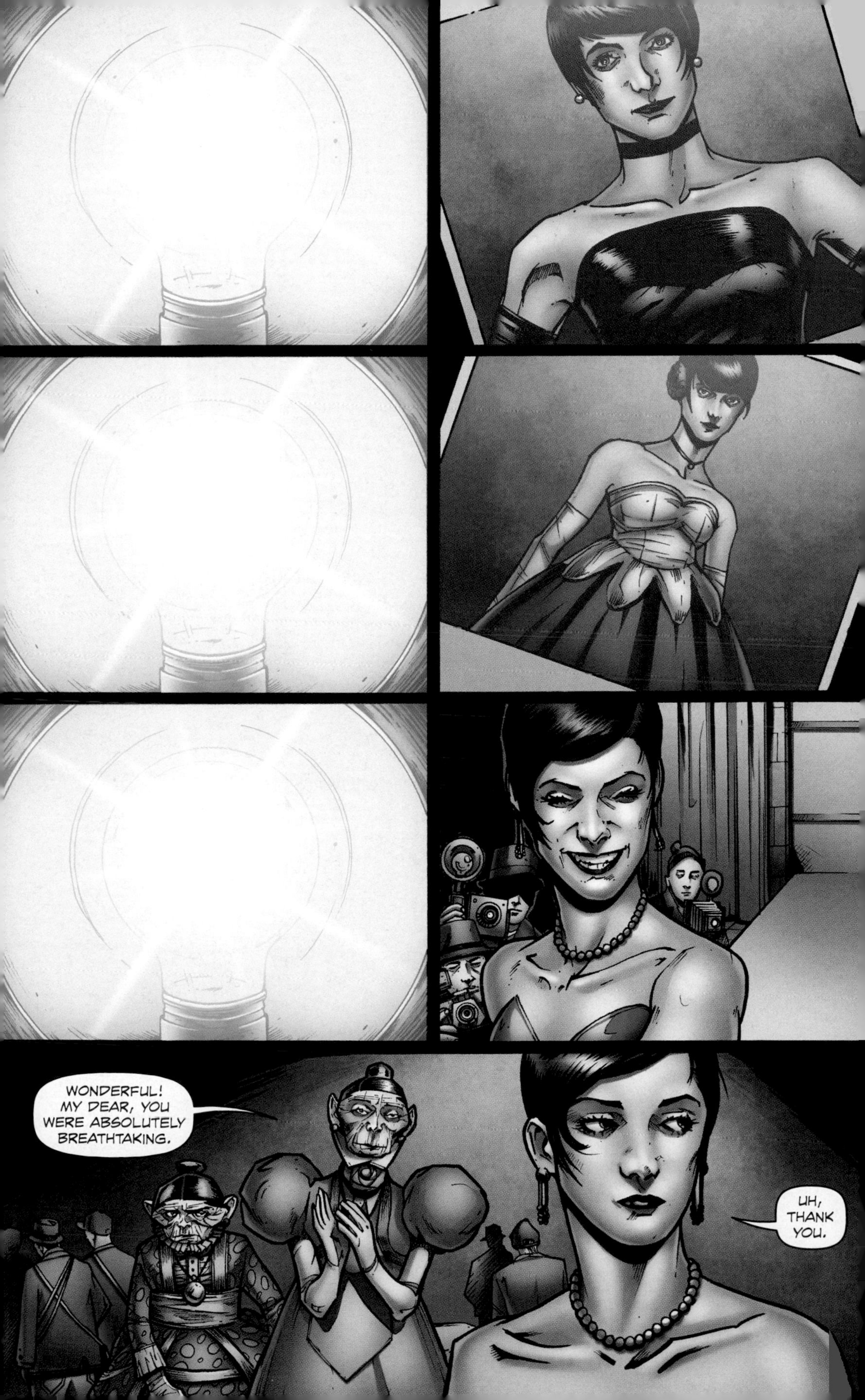
WONDERFUL! MY DEAR, YOU WERE ABSOLUTELY BREATHTAKING.
UH, THANK YOU.

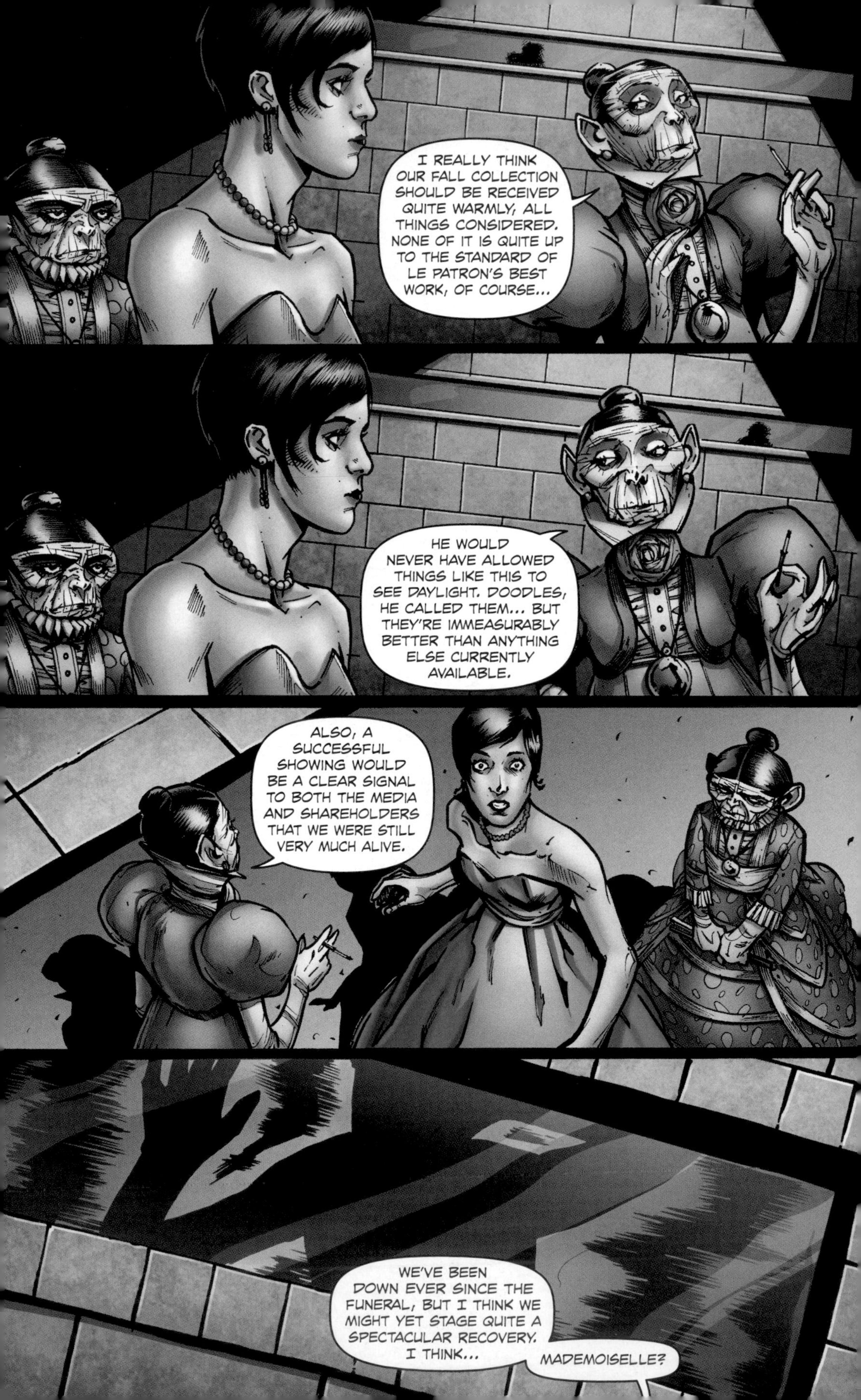
I REALLY THINK OUR FALL COLLECTION SHOULD BE RECEIVED QUITE WARMLY, ALL THINGS CONSIDERED. NONE OF IT IS QUITE UP TO THE STANDARD OF LE PATRON'S BEST WORK, OF COURSE...
HE WOULD NEVER HAVE ALLOWED THINGS LIKE THIS TO SEE DAYLIGHT. DOODLES, HE CALLED THEM... BUT THEY'RE IMMEASURABLY BETTER THAN ANYTHING ELSE CURRENTLY AVAILABLE.
ALSO, A SUCCESSFUL SHOWING WOULD BE A CLEAR SIGNAL TO BOTH THE MEDIA AND SHAREHOLDERS THAT WE WERE STILL VERY MUCH ALIVE.
WE'VE BEEN DOWN EVER SINCE THE FUNERAL, BUT I THINK WE MIGHT YET STAGE QUITE A SPECTACULAR RECOVERY. I THINK...
MADEMOISELLE?

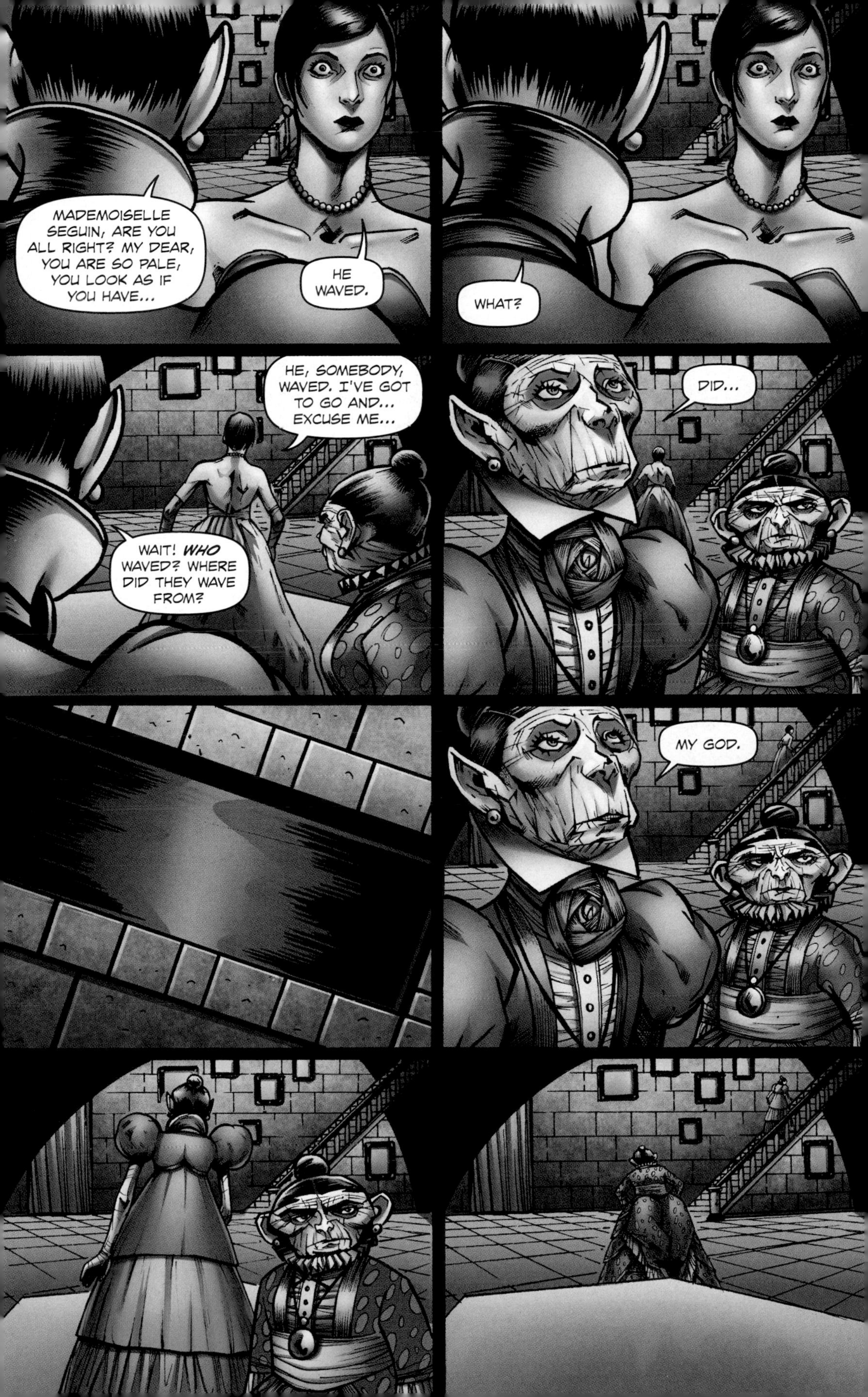
MADEMOISELLE SEGUIN, ARE YOU ALL RIGHT? MY DEAR, YOU ARE SO PALE, YOU LOOK AS IF YOU HAVE...
HE WAVED.
WHAT?
HE, SOMEBODY, WAVED. I'VE GOT TO GO AND... EXCUSE ME...
WAIT! *WHO* WAVED? WHERE DID THEY WAVE FROM?
DID...
MY GOD.

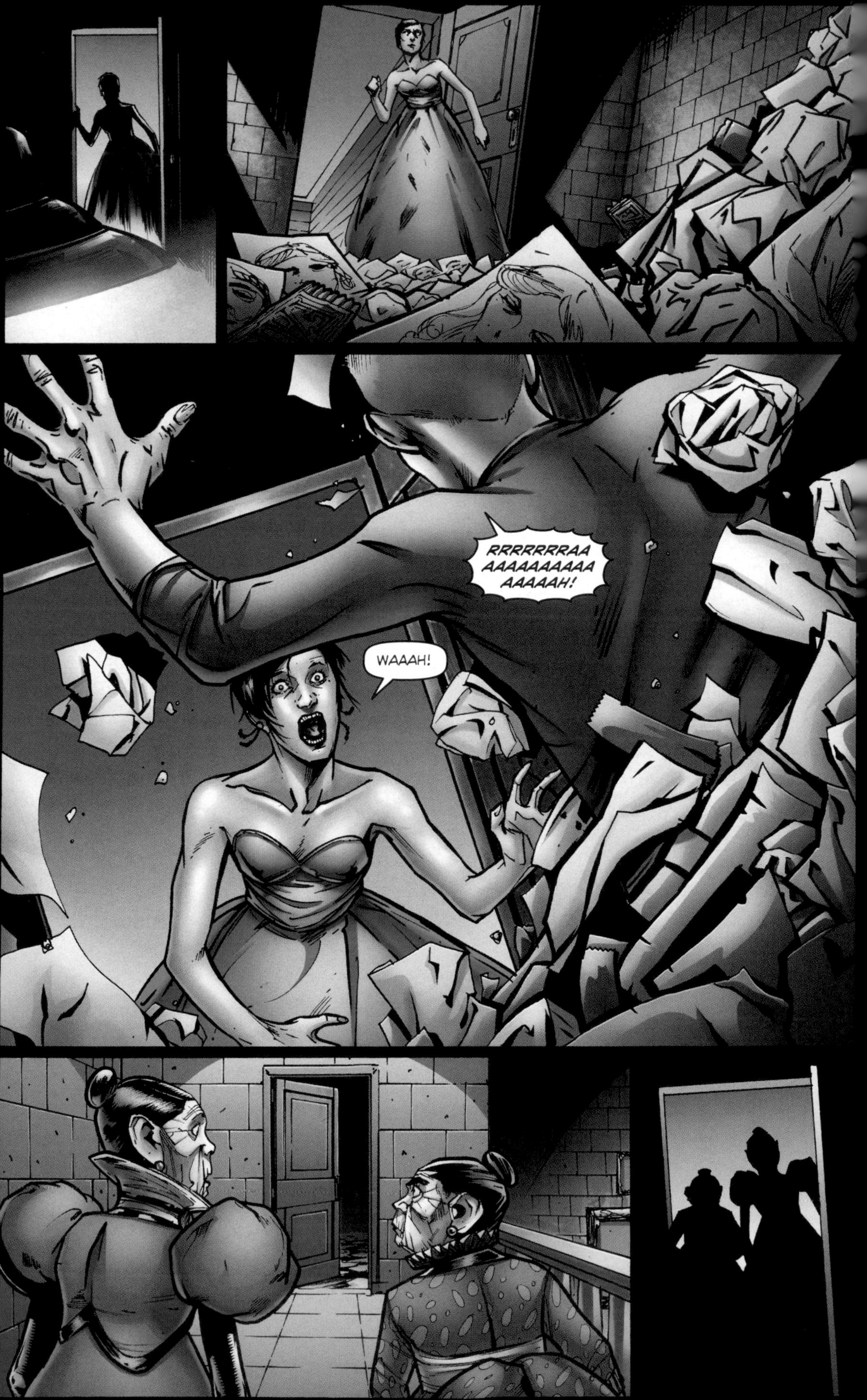
RRRRRRRAA AAAAAAAAAA AAAAAH!
WAAAH!

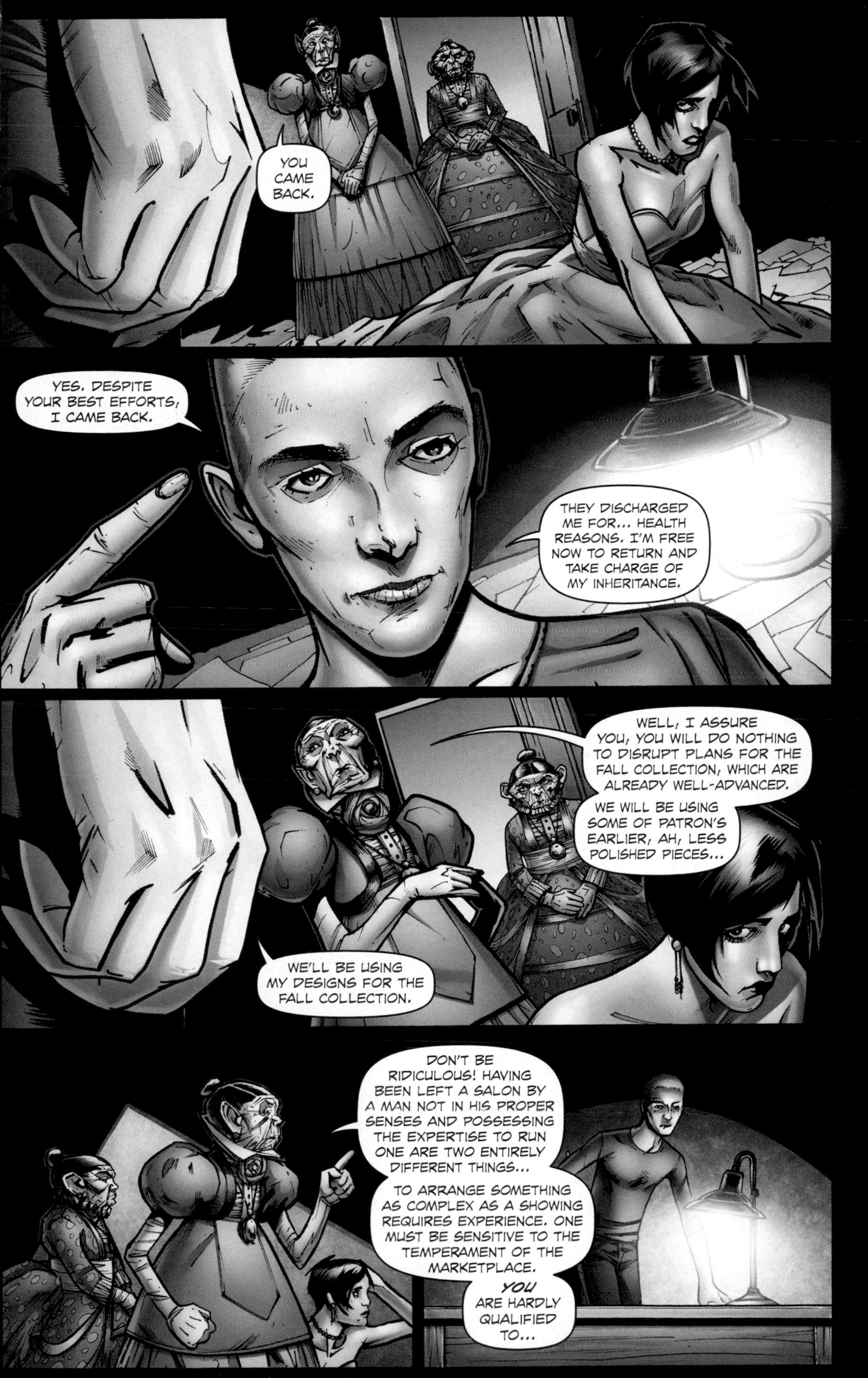
YOU CAME BACK.
YES. DESPITE YOUR BEST EFFORTS, I CAME BACK.
THEY DISCHARGED ME FOR... HEALTH REASONS. I'M FREE NOW TO RETURN AND TAKE CHARGE OF MY INHERITANCE.
WELL, I ASSURE YOU, YOU WILL DO NOTHING TO DISRUPT PLANS FOR THE FALL COLLECTION, WHICH ARE ALREADY WELL-ADVANCED.
WE WILL BE USING SOME OF PATRON'S EARLIER, AH, LESS POLISHED PIECES...
WE'LL BE USING MY DESIGNS FOR THE FALL COLLECTION.
DON'T BE RIDICULOUS! HAVING BEEN LEFT A SALON BY A MAN NOT IN HIS PROPER SENSES AND POSSESSING THE EXPERTISE TO RUN ONE ARE TWO ENTIRELY DIFFERENT THINGS...
TO ARRANGE SOMETHING AS COMPLEX AS A SHOWING REQUIRES EXPERIENCE. ONE MUST BE SENSITIVE TO THE TEMPERAMENT OF THE MARKETPLACE.
YOU ARE HARDLY QUALIFIED TO...

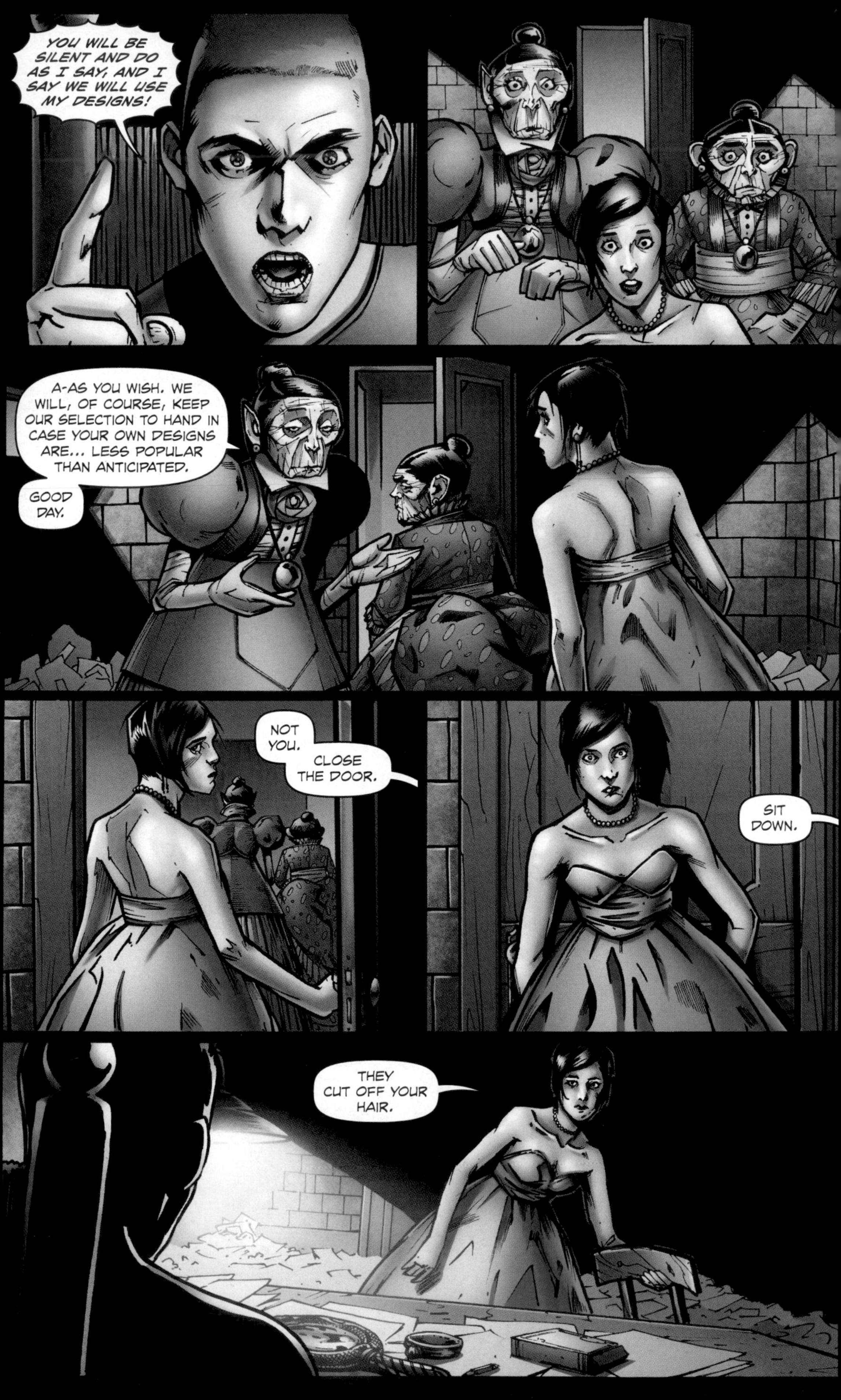
YOU WILL BE SILENT AND DO AS I SAY, AND I SAY WE WILL USE MY DESIGNS!
A-AS YOU WISH. WE WILL, OF COURSE, KEEP OUR SELECTION TO HAND IN CASE YOUR OWN DESIGNS ARE... LESS POPULAR THAN ANTICIPATED.
GOOD DAY.
NOT YOU.
CLOSE THE DOOR.
SIT DOWN.
THEY CUT OFF YOUR HAIR.

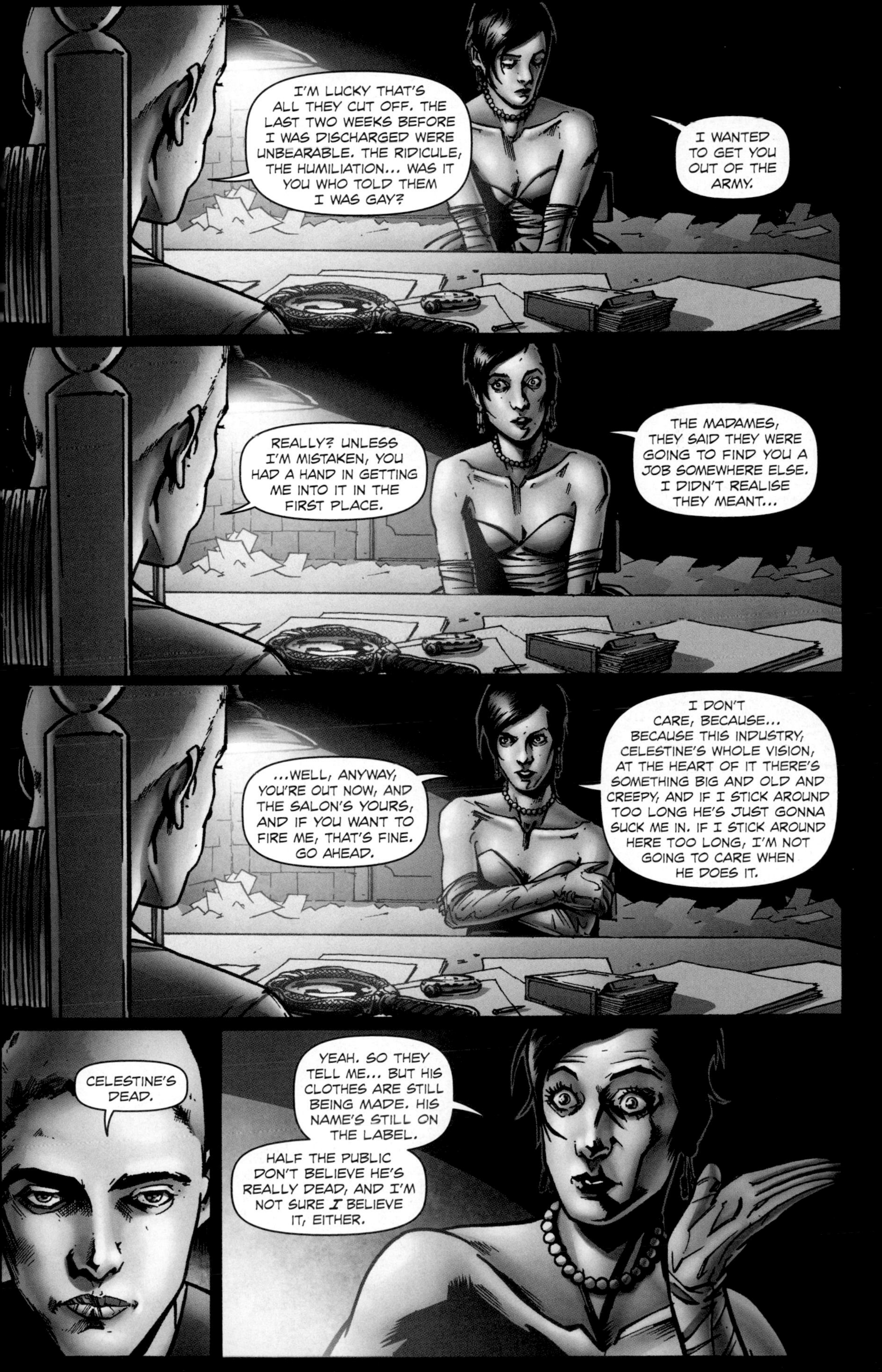
I'M LUCKY THAT'S ALL THEY CUT OFF. THE LAST TWO WEEKS BEFORE I WAS DISCHARGED WERE UNBEARABLE. THE RIDICULE, THE HUMILIATION... WAS IT YOU WHO TOLD THEM I WAS GAY?
I WANTED TO GET YOU OUT OF THE ARMY.
REALLY? UNLESS I'M MISTAKEN, YOU HAD A HAND IN GETTING ME INTO IT IN THE FIRST PLACE.
THE MADAMES, THEY SAID THEY WERE GOING TO FIND YOU A JOB SOMEWHERE ELSE. I DIDN'T REALISE THEY MEANT...
...WELL, ANYWAY, YOU'RE OUT NOW, AND THE SALON'S YOURS, AND IF YOU WANT TO FIRE ME, THAT'S FINE. GO AHEAD.
I DON'T CARE, BECAUSE... BECAUSE THIS INDUSTRY, CELESTINE'S WHOLE VISION, AT THE HEART OF IT THERE'S SOMETHING BIG AND OLD AND CREEPY, AND IF I STICK AROUND TOO LONG HE'S JUST GONNA SUCK ME IN. IF I STICK AROUND HERE TOO LONG, I'M NOT GOING TO CARE WHEN HE DOES IT.
CELESTINE'S DEAD.
YEAH. SO THEY TELL ME... BUT HIS CLOTHES ARE STILL BEING MADE. HIS NAME'S STILL ON THE LABEL.
HALF THE PUBLIC DON'T BELIEVE HE'S REALLY DEAD, AND I'M NOT SURE *I* BELIEVE IT, EITHER.

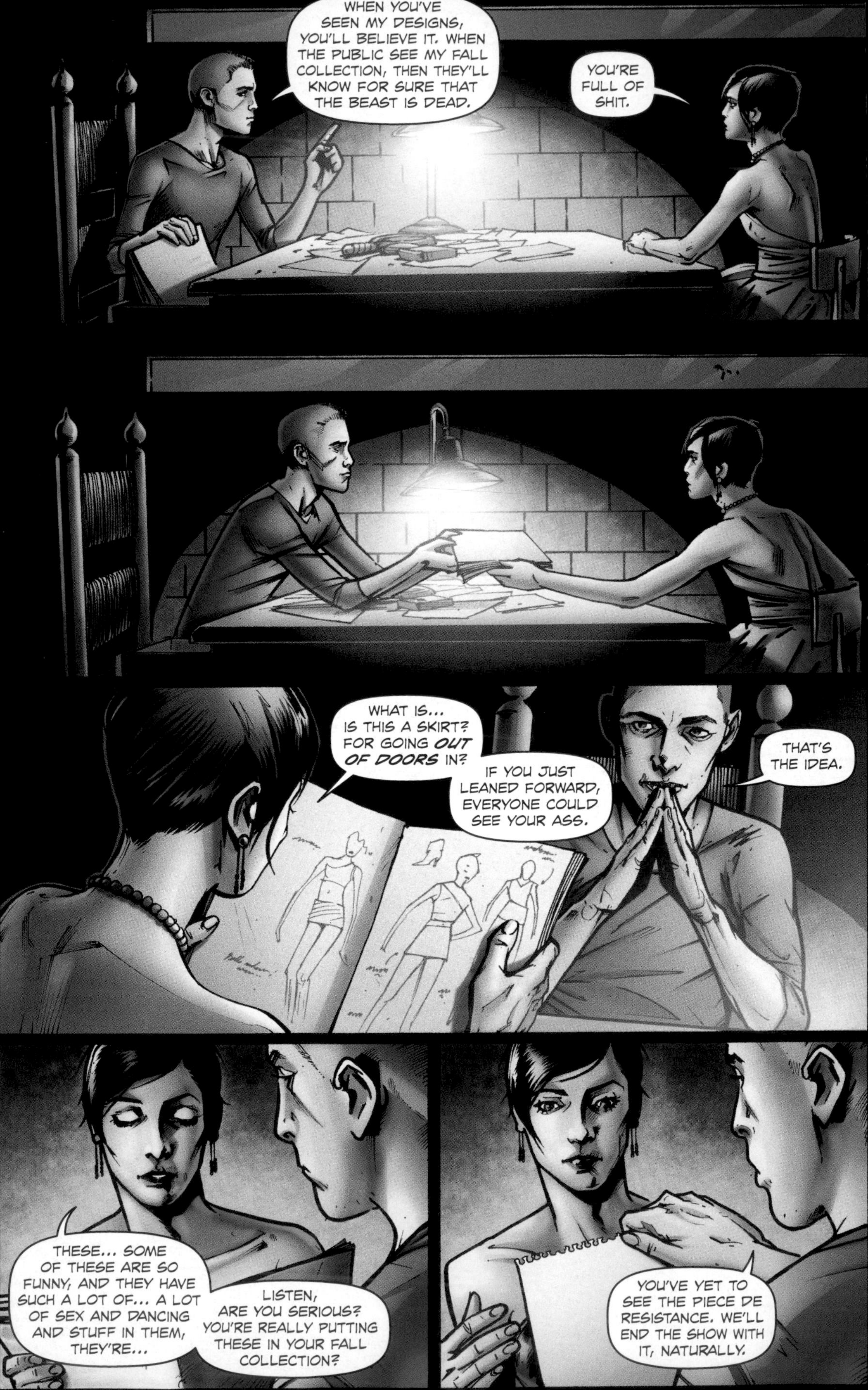
WHEN YOU'VE SEEN MY DESIGNS, YOU'LL BELIEVE IT. WHEN THE PUBLIC SEE MY FALL COLLECTION, THEN THEY'LL KNOW FOR SURE THAT THE BEAST IS DEAD.
YOU'RE FULL OF SHIT.
WHAT IS... IS THIS A SKIRT? FOR GOING *OUT OF DOORS* IN?
IF YOU JUST LEANED FORWARD, EVERYONE COULD SEE YOUR ASS.
THAT'S THE IDEA.
THESE... SOME OF THESE ARE SO FUNNY, AND THEY HAVE SUCH A LOT OF... A LOT OF SEX AND DANCING AND STUFF IN THEM, THEY'RE...
LISTEN, ARE YOU SERIOUS? YOU'RE REALLY PUTTING THESE IN YOUR FALL COLLECTION?
YOU'VE YET TO SEE THE PIECE DE RESISTANCE. WE'LL END THE SHOW WITH IT, NATURALLY.

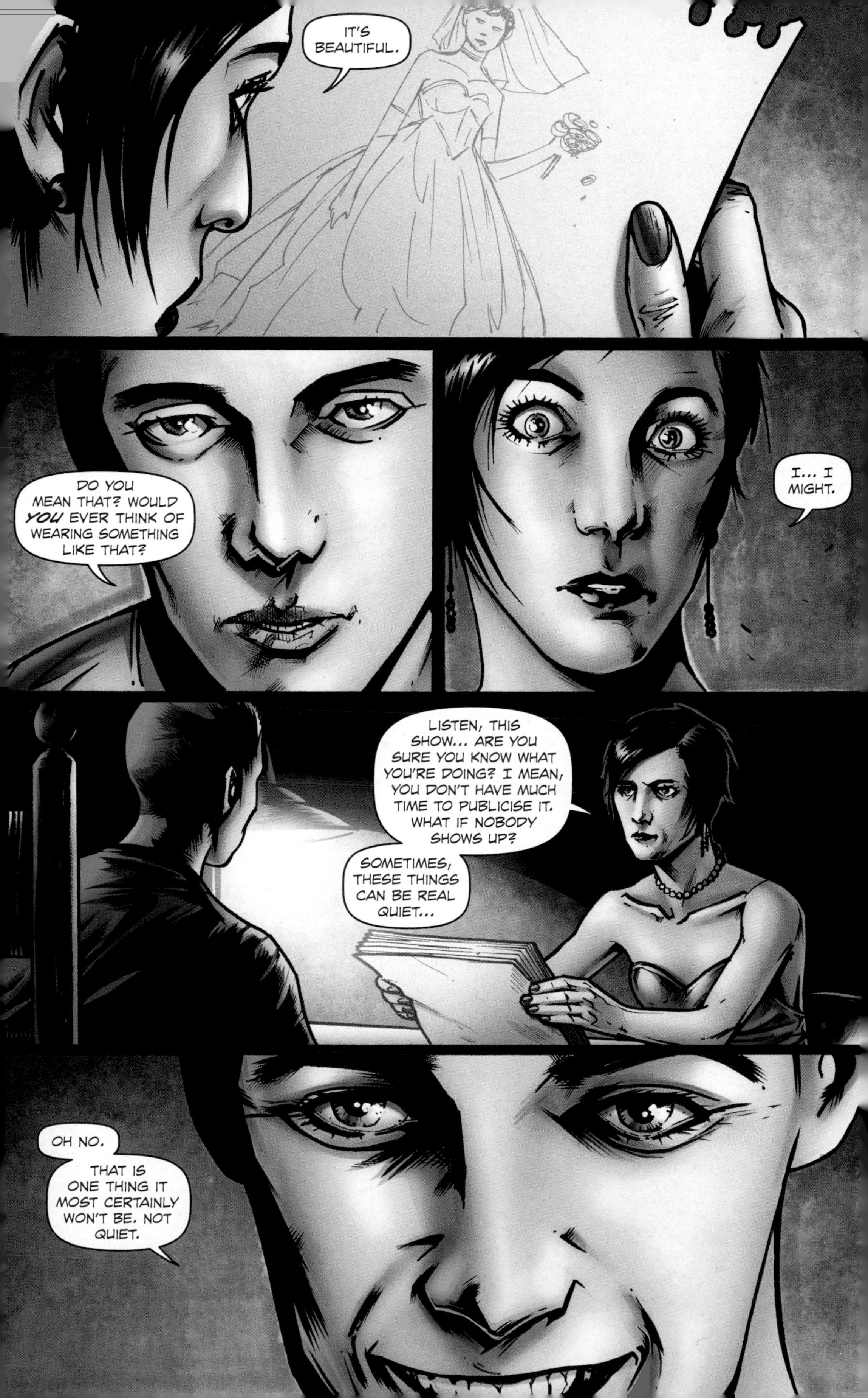
IT'S BEAUTIFUL.
DO YOU MEAN THAT? WOULD YOU EVER THINK OF WEARING SOMETHING LIKE THAT?
I... I MIGHT.
LISTEN, THIS SHOW... ARE YOU SURE YOU KNOW WHAT YOU'RE DOING? I MEAN, YOU DON'T HAVE MUCH TIME TO PUBLICISE IT. WHAT IF NOBODY SHOWS UP?
SOMETIMES, THESE THINGS CAN BE REAL QUIET...
OH NO.
THAT IS ONE THING IT MOST CERTAINLY WON'T BE. NOT QUIET.

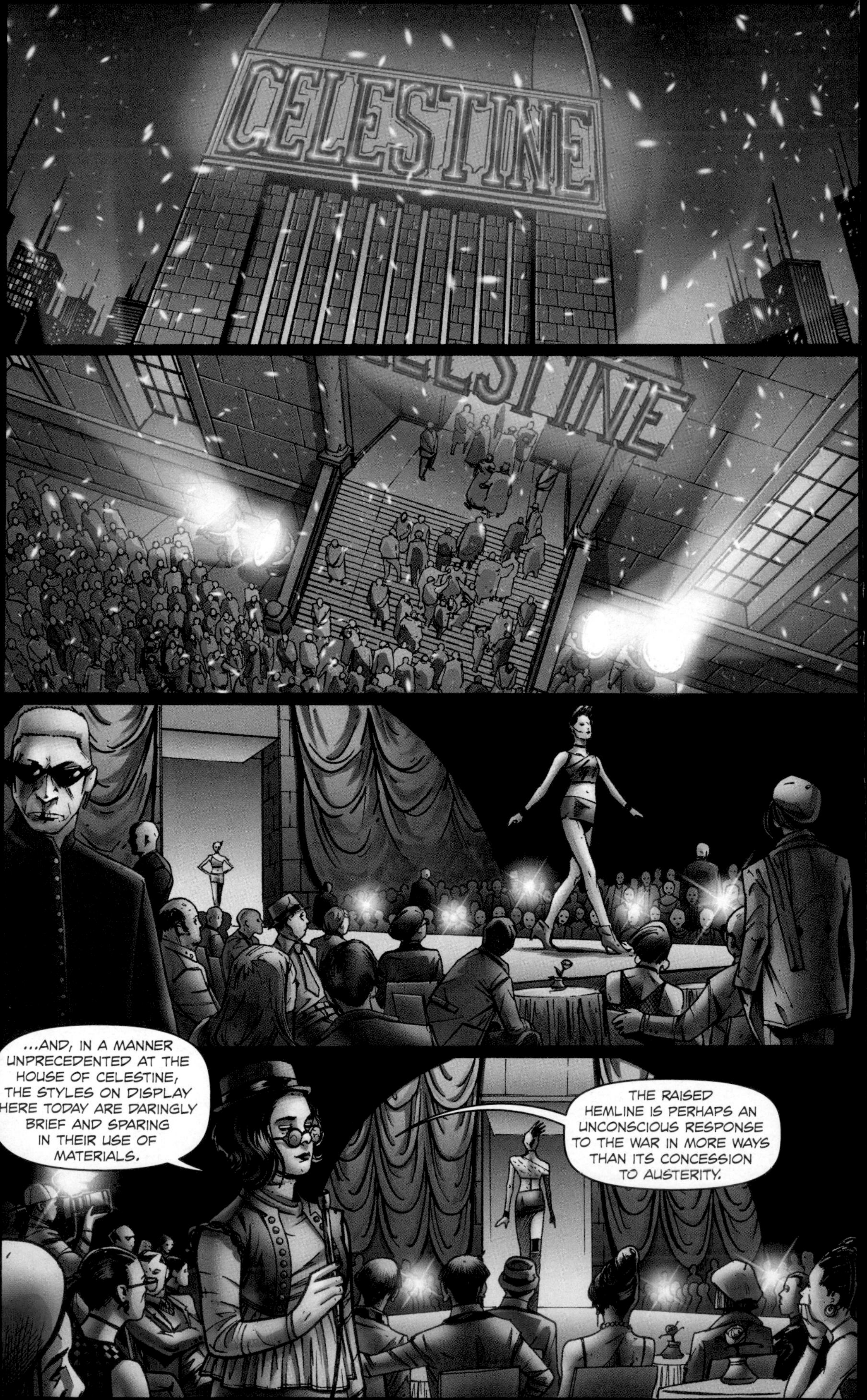
CELESTINE
...AND, IN A MANNER UNPRECEDENTED AT THE HOUSE OF CELESTINE, THE STYLES ON DISPLAY HERE TODAY ARE DARINGLY BRIEF AND SPARING IN THEIR USE OF MATERIALS.
THE RAISED HEMLINE IS PERHAPS AN UNCONSCIOUS RESPONSE TO THE WAR IN MORE WAYS THAN ITS CONCESSION TO AUSTERITY.

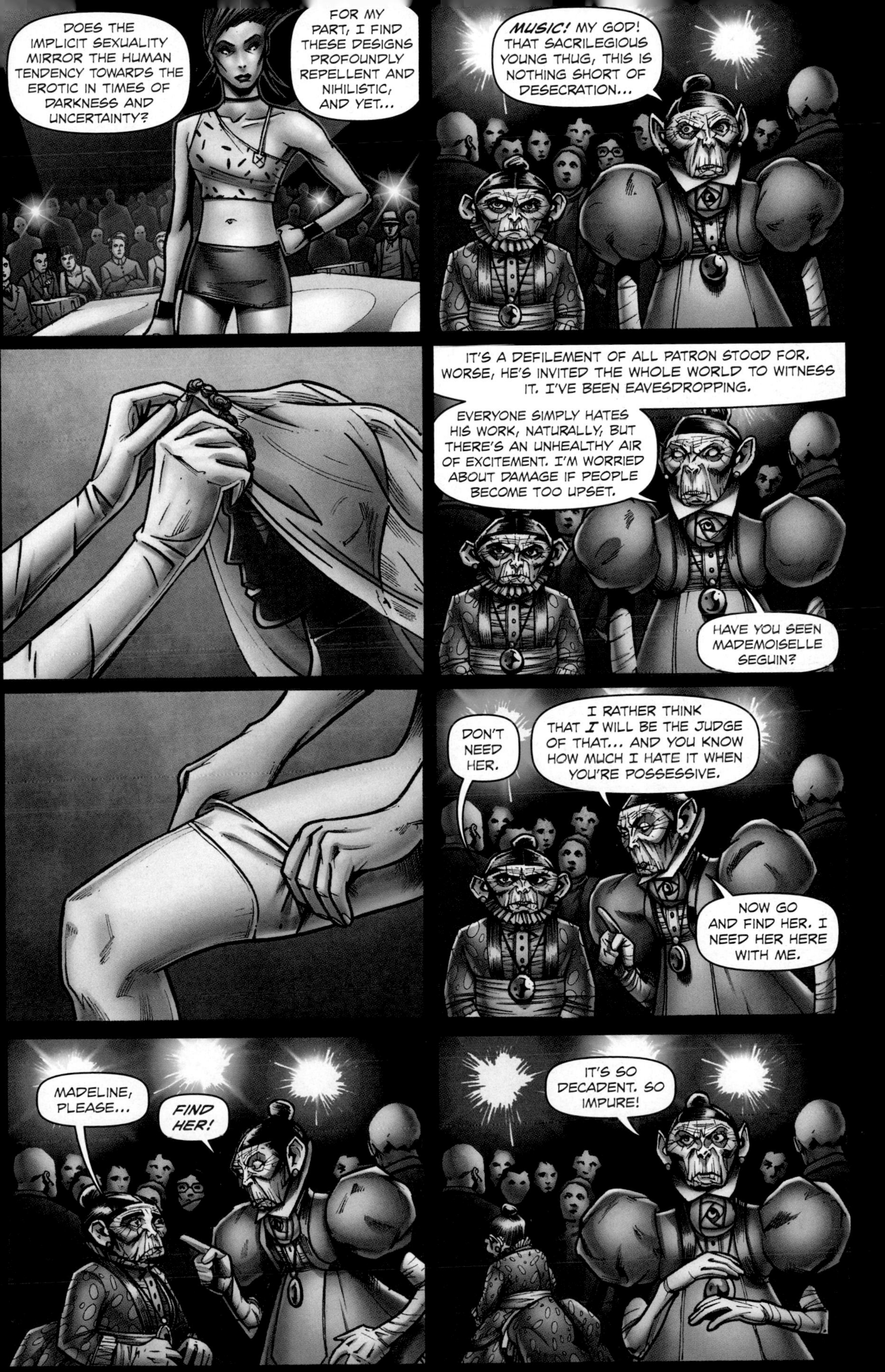
DOES THE IMPLICIT SEXUALITY MIRROR THE HUMAN TENDENCY TOWARDS THE EROTIC IN TIMES OF DARKNESS AND UNCERTAINTY?
FOR MY PART, I FIND THESE DESIGNS PROFOUNDLY REPELLENT AND NIHILISTIC, AND YET...
MUSIC! MY GOD! THAT SACRILEGIOUS YOUNG THUG, THIS IS NOTHING SHORT OF DESECRATION...
IT'S A DEFILEMENT OF ALL PATRON STOOD FOR. WORSE, HE'S INVITED THE WHOLE WORLD TO WITNESS IT. I'VE BEEN EAVESDROPPING.
EVERYONE SIMPLY HATES HIS WORK, NATURALLY, BUT THERE'S AN UNHEALTHY AIR OF EXCITEMENT. I'M WORRIED ABOUT DAMAGE IF PEOPLE BECOME TOO UPSET.
HAVE YOU SEEN MADEMOISELLE SEGUIN?
DON'T NEED HER.
I RATHER THINK THAT I WILL BE THE JUDGE OF THAT... AND YOU KNOW HOW MUCH I HATE IT WHEN YOU'RE POSSESSIVE.
NOW GO AND FIND HER. I NEED HER HERE WITH ME.
MADELINE, PLEASE...
FIND HER!
IT'S SO DECADENT. SO IMPURE!

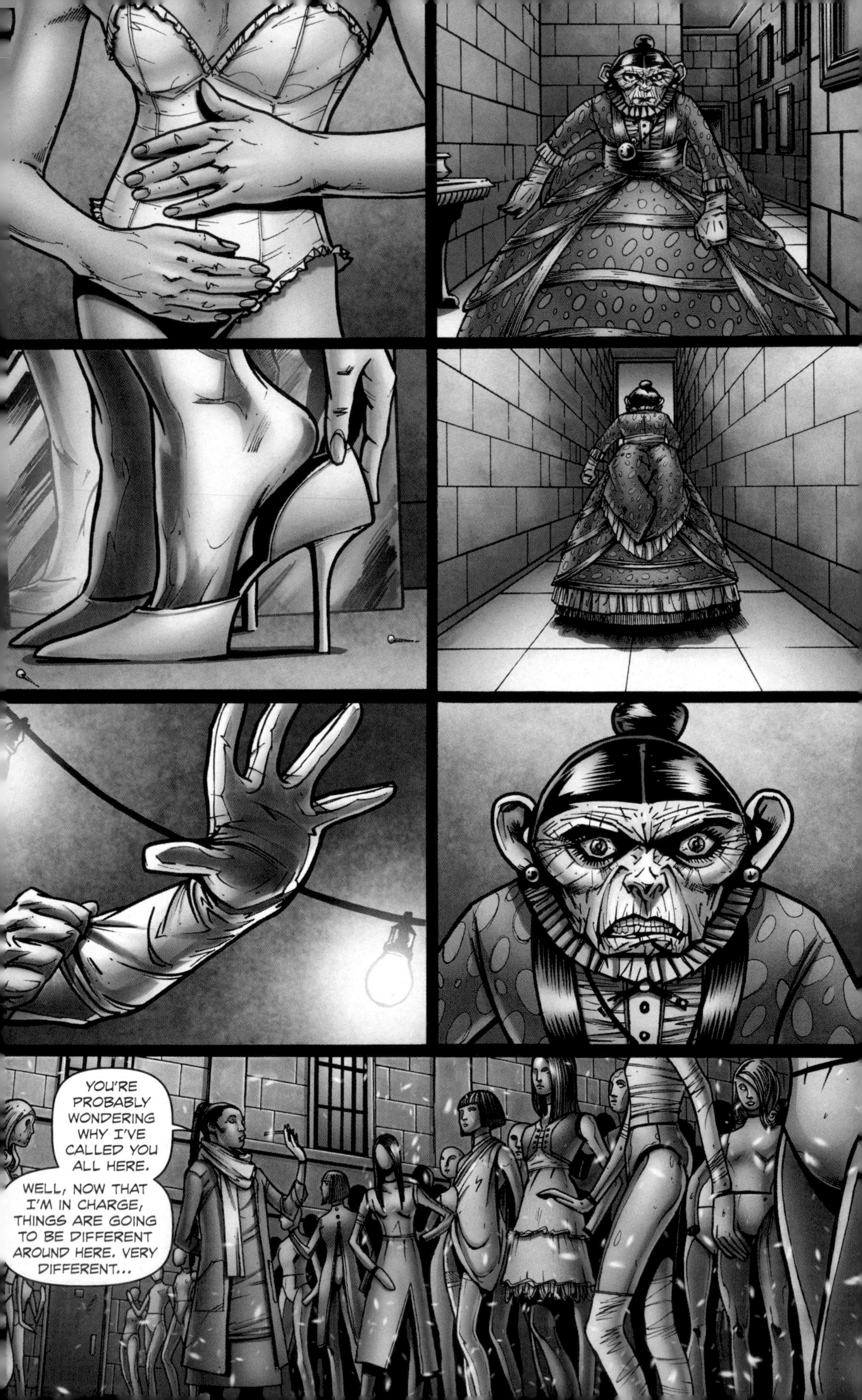
YOU'RE PROBABLY WONDERING WHY I'VE CALLED YOU ALL HERE.
WELL, NOW THAT I'M IN CHARGE, THINGS ARE GOING TO BE DIFFERENT AROUND HERE. VERY DIFFERENT...

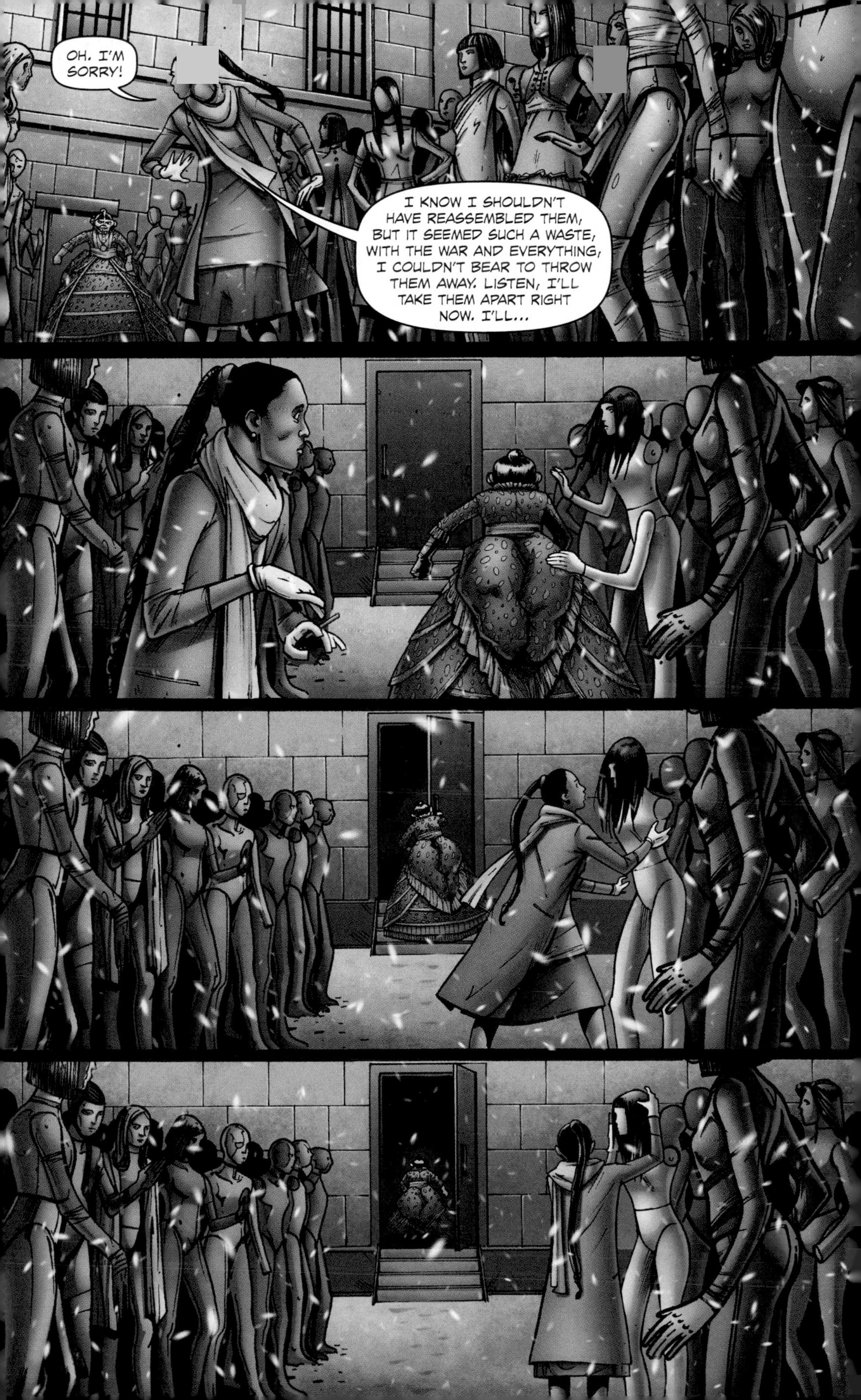
OH. I'M SORRY!
I KNOW I SHOULDN'T HAVE REASSEMBLED THEM, BUT IT SEEMED SUCH A WASTE, WITH THE WAR AND EVERYTHING, I COULDN'T BEAR TO THROW THEM AWAY. LISTEN, I'LL TAKE THEM APART RIGHT NOW. I'LL...

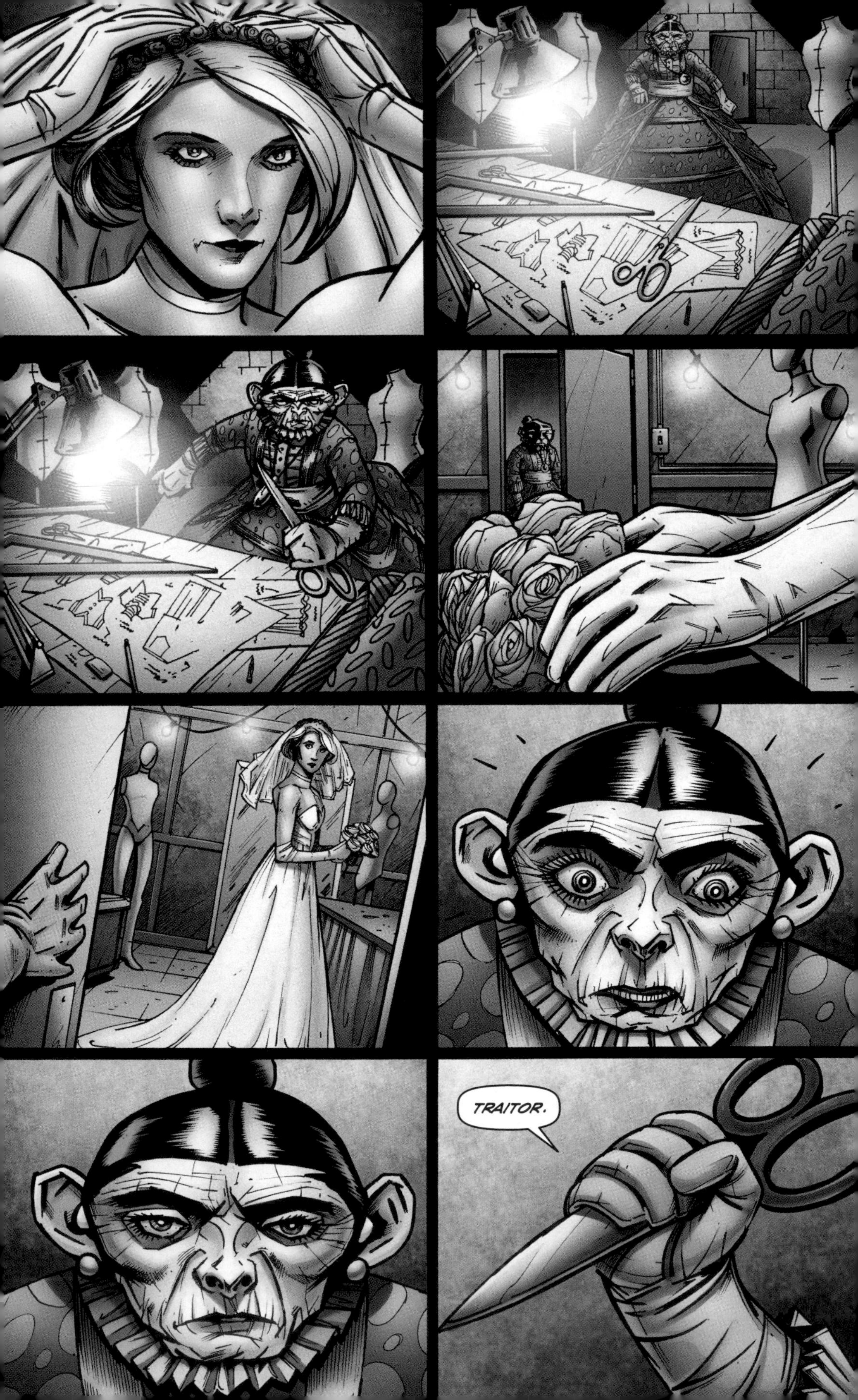
TRAITOR.

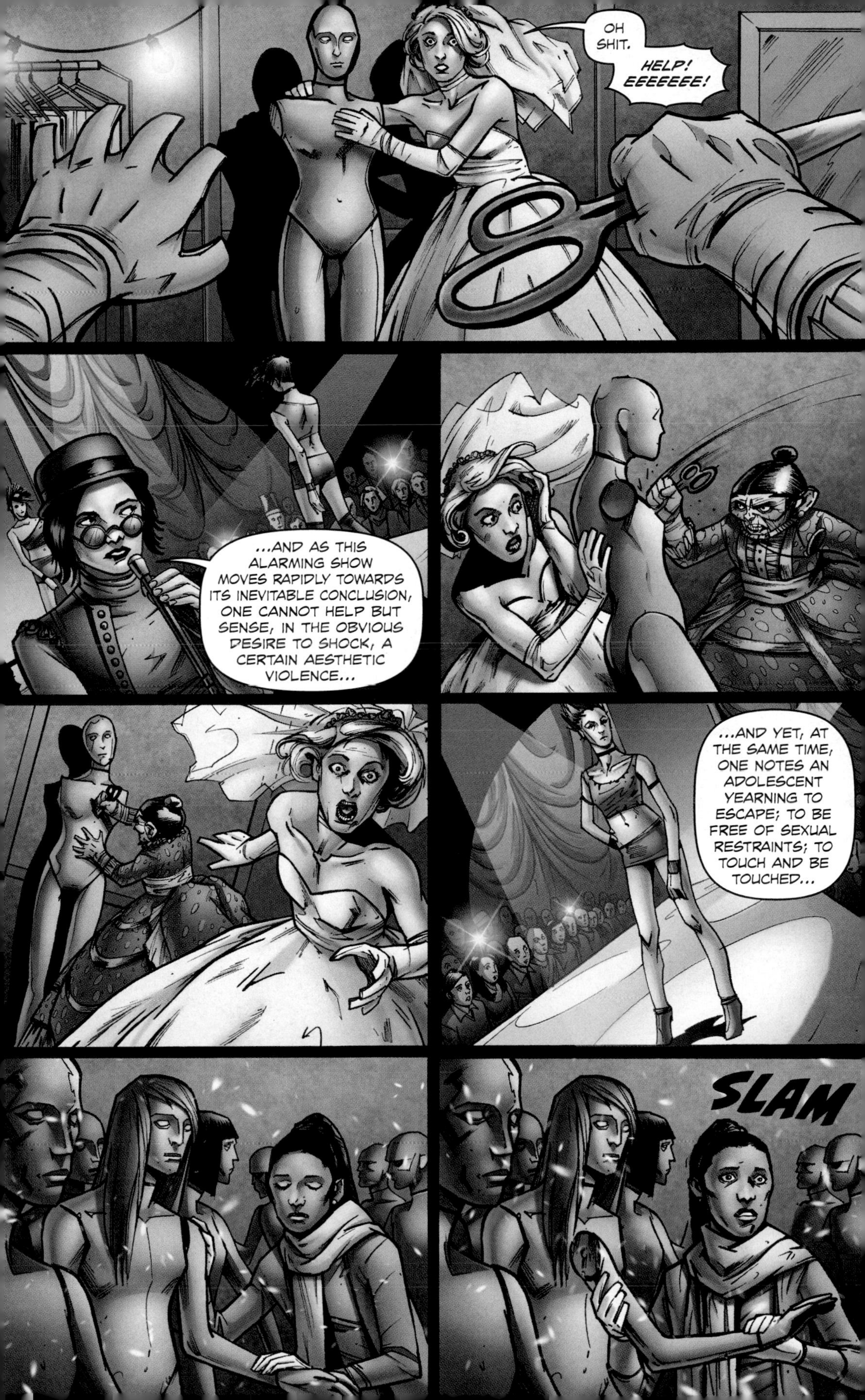
OH SHIT.
HELP! EEEEEEE!
...AND AS THIS ALARMING SHOW MOVES RAPIDLY TOWARDS ITS INEVITABLE CONCLUSION, ONE CANNOT HELP BUT SENSE, IN THE OBVIOUS DESIRE TO SHOCK, A CERTAIN AESTHETIC VIOLENCE...
...AND YET, AT THE SAME TIME, ONE NOTES AN ADOLESCENT YEARNING TO ESCAPE; TO BE FREE OF SEXUAL RESTRAINTS; TO TOUCH AND BE TOUCHED...
SLAM

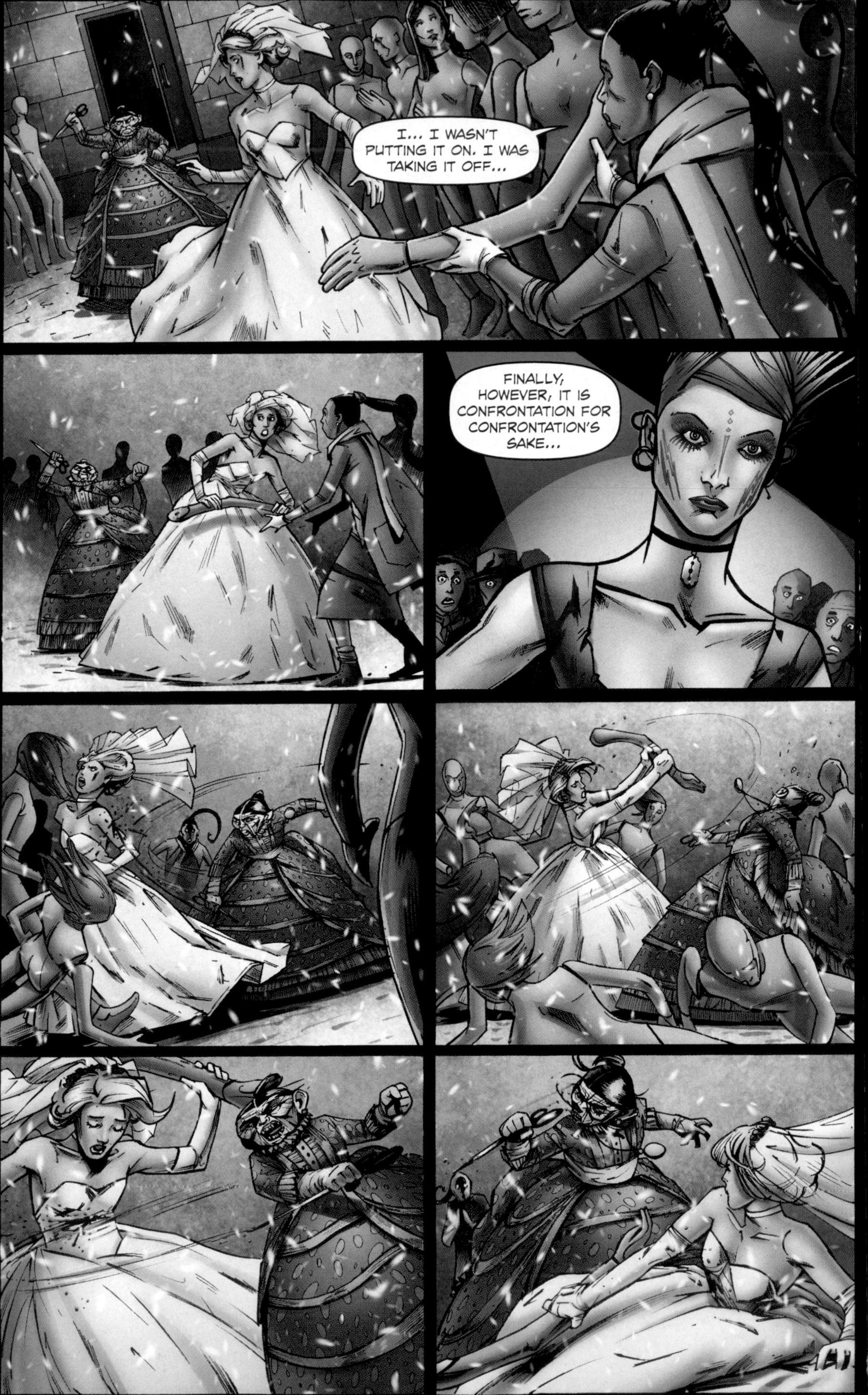
I... I WASN'T PUTTING IT ON. I WAS TAKING IT OFF...
FINALLY, HOWEVER, IT IS CONFRONTATION FOR CONFRONTATION'S SAKE...

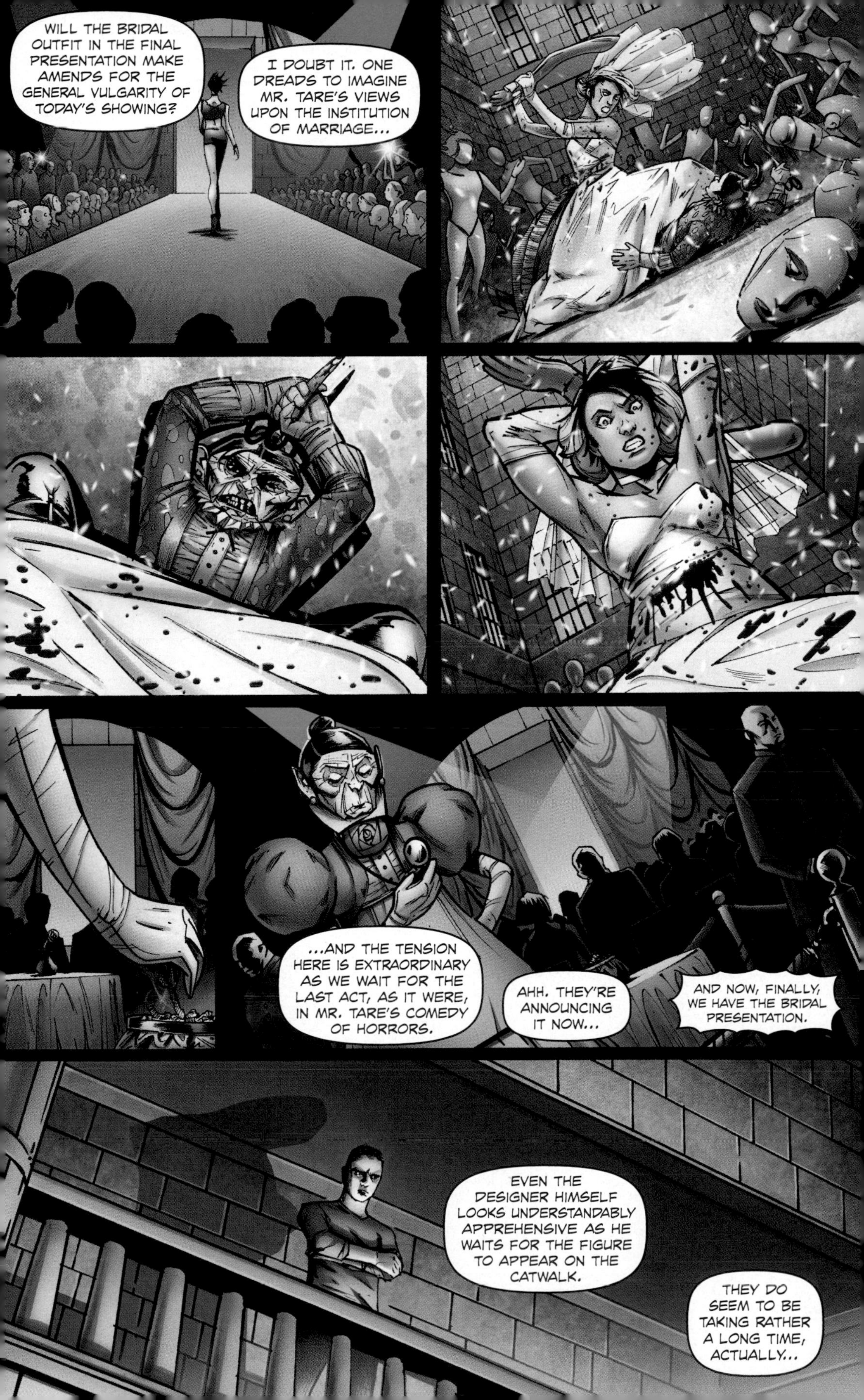
WILL THE BRIDAL OUTFIT IN THE FINAL PRESENTATION MAKE AMENDS FOR THE GENERAL VULGARITY OF TODAY'S SHOWING?
I DOUBT IT. ONE DREADS TO IMAGINE MR. TARE'S VIEWS UPON THE INSTITUTION OF MARRIAGE...
...AND THE TENSION HERE IS EXTRAORDINARY AS WE WAIT FOR THE LAST ACT, AS IT WERE, IN MR. TARE'S COMEDY OF HORRORS.
AHH. THEY'RE ANNOUNCING IT NOW...
AND NOW, FINALLY, WE HAVE THE BRIDAL PRESENTATION.
EVEN THE DESIGNER HIMSELF LOOKS UNDERSTANDABLY APPREHENSIVE AS HE WAITS FOR THE FIGURE TO APPEAR ON THE CATWALK.
THEY DO SEEM TO BE TAKING RATHER A LONG TIME, ACTUALLY...

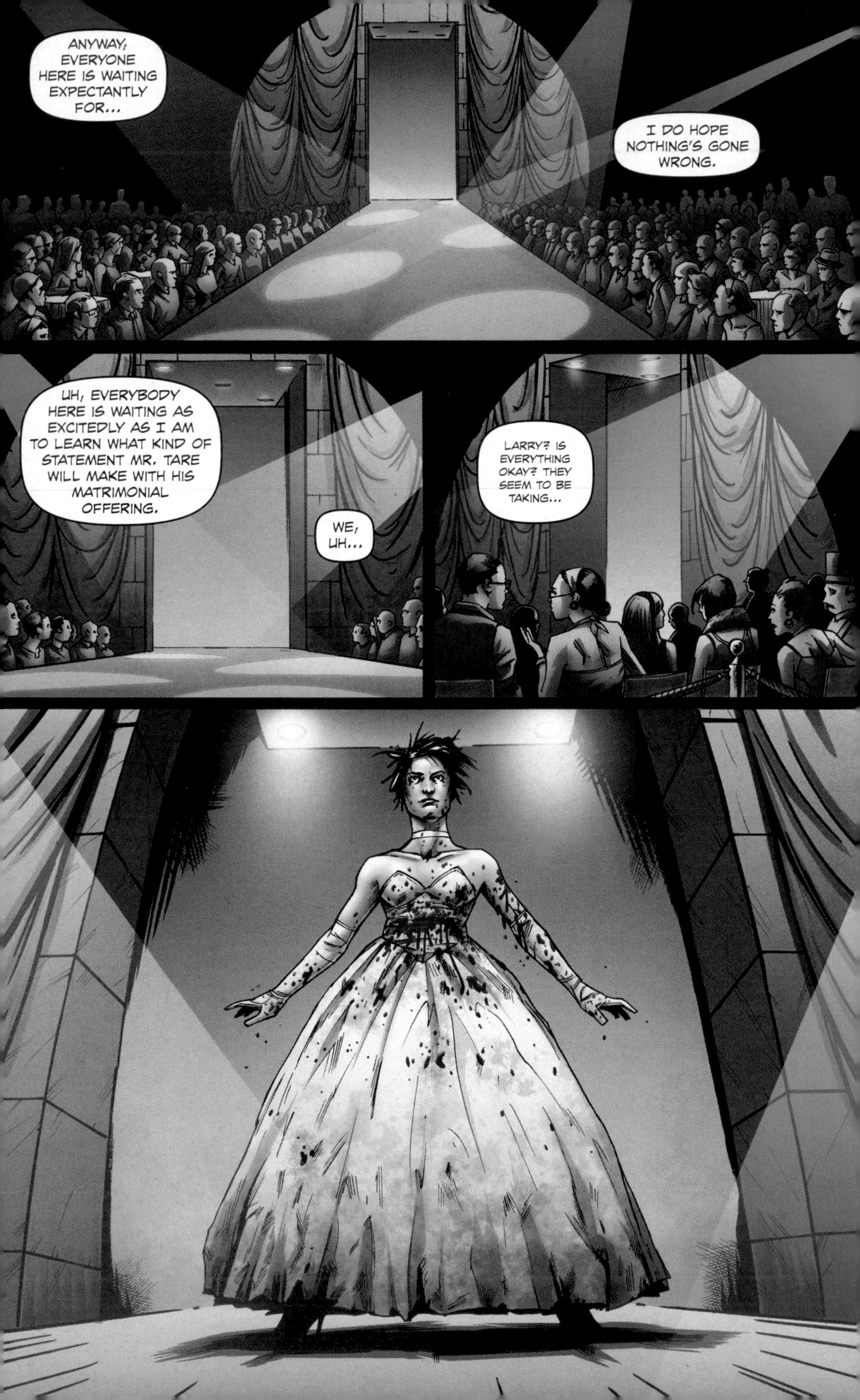
ANYWAY, EVERYONE HERE IS WAITING EXPECTANTLY FOR...
I DO HOPE NOTHING'S GONE WRONG.
UH, EVERYBODY HERE IS WAITING AS EXCITEDLY AS I AM TO LEARN WHAT KIND OF STATEMENT MR. TARE WILL MAKE WITH HIS MATRIMONIAL OFFERING.
WE, UH...
LARRY? IS EVERYTHING OKAY? THEY SEEM TO BE TAKING...

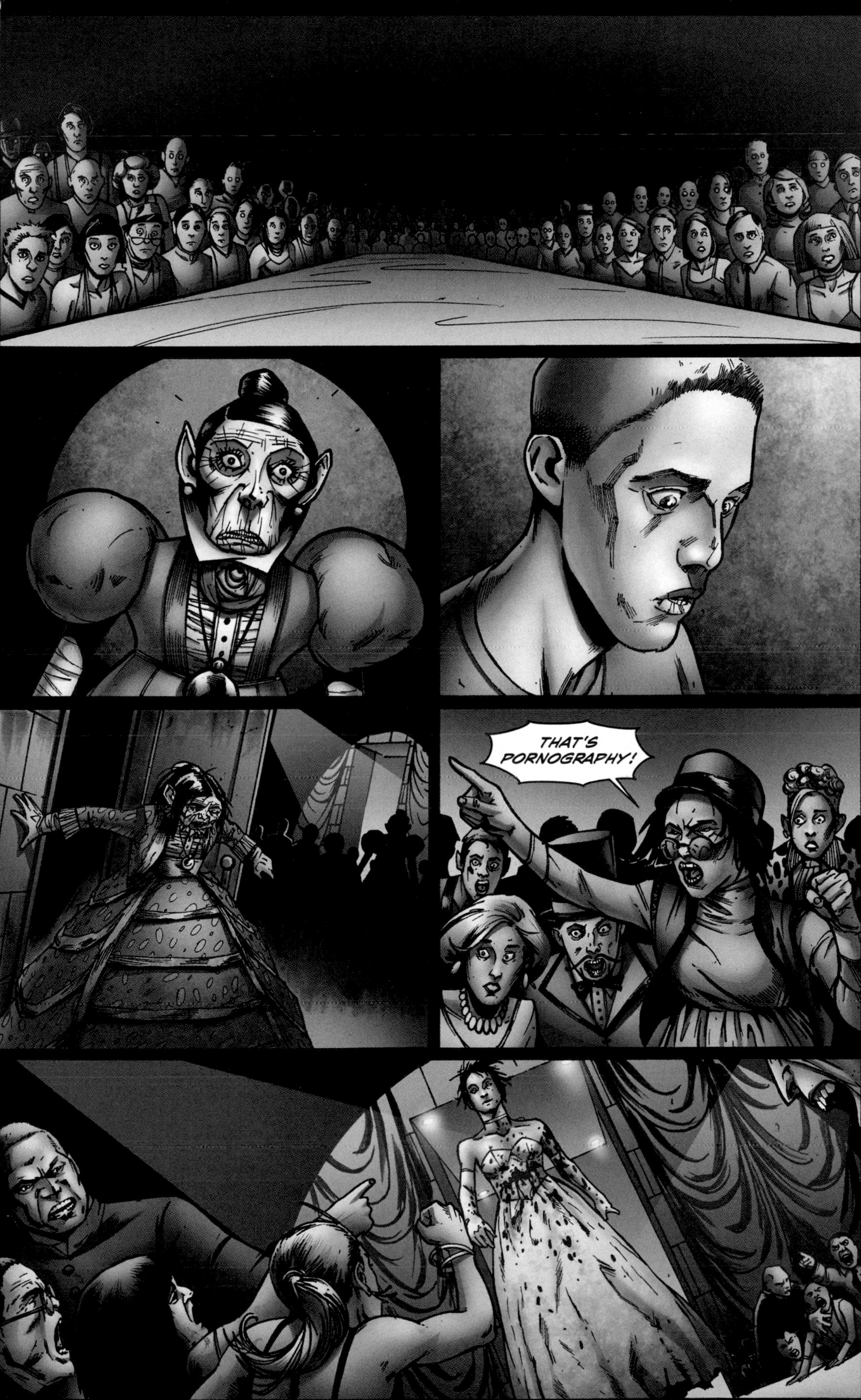
THAT'S PORNOGRAPHY!

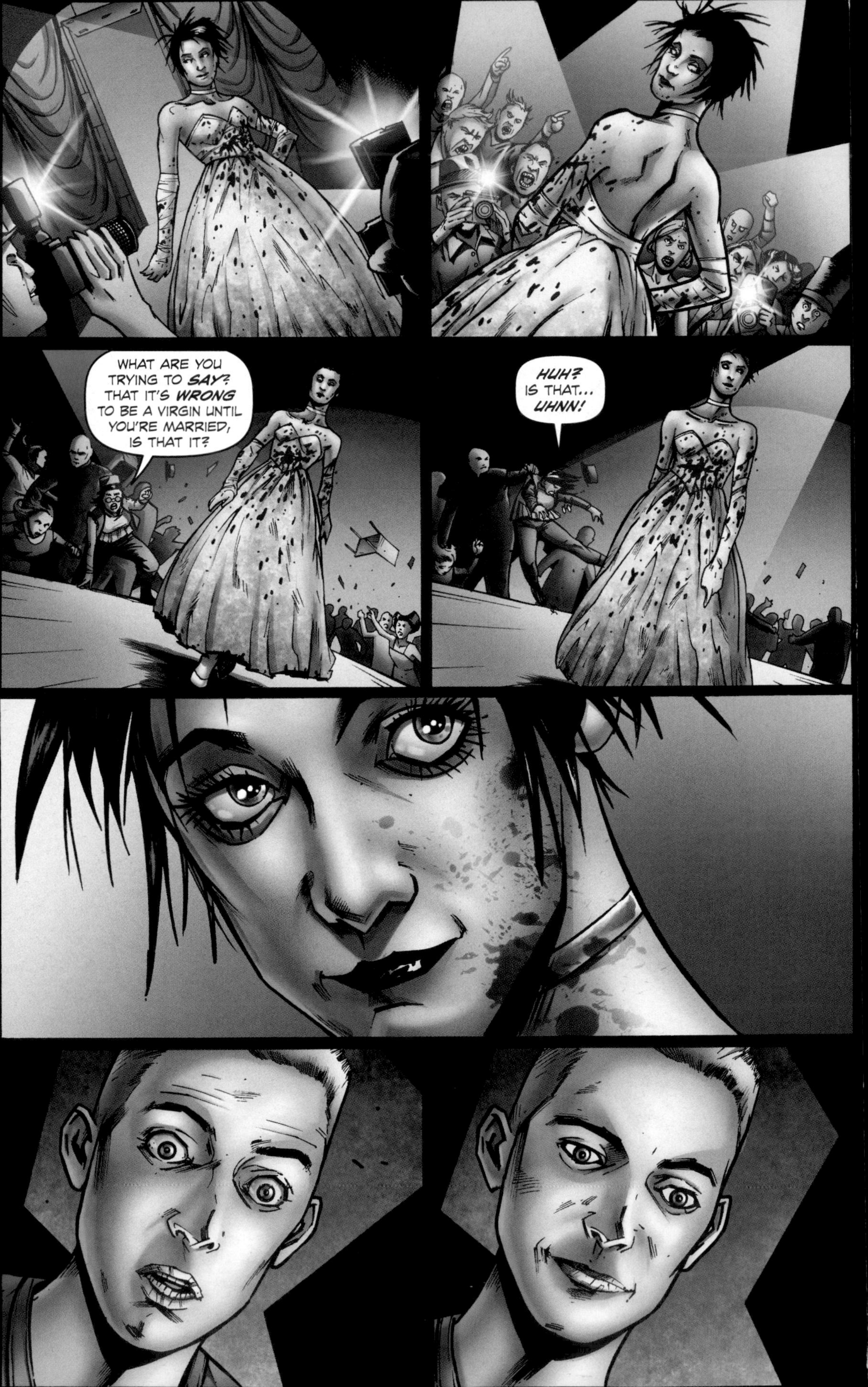
WHAT ARE YOU TRYING TO *SAY?* THAT IT'S *WRONG* TO BE A VIRGIN UNTIL YOU'RE MARRIED, IS THAT IT?
HUH? IS THAT... *UHNN!*

GEORGINA, PULL YOURSELF *TOGETHER!* THIS IS LIKE A *GODDAMNED* SCENE FROM THE *REVOLUTION* HERE AND WE HAVE TO FILE THE STORY...

LOOK AT THEM! THEY HATE THIS STUFF! THERE HASN'T BEEN A RIOT LIKE THIS SINCE *CELESTINE'S* FIRST SHOW. COME ON...

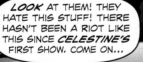

WHAT HAPPENED? YOU *STUPID COW*, HOW COULD YOU LET HER DO THAT?

YOU...

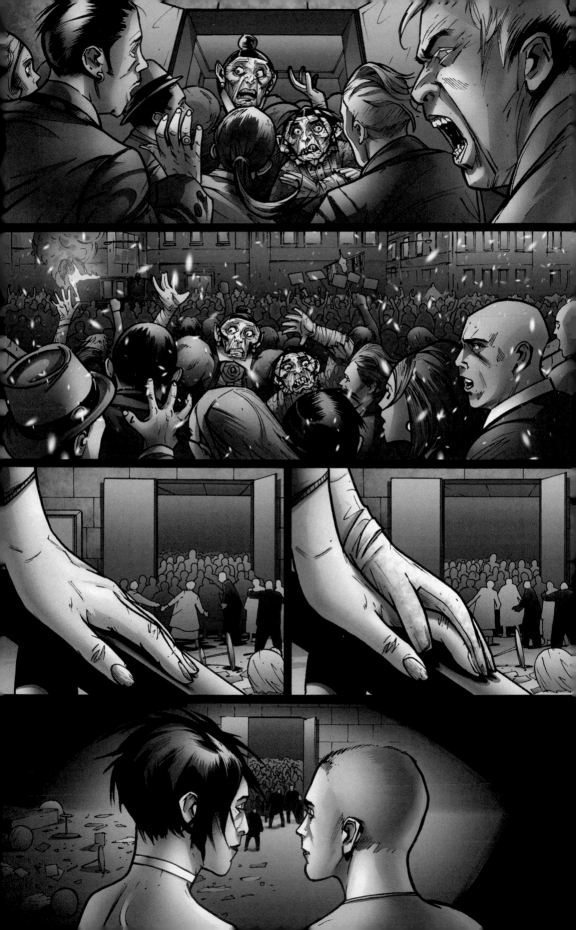

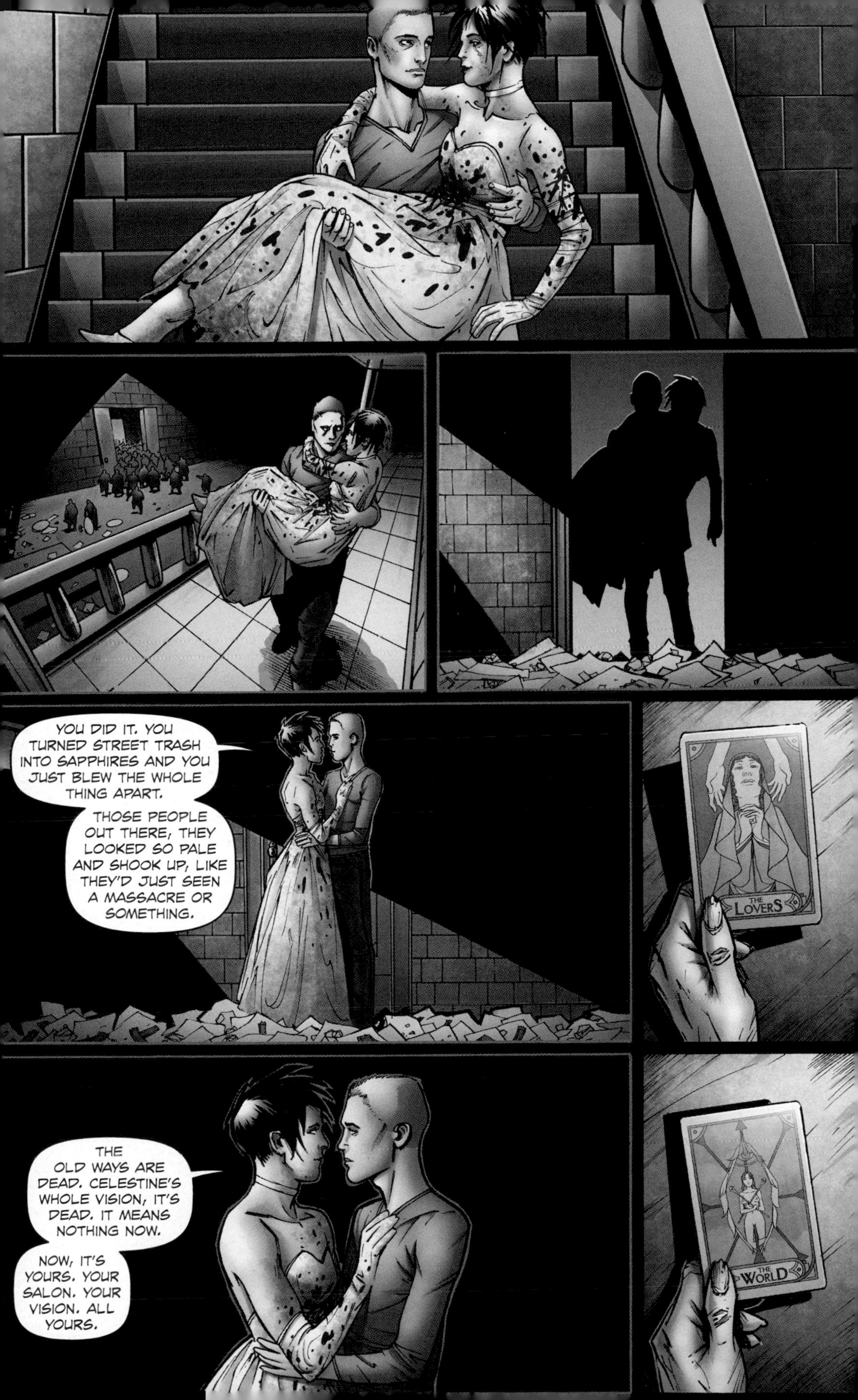
YOU DID IT. YOU TURNED STREET TRASH INTO SAPPHIRES AND YOU JUST BLEW THE WHOLE THING APART.
THOSE PEOPLE OUT THERE, THEY LOOKED SO PALE AND SHOOK UP, LIKE THEY'D JUST SEEN A MASSACRE OR SOMETHING.
THE LOVERS
THE OLD WAYS ARE DEAD. CELESTINE'S WHOLE VISION, IT'S DEAD. IT MEANS NOTHING NOW.
NOW, IT'S YOURS. YOUR SALON. YOUR VISION. ALL YOURS.
THE WORLD

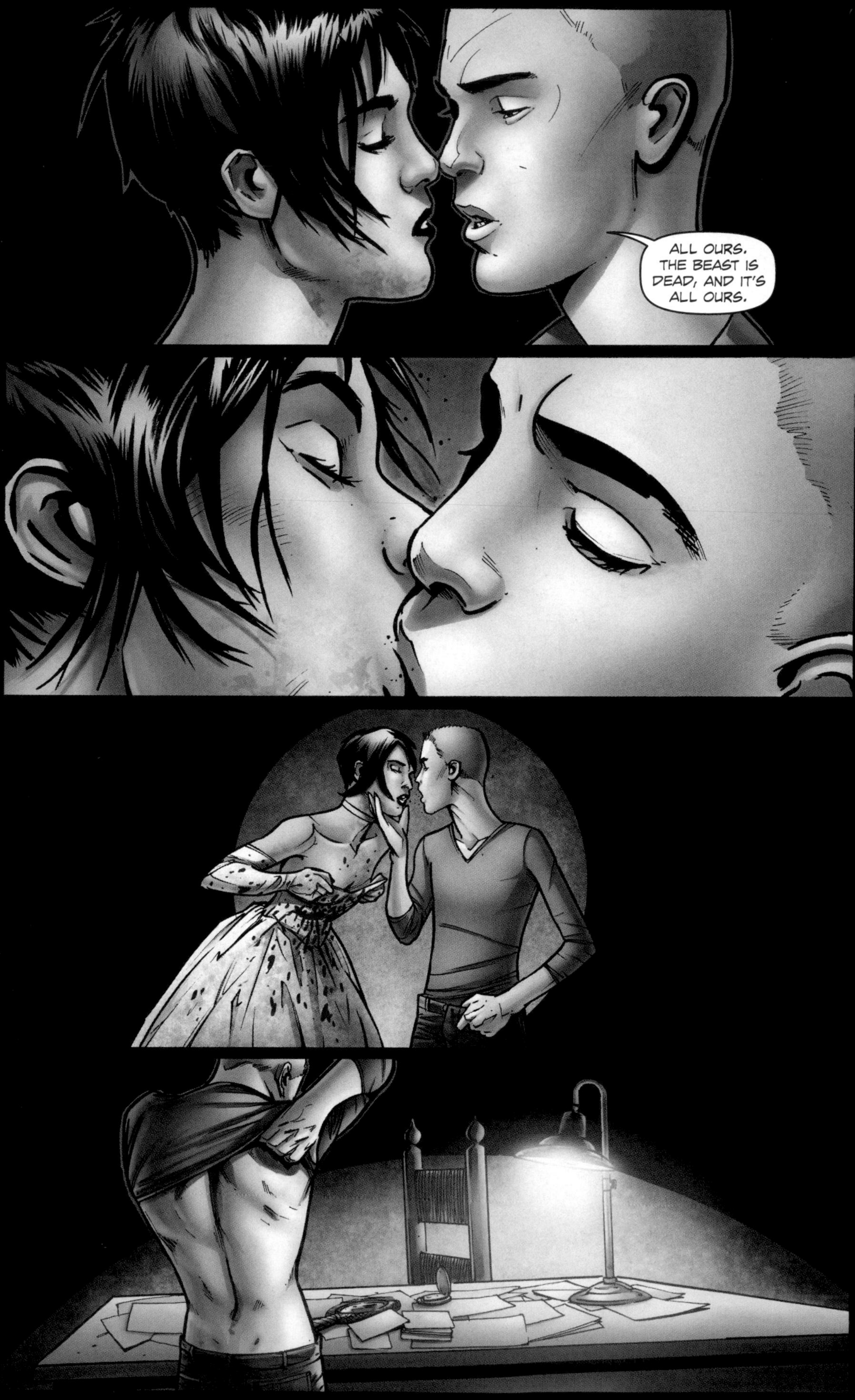
ALL OURS. THE BEAST IS DEAD, AND IT'S ALL OURS.

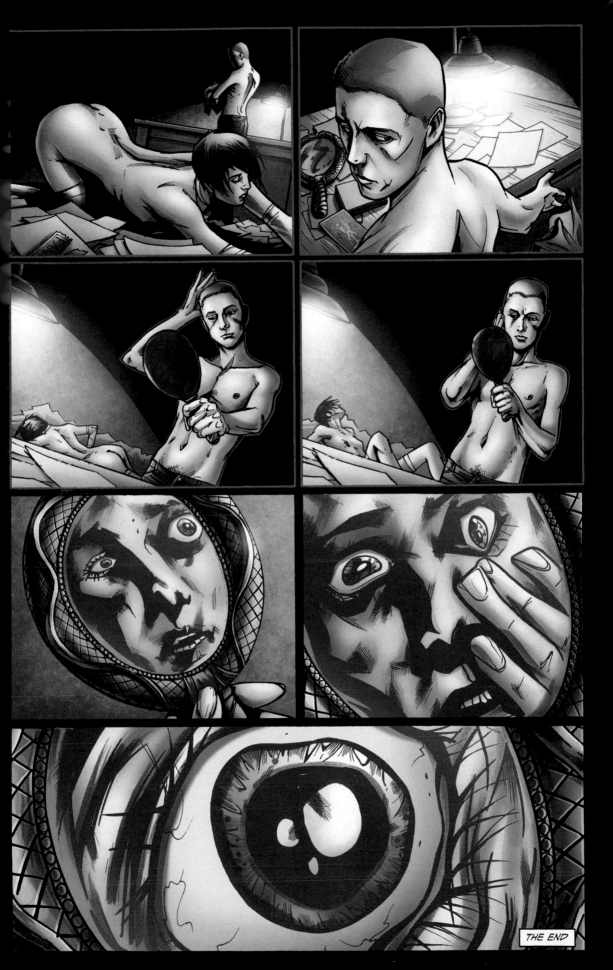

THE END

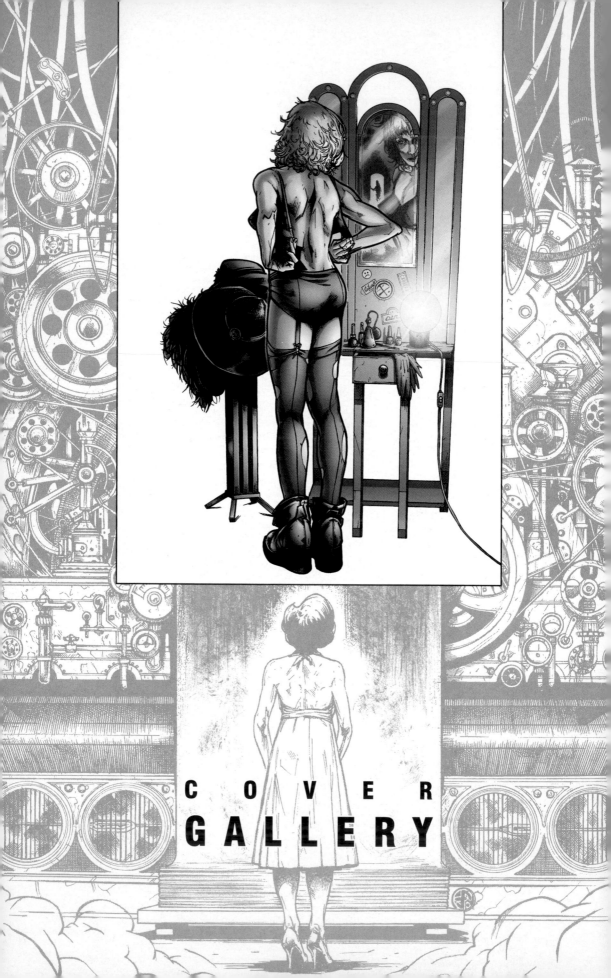

COVER
GALLERY

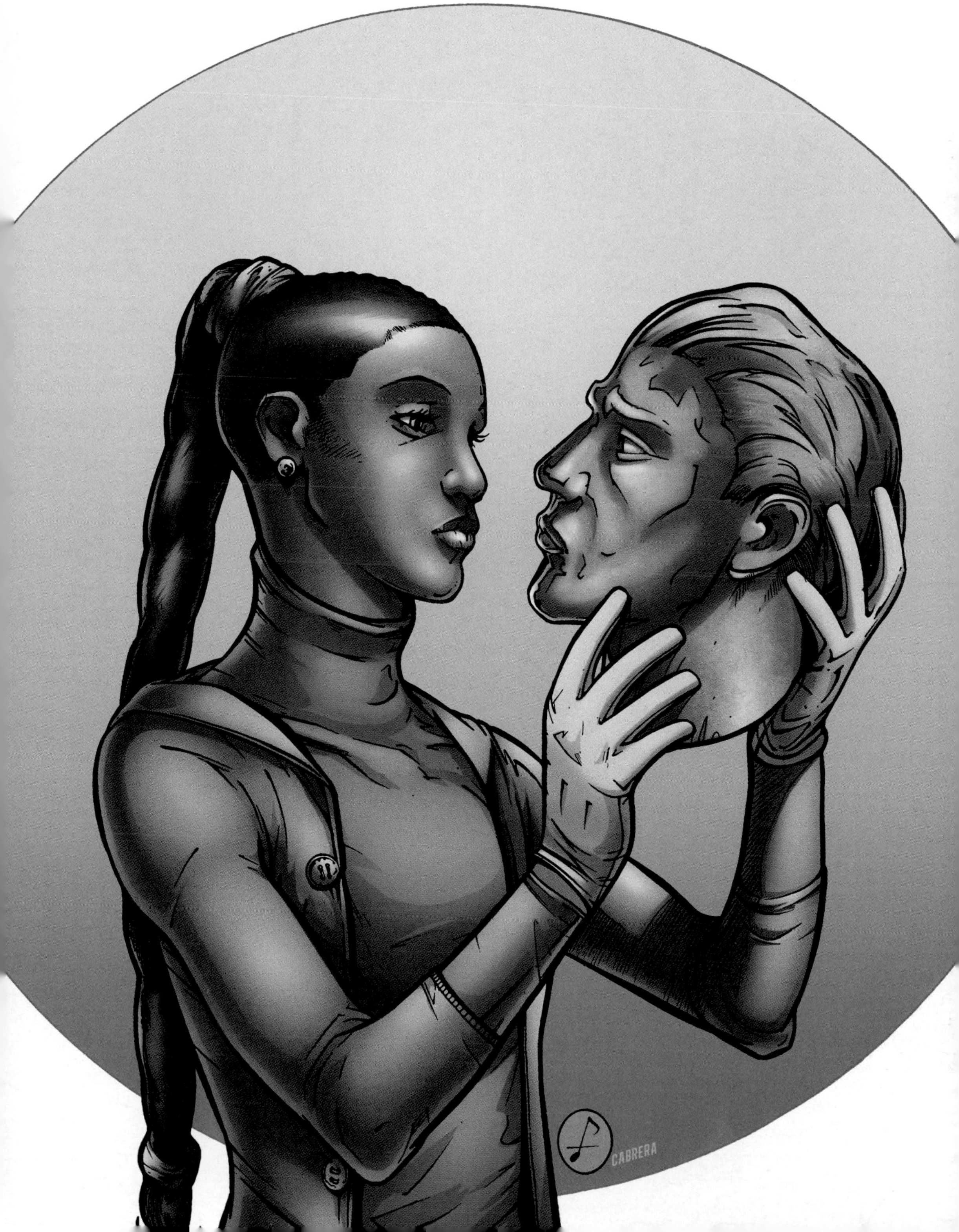
CABRERA

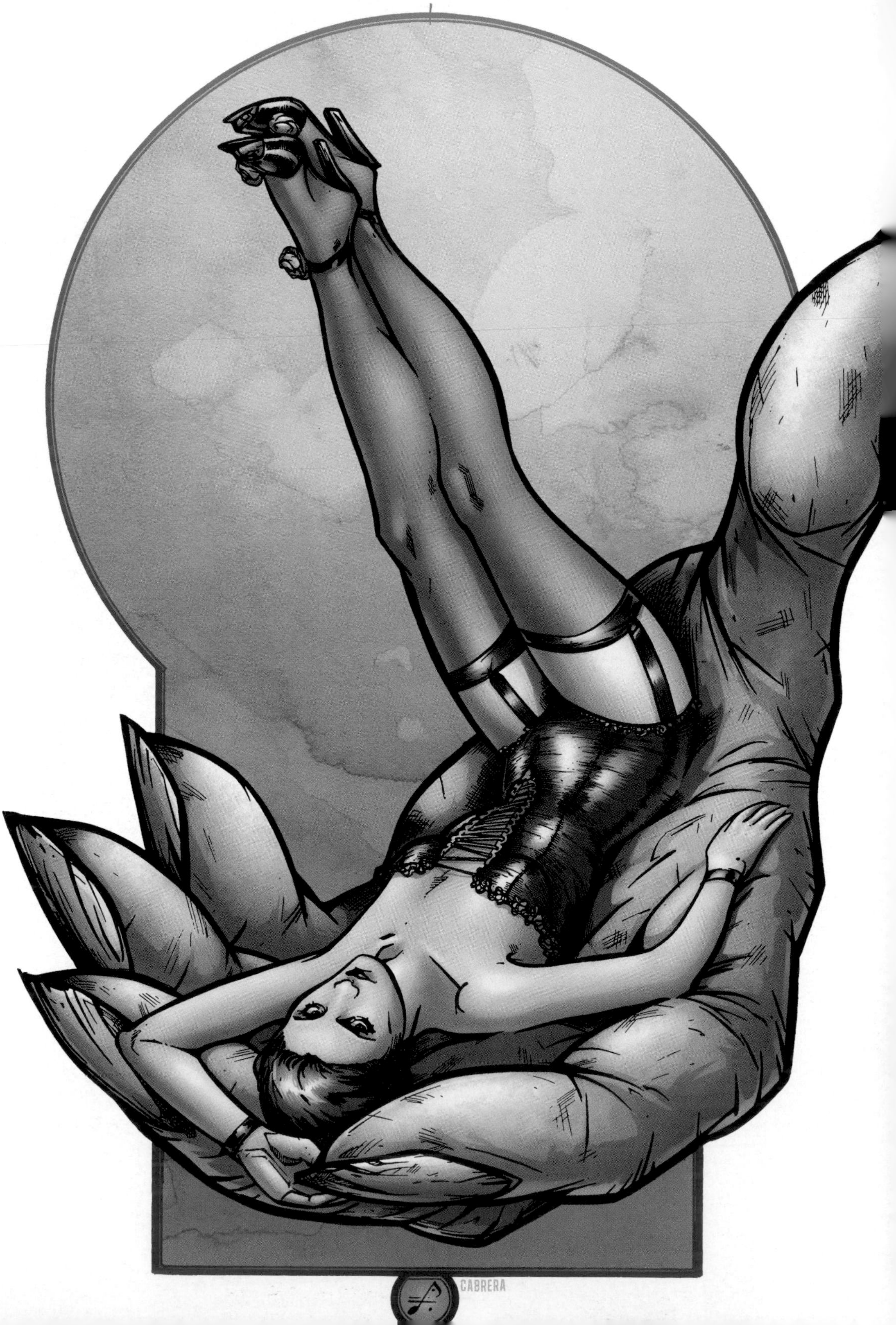
CABRERA

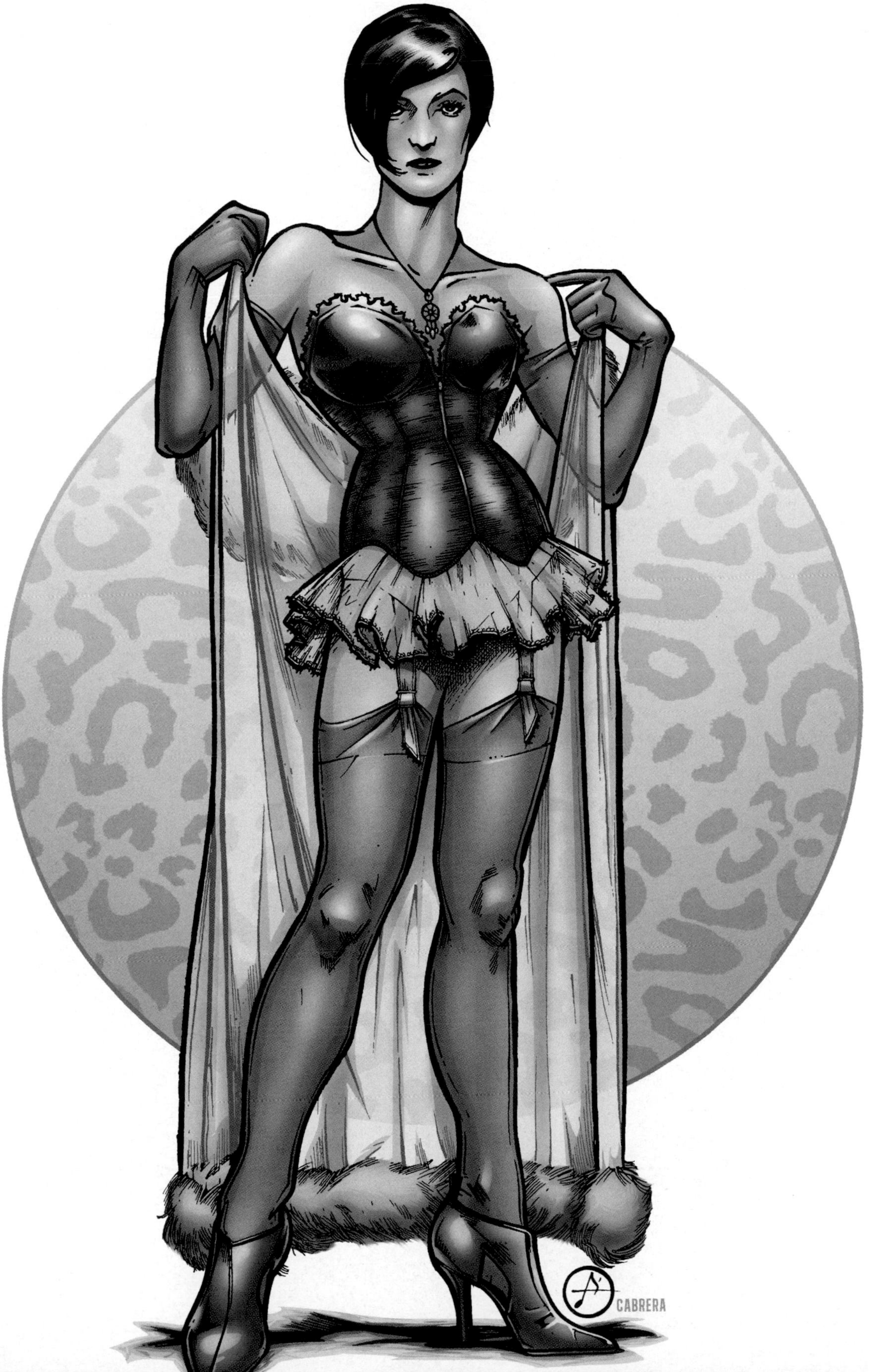
CABRERA

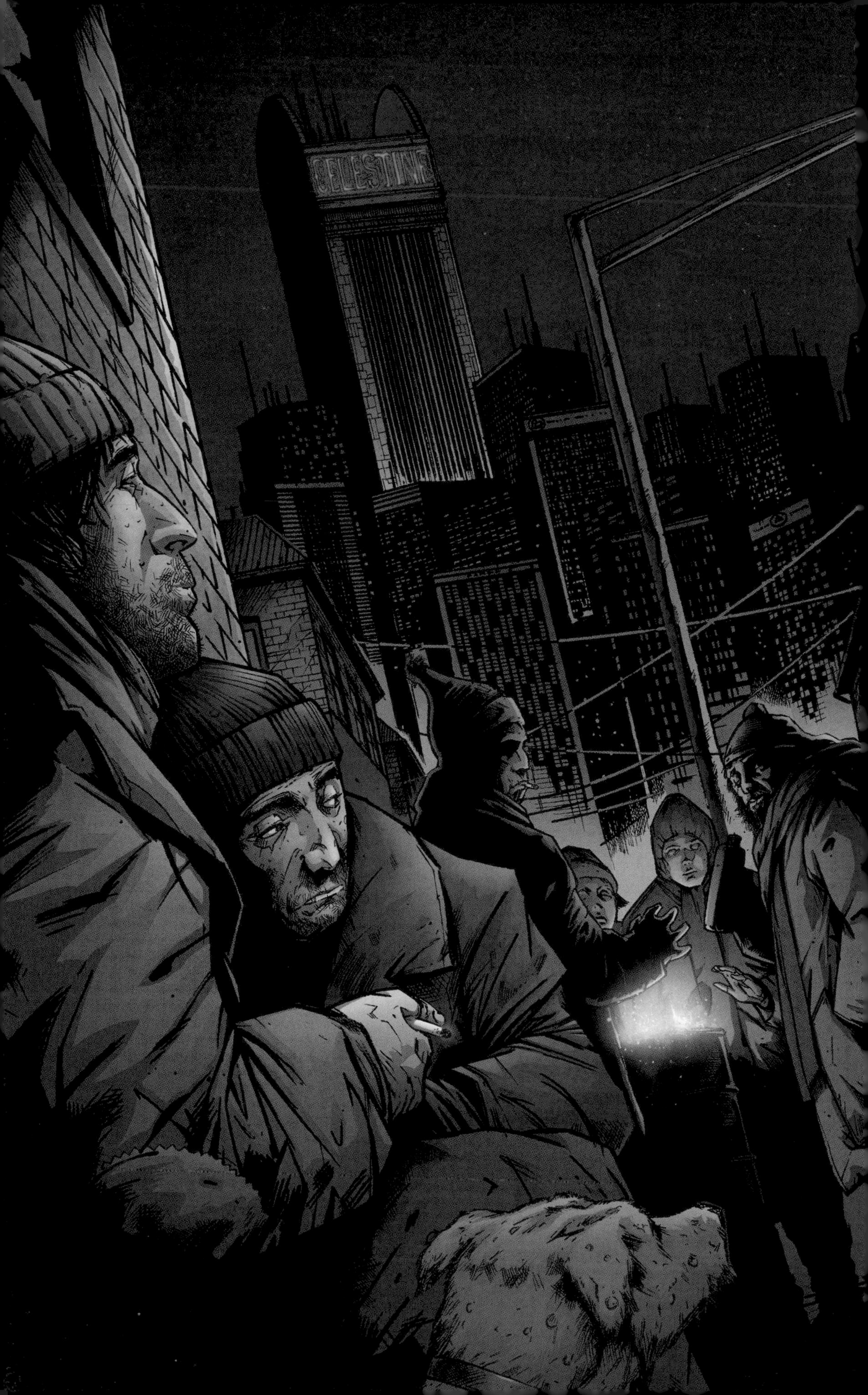
CELESTINE

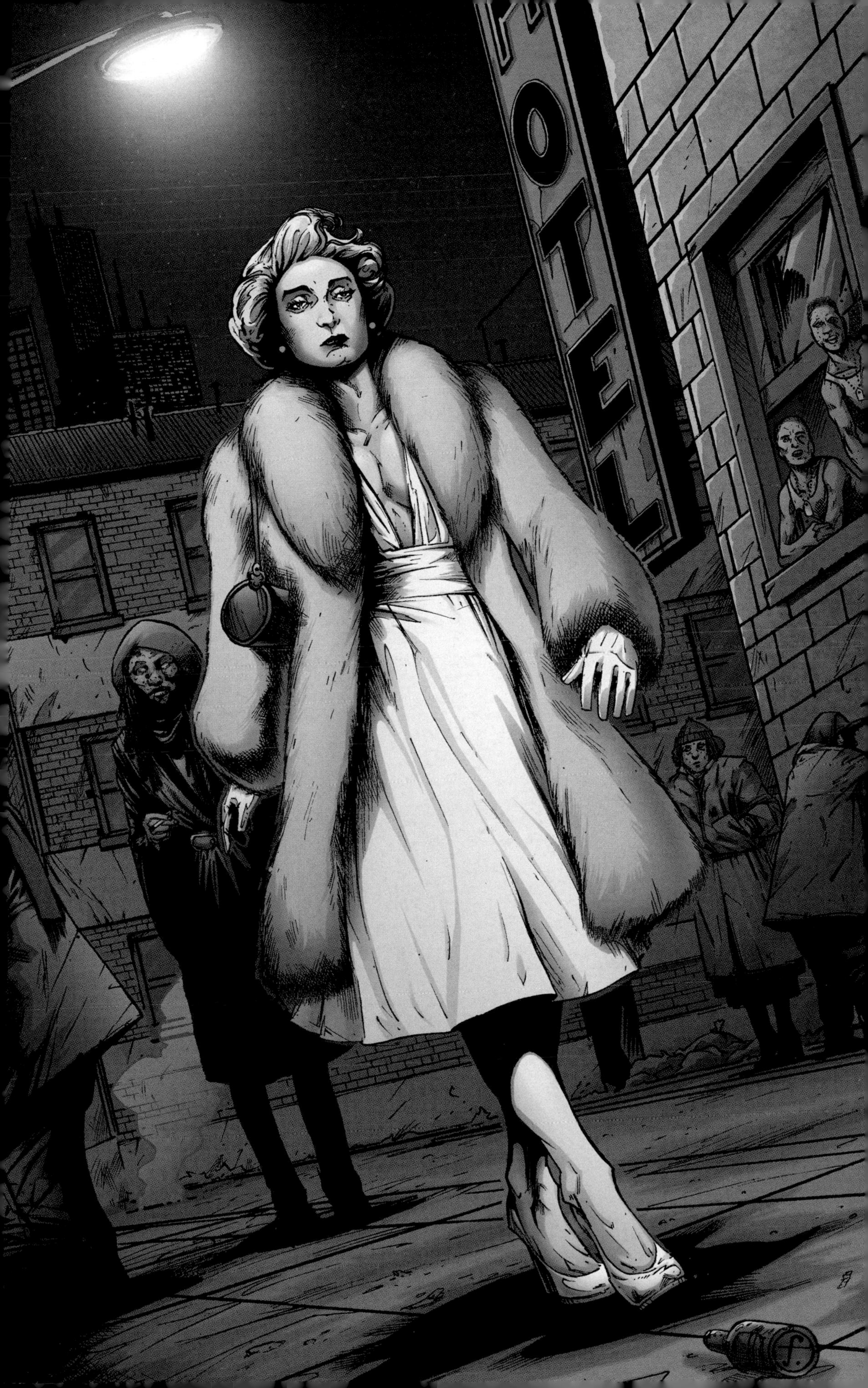
OTEL

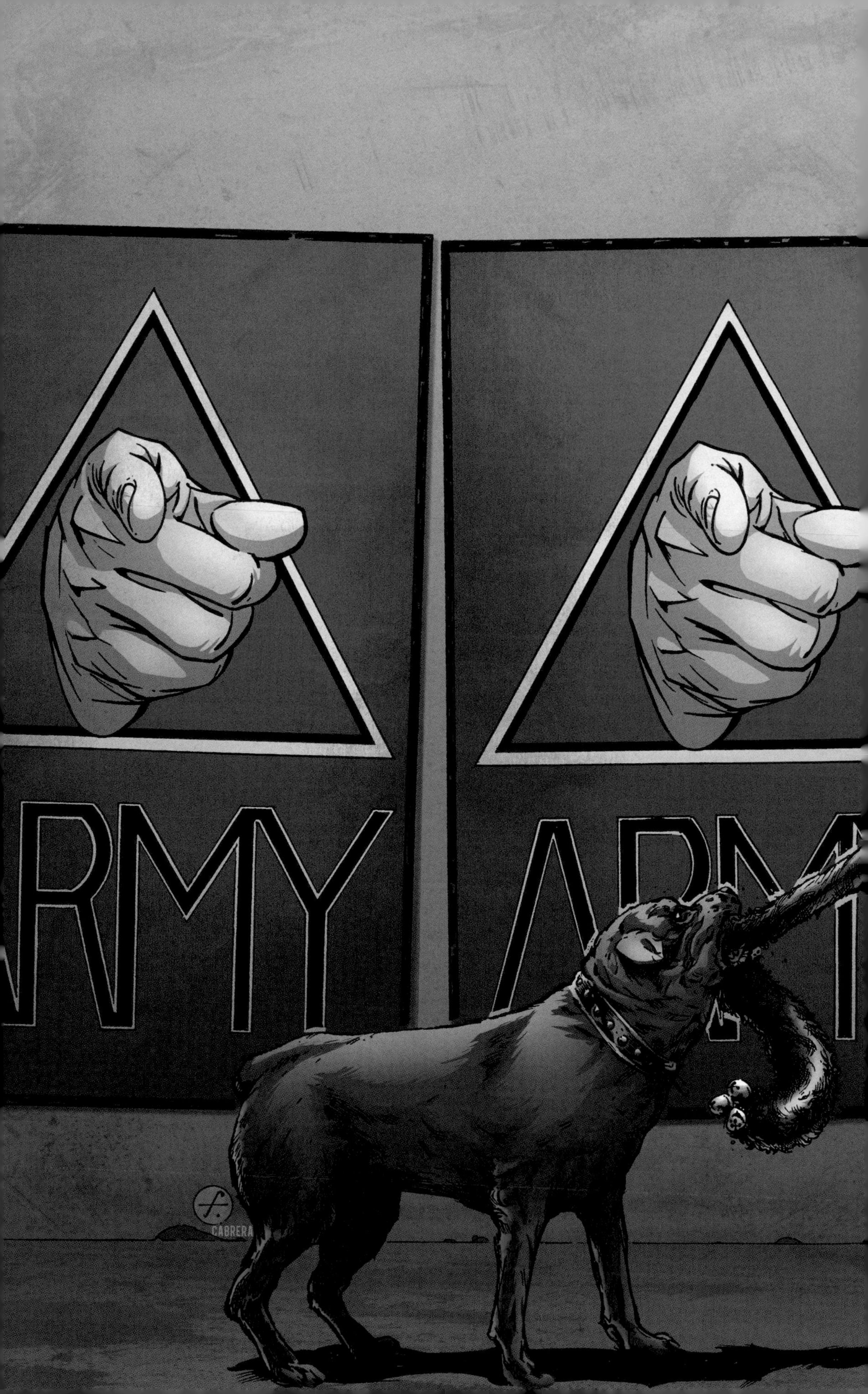
CABRERA

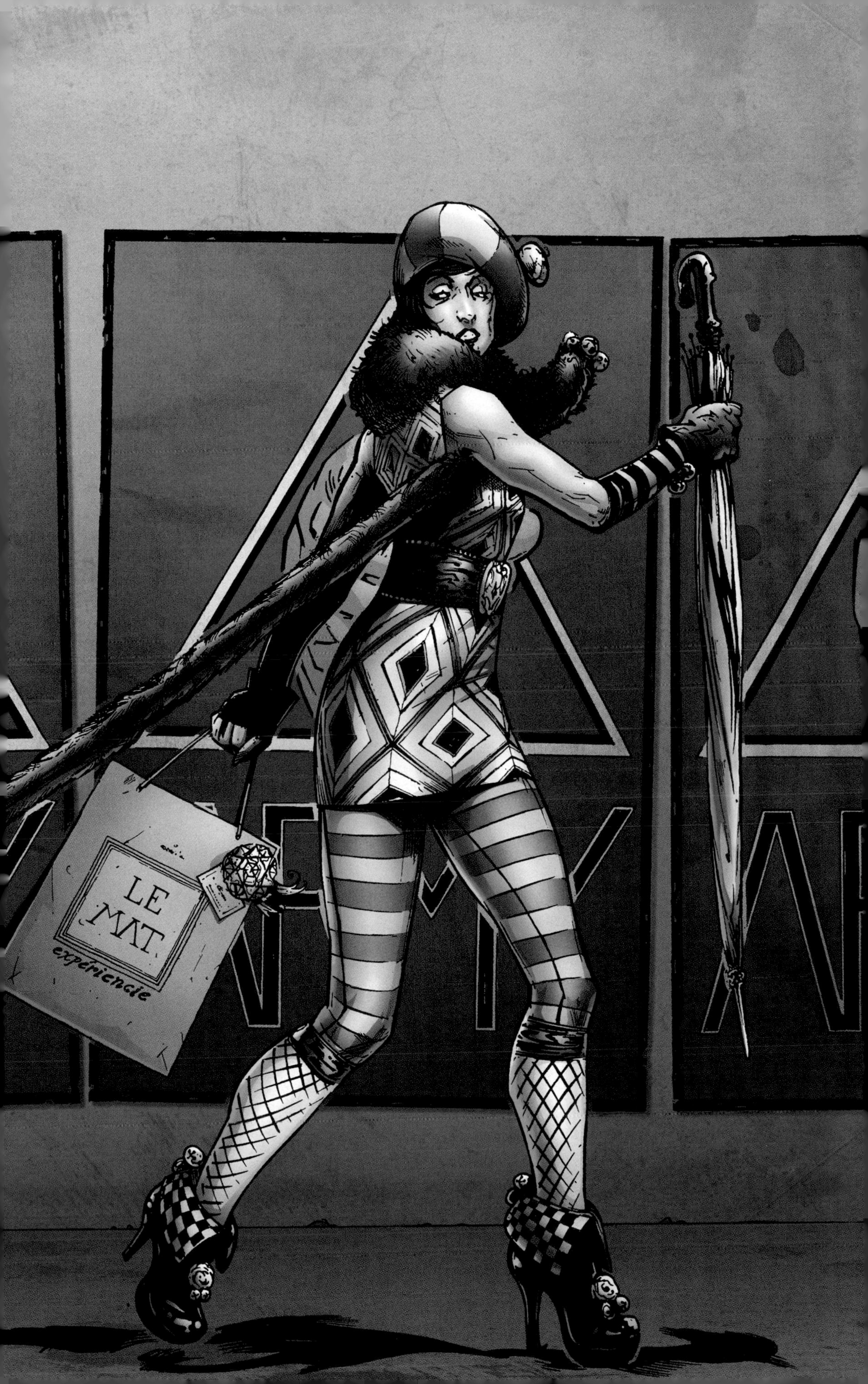
LE MAT
expériencie

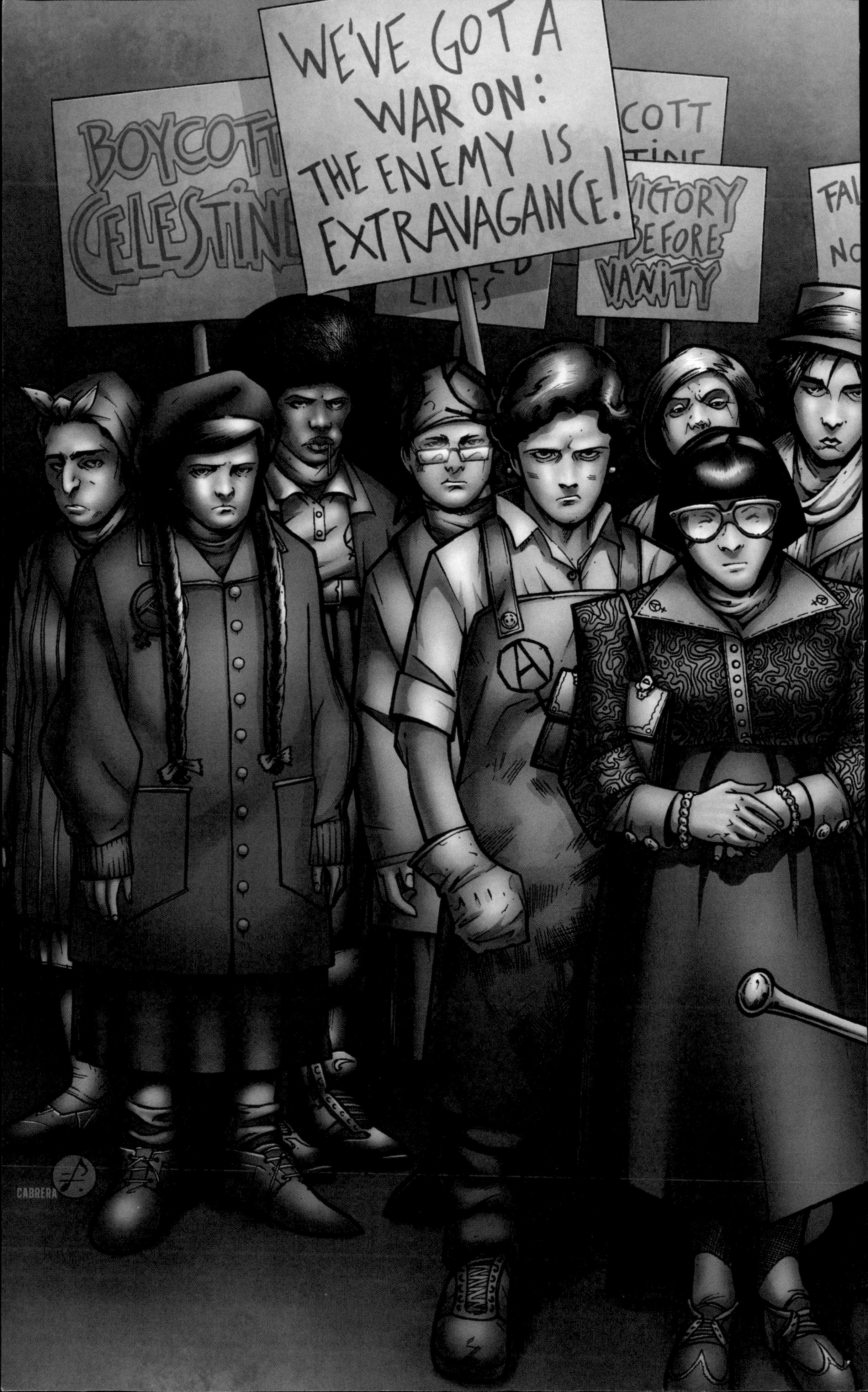

WE'VE GOT A WAR ON: THE ENEMY IS EXTRAVAGANCE!
VICTORY BEFORE VANITY
CABRERA

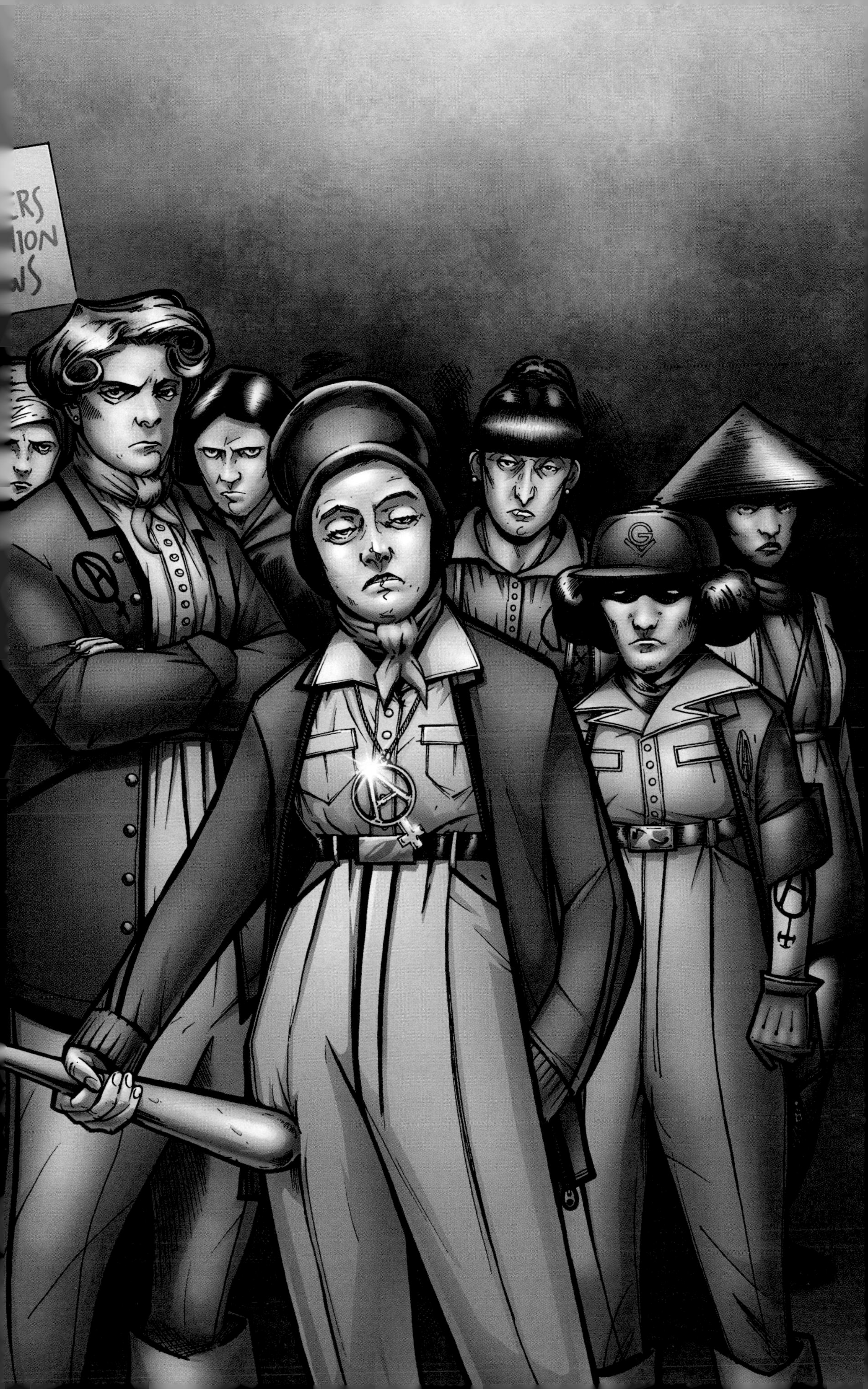

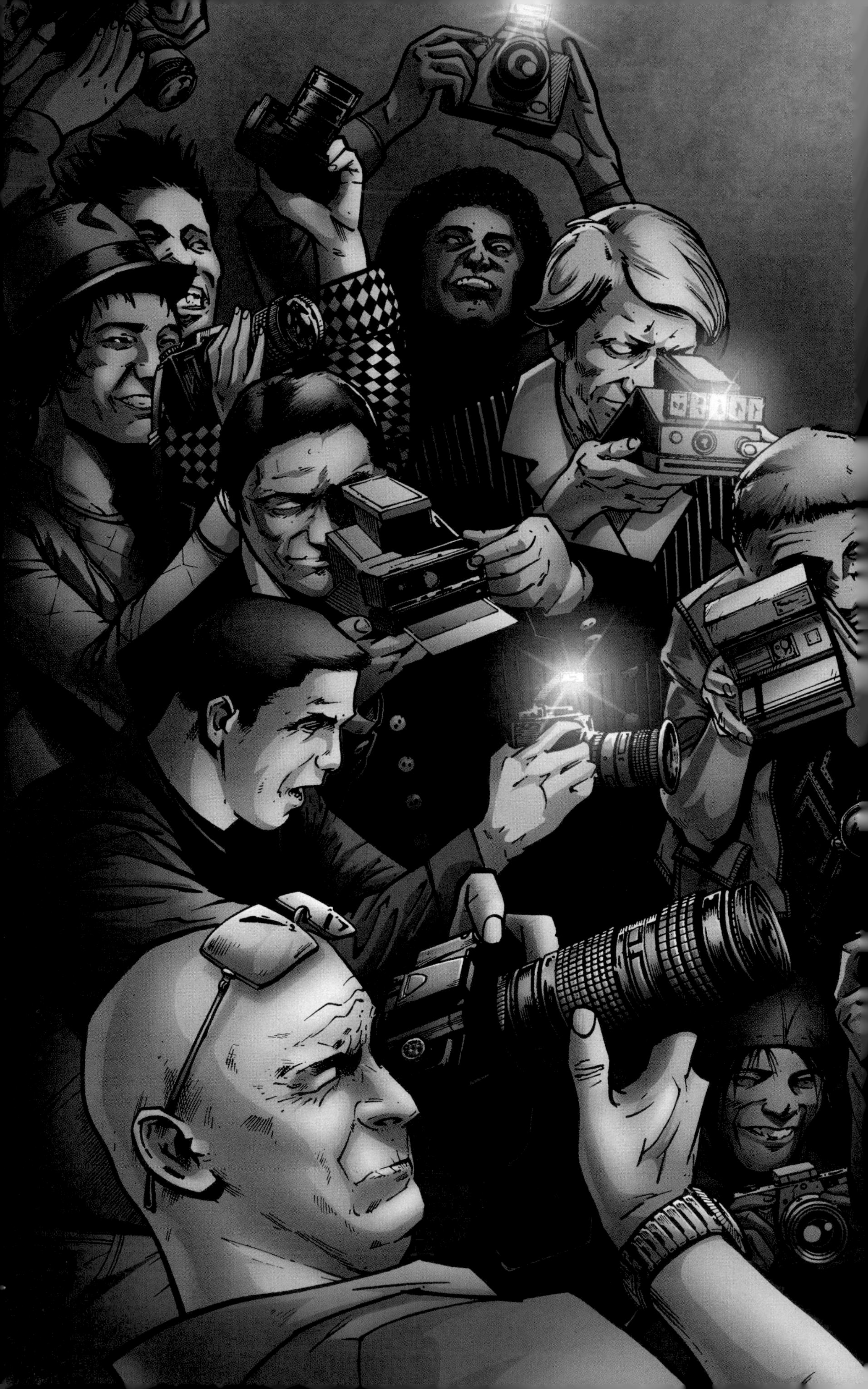

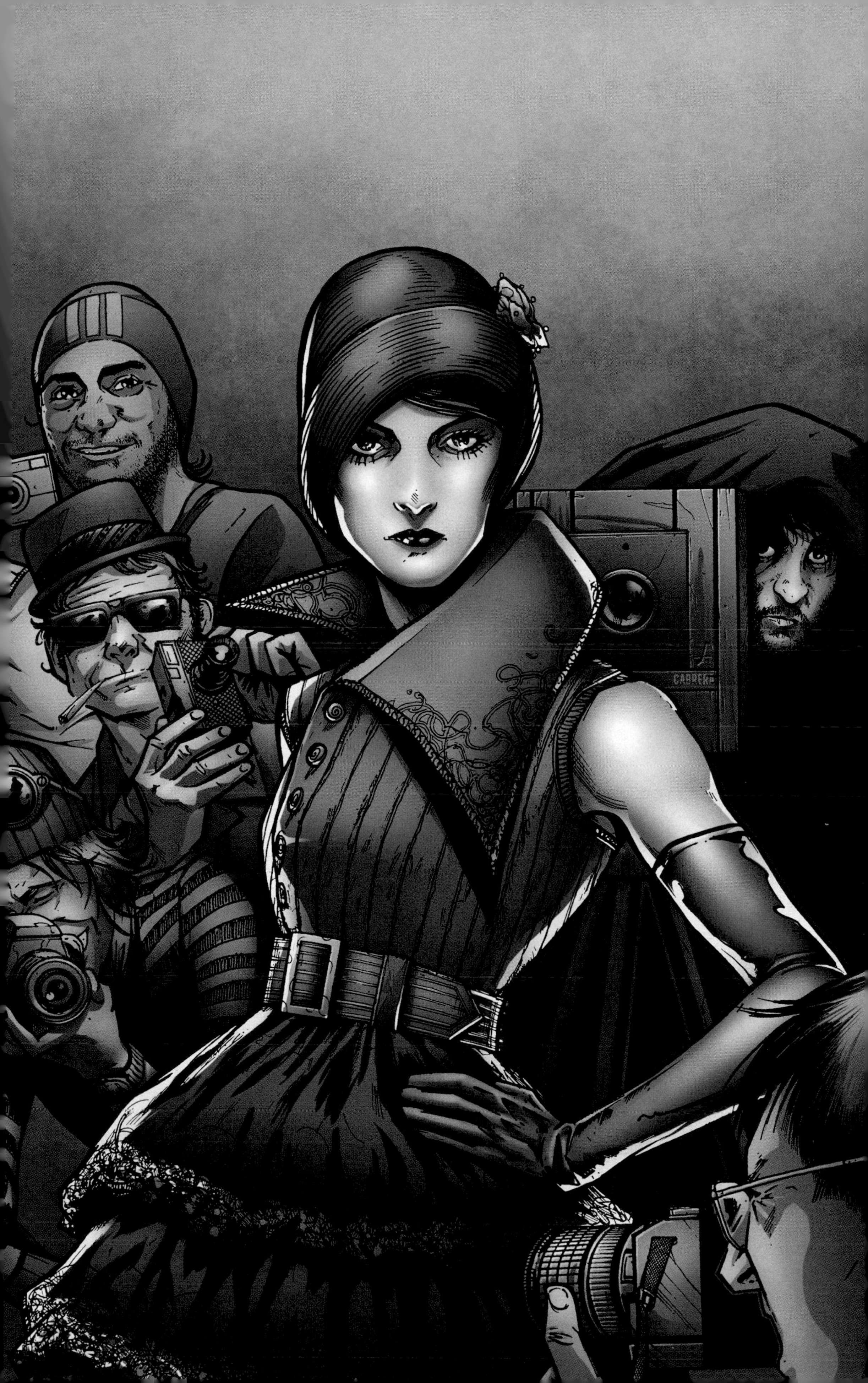

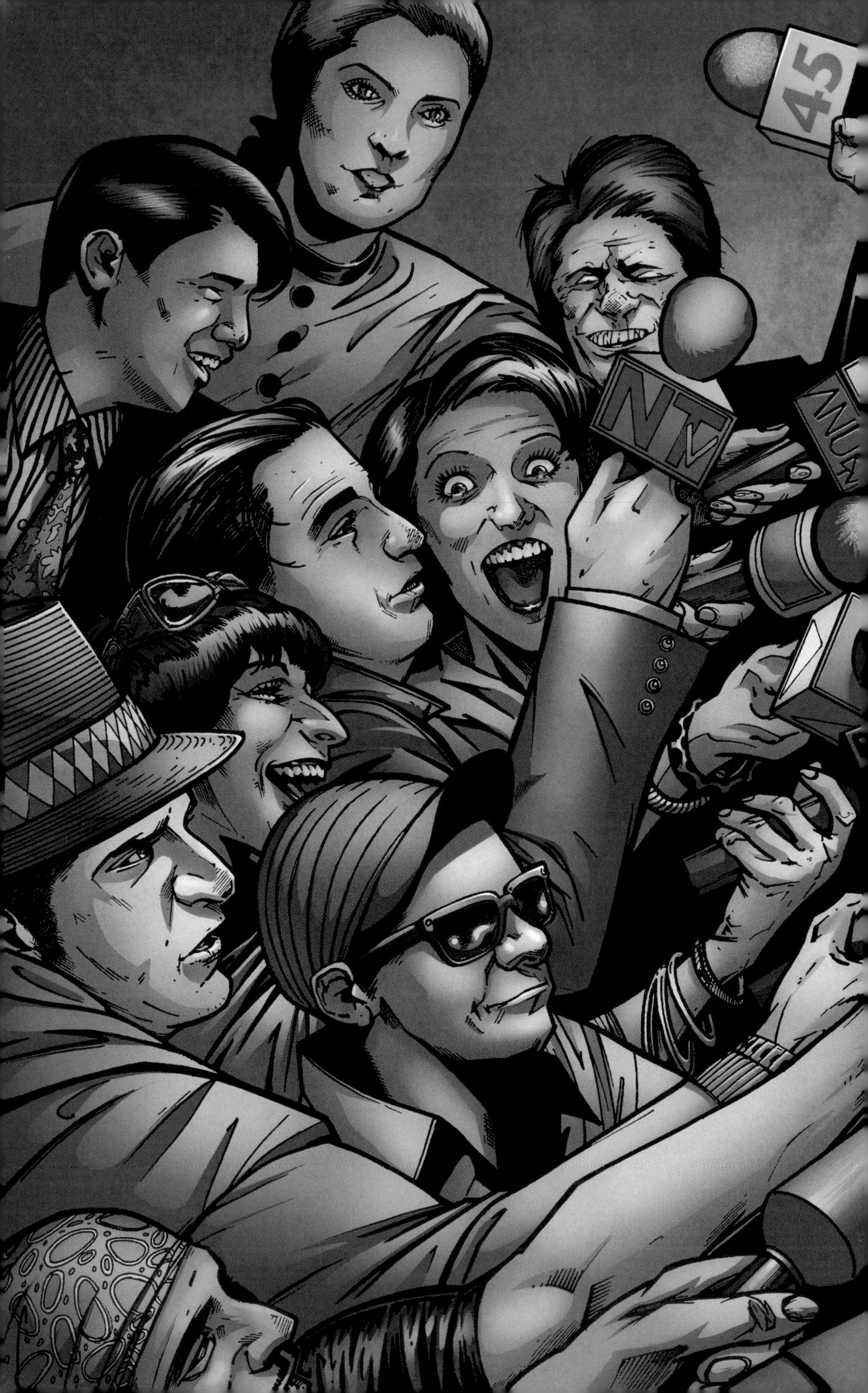
45

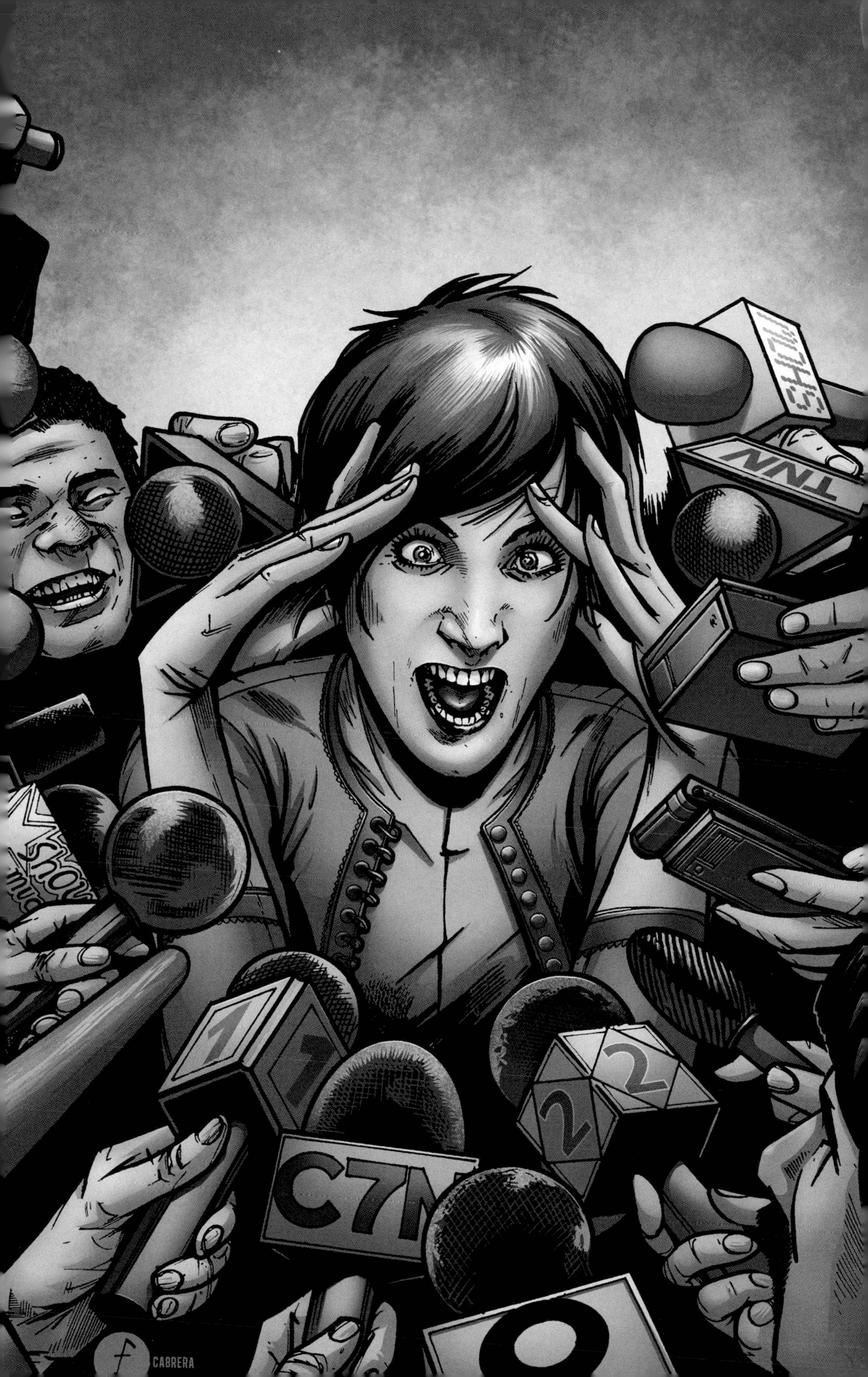
TNN
C7N
CABRERA

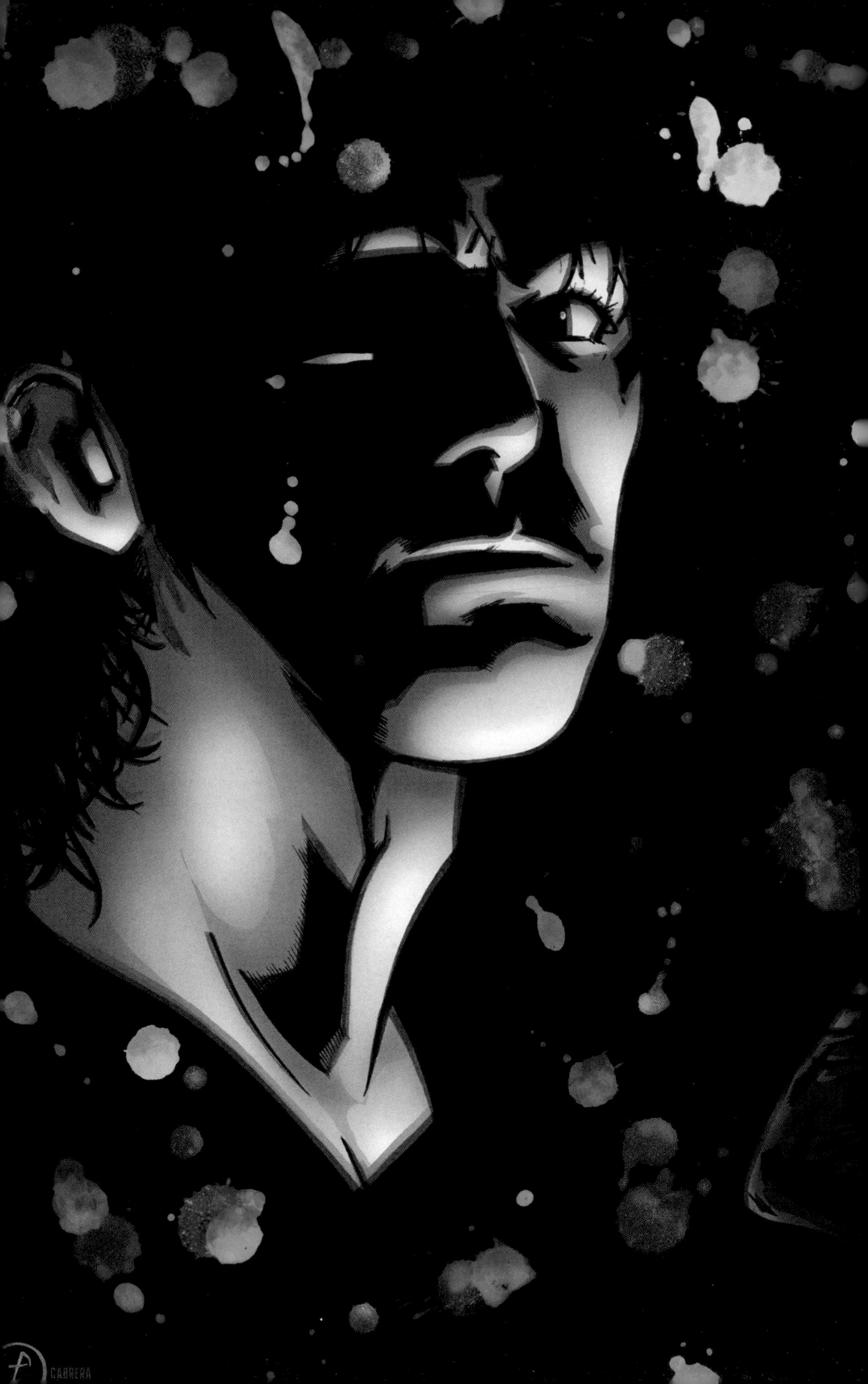
CABRERA

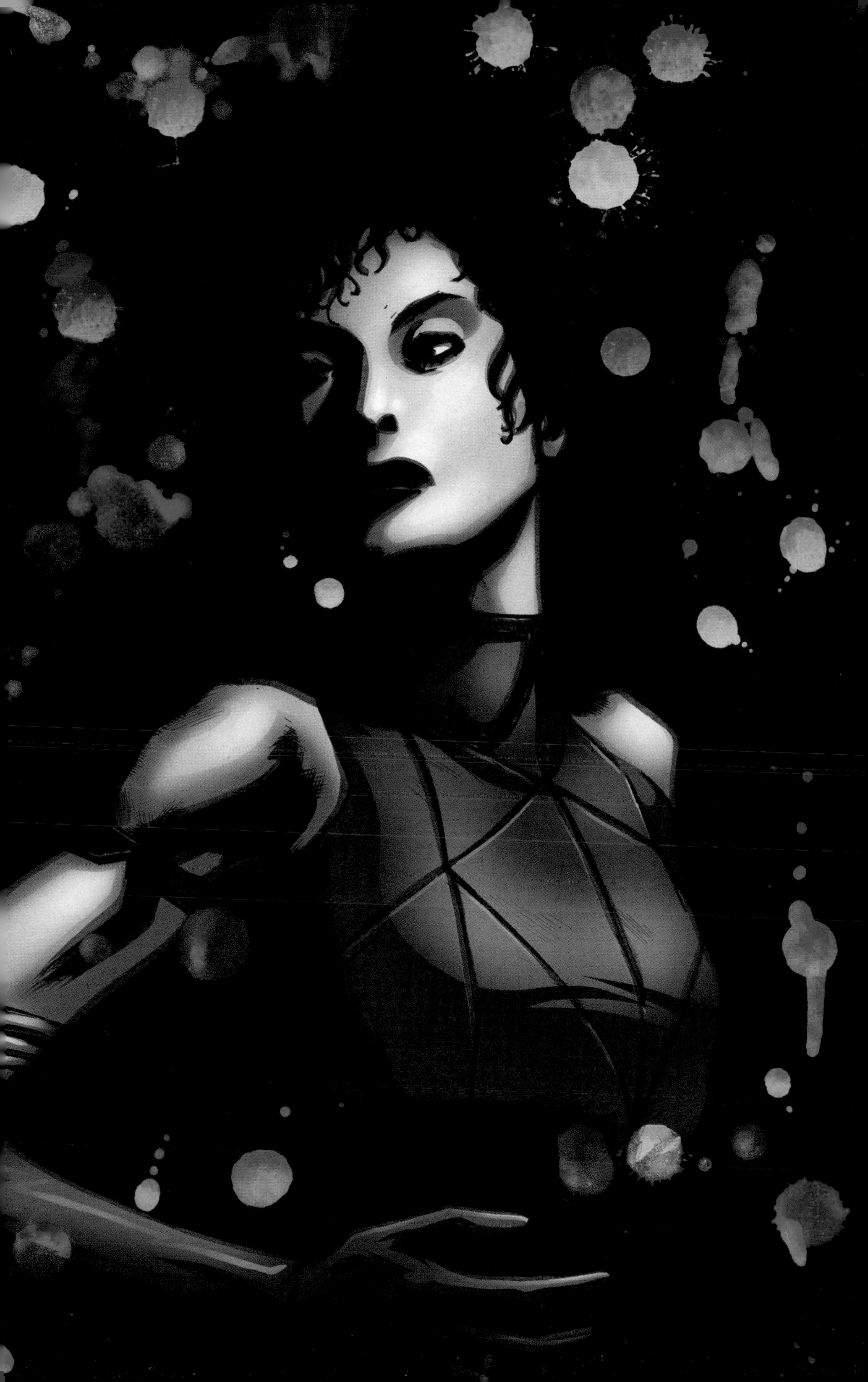

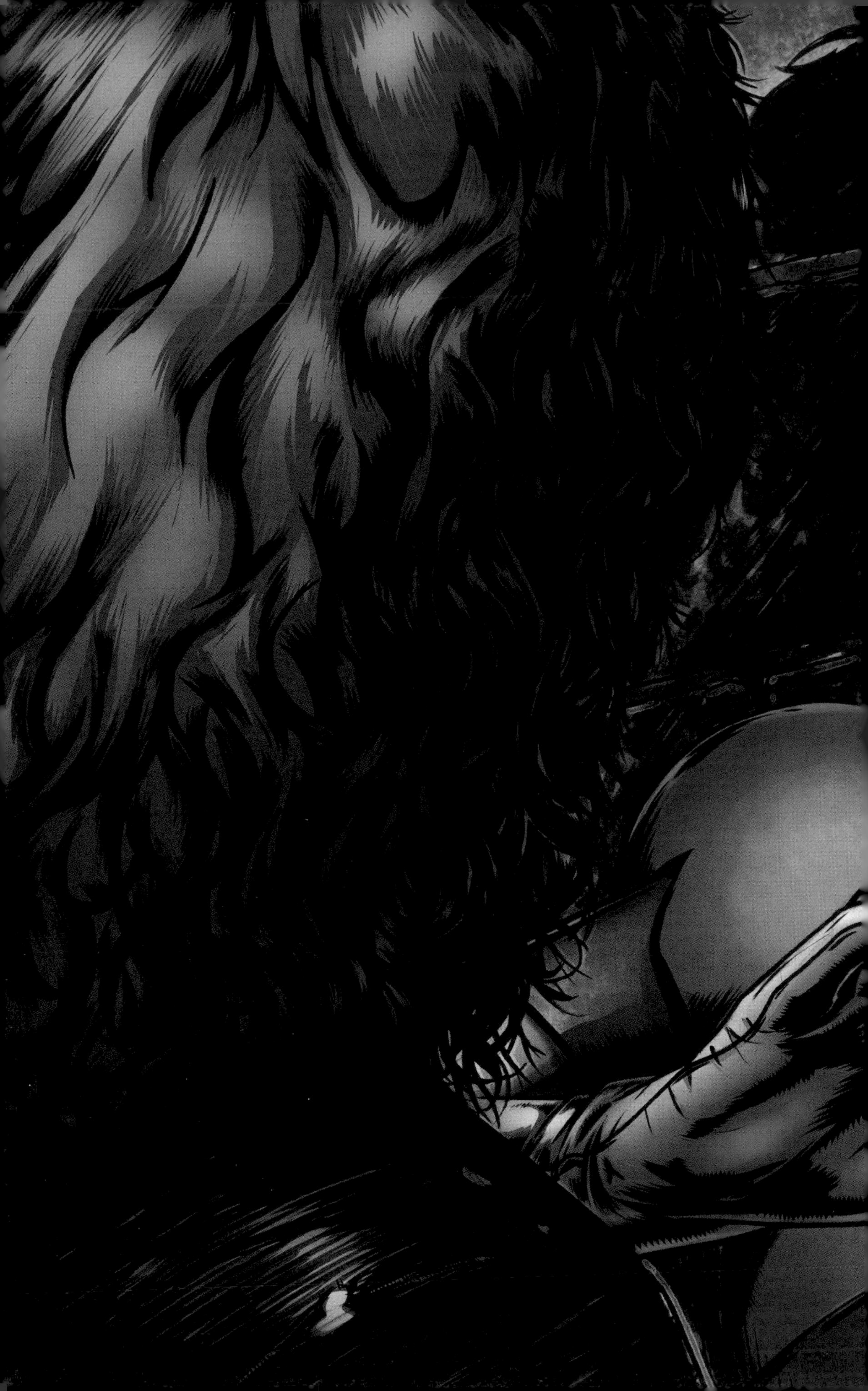

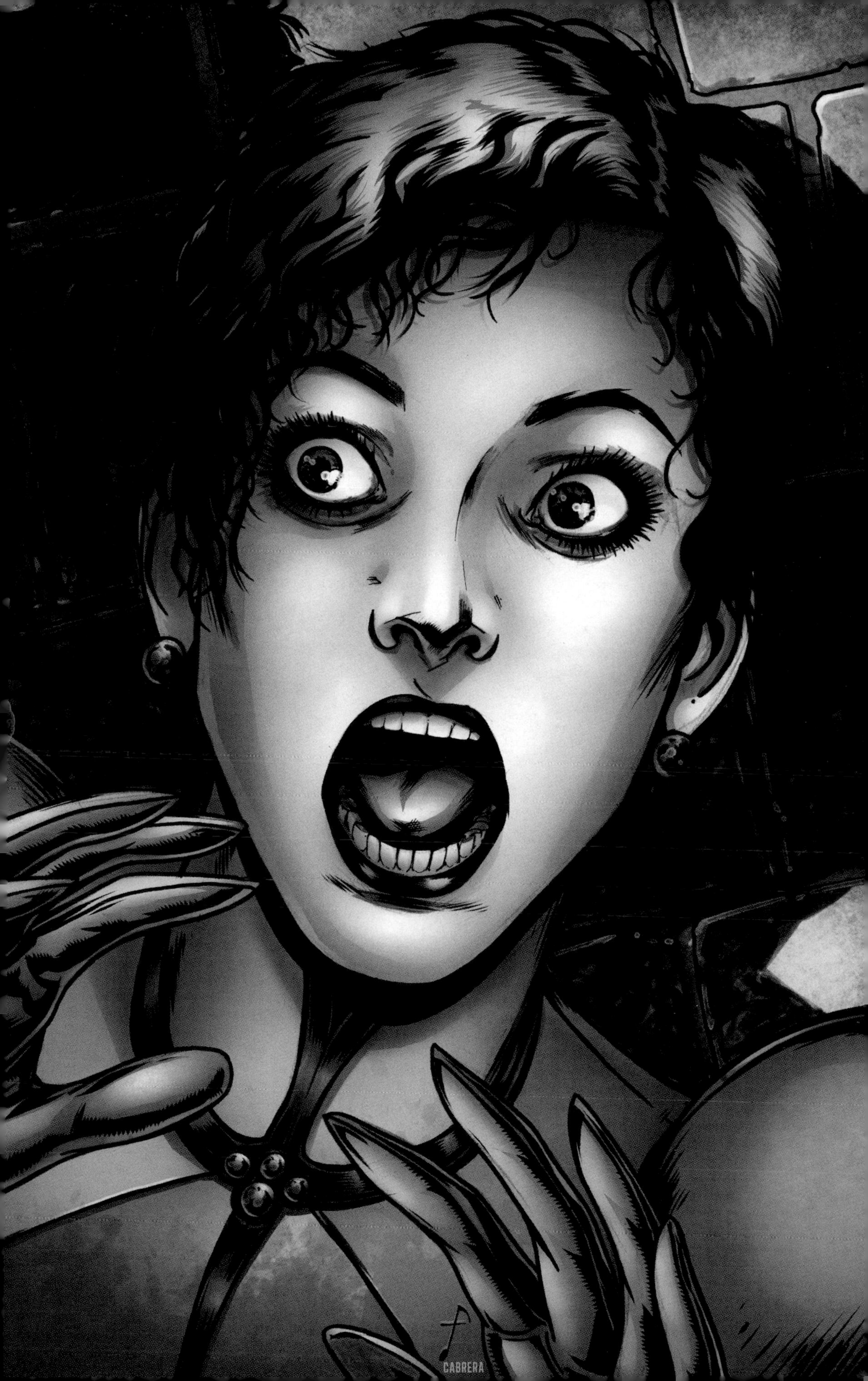
CABRERA

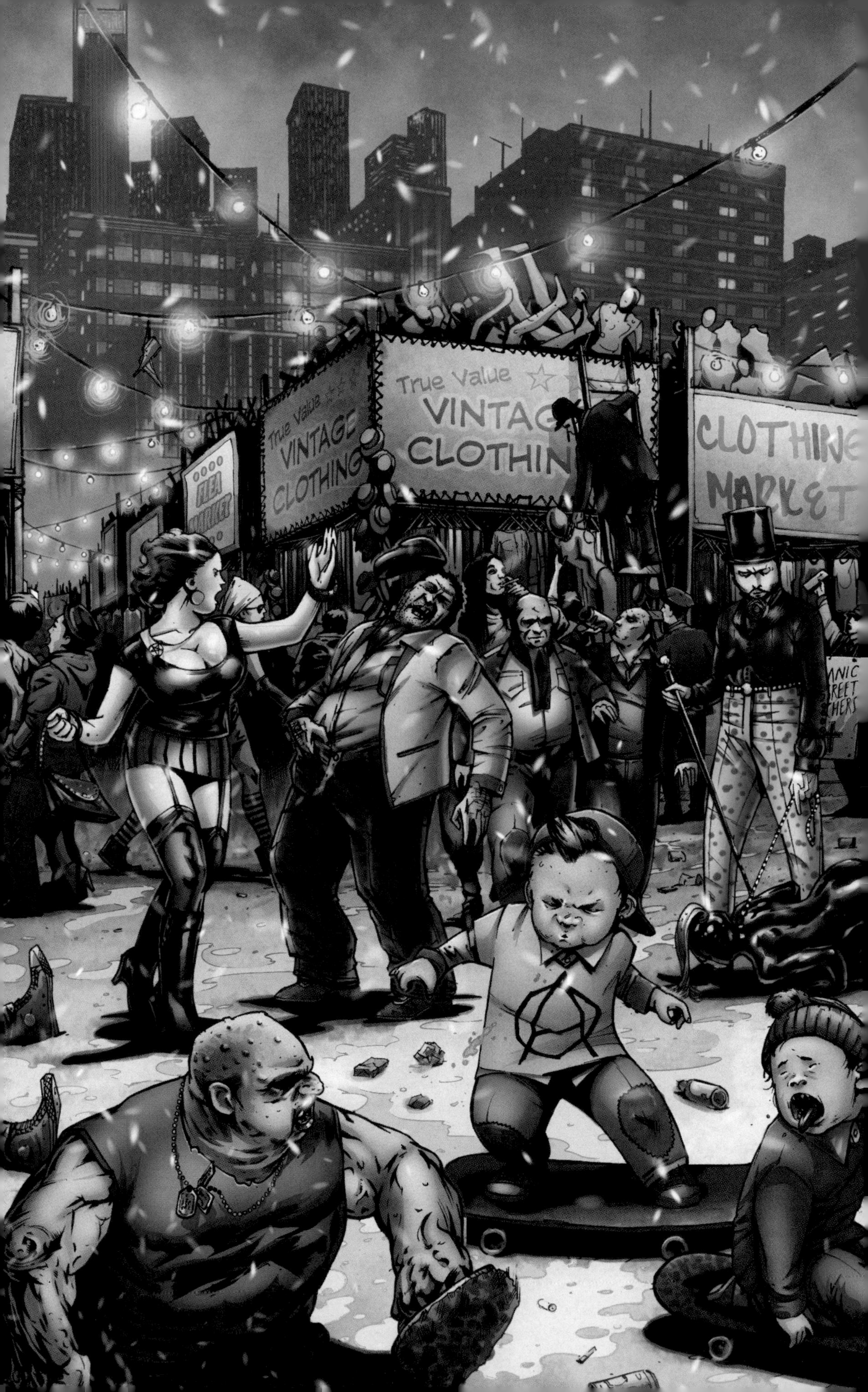

True Value VINTAGE CLOTHING
True Value VINTAG CLOTHIN
CLOTHING MARKET
FLEA MARKET

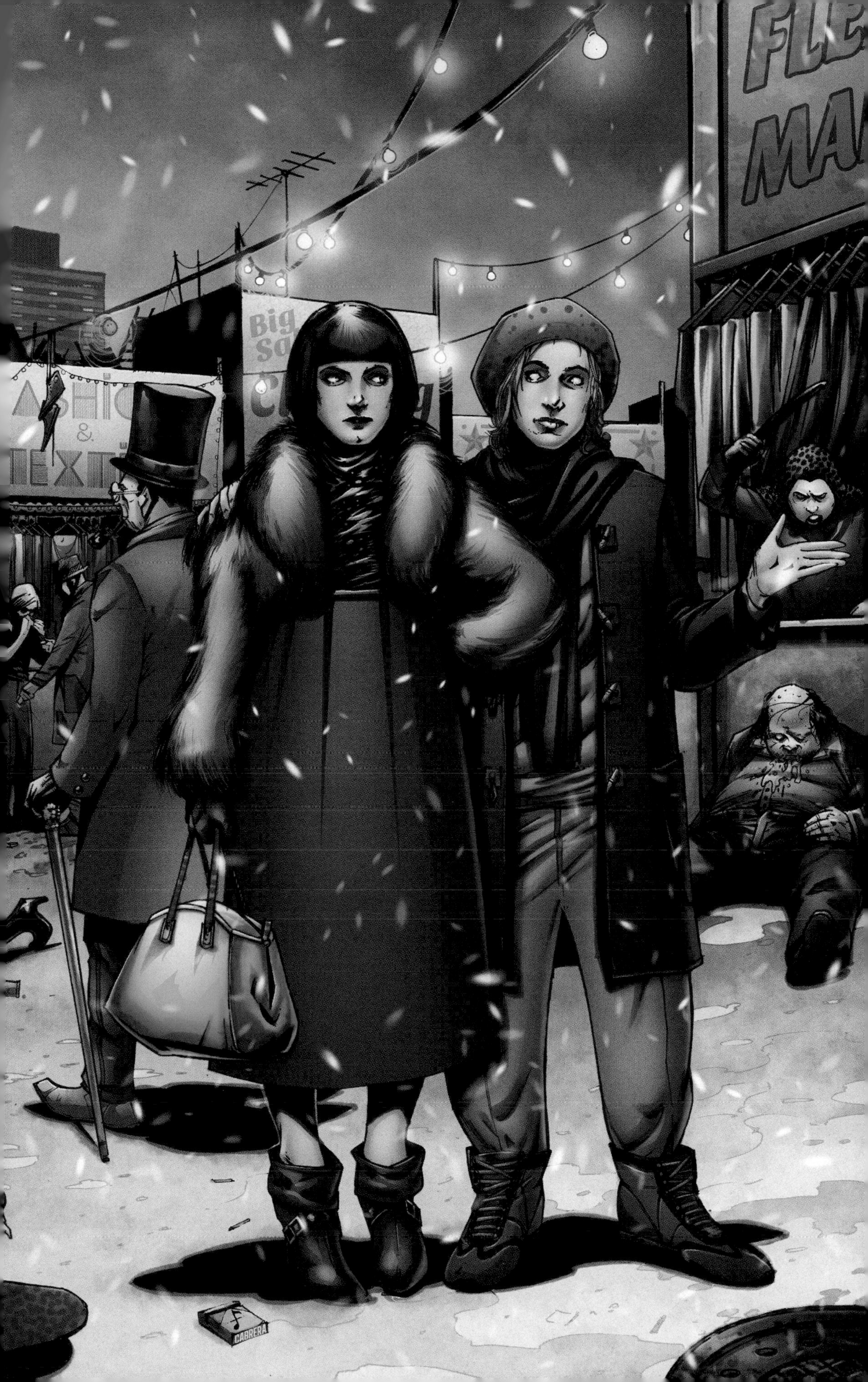
Big
CABRERA

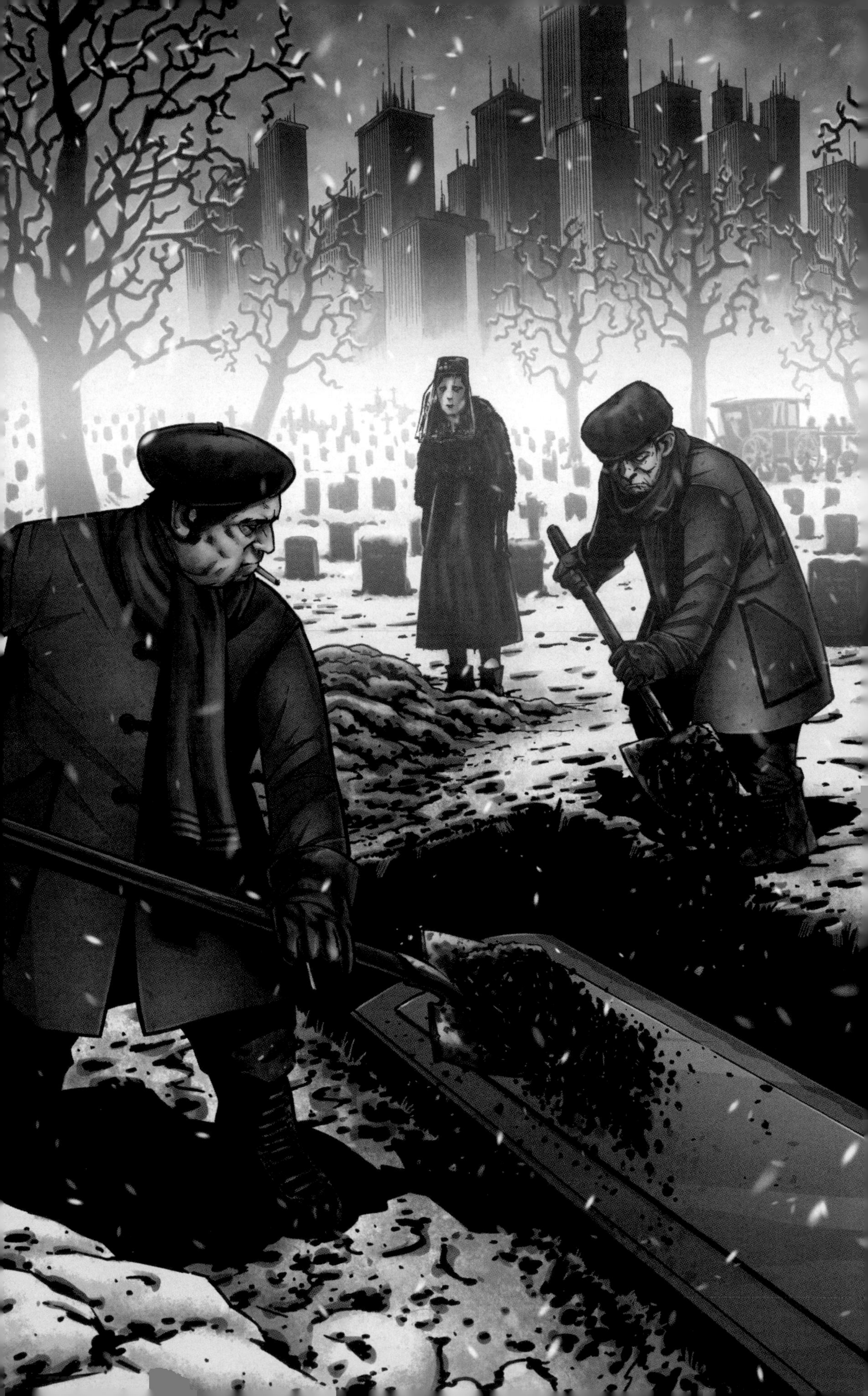

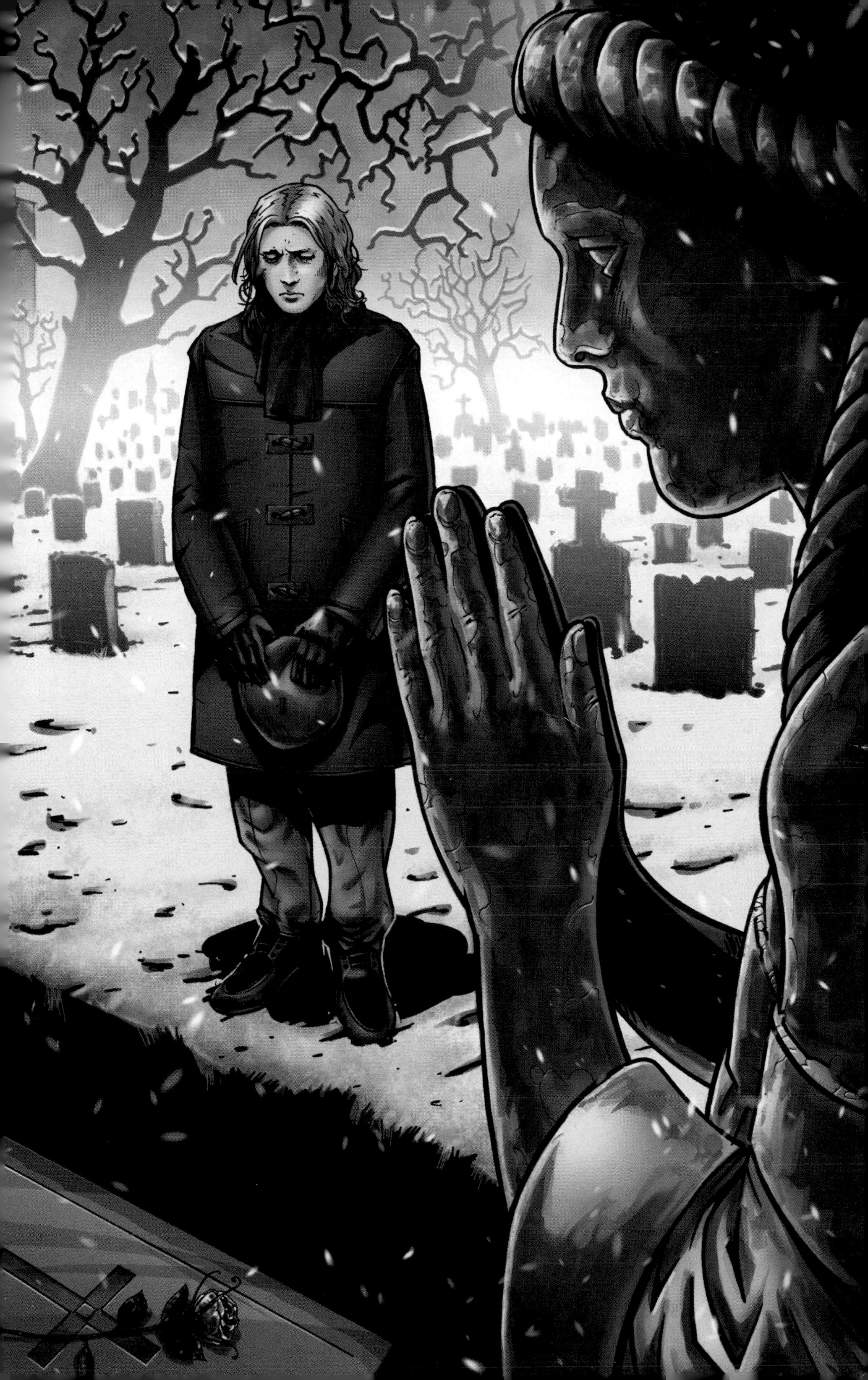

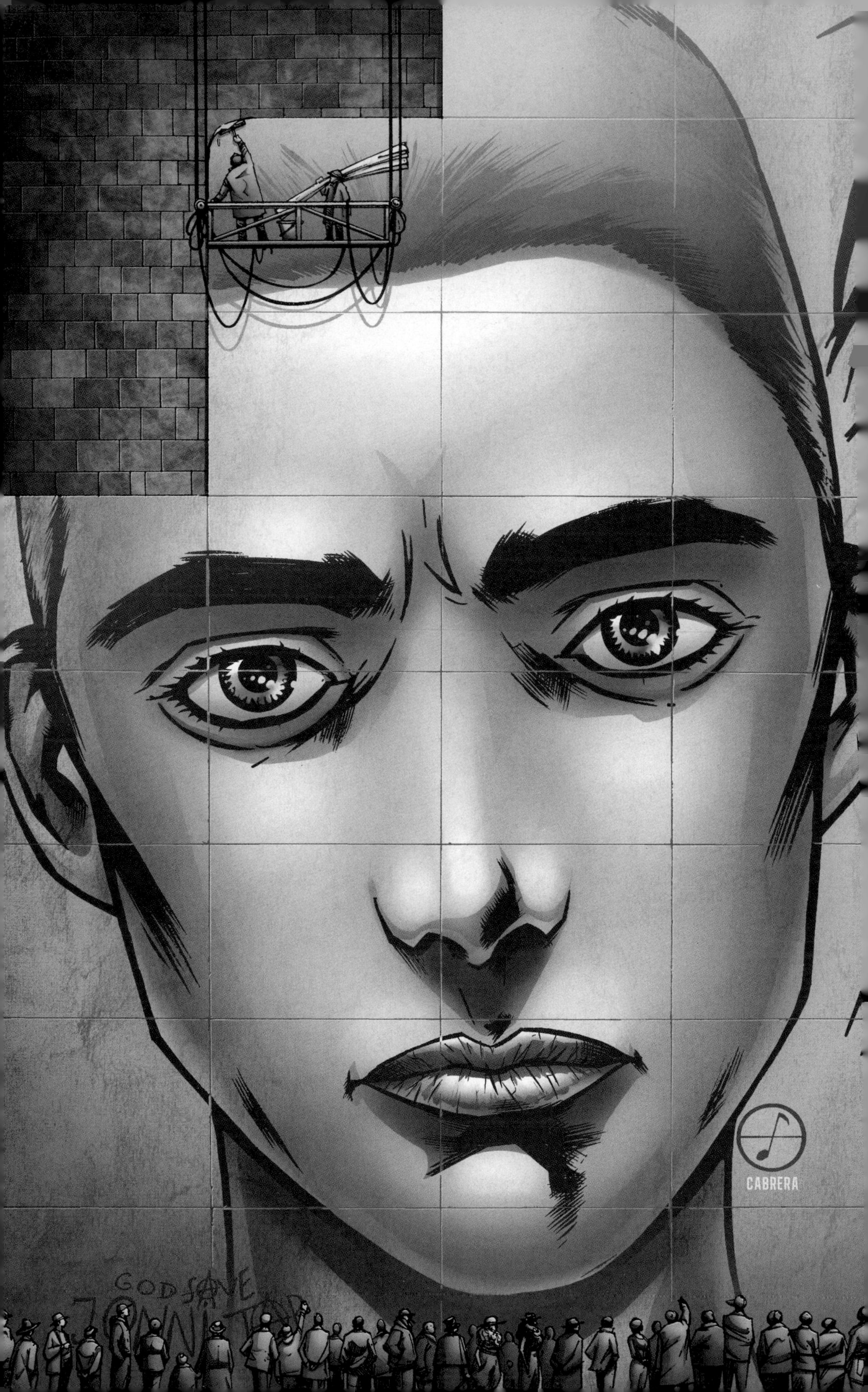
GOD SAVE
CABRERA

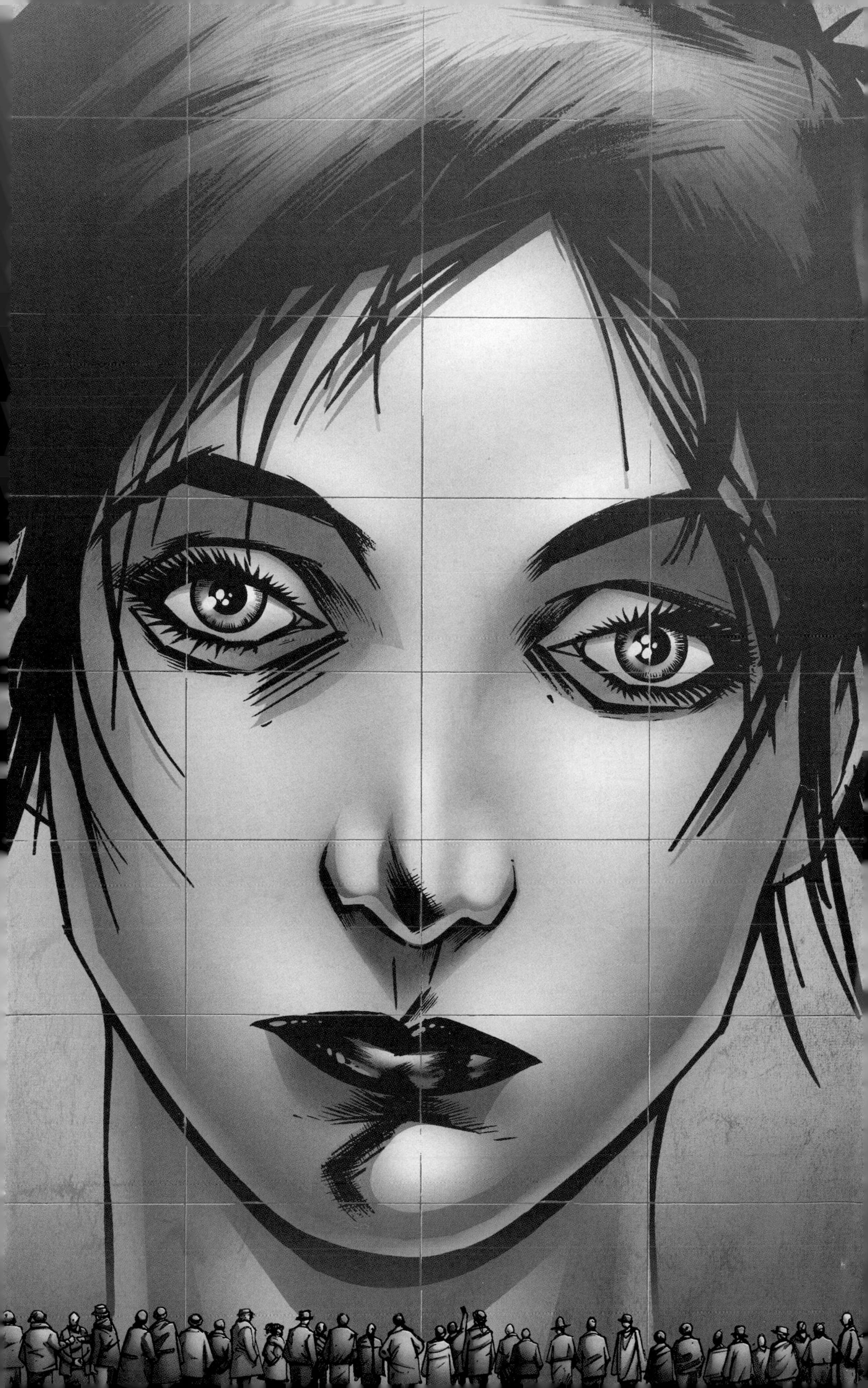

11/13 GRAPHIC

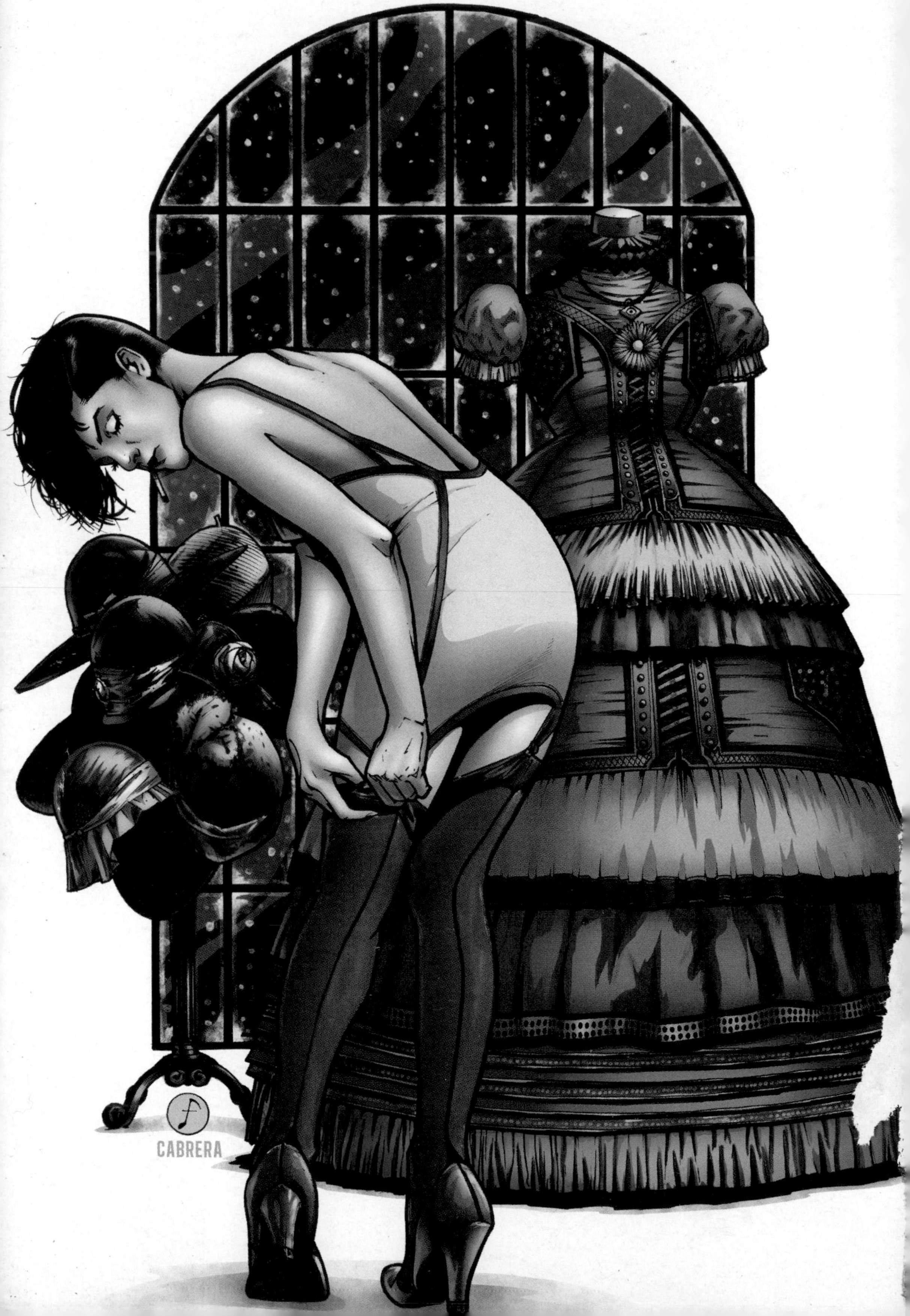
CABRERA